P9-ECN-467

MEMORY

*I dedicate this book to the memory of
my grandmothers, Miriam Halpert and Anna Schwartz.*

MEMORY

FOUNDATIONS AND APPLICATIONS

BENNETT L. SCHWARTZ
Florida International University

Los Angeles | London | New Delhi
Singapore | Washington DC

Copyright © 2011 by SAGE Publications, Inc.

All rights reserved. No part of this book may be reproduced or utilized in any form or by any means, electronic or mechanical, including photocopying, recording, or by any information storage and retrieval system, without permission in writing from the publisher.

For information:

SAGE Publications, Inc.
2455 Teller Road
Thousand Oaks, California 91320
E-mail: order@sagepub.com

SAGE Publications Ltd.
1 Oliver's Yard
55 City Road
London EC1Y 1SP
United Kingdom

SAGE Publications India Pvt. Ltd.
B 1/I 1 Mohan Cooperative Industrial Area
Mathura Road, New Delhi 110 044
India

SAGE Publications Asia-Pacific Pte. Ltd.
33 Pekin Street #02-01
Far East Square
Singapore 048763

Printed in the United States of America

Library of Congress Cataloging-in-Publication Data

Schwartz, Bennett L.
Memory: Foundations and applications / Bennett Schwartz.
    p. cm.
Includes bibliographical references and index.
ISBN 978-1-4129-7253-6 (pbk.)
  1. Memory. I. Title.

BF371.S445 2011
153.1′2—dc22   2010020001

This book is printed on acid-free paper.

10 11 12 13 14 10 9 8 7 6 5 4 3 2 1

Acquisitions Editor:	Christine Cardone
Editorial Assistant:	Sarita Sarak
Production Editor:	Eric Garner
Copy Editor:	Gillian Dickens
Typesetter:	C&M Digitals (P) Ltd.
Proofreader:	Joyce Li
Indexer:	Jean Casalegno
Cover Designer:	Candice Harman
Marketing Manager:	Stephanie Adams

Brief Contents

Detailed Contents

3   Working Memory   59

9   Metamemory   259

10   Memory Disorders   289

11   Memory in Childhood   323

Preface

It is hard to imagine an aspect of psychology more fundamental than memory. Without a functioning memory, all other cognitive functions—perception, learning, problem solving, and language—would be impossible. Emotion itself is informed and influenced by memory. Without a functioning memory, social interactions such as play, relationships, and work would be chaotic at best. For this reason, the study of memory has been important to psychologists from the very beginnings of psychology.

When I teach memory, the most common question that I receive from students is the following: How can I improve my own memory? However, memory textbooks seldom address this topic. Students learn about memory models, theories, a great many experiments, much about neuroscience, and the brain. These are all important if one is to understand how memory works, and these issues are well covered in this book. But *Memory: Foundations and Applications* is also designed to instruct students to apply these concepts to their everyday life and use them to improve their individual ability to learn and remember.

The classroom itself has changed in the past few years of higher education. Classes have companion websites, and in some cases, entire classes are online. College students have been downloading information from the Internet since they were in elementary school. However, textbooks in memory exist as if these resources did not exist. I wanted *Memory: Foundations and Applications* to capitalize on these sources of information. Thus, the book contains references to and links to websites where students can learn more about a particular topic or a particular individual's research. I believe that this approach will be conducive to the way modern students have grown accustom to learning. On the other hand, *Memory: Foundations and Applications* provides depth into the science and methodology of memory that may not be easily available from Internet sources. In the end, in most classes, there is still a professor in front of a classroom and a student reading a textbook. I wanted a textbook that provided depth and created interest in the field of memory, that is, a textbook that students would want to read. The balance between depth of understanding and ease of access is difficult in a world of super-information, but that is what I've strived for.

This book emphasizes the science of memory. It describes experiments, patients with memory disorders, the areas of the brain involved in memory, and the cognitive theory that links this research together. I have tried to write this book with students in mind—their concerns, interests, and curiosity. I hope—at the same time that this book emphasizes the science of memory—that it also tells a story about our search to understand our own minds and how we can benefit from that understanding.

ORGANIZATION AND CONTENT

Memory: Foundations and Applications is an accessible textbook on memory science presented in clear and understandable language. Each chapter begins with a discussion or exercise that engages the reader with an example or real-life incident that helps illustrate the relevance and importance of each chapter. This opener provides students with an appreciation for the topic and why scientists consider the topic important. Examples and applications of key concepts are integrated throughout the text in a way that students can appreciate the relevance to their lives.

Instead of having separate neuroscience sections, each chapter integrates findings from neuroscience. Topics such as the time course of brain activation during autobiographical memory, the regions of the brain involved in encoding, and the regions of the brain involved in monitoring are included in the flow of the chapters rather than in a separate section at the end of each chapter or a separate chapter entirely. Neuroscience is not simply presented as a map as to where memory processes occur but also how the neuroscience data can shape how we construct our theories.

Memory: Foundations and Applications is unique in its emphasis on applications, in educational situations, police investigations, courtrooms, memory clinics, and everyday life. These issues are also integrated within each chapter rather than kept separate from the development of theory and experiments. For example, the chapter on false memory discusses applications to legal proceedings. The chapter on memory and aging discusses the "use it or lose it" hypothesis. The chapter on amnesia discusses memory rehabilitation for patients with brain damage. And most chapters contain mnemonic hints, designed to help students become more efficient learners.

PEDAGOGICAL FEATURES

1. Important terms are highlighted in **bold.** This is useful when students outline their textbooks while studying for exams. It directs them to the parts of the book that are important for studying after the material has been understood.

2. **Mnemonic hints.** Almost every chapter contains highlighted *mnemonic hints.* These hints state succinctly how a particular concept can be applied to memory improvement. Chapter 13 ends with a list of all the mnemonic hints provided in the textbook.

3. **Interim summaries.** Every chapter except for Chapters 1 and 13 have interim summaries. These review the main points of the section, emphasize the important points, and provide organization that students can use in study.

4. **Key terms.** At the end of each chapter, I list the important terms introduced or reviewed in the chapter. Key terms include new definition, jargon, and concepts, as well as terms that may have been introduced in another chapter but are reviewed here. Students can use the "key terms" section as a way to review. Successfully defining the terms is the first step in mastering the material.

5. **Review questions.** At the end of each chapter are 10 review questions. Each question prompts the reader toward an understanding of one or more of the important ideas in the chapter. A student who can successfully answer all of the questions at the end of the chapter can be confident that he or she understands the main topics in that chapter.

ADDITIONAL RESOURCES

6. **Online resources.** Throughout each chapter are markers that indicate that there is additional content at sagepub.com. The links at sagepub.com will take readers to sites where they can get more information about a topic, learn about the research in a particular lab, or participate in a demonstration.

7. **Test bank.** Clear, unambiguous questions are available to professors using this textbook. Each question covers either factual knowledge from the text or conceptual knowledge based on the text. Many questions directly concern experiments discussed in the book.

8. **PowerPoint package.** A PowerPoint package has been designed to accompany the text. It parallels the textbook and highlights the important points. It can be modified by individual professors or used without modification.

ACKNOWLEDGMENTS

I need to thank many people at Sage Publications for their contribution to the development, writing, and production of *Memory: Foundations and Applications.* I am lucky to have been able to work with such talented and responsible people. I thank Christine Cardone for guiding this book to the finish line and seeing it published in a timely manner. I thank Lisa Cuevas Shaw for overseeing the production of this book, promoting patience when I might be reckless, and ensuring that the book was always high quality. I thank Acquisitions Editor Erik Evans for his enthusiasm and for his insight into the world of textbook publishing, from which the book benefitted immeasurably. I thank Sarita Sarak for always being willing to help me with any aspect of the book—from permissions to the artwork.

I also need to thank many colleagues and students who read parts of the textbook or gave me advice on what the important questions were in a particular topic. I thank my dissertation adviser Janet Metcalfe of Columbia University, who continues to advise and inspire me. I also thank George Wolford of Dartmouth College, a mentor par excellence. I thank Nate Kornell, Lisa Son, Bridgid Finn, John Dunlosky, Harlene Hayne, Rachel Herz, Steven M. Smith, Mike Toglia, Daniel Lehn, Anthony Prandi, Jeffrey Thomas, Leslie Frazier, and Endel Tulving for their advice and guidance in specific areas of the book. Jonathan Altman was always willing to be a sounding board for any idea, however silly, and give me technical advice. I thank Jack Frazier for providing illustrations.

Finally, I wish to thank two special people whose love for me and pride in me inspire me every day to do my best. They are my wife, Leslie Frazier, and my daughter, Sarina Schwartz.

—Bennett L. Schwartz

July 9, 2010

CHAPTER 1

Introduction to the Study of Memory

Remembering is a part of our every waking moment. Nearly everything we do throughout the day, including dreaming at night, involves memory. Consider the very act of waking up itself. As the alarm goes off, you must remember if you have an early appointment. If you do, you must get up right away, but if you do not, you can hit the snooze button and sleep a bit longer. Once you do get out of bed, even more is asked of your memory. Did you wear the same shirt on the same day last week? Would people notice? Are you going to the gym after classes? If so, do you need to bring workout clothes or are they already in your car? If you live in a dorm, you might try to remember if your roommate is in class already or trying to catch up on sleep. If you have a job, do you have any meetings that you cannot miss? These are just a few of the needs for memory within just a few moments of waking up. As the day proceeds, we have to remember how to drive to the university, the material for class that day, how to get from one classroom to another and what rooms are classes are in, where the car is parked so we can drive home, and the best route to get home in afternoon traffic. And this is just the beginning. You have to remember which friend you are meeting for lunch and where. Did this friend just break up with her boyfriend or are they back together? Remembering this is crucial in how you start your conversation with your friend. And, yes, did you forget that you had an exam in your social psychology class? You need to remember all the material you have been studying for the past few days. You can see how critical good memory performance is.

Memory also forms the basis of our views of our selves and our personalities. Think of how crucial your memory is to your sense of self and personality. Most of us, for example, like to think of ourselves as generous. But when was the last time you engaged in a truly generous act? Do you remember it? Being able to recall the characteristics of our own personality and back it up with actual memories is an important part of developing our sense of self. Certainly, early memories from childhood tend to be an important part of personality and sense of self as well. Almost all of us can describe poignant memories that shaped who we are today. For example, on the positive side, it might be the memory of a grandparent telling us to be confident and do our best, or it might be the memory of a teacher who inspired us in grade school. On the other hand, a memory of the first time you saw a dead body in an auto accident may be instrumental in keeping you a safe driver, or your memory of the events of 9/11 may shape your view of world politics. Each of us has important memories like these.

Another way to view the importance of memory in our society is to "google" it. I just did and got nearly half a billion hits. Now some of these deal with computer memory, not our own memory, but just a quick search of the web yields vast numbers of sites that offer ways in which to improve your memory. I am hoping that this book will help guide you to those based on scientific evidence.

Moreover, the thought of losing or forgetting certain memories is scary and painful. Imagine losing access to all the memories of your dear grandmother. These memories are "treasures" in a way more closely connected to our sense of self than any bracelet or ring. Losing these memories, even the bad ones, is seen as devastating. Capitalizing on this fear, movies abound in fictional tales of amnesiacs, who lose not just their ability to learn (common in amnesia in the real world) but also the memory of the personal past and hence their personalities (less common in the real world). What makes the amnesia plot compelling is the knowledge of how important the personal past is to the present self.

For students, memory is also one's livelihood. One's job is to learn and remember a myriad range of information. Facts, dates, authors, concepts, methodologies, hypotheses, theories, and philosophies all must be learned and remembered. Doing so efficiently is important to many students who have many conflicting obligations. One of the goals of this textbook is to help students use their memory more efficiently. Because learning and memory are a student's tools for advancement, managing one's learning is a valuable skill. So for a student, memory is even more crucial in daily life.

For this reason, students could potentially perform better in school with some training in the best ways to use their memory. However, students are seldom given any formal training in learning and memory, especially training supported by scientific research. We place tremendous demands on the memories of students. But, aside from the class that you are likely taking and this book, we provide little scientific information about how memory works and how we can improve upon our ability to encode, store, and retrieve information. One goal for this book is to provide students with some knowledge about the current state of memory science and what psychological science and neuroscience can tell us about the nature of human memory. Another goal in this book is to provide students with concrete ways of applying what we know from science to improve their own abilities to learn and remember. Yes, this book is a textbook, detailing the current state of memory science. As important as advice is on the topic of how to improve memory, first must come the science. Thus, more words in this textbook will be devoted to the science of memory than the wherewithal of memory improvement. But I hope that the students reading this book will be able to improve their own learning by gathering useful strategies from the sections on memory improvement as well as personalized strategies through your own interpretations of theory and data. Indeed, the final chapter is completely devoted to memory improvement. Some readers may want to read the last chapter first.

THE SCIENCE OF MEMORY

We will approach the study of human memory from a scientific perspective. What does the term *scientific perspective* mean? In a broad sense, science refers to a particular view of the world, one based on systematic observation, experimentation, and theory. Critical to science is an unbiased attitude. A scientist needs to be open to different points of view but follow his or her data to the most logical conclusions, which are based on evidence, not on his or her opinion. In science, a particular theory is useful only if careful and unbiased observations and experimentation support it. For psychological science, like biology, data derived from experiments constitute the building blocks of our theories. Our intuitions and guesses about the world have value, but in order to be science, they must be tested and verified via the scientific method (for further information on this topic, go to www.sagepub.com/schwartz).[1]

Empirical evidence is the product of scientific research. In order to be empirical evidence, it must be verifiable; that is, another scientist should be able to get the same results if he or she does the same or similar experiment. Empirical evidence is the building block for scientific theory. For example, in earth science, there is overwhelming empirical evidence that, as of 2011, the world's climate is warming. Yes, there are many warming deniers, but these deniers do not examine the empirical evidence. In contrast, empirical evidence, by itself, does not inform us how to act. For example, with respect to global warming, some may advocate making changes in human industrial activity so as to reduce this warming trend, whereas others may make claims that we have to adjust to it but do not need to eliminate the warming pattern. Both may agree on the basic empirical evidence—that globally, temperatures are rising—but disagree on what governments should do about it.

> **Empirical evidence:** the product of scientific research. In order to be empirical evidence, it must be verifiable; that is, another scientist should be able to get the same results if he or she does the same or similar experiment.

In memory science, empirical evidence is the results of experiments. For this reason, this textbook will devote much space and words to the methods and results of experiments. Interpretations of what these experiments mean may vary, and you may find different opinions in other textbooks out there, but you will find that we all rely on the same empirical evidence. These experiments form the basis of memory science. In making recommendations about ways in which to boost memory performance, I will rely on only those methods that have been put to the scientific test and for which empirical evidence is available. This is not to deny that there may be performance boosters out there that we do not know about yet, but this textbook will only include empirically tested sources. I will also try to make these principles easier to understand by giving examples and telling a story or two. But stories and anecdotes do not constitute science—although they may assist good pedagogy. So, please keep in mind the following: Experiments and empirical evidence form the basis of what we know about human memory from a scientific perspective.

The goal of memory science is to make generalizations about how memory works in the real world but by studying it under careful and controlled laboratory conditions. Thus, a researcher might be interested in how witnesses remember what they saw during a crime and how accurate their memory is for that event. But memory researchers cannot follow the police around and interview witnesses at the crime scenes as the police are trying to do their jobs. This would be neither good science nor helpful in running a criminal justice system. Nor can memory researchers "hang around" in places where crimes might occur. This would be dull tedious work because, except in movies, convenience stores are rather safe places, nor do brawls break out every night in every bar. And if the memory researcher were to witness a crime, it might also be dangerous for that researcher. We can, however, ask people to come to labs, where they may see an acted film clip of a convenience store robbery and then look at simulated mug shots. This, by and large, simulates the conditions that people might encounter when witnessing a crime but in a safe and controlled manner. The control involved also allows for careful experimentation, which produces valuable empirical evidence. Control over the conditions is not just a safety measure; as we will see, it also allows us to make causal connections between variables.

Memory researchers are occasionally able to conduct field studies in which they study memory in the real world, including memories for crimes (Yuille & Cutshall, 1986). These studies usually confirm what has occurred in the lab. One hundred twenty-five years of research in the lab on memory have yielded a strong body of knowledge that applies in the real world as well as the lab. Thus, in this book, we will focus on scientific research and assume that, by and large, what we learn in the lab is applicable in everyday life.

Before we spend most of the book discussing the latest data and most up-to-date theories, let's take a quick look at the history of memory science.

THE HISTORY OF MEMORY RESEARCH

Human beings have most likely been wondering about their own memories and how they work since prehistoric times. Early human beings have shown evidence of introspective behaviors as long ago as 40,000 years ago. We know from cave paintings as far afield as China, South Africa, and France that people were adorning themselves with body painting and jewelry, creating art, and presumably developing religious beliefs that long ago (see Figure 1.1). It is likely, though unproven, that some of their art reenacts memories of great hunting stories. Thus, it is likely that some of these Paleolithic people thought about their own memories.

Certainly, people have been writing about memory since the beginning of writing itself. Some of the oldest writing in the world records information about human memory. Ancient Egyptian medical manuals, known as Ebers Papyrus, from 1500 BCE (that is 3,500 years ago) describe the nature of memory deficits after injury (Scholl, 2002). Nearly 2,500 years ago, in classical Greece, Plato and Aristotle described theories of memory that sound surprisingly modern. Many philosophers and medical professionals wrote about the nature of memory during the ensuing millennia.

Memory metaphors are verbal models of how memory works. The great philosopher Plato (428–347 BCE) described two metaphors to account for memory. First, he compared human memory to a wax tablet. As learning occurs, information gets written into memory, as writing would get pressed into a wax tablet. Although the technology is outdated, this metaphor allows memory to be encoded, retrieved, and altered if the wax gets altered. Second, Plato also compared human memory retrieval to a bird cage. We reach our hands

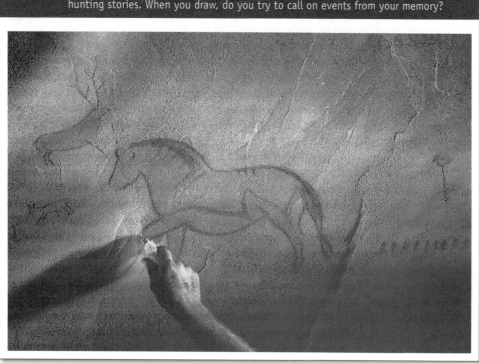

Figure 1.1   Cave painting. It is likely that some of prehistoric art reenacts memories of great hunting stories. When you draw, do you try to call on events from your memory?

into a cage to remove a bird, just as we reach into our memory to retrieve a particular event or item. Sometimes the memory may be difficult to retrieve, just as the bird may be difficult to catch. More recently, your author compared memory to a teenager's room. It may appear disorganized, but the person knows where to find things. Roediger (1980) provides an excellent review of memory metaphors throughout history.

Particularly influential in the later development of a scientific approach to memory were the British associationists. Philosophers such as John Locke and George Berkeley emphasized how the mind creates associations between one idea and another. Their philosophy shaped much of the original science on human memory. However, the scientific method was not applied to the study of memory until a mere 125 years ago when German psychologist Hermann Ebbinghaus (1885/1965) published a volume titled *Memory: A Contribution to Experimental Psychology.* So our history will start with him.

Hermann Ebbinghaus

Until Ebbinghaus published his book, experimental psychology had confined itself to exploring the nature of sensation and perception. Ebbinghaus was the first person to use scientific methods to study memory and, indeed, the first person to use the experimental method to address issues of higher cognition. Ebbinghaus is remembered today because he was the first memory psychologist but also because he established a number of principles of memory, which are still relevant today, both in terms of theory and application. Indeed, a number of his findings are directly applicable to the goals of memory improvement.

Most memory experiments today sample a large number of people. A memory experiment run on college students might test anywhere from 20 to 200 participants, depending on the nature of the experiment. Even studies today on special populations (infants, older adults, individuals with brain damage, etc.) will try to get at least several participants. But Ebbinghaus used only one test participant—himself. Of course, we now know that simply testing one person leads to questionable generalizations to others and is not necessarily a good way to conduct science. Luckily, although Ebbinghaus was a pioneering memory scientist, his own memory was rather ordinary. The experiments that he conducted on himself have since been tested on many other individuals, and what Ebbinghaus found in his 1885 study generalizes to other people.

Ebbinghaus taught himself lists of **nonsense syllables.** These nonsense syllables consisted of consonant-vowel-consonant trigrams, which lacked meaning in Ebbinghaus's native German. In English, nonsense syllable trigrams might be TOB or HIF. They are pronounceable as they follow the rules of English word formation, but they do not mean anything in everyday speech. Ebbinghaus created and studied more than 2,000 of these trigrams over the course of his experimental study. Ebbinghaus chose nonsense syllables over

> **Nonsense syllables**: meaningless phrases that can be given to participants to study that avoid the effect of meaning on memory (e.g., *wob*).

words because he did not want meaning to shade his results. He assumed that meaningful stimuli would be more memorable than nonmeaningful stimuli, and he wanted a set of material that did not differ with respect to meaning.

Ebbinghaus would prepare a list of nonsense syllables, perhaps a list of 20 items. Nonsense syllables were ordered into lists. Ebbinghaus constructed lists of nonsense syllables as short as 6 syllables and as long as 20. He would then study this list of items until he could free recall all of the nonsense syllables on the list. Later, he would test himself—to see how many trigrams he could remember from each list. Not surprisingly, he found it was easier to master the shorter lists than the longer ones. This is true of memory in general— shorter lists are easy to master than longer lists. I often wonder what his neighbors must have thought of this young eccentric, long-bearded philosophy professor endlessly reciting nonsense syllables in his garret in Berlin.

His next experiment was to vary the **retention interval** between when he studied a list and when he retrieved that list. A retention interval is the time between when an item is initially learned or encoded and when it is retrieved or remembered. In Ebbinghaus's case, he varied the time between his completion of mastering a particular list and when he tested himself again for that list. He found that the longer the retention interval, the more likely he was to forget items from that particular list. After a retention

> **Retention interval**: the amount of time that transpires between the learning of an event or material and when recall for that event or material occurs.

interval of just a few minutes, he might remember all of the syllables from a list. But if he waited a week, he might have forgotten a substantial number of items. This is another truism in memory—the longer the amount of time between learning and remembering, the more that will be forgotten.

Ebbinghaus measured this forgetting by looking at the **savings score.** Savings meant the reduction in the amount of time required to relearn the list. If it had initially taken 10 repetitions per item to learn the list, it might take only 5 repetitions to relearn the list. Even if he could no longer remember any items from a previously studied list, Ebbinghaus demonstrated savings; it took him less time to relearn the list than it had to learn the list initially. Although savings diminished with retention interval, no matter how long the retention interval was, there was always some evidence of savings. More recently, Bahrick (1984) showed that there are savings for high school Spanish and French even 25 years after the last time a student took those courses. The choice of measurement, namely savings, allowed Ebbinghaus to examine some other characteristics of memory as well.

> **Savings score:** the reduction in time required to relearn a previously mastered list.

Mnemonic Improvement Tip 1.1

Overlearning: If you need to master material, particular information without intrinsic meaning (e.g., the names of the parts of the brain), continue to study them even after you have mastered all of the material. The additional study will ensure that you remember the information for a longer amount of time. This may reduce the time you need to restudy information later in a cumulative final exam.

Ebbinghaus investigated the phenomenon of **overlearning.** Overlearning is defined as studying after material has been thoroughly learned. In some of his experiments, Ebbinghaus studied some lists until he mastered the list (that is, could recall all of the items), then put that list aside until it was time to test himself for that list. For other lists, he continued to study the list even after he scored 100% on retrieving it during practice. He even varied the amount of time that he studied a list after he had achieved 100% performance on that list. He found that if he overlearned a list, his forgetting curve was less steep. That is, if he studied past the point of mastery, his forgetting of that list was slowed considerably. Thus, if he had studied a list on Day 1 to 100% accuracy and then stopped, his performance on that list might be 50% the next day. However, if he overlearned the list on Day 1, his performance would be better, perhaps 75%, the next day. Thus, studying past the point of mastery led

> **Overlearning:** studying after material has been thoroughly learned.

to better long-term retention of that information. This principle has considerable generality and usefulness. If you want to really not forget something, keep studying it even after you have "gotten it."

Mnemonic Improvement Tip 1.2

Spacing effect: To maximize learning, study the same information at different times—don't "cram" all at once, but space your study over time both for individual items and for the entire set of material that you need to master. Remember an hour of study is not simply an hour of study. Spacing your study improves your study efficiency.

Massed practice: when all study occurs in one block of time.

Distributed practice: space your study out over time.

Spacing effect: more learning occurs when two study trials on the same information are spread out over time than when they occur successively.

Another variable studied by Ebbinghaus was the distribution of study time. For some lists, he studied the lists all at once until he mastered them (**massed practice**). For other lists, he distributed his study over a series of lists and a series of days (**distributed practice**). But he measured the amount of time and the number of rehearsals he needed to learn each list individually. Thus, even if he was distributing his practice over several lists on one day, he would record the time for each list separately. This allowed him later to compare how many rehearsals and how much time it took for him to master each list.

Ebbinghaus found that if he had studied a massed-practice or distributed-practice list the same amount of time (but under different schedules), there were different savings scores for the lists. The distributed lists demonstrated higher savings scores at the same level of practice. This is now called the **spacing effect,** or the advantage of distributed practice over massed practice. Even though equal amounts of time went into study, those lists that were spaced showed a higher savings score than those that were studied all at once. Morever, it took less total time to master a list that had been given distributed practice than one that received massed practice. This effect is also relevant today. Indeed, one of the crucial memory improvement hints given in the book is to take advantage of the spacing effect. Modern studies show that distributed practice can produce enormous boosts in the amount remembered per amount of time studied relative to massed practice. Indeed, if students can do only one thing to help their learning, it would be this one. And Ebbinghaus discovered it in the 19th century.

As you can see, Ebbinghaus's work is still important and relevant and provides the basis for the first two mnemonic improvement hints in the book. After finishing his studies on memory and writing his book on the topic, Ebbinghaus himself moved on to other interests and did not return to the study of memory. But for all those who followed, interested in the scientific pursuit of memory, Ebbinghaus laid the groundwork for memory science with solid methodology and important findings. For the complete text of Ebbinghaus's book, you can go to www.sagepub.com/schwartz.[2]

Mary Calkins

Shortly after the publication of Ebbinghaus's book, American psychologist Mary Calkins (who became the first woman president of the American Psychological Association) began her seminal study on the nature of associative learning, that is, how we pair new knowledge to existing knowledge. Calkins did this by examining **paired-associate learning.** Calkins (1894) had her participants study cue-target pairs of various types. In some cases, they were word-word pairs (e.g., *rain–cathedral*), but in others, they were syllables paired with word, syllables paired with pictures, and words paired with pictures. Calkins then gave the participant the first item from a pair and asked to recall the second item in the association. For example, if the participant had studied a word-word paired associate, such as *captain–carbon*, she presented the first word in a word-word pair (*captain*), and the participant would have to respond with the target, that is, the second word from the pair (*carbon*).

> **Paired-associate learning**: learning the association between two items, such as in language learning (e.g., learning the association between monkey–le singe).

Shortly after Calkins published her study, the behaviorist tradition would become dominant in American psychology. The behaviorists did not think memory was an appropriate topic of research, as memory is not a directly observable behavior. However, Calkins's methodology was easily carried over into this way of thinking, and thus learning research in this time period heavily relied on her methodology. Calkins's stimulus-response approach to memory preserved the importance of memory research in this period.

Calkins also made some significant discoveries concerning the nature of human memory. First, Calkins found that the greater the overlap between meaning in cue-target pairs, the easier it was for the participant to learn and retain the information. Prior familiarity with the cue-target pairs also helped learning. Thus, for example, it was easier for her American students to learn English-French word pairs than it was to learn English-Turkish word pairs because the French words were more familiar to her students, even if they did not know the meanings prior to the study (see Bower, 2000). Second, in her investigations of short-term memory, Calkins also discovered the **recency effect**—that is, in immediate recall (that is, when the test occurs right after learning), items that were most recently learned are remembered better than items from the middle of the list. For more on the life of Mary Calkins, go to www.sagepub.com/schwartz.[3]

> **Recency effect**: the observation that memory is usually superior for items at the end of a serial position curve; thought to be caused by the maintenance of those items in working memory.

Behaviorism

In the early 20th century, **behaviorism** was the predominant approach in American experimental psychology. Behaviorism took a somewhat paradoxical approach to learning and memory. Learning was a suitable topic of research because it was directly observable. However, memory, or the internal contents or stored information, is not directly observable. Thus, behaviorism focused on learning but deliberately ignored memory. Starting with the work of J. B. Watson (1913), behaviorism stipulated that psychology should focus only on observable verifiable behavior. Behaviorism emphasized the nature of environmental stimuli and their influence on the observable behavior of humans and other animals. Behaviorists did not consider the concepts of thought, mind, images, emotions, and memory to be the appropriate issues of psychological science because they could not be directly observed.

> **Behaviorism**: a school of psychology that focused on only the relation of environmental inputs and the observable behavior of organisms, including human beings.

Although contemporary cognitive psychologists no longer agree with these assumptions, behaviorism made important contributions to the study of learning, particularly in the areas of **classical conditioning** and **operant conditioning.** Classical conditioning occurs when a neutral stimulus is continually presented along with a stimulus that has a particular association. After enough repetition, the neutral stimulus acquires some of the characteristics of the other stimulus. For example, in many people, riding a roller coaster may trigger a nauseous response. Initially, the smell of diesel may be a neutral stimulus. But if a person rides enough diesel-powered rides, he or she may get nauseous at the smell of diesel alone, even if there is no dizzying ride in sight. Operant conditioning means that an animal learns to respond in a particular way because whenever the animal does respond in that way, it receives reinforcement or avoids punishment. Thus, a young child who makes requests without using the word *please* may have a request refused, but when he or she makes requests using the word *please,* the requests are granted. Both the punishment and the reinforcement will increase the likelihood that the child will utter "please" when making a request.

> **Classical conditioning**: a situation in which a relation exists between a stimulus (e.g., a ringing bell) and an outcome (e.g., getting food); the organism demonstrates behavior or response (e.g., salivating) that shows that the organism has learned the association between the stimulus and the outcome.
>
> **Operant conditioning**: organisms learn to emit responses or behaviors (e.g., pressing a bar), in response to a stimulus, to achieve desirable outcomes (e.g., getting food) or avoiding undesirable outcomes (e.g., getting electric shock).

These learning methods appear to be widespread across animals from the most simple to the most complex, including humans. Because of its commonness across animals, behaviorists often speculated that all learning was based on classical and operant conditioning. Indeed, with respect to human verbal memory, an attempt was made to understand memory in terms of these principles; it was labeled S-R psychology for stimulus-response (Bowers, 2000). By the 1960s, these S-R psychologists studying verbal learning started switching to cognitive models of memory. There were simply too many phenomena for which classical and operant conditioning were not enough to explain and that required thinking about internal memory states to predict.

Frederic Bartlett

Frederic Bartlett was a British psychologist who rejected the approach of behaviorism as well as the methodology of Ebbinghaus. In 1932, he published an important book titled *Remembering: A Study in Experimental and Social Psychology* (Bartlett, 1932). In contrast to Ebbinghaus, who emphasized "pure" memory uninfluenced by meaning, Bartlett considered the issue of meaning to be inseparable from the nature of human memory. As such, his studies focused on meaningful stimuli, like stories, and how expectations could subtly distort people's memory of these stories. For example, he had Cambridge University students read Native American folktales. When the English students retold the stories, they were biased in their retelling, in ways that revealed their particular culture. Inexplicable and magical aspects of the story tended to be replaced by more rational versions of the stories. Bartlett greatly influenced the emphasis on real-world memory and everyday issues that grew in memory research in the 1980s and continue today (Cohen, 1996). Bartlett's influence has also been felt in the recent interest in memory accuracy and its converse, false memory. For more information on Sir Frederic Bartlett, go to www.sagepub.com/schwartz.[4]

Endel Tulving

Tulving is a Canadian memory researcher, born in Estonia, who is now in his 80s and still very active in memory research (see Figure 1.2). Tulving served as an army translator for the U.S. and Canadian armies during World War II in Germany before immigrating to Canada. There, he attended the University of Toronto, and later, as a graduate student, he went to Harvard University. Eventually, he became a distinguished professor of psychology at the University of Toronto. Perhaps no scientist ever has made more meaningful and varied contributions to the science of memory than has Dr. Tulving. He has made innumerable contributions to the scientific study of memory over the years, starting in the 1950s and continuing to the present. Taking first the perspective of cognitive psychology and later cognitive neuroscience, Tulving has introduced to the field many of the theoretical ideas

Figure 1.2   Endel Tulving.

that all memory researchers now rely on. He is credited with developing the ideas behind encoding specificity (the idea that retrieval is better when it occurs in situations that match the conditions under which the memory was encoded). He is credited with the idea that long-term memory involves multiple systems. When he introduced the idea of multiple systems, it was roundly criticized. But today, it is universally accepted, in one form or another, by memory scientists. Tulving (1972) initially labeled these systems episodic memory (memory for personal events from one's life) and semantic memory (memory for facts). The theory has evolved considerably over the years, but the semantic/episodic distinction has stood the test of many empirical studies (Tulving, 1983, 1993, 2002). Both episodic memory and semantic memory are considered long-term memory systems, but they differ in the content of their representations, that is, what they are about. He also pioneered the study of the experience of memory, from how memories "feel" to us to the ways in which we monitor and control our own memory. In recent years, he has also become a leader in the field of cognitive neuroscience, focusing on the neural underpinnings of human memory. In this area, he has been instrumental in demonstrating the areas of the brain associated with remembering our personal past and exploring differences between the left and the right hemispheres. For more on the life of Endel Tulving, go to www.sagepub.com/schwartz.[5]

Cognitive Psychology

By the 1960s, memory scientists started finding the behaviorist models unable to explain many of the phenomena that they were starting to study, including why different variables affected short-term and long-term memory (L. R. Peterson & Peterson, 1959). Thus, memory scientists started switching from S-R models to models emanating from the new science of **cognitive psychology,** which emphasized the concepts of mind and internal representation of memories (Neisser, 1967). This change involved

> **Cognitive psychology**: an approach to psychology that emphasizes hidden mental processes.

two big features. First, cognitive psychology reopened the "black box" and allowed mental processes and "mind" to become appropriate topics of study. Second, it postulated that mental states are causal, not simply the by-products of behavior. Cognitive psychology proved useful in addressing issues of language, attention, and decision making, as well as memory, and continues to be a dominant force in psychological theory. For example, behaviorists were reluctant to address the issue of representation (or storage) in memory because it is a hidden process not directly observable through behavior. Theory in cognitive psychology has led to a variety of ways of addressing the issue of representation and studying it through careful experimentation.

At the core of theory in early cognitive psychology was the idea of the flow of information. For this reason, it often relied on an analogy to the computer in which information also moves and is transformed over time. For example, the study of encoding became the study of how information is transferred from short-term memory to long-term memory and how this process unfolds over time. The idea of the flow of information remains controversial. Many modern cognitive psychologists disagree with this view because the brain is a remarkably parallel device, doing many things at once as opposed to doing one thing at a time, albeit very fast.

Cognitive Neuroscience

Cognitive neuroscience is the study of the role of the brain in producing cognition. Traditionally, the correlation between brain processes and cognitive processes was studied by examining the cognitive deficits seen in patients with brain damage. Most recently, advances in neuroimaging techniques have led to tremendous gains in our knowledge of the biological processes involved in memory. Neuroimaging allows us to observe the intact living brain as it learns, remembers, communicates, and contemplates. The past 10 years of neuroimaging research have provided great progress in understanding both the workings of the brain and why certain memory processes are the way they are.

> **Cognitive neuroscience:** the study of the role of the brain in producing cognition.

For example, Martin Conway and his colleagues (Conway, Pleydell-Pearce, Whitecross, & Sharpe, 2003) conducted a study in which they examined the relation between regions within the brain and retrieval of autobiographical events. Think about an event that happened recently to you, such as visiting the zoo. What areas of the brain become active as you contemplate your memory of the trip? This is what Conway and his colleagues were interested in.

Conway et al. (2003) studied this phenomenon by asking people to remember particular events while imaging equipment was monitoring their brains. To be more specific, the participants thought of the first personal memory that a particular word evoked. The cue word was provided to the participants by the researchers. Thus, in response to the word *rock,* an individual might remember his recent visit to the local rock-climbing gym and remember his satisfaction at completing a particularly difficult route. In response to the word *church,* a participant might remember her sister's wedding ceremony and how beautiful the church looked that day. Using a neuroimaging technique called EEG (electroencephalography), Conway et al. followed the path of memory retrieval as it played out in the brain.

Conway et al. (2003) found that immediately after the presentation of the word, areas in the prefrontal cortex (the very front of the brain, just under your forehead) of the brain became active. Conway et al. interpreted this to indicate that this was the brain going into "retrieval mode." At just about the point people indicated that they "had the memory," areas in the occipital lobe (in the back of the brain; associated with vision) became active. That is, the visual imagery associated with a particular memory was apparent in the EEG patterns. At the same time, areas in the hippocampus (associated with memory encoding and retrieval) also became active. Thus, Conway et al. were able to map out both in time and space the pattern of retrieval in the brain and correlate it with how people remember autobiographical events (see Figure 1.3). Moreover, Conway et al. also compared real memories with imagined events. The imagined events never occurred, but the participants were asked to produce plausible imagined events. The imagined events had much more activation in the prefrontal lobes than did the real events and less activation in visual areas of the brain. Thus, it may even be possible to distinguish real and false memories from their signature patterns during neuroimaging. The integration of cognitive memory theory with neuroscience is revolutionizing the way we think about memory.

Figure 1.3 EEG graph.

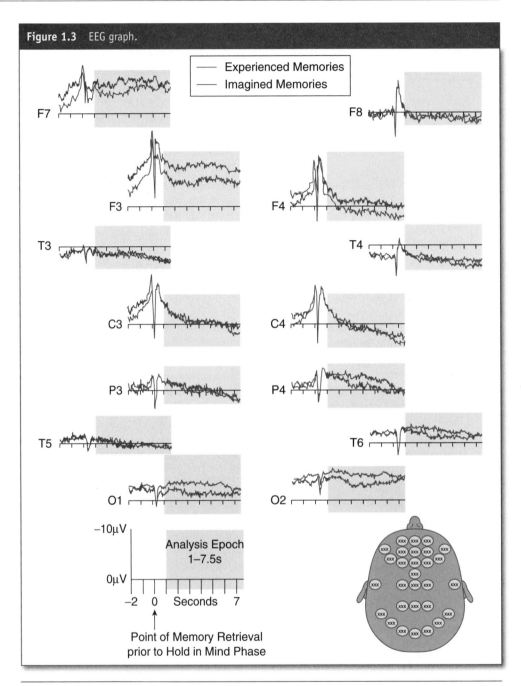

Slow potentials observed when experienced and imagined memories were held in mind over a 7.5s period. Electrolytes are displayed. Note that experienced memories are associated with greater posterior activity.

SOURCE: Conway et al. (2003).

METHODS OF STUDYING MEMORY

We all feel familiar with the workings of our own memories. One individual might report that she never remembers her family member's birthdays. Another individual might tell you that he is not good at remembering faces. Yet, a third will tell you that she has "photographic memory" and can simply look at a page on a textbook and recite all the information on it from memory (this is typically illusory, but more on that in Chapter 5). As memory scientists, however, we cannot simply rely on people's stories and anecdotes. Instead, we conduct experiments, which measure memory abilities under different conditions. We test to see if all those who claim to have photographic memories really can remember what is on a page of text after one or more casual glances. We test to see how good people are, in general, at recognizing faces and then can objectively tell your friend whether he is indeed above or below the average in remembering faces. In short, to study memory objectively, we must apply the scientific method. By applying the scientific method, we can make generalizations about how memory works in general in human beings and also get reasonable approximations to the extent to which there are measurable individual differences. The key to this enterprise is the experiment.

> **Experiment**: set of observations that occur under controlled circumstances determined by the experimenter.

An **experiment** is set of observations that occur under controlled circumstances determined by the experimenter. The controlled circumstances mean that the researcher strives to maintain a situation in which he or she has control over what a subject sees, hears, or can potentially remember. The control allows the researcher to focus on one select issue (say, distributed practice vs. massed practice) at a time. By keeping other conditions constant, the researcher can determine if distributed practice is truly better than massed practice.

The experimenter does this by looking at the effects of independent variables on dependent variables. **Independent variables** are the factors that the experimenter manipulates among different conditions. For example, to use a simplified hypothetical example, if an experimenter is interested in whether Starbuck's coffee can improve memory, he or she can manipulate the amount of coffee given to different groups of participants. Thus, the amount of coffee consumed is the independent variable. Each group receives the same list of words to remember. Thus, one group of people might not get any coffee in advance of studying the list of words. This group is called the control group. A second group might get one cup of coffee in advance of studying the list of words. And a third group might get four cups of coffee in advance of

> **Independent variable**: independent variables are the factors that the experimenter manipulates among different conditions.

studying the list of words. The second and third groups are considered the experimental groups and are compared to each other and to the control group. Another way of saying this is that there is an independent variable (amount of coffee consumed) with three levels (zero cups, one cup, and four cups). Some time after study, we then test the people to see how much they can remember from the list.

> **Dependent variable**: dependent variables are the observations that we measure or record in response to the independent variable.

Dependent variables are the observations that we measure or record in response to the independent variable. In the Starbuck's experiment, the dependent variable is the amount of words recalled from the study list by the participants. As memory researchers, we are interested in the effects of the independent variable (amount of coffee consumed) on the dependent variable (amount of words remembered). So, we measure the amount of words remembered for each participant in each condition. We can then statistically compare the outcomes in each condition. The statistical comparison can then inform us if Starbuck's coffee does help us remember words on lists and if too much coffee (i.e., four cups) just makes us too jittery to concentrate on anything (see Figure 1.4). In memory science, we will see a few dependent variables used extensively in the work described in this book. These dependent variables include recall, recognition, and a variety of judgments.

A number of features must be included in an experiment to make it a good scientific study. First, **random assignment** means that any particular person is equally likely to be assigned to any of the conditions. Usually, a random-number generator assigns any individual to one of the possible groups. In the coffee experiment, you would not want to put the people who you know are good at memory in the four-cup condition, as their propensity to remember well would bias the results. You want a representative sample of people

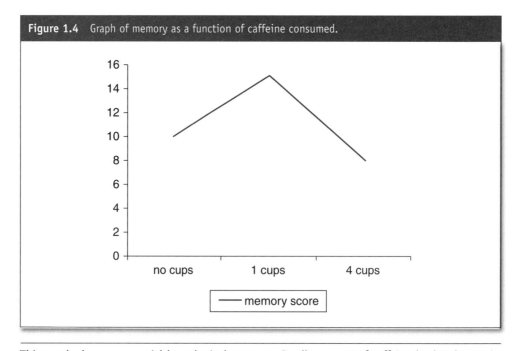

Figure 1.4   Graph of memory as a function of caffeine consumed.

This graph shows a potential hypothetical outcome. Small amounts of caffeine lead to boosts in memory, but a larger amount hurts memory. In fact, research shows that caffeine can hurt memory even at smaller amounts. The y-axis is the number of words recalled.

Random assignment: any particular participant is equally likely to be assigned to any of the conditions.

Double-blind procedure: neither the tester nor the participant should know what condition that participant is in.

who are good and poor at memory in each condition. The best way to do this is to assign each person randomly to one of the conditions. Second, the participants should not know what you expect to find in the experiment until after the experiment is over. Even the most honest participants may slightly alter their concentration or attention to satisfy (or perhaps disrupt the experiment) if they know what the experimenter wants to find. Third, as best as possible, the person actually running the experiment should not know what condition each participant is in. So the person actually administering the memory test should not know if an individual had zero, one, or four cups of coffee, as this too might introduce subtle bias into the experiment. These last two concerns make up what is called a **double-blind procedure,** that is, neither the tester nor the participant should know what condition that person is in.

When these conditions are met, our experiment will test only the independent variable or variables that we are interested in studying. We can be sure that other extraneous factors have been controlled for by randomizing the assignment of participant to condition and by keeping both the participants and the experimenters unaware of what condition they are in. This allows us to be confident that any differences we get between conditions are a function of the independent variable. Thus, we can safely conclude what are the effects of caffeine on the learning of the list.

In memory research, it is also crucial to have good dependent measures. Because we are interested in memory, we need good tests of memory. These tests are the dependent variables in the experiments on memory. Thus, scientists have developed a large set of memory measures so that researchers can choose the right dependent variable for their experiment. The next section will review these common measures, which we will see throughout the book.

MEMORY MEASURES

Recall

Recall means that a person must generate the target memory. That is, **recall** is the producing of a memory or a part of one that was not already presented. For recall, a person

Recall: a person must generate the target memory based on cues, but without seeing or hearing the actual target memory.

must speak or write the remembered items without seeing them in advance. In some cases, a recall test might involve reenacting a physical event as well. Recall can be free recall, in which you are given a global cue to remember a particular memory or set of memories. "Tell me about your childhood," "what were all the words on the study list," "write two paragraphs about the fall of the Peloponnesian war," and "describe everything you saw at the scene of the crime" are examples of free recall. The cue "tell me about your childhood" provides no information about one's childhood.

Thus, all the information recalled is freely selected by the rememberer. In memory experiments, free recall is more likely to be of the "write down all the words from the list" variety. Cued recall occurs when you are given a specific cue to remember a specific memory. Cued recall includes questions like, "What is your middle initial?" "What word went with *pasture* on the study list?" "In what year was the Greek philosopher Aristotle born?" and "What color car were the bank robbers driving?"

Cued recall is also a common technique in memory experiments. It is useful in looking at association in memory, that is, the connection between two ideas of two memories. Thus, for a student learning French, a person must associate the English and the French words, as in *dog–chien*. In a cued recall test, you might receive the English word (*dog*) and be asked to recall the French word.

Recognition

Recognition means matching one's memory to a presented choice. Rather than having to produce the item itself, the person must match what is stored in the memory with what he

> **Recognition**: person must identify the target memory from presented item(s).

or she sees in the list. Recognition can be old/new recognition, in which the person has to decide if an item was on the study list. If the participants saw the word *pasture* on the study list, they would need to indicate that by saying "old," whereas if the participants had not seen the word, they would indicate that by saying "new." Recognition can also be forced-choice recognition, also known as multiple-choice recognition. In this case, a question is asked with a series of possible answers. Using the earlier examples, we could ask a recognition question such as, "In what year was Aristotle born? (a) 502 CE, (b) 5 CE, (c) 384 BCE, (d) 672 BCE. (The correct answer is 384 BCE.) A police lineup is technically a recognition test as the witness can see all of the possible suspects. Most police lineups, however, are not forced. The witness can say "not there" if none of the suspects match his or her memory. The key difference between recall and recognition is that in recall, the person must generate the memory, whereas in recognition, the person must match what is in his or her memory with what he or she sees in front.

Implicit Memory Tests

Implicit memory tests are tests that draw on the nonconscious aspects of memory. That is, memory is tested without the person being conscious of the fact that his or her memory is being assessed. In some cases, the participant may not have conscious access to the memory at all, although this is not required for the task to be classified as implicit.

To give an example, something as simple as a spelling test can be used as an implicit memory test. Eich (1984) presented two streams of stimuli, one to each ear of his participants. The participants were directed to attend to one of the two stimuli and to ignore the other. Decades of research on attention demonstrate that people are very good at focusing on one message and ignoring the other. In Eich's study, in a test of free recall, the participants remembered very little to nothing at all of the unattended stimuli. However, Eich found that even though they could not consciously recall the items presented to the unattended ear, there must have been some memory of them because it biased their spelling of homophones (words with different meanings that sound the same but are spelled differently). Some of the items presented to the ignored ear were sentences like, "The men took photographs of the grizzly bear," and "The fencers flashed their swords of cold steel at each other." During the spelling test, participants were read aloud words to spell, including *bare/bear* and *steal/steel*. No instructions were given as to how to choose which of two spellings they should use. Participants who had heard these words were more likely to spell them according to the given context, even though they could not consciously remember having heard the words. That is, relative to control participants who had not heard the words being presented to the unattended ear, those who had were more likely to spell *steal/steel* as *steel* and *bear/bare* as *bear*. This increase (or decrease) in performance based on some prior processing is known as *priming* (see Jacoby, 1991).

> **Implicit memory tests**: tests that draw on the nonconscious aspects of memory.

Source Judgments

Source judgments are our attributions of where or from whom we learned something. Thus, I know that the first European settlers introduced rabbits to Australia. However, I cannot recall who told me this, where I read it, or when or where I may have seen this on a nature television show. In many cases, remembering the source is vital to your appraisal of the memory. We must remember where or from whom we heard the information. Consider a situation in which, while gossiping with a friend, you mention that the actress Cameron Diaz is having a baby. Your friend asks, "Where did you hear that?" In such gossip, the source of a memory is important. If you read it in a tabloid newspaper, such as the *National Enquirer,* it may be of dubious validity. However, if you saw in on CNN, it is more likely to be true (but no less any of your business). Source judgments are decisions researchers ask people to make regarding from whom they heard information (Foley & Foley, 2007). In some experiments, for example, two individuals, one male and one female, may read a list of words. The two readers alternate, each one reading one word, and then the other one reads a word. Later, participants must recall not only the words but also which speaker said which one. Related to source judgments is the concept of **reality monitoring.** Reality monitoring refers to our ability to distinguish whether our memory is of a real or an imagined event. Each of us may have memories of fantasies (being elected president, for example), but it is important to recognize these memories as being internally generated rather than based on real events.

> **Source judgments**: our attributions of where or from whom we learned something.
>
> **Reality monitoring**: refers to our ability to distinguish whether our memory is of a real event or of an imagined event.

Metamemory Judgments

Metamemory means our knowledge and awareness of our own memory processes. Metamemory judgments are the ratings or decisions we make concerning what we know about our memory processes. Metamemory includes our knowledge of our own strengths and weaknesses about our memory (when we say, "I am good at remembering faces," we are making a metamemory statement). A tip-of-the-tongue state is also a metamemory judgment; we are confident that an unrecalled word will be recalled (Schwartz, 2002). Usually, in memory experiments, the metamemory judgments refer to whether we think we can learn or retrieve a particular item. Judgments of learning are predictions of the likelihood of remembering an item that we make as we study the items. We can then ascertain if these judgments are accurate by later correlating them with actual memory performance. Other metamemory judgments include ease-of-learning judgments, confidence judgments, feelings of knowing, and tip-of-the-tongue states. Metamemory will be covered extensively in Chapter 9.

> **Metamemory**: our knowledge and awareness of our own memory processes.

These five categories (recall, recognition, implicit memory tests, source judgments, metamemory judgments) make up the vast majority of measures that memory scientists use to study human memory. Almost every behavioral experiment that we will cover in this book makes use of one of these five techniques. So make sure you know what they are and what they mean now! The next three methods are drawn from the neuroscience/neuroimaging perspective on memory research.

Neuropsychology

The study of patients with brain damage has a long and distinguished history (Feinberg & Farah, 2000). Indeed, ancient Egyptian doctors noted that blows to specific areas of the head resulted in characteristic damage. Nowadays, the goal of neuropsychological research is to correlate the specific area of brain damage with the cognitive or behavioral deficits seen in a particular patient. You can see the change in language behaviors based on damage to an area of the brain called Broca's area (go to www.sagepub.com/schwartz).[6] For many patients, the damage is too wide, too diffuse, or too minor to be of interest to neuropsychologists. But if the damage is relatively restricted, whatever behavioral changes occur in a patient can be linked to that area of the brain. For example, a patient who has damage to the hippocampus (a small part of the brain in the limbic system) will show deficits in learning new information but not in retrieving information that is already well learned. Thus, we can conclude that the hippocampus is involved in the encoding of new events. Another patient might have damage restricted to areas of the right frontal lobe, which will result in difficulties in remembering the source of information. In this way, by probing the nature of brain damage, we can develop a model of the relation between particular brain region and memory function. Unfortunately, strokes, tumors, auto accidents, and war injuries will be with us for the foreseeable future.

> **Neuropsychology**: the study of patients with brain damage.

Thus, **neuropsychology** will continue to have a role in both learning from these patients and, it is hoped, learning to help these people recover.

Animal Models

Many animals, including most mammals and birds, have complex brains. Many of the structures involved in memory are common across these animals. For example, the hippocampus is involved in memory in both mammals and birds, even though their common ancestor lived long before the dinosaurs went extinct. Animals can be used in simple behavioral experiment because, in general, their memory systems are less complex than ours. In the past, animals, particularly rats and rhesus monkeys, have been used for single-cell recording. In single-cell recording, electrodes are inserted into individual neurons in the animal's brain. Then researchers can determine what kinds of stimuli elicit responses in that cell. Animals have also been used for lesion studies, in which parts of their brain are surgically removed. Because both of these methods involve invasive and potentially painful procedures, they are now used only for medically critical experiments.

Neuroimaging

Neuroimaging techniques are advanced technologies that allow us to visually examine intact human brains. This area has seen marked growth in recent years and will be one of the issues that we focus on in Chapter 2. These techniques allow scientists to correlate behavior with function in the brain in normal active brains. Indeed, modern neuroimaging techniques allow us to trace the flow of information in the brain as individual people think. As of yet, they cannot tell what a person is thinking, but when a person reports what he or she is thinking, there seem to be reliable correlations between that person's reports and particular parts of the brain. Neuroimaging techniques have been used to investigate memory, perception, language, and emotion. Two goals of neuroimaging are to determine where things happen in the brain. For this, neuroimaging can develop detailed spatial maps of the brain and which areas are active during which cognitive task. Another goal is to determine the flow of activity in the brain over time. For this, neuroimaging must be able to take quick successive pictures of the brain in order to determine the time course of processes in the brain. It is important to note that no serious scholar of memory would argue that the brain is not responsible for cognitive processes. Therefore, for some cognitive psychologists, knowing where in the brain particular processes operate is less interesting than why they operate the way they do.

> **Neuroimaging:** refers to a set of techniques that allows researchers to make detailed maps of the human brain and assign functions to particular regions in the brain.

There are three major techniques used in neuroimaging today.

1. **EEG (electroencephalography):** measures the electrical output of the brain. Electrodes are placed on various places on the scalp, sometimes as many as 64 electrodes. Each electrode can then pick up a signal from the total electrical output. However, areas

EEG (electroencephalography): using electrodes to measure the electrical output of the brain.

of the brain that are active will generate more electric output in total than those that do not. Thus, we can see where things are happening in the brain by comparing these outputs. Because the electrodes pick up a continuous electric signal, measurements can be made very quickly, in fact, on the order of every millisecond (1/1,000th of a second). Therefore, EEG provides an excellent way of measuring the changes that happen in the brain as a person engages in a memory task.

2. **PET (positron emission tomography).** In PET, a small radioactive tracer is injected into a person's bloodstream. The radioactive tracer travels in the bloodstream to all areas of the body, including the brain. Areas of the brain that are active will require more blood than areas that are resting. This is the fundamental assumption of neuroimaging—that blood flows to areas of the brain that are active. Therefore, more radioactivity will be drawn to active regions of the brain. A complex X-ray-like camera measures the emission of the radioactivity and determines where it is coming from in the brain. From this, researchers can determine what areas of the brain are active during different memory processes. PET is very good at making spatial maps of the brain and pinpointing where in the brain activity is taking place. However, successive images can be made only every 30 seconds, so it is not helpful in determining the flow of information in the brain.

PET (positron emission tomography): radioactive chemicals are placed in the blood, which allows scientists to obtain a three-dimensional image of the intact brain.

3. MRI and **fMRI** (magnetic resonance imagery and functional magnetic resonance imagery). In this technique, people are put in large magnetic fields, which align the molecules in the brain. Then as blood flows into areas of the brain, the molecules' organization is disrupted. A specialized camera detects this disruption. In the fMRI technique, it is the oxygen molecules in the blood that are traced. This allows the technique to measure which areas of the brain are more active during any particular cognitive task. Because fMRI can take another picture every half of a second, the technique permits the researcher to determine both where in the brain a particular memory function is taking place and how it changes over time. Thus, fMRI has the advantage of both EEG and PET, although it is still slower than EEG. It is also safer than PET because no radioactivity is involved. Its only current drawback is its expense and that you cannot place electronic devices such as computers into the magnetic field without totally destroying the electronic device. For a video clip showing fMRI, go to www.sagepub.com/schwartz.[7]

fMRI: magnetic fields create a three-dimensional image of the brain, which can capture both the structure and function of the brain.

Throughout the book, we will be discussing research generated from each of these three neuroimaging techniques. The fMRI technique is currently the state of the art in neuroimaging. It is providing insight into the workings of the brain not just for memory but almost all areas of human thinking and emotion (see Figure 1.5).

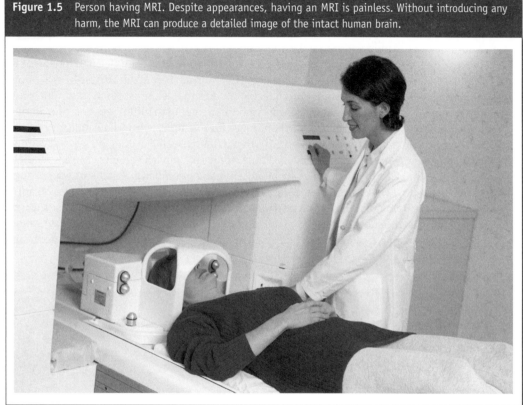

Figure 1.5 Person having MRI. Despite appearances, having an MRI is painless. Without introducing any harm, the MRI can produce a detailed image of the intact human brain.

MEMORY IMPROVEMENT

One of the themes of this book is that you can use the principles advanced in this textbook to improve your own ability to learn and remember. Memory science has found a great many ways in which learning efficiency can be improved and memory can be enhanced. However, the first point to be made is that there is no memory magic bullet— no one sentence that I can write that will transform you, the reader, into a mnemonic marvel. Nor is there a pill that your doctor can prescribe that will radically improve your ability to remember information. To state bluntly a point that will be repeated throughout the book: Memory improvement is hard work! Yet, the hard work can be directed in thoughtful and informed ways in order to be more efficient. Memory science knows a lot about what makes for good learning and good remembering. The informed student can apply much of this information to his or her schoolwork or other aspects of daily life that require remembering.

When discussing memory improvement, it is important to begin the discussion of types of memory. Chapter 3 will outline the current theories concerning how many different memory systems human beings actually have. Although there is some debate as to exactly where to draw the lines between one memory system and another, it is now abundantly clear that not all memory is alike. Indeed, the research suggests that there are a number of systems of memory with different neurological underpinnings (Schacter, 2007). For example, the learning and remembering required to play the violin is very different from the learning and remembering required to master the rules of spoken German (or any other language). The rules that govern remembering the individual events from our lives are quite different from the learning and remembering of facts that we must learn in school. Thus, the principles that govern memory improvement are going to differ between one domain and another. Use of visual imagery mnemonics, for example, is useful for mastering new-language vocabulary (Thomas & Wang, 1996) but of no use in learning to play a new musical instrument. Similarly, using linkword mnemonics to help learn name-face associations is useful, but linkword mnemonics will not help you remember the name of your kindergarten teacher when somebody asks you. Having said that, a number of principles do apply across a wide domain of memory systems. The spacing effect, described in the section on Ebbinghaus, is one such example. Spaced rehearsal is helpful for remembering facts about the world, learning a skilled task such as typing or playing a musical instrument, and remembering landmark events from one's life.

Mnemonic Improvement Tip 1.3

There is no magic bullet for memory. Good memory requires hard work.

While students are usually chiefly concerned about ways in which they can improve their ability to remember raw information, older adults are often more concerned about the failings of another aspect of memory, known as prospective memory. **Prospective memory** is memory for the things we need to do in the future. This is not some weird science fiction–type thing. It refers to the fact that we need to remember our future plans. Parents have to remember to pick up their kids at school, employees have to remember to pick up the mail from the mailroom, chefs have to remember exactly what time to take the soufflé out of the oven, and husbands must remember to put the garbage out on the curb. And perhaps most important, individuals requiring medication must remember to take their medication at the prescribed time of day. In other words, prospective memory is about remembering intentions (McDaniel & Einstein, 2007). McDaniel and Einstein made a series of recommendations as to how we can improve our prospective memory. However, most of their recommendations involve the extensive use of external cues. That is, if you need to remember to pick up your kids at school (perhaps normally your spouse's task), you can carry a photograph around of them. Place it (in your pocket) where you will keep coming across it. The constant reminder will help you to remember your intention even if you are a chef and busy with your soufflé. Similarly, if you have

Prospective memory: memory for the things we need to do in the future.

to remember to return a particular book to the library, place it by your car keys the night before. When you look for your keys to drive to school, you will also find the book you need to return to the library. Once you are in your car, place it in the passenger seat, so you see it and won't drive to school or work without stopping at the library (for further information on this topic, go to www.sagepub.com/schwartz).[8]

We can improve our memories. In this book, I hope to offer a number of ways in which memory science has shown that memories can be improved. However, I will reiterate the following point: Memory improvement is an active process. It doesn't just happen; we have to work to make it happen. Indeed, both of the recommendations made in this chapter require active memory improvement. We must think about how to distribute our learning; it requires a little planning. And taking advantage of external cues also requires us to work a little. We have to think about our routines and use them to our advantage. Last, in this chapter, I will present four themes, which will be returned to repeatedly throughout the book. Each theme represents an important concept in memory theory and practice (for further information on this topic, go to www.sagepub.com/schwartz).[9]

Mnemonic Improvement Tip 1.4

External cues can help. But external cues require action. You must place them in your environment.

THEMES FOR THE BOOK

1. Learning and remembering are active processes. Human beings are learning animals. Learning is what we do best. Human beings can learn to knit sweaters in intricate patterns, and we can learn to negotiate small kayaks down ferocious whitewater that would drown the untrained person. Some human beings memorize the Bible or the Koran, whereas others can tell you the complex ingredients to a crème brûlée. But little if any of this learning happens passively. The person who learns and remembers best is the person who seeks out opportunities to learn, who rehearses the information, and who teaches to others. Throughout this book, I will make note of how the active learner who employs strategies, relates information to himself or herself, organizes information, and employs metamemory strategies winds up learning a lot more than those who do not.

2. Learning and remembering have a biological/neurological basis. Our brains are our biological organ of learning and remembering. In the past two decades, with the advent of neuroimaging, there has been tremendous growth in our understanding of how the brain works, particularly with respect to learning and memory. Our understanding of behavior, memory, and cognition has guided much of this neuroscience research, and in turn, neuroscience is now guiding the questions we ask of our memory systems. Chapter 2 will provide an overview of what we know of the neurological basis of memory,

and then each chapter will discuss the specifics of a particular aspect of memory and how it plays out in the brain.

3. Memory has multiple components, which act in different ways. We have many different kinds of memory. We have memory for the individual events from our lives, for the words of our native languages, for the geography of our home and surrounding areas, and for the music we love. We hold some memories, like the phone number of the pizza place as we dial it, for very short periods of time, whereas other memories such as an individual's wedding ceremony or the time you hit a home run in little league may last a lifetime. We have several different neurocognitive systems to handle these different kinds of memory. Chapters 3 and 4 will explore the nature of these memory systems.

4. Learning and remembering can be improved. By applying many of the facts, theories, and ideas of memory science, we can improve our ability to learn and remember. Many of these are ways of managing our existing resources and efficiently using our time. We can apply a number of principles consciously to both our efforts to learn information and our efforts to remember information. In each chapter, there will be memory hints, which are based on the research discussed. Each hint will provide a method whereby you can improve some aspect of learning and remembering. And then, in Chapter 9, an entire chapter will be spent on the topic.

SUMMARY

Understanding the science and practice of memory is the overarching goal of this book. Memory is an essential component of our cognitive systems and indeed our sense of who we are. This book addresses the science of memory, what we know from both the point of view of cognitive psychology and from cognitive neuroscience. In both domains, established methodologies allow us to analyze and think about memory research. From this research, we can draw practical applications that will allow each of us to improve and make more efficient our own learning. We also reviewed the history of the field, starting with the seminal work of Hermann Ebbinghaus. Ebbinghaus established a number of key findings, including aspects that benefit memory performance. Following Ebbinghaus, Mary Calkins, Frederic Bartlett, and Endel Tulving defined the future of memory along with bigger schools of thought, such as behaviorism, cognitive psychology, and cognitive neuroscience. This chapter also reviewed the fundamental techniques used to study memory from behavioral measures such as recall, recognition, and metamemory judgments to neuroscience methods, such as fMRI and PET. Four overarching themes were introduced, focusing on the active nature of learning and remembering, its status as a biological process, that memory is composed of multiple systems, and that we can use principles of learning and remembering to improve our individual ability to learn and remember. With this in mind, we will begin our exploration of the fascinating world of human memory.

KEY TERMS

Empirical evidence

Nonsense syllables

Retention interval

Savings score

Overlearning

Spacing effect

Massed practice

Distributive practice

Paired-associate learning

Recency effect

Behaviorism

Classical conditioning

Operant conditioning

Cognitive psychology

Cognitive neuroscience

Experiment

Independent variable

Dependent variable

Random assignment

Double-blind procedure

Recall

Recognition

Implicit memory tests

Source judgments

Reality monitoring

Metamemory

Neuroimaging

Neuropsychology

EEG (electroencephalography)

PET (positron emission tomography)

fMRI

Prospective memory

REVIEW QUESTIONS

1. Who was Hermann Ebbinghaus, and what were his important contributions to memory science?

2. How can the spacing effect be used to improve memory?

3. How did the contributions to modern memory science of behaviorism and cognitive psychology differ?

4. What are the key components of a memory experiment?

5. What is the difference between recall and recognition?

6. What are source judgments? What are metamemory judgments?

7. How does studying neuropsychological patients aid in understanding the nature of memory and the brain?

8. What are the three techniques of neuroimaging? What are the advantages and disadvantages of each?

9. What is prospective memory?

10. What are the four themes of the book? Why are they important?

ONLINE RESOURCES

1. For a good website on the general philosophy of science, go to http://teacher.pas.rochester.edu/phy_labs/appendixe/appendixe.html.

2. For Hermann Ebbinghaus's book, see http://psychclassics.yorku.ca/Ebbinghaus.

3. For more on Mary Calkins, go to http://www.webster.edu/ ~ woolflm/marycalkins.html.

4. For more on Frederic Bartlett, go to http://www.ppsis.cam.ac.uk/bartlett.

5. For more on Endel Tulving, go to http://www.science.ca/scientists/scientistprofile.php?pID=20.

6. See a patient with Broca's aphasia at http://www.youtube.com/watch?v=f2IiMEbMnPM.

7. For a video depicting fMRI, go to http://www.youtube.com/watch?v=PYg09mPA8fA.

8. For the latest on memory research, go to http://www.memoryarena.com/resources.

9. For the latest research on applications of memory, go to http://www.sarmac.org/index.htm.

Go to www.sagepub.com/schwartz for additional exercises and study resources. Select **Chapter 1, Introduction to the Study of Memory** for chapter-specific resources.

CHAPTER 2

Memory and the Brain

The word *brain* really means different things to different people. In everyday usage, the word *brain* is nearly synonymous with the word *mind*. We say that we have something "in our brain that we cannot get out," meaning we have been thinking about something. You call someone a "brain" if you think that his or her intelligence is that person's chief characteristic. However, underlying this metaphor is the certainty that the brain is the biological organ responsible for thinking, memory, reasoning, and language. In this chapter, we will explore the science of how the brain produces memory.

For a neurosurgeon, the brain is a mass of soft tissue inside the head that has to be handled very carefully when damaged. The brain itself has no pain receptors, so neurosurgeons are less concerned about anesthesia than other doctors. However, the brain is surrounded and infused with millions of blood vessels, so surgeons must be very careful when probing around the brain, lest they accidentally induce a hemorrhage. Neurosurgeons understand the critical nature of the human brain for what it is to be human, yet for a surgeon, its identity is a biological tissue.

For a cognitive neuroscientist, the brain is a complex assortment of separate areas and regions, each of which has its own unique function. For example, the frontal regions are for planning, thinking, and monitoring, while the back of the brain processes vision. Viewed this way, the brain is not really one organ but many dozens of distinct regions each with its own appearance, its own micro-anatomy, and its own function. In each way of looking at the brain, however, is the assumption that the biological organ located inside the skull is the organ directly involved in memory, language, and thought. It was not always thus. Aristotle famously mistook the heart as the organ of thought and thought that the brain was merely for cooling the blood. This theory has long since been discredited; any physician who advanced such a notion today would find himself or herself without patients very quickly.

We live in an age in which we are at the cusp of tremendous breakthroughs in our understanding of the relation of brain and cognition (Sylwester, 2005). Recent technological advances have provided unrivaled methods for examining how the brain works and how memories are formed, stored, and retrieved. Most of these advances come from neuroimaging technology, which allows us to peer inside the normal functioning brain. Despite these advances, however, much still remains a mystery, and neuroscientists will be researching the correlation between brain function and memory processes for many years to come.

Nonetheless, this chapter would have been much less detailed if it had been written 10 years ago. We are in the midst of a neuroimaging revolution, and we know much about brain function because of it. And for a number of reasons, research on the cognitive neuroscience of memory has been leading the way.

OLD QUESTIONS, NEW ANSWERS

To introduce the neuroscience of memory, we will start with one of the older questions in this area—namely, where in the brain are memories stored? This question is of interest for a number of reasons. First, it is a deeply philosophical question; how is it that this brain stuff (shortly to be called neurons) can contain information about the taste of oranges, the name of the 10th president of the United States, and the image of one's long-departed great-grandmother? Second, it is an important practical question. If there are certain areas of the brain that store memories, then we need to respect these areas when probing the brain during neurosurgery. The consensual wisdom on this topic for some time is that memories are not stored in any particular location in the brain but are distributed throughout the brain. The memory of your great-grandmother is stored in many parts of the brain—her image is in your visual cortex, her voice is in your auditory cortex, and the emotions from childhood her memory elicits are in yet other areas of the cortex. Fourth, this consensual wisdom has been challenged. We will briefly review some data that support the idea that specific areas of the brain are for specific memories. These data are based on neuroimaging techniques using the newest and most sophisticated technology.

Many years ago, Karl Lashley labeled this question the "search for the engram"—the engram being the physical unit of storage of a memory (Schacter, 2001). For example, when you learn that "Bratislava is the capital of Slovakia," there must be some change in the brain that marks this new information. If somebody asks you what the capital of Slovakia is, the question activates the engram, which stores the association between the names "Bratislava" and "Slovakia." Lashley suspected that there might be specific cells or groups of cells that transform when new information has been acquired. He spent his entire career looking for these memory-specific cells but never found any. Finally, at the end of his career, Lashley was forced into concluding that there are no engrams—that memory representation occurs because of a connection between disparate areas in the brain. Nowadays, there is good evidence to support this idea. The Conway et al. (2003) study discussed in Chapter 1, which shows that visual areas of the brain are activated during autobiographical recall, supports this idea. Thus, the current view is that that stored memories are distributed throughout the brain and have more to do with connections across spatially separate areas of the brain than in any specific area. Thus, the memory of your great-grandmother is the result of axonal connections between areas in the visual brain, auditory brain, emotion centers, and perhaps many others.

Engram: the hypothetical physical unit of storage of a memory.

This was the conventional wisdom from Lashley's time to the present. However, Quiroga, Reddy, Kreiman, Koch, and Fried (2005), using functional magnetic resonance imaging (fMRI) technology, which was never available to Lashley, apparently has found specific areas in the brain that seem to support very specific knowledge structures. In Quiroga et al.'s studies, people see photographs or printed names of various celebrities while the fMRI is scanning their brains. In general, the photographs elicit greater responses in the visual areas of the brain, whereas the printed names evoke responses in areas of the brain involved in reading. But embedded in the temporal lobe, Quiroga et al. found areas of the brain that respond specifically to information about particular people. That is, these areas of the brain respond selectively to either the picture or the name of one celebrity but not another celebrity. For example, many of Quiroga et al.'s participants actually had "Halle Berry" areas of the brain, that is, neurons that respond to her name or her photograph, even across a range of characters from movies. Nearby the Halle Berry is a "Harrison Ford" area, which responds to his name and his picture, but much less so than to Halle Berry. The specificity of these areas to the recognition of individual people makes it look like there just may be engrams after all. There are many who question these data. In fact, many think that there are other explanations of Quiroga et al.'s data and that citing their findings as support of an engram theory is premature. However, Quiroga et al.'s study has definitely raised the possibility that Lashley's search may not have been in vain. There may be engrams after all. Still, most researchers think that memory storage is widely distributed across the brain and that distributed models such as that of Farah and McClelland (1991) offer better explanations.

BRAIN AND MEMORY

Understanding how the brain forms, stores, and retrieves memory has tremendous practical applications in educational and medical settings because learning is such an important human process. First, consider the medical implications of understanding brain-memory relationships. In particular, knowing how the brain forms memories means that we may be better able to intervene in memory loss, especially the memory loss associated with pathological aging, such as Alzheimer's disease. **Alzheimer's disease** is one of many dementia-type illnesses that are more common in older adults than they are in younger adults. Roughly 26 million people now have Alzheimer's, and that number is likely to quadruple in the next 40 years (Brookmeyer, Johnson, Ziegler-Graham, & Arrighi, 2007). Alzheimer's disease (go to www.sagepub.com/schwartz[1] for more information) is a terminal illness whose initial signature is the development of amnesic (memory loss) symptoms. It is a disease that affects the brain, clearly illustrating the brain-memory relation. Early Alzheimer's patients have trouble learning new information and retrieving recent events. Later stage Alzheimer's involves the loss of knowledge of the past and eventually the identity of close relatives. Understanding the neural processes of memory will help medical research to be able to prevent Alzheimer's or alleviate the symptoms of those with the disease. Preventing Alzheimer's will have enormous consequences for untold millions and relieve fear among many who would never develop it.

> **Alzheimer's disease**: one of many dementia-type illnesses that are more common in older adults than they are in younger adults. Memory is the first deficit detected in this disease.

Normal aging is also characterized by memory loss, albeit mild compared to the ravages of Alzheimer's. Much of this loss is correlated to changes in the brain. Therefore, even for normal older adults, understanding brain-memory relationships could wind up benefiting them.

Memory deficits are also a common symptom of **traumatic brain injuries** (TBIs; for more information, go to www.sagepub.com/schwartz).[2] TBIs occur when the brain violently and suddenly hits a hard object, such as an automobile windshield. These are usually called closed-head injuries because the windshield seldom completely cracks the skull. TBIs often can occur in open-head injuries as well, such as when the brain is penetrated by an object such as a bullet. In many cases, the closed-head injury can result in greater damage to the brain than the open-head injury. According to the CDC (Centers for Disease Control and Prevention, 2010), 1.7 million people suffer TBIs every year. Most of these are minor, but 50,000 a year are fatal.

> **Traumatic brain injuries**: sudden and devastating injuries to the brain.

The biggest source of TBIs is from motor vehicle crashes. In fact, 17% of TBIs result from motor vehicle crashes (Centers for Disease Control and Prevention, 2010). TBIs are a leading cause of death among young adults, particularly among young male adults. In many severe auto accidents, the head strikes the windshield, causing damage to the prefrontal lobes of the brain. This damage to the frontal lobe can result in long-term deficits in memory, emotional complications, and difficulties in planning and organization. In addition, temporal lobe areas may also be damaged, causing further memory complications. The counter-coup (that is, the blow to the back of the head) may bring damage to the occipital lobe, resulting in visual deficits as well. Better understanding of the nature of memory in the brain could bring much-needed relief to these individuals as well. In the near term, however, buckle up and don't disconnect your airbag!

The care and treatment of patients with brain damage falls in the domain of **clinical neuropsychology**. Since most auto accident victims are young adults with long lives in front of them, the treatment and rehabilitation of TBIs is of tremendous social importance in our autocentric culture. Therefore, clinical neuropsychology focuses on rehabilitation and restoration of cognitive skills for auto accident victims. However, due to the usual pattern of widespread damage in an auto accident, auto accident victims are seldom used in research examining the relation of brain and behavior.

> **Clinical neuropsychology**: the practice of helping brain-damaged patients recover and cope with their injuries.

Alzheimer's and TBIs are two major sources of individuals with memory-related brain damage. But there are other sources as well. Strokes affect the brains of many older adults, as do tumors. Each of these may create deficits in memory. We will return to each of these phenomena in this book—as understanding memory deficits are an important part of memory science. But the primary goal of this chapter is to understand how the brain processes result in the cognitive processes of memory. It is therefore important to begin with an understanding of the underlying structure in the brain.

NEURONS

Our brains contain billions of microscopic cells called **neurons.** Neurons are biological cells that specialize in the transmission and retention of information (see Figure 2.1). As such, neurons are the basic building block of both our brain and our entire nervous system. Neurons form huge networks of communicating cells in the brain and also connect to neurons in the nerves and muscles of the body. They innervate all of the sensory systems and muscular systems and allow us to move, see, think, and remember. Understanding memory or any other cognitive process requires a fundamental understanding of how neurons transmit information. To understand how they transmit information, you must first understand their basic anatomy.

> **Neurons**: biological cells that specialize in the transmission and retention of information.

Figure 2.1   A typical neuron.

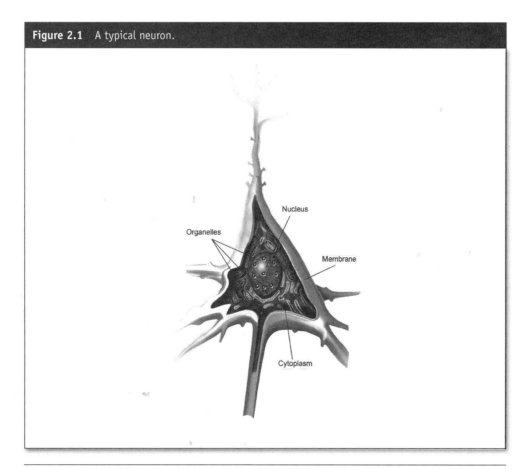

SOURCE: B. Garrett (2009).

Like all biological cells, the neuron contains a nucleus, which houses the individual's chromosomes. The chromosomes contain the genes, which contain each individual's DNA. Surrounding the nucleus is the soma or cell body. The soma contains all the apparatuses that keep the cell working, such as mitochondria and other organelles. In this way, neurons are similar to all other cells of the human body. What make neurons unique are the fibers that extend outward from the soma. These fibers allow neurons to conduct the transmission of information from one part of the brain or nervous system to another part of the brain or nervous system. There are two types of fibers, one that leads into the neuron and one that leads out of the neuron. Each of these fibers conducts electricity, although each fiber does so in a different manner. Indeed, the transmission of information in the brain occurs through small electric currents racing through the neurons of the brain.

The part of the neuron that receives information from other neurons is the **dendrite.** Any neuron may have many hundreds of dendrites, each one receiving different pulses from other neurons. Some of these pulses may make the voltage higher within the cell, and some of the pulses may make the voltage lower in the cell. The voltage refers to the electrical potential of the cell. The various inputs sum at the soma and determine the electrical state of that neuron at that particular instant of time. This sum total of electric input at any given time can then cause that particular cell to start a signal to other cells. The message leaves the cell via the other unique fiber in the neuron.

> **Dendrites**: the part of the neuron that receives information from other neurons or from sensory receptors.

Each neuron has only one **axon,** which transmits messages to other neurons. A neuron has only one axon, but it may branch out and be connected to many hundreds of other neurons. But each of those neurons gets the same electrical pulse as all the others because the cell has only one axon. Transmission in an axon is an electrochemical process called an **action potential.** This is because transmission of electricity along the axon is not simply like a wire. Chemical processes keep the message strong regardless of the length of the axon.

> **Axons**: the part of the neuron that sends information to other neurons.
>
> **Action potentials**: the electrochemical process of transmission in an axon.

The axon of one neuron does not actually touch the dendrite of the next neuron. A gap exists between the two neurons, called the **synapse.** The synapse is extremely small—but electricity does not pass from the axon of one cell to the dendrite of the next. Instead, the transfer of information from one neuron to the next occurs chemically, rather than electrically. The axon does so in the following manner. At the end of the axon are little nodules called **terminal buttons.** When the electrical signal reaches the terminal buttons, the signal triggers the terminal buttons to release **neurotransmitters,** which

> **Synapses**: gaps between the axon of one neuron and the dendrite of the next neuron, in which transmission occurs via neurotransmitters.
>
> **Terminal buttons**: the ends of axon that hold neurotransmitters.
>
> **Neurotransmitters**: chemicals (such as dopamine), which cross the synapse and induce an electric flow in the next neuron.

are chemicals (such as dopamine) that cross the synapse and induce an electric flow in the next cell (see Figures 2.2 and 2.3). Thus, the flow of information in the neurons is both chemical and electrical.

A few important things to note about this process are as follows. First, transmission of information in the dendrites is electrical. The longer dendrites will show a greater loss of electrical power than will shorter dendrites. This is similar to the transmission of electricity through power lines. More energy is lost when the electricity is transported over long distances than over short distances. As such, dendrites tend to be very short. Because the flow of information in the dendrite is electrical, it is also extremely fast. Indeed, in terms of the size of biological organisms, transmission in the dendrites is said to be instantaneous.

Transmission of information in the axons is electrochemical. It is electrical over very short segments but then gets a power boost (called action potentials) via a chemical process as it moves down the axon. This allows axons to be quite long (indeed, you have 1-meter-long axons going up your spinal cord), as the action potentials keep the electric potential constant as it flows along the axon. However, because of these action potentials, information

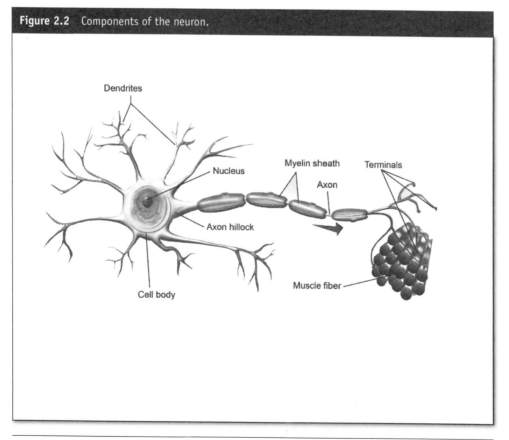

Figure 2.2   Components of the neuron.

SOURCE: B. Garrett (2009).

Figure 2.3   The synapse.

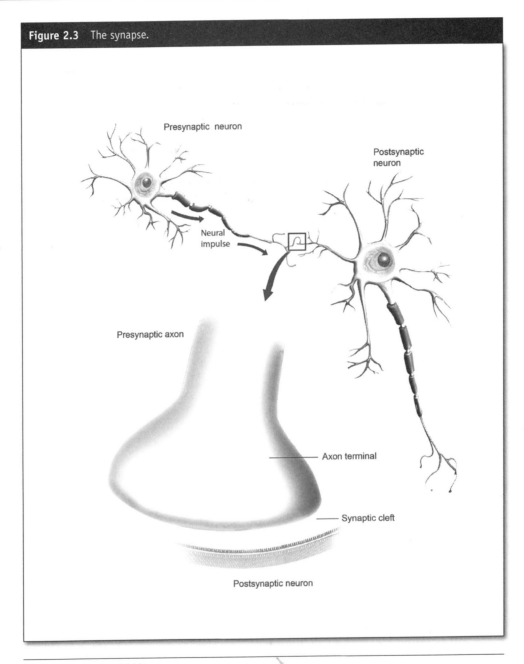

SOURCE: B. Garrett (2009).

flow in the axon is relatively slow (sometimes as slow as 10 meters per second). Incidentally, it is likely the slowness of axon transmission that caused big animals such as dinosaurs to evolve a second "brain" (really a large nerve ganglion) in their tail. Finally, transmission of information is completely chemical at the synapse when neurotransmitters carry the information from one axon to the next dendrite. This transmission also slows down the general speed of neural transmission.

Most axons are coated with a myelin sheath, which speeds the flow of information in the axons. Myelin is a fatty substance, which acts as an insulator would to a copper wire. The myelin, therefore, allows the electric signal to travel faster along the axon. The loss of myelin along human axons is associated with the disease known as **multiple sclerosis** (MS). The loss of movement and coordination seen in MS is because of the slowdown of information flowing through the axons.

> **Multiple sclerosis**: a disease caused by the loss of myelin along human axons.

Neurotransmitters

The brain and nervous system make use of many different neurotransmitters depending on the type of neuron and the part of the brain. Neurotransmitters are proteins produced by the nervous system. To be classified as a neurotransmitter, a chemical must bridge the synapse and induce an electric current in a dendrite. Neurotransmitters may either excite the dendrite or inhibit it, and the same neurotransmitter may be excitatory or inhibitory in different neural circuits. Neurotransmitters that increase activity in the neuron are said to be excitatory. In contrast, neurotransmitters that decrease activity in the neuron are said to be inhibitory. That is, inhibition causes the neuron to make fewer action potentials rather than more. Common neurotransmitters include dopamine, acetylcholine, serotonin, gamma-aminobutyric acid (GABA), and norepinephrine. GABA is the most commonly used neurotransmitter in the human brain. Acetylcholine is used by neurons that innervate and control our muscles.

If some of these chemicals' names seem familiar to you, it is because of their importance. Many neurological diseases are associated with malfunction of the systems that produce these chemicals. Moreover, many psychiatric conditions are treated by altering the process by which neurotransmitters are produced in the body. Finally, orally consumed drugs can alter the functioning of many of these neurotransmitters. Indeed, many of the drugs we consume (both legal and illegal) affect the function of the brain by changing the chemistry at the synapse. This section will provide just a few examples of this, but there are many more.

In Parkinson's disease, for example, a part of the brain (the **substantia nigra**) is no longer able to produce enough dopamine. This loss of dopamine then results in the characteristic disorders of movement associated with Parkinson's. Patients with Parkinson's disease may have difficulties initiating movements, frozen facial expressions, and tics about which they are not aware. If left untreated, the symptoms get worse as the disease progresses. However, there are medicines available that can control the symptoms—at least to some extent.

> **Substantia nigra**: a part of the brain that produces dopamine. In Parkinson's disease, this brain region does not produce enough dopamine.

The medicine given to patients with Parkinson's disease contains a precursor of dopamine, which the body can convert into dopamine. This gives patients with Parkinson's disease short-term reduction of their symptoms. The medicine can be given to constantly replenish the dopamine in the synapses.

Many illegal drugs affect the brain by altering the transmission of neurotransmitters at the synapse. Serotonin, for example, is used in the circuits that regulate mood. The drug ecstasy (MDMA) affects people's moods by affecting the release of serotonin at the synapse. Cocaine blocks the flow of dopamine. LSD (lysergic acid diethylamide) is a powerful hallucinogenic drug. Not used much by the youth of today, it was popular in the United States during the 1960s. LSD affects both dopamine and serotonin channels, increasing the release of neurotransmitters by axons in sensory areas of the brain. This increase of activity in sensory areas is responsible for the strong visual illusions, auditory illusions, and even illusions of balance that occur when a person is under the influence of LSD.

Legal drugs can also affect neurotransmitters. Caffeine—common in coffee and tea—affects neurotransmitters in neurons, which innervate our muscles. Caffeine also causes the release of the neurotransmitter dopamine in our **prefrontal cortex.** Nicotine increases the activation of neurons that innervate our muscles. This is why some baseball players used to chew tobacco. The influx of nicotine into the nervous system allowed them to react just a tad faster to an incoming fastball. Chocolate induces additional release of serotonin.

> **Prefrontal cortex:** the part of the frontal lobe most associated with higher emotion and memory.

Sensory systems have specialized neurons called receptor cells. These neurons have essentially modified their dendrites. Instead of receiving information from other neurons, these cells transform physical energy, such as light, into an electrochemical neural signal. For example, the rods and cones on the retina of the eye respond to light by converting the light (electromagnetic energy) into a neural signal, which travels up the optic nerve and synapses in the brain (go to www.sagepub.com/schwartz for more information).[3]

Learning at the Cellular Level

Few scientific facts are more certain than the fact that the brain uses its neurons to transmit information. The neuroanatomy described above has resulted from the painstaking research of many neuroscientists, some of whom have received Nobel Prizes for their effort. However, understanding how these neurons encode and represent information—that is, memory—is still just being unraveled. We know much about processes that are involved in learning but little about how these relate to higher order organization of memory. Thus, what happens in the brain and to the brain when we learn something new is still an area of great mystery and dispute. Some researchers have examined what might be happening at a neural level when learning takes place. One possible cellular mechanism of learning is called long-term potentiation.

Long-term potentiation occurs when there has been a consistent pattern of activation between two connected neurons. What does this mean? Think of two neurons connected to each other. The axon of one transmits a message to the synapse between them. Neurotransmitters forge the gap between the two. The dendrite of the second neuron picks

Long-term potentiation: the lowering of the threshold at which a postsynaptic dendrite will begin sending an electric signal.

up the signal and fires along to its next cell. Now, the rate of action potentials along the axon determines how much neurotransmitters will be released. The amount of neurotransmitters crossing the synapse determines how much of a signal will be initiated in the dendrite of the second cell. Usually, more neurotransmitter release means more of a signal in the dendrite. However, long-term potentiation means that constant signaling between these two cells will lower the amount of neurotransmitters needed to elicit a signal in the dendrite of the second cell. Thus, a change in the rate of firing in the second cell is caused by the experience of that cell. Thus, long-term potentiation is one possible model for learning at the level of the neuron. With this possible cellular basis for learning, we will leave our discussion of the microscopic and consider the gross anatomy of the human brain (go to www.sagepub.com/schwartz for more information).[4]

STRUCTURES OF THE HUMAN BRAIN

The human brain is an incredibly complex biological organ containing more than 100 billion neurons (Murre & Sturdy, 1995). In addition to the neurons themselves are many other cells that support the functioning of the neurons. The brain weighs about 1,300 to 1,400 grams (3 pounds), larger than all other primate brains but smaller than those of dolphins, whales, and elephants. Even though the brain represents only about 2% of the average human's body weight, it is an energy-intensive organ, using about 25% of the oxygen used by the body at any given moment. For this reason, the brain is heavily profused by a large blood supply, necessary to provide all that oxygen for the brain.

In earlier times, the brain was thought of as a single organ, in which areas within the brain were equally involved in all of its functions. We now know that the brain is composed of many separate anatomical and functional areas. In this section, we will review some of the main anatomical regions of the brain, explore what their function is, and describe how this relates to learning and memory (see Figure 2.4). This is not a textbook in neuroanatomy; thus, our tour of the brain's anatomy will be merely an incomplete sketch of the incredible complexity of the brain's organization.

First, the brain is divisible into two symmetrical halves, oriented in the left-right direction. These are the **right hemisphere** and the **left hemisphere.** With respect to human cognition, the left and right hemispheres do tend to have specific specializations, with the left hemisphere in particular being devoted to language and, with respect to memory, the interaction of language and memory. The right hemisphere is heavily involved in spatial cognition—that is, our understanding

Right hemisphere/left hemisphere: the brain is divisible into two symmetrical halves, oriented in the left-right direction.

of space around us. The right hemisphere also allows us to process music. Although hemispheric specialization is the rule in human brains, there is also great overlap in function

Figure 2.4 Gross anatomy of the human brain.

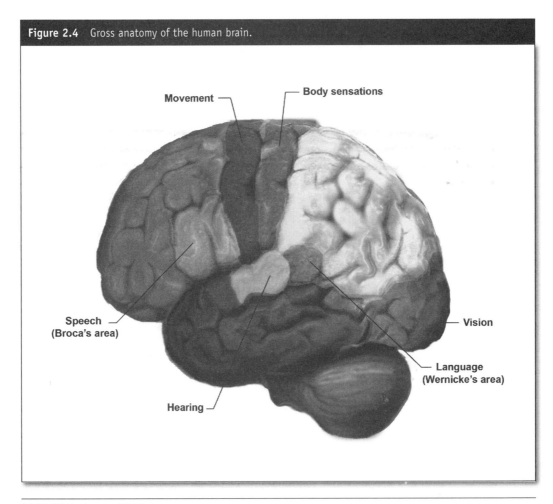

SOURCE: B. Garrett (2009).

and considerable cross-talk between the two hemispheres. Therefore, the popular distinction between "left-brained people" (logical, verbal, and cold) and "right-brained people" (emotional, musical, and warm) has no reality in the brain. Indeed, modern neuroimaging is showing that although the left and right hemispheres are anatomically separate, functionally, with respect to higher cognition, there is less hemispheric specialization than previously thought.

In the top-to-bottom direction, the brain is divided into cortical (the surface of the brain) and subcortical (below the surface) structures. Subcortical structures are the many areas of the brain that rest below the brain's surface. These are "evolutionarily old" areas of the brain that we, by and large, share with nonhuman animals. Subcortical structures are critical in maintaining basic life functions. They control the regulation of heartbeat, breathing, hunger, thirst, sleep, and many aspects of movement. Some subcortical areas

Cerebral cortex: the outer layer of the brain most associated with higher cognitive and emotional functioning.

are also involved in memory and in emotion. We will focus on those areas in this chapter. The thin top layer of the brain (see Figure 2.4) is the **cerebral cortex,** which is most closely associated with the processes that we study in psychology. Language, memory, complex emotion, creativity, problem solving, and music (to name a few) are all largely a function of this thin crust of the brain. It is our large cerebral cortex that also distinguishes our brains from those of other species. In this chapter, we will consider only those areas of the brain that are involved in memory function. Suffice it to say that the brain regulates everything we do externally, internally, consciously, and unconsciously. But our focus is memory. At the level of large-scale anatomy of the brain, memory functions appear to be most critical in the subcortical structures, the hippocampus, and the amygdala and in the frontal and temporal lobes of the cortex. We will review these areas next.

Subcortical Structures

Hippocampus. The **hippocampus** (see Figure 2.5) is in a network of the brain called the **limbic system,** located in and below the medial temporal lobe (a part of the temporal lobe just behind your ear). The hippocampus is considered a subcortical structure. Like most brain structures, it is bilateral—that is, there is one hippocampus on each side of the brain. To some (although not your author), its physical shape is reminiscent of a seahorse, hence the name "hippocampus," which means "seahorse" in Greek. The main function of the limbic system seems to revolve around both memory and emotion, but the hippocampus is a structure very much associated with memory. In particular, the hippocampus appears to be an important part of the circuit, which encodes new memories, both conscious and unconscious. It does not, however, appear to be involved in the storage or representation of information in memory. However, when we retrieve information, the hippocampus does become activated. Interestingly, the hippocampus is involved in memory across a wide range of species. Rats, monkeys, and songbirds all have hippocampuses that are involved in memory. Thus, it is likely that the hippocampus has served a memory function for an extremely long time during the evolution of animal life on earth.

Hippocampus: an area of the brain associated with learning and memory. Damage can cause anterograde amnesia.

Limbic system: set of brain structures, located just beneath the cerebral cortex. It includes the hypothalamus, the hippocampus, and the amygdala. The limbic system functions as an important area for both memory and emotion.

In humans, damage to the hippocampus can cause **amnesia** (that is, acquired memory loss). In particular, damage to the hippocampus causes difficulties in acquiring new information. Some research suggests that, in humans, the left hippocampus takes on more responsibility for verbal memory, whereas the right hemisphere is more involved in the memory for the spatial world around us and directions within the world (Amaral &

Figure 2.5   The hippocampus.

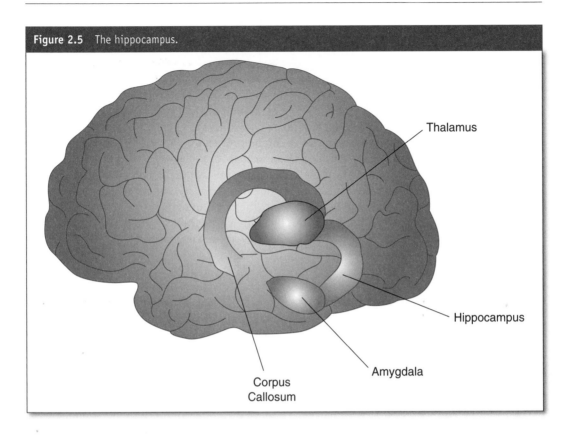

Thalamus

Hippocampus

Amygdala

Corpus
Callosum

Amnesia: memory deficits acquired through brain damage.

Lavenex, 2007). There is a parallel in bird memory. Research with a variety of bird species shows that the left hemisphere is responsible for the memory of song, whereas the right hemisphere is responsible for the memory of migratory routes (Colombo & Broadbent, 2000). Birds with either the left or right hippocampus damaged become amnesic as well. If the left hemisphere is damaged, they can no longer sing, but if the right hippocampus is damaged, they do not fly south properly in the winter (or whatever their migratory pattern is). Similarly, data show that in humans, damage to the left hippocampus is more likely to affect memory for stories and words, but damage to the right hemisphere will affect memory for directions and pictures.

Amygdala: a part of the brain critical in emotional learning, fear, and memory.

Hypothalamus: an area of the brain associated with basic emotions.

Amygdala. The amygdala is also in the limbic system (amygdala means "almond" in Greek). The amygdala appears to have an important role in connecting features of memory with aspects of emotion. It is highly connected to the hippocampus, consistent with its role in memory and also with the **hypothalamus,** an area of the brain associated with basic emotions. Because of these connections, the amygdala is associated with both fear conditioning and emotional learning.

Diencephalon. This part of the brain includes the structure known as the thalamus and the hypothalamus. The **thalamus,** in particular, is an area of the brain heavily connected to other areas of the brain. It appears to serve as a routing center, connecting disparate parts of the brain. Parts of the thalamus are crucial in the transmission of information from our sensory organs (eyes and ears, for example) to the cortical areas responsible for sensation. With respect to memory, the **diencephalon** includes massive connections between the medial temporal lobes and the hippocampus with the prefrontal lobes, which are involved in memory as well. Damage to the diencephalon can incur tremendous costs in terms of memory deficits. The amnesic syndrome associated with Korsakoff's disease is associated with damage to the diencephalon. We will discuss Korsakoff's disease in Chapter 10. Korsakoff's disease involves deficits in new learning, deficits in retrieving well-stored information, and an impairment in the ability to distinguish between true and false memories.

> **Thalamus**: an area of the brain heavily connected to other areas of the brain. It appears to serve as a routing center, connecting disparate parts of the brain.
>
> **Diencephalon**: the part of the brain that includes the thalamus and hypothalamus. It serves as an important relay point in the human memory circuit.

Cortical Areas of the Brain Associated With Memory

The cerebral cortex consists of four main anatomical areas: the frontal lobe, the temporal lobe, the parietal lobe, and the occipital lobe (see Figure 2.6). Each area is named to agree with the name of the skull bone under which it lies. Each of these lobes is bilateral—that is, there is one on the left side and one on the right side of the brain.

The cerebral cortex, or simply cortex, is the evolutionarily most recent area of the brain and the area of the brain most different in humans than in other animals. In particular, the **frontal lobe** marks humans apart from other primates, especially the areas most anterior (i.e., toward the front) in the brain, usually referred to as the prefrontal areas. The surface of the human cortex is very wrinkly. These wrinkles allow the brain to pack more surface area of cortex inside the skull.

> **Frontal lobe**: the most anterior part of the cerebral cortex associated with higher emotion, decision making, metacognition, and memory.

The function of the occipital lobe is visual processing. With respect to memory, this area of the brain is important in providing visual imagery when people remember events from their lives or what people or visual scenes look like. Therefore, when you recall what Brad Pitt looked like in *Benjamin Button,* your visual cortex will become activated. Similarly, when you think about the time you saw the

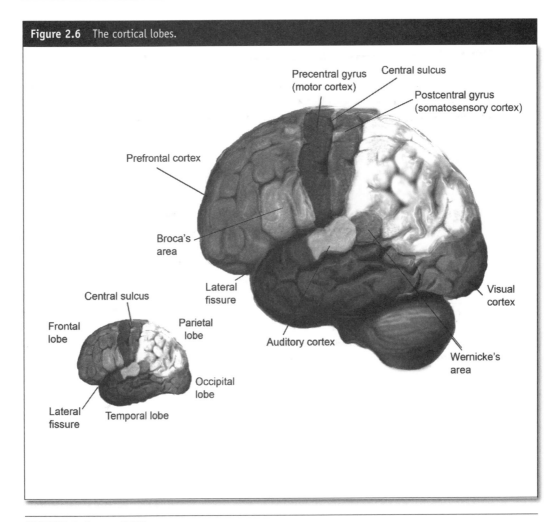

Figure 2.6 The cortical lobes.

SOURCE: B. Garrett (2009).

Mona Lisa at the Louvre Museum in Paris, your visual cortex will become activated. Interestingly, the occipital lobe is also involved in more basic visual memory. V4 is an area of the brain involved in color processing. Patients with damage to this area forget the colors associated with objects. For example, a patient will forget that ripe bananas are yellow.

The two main functions of the parietal lobe are somatosensory perception and attention. Somatosensory perception refers to our various senses of touch (fine touch, pain, heat, cold, and pressure). This area of the parietal lobe is located toward the front of the parietal lobe, adjacent to the frontal lobe. Toward the back of the parietal lobe, near the occipital lobe, are networks engaged in spatial attention in the right hemisphere and attention to verbal material in the left hemisphere.

Occipital—vision

Parietal—somatosensory; attention

Temporal—audition, language, memory

Frontal—higher emotion, decision making, metacognition, memory

The two lobes most directly involved in memory processing are the temporal lobes and the frontal lobes.

Temporal lobe: a part of the cerebral cortex associated with learning, memory, audition, and language.

Medial temporal lobes: a cortical area of the brain in the temporal lobes associated with learning and memory. Damage can cause anterograde amnesia.

Temporal Lobes. The areas of the **temporal lobe** most involved in memory processing are the areas directly adjacent to the hippocampus. These areas are called the medial temporal cortex. Like the hippocampus, the **medial temporal lobe** appears to be involved in the encoding of information into memory but not in the actual storage or representation of that information. In humans, there is some evidence that the left temporal lobe is more involved in the processing of verbal information and the right temporal lobe is more involved in the processing of spatial information. Damage to the medial temporal lobe produces amnesia similar to that seen with hippocampus damage. Other areas of the temporal lobe are involved in language, auditory processing, and interpreting and labeling visual images.

Frontal Lobes. The areas of the frontal lobe most involved in memory are the areas most anterior (i.e., to the front) of the brain called the prefrontal areas. The function of these prefrontal areas includes initiating memory (starting the conscious process of remembering). It also includes source monitoring, that is, determining from what source a memory came. Source monitoring means being able to distinguish if a memory is a personally experienced event or something someone told you. Source monitoring includes reality monitoring, which means distinguishing between fact and imagination. For example, one might have a vivid memory of surfing big waves in Hawaii but then realize this is a memory of dreaming that one participated in such an activity, rather than a memory of actually surfing. Patients with damage to the prefrontal lobes are known to confabulate (telling untruths but not knowing they are untrue). The confabulation occurs because they cannot distinguish real memories from fantasies, as in the example above. The prefrontal lobes are also associated with metamemory and self-regulation. Metamemory involves our awareness and knowledge of our own memory, and self-regulation involves our control of our memory system. The prefrontal lobes have other functions aside from the regulation of memory. They are also involved in higher emotion (i.e., jealousy, respect) and various aspects of problem solving and creativity.

That concludes our brief sketch of neuroanatomy. As we delve in greater detail into the cognitive psychology of memory, we will touch on the underlying neuroanatomy when the relation between memory function and brain anatomy is known. In these sections, greater detail on the anatomy-functional relations will be provided. Next we turn to the great tools for learning about memory and the brain—namely, neuroimaging and neuropsychology.

INTERIM SUMMARY

The brain is a remarkably complex organ, composed of many intersecting parts and layers. Fundamental to the study of memory and the brain is its division into left and right hemispheres and its division into cortical and subcortical areas. The left and right hemispheres of the cortex have slightly different functions. The right hemisphere is more likely to take on roles related to spatial memory, to imagery, and to music, whereas the left hemisphere focuses on language and verbal learning. The cortical areas of the brain tend to be involved in higher levels of memory processing, whereas the subcortical areas, such as the hippocampus, are more involved directly in encoding or, as in the case of the amygdala, emotion and emotional learning.

NEUROIMAGING

The first decade of the 21st century has truly been the "decade of the brain." Improvements in technology and lowering of costs have allowed memory researchers to employ modern neuroimaging techniques to explore the relation between memory processes and the physical brain in ways in which researchers even in the 1990s would not have thought possible. We are beginning to get good snapshots of not only where in the brain various processes occur but how these processes unfold over time (Conway et al., 2003). **Neuroimaging** is the technology that allows us to create images that demonstrate which regions of the brain are working during a particular memory or cognitive task. In this section, we will give a rudimentary

Neuroimaging: refers to a set of techniques that allows researchers to make detailed maps of the human brain and assign functions to particular regions in the brain.

description of how the technology works and then focus on what the technique can tell us about human memory. It is always worth keeping in mind, though, that neuroimaging is a correlational technique. It shows correlations between cognitive performance and areas of the brain that are active. This does not necessarily mean that these areas cause the activity. Three main neuroimaging techniques are outlined here: EEG, PET, and fMRI.

EEG (Electroencephalography)

EEG (electroencephalography) is the oldest of the neuroimaging techniques, dating back into the 1940s. EEG technology is based on the fact that neurons conduct electricity. This electrical conduction can be measured by sensitive electrodes, which are placed on the skull of a person. As electrical activity moves from one area of the brain to another, it can be measured as distinct "waves" of electrical activity (see Figure 2.7). In particular tasks, some areas of the brain will be more active. This activity will produce a larger wave of electricity, which EEG can detect. More important today is that the electrical activity of the brain can be measured every millisecond (1/1,000th of a second). Therefore, EEG is very sensitive to changes in time in the brain. However, even when 64 electrodes are placed on the skull, EEG is not as good as the other techniques at developing maps as to where processes occur in the brain.

Figure 2.7   EEG patterns. When an EEG is recorded on paper, it produces a pattern that looks like this. Although the EEG measures the electrical activity of millions of neurons, it can be used to make reliable inferences about brain function.

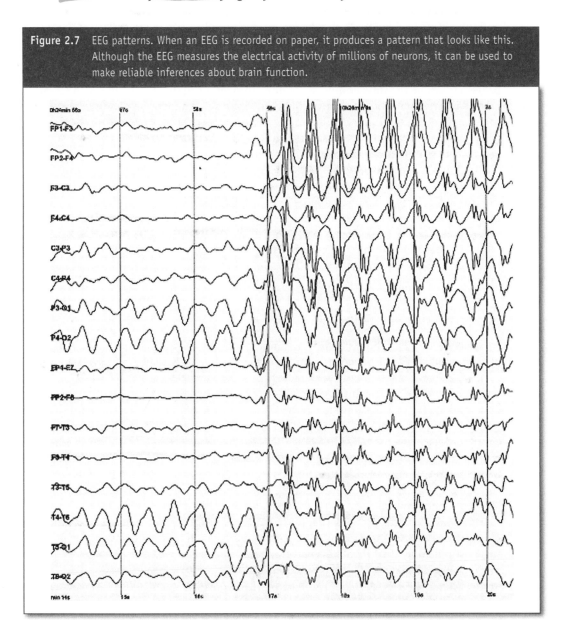

During sleep, our brains produce characteristic electric waves, whose form can be captured by the EEG. These waves are associated with the various stages of sleep (Massimini et al., 2005). EEG is also important in the diagnosis of epilepsy.

To study memory, researchers use a particular method called the event-related potential (ERP). In the ERP technique, EEGs are measured in response to particular stimuli (or events). The EEG starts recording when the stimulus is presented to a participant. It continues for the duration of the trial. The stimulus is then presented in many trials, and the EEGs are then averaged across the trials to eliminate the random activity that may be present during any given trial. What remains is a very clear wave. Once the trials have been averaged together, the resulting data can present a picture as to how electrical activity changes over time in response to the stimulus. Event-related potential can be used to probe the time course of cognitive processes in the brain. One such example involves a brainwave known as the p300. We discuss this here as an example of the usefulness of the technique. For example, when presenting words during a memory experiment, a particular wave occurs about 300 milliseconds after the stimulus is presented. It is called the p300 because it is a positive change in voltage. In a famous paradigm (known as the **von Restorff effect**), a list of words is presented to a participant. All but one of the words are from the same category. The out-of-category word is called the von Restorff item or the oddball. For example, the oddball item might be the name of a city in California among a list of names of kinds of fish. The p300 part of the event-related potential is distinctly higher for the oddball item than it is for in-category items (Metcalfe, 1993). Being able to see in the ERP exactly where the p300 is and how it correlates to the person's memory allows researchers to make a hypothesis about how memory is processed in the brain.

Positron Emission Tomography (PET)

Positron emission tomography (PET) technology allows scientists to get a detailed image of a living human brain without having to damage any living tissue. It does involve, however, injecting a small amount of a radioactive substance into a person's blood, which does have potentially negative effects. Therefore, it is not a procedure that should be done repeatedly. PET is useful for both medical purposes (it can pinpoint a tumor) and research because it can isolate functional areas of the brain. PET offers, relative to earlier techniques, a superior ability to determine where in the brain a particular function is occurring. However, it does not allow for the detailed description of how in time information is changing in the brain. This is because it requires about 30 seconds of exposure to get a good image of the brain. Thus, activity in the brain is blurred over a 30-second window.

PET is based on a simple assumption: that areas of the brain that are being used will require more blood. Your brain is a biological organ, which is powered by the oxygen and sugars supplied by the blood. Because neurons that are active will require more oxygen, the body should send more blood to those neurons that are engaged in any particular cognitive, emotional, or behavioral task. Therefore, if you can trace where the blood is going to during a particular memory or cognitive task, then you can correlate that area of the brain with that particular cognitive function. Thus, if you can measure to what parts of the brain the blood is flowing during a particular memory process, you know that the area of the brain is critical for that process.

In PET, a small amount of radioactive tracer is injected into the blood of a willing volunteer. The tracer travels through the bloodstream to all parts of the body and brain. However, the areas of the brain that are active will draw more blood from the circulatory system. Thus, greater amounts of the radioactive tracer will go to areas of the brain that are more active than to those that are less active. PET scans use complex measurements to determine which areas of the brain are emitting more radioactivity. Those areas that are more "radioactive" are associated with whatever cognitive task the volunteer is engaging in.

PET allows for very precise maps of the brain to be drawn. Increased activity is often restricted to very small regions of the brain, which can be determined via the PET. Cabeza and Nyberg (1997) used PET technology to isolate hemispheric differences in memory processing. They showed that when people were actively trying to learn new information—as opposed to passively registering information—there was increased activity in both the hippocampus and areas of the left frontal lobe. During retrieval, however, right frontal regions were more active. Other studies show that the right prefrontal lobe is more involved in retrieving events from your personal past, whereas the left prefrontal lobe is more involved in encoding new verbal information (go to www.sagepub.com/schwartz[5] for more information on PET technology).

Functional Magnetic Resonance Imaging (fMRI)

MRIs are now the medical and research standard. Functional magnetic resonance imaging (fMRI) is the state of the art for cognitive neuroscience research. MRIs, like PET, allow for complex imaging of the brain without any invasive procedures. And today, MRIs are both safer and better at imaging than PET, as they involve no radiation. Magnetic resonance imaging is a common medical tool to examine structural damage in internal organs. It is routinely used to detect tumors, growths, and other damage in the brain. The term *MRI* means a structural MRI—these images are used to produce a detailed picture of the intact human brain. MRIs are of use medically, if you want to known where tumors or brain damage occur in the brain. They can also specify individual differences in the brain. As such, structural MRIs are useful for medical diagnosis and procedure. fMRI refers to a variant that tracks where in the brain particular functional components occur. That is, fMRIs track blood flow and thus can determine where in the brain certain processes are. The blood flow scan can be superimposed on MRI to reveal the structure responsible. Thus, in addition to acquiring a structural map, the fMRI can show dynamic changes in the brain (see Figure 2.8).

MRI works because different molecules in the brain react differently when placed in an extremely strong magnetic field. For structural images of the brain, typical of an MRI, the detector looks for changes in structures in water molecules in the brain. For fMRI, which has been developed to specify cognition-brain region correlations, the detector looks for changes in blood flow, much as PET does. Neither MRI nor fMRI require the introduction of harmful radioactive chemicals, and at present, there are no known adverse effects of the magnet itself. MRIs and fMRIs offer also much greater spatial resolution of where events take place in the brain than any other neuroimaging technique. fMRI can rescan the brain every .5 seconds, thus offering a much better time window than does PET, although still not as good as the EEG technology.

Research using fMRI technology has far-reaching consequences. As an example of the power of fMRI to answer previously unanswered question, Koshino et al. (2008) were interested in the differences in working or short-term memory for faces in autistic individuals. Autism is a disorder in which people may have linguistic, social, and emotional problems. Working memory is the memory system that handles information over short periods of time and that we currently have accessible in consciousness. It turns out that autistic individuals have a deficit in remembering faces, and Koshino and colleagues wanted to determine if it was a perceptual phenomenon or a memory one. If it is a perceptual phenomenon, the autistic individuals would have difficulties seeing the faces, which would show up in the fMRI as decreased activity in the areas associated with vision. If it is a memory phenomenon, the autistic individuals would see the face but then have difficulties matching it later. This would show up in the fMRI as a decrease in activation in memory areas of the brain. Koshino et al. asked people with and without autism to match faces while being monitoring by an fMRI. They found that, relative to the normal controls, the autistic individuals showed lower levels of activation in areas of the left prefrontal lobe, known to be involved in working memory. Thus, the neuroimaging data support the memory interpretation of this deficit in autism. For more on this study, go to www.sagepub.com/schwartz.[6]

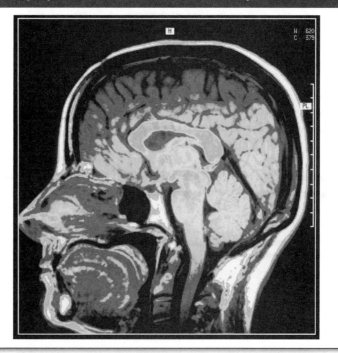

Figure 2.8 The brain as seen through an MRI. This image shows the brain from the side. Can you identify any areas of the brain associated with memory?

NEUROPSYCHOLOGY: MEMORY DEFICITS AND AMNESIA

The oldest methodology for examining the relation between memory and the brain is examining patients with brain damage. This is because examining patients with neuropsychological deficits does not require technology. Researchers must locate patients who have suffered brain damage, which is not a difficult task, and then observe the cognitive and behavioral deficits in the patients. Going back to the famous case of Phineas Gage in 1848, research has been directed at how brain damage affects cognition and behavior (Fleischman, 2002). Gage was a foreman on a railroad crew who was severely injured in a railroad construction accident. A poorly timed dynamite blast shot a medal rod through his frontal lobe. Although he survived the accident and lived many more years, the resulting brain injury changed his cognitive and emotional abilities, as well as drastically altered his personality. The study of the change in his behavior as a result of this accident set the stage for the development of neuropsychology. The research goal of neuropsychology is to correlate behavioral deficits or cognitive changes with the area of the brain that is damaged. The assumption, then, is that the damaged area of the brain is normally involved in the function of the affected behavior or cognitive ability.

Just over 100 years after Gage, in September 1953, a 27-year-old man known as HM underwent a risky and experimental surgery to alleviate symptoms of debilitating and extreme epilepsy. During the surgery, parts of his medial temporal lobe were removed on both sides, including most of both of his hippocampuses. As a direct result of the surgical procedure, HM suffered from strong **anterograde amnesia,** that is, a deficit in learning and retaining new information. This means he could not learn new facts, such as memorizing a phone number. He also suffered some but relatively mild **retrograde amnesia,** that is, the loss of memory of events before the injury. That is, he could remember events and facts from his life prior to the surgery no worse than a normal adult. While this surgery has never been repeated on any other human being, HM's memory was studied extensively for the next 50 years (Corkin, 2002). HM passed away in 2008 at the age of 82. Although his ability to encode new events into episodic memory was strongly affected, research showed that his working memory (short-term memory) and procedural learning (skills) were largely intact.

> **Anterograde amnesia**: an inability to form new memories following brain damage.
>
> **Retrograde amnesia**: when patients lose the ability to retrieve memories of events prior to brain damage.

Many other patients have been studied since then. These patients have varied from having very mild amnesia, just barely different from the memory of normal people without brain damage, to very severe. Moreover, the particular pattern of deficits is different in each patient, and the pattern of these deficits can be linked to where in the brain the damage occurs in that patient.

Neuropsychological studies allow researchers to examine the relation of deficits in cognition and behavior with the locus of damage within the person's brain. In fact, most brain damage is fairly diffuse, spread around large areas of the brain. However, in some cases, often the result of bullet wounds, strokes, or indeed surgery, as seen in the case of HM, the damage can be quite localized, allowing clear correlations to be drawn between the memory deficits and the brain damage. We will examine amnesia and other effects of brain damage on memory in detail in Chapter 10. The website sagepub.com/Schwartz has links to neuropsychological research (go to www.sagepub .com/schwartz).[7]

CHEMICAL ENHANCEMENT OF MEMORY

From an early age, children in our society are warned of the dangers of illegal drug use. Paradoxically, over-the-counter drugs, prescription drugs, and legally available brain-altering drugs are ever present in our society. Indeed, there are few illegal drugs that have such a profound effect on our nervous system as these three legal drugs—caffeine, alcohol, and nicotine.

We take drugs when we have a cold, drugs to keep us happy, drugs to wake us up, and drugs to help us sleep. So it is not surprising that many people wonder if they can take drugs—legal or otherwise—that will help them remember new information. Unfortunately, the empirical data are mixed here. There are drugs that we can take that improve our memory, but most of them work by improving our alertness, influencing how long we can stay awake and focused, rather than memory per se. On the other hand, there is no doubt that there are drugs that prevent the formation of new memories. Indeed, these drugs may be considered to induce temporary amnesic symptoms. Some of these drugs—the antianxiety benzodiazepines—are widely prescribed and available.

The only prescription drugs available to improve memory are **cholinergics** (McDaniel, Maier, & Einstein, 2002). Although there is no evidence that these drugs improve memory in healthy individuals, they have been shown to boost memory performance in those who suffer from memory disorders such as Alzheimer's. They do so by providing chemicals that serve as precursors to vital neurotransmitters in the human brain. Because many memory circuits use the neurotransmitter acetylcholine, the cholinergics provide acetylcholine precursors. The first available drug in this category was piracetam; it is now not regulated in the United States but is available with a prescription in most of Europe.

Cholinergics: drugs prescribed to patients with Alzheimer's disease that alleviate memory loss in early phases of the disease.

The data on caffeine, the active drug in common products such as coffee and colas, are mixed. Some data show that caffeine improves memory, whereas others point to decrements (Lesk & Womble, 2004). In any case, the advantage that caffeine may offer to memory is allowing an individual to study longer before falling asleep, rather than making the actual learning process more efficient. Indeed, new research suggests that caffeine, although it may help people study by allowing them to remain awake longer, reduces the efficiency of learning (Mednick, Cai, Kanady, & Drummond, 2008). That is, caffeine may hurt learning by making the number of items learned per unit of time actually less. However, caffeine may benefit memory by giving us more awake time to study.

On the herbal side, the leaves of the ginkgo tree have been used for generations and generations as a memory enhancer. It is marketed as such in health food stores, herbal stores, and even supermarkets. Marketers are allowed to do this because the extract from ginkgo is not considered a medicine. However, virtually no data demonstrate any positive effects that this herb has on memory (Elsabagh, Hartley, Ali, Williamson, & File, 2005). Thus, it is likely that, like many "folk" remedies, ginkgo only works via the placebo effect.

In short, there really does not yet exist a "memory drug," that is, a simple pill that can increase your memory skills without affecting other aspects of your cognition or emotion. There are drugs that clearly interfere with memory, causing temporary amnesia.

Benzodiazepines, such as diazepam (i.e., Valium), lorazepam, triazolam, and midazolam, are the most commonly consumed drugs in the world because of their effects on anxiety, insomnia, and muscle relaxation (Kaplan, 2005). However, they are also strong amnesia-inducing drugs, especially within the episodic memory domain. Episodic memory refers to the memory for individual events from a person's life. Many benzodiazepines also affect semantic memory, or our knowledge of the world. The benzodiazepines that are the most commonly studied in cognitive research are diazepam, lorazepam, and midazolam. The pattern of memory impairment differs slightly from one benzodiazepine to another, but all of the benzodiazepines impair the learning of new information, creating temporary anterograde amnesia (Danion, 1994).

> **Benzodiazepines**: drugs that are used usually because of their effects on anxiety, insomnia, and muscle relaxation. However, they are also strong amnesia-inducing drugs, especially within the episodic memory domain.

OLFACTION, MEMORY, AND THE BRAIN

Olfaction refers to our sense of smell. Human beings have long been aware of the intimate relation between the sense of smell and memory, particularly the retrieval of highly personal autobiographical memory. Most people can describe the relation of a particular smell to some salient event from their life (Herz, 2007). For example, the smell of naphthalene (mothballs) always reminds your author of visits to his grandmother's apartment as a young child. The famous writer Proust describes how the scent of a French pastry called a madeleine transported him back to his childhood in the south of France (Proust, 1928). Many people report associations between a particular perfume or cologne with a girlfriend or boyfriend, even if the relationship ended years ago. As is clear from the examples, the connection between memory and smell is also connected to emotion. The memories elicited by odor are usually highly emotional memories.

The neural reason for this strong connection between our senses of smell, emotion, and our memories rests in the limbic system. The limbic system is involved in both memory and emotion but is also the primary area for processing odors. Located within the limbic system is the **olfactory bulb,** the primary organ in the brain for processing odors. It receives input directly from the olfactory nerves coming from the hair cells in the nose.

> **Olfactory bulb**: the primary organ in the brain for processing odors.

Only after information passes through the olfactory bulb does it go to higher areas of the brain in the cortex. But the olfactory bulb is heavily connected neurally to two important memory centers in the limbic system, the hippocampus and the amygdala. These strong connections provide the neural basis for the strong association between odors and both memory and emotion. Interestingly, it is only after these connections between the olfactory bulb and the limbic system occur that information is processed by the olfactory cortex and other areas in the prefrontal lobe. This may account for the "gut" feeling that is characteristic of these strong odor-memory-emotion associations (Herz, 2005). For more on research on memory and olfaction, go to www.sagepub.com/schwartz.[8]

MEMORY, MUSIC, AND THE BRAIN

In many ways, music has similar effects on memory. A particular song may remind you of a long-ago dance with your high school sweetheart. Another song will rouse memories of the good old days in college. Yet another song may bring back pleasant childhood memories. In addition, many performers develop powerful abilities to learn and remember music. I have seen professional pianists play for hours straight without consulting sheet music. The sheer number of finger movements that must be memorized to accomplish this task is enormous. How is it that musicians are able to remember so much and retrieve it while playing?

These intuitions have been documented in the psychological laboratory. Janata, Tomic, and Rakowski (2007) played segments from a large set of popular songs to participants in their experiment. The participants were asked to describe any autobiographical memories or any emotions that were elicited by the songs. More than 30% of songs, on average, elicited memories or feeling of nostalgia in each participant. In some cases, the participants reported vivid memories or strong emotions.

We also know that, unlike language, musical perception is mainly processed in the right hemisphere of the brain. In many professional musicians, however, hearing or playing music activates both the left and the right hemispheres equally. Many cortical areas and nearly every cortical lobe are involved in some aspect of music. Whereas the occipital lobe (vision) is mainly sidelined (except for reading music), the other three main cortical lobes all have important roles in the processing of music. The temporal lobes house the auditory cortex, the first area of the brain that processes sounds, including musical sounds. The sensory cortex in the parietal lobe is essential in providing feedback in playing an instrument or in dancing. And the prefrontal cortex is necessary in interpreting and appreciating music (see Levitin, 2006).

The brain is able to create powerful memories of music. This can be seen in our ability to make auditory images of music. Most of us can mentally "play" a song without any actual music or voices occurring. Imagine the opening strains of Beethoven's Fifth Symphony, and you probably hear an orchestra. Imagine Billy Joel singing "Piano Man" and you probably "hear" his raspy voice. Indeed, research shows that auditory centers in the brain are just as active when you are imagining music as when you actually hear music (Janata, 2001). To have such strong imagery, we must have an accurate memory of the song, what it sounds like, and how one singer's voice differs from another. For most current students, of course, the musical selections in the example will not trigger strong autobiographical memories, but they might for older adults. Thus, the connection between music and autobiographical memory is also important. Thus, like with olfaction, there are strong connections between memory and music, which we are beginning to understand are rooted in connections in the brain. For more on music and the brain, go to www.sagepub.com/schwartz.[9]

SUMMARY

The cognitive psychology of memory is increasingly becoming influenced by the neuroscience of memory, forming the hybrid field known as cognitive neuroscience. Cognitive neuroscience is the science that examines the relation between brain anatomy and cognitive function. Foremost in this field are the successes of neuroimaging, which have greatly contributed to our understanding of how the brain creates, represents, interprets, and retrieves memories. At the level of cells, the brain is composed of billions of neurons, which talk to each other electrically. At higher levels, there are several key components of the brain involved in memory, including the amygdala, the hippocampus, the diencephalon, the medial temporal lobes, and areas in the prefrontal lobes. Damage to these areas of the brain can cause various forms of amnesia, or disorders of memory. Neuroimaging studies reveal how these areas are active during memory processes. There are three main neuroimaging techniques: PET scans, MRI and fMRI, and EEG. Each technique has different advantages and disadvantages, although fMRI has become the state of the art in cognitive neuroscience.

The brain uses chemicals called neurotransmitters to bridge the gap in the synapse between cells. Neurotransmitter function can be influenced by drugs. Some drugs, such as benzodiazepines, interfere with memory processing, but the search continues for drugs that can improve memory performance directly. We also discussed the neural explanation for why such a strong connection exists between some odors and certain strong autobiographical memories. Finally, we concluded with a brief section on the intersection between music and memory and the how this relation occurs in the brain.

KEY TERMS

Engram

Alzheimer's disease

Traumatic brain injuries

Clinical neuropsychology

Neurons

Dendrites

Axons

Action potentials

Synapses

Terminal buttons

Neurotransmitters

Multiple sclerosis

Substantia nigra

Prefrontal cortex

Long-term potentiation

Right hemisphere/
left hemisphere

Cerebral cortex

Hippocampus

Limbic system

Amnesia

Amygdala

Hypothalamus

Thalamus

Diencephalon

Frontal lobe

Temporal lobe

Medial temporal lobes

Neuroimaging

Anterograde amnesia

Retrograde amnesia

Cholinergics

Benzodiazepines

Olfactory bulb

REVIEW QUESTIONS

1. What is meant by the term *engram?* What did Lashley hope to achieve by identifying it? How does the Quiroga et al. (2005) experiment relate to the concept of the engram?

2. What is a traumatic brain injury?

3. Describe the flow of information through the neuron, including how information is transmitted through the axon, dendrite, and synapse. Include the purpose of neurotransmitters.

4. What is long-term potentiation?

5. Describe the functional significance of each of the following brain regions: (1) hippocampus, (2) amygdala, (3) diencephalon, (3) temporal lobe, and (4) frontal lobe.

6. How does the EEG measure activity in the brain? What is the EEG good for?

7. What advantages does fMRI have over EEG and PET technology?

8. What is amnesia? What is the difference between anterograde and retrograde amnesia?

9. How do benzodiazepines affect memory? How do cholinergics affect memory?

10. Why is the olfactory (sense of smell) system so tied to emotion and memory?

ONLINE RESOURCES

1. For more on Alzheimer's disease, see http://www.alz.org/index.asp.

2. For more on traumatic brain injuries, see http://www.traumaticbraininjury.com.

3. For more on neurotransmitters, go to http://faculty.washington.edu/chudler/chnt1.html or http://www.neurotransmitter.net.

4. For more information on cellular neuroscience, go to http://www.estrellamountain.edu/faculty/farabee/biobk/BioBookNERV.html.

5. For more on PET scans, go to http://www.radiologyinfo.org/en/info.cfm?PG=pet.

6. For the complete article on fMRI in autism, go to http://cercor.oxfordjournals.org/cgi/content/abstract/18/2/289.

7. For more information on neuropsychology, go to http://www.neuropsychologycentral.com.

8. For more on research on memory and olfaction, go to http://www.rachelherz.com.

9. For more on music and the brain, go to http://faculty.washington.edu/chudler/music.html.

 Go to www.sagepub.com/schwartz for additional exercises and study resources. Select **Chapter 2, Memory and the Brain** for chapter-specific resources.

CHAPTER 3

Working Memory

Imagine you are driving your car to a friend's house. You've never been there before, so you are on your cell phone (hands free, of course) with your friend. She is giving you directions. "Make a left onto Martin Luther King Boulevard, go straight for 2 miles, and then, when you are just past the university, make a right onto Canseco Street." Your friend gets another call, signs off, and you are on your own. Will you remember those directions? You are not sure, so you decide to repeat the directions over and over until you get to Canseco Street. If you choose to do this, you would not be alone. What many people do is mentally rehearse those directions, to keep them fresh, available, that is, in our **working memory** until we do not need them anymore. "Left on MLK, 2 miles, right on Canseco" might keep running through your head. The goal of rehearsing is to keep information in working memory, the active contents of our consciousness.

> **Working memory**: the neural structures and cognitive processes that maintain the accessibility of information for short periods of time in an active conscious state.

Working memory systems are the neurocognitive systems that allow us to maintain information over short periods of time. It used to be called short-term memory, but for a number of reasons, that term has fallen out of favor. The concept of working memory is important for practical reasons; you need to remember directions, the phone number to the pizza shop, and where you just put your car keys. However, working memory is also one of the most philosophically loaded terms in modern experimental psychology. Most cognitive psychologists today think of working memory as the active contents of consciousness. Working memory indeed can be considered consciousness itself. That is, whatever you are conscious of right now (hopefully this paragraph) is exactly what your working memory is representing right now. Direct your attention to the television running in the background or your roommate's game of Nintendo, and this paragraph will cease to be maintained in working memory, as your attention and conscious awareness are directed elsewhere.

WHAT IS WORKING MEMORY?

Although there is still much controversy about the theories used to describe what working memory is and explain how it works, there are some basic tenets about which almost all cognitive scientists would agree. Working memory is the following:

1. A short-term memory system. That is, working memory's function is to temporarily hold information over a short period of time. Estimates of this time period may vary, but most estimates run somewhere between 15 and 30 seconds (½ minute). If information is continually refreshed or rehearsed, it can be maintained indefinitely in working memory. However, as soon as the retrieval stops, information will be lost from working memory within that time. However, the process by which information is lost from working memory has to do with interference, not time, per se. In contrast, long-term memory can store information from minutes to years to an entire lifetime.

2. A limited capacity system. Working memory can only hold so much information. Miller (1956) identified short-term memory as maintaining about seven units of information. Research since has modified this conception of working memory, yet nonetheless, only a small finite amount of information can be active at any particular point in time. This contrasts with long-term memory, which appears to have a virtually limitless capacity. That it, research has never been able to document the maximum amount that human long-term memory can hold.

3. The current contents of working memory are thought to be equivalent to conscious awareness.

The clear contrast here of working memory is the typical conceptualization of long-term memory. Working memory maintains information for brief periods of time in an active conscious state. In contrast, long-term memory stores information for long periods of disuse before being activated when called for. Working memory can maintain only a limited number of items in conscious awareness at any point in time. Long-term memory is seemingly limitless. Indeed, most research suggests that the more someone knows, the easier it is for that person to learn more. Despite some popular misconceptions to the contrary, it is impossible to "fill up" one's long-term memory, as if it were a gas tank. Finally, what is in our working memory is that which we are thinking about now. In long-term memory, there may be information we have not thought of for years and that may be very difficult to actually retrieve into an active form.

SOME TERMINOLOGICAL CLARIFICATIONS

Prior to the late 1980s (Baddeley, 1986), the term **short-term memory** was used more often to describe the phenomena covered in this chapter. The names used to identify what we currently refer to as "working memory" have evolved over time. Cognitive psychologists now seldom use the term *short-term memory*. First, it is associated with theory that is no longer considered to be correct. Second, the term *short-term memory* is now used in everyday speech

Short-term memory: an older term used to describe the memory system that holds information for a short period of time, up to 15 seconds.

Primary memory: a term used to mean short-term memory.

in a way that is different from its former use in psychology. As a consequence, nowadays, memory science prefers the term *working memory*. **Primary memory** was the term originally used by William James to refer to working memory and has been used by some researchers since then (James, 1890; see Purdy, Markham, Schwartz, & Gordon, 2001). This term also fell out of favor because current conceptions of working memory postulate that it is both the active area where we

rehearse new information and the area that holds information after it has been retrieved from long-term memory. Thus, it is neither primary nor secondary to long-term memory. Go to www.sagepub.com/schwartz[1] for more information on William James.

Some of you may have already taken a course in comparative psychology (the study of animal behavior). Many animal behavior researchers are interested in animal memory systems and how they compare to each other and to human memory. Animal behavior researchers use the term *working memory*, but they use the term in a slightly different manner. In animal memory research, the term *working memory* refers to memory of the most recent trial, regardless of the time course of that memory (see Shettleworth, 2010; also see www.sagepub.com/schwartz[2] for more information). This is quite different from its usage in human memory research. In keeping with current terminology, this textbook will use the term *working memory* in the manner in which it is used in the study of human memory.

Working memory is also sometimes confused with **sensory memory.** Sensory memory refers to a very brief memory system that holds literal information for a fraction of a second to allow cognitive processing. Unlike working memory, sensory memory occurs prior to conscious access. Sensory memory is thought to be composed of separate memory systems for each perceptual system. **Iconic memory** is visual sensory memory, whereas **echoic memory** is auditory sensory memory. Sperling (1960) demonstrated the hypothetical existence of iconic memory. Participants were shown a matrix of 12 letters in a 4 × 3 grid for a brief period of time. When asked to retrieve all of the letters, they could only recall about 5 letters. However, when they were cued for a particular line, they could remember 3 from that line. This suggests that 9 letters were accessible visually at the time of recall and that the poor recall when asked for all the letters was a consequence of working memory problems, not sensory deficits. Thus, sensory memory is a low-level system separate from short-term memory.

Sensory memory: a very brief memory system that holds literal information for a fraction of a second to allow cognitive processing.

Iconic memory: visual sensory memory.

Echoic memory: auditory sensory memory.

WORKING MEMORY CAPACITY

Here's the phone number for the best pizzeria in the city: 555–3756. Most of us have no problem juggling that 7-digit number in our head. We repeat the numbers over and over until we dial the number and get our "everything but anchovies" pizza (see Figure 3.1). Now consider when you also have to remember an unfamiliar area code. Now the number is 555–520–3756 (please do not dial this number; the numbers were chosen randomly). Try mentally rehearsing that number. It is likely that you will have forgotten bits of it by the time you actually get to your telephone. The task of remembering the numbers becomes much more difficult for most of us as the number of digits passes seven.

George Miller (1956) argued that the **capacity** of human working (or primary, to use Miller's terms) is, on average, seven items of information. Indeed, he described the "magic number 7" as critical to working memory. It was his view that working memory could hold 7 ± 2 "items" at any point in time (we shall return to the concept of items shortly). This makes the 7-digit number relatively easy but the slightly longer 10-digit number extremely difficult. For most people, remembering a 9-digit Social Security number on the first try is very difficult. The "plus or minus 2" refers to individual differences in the capacity of working memory. Some of us may have slightly bigger or smaller working memory capacities.

Capacity: the amount of information that can be maintained in working memory.

Figure 3.1   You will need to remember the digits of the phone number before you can have this mouth-watering pizza delivered to you.

Digit span task: a task in which a person must remember a list of digits presented by an experimenter.

One of the chief methods employed to look at the capacity of working memory is called the **digit span task,** a standard test in the memory researcher's toolkit. The digit span task is very similar to trying to remember the digits in the phone number for the pizza restaurant. The digit span task is deceptively easy but very valuable as a research tool. In the digit span task, an experimenter reads a list of numbers to a willing participant or group of participants. As soon as the list is read, the participants must repeat back the numerals in order, either by reading them or writing them. The experimenter can then vary the number of digits that he or she reads to the participants. The ability to recall the digits can be examined as a function of how long the set was. See the demonstration below and try it yourself.

Demonstration: Try your hand at the following digit sequences. Read them. Then close the book and try to repeat them.

5-digit: 9 0 3 0 7

6-digit: 4 8 6 2 9 1

7-digit: 6 7 8 5 2 3 0

8-digit: 1 9 5 7 5 0 4 6

10-digit: 1 9 0 7 3 7 3 8 2 9

12-digit: 4 1 5 3 6 7 5 8 1 8 5 6

The results show that average (arithmetic mean) performance is just about 7 digits, consistent with Miller's "magic" number. Given that educated and younger people tend to have longer digit spans than less educated and older people, it is likely that college students doing this demonstration will find 7 digits relatively easy and get the 8-digit sequence. But for most college students, the 10-digit sequence is out of their range.

Let's return to the concept of an "item." Miller (1956) suggested that the capacity of working memory was about seven items. For Miller, however, the word *item* was intentionally vague. Indeed, he argued that a lot of information could be packed into a single item. That is, people can use strategies to make each item of information decomposable into several parts.

Chunk: memory unit consisting of related components.

For example, rather than remembering the number sequence 6-1-9 as three digits, each a unit of information, participants could simply rehearse San Diego. Then, when it is time to retrieve the digits, the item "San Diego" could be converted into 6-1-9 because 619 is the area code for that city. Using this strategy is called **chunking.** Miller introduced the word *chunk* to represent the basic unit of information in working memory. A chunk is a memory unit consisting of related components (Cowan, 2001).

There are many strategies individuals can use to chunk digits in a digit span task. You can use area codes, home addresses, and even the jersey numbers of your favorite athletes. For example, another sequence—2-3—can be encoded as "LeBron James" (or Michael Jordan, for those of us who are older) rather than two digits. In this way, we can extend our working memory capacity by using more and more informative chunking strategies. For example, your author can remember up to 14 digits by taking each 2-digit sequence and processing it as a jersey number for a famous athlete.

Mnemonic Improvement Tip 3.1

If you need to keep arbitrary lists of information accessible in working memory, use chunking strategies as best you can. Try to encode multiple items of information using a common associative strategy. Use well-learned information to guide your chunking strategy. Chunking is useful in ordinary learning tasks that involve working memory, such as remembering phone numbers, keeping directions in mind, and remembering the names of new auquaintances.

In a classic demonstration of how effective chunking can be, Anders Ericsson and his colleagues trained an average first-year college student in digit span tasks (Ericsson, Chase, & Faloon, 1980). At the start, the first-year college student had a normal digit span of about 7 numbers. The experimenters did not suggest a method to him. They just gave him lots of practice. However, by the end of a year of training, the young man had an 80-number digit span! That is, someone could read off a list of 80 straight numbers, and he'd repeat them all right back to you without any mistakes. How could this man with a normal digit span increase his abilities so dramatically over the course of an academic year?

First, it was his job—he spent about 10 hours a week for 40 weeks engaging in digit spans tasks. That is a lot of practice and hard work. But it was not simply practice—the student used a complex mnemonic chunking strategy to build his digit span. The young man was a star runner on the university track team. He therefore chunked numbers together by thinking of them in terms of times in track-and-field races. The sequence 1-9-1-9 might be encoded as "world record in 200-meter dash." The sequence 3-4-3 might be remembered as near world record pace for the mile race. Because most of these sequences were already stored in his long-term memory, he was able to apply them to the new digit sequences (Ericsson et al., 1980). The complex chunking strategy combined with lots of practice made a mnemonist out of this young runner. Just to be sure, there was not something unique about this young man; Ericsson and colleagues employed another runner from the track team the next year and gave him the same amount of practice using the same chunking strategy. This participant went from a normal 7-digit span to a 70-digit span over the course of the experiment. The implication is that anyone can use chunking strategies to boost their performance (see Ericsson, 2003). For more on Ericsson's work, go to www.sagepub.com/schwartz.[3]

Pronunciation Time

Regardless of one's ability to chunk information, most of us are still constrained by the fact that working memory usually can contain only about seven items, even if these items can be chunked. Therefore, the extraordinary digit spans of these participants do not take away from Miller's basic finding—that seven items is the average amount of information in working memory. However, there is more to working memory capacity than just the number of items in a chunk. There are other processes important in determining the capacity of working memory. One such factor is phonological processing, also called pronunciation time. **Pronunciation time** refers to the amount of time it would take to say aloud the items being rehearsed in working memory. That is, the limit on working memory is the number of words that can be pronounced, either aloud or subvocally, in about 1.5 seconds (Schweickert & Boruff, 1986). For digits in American English, most of us can say seven digits in 1.5 seconds. For example, words that take longer (that is, take longer to pronounce) require more of working memory than do shorter words. For example, you can maintain the names of European cities with one syllable (Prague, Nice, Rome, Bruge) more easily in working memory than the names of European cities with multiple syllables (Amsterdam, Bratislava, Barcelona, Manchester). For another example, consider the names of trees. Try to keep the following words rehearsed in working memory: oak, birch, pine, palm. Then try to keep the following words rehearsed in working memory: eucalyptus, bottlebrush, Poinciana, sycamore. This is also referred to as the **word length effect.** Most of us will find it easier to maintain the short names for trees in working memory than the longer ones.

> **Pronunciation time**: the amount of time it would take to say aloud the items being rehearsed in working memory.
>
> **Word length effect**: longer words are more difficult to maintain in working memory than shorter words.

To test the effect of word length, Ellis and Hennely (1980) looked at digit spans in children in the United Kingdom. They focused their testing in the part of Great Britain called Wales. In Wales, there are many people for whom their first language is not English but Welsh (a Celtic language). As a consequence, there is a population of Welsh-English bilinguals. In Welsh, the words for digits take longer to pronounce because many of the vowels are longer than they are in English. Therefore, it takes more time to count from 1 to 10 as fast as one can in Welsh compared to English. Ellis and Hennely examined digit spans in Welsh-English bilingual children. Consistently, the children's digit span was longer in English than it was in Welsh. Because the words mean the same thing in both languages and because most of the students were more fluent in Welsh, the difference in digit spans must be because, at least for the names of the digits, one can say them faster in English than in Welsh.

A short time later, a second study confirmed this finding, but using different languages. Navah-Benjamin and Ayres (1986) also made use of the fact that different digits take a different amount of time to say in different languages. For example, in English, the numeral "1" is pronounced "one," which is one syllable. In Spanish, however, the numeral "1" is pronounced "uno," which is two syllables and takes a little more time to say. Therefore, "uno" should occupy slightly more of the capacity of working memory than "one" does. Navah-Benjamin and Ayres tested students at a university in Israel, where they were able to examine fluent speakers of four languages, English, Spanish, Hebrew, and Arabic. In terms of pronunciation time, it takes the least amount of time to count from 1 to 10 in English and the most amount of time to count from 1 to 10 in Arabic. Spanish is slightly faster than

Hebrew. ~~When the digit span task was presented to speakers of each language, the digit spans reflected the pronunciation times.~~ The digit spans were longest in English, followed ~~by, in order, Spanish, Hebrew, and Arabic~~ (see Figure 3.2). This decrease in digit spans is related to the increase in pronunciation time of the digits in each language. Therefore, the pronunciation time is clearly relevant in evaluating the capacity of working memory.

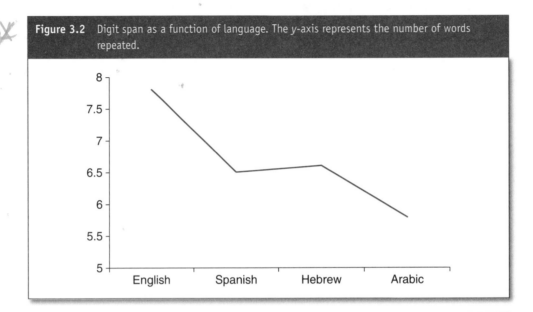

Figure 3.2   Digit span as a function of language. The y-axis represents the number of words repeated.

SOURCE: Based on Navah-Benjamin and Ayres (1986).

THE DURATION OF INFORMATION IN WORKING MEMORY

Working memory is designed to hold information for only brief periods of time. As such, perhaps the most frustrating of memory experiences is the rapid loss of information from working memory. Consider having just heard the phone number of your client on your answering machine. Before you can write the entire number down, you have lost the first three digits. For professors, working memory often constrains the efficiency with which we learn the names of new students. For example, I try to learn the names of many new students on the first few days of class each semester. I am well aware how insulting it can be when somebody forgets your name immediately even when they can sympathize with the name learner's dilemma. A student may introduce herself as "Christina Rodriguez, a sophomore, from South Miami, Florida. Majoring in psychology." I look at her face and silently repeat the name to myself. Then the next student introduces himself or herself. After a few more students, I look back at the first person, and I have no recollection of the name she just spoke mere minutes before. This is because the information pertaining to Christina Rodriguez is no longer in working memory, having been replaced by subsequent names. Because I failed to transfer her name to long-term memory, the subsequent names, faces, and other information have displaced the information in my working memory, leaving me with a complete blank on the student's name. Because the information was never encoded into long-term memory, it can no longer be recalled.

This leads us to one of the earliest issues tackled by cognitive psychologists. How long does information persist in working memory? And, the intimately related question, what causes forgetting from working memory?

To address the first question, the short answer is that it depends. And what it depends on is rehearsal. **Rehearsal** here means actively maintaining the items in working memory by repeating it over and over (**maintenance rehearsal**) or by elaborating on the item to some other concept (**elaborative rehearsal**). If you wish to maintain a new name in working memory, you can simply continue to mentally rehearse it. For example, as long as I am repeating the name "Christina Rodriguez" over and over, I can maintain that name in working memory. Indeed, if I continuously repeat it, I can keep that name for hours in my working memory. However, as soon as my thoughts drift off elsewhere, that new information replaces the name in working memory. Elaborative rehearsal means associating the item in working memory to existing long-term memory structures. So, for

Rehearsal: actively maintaining the items in working memory by repeating them over and over (maintenance rehearsal) or by elaborating on the item to some other concept (elaborative rehearsal).

Maintenance rehearsal: repeating information over and over.

Elaborative rehearsal: processing the meaning of information in working memory.

example, if instead of repeating the name over and over, I thought about how Ms. Rodriguez looked like other people I know with the same first name or same last name, or even whether she looks honest or not to me, I engage in elaborative rehearsal. Elaborative rehearsal takes more attention but produces better encoding into long-term memory. Elaborative rehearsal is good for encoding the information into long-term memory. It creates more retrieval cues that are useful for later recall. However, maintenance rehearsal guarantees the information will remain in working memory. Our focus in this chapter is on working memory.

Once you stop maintenance rehearsal, there is only a limited amount of time before information is forgotten (or replaced) in working memory. When you move on from "Christina Rodriguez" to "Sanjay Gupta," it is the new name that is now being maintained in working memory rather than the old one. Therefore, one important question is, what is the rate of forgetting once you stop rehearsing the information?

Most estimates of the duration of information unrehearsed in working memory are of the order of between 15 and 30 seconds. Almost all cognitive psychologists would agree that, if you remember something *after not thinking about it* for one minute, you are essentially retrieving that information from long-term memory, not working memory. However, what really seems to matter is not how long information goes unrehearsed but what information becomes activated that interferes with it. That is, if we could somehow keep our minds completely blank, information might not spontaneously decay from working memory. Keeping our minds blank like this while awake is notoriously difficult. And new information is always entering working memory.

Duration of information in working memory: the amount of time in which information will remain in working memory if not rehearsed.

The basis of the estimate of the **duration of information in working memory** comes from two classic demonstrations done by John Brown (1958) in the United Kingdom and Lloyd and Margaret Peterson in the United States (1959). The two groups were working largely independently of each other but published similar experiments within months of each other. Both researchers were interested in forgetting from working memory but also demonstrated the duration of information in working memory (or what they referred to as primary memory).

In their experimental paradigms, participants were given three words to remember (i.e., apple, hammer, shell). Following the presentation of the three words, the participants were given a number, such as 417, and asked to count backward by three from that number (i.e., 417, 414, 411, 408, etc.). This task served as a **rehearsal prevention task,** preventing participants from repeating the words previously shown. The research teams then varied the amount of time required to count backward. In some conditions, the participant might only count backward by threes for 3 seconds, but in other conditions, the participant might be required to count backward for 2 minutes. After the rehearsal prevention period was over, the participants were expected to retrieve the three words given to them prior to rehearsal to prevention. After retrieving the three words, the participants were given three new words to remember and then given a new number from which to start counting backward. In this way, the researchers could look at the effect of the amount of time spent on rehearsal prevention and the recall of the words.

Rehearsal prevention task: a task that prevents a participant from maintaining information in working memory.

The findings are illustrated graphically in Figure 3.3. The more time spent in the rehearsal prevention task led to lower recall of the initial words presented. Indeed, much forgetting occurs even after just 5 seconds of rehearsal prevention. L. R. Peterson and Peterson (1959) estimated that within 18 seconds, all information stored in working memory was lost, and only information that had somehow gotten into long-term memory accounted for the 20% recall. They note that by 18 seconds, the curve had hit an asymptote (flattened out) and remained essentially the same even at much longer retention intervals.

It should be noted that typically, even at longer retention intervals, the participants remembered all three words from the very first trial. Apparently, the number counting did not produce sufficient interference on the first trial, as these items were easy to encode into long-term memory. However, on subsequent trials, memory for the words was interfered with by the combination of words from earlier trials combined with the number counting. Thus, the results shown in Figure 3.3 are the function of the average across many trials.

Both the Petersons and Brown favored an explanation based on decay; that is, information not being rehearsed simply naturally vanishes or decays after 20 seconds or so. However, subsequent research strongly supports an explanation based on interference.

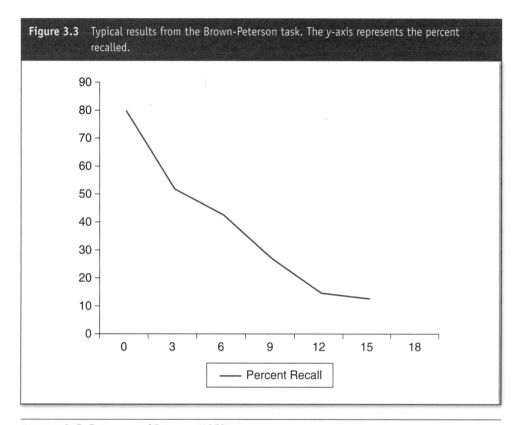

Figure 3.3 Typical results from the Brown-Peterson task. The y-axis represents the percent recalled.

SOURCE: L. R. Peterson and Peterson (1959).

Interference: new information enters working memory and displaces information already present.

Interference means that new information enters working memory and displaces information already present. Because the capacity of working memory is limited, new information will necessarily displace old information. In the case of the Brown-Peterson-Peterson experiment, the numbers being spoken during the rehearsal prevention task are entering working memory and displacing the words that the participant initially was asked to remember. The more time spent counting backward, the more likely those words will be displaced by the interfering numbers. Thus, the best explanation for the results is that the numbers being spoken during rehearsal prevention replace the words in working memory, thus interfering with their presence in working memory. Indeed, a few years later, Keppel and Underwood (1962) showed that part of the interference that created forgetting in working memory came not simply from the rehearsal prevention but also from previous to-be-remembered items. Keppel and Underwood showed that on the first trial, participants could remember all of words, even when the retention interval was long. However, as more trials occurred, it was more difficult for participants to remember digits at any retention interval because earlier items were not interfering with later items. Thus, interference played a bigger role in forgetting than did decay.

Another classic experiment also demonstrated the role of interference in working memory. Waugh and Norman (1965) presented participants with a sequential list of 16 digits. After viewing all 16 digits, the participants were presented with one of the digits that they had seen in the list. Their task was to recall the digit that occurred just prior to the probe digit during the sequence. In other words, if part of the sequence was 1-5-6-2-9, and the probe digit was 6, the participant should reply with the digit "5." Waugh and Norman could then examine performance on this task as function of where in the sequence the probe digit was. If more digits occurred after the probe, then more new digits are likely to interfere with and replace the memory of the probe digit and the digit that preceded it. If the probe digit occurred toward the end of the sequence, there should be less information to interfere with, and therefore memory of the digit that preceded it should be better. This is exactly what Waugh and Norman found—the fewer items that followed the probe digit, the better memory was for the item that preceded it. This cemented the view that forgetting from working memory originates from interference.

THE SERIAL POSITION CURVE AND ITS IMPLICATION FOR WORKING MEMORY

In light of what we know now about the functioning of the brain and memory, it is quite clear that separate neurocognitive memory systems handle different kinds of information. For example, memory should be divided into short-term memory systems and long-term memory systems. With respect to long-term memory, most researchers agree on the distinction between semantic and episodic memory. However, 50 years ago, on the basis of the principle of parsimony (that is, opt for the simplest theory when possible), many researchers argued that the brain had just one memory system that could be used in many different ways. Thus, one of the goals of early researchers in the field of working memory was to show how it was different from long-term memory. Some of the earliest evidence for the separation of working memory from long-term memory came from a deceptively simple procedure, called "free recall," and its measurement, the **serial position curve.**

> **Serial position curve**: the observation that participants remember items well from the beginning and end of a list but not from the middle.

In a free recall test, participants are read (or read themselves) a list of words, usually randomly chosen and with little associative structure. Immediately following the reading of the list, participants are asked to recall (usually by writing down) as many of the words as possible. As you can see, nothing could be simpler. Yet, this test is quite powerful. For more information on serial position curves, go to www.sagepub.com/schwartz.[4]

Demonstration: Read aloud the following words. Immediately after reading the words, write down as many as you can. Then plot your recall as a function of input order.

1. medal
2. paintbrush
3. typewriter
4. sofa
5. cushion
6. pasture
7. clock

8. dragon
9. captain
10. carbon
11. lawyer
12. bubble
13. lemon
14. fountain

15. mask
16. lunch
17. water
18. racket
19. market
20. folder

Now write all the words.

After the participants can no longer recall any more words from the list, the experimenters can examine the amount recalled as a function of serial position, that is, the order with which they appeared on the list. So the first word on the list in the demonstration is *medal.* The experiments would examine the percentage of participants who successfully recalled the word *medal* at serial position 1. The experimenters then examine recall at the next serial position, that is, for the word *paintbrush* in the list above. Thus, the percent recall can be examined as a function of what serial position a word occupies in a given list. The standard result of such a test is illustrated in Figure 3.4. For an online demonstration, go to www.sagepub.com/schwartz.[5]

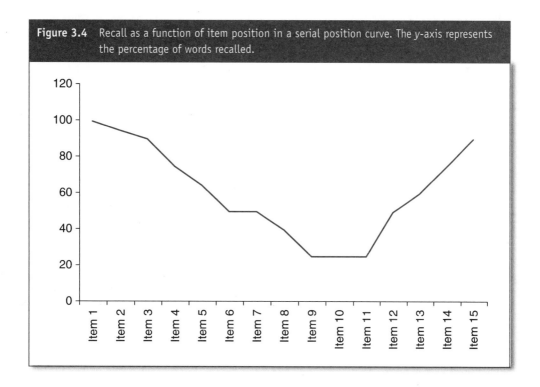

Figure 3.4 Recall as a function of item position in a serial position curve. The *y*-axis represents the percentage of words recalled.

Primacy effect: the observation that memory is usually superior for items at the beginning of a serial position curve; thought to be caused by the encoding of those items into long-term memory.

Recency effect: the observation that memory is usually superior for items at the end of a serial position curve; thought to be caused by the maintenance of those items in working memory.

There are a few important aspects of the serial position curve. First, you can see that recall is very good for the first few items on the list. This effect is called the **primacy effect.** You then see a big dip in performance for items in the middle of the list. Then right at the end of the list, the words become easier to recall again. This good performance for words at the end of the list is called the **recency effect.** Primacy and recency effects can be seen under a wide range of conditions in which people must recall words or other items immediately. Indeed, even monkeys and other primates show primacy and recency effects in experiments that test them for serial memory (Buchanan, Gill, & Braggio, 1981; Wright, Santiago, & Sands, 1984).

Primacy effects appear to result from the encoding of information into long-term memory, even though the memory test may be less than a minute after the participants originally heard the words. Much research now supports this point of view. In terms of people's self-report, many participants describe trying to remember the words by constructing a story. For example, they might think of a story in which a medal is awarded to a person who invented a paintbrush key on a typewriter, which can be used on the sofa. The elaborative encoding necessary to create this story is the kind of encoding that promotes storage in long-term memory. There is now also considerable empirical data that support the idea that the primacy effect occurs because of encoding into long-term memory.

First, mistakes made on early items tend to be related to their meaning, a key component of representation in long-term memory. For example, *medal* might be mistakenly recalled as *award,* whereas *paintbrush* might be remembered as "toothbrush." The mistake here is because we encode information into long-term memory mostly in terms of what the information means. Because *medal* and *award* overlap considerably in meaning, errors of this sort tend to be thought of as resulting from long-term memory. Mistakes from working memory, as we will see, tend to come from sensory confusions.

Second, there are data from experiments in which the researchers come back much later and ask participants to remember what was on the lists they had seen previously. In some cases, these surprise tests may be 24 hours later, a week later, or an entire year later. Interestingly, although recency effects are no longer apparent, primacy effects still exist. Participants may still remember the first few words from the list a year later! This retrieval is clearly mediated by long-term memory.

Third, variables that interfere with long-term memory level reduce the primacy effect. One such variable is the rate at which words are presented. This interferes with elaborative encoding, leading to worse long-term memory. Consider the idea of constructing a story to link the words. This requires a certain amount of time. If that time is reduced, it may be more difficult to construct the story. Therefore, reduced time for each word will prevent the ability of participants to use elaborative encoding. Because they cannot use elaborative encoding, it will be more difficult to encode the first few items into long-term memory. As such, reducing the amount of time per word lowers the primacy effect in free recall studies.

In contrast, the rapid presentation of words has no effect or helps the recency part of the curve, caused by working memory.

Recency effects appear to be based on retrieval from working memory. As with the primacy effect, there is now a great deal of research that supports this idea. Think about doing the task yourself. If the first few items you wrote down were the last items, you were probably likely to remember several of them. If, however, you tried to recall the list in order from start to finish, you probably did not recall the last two or three words from the list. Like with the primacy effect, there is now much evidence to support the view that the recency effect is due to working memory.

First, if you ask the participants to wait 30 seconds (that is, if you introduce a retention interval) before writing down the words that they can recall, the recency effect disappears. However, this delay does not affect the primacy effect at all. This is because the participants' working memory is now engaged in other activities, causing interference with the items at the end of the list, which were the last list items to be there. This effect is stronger if you give participants a rehearsal prevention task, so that they cannot rehearse the last few items in working memory before the test. Items recalled from the beginning of the list are in long-term memory, so the extra 30 seconds does not affect their strength in memory. Second, errors in the recency effect part of the serial position curve tend to be based on sensory errors, either visual or auditory. For example, *folder* might be recalled as *bolder,* or *market* might be recalled as *markup.* This kind of mistake is characteristic of working memory, which is more dependent on sensory characteristics than is long-term memory. Third, participants who write down the words from the recency portion of the curve first remember more total items than those who try to retrieve the words in order. Participants who retrieve in order remember the words from early in the list based on long-term memory, but by the time they get to the end of the list, those words have already been eliminated from working memory.

For this reason, the serial position curve—the graph that shows good memory for both the beginning of the list and the end of the list—in immediate free recall tests demonstrates that working memory and long-term memory have different properties. Variables that affect the primacy effect are variables that affect long-term memory. These variables do not influence the recency effect in free recall. By contrast, the variables that affect the recency effect are variables implicated in working memory and do not affect the primacy effect.

In free recall of recently presented lists, the recency effect is due to retrieval from working memory. But it turns out the primacy and recency effects are not just restricted to free recall of lists of randomly grouped words. Both primacy and recency effects exist in other memory situations as well, including situations in which the retrieval is strictly from long-term memory. For example, try writing down the names of as many U.S. presidents as you can. Take a moment away from the textbook now—so you don't see any of the names below. It turns out that recalling the names of the U.S. presidents shows a primacy effect and recency effect. Most people remember Washington, Adams, and Jefferson, on one hand, and Clinton, Bush, and Obama on the other. However, few people will get Chester Alan Arthur or Grover Cleveland, in the middle of the list. So remembering the first presidents is equivalent to the primacy effect, whereas the recall of the most recent presidents can be considered a recency effect (Roediger & Crowder, 1976). Another example comes from watching the advertisements during the Super Bowl. The advertisements have become almost as important part of the show as the actual football game itself. But which advertisements are remembered the best (an important piece of information for the advertisers, who are paying a tremendous amount of money for airtime)? It turns out that primacy and recency effects can also be seen in the memory of TV ads. The ones at the beginning and the ones at the end are recalled better than those from the middle of the game (Brunel & Nelson, 2003). Primacy and recency effects are also seen in the retention of information from academic classes. Information from the beginning of the semester and the end of the semester is remembered better than information from the middle of the semester (Conway, Cohen, & Stanhope, 1992).

INTERIM SUMMARY

Working memory is a short-term memory system, which can hold information for a short period of time for conscious introspection. Originally, it was thought to hold about seven items, but more recent views of working memory suggest that other factors such as word length and pronunciation time also affect the amount that can be maintained in working memory. If unrehearsed, information will fade from working memory in approximately 15 to 30 seconds. When people learn a list of words and then have to recall them immediately after presentation, the recency effect is caused by retrieval from working memory, whereas the primacy effect is caused because the early items in the list are the ones that enter long-term memory most quickly. Variables that affect working memory affect the recency portion of the serial position curve. Errors here will reflect working memory processes. However, serial position curves are common in memory, and primacy and recency effects can also occur in retrieval from solely long-term memory.

THE WORKING MEMORY MODEL OF BADDELEY

Alan Baddeley is a British memory psychologist who has contributed to many areas in psychology. His single most influential theory is his theory of working memory (1986, 2007; Baddeley & Hitch, 1974). Baddeley and his theory are probably most responsible for the change of terminology from short-term to working memory. For Baddeley, the term *working memory* more genuinely reflected what working memory is for—the active contents of consciousness. But there is another aspect of Baddeley's working memory theory that makes it different from the theories of short-term memory that came before it—that there are actual multiple working memory systems. He called these systems subsystems or "slave" systems. However, for all intents and purposes, what he proposed is that we have separate working memory systems for each major perceptual modality. He called visual working memory the **visuospatial sketchpad,** and he called auditory working memory the

Visuospatial sketchpad: visual working memory.

Phonological loop: auditory working memory.

Episodic buffer: coordinates overlap between the auditory and visual systems.

Central executive: the attentional mechanism of working memory.

phonological loop (Baddeley, 1986). In the latest versions of the model, Baddeley also introduced another system called the **episodic buffer,** which coordinates overlap between the auditory and visual systems (Baddeley, 2007). The episodic buffer is also the link between working memory and long-term memory. Coordinating the activities of these two systems is an attentional mechanism that he called the **central executive** (see Figure 3.5). We will now examine what each of these terms means and what evidence exists to support the theoretical constructs developed by Baddeley and his colleagues over the past 30 years.

Mnemonic Improvement Tip 3.2

Keeping your working memory sharp can lead to general cognitive well-being. Practicing digit spans can be considered mental exercise.

Figure 3.5   Baddeley's working memory model.

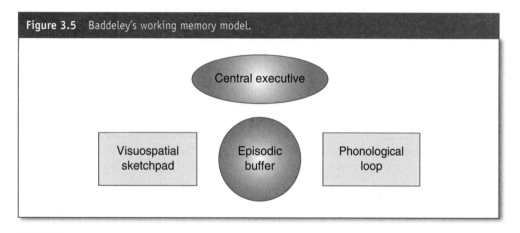

SOURCE: Baddeley (2000).

Baddeley originally stumbled onto the concept that working memory must have multiple components. He and his colleagues were working on experiments in which they were asking participants to engage in two working memory tasks at the same time. In all the old models, there should be interference between the two tasks, leading to diminished performance in at least one, if not both, tasks. What they discovered, in contrast to the theory at the time, is that this is not always the case. In some instances, people can successfully do two working memory tasks at the same time without interference. That is, they can be successful at both tasks. Consider the visual working memory required to drive a car. Your attention must be on the road. However, this does not prevent you from devoting auditory working memory to listening to a CD or talking to a passenger. Similarly, in a psychological experiment, a participant can track a moving arrow on a screen and rehearse digits without a deficit in the ability to do either task.

Concurrent tasks: tasks to be done simultaneously.

The first published evidence to support the idea that working memory was not unitary and might consist of multiple systems goes back to a landmark study by Baddeley and Hitch (1974). In the study, participants were given strings of digits to remember. These strings varied from simply one number to as many as eight. Thus, essentially, this task was a digit span task, some of which were trivially easy and others more difficult. The catch was that Baddeley and Hitch also gave their participants a **concurrent task** (a task to be done simultaneously with the first task). In the concurrent task, the participants had to judge whether simple sentences were correct. The participant might see the letters JK, and underneath would be a statement, "The J is before the K" (true) or they might see "The K is before the J" (false).

Based on earlier conceptions of working memory, you might expect that the concurrent task would provide an additional burden to working memory and interfere with the recall in the digit span task. However, that is not what Baddeley and Hitch (1974) found in this experiment. Instead, there was almost no overlap between the two tasks. The retrieval of digits was just as good as it would have been without a concurrent task, and participants did as well on the concurrent task when they were rehearsing eight digits as they did when they rehearsed only one digit. That is, there was no interference between the two tasks. For these two tasks, the participants really could do two things simultaneously.

These results are interpretable when one thinks of the visuospatial sketchpad and the phonological loop as separate systems. The phonological loop was sufficient to handle the digit span task, whereas the visuospatial sketchpad was sufficient to handle the reading and processing of the simple reasoning task. Because both of these components did not need to tax the attentional mechanism (the central executive), both tasks could be done at the same time without any interference. Thus, this study counts as evidence that visual and auditory working memory can function independent of each other, as there was no interference between them.

In another experiment specifically designed to test this model of working memory, Logie (1986) asked participants to learn paired associates (digit word pairs, such as 23-typewriter or 12-candlestick). Some participants were instructed to use a visual strategy to encode the words (that is, to employ the visuospatial sketchpad by making a mental image of the association), whereas other participants were instructed to use rote encoding (to employ the phonological loop). In the concurrent task, Logie either presented pictures (visual) or required participants to listen to names (auditory). The participants merely had to see or hear the items—they were not required to encode them. Nonetheless, the results were striking; the visual concurrent task interfered with the learning of paired associates when the associates were learned using the visual strategy, and the auditory concurrent task interfered with learning of the paired associates when the associates were being learned using the rote encoding. In contrast, the cross-sensory interference was much less. Looking at pictures did not interfere with rote encoding, and hearing names did not interfere with the visual learning strategy. To restate the findings another way, when the learning task required visual imagery, viewing pictures interfered with learning, but hearing words did not. When the task required auditory processing, hearing words interfered with learning but seeing pictures did not.

Now let us contrast the Baddeley and Hitch (1974) and Logie (1986) data with another experiment. L. R. Peterson and Johnson (1971) also did a digit span task with a simultaneously performed concurrent task. Peterson and Johnson asked participants to repeat simple words over and over (e.g., *the, the, the, the . . .*) while they were also supposed to be rehearsing the digits for the digit span task. Because both tasks now involve the phonological loop, this concurrent task did reduce the number of digits that could be remembered. This kind of interference is called **articulatory suppression.** You might think that silently repeating the word *the* would not interfere with processing, as it is such an easy task. But because it requires some use of the phonological loop, it does interfere with other tasks that employ the phonological loop.

> **Articulatory suppression**: a concurrent task that prevents the participants from engaging in rehearsal within the phonological loop.

Thus, a basic principle can be derived from these experiments. As long as the attentional demands are not too great, visual working memory (visuospatial sketchpad) tasks should not interfere with auditory working memory (phonological loop) tasks. By the same token, auditory working memory tasks should not interfere with visual working memory tasks. In contrast, even relatively easy tasks within the same working memory system will interfere with each other. That is, two auditory working memory tasks will interfere with each other, and two visual working memory tasks will interfere with each other.

WORKING MEMORY SYSTEMS

The Phonological Loop

The phonological loop is our auditory working memory system. It stores sounds, particularly language sounds, for a short period of time. In this way, it is like an "inner ear" that stores the sounds we hear in a most literal format until we can process them in terms of their meaning and store them in long-term memory. Most of our earlier discussion of working memory really concerned the phonological loop.

In keeping with the principle of parsimony, it is important for researchers to demonstrate the need for a new theoretical construct. Thus, the onus of evidence fell on those researchers who argue that working memory is composed of multiple systems rather than a single system. So let's consider evidence from experiments that was specifically designed to test Baddeley's theories.

We'll start with evidence from the neuropsychological domain. Vallar and Baddeley (1984) examined a patient with selective damage to the phonological loop. The patient tested normally in most areas of cognitive functioning. However, her working memory, as measured by digit spans, was severely impaired. Moreover, she did not show the word length effect. This means that longer words were not more difficult to keep in working memory than shorter words. Vallar and Baddeley claim that this occurred because whatever words she could recall were coming from the sketchpad rather than the loop. The longer words may have taken longer to pronounce, but because she was not using the phonological loop, whatever she did retain in working memory was based on visual processing. Her working memory was also unaffected by phonological similarity (that is, words that sound similar), also suggesting that it was only the phonological loop that was affected and not the sketchpad.

From the cognitive domain, we have already discussed the initial findings of Baddeley and Hitch (1974), which support the distinction between the phonological loop and the visuospatial sketchpad. Other evidence that supports the existence of a phonological loop comes from the research on irrelevant speech. The irrelevant speech effect refers to the observation that the phonological loop is mildly impaired when there is background talking going on. Irrelevant speech affects performance on phonological loop tasks but not visuospatial sketchpad tasks. For example, Salame and Baddeley (1989) asked participants to maintain information in working memory while listening to either singing, music without singing, or no sounds at all (see Figure 3.6). The silent group performed the best on the working memory task, but the group that listened to music without singing outperformed the group that listened to singing. Thus, sounds of any nature, particularly meaningful sounds, interfere with our ability to maintain information in the phonological loop. Of course, the results of Salame and Baddeley have implications for mnemonic improvement as well—studying in a quiet room leads to a more efficient environment for learning. This has implications for the so-called Mozart effect. In fact, research suggests that listening to Mozart did not have positive effects on immediate learning of spatial information (T. L. Wilson & Brown, 1997).

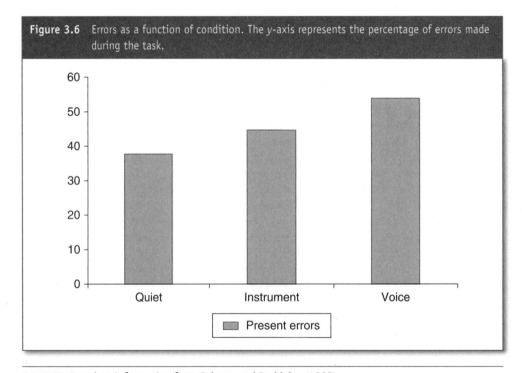

Figure 3.6   Errors as a function of condition. The y-axis represents the percentage of errors made during the task.

SOURCE: Based on information from Salame and Baddeley (1989).

Visuospatial Sketchpad

The visuospatial sketchpad stores visual and spatial information for short amounts of time in the activated contents of consciousness. It is largely independent of the phonological loop as long as attentional demands are low. We experience the visuospatial sketchpad when we retrieve what a person looks like. If you have a mental image of your best friend's face in your mind's eye, it is being represented in your visuospatial sketchpad. If you glance briefly at a map while driving and then try to figure out where you are supposed to get off the highway, you are using your visuospatial sketchpad to represent that information.

As we have seen in the experiments described above, phonological processing does not interfere with visual working memory. Nor does visual processing interfere with the phonological loop. Another example of this that focuses on the visuospatial sketchpad comes from an experiment done by Lee Brooks (1968). Brooks's original purpose was to explore the nature of imagery, but his experiment provides an excellent example of the independence of the visuospatial sketchpad. Brooks asked participants to imagine letters that were not actually present, such as the letter F (see Figure 3.7). Because participants were asked to make a visual image, we can assume that the representation of this image is being held in the visuospatial sketchpad. Keep in mind that the participants could not actually see the letter—they only had a mental image with which to base their decisions. Participants were then asked to make judgments about the letter, such as whether the angle of the letter was obtuse (greater than 180 degrees) or acute (less than 180 degrees). Participants had to rely on their image of the letter and were not allowed to draw one. Most participants found this task challenging yet possible.

The important experimental manipulation concerned how participants made their responses. Responses were made by speaking the answers aloud, tapping them out with their hands (i.e., one tap for "yes"; two taps for "no"), or pointing to a field with an array of *y*s for "yes" and *n*s for "no." Note that neither speaking nor tapping requires use of the visuospatial sketchpad. Thus, these response options should not interfere with the imagery task. Pointing to letters on a display in front of them does require visual processing. Thus, the pointing response also employs the visuospatial sketchpad. In fact, participants were more accurate and faster when they had to speak the answer or tap the answer than when they were pointing to the array. Thus, only the visual task interfered with the imagery task. This happens because the pointing task makes use of the visuospatial sketchpad as well as the imagery task. Because of the interference, performance decreases.

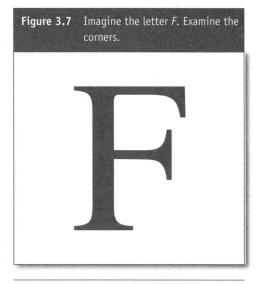

Figure 3.7 Imagine the letter F. Examine the corners.

SOURCE: Based on Brooks (1968).

The Episodic Buffer

Baddeley (2000) added a further component to his model called the episodic buffer. Baddeley introduced this theoretical concept because he thought his earlier version of the model did not adequately account for all the data in the field. The episodic buffer maintains information after it has been processed in the phonological loop and the visuospatial sketchpad as well as information from long-term memory. In this way, the episodic buffer is a multimodal system. This allows the episodic buffer to provide needed meaning or semantic-based information to the working memory system. For example, when you retrieve information, such as the directions to your cousin's apartment, this information is briefly maintained in the buffer before it is converted into directions (in the phonological loop) or a visual map (in the visuospatial sketchpad). The buffer also allows new information to be integrated before it reaches long-term memory. For example, a scene being processed by the visuospatial sketchpad will be encoded for meaning in the buffer before it is stored in long-term episodic memory. The only current evidence for the episodic buffer comes from amnesic patients who have very impaired encoding into long-term memory but normal working memory (Baddeley & Wilson, 2002). However, when encoding stories, they seem to be able maintain more than seven items of information in mind while reading the stories. They forget the stories later (the patients have amnesia), but their "intermediate memory" extends past what and how long working memory usually processes. Baddeley and Wilson (2002) argue that this is because of the integrated nature of the episodic buffer. Future research will determine if this component makes accurate predictions about human memory performance.

The Central Executive

The central executive is an attentional system that supervises and coordinates the actions of the other working memory components. In early versions of Baddeley's theory, the central executive received much less attention than the phonological loop and the visuospatial sketchpad. However, over the past few years, this component has been investigated with vigor and success. The goal of the central executive is to allocate limited attentional resources to the working memory subsystems. Most researchers think of the central executive as part of a broader supervisory network, probably located in the frontal lobes, which has many other roles in cognition in addition to coordinating working memory.

One interesting study designed to probe the role of the central executive with respect to working memory comes from the work of Teasdale et al. (1995). They asked participants to generate random numbers at a rate of one number per second. This is not as easy as it seems. You must regulate the generation of numbers to ensure that you are not making any obvious pattern. You must also do it in rhythm. If you try it yourself, you will find it does require attention, that is, a little bit of focus to make sure a clear pattern is not developing and that you are keeping up the beat. Teasdale et al. probed participants at intervals about every 2 minutes and asked them what they were thinking about. When participants reported "daydreaming" (not surprising giving the repetitive nature of the random-number generation task), their patterns tended to be nonrandom (i.e., noticeable sequences, such as 1, 2, 4, 8). When they reported concentration on the task, their numbers were better approximations of randomness. Thus, when people's attention was diverted, as when they were daydreaming, there were insufficient attentional resources left to devote to the number generation task. The implication is that the central executive—when directing attention to the task—allowed participants to better produce the digits into working memory. We will consider other aspects of the role executive functions have on memory in subsequent chapters.

WORKING MEMORY AND THE BRAIN

Working memory has also become the intense focus of cognitive neuroscientists recently, with the central executive of particular interest and importance. Baddeley's (2007) multiple-component model has found great support in brain-based studies. Indeed, the phonological loop, the visuospatial sketchpad, and the central executive appear not to be based on fine distinctions in areas of adjacent cortex but seemingly housed in different lobes of the cerebral cortex! So let's start looking at the correlations between behavioral measures of working memory and the brain. We will start with a neuropsychological study and then consider the more recent neuroimaging research.

Warrington and Shallice (1969) studied a young brain-damaged man identified in their paper by the initials KF. KF's brain was injured as the result of a motorcycle accident in England. KF's long-term memory was unaffected, both in terms of new learning and retrieving prior knowledge. However, his working memory was severely impaired. On a digit span task, he could not recall spans longer than two digits when tested auditorily! Even when tested visually, he still only had a digit span of four. This suggests that the problem was more with the phonological loop than with the visuospatial sketchpad. Think about this—if you read out the numbers 5-8-9, he would not be able to repeat them back to you. Subsequent examination of his brain confirmed this pattern—KF's damage was in the left temporal lobe, in areas typically associated with language.

Warrington and Shallice (1969) did not have Baddeley's model yet to work with, but the early neuroimaging researchers did. In fact, Jonides (1995), in one of the earliest positron emission tomography (PET) studies to look at memory phenomena, tested Baddeley's model. Jonides examined the brains of participants engaged in tasks designed to measure the phonological loop or the visuospatial sketchpad. In the task designed to examine the phonological loop, participants watched a sequence of letters at a rate of one letter every 3 seconds. If a given letter was the same as one two spaces back (i.e., 6 seconds ago), the participant indicated this by saying yes. If not, the participant said no. Most people will do this task by mentally rehearsing the digits as they appear. Thus, even though the presentation is visual, it is sensible to consider this a task for the phonological loop. To occupy the visuospatial sketchpad, participants saw three dots presented in different locations for a 200-msec interval. The dots then disappeared, and 3 seconds later, a circle appeared. The participants then indicated if this circle marked a spot where one of the dots had been just prior.

The PET data showed that the two tasks led to different patterns of activation in the cerebral cortex. The phonological loop task was associated with activity in Broca's area of the left frontal lobe (known as an important area in speech) as well as areas in the left parietal lobe. In contrast, the visuospatial sketchpad task led to activation in the right occipital lobe (visual processing) as well as the right parietal and right prefrontal lobes. Thus, the distinction between the visuospatial sketchpad and the phonological loop is supported by PET studies, which show different activation patterns for each task (see Jonides, Lacey, & Nee, 2005).

Neuroimaging data are also demonstrating that the central executive is an important component of working memory. Areas of the prefrontal cortex that are known to be involved in other attentional or monitoring tasks also appear to be active during working memory tasks, including digit span and other verbal working memory tasks. For example, PET studies and functional magnetic resonance imaging (fMRI) studies confer that verbal working memory tasks activate the right dorsolateral prefrontal cortex (Ruchkin, Grafman, Cameron, & Berndt, 2003; Rypma & D'Esposito, 2003) as well as the anterior cingulate (Otsuka & Osaka, 2005). The anterior cingulate is also located in the prefrontal regions of the brain. Both of these brain regions (right dorsolateral prefrontal cortex and anterior cingulate) are important in self-regulation, attention, and cognitive monitoring as well as verbal working memory.

Thus, the pattern of activity that emerges from the neuroimaging studies is the following. The phonological loop is mainly housed in the language-related areas of the brain, particularly in areas associated with the production of speech. The visuospatial sketchpad appears to be located in areas of the right hemisphere, associated with vision and spatial skills. Finally, the central executive is centered in prefrontal regions of the brain, which are also active in planning, monitoring, and other executive cognitive functions.

APPLICATIONS OF WORKING MEMORY

Reading Fluency

When we read, we are using our working memory. In fact, your working memory—at this very moment—is holding the words and ideas in this sentence so that you can understand this sentence. Consider how difficult it must have been for the patient KF to read, given he could only keep two words in his working memory at any particular time. It is likely that his reading was slow and laborious. Given how important working memory is to reading, it is likely that there may be some connection between working memory capacity and reading ability. Indeed, in children just becoming fluent readers (age 12), there is a clear correlation between the capacity of working memory and fluency of reading (Daneman & Carpenter, 1980). That is, if the child can maintain more information in his or her working memory, he or she can understand the material quicker with less "looking back." Stated another way, the better a child's working memory is, the better his or her reading ability is.

Daneman and Carpenter (1980) asked young participants to read sentences and process them for meaning. They were then asked questions about the meaning of the passage and asked to retrieve as many words as they could from the end of the last sentence. They found that participants who could retrieve more of the last few words also scored higher on comprehension. This advantage continues into college. Daneman and Hannon (2001) found that people with high working memory capacity did better than those with lower working memory capacity on their SAT tests.

Verbal Fluency

Engle (2002) also argued that working memory capacity was related to verbal fluency—that is, the ability to speak fluently without pausing. In other words, those of us who intrude frequent "uhs" or "hmms" in our speech are likely to have less efficient working memory than those who are less likely to make these errors. Engle argued that those with larger working memory capacities were also those who spoke with fewer pauses. To test this, Engle and his colleagues divided students into groups with high working memory scores and those with lower working memory scores. The group with the higher working memory scores was able to generate more examples in a given category (e.g., tools) during a particular time period than those with lower working memory scores.

ADHD

Some studies have shown that children with attention deficit disorders have weaker working memory capacity than normal controls (Klingberg, Forssberg, & Westerberg, 2002). However, this is reversible. Children with attention deficit hyperactivity disorder (ADHD) who receive training and practice in working memory tasks can improve their working memory capacity. Training of working memory in unimpaired individuals can also lead to an improvement in capacity, which may lead to improvements in test scores, including IQ tests (Oleson, Westerberg, & Klingberg, 2004).

> **Reading fluency**: the ability to read at speeds sufficient to process and understand written material.
>
> **Verbal fluency**: the ability to talk without pausing or stopping.

Alzheimer's Disease

Alzheimer's disease is often hard to diagnose. Its early symptoms are difficult to distinguish from other forms of amnesia. However, unlike amnesia that results directly from damage to the medial temporal lobe, in which there is no deficit in working memory, Alzheimer's disease is accompanied by a deficit in working memory (Caza & Belleville, 2008). Therefore, Alzheimer's can be distinguished during its early phases from other organic deficits by examining working memory performance.

Cell Phones and Working Memory

When cell phones became such a staple of modern life, there was some initial concern that the chronic and intense exposure to the low-level radiofrequency electromagnetic fields produced by cell phones could produce some interference with normal cognitive functioning. Cinel,

Boldini, Fox, and Russo (2008) found, to the contrary, that exposure to such fields does not interfere with working memory performance. So rest assure, although you may still not want to talk on your cell phone during class (or church), it will not affect your working memory.

SUMMARY

Working memory refers to the neural structures and cognitive processes that maintain the accessibility of information for short periods of time in an active conscious state. Working memory holds a small amount of information at any one time, which can be maintained by rehearsal. Rehearsal refers to the active repetition of information in conscious awareness. *Working memory* is the current term, while previous generations referred to this phenomenon by the name *short-term memory*. Working memory capacity can be measured by the digit span task or by the recency effect in serial position curves. Most estimates of the capacity of working memory indicate that we can maintain about seven items. However, this is modulated by the length of the words we are maintaining in working memory. Words that take less time to pronounce are easier to maintain in working memory. In free recall of serial lists, the primacy effect is associated with long-term memory, whereas the recency effect is associated with working memory. Most recently, working memory is thought to consist of several subsystems, including the visuospatial sketchpad, the phonological loop, the episodic buffer, and the central executive. Each subsystem is responsible for one aspect of the working memory process, with the central executive coordinating among them. Areas in the prefrontal and medial temporal lobes appear to be the neural regions mediating working memory. Working memory is linked to **reading fluency** and **verbal fluency.** It is impaired in both individuals with ADHD in childhood and Alzheimer's disease in older adults (see also www.sagepub.com/schwartz[5, 6]).

KEY TERMS

Working memory	Word length effect	Recency effect
Short-term memory	Rehearsal	Visuospatial sketchpad
Primary memory	Maintenance rehearsal	Phonological loop
Sensory memory	Elaborative rehearsal	Episodic buffer
Iconic memory	Duration of information in working memory	Central executive
Echoic memory		
Capacity	Rehearsal prevention task	Concurrent tasks
Digit span task	Interference	Articulatory suppression
Chunking	Serial position curve	Reading fluency
Pronunciation time	Primacy effect	Verbal fluency

REVIEW QUESTIONS

1. Why is working memory considered to be the active contents of consciousness? How does the concept of working memory differ from the concept of short-term memory?

2. Describe three main differences between working memory and long-term memory.

3. How does the digit span task measure working memory? How is it modified by the pronunciation time effect?

4. How did Naveh-Benjamin and his colleagues demonstrate the importance of pronunciation time on the capacity of working memory?

5. How is the serial position curve measured?

6. Describe one variable that affects the primacy portion of the curve and one variable that affects the recency portion of the curve.

7. What evidence supports the idea that the visuospatial sketchpad and the phonological loop are separate subsystems in working memory?

8. What is the role of the central executive in working memory?

9. What neuropsychological evidence exists to support the notion that working memory is a distinct memory system separate from long-term memory?

10. How is working memory related to reading ability?

ONLINE RESOURCES

1. For information on William James, go to http://www.des.emory.edu/mfp/james.html.

2. For animal working memory, see http://www.psych.utoronto.ca/users/shettle/sararsch .html#animalperceptionmemory.

3. For more on Ericsson's work, go to http://www.psy.fsu.edu/faculty/ericsson/ericsson.hp.html.

4. For a demonstration of serial position, go to http://cat.xula.edu/thinker/memory/working/serial.

5. For information on Alan Baddeley, go to http://www.york.ac.uk/depts/psych/www/people/ biogs/ab50.html.

6. For a nice overview of working memory, go to http://cat.xula.edu/thinker/memory/working.

7. For another nice cite on working memory, go to http://www.workingmemory.org.

 Go to www.sagepub.com/schwartz for additional exercises and study resources. Select **Chapter 3, Working Memory** for chapter-specific resources.

CHAPTER 4

Episodic Memory

Remember some of the important and significant events from your life. Think about your high school graduation ceremony or when you and your significant other agreed to get married. Also think of more mundane information—have you brushed your teeth yet today? Was your professor drinking Coca-Cola or Pepsi this morning? Did you go to the gym, and what exercises did you do there? Each of these represents the memory of a specific event from your life. In some cases, they happened years ago and are very important, whereas in other cases, they just happened this morning and are much less important. But each event happened in the past, and it only happened once, and yet we can relive and feel again what we felt then. This is the hallmark of episodic memory—our long-term memory for the personal events from our lives. These events may have taken place only a few minutes ago, or they may have occurred a lifetime ago. But the manner in which we represent them in memory is surprisingly similar. Many memory theorists today think that long-term memory is also divided into systems—each designed to handle different kinds of information. Starting with the work of Endel Tulving (discussed in Chapter 1), many memory researchers think we have a unique neurocognitive system, known as episodic memory, designed to store and retrieve the unique events of our lives (Tulving, 2002).

Unlike working memory, which stores only a small amount of information, long-term memory systems, such as episodic memory, must be able to store a tremendous amount of information. For any particular event, one must remember when the event took place, where it took place, what was involved in the event, and who was present. It may also be important to remember what our emotions were and what the outcome was. We need to store this information for all of the thousands and thousands of events that we participate in over the course of our lives. Thus, finding a way to store or represent all this information is crucial for episodic and other long-term memory systems. Let's take a look at the memory taxonomy theorized by Endel Tulving and then see if holds up to experimental scrutiny.

Tulving hypothesized that there is an important difference between two functional aspects of memory: knowledge of the world (semantic memory) and memory of personal events (episodic memory). (See Table 4.1.) For Tulving, semantic memory means impersonal knowledge that we acquire about the world. In most cases, we do not remember when and how we learned that information. Episodic memory is our personal memory for the events from our lives. Thus, for example, the memory of your high school graduation ceremony is stored in your episodic memory. Or the memory of using the Stairmaster this morning is stored in episodic memory. On the other hand, semantic memory encompasses our knowledge of the world. For example, your knowledge that George Washington was the first president of the United States is stored in semantic memory. Your knowledge that London is the capital of Great Britain is stored in semantic memory. Episodic and semantic memory, therefore, differ in the *content* of what is represented, in the personal meaning to the individual, and the emotions it inspires, but Tulving's assertion is that we have different neurocognitive systems for episodic and semantic memory. That is, Tulving claimed that our brains have different systems that operate according to different principles for episodic and semantic memory. When Tulving first proposed this point of view in the early 1970s, it was met with great skepticism. However, there is now a considerable amount of evidence supporting both the cognitive and neural basis for this hypothesis.

Let's start with semantic memory. **Semantic memory** is the neurocognitive memory system that encodes, stores, and retrieves information concerning knowledge of the world. The contents of semantic memory are the facts, stories, words, and associations we make as we learn about our world. Semantic memory is potentially impersonal in that many of the facts that we store in it are detached from our actual experience, and we may not remember when and where we learned these facts. Moreover, we are more likely to express our memory by saying "I know" rather than "I remember" for semantic memories than for episodic memories. Each individual person stores thousands upon thousands of semantic memories. For example, that the pop star "Hannah Montana" is played by the actress Miley Cyrus is an

> **Semantic memory**: the neurocognitive memory system that encodes, stores, and retrieves information concerning knowledge of the world.

Table 4.1 Differences between episodic and semantic memory.

Characteristics	Episodic Memory	Semantic Memory
Type of information stored	Personally experienced events	General facts
Unit of information	Events or episodes	Facts, ideas, concepts
Mental experience	"Mental time travel"/remembering	"Knowledge of facts"/knowing
Neural regions/retrieval: frontal lobe	Right prefrontal	Left prefrontal
Neural regions: temporal lobe	Medial temporal lobes	Medial temporal lobes

example of knowledge about the world. "Angela Merkel" was chancellor of Germany in 2010 is also stored in semantic memory. So are facts such as "Pittsburgh is east of Miami," "Vegans do not eat eggs," and "Casey Kasem was the original voice of Shaggy on Scooby Doo." In addition, we may also have semantic memory that does reference ourselves. Thus, you can say, "I went to South Valley Elementary School" without actually thinking about any particular experience in elementary school. Most of us also know our birthday, even though we do not remember being born. We will continue our discussion of semantic memory in Chapter 5. For now, it is presented just to contrast with episodic memory.

Episodic memory is the neurocognitive memory system that encodes, stores, and retrieves memories of our personal individual experiences. Episodic memory is the system responsible for encoding the *what, when,* and *where* of an event and representing the past-ness of the event. This means we are sure the event is past and not occurring at present. Moreover, the memory pertains to the past rather than the present. For example, you may remember shaking President Obama's hand at a campaign rally. You attribute this to the past and will continue to do so even after someone else becomes president. In addition, you are likely to remember the where (on your college campus) and the when (while he was running for president) as well as the what (shaking hands with the president). Episodic memories are usually characterized by feelings of "remembering" rather than knowing. In order for it to be an episodic memory, it must be directly based on personal experiences that you have had. For example, remembering the time I saw an iguana fall out of a tree and land directly in front of me is an example of episodic memory. So is the memory of the time I drove a rented convertible Ford Mustang from the airport to my hotel in San Francisco. Episodic memories can be big events from one's life (remembering the moment when you say "I do" in a wedding ceremony) to small events from your life (remembering the act of pouring cereal during this morning's breakfast). Episodic memory even includes **flashbulb memories,** those highly salient memories people have of their own circumstances during major public events. Anyone who was older than age 6 or so on September 11, 2001, probably remembers what they were doing and where they were when they heard the news of the terrorist attacks that day.

Note some of the functional differences between the two systems. Semantic memory need not be personal. Indeed, we can have semantic memories concerning events that occurred long before we were born. For example, you probably know that George Washington was the first president of the United States, even though it happened hundreds of years before your birth. On the other hand, episodic memories are always *personal experiences.* Thus, I remember my visit to the Washington monument in which my umbrella was blown out by the wind while running to my car in a thunderstorm. Furthermore, semantic memories are usually not emotionally tinged. I may know that an earthquake in Turkey killed tens of thousands of people, but that fact alone may not elicit emotion. It is only when I retrieve my own episodic memory of seeing television news coverage of the

> **Episodic memory**: the neurocognitive memory system that encodes, stores, and retrieves memories of our personal individual experiences.
>
> **Flashbulb memories**: highly confident personal memories of surprising events. In order to study them, researchers have focused on the memory of public tragedies.

tragedy that emotion becomes involved. Emotion is an essential component of many episodic memories. Anguish, anger, and grief are all vital components to most of our flash-bulb memories of 9/11. On the positive side, happiness is (usually) a key component of memories of wedding ceremonies.

Another difference, however subtle, is that episodic memories necessarily are concerned about the past, whereas semantic memories usually concern the present. So the knowledge (semantic memory) that saiten is used as a meat substitute by vegans is usually retrieved when somebody wants information from the rememberer about the current state of the world, such as what to expect at a vegan restaurant. With semantic memory, we might retrieve "Dr. Hughes's office is on the fourth floor of Silsby Hall" because we want to direct someone to Dr. Hughes right now. Thus, semantic memory uses memory to serve our present purposes. In this way, it is important to update semantic memory. If Dr. Hughes moves his office from the fourth floor of Silsby Hall to the third floor of Moore Hall, I have to update memory in order to direct people to the right office. In contrast, episodic memory truly concerns the past. We want people to know not that a vegan restaurant exists but that we ate there last week and had a delicious dinner and a fun time with friends. You retrieve your day of snorkeling in Cozumel, and you want to reexperience the peacefulness and beauty of the event. In episodic memory, the emphasis is on the past rather than the present (Tulving & Lepage, 2000). Indeed, Tulving has called episodic memory "mental time travel." Episodic memory is also a highly social phenomenon. We want to share our episodic memories with our friends and family. Indeed, we all know someone who shares his episodic memories too often. By the fifth time you have heard the same story about his giant meal on the cruise ship, you cannot wait to get away. In a more positive vein, when you meet old friends whom you may not have seen or spoken with in some time, you are likely to start reminiscing about old times, that is, sharing your common memories of exciting, fun, and embarrassing experiences that you shared in common.

Later in the text, we will consider autobiographical memory. The term *autobiographical memory* means the memories we have of our own lives. Autobiographical memory is not associated with any individual particular neurocognitive system in the way that episodic and semantic memory are. In fact, autobiographical memory is a combination of episodic memory and self-referential semantic memories. That is, our memory of our lives is composed of both our memory for events from our lives and the facts of our lives, some of which may not be based on the memory of individual experiences. For example, you may know the details concerning your birth, such as what city you were born in, what hospital, your actual birthday, and similar details for a sibling born a year or two after yourself. These memories are semantic in nature, as you were too young to encode them yourself episodically. Your knowledge of them is semantic knowledge, not episodic memory. Similarly, you may have information about your personality—that you are kind and generous, even when you are not thinking about a particular event in which you acted kindly or generously. In semantic memory, we may form categories concerning our lives, such as "when I was in high school," which do not necessitate any episodic memories of being in high school, although they may facilitate their retrieval. Therefore, do not confuse autobiographical memory with episodic memory. The terms have two distinct meanings. We will focus on autobiographical memory in Chapter 7.

EVIDENCE FOR THE DISTINCTION

When Tulving first proposed the distinction between episodic and semantic memory, it was a largely unsubstantiated hypothesis (Tulving, 1972, 1983). It made some intuitive sense, but there was little evidence to demonstrate that semantic and episodic memory form distinct systems. Today, there is a large body of evidence to support the reality of this distinction, some of it coming from cognitive psychology and much of it coming from the neuropsychological and neuroimaging domain.

Behavioral Evidence

We have already pointed out that many of us prefer the expression "I know" to describe a semantic memory but "I remember" to describe an episodic memory. Tulving (1983) thought this distinction was important and that the feeling captures some underlying difference between the two mental states. Indeed, the distinction between know and remember is made in most languages (e.g., *savoir* and *connaître* in French). Now the boundaries between "I know" and "I remember" are flexible. No one would look at you oddly if you said, "I know where and who I was with when I saw Michael Phelps get his eight gold medals in the Olympics." However, it connotes something different than if you said, "I remember where and who I was with when I saw Michael Phelps get his eight gold medals in the Olympics." The latter is clearly more personal and "episodic."

Tulving (1985) devised a test in which people were asked if they "remembered" information or if they "knew" information and then examined whether different experimental variables affected the two subjective states in different ways. In this context, "remembered" meant that you could retrieve the personal context in which you encountered the information. Remembering also meant an experience of "mental time travel," that is, that the participant was aware of the past. In contrast, "know" judgments were simply declarations that the information was accessible in memory. "Know" judgments are about what the person knows now, not about the past per se. If you learn a list of unrelated words (e.g., *dog, fork, pasture, compass, omnivore,* etc.), when you see one of the words later, what factors will cause you to experience that you "know" that the word was on the list versus that you "remember" that the word was on the list?

Consider an experiment in which you study some words by focusing on what the words mean. We shall see shortly that this leads to good recall of those words. In another condition, however, you study some words by focusing on what color the word is printed in. Later, you are asked to recognize the words from distractors and also asked to distinguish if you "remember" (henceforth R judgments) or "know" (henceforth K judgments) the words. Research shows that K judgments occur equally often when you study for meaning and when you study for visual characteristics. However, R judgments are much more common for meaning-based learning than for visual-based learning (see Gardiner, 2002). In contrast, studying words versus nonwords does not affect the number of R judgments, but nonwords are much more likely to receive K judgments than words. These and other experimental variables show that R judgments and K judgments are influenced by different factors.

These data led Tulving and many other researchers to conclude that **remember judgments** are more likely to accompany episodic events, whereas **know judgments** (sometimes

> **Remember/know judgments**: a task in which participants determine the feeling of memories by assigning them categories of "remember" or "know."

pronounced "kih-no," to differentiate it from "no," that is, don't remember judgments) are more likely to accompany semantic knowledge. These subjective variables, that is, how participants feel, are correlated with many objective variables, that is, how they behave in experiments.

Neuropsychological Evidence

Neuropsychology refers to the relation between brain damage and memory and cognitive deficits. Research in this area now shows that both episodic memory and semantic memory can be impaired by brain damage but that there can be impairment to one form of memory but not to the other. First, memory impairment occurs much more often for episodic memory. Semantic memory amnesia is, in fact, quite rare. Second, memory impairment following brain damage is usually much greater for episodic memory than for semantic memory. In many cases, amnesic patients can lose much of the access to their episodic memories but without substantial impairment of retrieval from semantic memory, although they still may have impaired encoding into semantic memory. These patients will still recall many facts about the world but will suffer impairments in remembering events from their lives.

Consider the case of the amnesic patient KC, studied originally by Tulving (Rosenbaum et al., 2005). KC suffered extensive brain damage following a terrible motorcycle accident. During testing, KC could retrieve information from semantic memory essentially normally. He was able to list all the teams that had won the Stanley Cup in hockey over the previous 10 years, for example. He could also tell you how a car engine worked and how to repair one. However, retrieval from episodic memory was severely impaired. He could not remember any details of his life at all, none of the times he had fixed cars, none of his previous motorcycle crashes, or even the details concerning the tragic death of his brother. Nor could he form new episodic memories. Thus, with KC, we see that both encoding and retrieval from episodic memory can occur without damage to semantic memory. These patients point to an important neurological difference between semantic and episodic memory. To see KC for yourself, go to the following YouTube site: www.sagepub.com/schwartz.[1]

Vargha-Khadem et al. (1997) studied patients who had what they called **developmental amnesia.** Unlike HM (see Chapter 2) or KC, these patients did not have traumatic brain injuries, at least none of which that they or their doctors were aware. Nonetheless, they appear to be impaired at encoding new episodic events and retrieving events from their lives. Nonetheless, they learn new facts about the world, that is, they learn semantic information, normally. Thus, it seems that their deficits are solely in the episodic memory system. Therefore, based on patterns of deficits seen in neuropsychological patients, there is the potential for a **dissociation** between episodic and semantic memory. Dissociation means that brain damage (or an experimental variable) can affect one cognitive system but

> **Developmental amnesia**: a congenital memory deficit, usually restrictive to episodic memory.
>
> **Dissociation**: brain damage (or an experimental variable) can affect one cognitive system but leave another one intact.

leave another one intact. In this case, brain damage impairs episodic memory without affecting semantic memory. For more information on developmental amnesia, go to www.sagepub.com/schwartz.[2]

Evidence From Neuroimaging

The *neuro* in the term *neurocognitive systems of memory* was given a giant boost when people began looking at differences between episodic and semantic memory using modern neuroimaging techniques. Although there is some overlap in terms of neural regions during both kinds of memory tasks, there are also great differences. It is these differences that are now the best support to the claim that episodic and semantic memory are different neurocognitive systems. We will examine a typical neuroimaging experiment on this topic.

Tulving and his colleagues conducted a series of important positron emission tomography (PET) studies on the episodic/semantic distinction (see Habib, McIntosh, Wheeler, & Tulving, 2003). As a consequence, they derived the **HERA (hemispheric encoding/retrieval asymmetry)** model of memory. The HERA model states that the left hemisphere has greater involvement in semantic memory but that the right hemisphere has greater involvement with episodic memory. They tested this idea by giving participants cue words and then asking them to retrieve a specific event from their life elicited by the cue (episodic memory) or a fact about the world elicited by the cue (semantic memory). However, in these studies, the recollection of past events occurred while the PET scan was on, monitoring their brain output. In another condition, the participants were asked to recall facts they knew were associated with the cue word. This method elicited semantic memories. Habib et al. (2003) discovered a number of important facts about the brain and memory. First, research found that the left prefrontal cortex was more involved in the retrieval of information from semantic memory, whereas the right prefrontal cortex is more involved in the retrieval of episodic memory. Second, the researchers asked participants to encode episodic events or learn new facts. With respect to encoding in episodic memory, the left prefrontal lobe is more involved than the right prefrontal lobe. This asymmetry does not appear for semantic memory. Thus, although semantic and episodic memory may share many features in common, they have different underlying neural networks in the brain. To summarize, the neuroimaging data are consistent with the behavioral data; episodic memory and semantic memory are likely the products of different neurocognitive systems.

> **HERA (hemispheric encoding/retrieval asymmetry):** the theory that the right hemisphere is more involved in the retrieval of events from episodic memory and that the left hemisphere is more involved in the retrieval of events from semantic memory.

MEMORY PROCESSES: ENCODING, REPRESENTATION, AND RETRIEVAL

Both episodic and semantic memory can be divided into three important processes that are necessary for any memory system: encoding, representation, and retrieval. **Encoding** refers to the learning process, that is, how information is initially encountered

Encoding: the learning process, that is, how information is initially encountered and learned.

Representation: the storage of information in memory when that information is not in use.

Retrieval: the process of how we activate information from long-term memory and access it when we need it.

and learned. **Representation** is how we store information when it is not currently in use. **Retrieval** is the process of how we activate information from long-term memory and access it when we need it. There is strong overlap in how semantic memory and episodic memory accomplish these goals on a cognitive level. In this chapter, only encoding and retrieval in episodic memory will be covered. Representation and semantic memory will be discussed in Chapter 5.

Encoding in Episodic Memory

Encoding is the process by which we learn—that is, we perceive the world and process that information into memory. Encoding can also occur when we commit something we are imagining to memory. Thus, when someone you have just met tells you her name, you encode that name so that you can remember her later. When you go skydiving for the first time, you encode all the exciting experiences you have so that you can relive them later. Because encoding is the first step in the memory process, we will consider it first.

How do we transform information into a memory representation? Consider learning a new fact: Winnipeg is a city in Manitoba, Canada. We first must be able to perceive the letters and then understand the words. Then somehow we must be able to transform that sentence into some kind of neurocognitive code. This is not some esoteric question: Encoding is what we must to do to master the material we need to learn at school or work. Thus, we will start with one of the important theoretical perspectives on examining encoding.

Levels of Processing

Levels of processing means that more meaningful handling of information leads to better encoding of that information. It is one of the most successful theoretical constructs in memory research to date. Levels of processing applies to both encoding into episodic memory and to semantic memory. Two University of Toronto memory researchers named Fergus Craik and Robert Lockhart developed the theory in the early 1970s (Craik & Lockhart, 1972). Although they originally presented it as a theory that would allow for short-term memory and long-term memory to be considered two different processes of the same system, nowadays, levels-of-processing theory provides the basis of much of what we know about encoding. For an alternate view of levels of processing, go to www.sagepub.com/schwartz.[3]

Levels of processing: more meaningful handling of information leads to better encoding of that information.

Craik and Lockhart (1972) were interested not in intentional learning but in incidental learning. **Incidental learning** means that people encode information not by actively trying to remember but rather as a by-product of perceiving and understanding the world. In

Incidental learning: people encode information not by actively trying to remember but rather as by-product of perceiving and understanding the world.

Intentional learning: people actively engage in learning information because they know that their memories may be tested.

incidental learning, the goal is not to encode information. Rather, it occurs as a by-product of other processes. Incidental learning contrasts with intentional learning. **Intentional learning** means that people actively engage in learning information because they know that their memories may be tested. In intentional learning, we want to remember something and work hard to do so (see Figure 4.1).

Craik and Lockhart (1972) considered incidental learning to be an important aspect of cognition. They argued that much of our learning in ordinary life is, in fact, incidental learning. They claimed that most of our knowledge and memory is based not on explicit memorization but on incidental learning, which comes about just by processing the events and information we need. For example, we don't normally say to ourselves, "I have to remember how to get to Johnny's house," or "I have to remember how to chop the onions just right," or even, "I have to remember the plot of that great new movie we just saw." Yet in each case, you encode something, such as the directions, the recipe, and the plot, even though you were not specifically studying this information as you might do for a test in a college class. Another example is when a friend is coming over for dinner. You try to remember what that person likes to eat and perhaps what you served the last time that he or she was at your house for dinner. You probably never sat down with a notebook and recorded your friend's dining preferences, but if that person is a good friend, you have incidentally learned his or her favorite foods. Thus, at least some, if not most, of our learning occurs incidentally without our intention to remember. Therefore, in their experiments, Craik and Lockhart decided to use incidental learning.

Craik and Lockhart (1972) argued that our attentional resources are limited, so we can focus on only some aspects of any particular stimulus. However, people can control what aspects of the stimulus on which they are focusing. For example, when reading a novel, we can focus on the quality of the writing, the excitement of the plot, and the development of the characters. But it is usually difficult to concentrate on all of these aspects of reading a novel at once. This is where the idea of levels of processing fits in. The level of processing refers to the idea that the manner in which information is first encountered and rehearsed leads to a different depth of processing. **Elaborative rehearsal** leads to deeper processing, and **maintenance rehearsal** leads to shallow processing. Thus, when reading a novel, if you only pay attention to the size of the type, whether the book is old or new, or what designs are on the cover, you are processing your reading at a

Elaborative rehearsal: processing the meaning of information in working memory.

Maintenance rehearsal: repeating information over and over.

Deep processing vs. shallow processing: when we process more deeply, that is, using elaborative or meaningful processing, we will be more likely to remember the information processed. When we process more shallowly, that is, using maintenance rehearsal or processing for sensory characteristics, we will remember less of the information processed.

Figure 4.1 Most learning is not intentional, as it is for these students. This contrasts with learning in school, in which students make great efforts to master large amounts of material.

shallow level. If you are reading the book and trying to connect the plot to ideas about the world, how it applies to your life, and if the book is enjoyable or not, this is considered **deep processing.** If you are listening to someone speak, deep processing means attending to the message of the speaker. **Shallow processing** would include attending to his or her accent, whether or not the speaker had a deep or high-pitched voice, or how he or she pronounced the letter *r*. In real life, we normally are expected to pay attention to meaning, but there may be some circumstances when the lower level processing is more important.

Craik and Lockhart (1972) then derived the following hypothesis. When we process more deeply, that is, using elaborative or meaningful processing, we will be more likely to remember the information processed. When we process more shallowly, that is, using maintenance rehearsal or processing for sensory characteristics, we will remember less of the information processed. In retrospect of nearly 40 years, these ideas appear to be relatively straightforward. But at the time, it offered a new way of looking at memory. It also has very clear implications for memory improvement: Process more deeply and you will remember more of what you are studying.

To test this hypothesis, Craik teamed up with Endel Tulving to create what is now considered a landmark study (Craik & Tulving, 1975). In a series of experiments, Craik and Tulving employed a number of new methods, which became standard in much research to follow over the past three decades. First, they wanted their participants to encode the information through incidental learning because this approximates many real-life situations. Therefore, they did not tell the participants that their memory would be tested later. Second, they wanted the participants to encode some ideas through shallow or sensory-level processing and other items through deep or meaning-based processing. To accomplish both of these objectives, Craik and Tulving employed **orienting tasks.** An orienting task directs the participant's attention to some aspect of the stimuli—either deep or shallow—but does not alert the participant to the potential of a later memory test. In the orienting task, participants thought that they were being tested on the speed at which they could perform simple tasks involving words. They were not told that their memory for these words would be tested later. For example, the participant might see the word *beetle* and have to decide whether it was written in all capital letters or not. This would be a shallow or sensory task. A deep or meaning-based task involved asking something about the meaning. Therefore, deciding whether a "beetle" is an example of an animal is a meaning-based task. It is easy—but it requires the participants to think about the meaning of the word. These tasks force people into processing at either the shallow or deep level but do not alert the participants to the fact that their memory will subsequently be tested. Participants are later surprised when given a test of recognition or recall for the words they worked on.

> **Orienting tasks**: directs the participant's attention to some aspect of the stimuli—either deep or shallow—but does not alert the participant to the potential of a later memory test.

In the experiments, participants were first asked a question (the orienting task). They were then presented visually with a word and asked to answer the question with a yes or no answer. Some of the questions concerned physical characteristics of the printed word (visual-shallow), some of the questions concerned what the word sounded like (auditory-shallow), and others were concerned with the meaning of the word (deep-meaning based).

For example, the word might be *chip*.

Visual-shallow: Does the word have any capital letters?   NO

Auditory-shallow: Does the word rhyme with "skip"?   YES

Meaningful: Does it fit in the following sentence: "The boys were only allowed to eat one potato ___ each"?   YES

The experimental hypothesis was that deeper processing should lead to better retention of the words than shallow processing. In terms of the experiment, this means that the meaningful orienting task would produce better recall or recognition performance than the shallow processing, even though the participants were not trying to remember in any condition. And indeed, this is precisely what Craik and Tulving (1975) found in their experiment (see Figure 4.2). When the participants were given surprise recognition test or a surprise recall test, the items that had been encoded with meaningful or deep processing were remembered better than those items that had been encoded with shallow processing.

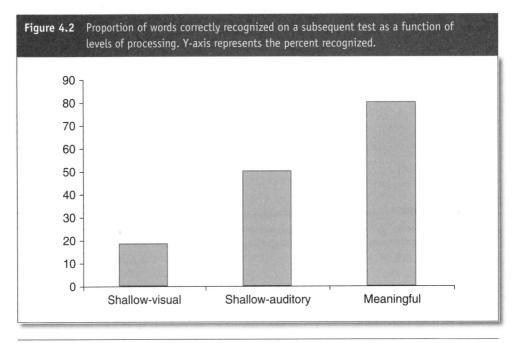

Figure 4.2   Proportion of words correctly recognized on a subsequent test as a function of levels of processing. Y-axis represents the percent recognized.

SOURCE: Based on Craik and Tulving (1975).

Mnemonic Improvement Tip 4.1

When learning new information, use elaborative or meaning-based encoding techniques. Elaborative encoding or deep encoding leads to stronger memory representations. Elaborative encoding can be idiosyncratic, but one of the best meaning-based techniques is to relate the information to one's own personal life.

The idea of levels of processing has many implications and applications. First of all, it implies that simply using deep or meaning-based encoding strategies can improve memory without any additional investment of time and effort. This can be very useful for students who must master large amounts of materials in relatively short periods of time. Many literature students have to read many books and remember much of the details in a very short period of time. Thus, it is important for these students to determine ways in which to remember the details. Consider preparing for a quiz on a novel. Concentrating on the ideas in the novel (probably what your literature professor is after anyway) will help you remember the details about the book that you need to know for the quiz. It's a win-win. The ultimate goal is to understand the novel, the author's intentions, and how they play out in the plot and the characters. By focusing on the big picture, details follow.

Deep levels of processing can also improve memory in areas in which you might not think it would help. The levels-of-processing framework also predicts how well people can remember faces. Deeper levels of processing lead to better memory for faces. Sporer (1991) showed that people were better at recognizing faces if they had first processed them in terms of whether or not the face looked "honest" than if they had processed them in terms of whether or not the person had a wide nose. Judging for honesty is very similar to the meaning-based processing we have been discussing, whereas judging the physical characteristics of the face is clearly shallow processing. Although most of us would agree we should not judge a person's honesty by how they look, doing so allowed the participants to remember those faces later.

Levels of processing has had its critics as well. One major criticism is that the theory is circular, that is, anything that produces good memory performance is thought to be deep processing. In this view, deep processing is not defined separately from good memory performance. Aware of this possibility, Fisher and Craik (1977) showed that under some conditions, deep processing produced worse memory performance than did shallow processing. The key was in the test. If the test required the participant to recall perceptual details (i.e., the color of a written word), then processing for color led to better recall than did processing for meaning. Thus, deep processing was defined independently of its positive effect on memory. Nonetheless, this was an important criticism of levels of processing that researchers still evoke today.

Applications of Levels of Processing

Levels of processing is a powerful tool in investigating differences in encoding. It predicts memory performance under a wide variety of situations. Indeed, any variable that increases the meaning-based processing of a to-be-learned item will also increase that item's memorability. Thus, when learning a new language, placing a new vocabulary term in a sentence produces better learning than simply repeating the word and its definition over and over. There are a number of extensions of levels of processing that we will discuss here: the self-reference effect, survival processing, the generation effect, organization, and distinctiveness. All of these effects work because they produced deeper or more meaningful processing. Some critics of levels of processing point out that researchers call "meaningful" whichever processing leads to good memory recall. See if you can apply this criticism to each of the applications.

The Self-Reference Effect

> **Self-reference effect**: the observation that linking to-be-learned information to personally relevant information about oneself creates strong encoding.

The **self-reference effect** refers to the observation that linking to-be-learned information to personally relevant information about oneself creates strong encoding. To demonstrate the self-reference effect, T. B. Rogers, Kuiper, and Kirker (1977) found that relating information to oneself was particularly useful in creating strongly encoding memory traces. More recently, Kelley et al. (2002) showed that words that referred to personality traits were more likely to be recalled if the person applied that trait to himself or herself than if he or she did not. Kelley et al. also found that when people applied these traits to themselves during encoding, there was increased activity in the prefrontal cortex, including the anterior cingulate, as measured by functional magnetic resonance imaging (fMRI). The anterior cingulate is an area in the prefrontal lobe associated with novelty, surprise, and cognitive conflict (Botvinick, 2007). Activating this area makes a stimulus particularly distinctive.

Survival Processing

Imagine you are lost in the desert without food or water or a compass to guide you back to civilization. You must survive on your own, using the plants and animals you find and avoiding predators, such as the mountain lion, hiding behind every boulder. What would be useful to you under such circumstances? A radio? Opium? A priest? Talk about personal relevance! Nairne, Thompson, and Pandeirada (2007) asked participants to rate a group of unrelated words in terms of how relevant these words were to surviving on grasslands of a foreign land. They compared subsequent memory for these words with words that had been learned using a variety of other orienting tasks, including rating the words for pleasantness, usually considered a deep level of processing because it focuses participants on the meaning of words. Surprisingly, the survival scenario led to 10% better recall than did the pleasantness judgments or judgments about surviving in a city. This has now been replicated several times. Weinstein, Buck, and Roediger (2008) also asked participants to encode a list of unrelated words while thinking about how they would survive on grasslands much like the savannahs of Africa. This encoding strategy was then compared to other less engaging scenarios. Weinstein et al. found that the grasslands survival strategy was a powerful one, leading to better memory performance than the other conditions (see Figure 4.3). Nairne and Pandeirada (2008) argued that these results suggest that memory may have evolved to help early humans survive on the African savannahs hundreds of thousands of years ago (although very few other researchers, including Weinstein et al., accept this explanation). So, the next time you have to study for a test, imagine you are studying in the African savannah surrounded by ferocious lions. You may just do better on that test than you would have, and it may be fun as well. Nairn and Pandierada define this type of processing as **survival processing.**

> **Survival processing:** processing information in terms of its value to surviving in the wild is a surprisingly effective manner in which to encode information.

In terms of our current concerns, survival processing can be considered almost the "ultimate" deep-level processing. It instantly focuses you on the meaning of the words. For what possible purpose could a "priest" help me survive in the desert? Well, he could perform last rites if I cannot find enough water. Opium? It might be useful if I have to walk a long distance in the intense discomfort caused by the heat and lack of water. What about a radio? Now, that's useful—I could find out the direction to the nearest town, where help would be waiting. Thus, processing for survival rivets our attention on the meaning of

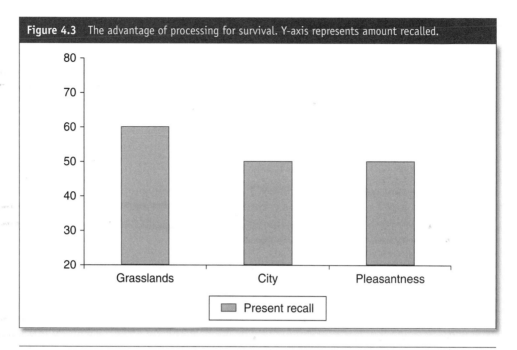

Figure 4.3   The advantage of processing for survival. Y-axis represents amount recalled.

SOURCE: Based on Nairne, Thompson, and Pandeirada (2007).

words and therefore promotes deep processing in a way few other tasks can match. However, it remains to be seen if survival processing generalizes beyond the learning of unrelated lists.

The Generation Effect

According to the levels-of-processing framework, anything we do to increase elaborative or meaning-based processing will strengthen an item in long-term memory. Furthermore, as we have seen in the self-reference effect and survival processing, relating information to oneself is a particularly successful way of enhancing the strength of memories. The **generation effect** refers to the fact that memory is better when we generate associations ourselves than when we simply read them. Slameka and Graf

Generation effect: memory is better when we generate associations ourselves than when we simply read them.

(1978) demonstrated this effect in a particularly clever way. They controlled the material so that generating items would be trivially easy, as easy as it was to simply read the materials. If memory performance was better for the generated items, it would not be the result of the extra effort used to generate the items but because the person generated the items himself or herself. Here is how they did it:

Participants in this experiment knew that their memory for associations would be tested, so it was intentional learning, not incidental learning. They also knew that they would see the left-hand cue of a paired associate and have to remember the right-hand target. However, they encoded the items in one of two ways. In the read condition, they simply read the pair of items, but in the generate condition, they followed a rule, which allowed them to generate the items.

Read condition: rose—hose

Generate condition: mash–cr____ (rhyme).

The generate condition is rather easy. Almost all participants successfully generated the expected target without error. As you can see, it takes little mental effort to generate the word *crash*. Yet the effect on memory performance was profound. Recall of the target words was 28% better in the generate condition (see Figure 4.4).

This effect is not limited to paired associates in the laboratory. It also works in real-world settings. For example, Butler and Roediger (2007) tested it in a simulated classroom setting. Participants viewed three lectures on different topics over three consecutive days. Many of you are taking a class that meets Mondays, Wednesdays, and Fridays. The experiment mirrors that learning situation. After each lecture, some "students" received a lecture summary (equivalent to the read condition), whereas other "students" received short-answer tests (equivalent to the generate condition) with feedback given to the participants on half of their answers. A final control group of participants did not get a summary or receive a short-answer test. One month later, the participants returned and took a test on the materials

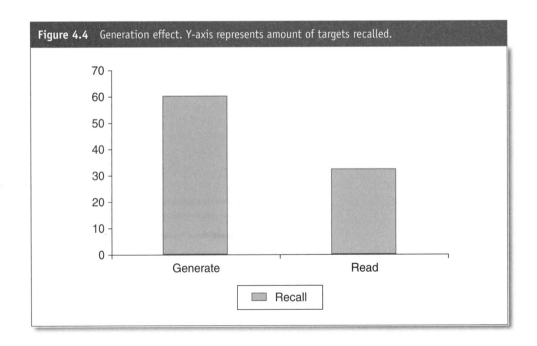

Figure 4.4   Generation effect. Y-axis represents amount of targets recalled.

covered in the lectures. The group that performed the best on this final test was the group that had been given a short-answer test, that is, the group that had to generate the answers. Thus, in real-world learning situations, generating items can lead to the best memory performance as well as in typical laboratory conditions.

Mnemonic Improvement Tip 4.2

The generation effect: Generating answers yourself is a more powerful memory aid than simply reading answers. This can be a very effective studying tool. Rather than simply reading and rereading the material, writing it yourself and generating the answer leads to stronger memory traces and better long-term performance.

> **Enactment effect**: performed tasks are remembered better than those that are simply read about.

A related effect is called the **enactment effect.** According to the enactment effect, performed tasks are remembered better than those that are simply read about (Helstrup, 2004). That is, actually bending a paperclip is better than reading "bending a paperclip" for remembering this activity at a subsequent time period. Interestingly, this effect appears to be mediated by the parietal lobe rather than the normal areas of the brain involved in memory, the prefrontal and temporal lobes (Russ, Mack, Grama, Lanfermann, & Knoff, 2003).

Organization

Organization means imposing a meaningful structure on to-be-learned material. Applying organization to new learning causes the learner to focus on the meaning of the material and thus increases the depth of processing. Thus, organizing what we learn into categories and meaning-based connections is also a powerful way to improve encoding. Think about doing a memory experiment. If you encounter a random list of words in a memory experiment, divide them into categories and try to use the categories to help you remember the words. If you have to study for a history test on the French Revolution, you could divide it up into information that came before the overthrow of the king and information after, or you could divide it by separating those historical figures who supported the monarchy versus those who favored the republic. Tulving (1962) points out that the best organizational strategies are the ones that rely on the person's own subjective experience.

> **Organization**: imposing a meaningful structure on to-be-learned material.

Mnemonic Improvement Tip 4.3

Another potent memory aid is organization. You can use both standard and subjective strategies to organize information. Organization leads to deeper processing, which leads to more strongly encoded memories.

Distinctiveness

Another feature that causes learners to focus on the meaning is to focus on the unique distinctive meaning of each item. In contrast to organization, in which we group items together based on meaning, **distinctiveness** implies that we search for the unique meaning for each item. Thus, even though organization and distinctiveness are opposites (one focuses on uniqueness of a stimulus, whereas the other focuses on commonalities among stimuli) in some respects, they both focus the learner on meaning and therefore increase the depth of

Distinctiveness: we search for the unique meaning for each item. Focusing on distinctive aspects of a stimulus causes comparatively good memory performance.

processing. Deeper processing leads to better encoding.

The study of the effect of distinctiveness on memory has an interesting history. Hedwig von Restorff, in 1933, published an important paper on the effects of distinctiveness in memory encoding. Since her seminal research, the **von Restorff effect** means the advantage in memory that distinctive items have over less distinctive items. Consider the following list of words: jump, hop, fly, swim, crawl, putter, **VOMIT**, run, skip, skate, flip. It is likely that the word *vomit* will stand out. Why? Well, all the other words are neutral or pleasant words, but *vomit* is a decidedly unpleasant word. In addition, all of the other words convey a manner of motion, quite different from the motion

von Restorff effect: advantage in memory that distinctive items have over less distinctive items.

involved in the word *vomit* (grossed you out yet?). All the other words do not normally evoke strong emotions, whereas the word *vomit* can evoke strong emotions. Finally, the word *vomit*, unlike the other words in the list, is in green, bold, italics, and all caps, which further enhance its distinctiveness. Indeed, although you may consider your author crude by using this example, I have virtually guaranteed that you will never forget the von Restorff effect. The goal here is to make one item in the list undeniably distinctive from the rest. von Restorff showed that the distinctive item was remembered better than a category-consistent word placed in the same serial position.

So let's consider the von Restorff effect in more depth (also known by the term *isolation effect*) as well as the general variable of distinctiveness. In the von Restorff effect, participants are given a list of words to commit to memory. The words on the list are homogeneous along one dimension, except for one word, which differs from the rest in terms of category, color, size, and so on. For example, participants might study the names of 11 birds (e.g., sparrow, pigeon, owl, jay, etc.) but also see the name of one boat (e.g., kayak). The typical finding is that the isolated word or distinctive word is recalled much better than a within-category word in the same serial position. This occurs regardless of the dimension on which the word differs from the others.

However, we do not have to rely on distinctiveness being provided for us. We can focus on distinctive aspects of material that we need to remember. Consider learning the people in your new study group. Look for distinctive aspects of a person's name or face. For example, if a person has a unibrow (hair connecting each eyebrow), try to use that distinct feature into a way of remembering that person and his (hopefully) name. If the person has an unusual name (e.g., Dweezel), that helps, but if this person doesn't (e.g., Christina), find a way to make it distinctive ("Christina the ballerina").

Mnemonic Improvement Tip 4.4

Distinctiveness also provides another variable that can improve memory. Focusing on distinctive aspects of to-be-remembered items improves memory greatly. This is applicable to learning school information, faces, and names of people.

Like the other variables that influence encoding, distinctiveness works by accentuating an aspect of meaning in the distinctive stimuli. This in turn increases the depth of processing, leading to better encoding of that item. In this section, we have seen that one of the key elements of encoding is meaning-based processing. What we learn from a particular experience is its meaning. This is what is generally relevant to us later, so adaptive memory focuses on meaning. We now turn to the other aspect of memory, retrieval—that is, how do we access information that we already have encoded?

INTERIM SUMMARY

Episodic memory is a form of "mental time travel." This differentiates it from semantic memory, the representations we have of "facts." A generation of research now shows that episodic memory is a distinct neurocognitive system. This research includes behavioral evidence, neuroimaging, and neuropsychology. Encoding into long-term memory is based on meaningful processing. The levels-of-processing framework shows that deeper processing leads to better encoding into long-term episodic memory. Many factors that increase meaningful processing also lead to better encoding. These include the self-reference effect, survival processing, the generation effect, organization, and distinctiveness.

Retrieval From Episodic Memory

Retrieval is the process by which information is recovered from memory. In episodic memory, we retrieve events—that is, specific individual happenings from our lives. Events can include memories of what people said or did, visual images, and emotions as to how we felt. Information about the event can include when it occurred or how long ago, where it took place, and its significance to the person doing the remembering. We have many memories stored in episodic memory—the issue is, how do we access them?

Think of a computer. Inside it, many millions of bits of information are stored. Perhaps some of this memory is of the paper that you have due in your human memory class. In fact, you may have written a wonderful paper on Baddeley's theory of working memory. However, the paper is no good to you when the computer is turned off and stowed away. You can't say to your professor, "I have the paper—it is on my computer, but you can't see it." In order for that computer file to be any good, you and the computer must be able to access it and then print it, upload it to your professor's website, or email it to him. All of these activities are acts of retrieval. Memory is only as good as the retrieval system that allows us to draw information from it. Episodic memory is no exception.

Retrieval is the process whereby information is recovered and brought to consciousness in working memory. An important feature of retrieval is that it must be accurate. From all the information stored in memory, we must get exactly the memory sought. If you are asked about your dietary restrictions and your respond with "walnuts" when it is "peanuts" that you are allergic to, this can have important and negative consequences. If you are asked to describe your high school graduation by a classmate who missed it and instead you retrieve the memory of your sister's graduation, you might not be able to help that person learn about the event. Similarly, when a parent accidentally calls one child by the name of another child in the family, he or she is not indicating that the right names have been forgotten. Last, if you need to retrieve the name of your current significant other and you instead call that person by the name of your last boyfriend or girlfriend, you may not have that friend anymore. Sometimes accurate retrieval is really important! Therefore, we need a memory system that is precise as possible in retrieving the correct memory.

Not only must retrieval be accurate, but it must also be fast. The waiter is busy and has other tables to get to and cannot wait forever for you say that you are allergic to peanuts. Moreover, if you want your classmate to be interested in your story from high school graduation, you must be able to tell the story without too many pauses. Consider a time when you were sure you knew someone's name but you could not think of it at the moment. When the person leaves later, you remember the name. The embarrassment of not knowing your acquaintance's name is the cost of a too-slow retrieval system. So we need a retrieval system that is both fast and accurate.

One of the ways in which we achieve both speed and accuracy is to keep memories that we are likely to retrieve more accessible to recall than others we are less likely to need to remember. What determines what we are likely to need to retrieve? It is likely that we will need to retrieve information that we have retrieved recently and information that is stored strongly in memory (Bjork & Bjork, 1992). An important theoretical distinction here is the difference between availability and accessibility.

Availability refers to all information present in the memory system. That is, everything that you have stored in your episodic memory! Availability can never be directly measured because, although all of this information may be stored in memory, we can never retrieve

> **Availability**: all information present in the memory system.
>
> **Accessibility**: that part of our stored memories that we can retrieve under the present conditions.

it all at any particular time. In contrast, **accessibility** refers to that part of our stored memories that we can retrieve under the present conditions. At any given time, we may be able to access only some of our memories but not all of them. Thus, availability and accessibility are very different concepts. As it turns out, the key to ensuring that a memory is accessible is having the right retrieval cue. Why some information is accessible and other stored information (available) is not is the important question of this section. Consider the following anecdote.

Several years ago, I lived next door to a neighbor who was a retired civil engineer, who we will call Mr. Rojas (not his real name). Mr. Rojas had come from Cuba to attend college in the United States in the late 1950s. When the Cuban revolution catapulted Fidel Castro to power, Mr. Rojas was unable to return safely to Cuba. He continued with graduate school and became a very successful engineer in the United Sates. Shortly after I moved in next to Mr. Rojas and his wife, his brother died. His brother had remained behind in Cuba and had become a prominent government official. Because Mr. Rojas opposed the communists, they had seldom spoken or seen each other in all those years. Yet, Mr. Rojas returned to Cuba for the very first time in nearly 50 years to attend the funeral of his brother.

When Mr. Rojas returned to Miami, he described to me the incredible wave of memories he had experienced when he returned to his hometown for the first time in so many years. Many events, which he had not thought of in years, came flooding back to him. There was the place where his father had taught him how to ride a bicycle. There was the place where he and his girlfriend had snuck off to so they could be alone. For Mr. Rojas, returning to the land of his childhood provided the cues to remember events, which he doubted he would ever have thought of in his adult world back in the United States.

Most of us will fortunately never be in the strange position of Mr. Rojas, but all you need do to experience what he did is to return to your high school (assuming you have not visited since starting college). You too will likely remember many things you have not thought of in a long time. Other readers may have moved from one town to another when they were quite young. A trip back to the early town will bring back a flood of memories of events not thought of in years.

This is the essence of the concept of **retrieval cues.** We use information present in our current environment—that is, retrieval cues—to trigger our memories of past events. Therefore, it is the presence of the right retrieval cues that activates or makes accessible a particular memory. As we will discuss shortly, geographic location may serve as a retrieval cue. Remove Mr. Rojas from his hometown, and

> **Retrieval cues**: we use information present in our current environment, that is, retrieval cues, to trigger our memories of past events.

he will not remember his bicycle lesson. Place him back in it, and he vividly remembers his father helping his with his balance all those years ago.

In terms of practical issues of memory, nothing could be more important than this principle. Retrieval cues matter! If you want to remember something important, structure your environment such that ample cues are around to trigger this memory (or, technically, to make this memory accessible). This is the basis of many memory strategies, such as tying a string around your finger to remind you to do a task, such as feeding your neighbor's cat. Very little in your house, apartment, or car may exist to remind you of Fluffy next door. However, remembering to feed her is important because (1) you don't want the cat to starve, and (2) you don't want to disappoint your neighbor. So you tie the string around your finger to serve as a retrieval cue to go next door and open a can of tuna for Fluffy. Whenever you glance at your finger, you remember your obligation. Setting the timer on the oven serves a similar person for your own feeding. When the timer goes off, the sound reminds us that it is now time to take the soufflé out of the oven and let it cool for dinner. How many times have you burned something because you forgot to take it out of the oven?

Mnemonic Improvement Tip 4.5

Retrieval cues are the single most important feature of remembering. If you need to remember something important, structure your environment such that many cues are accessible to help trigger your memory.

Because retrieval cues are so important to memory, it is critical to understand some of the factors that lead to good cues. The assertion here is that good cues are items, information, and events present in the environment that are highly linked, associated, or connected to the event or idea you need to remember. A mistake I frequently make while learning names of new students every semester is focusing on learning first name–last name associations. I may know that Isabel goes with Sanchez, but I fail to make the connection between the name and the face or physical appearance. And it is this association that I must learn if I want to be able or remember people by name. There are a number of factors that aid in making these good retrieval cues. Many of them are grouped under the heading of the encoding specificity principle.

Encoding Specificity

Encoding specificity means that retrieval of information from memory will be maximized when the conditions at retrieval match the conditions at encoding. That is, recall or recognition of information will be easier, faster, and greater in amount when there is overlap between conditions of retrieval and encoding (D. M. Thompson & Tulving, 1970). Conditions can mean the physical location of the person and his or her mental state, emotional state, or even physiological state. It is

> Encoding specificity: retrieval of information from memory will be maximized when the conditions at retrieval match the conditions at encoding.

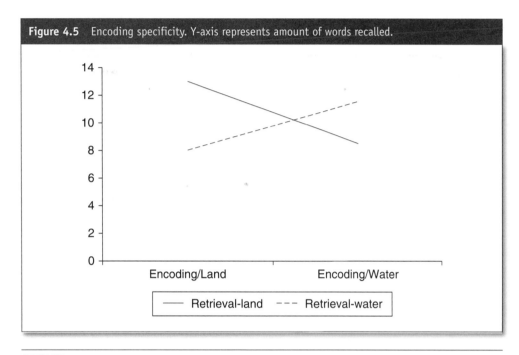

Figure 4.5   Encoding specificity. Y-axis represents amount of words recalled.

SOURCE: Based on Godden and Baddeley (1975).

likely that when we encode information at the time of learning, we make use of all the available associations. Therefore, we may associate the newly learned information with aspects of our mood, aspects of environment, and even the presence or absence of drugs in our body. For example, if we study for a test when we are feeling angry, we will actually do better on the test if we are also angry at the time we take the test. If we have a conversation with a friend in the bookstore café, we will better remember that conversation if we try to recall it while in the same café. The encoding specificity principle is observable across a great many different circumstances. Its effect can also be quite strong. Let's take a look at some of the circumstances under which the encoding specificity can be observed.

Research on the encoding specificity principle takes the following form. Participants encode information under one of two conditions. Then, after a retention interval, the participants return to either the same condition or the opposite condition and then attempt to retrieve the information that they encoded. The typical pattern of data is that people recall better when they encode and retrieve under the same conditions.

Our first example of this form of experiment is a now-classic study on this phenomenon done by two British researchers, Godden and Baddeley (1975), who studied British naval divers. The participants were all trained scuba divers who were quite comfortable in scuba gear working underwater. Godden and Baddeley asked half of the divers to learn a list of words on a waterproof whiteboard anchored 15 feet underwater. The other half of the participants studied the same list of words on land. This is called the encoding manipulation—that is, the researchers established two contexts at the time of encoding, land and water.

Each encoding group was divided into two groups, a group that retrieved the words on land and a group that retrieved the words underwater by writing the list of words on the underwater whiteboard. This was the retrieval manipulation with two conditions, retrieving underwater and retrieving on land. Therefore, there were four conditions in total: encoding on land/encoding on land, encoding on land/retrieving underwater, encoding underwater/retrieving underwater, and encoding underwater/retrieving on land. The results can be seen in Figure 4.5.

As you can see in Figure 4.5, the divers recalled more words when the conditions at test (retrieval) matched the conditions at learning (encoding). That is, when participants studied and retrieved only on land or only underwater, recall was better than when the conditions mismatched. This is the essence of the encoding specificity principle. The closer you are to your physical and mental state when you try to retrieve something, the more likely you will succeed.

Scuba diving is now a vastly popular recreational activity, despite its inherent dangers. Many people find it extremely relaxing, particularly if they are diving on beautiful coral reefs (see Figure 4.6). A frequent comment heard on dive boats is how all one's troubles and stressors seem to melt away once you submerge under the ocean's waves. It is possible that encoding specificity has something to do with this. When you are in an environment completely surrounded by corals, sponges, angelfish, and parrotfish, it is likely that is more difficult than normal to think of grades, student loans, parking tickets, arguments with boy-girlfriends, and, if you are bit older, mortgages, health insurance premiums, and car payments.

Figure 4.6   Scuba diving is a very relaxing activity for many people. Could it be that people find it relaxing because it is difficult to retrieve normal stressful events while in such a different environment?

State-dependent memory: when encoding specificity is applied to internal human states such as drug state or mood states.

When encoding specificity is applied to internal human states such as drug state or mood states, it is also referred to as **state-dependent memory.** In one of the more daring demonstrations of state-dependent learning and the encoding specificity principle, Eich, Weingartner, Stillman, and Gillian (1975) examined the influence of marijuana on people's memory. In an ad in the University of British Columbia newspaper, they recruited smokers to participate in his study. On Day 1, the participants were given either a marijuana cigarette to smoke or a tobacco cigarette. The researchers then waited about an hour for the drugs (THC and nicotine, respectively) from each of the cigarettes to enter the participant's bloodstream. Then the participants were given a list of unrelated words to study, as we have seen in many experiments already. The participants were then dismissed and asked to refrain from smoking for the ensuring 48 hours. This was important to ensure that the drugs would be eliminated from the participants' bloodstream when they returned for recall. When the participants returned, they were again given a cigarette to smoke. Of the participants who had originally smoked marijuana, half again smoked marijuana, and half smoked tobacco. Of the participants who had originally smoked a tobacco cigarette, half again smoked tobacco and half smoked marijuana.

The results were strikingly similar to those from Godden and Baddeley (1975). That is, the conditions in which encoding and retrieval were matched led to the best recall (see Figure 4.7). In this case, the two conditions that led to the best recall were when the participants had

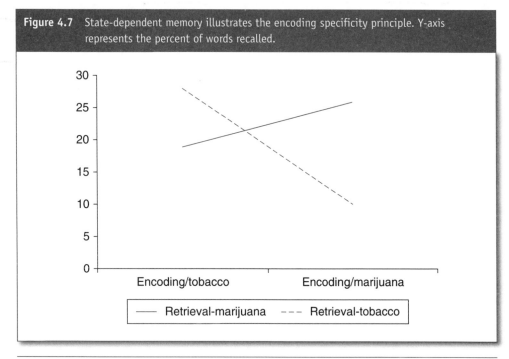

Figure 4.7   State-dependent memory illustrates the encoding specificity principle. Y-axis represents the percent of words recalled.

SOURCE: Eich et al. (1975).

smoked the same drug at both encoding and retrieval, the marijuana/marijuana condition and the tobacco/tobacco condition. The mismatched conditions in which the people smoked different drugs at different times led to more poor recall. Eich (in press) has also found similar results for alcohol (also see Goodwin, Powell, Bremer, Hoine, & Stern, 1969). Thus, encoding specificity also holds for drug-induced cognitive-emotional conditions.

I will note here that tobacco, marijuana, and alcohol are very unhealthy. Indeed, long-term use of marijuana has been shown to cause deficits in memory performance. Smoking cigarettes increases your likelihood of dying of lung cancer 400 times. It also causes heart disease, asthma, emphysema, and glaucoma and increases the likelihood of strokes. So I do not recommend starting with either of these drugs. However, if you smoke when you study for a test, you should probably smoke just before you go into a test.

So far, we have seen place-dependent memory in the navy diver experiment and drug-dependent memory in the Eich studies. Encoding specificity also applies to mood-dependent memory.

In another experiment from Eich's lab, Eich and Metcalfe (1989) examined if mood states were subject to the encoding specificity principle. Like the earlier studies, they had two encoding condition crossed with two retrieval conditions. In their study, they tested normal Canadian college students by inducing them into either happy or sad moods by having them listen to either happy or sad music. The experimenters instructed the students to think about pleasant or unpleasant incidents while listening to the music. This was sufficient to induce most of the students into a happy or sad mood, depending on which music they had listened to. Eich and Metcalfe waited until students reached a predetermined level of mood and then asked them to learn a list of paired associates (e.g., silver-gold). The students returned to the lab 2 days later and were again induced into either a happy or sad mood. Half of the participants who had studied while sad studied again while sad, whereas half of the participants who had studied while happy studied again while happy. Again, consistent with the earlier data, cued recall was better when the participants were in the same mood as when they learned the paired associates. Thus, if the participants had been sad at encoding, they recalled more when they were also sad at test, and if the participants had been happy at retrieval, they recalled more when they were also happy at test. Eich and Metcalfe called this pattern mood dependence, but you can see that it is practically identical to the other encoding specificity effects. Figure 4.8 demonstrates this.

Mnemonic Improvement Tip 4.6

Make use of the encoding specificity principle. If you know you are going to be tested on to-be-learned material, such as preparing for an exam, you can aid your preparation by looking for ways to make your study conditions actually match your test conditions. If you are usually nervous when you take exams, review your notes when you are feeling nervous about something else. Make sure to study during the same mood/chemical condition as when you take the test. Spend a few minutes studying in the room in which you are going to take the test. All of these activities will allow encoding specificity to work for you: Your test conditions will be similar to your learning conditions.

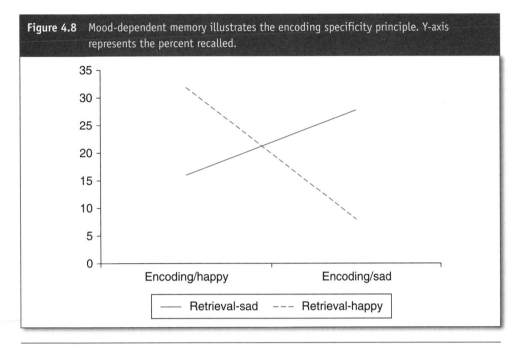

Figure 4.8   Mood-dependent memory illustrates the encoding specificity principle. Y-axis represents the percent recalled.

SOURCE: Eich and Metcalfe (1989).

Mood congruence: people are more likely to remember events or information that is positive when they are in a positive mood and more likely to remember events or information that is negative when they are in a negative mood.

A related phenomenon to mood dependence is called mood-congruent memory. **Mood congruence** means that you are more likely to remember events or information that is positive when you are in a positive mood and more likely to remember events or information that is negative when you are in a negative mood. For example, if you have just had an argument with your boyfriend or girlfriend, you are likely to remember negative things about that person, perhaps all the reasons you might want to go looking for a new intimate friend. On the other hand, while you are walking down the beach in the moonlight, you may be more likely to think of all the reasons you love that person. Many studies support the idea that we remember mood-congruent information more than mood-incongruent information (Blaney, 1986).

Transfer-appropriate processing: retrieval will be stronger when the cognitive processes present at the time of retrieval are most similar to the ones that were present at the time of encoding.

A concept closely related to encoding specificity is the idea of **transfer-appropriate processing**. Transfer-appropriate processing is a more general term than encoding specificity as it applies to cognitive processes other than memory. In the context of memory, it means that retrieval will be stronger when the cognitive processes present at the time of retrieval are most similar to the ones that were present at the time of encoding. Thus, a word like *jam* will be retrieved better when *grape* is given as a retrieval cue if the word was originally encoded with *strawberry* than with *traffic*.

Inhibition in Episodic Memory

Consider the following situation. You are visiting all the universities that have accepted you to medical school (congratulations!). This is something you always wanted to achieve, so choosing the right medical school is a very important decision. So you embark on a tour to visit all the potential schools. On each of the next several days, you will be staying in a different hotel in a different city adjacent to a different university. When you check into the Tipton Hotel in Boston, you are assigned room number 653. When you leave to visit the medical schools that you have been accepted to in Boston, remembering your hotel room number is vital information. When you return and are tired, you don't want to waste time waiting for a clerk to look up your number. However, once you leave Boston on your way to the Big Blue Bug Motel in Providence, Rhode Island, the number "653" is no longer important. What becomes important is your new room number, Suite 54, at the Big Blue Bug. When you return from your visit to the medical school in Providence, you don't want to mistakenly misremember the room number from the Tipton; you need your suite number at the Big Blue Bug. Therefore, it is actually adaptive to forget your room number from the Tipton as soon as you check out, so that it will not interfere with your retrieval of the room number at the Big Blue Bug. And indeed, our memory systems have such an inhibitory mechanism.

Second, consider the situation of a veteran returning home from the battlefields of Iraq or some other war. He or she may wish to return to normal life and not be reminded of the horrors that the soldier witnessed during war. Blocking out these painful memories is an important part of normal adjustment to civilian life. Indeed, one of the major symptoms of posttraumatic stress disorder (PTSD) is the constant recurrence of unbidden memories. This symptom of PTSD is really a failure of the inhibitory mechanism to prevent the retrieval of unwanted memories. Thus, in situations both relatively trivial (remembering your hotel number) and life shattering (memories of wartime battles), inhibiting the retrieval of information can often be just as crucial as retrieval itself. Therefore, an effective inhibition system is important to proper memory functioning (M. C. Anderson, 2007).

The importance of inhibition to memory function is currently drawing support from cognitive neuroscience. There appear to be specific areas of the brain devoted in inhibiting unwanted memories. M. C. Anderson, Bjork, and Bjork (2004), using fMRI technology, showed that areas of the prefrontal lobe were particularly active when participants were actively trying to block out unwanted memories. This suggests that the failure to inhibit painful memories, seen in PTSD, may be the result of improper functioning of the prefrontal lobe. As we will see throughout our discussion of memory, the prefrontal lobes are involved in many aspects of memory that have to do with control of memory, monitoring of memory, and inhibition of responses (Thompson-Schill, Ramscar, & Chrysikou, 2009). In this way, the prefrontal lobes are said to have a supervisory role in memory.

Inhibition: the mechanism that actively interferes with and reduces the likelihood of recall of particular information.

Retrieval-induced inhibition: when recently retrieved information interferes with the retrieval of other related information.

Inhibition is a mechanism that actively interferes with and reduces the likelihood of recall of particular information. What allows us to inhibit information that we don't want to remember? For many of us, it seems that as soon as we decide we don't want to think of something (that catchy jingle from the McDonald's commercial, for example), it turns out we can't think of anything else. Thus, a reasonable question is, what processes allow us to inhibit information we want to forget? It turns out the act of retrieving some information can inhibit the retrieval of other related information (M. C. Anderson, 2007). That is, when people repeatedly retrieve certain information, it actually makes it more difficult to retrieve other related information. In this way, constantly recalling your current suite number at the Big Blue Bug will inhibit retrieval of your room number at the Tipton. Consider the following experiment demonstrating what M. C. Anderson et al. (1994) called **retrieval-induced inhibition**.

Retrieval-Induced Inhibition

M. C. Anderson et al. (1994) gave participants word lists within a particular category to study and asked them to engage in extended retrieval practice (see Figure 4.9). For example, if the category is vegetables, the participants might study *squash, carrots, cucumbers, and broccoli*. Retrieval practice involves repeated retrieval of certain items. Thus, a participant sees vegetables: car___ and vegetables: broc____ and has to retrieve the words *carrot* and *broccoli*. In contrast, you can also have unpracticed items in the category if you do not see this pattern for squash and cucumbers. Thus, within the category of "vegetables," you can have practiced items (carrot, broccoli) and unpracticed items (squash, cucumber). Anderson et al. also had categories for which participants engaged in no retrieval practice on any items. That is, they read through the category initially once but then did not engage in retrieval practice.

The question asked by M. C. Anderson et al. (1994) was whether or not the repeated retrieval of some items would later inhibit the retrieval of later related items for which retrieval practice had not taken place. Thus, after the retrieval practice sessions, the participants were asked to free recall the examples from each category. Consider another example. Anderson et al. presented the participants with long lists of category examples from several categories (Fish—trout, herring, barracuda, etc.). Participants were then given practice retrieving some examples from that category (e.g., Fish—trout) but not others from that category (Fish—herring). Other categories (Trees—hemlock, oak, palm, pine) did not receive any practice. Participants retrieved these examples up to three times before the final test was given. The final test was a free-recall test in which participants were asked to recall of the originally studied examples from each category. The results seem complex, but a brief inspection of Figure 4.9 shows that they are really quite straightforward. Consider first the practiced category (e.g., Fish). There are two types of words in a practiced category:

examples that have been practiced (labeled RP+) and examples that have not been practiced (labeled RP–). Participants also engage in final recall for the unpracticed category (trees, labeled NRP), which they saw initially but were not asked to practice.

The prediction from retrieval inhibition is that the RP– items (unpracticed members of the practiced category) will be inhibited by the constant retrieval of the RP+ items. Therefore, the RP+ items will not simply be better recalled than the RP– items, but because the RP– items are inhibited, their recall will go below the baseline control condition provided by the NRP items. Thus, if retrieval inhibition is real, the NRP items should be better remembered than the RP– items.

RP+ = target items from practiced category that were practiced.

RP– = target items from practiced category that were unpracticed.

NRP = target items from the nonpracticed condition.

Retrieval-induced forgetting demonstrates inhibition. This is because RP– items are recalled worse than NRP items despite the fact that each was viewed equally often in the experiment. The only difference is that other items in the RP category were repeated. Thus, this represents an inhibitory effect because the RP– items are recalled at a lower rate than control items. What causes the inhibition? Well, the RP+ items are remembered well, better than the other two conditions. So it is the act of retrieving RP+ items that drives down RP– items, thus demonstrating that the act of retrieval is causing the inhibition.

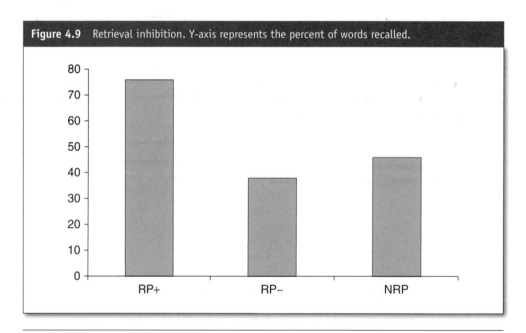

Figure 4.9 Retrieval inhibition. Y-axis represents the percent of words recalled.

SOURCE: M. C. Anderson, Bjork, and Bjork (1994).

What is the implication for real-world memory? It supports the idea that refreshing the memory of your current hotel room number will make it less likely that you will accidentally go to the room number of last night's hotel. It is also potentially useful in treating patients with PTSD. Therapy that encourages patients to recall related but non-traumatic wartime memories may work to inhibit the unbidden retrieval of the traumatic ones.

Part-Set Cueing

Inhibition can be seen in other experimental paradigms as well. Consider part-set cueing. **Part-set cueing** occurs when you study some of the information in a set of already learned information but not all of it. When you are asked to retrieve that information later, your memory for the part you studied will be better than if you had not studied, but your memory will actually be worse for the section of the information that you did not study than if you had not studied the other set of the list (Basden,

> **Part-set cueing**: occurs when people study some of the information in a set of already learned information but not all of it.

Basden, & Morales, 2003). This is likely to sound confusing, so let us consider an example. Most of us are familiar with the 50 states of the United States. If asked to recall them, you might fall short of writing down all 50, but then when someone prompts you with "Oklahoma," "Idaho," or "Delaware," it is likely that you would likely recognize these names as states. "Guam," "Quebec," and "Panama" would be rejected as names of U.S. states. Now consider you are given 25 names of states to review and study. These 25 states are listed below.

1. Washington	9. Connecticut	17. Indiana
2. Florida	10. Arizona	18. Kentucky
3. New Hampshire	11. Missouri	19. West Virginia
4. Minnesota	12. Virginia	20. Wisconsin
5. Oklahoma	13. South Dakota	21. New York
6. North Dakota	14. Delaware	22. Georgia
7. Alabama	15. Michigan	23. New Mexico
8. Idaho	16. New Jersey	24. Kansas
		25. Illinois

Now find a separate piece of paper and try to write down all 50 states of the United States. You will find that you will remember the above 25 rather well but will not do as well for the 25 not listed above. In fact, if you compare your retrieval of the 25 not on the above list to people who did not study at all, your performance will be, on average, worse than theirs. Nickerson (1984) did a version of this experiment and found inhibition for the unpracticed items. This is called part-set cueing.

DIRECTED FORGETTING

What happens when someone—your boyfriend/girlfriend, brother or sister, parent, teacher, or boss—tells you to forget something? "Just forget I dented the car, Dad. I'll get it fixed and you don't have to worry about it." "Forget how much money I spent on your birthday present—just enjoy it." "Forget that the Yankees just lost and come help me with the laundry." "Forget the scary parts of the movie and just focus on the happy ending." Most of us would consider these requests futile. No matter how much your father may want to forget that you dented his car, he is not going to forget. Next time, you'll have to take the 10-year-old station wagon instead of the brand-new convertible. However, research does demonstrate that, under the right conditions, it is possible to forget the material that you want to forget. This form of forgetting is called **directed forgetting.**

> **Directed forgetting**: the inhibition in memory that occurs when people are asked to forget some information but not other information.

Interesting, specific instructions to forget information can inhibit the retrieval of that information (see Bjork, 1992; Bjork & Bjork, 1992). In a typical directed-forgetting paradigm, participants are given a list of words to remember. Then, the experimenter feigns that he or she has made a mistake, instructs the participant to forget that list, and then gives the participant a new list to remember. In the control condition, a participant is given one list to remember, some incidental instructions, and then a new list to study but is not told to forget the first list. The final test is for the first list for each group. The question is, is there a difference between the group that was explicitly told to forget the first list and the group that was not?

Results show that the group given the instructions to forget show more poor recall performance than does the group not given instructions to forget. It is not a large effect but has been demonstrated at a statistically significant level in many experiments (see Bjork & Bjork, 1992). Simply giving people instructions to forget material does result in less complete recall. Interestingly, though, this does not mean the material is entirely forgotten. If you switch from a recall test to a recognition test, the performance of the "forget" group and the control group is the same. However, recent research suggests that directed forgetting can occur even in recognition performance (Sahakyan, Waldum, Benjamin, & Bickett, 2009). Therefore, it is likely that this inhibition is at least partially under conscious control. For more information on the Bjorks' research, go to www.sagepub.com/schwartz.[4]

PROSPECTIVE MEMORY

Memory does not only concern remembering the past. Remembering what lies in the future is also important. To be successful on any given day, students must remember what classes they have that day and when they meet. Parents must remember to pick up their children from school. Airline pilots must remember to turn off the autopilot at the right time and manually land the plane. Patients must remember when to take their medications. All of these tasks involve remembering actions or intentions that will take place in the future. This is the domain of prospective memory. **Prospective memory** is memory for the things we need to do in the future. Prospective memory is, in some ways, the flip side of episodic memory. In episodic memory, the goal is to retrieve past events, whereas in prospective memory, the goal is to retrieve future events. Episodic memories usually concern what happened at a particular point in the past, whereas prospective memory usually concerns what will happen at a particular point in the future.

> **Prospective memory**: memory for the things we need to do in the future.

Prospective memory can be studied by using both laboratory methods and field methods. In the lab, participants are asked to remember to do something during the experiment and then they are kept busy doing other activities. The experimenter can then observe if the participant remembers to do the task at the appointed time. In one early experiment on prospective memory, Harris and Wilkens (1982) invited participants to watch a 2-hour movie, which most participants reported enjoying. However, they were supposed to pick up cards and display them to a camera at specified intervals throughout the movie. There was no clock present to remind them of when it was the right time to show the cards. Therefore, the participants needed to rely on memory to allow them to do the prospective task. Another early experiment on the topic involved baking cupcakes (Ceci & Bronfenbrenner, 1985). Children needed to remember when to take cupcakes out of the oven. Successful children checked the time at decreasing intervals in advance while the cookies were in the oven, thus continually reminding themselves about the task at hand. To summarize, a prospective memory task consists of the following. Participants are given a designated target task, such as remembering to remove the cupcakes from the oven. Then, participants are kept occupied with other tasks. This is intended to remove the designated target task from working memory. Finally, performance is measured by looking at how often participants actually perform the target task (see McDaniel & Einstein, 2007).

Some retrospective memory tasks are event based—that is, they require participants to perform an action when a particular event occurs. In event-based retrospective memory, a particular cue—not a specific time—lets you know when to perform the remembered task. Thus, you might have to relay a phone message to your mother when she gets home. Other retrospective memory tasks are time based. In these tasks, you must remember to do a particular activity at a particular time. Thus, you might be required to put the cookies in the oven at exactly 5:00 p.m. (Hicks, Marsh, & Cook, 2005).

When people have little else to do, they are usually good at prospective memory tasks. That is, if you need to pick up a file at work at 10:00 a.m. and you have nothing else to do that day at work, your likelihood of remembering the future task is high. However, when there are competing attentional demands, prospective memory performance can decline rapidly (Marsh & Hicks, 1998). That is, if you have a busy morning of other tasks, it is easier to forget to leave for the file room and pick up the specified file at just the right time. It is likely that the explanation for this phenomenon has to do with the interaction of prospective memory and working memory. Acting on prospective memory appears to draw on working memory's central executive. When the central executive is absorbed in other tasks, participants are less able to recall when they have to perform a particular event. When the competing tasks tap the visuospatial sketchpad or the phonological loop, there is no decrease in prospective memory performance. It is likely that situation in which participants can monitor the proximity of having to do the to-be-performed event while doing other tasks also influences whether the intended task will be performed (Marsh, Hicks, & Cook, 2006).

Because of the importance of attention and the central executive in prospective memory, neuroscience has focused on the role of the prefrontal cortex in prospective memory. Indeed, converging evidence supports the hypothesis that the prefrontal lobe is critical in performing prospective memory tasks. For example, Simons, Scholvinck, Gilbert, Frith, and Burgess (2006) used fMRI technology to examine the brain during prospective memory tasks. They compared brain activity during a control task with brain activity when participants had to maintain a future intention using prospective memory. Under these conditions, there was more activity in both the left and right prefrontal lobes for the task involving prospective memory relative to the one with no prospective memory. The fMRI study is consistent with neuropsychological studies, which show that patients with damage to the prefrontal lobe may have deficits in prospective memory (McDaniel & Einstein, 2007).

In everyday life, prospective memory is important. Each day, most of us have many future actions planned. Failure to retrieve them may result in costly mistakes. Think of a doctor who forgets his or her intention to remove a surgical clip from a patient. The failure to remember this task may severely imperil the patient's health. A patient who forgets his or her intention to take needed medications may also be endangering health. An air traffic controller who forgets his or her intention to warn a pilot about incoming weather endangers many more lives. Thus, developing ways of studying and ultimately improving prospective memory is an important task for memory science.

SUMMARY

Episodic memory is a system of memory than encodes, stores, and retrieves individual events from our personal lives. It contrasts with semantic memory, which is knowledge of the world. Substantial evidence now exists to support the idea that these two forms of memory are subserved by separate neurocognitive systems. Encoding into episodic memory is aided by principles that lead to deeper encoding. The levels-of-processing framework specifies that any factor that leads to deeper or more meaning-based encoding will lead to better retention of that event or information. Relating the information to oneself, to survival, or by organizing it or recognizing distinct aspects of the to-be-remembered event leads to better encoding. On the retrieval side, memory is dependent on retrieval cues, the environmental triggers that allow us to access stored information. With respect to retrieval, encoding specificity means that when the psychological and physical conditions at retrieval match those of encoding, there will be more retrieval cues around, and hence memory performance will improve. This includes external physical landscapes, internal drug states, and internal mood states. Inhibition revolves around the idea that sometimes it is adaptive to forget. Retrieval-induced inhibition shows that when we frequently retrieve some information, it actually inhibits the retrieval of related information. Part-set cueing demonstrates that studying part of a list may actually make it more difficult to recall the rest of the list. Directed-forgetting studies show that explicit directions to forget some material actually cause recall performance to decline. Prospective memory refers to our memory for future intentions, rather than events from the past. Prospective memory appears to be directed by mechanisms in the frontal lobes. When attention is distracted from the intended task, prospective memory can suffer.

KEY TERMS

Semantic memory

Episodic memory

Flashbulb memories

Remember/know judgments

Developmental amnesia

Dissociation

HERA (hemispheric encoding/retrieval asymmetry)

Encoding

Representation

Retrieval

Levels of processing

Incidental learning

Intentional learning

Elaborative rehearsal

Maintenance rehearsal

Deep processing vs. shallow processing

Orienting tasks

Self-reference effect

Survival processing

Generation effect

Enactment effect

Organization

Distinctiveness

von Restorff effect

Availability

Accessibility

Retrieval cues

Encoding specificity

State-dependent memory

Mood congruence

Transfer-appropriate processing

Inhibition

Retrieval-induced inhibition

Part-set cueing

Directed forgetting

Prospective memory

REVIEW QUESTIONS

1. What are the differences between episodic and semantic memory? What kinds of memory does each refer to?

2. List three reasons why episodic memory and semantic memory are considered separate neurocognitive systems.

3. What is meant by the term *levels of processing?* Describe an experiment that supports the hypotheses put forth by levels of processing.

4. What is incidental learning? How does it differ from intentional learning?

5. What is survival processing? What experiment was done to demonstrate it?

6. What is the generation effect? How does it improve memory?

7. What is the von Restorff effect? How is it linked to distinctiveness?

8. What is the theoretical difference between availability and accessibility?

9. What is encoding specificity? Describe an experiment that supports its contentions.

10. What is retrieval-induced inhibition? How has it been tested in experiments?

ONLINE RESOURCES

1. To see KC the amnesic patient, go to the following YouTube site: http://www.youtube.com/watch?v=tXHk0a3RvLc.

2. For more information on developmental amnesia, go to http://www.bbc.co.uk/radio4/memory/programmes/me_and_my_memory2.shtml.

3. For an alternate view of levels of processing, go to http://www.uark.edu/misc/lampinen/LOP.html.

4. For more on the work of the Bjorks, go to http://bjorklab.psych.ucla.edu.

Go to www.sagepub.com/schwartz for additional exercises and study resources. Select **Chapter 4, Episodic Memory** for chapter-specific resources.

CHAPTER 5

Semantic and Lexical Memory

Think of the many things that you have learned in school. In economics, you learned that prices are determined by supply and demand. In physics, you learned that electricity and magnetism are related. In literature, you learned that T. S. Elliot was a famous poet. In music, you learned that Debussy was an impressionist composer. Also think of the things you know that you have learned elsewhere. You have learned the function of your car's carburetor, you have learned that in double-knitting two or more yarns are alternated, and you have learned that hybrid cars use less gas and emit less greenhouse gases than normal cars. You also learned that Republican George Bush won the U.S. presidential election in 2000 and that Democrat Barack Obama won it in 2008. You may also know the name of the current prime minister of Great Britain (David Cameron). You may also know that Jessica Simpson gained 20 pounds and that Alex Rodriguez (the baseball player) had an affair with the singer known as Madonna. These facts about the world are not things that you are born knowing. We learn them as we go and need a memory system to store them until we need them.

Our memory for knowledge of the world—from knitting to literature to politics to gossip—is called semantic memory. Semantic memory is broadly defined as general knowledge of the world. Semantic memory includes our knowledge of history, sports, ideas, geography, pop culture, and even music. As such, it covers a broad range of topics, only some of which we will be able to address here. What unites these topics is that the memory involved is stored in a common representational system. Semantic memory is thought of as a separate neurocognitive system than episodic memory, which we discussed in the last chapter. Recall that episodic memory has a temporal dynamic—we attribute retrieval from episodic memory to the past. In semantic memory, we attribute retrieval of information to be true about the world. In this chapter, we will consider how people represent information into semantic memory as well as issues of encoding and retrieval.

This chapter will also consider another and separate form of memory, known as lexical memory. In the second half of this chapter, our memory for the structure of language will

> **Lexical memory (lexicon):** our mental dictionary, a representational system for the words of our language.

be considered. Our use of language requires a large representational system with an extremely efficient retrieval system. We must be able to retrieve particular words from a huge supply of them at a moment's notice, each and every time we speak or write. For example, think of the last conversation you had before you sat down to read this book. Or think of the last email message you sent before you started reading. Memory for words and grammar is needed for these tasks as well. You have to remember words and what they mean. You have to remember how to pronounce the words if you are talking and spell the words if you are writing. You must remember how words are strung together into acceptable English sentences. You may be asked to translate a passage of this book into another language so that your grandmother can understand what you are learning. This invokes even greater memory demands on those of you who are bilingual or multilingual. **Lexical memory** (also known as the **lexicon**) is our mental dictionary, a representational system for the words of our language. Lexical memory is also considered a separate neurocognitive system from semantic (and episodic memory). There is much overlap between what is meant by semantic memory and what is meant by lexical memory. However, semantic memory is usually studied by researchers interested in memory, and lexical memory is usually studied by researchers interested in language. Lexical memory is a form of memory and therefore is relevant here.

Psycholinguists are interested in the structure of the representational system involved in lexical memory for a number of reasons. First, lexical memory must maintain a huge number of items (words and rules of grammar) stored in memory. Second, access to these items must be extremely fast in order to support normal speech and normal speech comprehension. Given that human beings start life knowing no words at all, the encoding of words into lexical memory is also of great interest as young children acquire vocabulary at astonishing rates.

SEMANTIC MEMORY

Semantic memory is a broad term. It includes all kinds of knowledge that we acquire and requires a representational system to maintain. As such, semantic memory informs many of the decisions we make on an ordinary basis, from understanding what we read, to informing how we vote, to deciding how to make a delicious homemade pizza, to determining how we earn a living.

ASSOCIATIVE STRUCTURES IN SEMANTIC MEMORY

As the above examples illustrate, each of us has countless facts about the world. One goal for memory researchers is to try to model how all this information is represented by one's cognitive systems (not to mention how they are physically stored by the brain). To achieve this goal, most theorists have focused on associative models of semantic memory. An

Associative model: we represent information in semantic memory in terms of connections among units of information. A
node is the unit of memory, which is then
connected to other nodes.

associative model means that we represent information in semantic memory in terms of connections among units of information (see Figure 5.1).
A node is the unit of memory, which is then connected to other nodes. For example, you might
have a node for the 18th-century British philosopher George Berkeley, who championed the ideas
of associationism. The node for the memory of this
philosopher might be linked to the node for John Locke (another associationist philosopher) and
to the node for Charles Barkley, the star basketball player for the Philadelphia 76'ers in the 1980s
and 1990s. Nodes may be strongly connected, as in the Berkeley-Locke connection, or less
strongly connected, as in the Berkeley-Barkley connection. Eventually, as the activation spreads
to multiple nodes, it fades, and we can no longer see the trail of activation. Thus, in association
models of semantic memory, our memory is a web of interconnected ideas and facts. For more
on the life of George Berkeley, go to www.sagepub.com/schwartz.[1]

Spreading activation: refers to the transfer
of activation from one node to an associated node.

Semantic network models posit that retrieval
takes place when one node is activated based on
the input from a cue. Once a node is activated, this
activation will spread to existing associated nodes
(Collins & Loftus, 1975). The term **spreading
activation** refers to the transfer of activation from

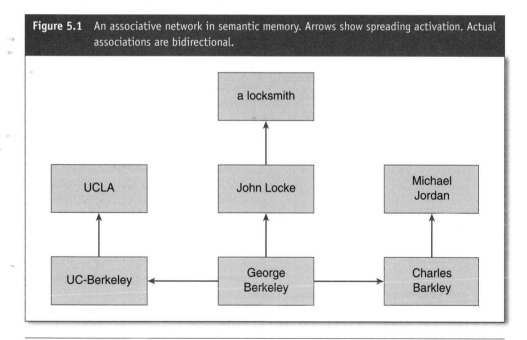

Figure 5.1 An associative network in semantic memory. Arrows show spreading activation. Actual
associations are bidirectional.

SOURCE: Based on theory by Collins and Loftus (1975).

one node to an associated node. For example, if you are asked, "Who was the British philosopher most noted for his theories of associationism and his theory that the minds starts as a blank slate?" this should activate the node in memory for "John Locke." Activating the node for John Locke can lead to the spoken response of, "Of course, I know that one, it's that bloke from Somerset England, John Locke." The current thinking in cognitive psychology is that activation spreads—that is, as soon as the node for John Locke is activated, some, but a lesser amount of activation, spreads to the node for George Berkeley because the nodes for Berkeley and Locke are connected. In turn, some activation spreads to the node for Charles Barkley. Thus, activation spreads from one node to the next when one node is activated. However, an important component of these models is that activation weakens as it spreads from node to node. Thus, "Charles Barkley" will be less activated than "George Berkeley." Thus, it is likely that the activation will not spread further than "Barkley" (say, failing to activate any other basketball knowledge).

SEMANTIC PRIMING AND LEXICAL DECISION TASKS

This theoretical architecture has been repeatedly put through experimental testing and, by and large, is generally supported by the data. One of the main methods of testing this model is **semantic priming.** The basic idea of semantic priming is as follows. When a particular node is activated (e.g., by hearing "John Locke)," that activation will spread to associated nodes, including the one for George Berkeley. Similarly, if one reads the word *tiger,* activation should spread to related nodes for concepts such as "striped" and "lion." This activation of these additional nodes should make it easier for the person to process the associated items. Thus, we should respond faster to the name George Berkeley if we have just heard the name John Locke. We should respond faster to the word *lion* if we have just heard the word *tiger.*

> **Semantic priming:** the effect of one word or idea on the processing of a related word or idea. A related word will activate a target item and allow it to be processed more quickly.

In experimental situations, this is measured by use of a **lexical decision task.** In a lexical decision task, participants must judge as quickly as they can whether a string of letters is a word or not (Meyer & Schvanevelt, 1976). For example, the words *doctor* and *cranberry* should elicit a response of yes, but the nonsense string *xffxere* should elicit a response of no. Possible words that are not used in English such as *pluckban* or *scrawps* should also elicit a response of no. Participants are asked to make such judgments as quickly as they can so that reaction times can be measured. Typically, a young adult in college can make these decisions in under half of a second. The following website allows you to participate in an online lexical decision task experiment; go to www.sagepub .com/schwartz.[2]

> **Lexical decision task:** a cognitive task in which participants judge if a string of letters is a word as quickly as they can.

Semantic priming can then be added to the lexical decision task. Participants still have to judge if a string of letters is a word, but now that string is preceded by a prime, which is also usually a word but may be picture as well. Primes may be related or unrelated to the to-be-judged words. For example, if the target word is *doctor,* a related prime is *nurse,* and an unrelated prime is *gumball.* Research consistently shows that the related primes produce faster and easier processing of the target word. This translates into faster reaction times in the lexical decision for words preceded by related primes than those preceded by unrelated primes (McNamara, 2005; Meyer & Schvaneveldt, 1971). Semantic priming is different from subliminal priming. In subliminal priming, the participant is not consciously aware of the stimuli that are affecting his or her behavior (Marcel, 1983). Semantic priming occurs because the participant processes the prime.

Spreading activation states that activation will move from one node to the next. Thus, *nurse* will prime *doctor,* which is associated with the word *lawyer.* Thus, this model predicts that a word like *nurse* will also show some small priming effect on a second-order association. The smaller amount of priming occurs because activation spreads and dissipates. Anticipating how much priming occurs is important for developing quantitative (mathematical) models of how priming occurs. This kind of priming is called *mediated priming.* Mediated priming occurs when the prime word is related to a word, which is also related to the target word. For example, if the target word is *lion,* then the word *stripes* will prime it. The reason being is that *stripes* is associated with *tiger,* and *tiger* is associated with *lion.* Therefore, preceding *lion* with *stripes* allows for faster processing (McNamara & Altarriba, 1988). In a recent study on mediated priming, Duñabeitia, Carreiras, and Perea (2008) showed that mediated priming could also cross over from semantic characteristics to phonological characteristics. That is, the first link in the priming is semantic (*lion* to *tiger*), but the second link is phonological, that is, sound related (*tiger* to *Geiger*). In a similar way, *John Locke* can prime *Charles Barkley* through *George Berkeley.*

SENTENCE VERIFICATION TASKS

Another manner in which spreading activation of association networks has been experimentally tested is by looking at sentence verification tasks. In a **sentence verification task,** participants are asked to decide as quickly as possible if a sentence is true or false. Thus, a sentence such as "All men are mortal" should be judged to be true, whereas a sentence such as "Hawaii is located in the Atlantic Ocean" should be judged to be false. According to the model of spreading activation, sentences reflecting closely linked nodes will be verified faster than sentences reflecting distantly linked nodes. This is likely because the activation can spread from one node to a nearby node faster than it can spread to a more distant node. For example, the sentence "Tigers have stripes" should be verified faster than an equally true sentence that reflects a more distant association, such as "Tigers have lungs." Collins and Quillian (1969) reasoned that characteristics that are unique

> **Sentence verification tasks:** participants are asked to decide as quickly as possible if a sentence is true or false.

to a particular item will be closely linked in associative space, whereas characteristics that are shared with other items will be more distantly linked. That is, *stripes* will be stored closely to *tiger,* but *lungs* will be linked through a common link to "land animals." Therefore, if spreading activation is correct, "tigers have stripes" is faster to verify than "tigers have lungs." In their experiment, this prediction turned out to be correct; closer associations led to faster verification times.

Therefore, it is a reasonable conclusion that semantic memory is organized into some associative network. In this associative network, information is linked together with varying strengths and at varying distances. Strong connective links or close links lead to much shared activation, whereas weaker links or more distant links lead to less shared activation. When a particular node is activated, that activation spreads to other adjacent links. In the next section, we will expand on the notion of associative structure in semantic memory and discuss how items in semantic memory are bound together into categories and concepts. The basic idea of an associative structure is similar, but now the goal is to understand how the mind constructs categories.

CATEGORIES AND CONCEPTS

Concepts and categories are important ideas in semantic memory. These are two terms borrowed from everyday usage, but their definitions within cognitive psychology are quite specific. A **concept** is a mental construct that contains information associated with a specific idea. That is, a concept is a mental representation of an idea. A **category** is a mental construct referring to a set of objects or ideas that are grouped together or are associated with each other. That is, a category usually refers to things that are similar in some respect. Thus, categories can include the items that are grouped together, such as tools, furniture, flowering plants, forms of government, or Mexican Americans. Note the flexibility of a category. A hammer has little in common with a pressure cleaner except that they are both used to maintain order in a household. The category "Mexican American" means all people in the United States who share a common origin in Mexico. It says nothing about how old they are, what they look like, what language they speak, where they live, their socioeconomic status, or which political parties they prefer.

> **Concept:** mental construct that contains information associated with a specific idea.
>
> **Category:** mental construct referring to a set of objects or ideas that are grouped together or are associated with each other.

Concepts can refer to our mental representations of categories. For example, the concept of a "tool" is our mental representation of the characteristics that tools share (by and large, as we will see). However, *concept* is a broader term than *categories*. For example, concepts such as truth, love, and literacy are abstract concepts not easily translated into categories. Categories tend to be more concrete, such as things that are true, the reasons we love, and literacy rates among Western countries. It is your semantic memory system that stores concepts and categories and allows you to access them when you need to. It is important for cognitive systems to be able to categorize material. It allows us to organize information and understand it.

Because of the complexity of concepts and the need for spreading activation networks to account for them, cognitive neuroscientists expected that representation of concepts would be widely distributed throughout the brain. Activating a concept may draw on a great many different brain regions. Kuchinke, van der Meer, and Krueger (2009) examined decisions made about whether two objects belonged to the same category while monitoring participants using functional magnetic resonance imaging (fMRI). They found a wide distribution of brain areas became active, including areas in the frontal lobes and in the temporal lobes. Because they were dealing with linguistic concepts, there was a decided emphasis on the left hemisphere, but areas in the right hemisphere were activated as well.

Categories Are Fuzzy

At first, a category seems like a concrete entity. Tools, furniture, literacy rates, and Mexican Americans all seem like fairly straightforward categories. But each category has fuzzy boundaries. Consider the category of tools. Clearly, hammers and pressure cleaners are tools, despite the differences in what they are used for and how they operate. But is a pickle jar a tool? Looking up the word *tool* in a dictionary might yield something like this: a device that helps us accomplish a task. Using this definition, a pickle jar certainly is a tool. It is human-made objects whose function is to store pickles, something that would be much more difficult to do without one. Yet, to most of us, a pickle jar does not quite fit into our mental category of tools. It is too passive—it just sits there holding pickles. Tools need to be wielded. Tools are macho things like axes, hammers, and blowtorches, and a pickle jar is not quite one of them.

Consider the category of Mexican American. More straightforward? Clearly, someone whose parents were born in Guadalajara, grew up speaking Spanish, and has a last name of Garcia, fits into our category of Mexican American. What about Californians whose ancestors lived in California while it was still part of Mexico? And what about the blond-haired blue-eyed child, born in Massachusetts, whose grandmother lived in Mexico City for 10 years after escaping the Nazis in Germany, became a Mexican citizen, but then moved to Boston and raised her children there? Mexican American?

There are other ways of looking at boundary conditions as well. For example, function is an important defining feature of many concepts. Thus, for tools, function—that they aid humans in tasks—is at the heart of what a tool is (see Figure 5.2). What happens when an object is no longer able to serve that function? What about broken tools? Is a pressure cleaner that is out of gas a tool? Is a broken hammer a tool? They cannot serve the function of being a tool even though they still resemble tools. Which is more important for the definition of a tool—its function or its appearance? Consider the concept "bachelor," which refers to an unmarried adult male. Certainly, an unmarried sexually active heterosexual male at the age of 40 who lives alone is a bachelor. But there are unmarried heterosexual adult males who would not be considered bachelors—Catholic priests, for example. One might choose to revise the definition of "bachelor" to mean heterosexual unmarried adult men who have not taken vows of celibacy. But then there are widowers and divorcees. Do they revert to bachelorhood? Without belaboring this example, suffice it so say that boundary conditions are important in defining categories.

Figure 5.2 All these implements are a part of a common category, tools. What does an object have to be in order to be considered a tool? Is an aspirin a tool? Is a computer a tool?

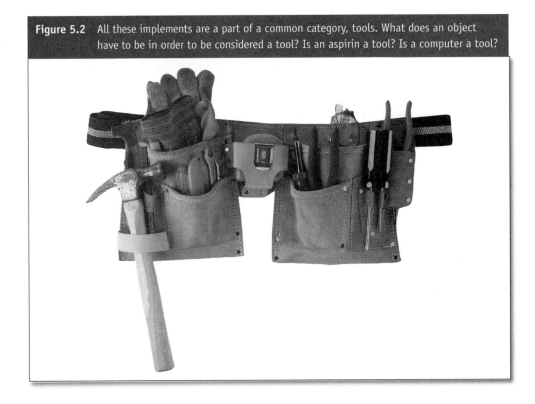

Because of these boundary conditions, researchers think of categories as complex and related to each other in multiple ways. The complexity of categories seems to be clear in the way memory is organized for categories. One variable that appears to have psychological reality here is called **levels of categorization.** Levels of categorization means that categories are nested structures in which the level of organization is important in defining the category. There are three such levels: basic, subordinate, and superordinate (Rosch & Mervis, 1975). The basic level is the most common level of categories and the one we are most likely to invoke. For example, tools is a basic-level category for most people (with power tools being subordinate and human implements being superordinate). The subordinate level allows for more specific or specialized categories to be formed, such as power tools and first-generation Mexican Americans to be considered. Superordinate categories are higher order categories, which include general information, which include many more common categories. Thus, human-made implements and all "ethnic" Americans are two such superordinate categories.

Levels of categorization are fluid, depending on a person's expertise. For example, for most of us, "cat" might be the basic-level category and "Scottish fold" might be the subordinate

> **Levels of categorization:** categories are nested structures in which the level of organization is important in defining the category. There are three such levels: basic, subordinate, and superordinate.

category. But for a cat fancier who takes his or her cats to shows across the country, "cat" might assume a superordinate classification, as the person endlessly discusses the variants between various types of purebred cats. For the cat fancier, "Scottish fold" takes on the basic-level classification, and the differences between American short-hair Scottish folds and European piebald Scottish folds become the subordinate category (see Figure 5.3).

Levels of categorization have a psychological reality. Research has demonstrated that basic-level information is retrieved faster than subordinate or superordinate information (T. T. Rogers & McClelland, 2004; Rosch, Mervis, Gray, Johnson, & Boyes-Braem, 1976). Indeed, when we see an object, we tend to use the basic level first. For example, we call the object on your desk generally a "computer," not a "Powerbook G4 Macintosh laptop computer." Furthermore, different levels of categorization are associated with different areas of the brain. Kosslyn, Alpert, and Thompson (1995)

Figure 5.3   A Scottish fold. At a basic level, we call this animal a cat. For most of us, "Scottish fold" is a subordinate category, and "mammal" is a superordinate category.

used positron emission tomography (PET) technology to examine categorization. They did so by asking participants to match picture to words. Thus, a picture of a dog was accompanied by three words: *animal* (superordinate), *dog* (basic), and *miniature poodle* (subordinate). They showed that superordinate levels are more likely to activate the prefrontal cortex than basic-level categories. In contrast, when people choose subordinate categories, there is more activity in the parietal lobe of the brain. It is possible that superordinate categories cause people to reason about the category or have to remember more features. This may tax the prefrontal lobe, whereas it is likely that the subordinate level draws on more sensory representations, thus drawing on the parietal lobe.

Family Resemblance

Categories are inherently fuzzy in nature. Nearly every natural category will defy a definition and will have members that differ from the "mainstream." Think of the category "Mexican American." A U.S. citizen living in San Diego, named Garcia, and fluent in Spanish is a typical Mexican American. However, the grandson of the German immigrant

> **Family resemblance**: membership in a category may be defined by each item's general similarity to other members in the category rather than by a specific list of features.

who lived briefly in Mexico before moving to the United Sates is a less typical Mexican American. **Family resemblance** means that membership in a category may be defined by each item's general similarity to other members in the category rather than by a specific list of features (Rosch & Mervis, 1975). Family resemblance takes into account that many categories are multimodal; there are many characteristics that apply. For example, think of the category "bird." When we consider birds from a purely zoological understanding, both penguins and ostriches are every bit as much of a bird as is a sparrow, a robin, or an eagle. Yet, because penguins and ostriches vary from most birds in many respects (most notably, flying), they are often considered less central members of the category.

Because of the complexity of categories and their fuzzy boundary conditions, cognitive psychologists have found it necessary to create models as to how concepts and categories are represented in semantic memory. The next section will describe the major models that have been advanced to account for the representation of categories.

Prototype Theory

A prototype is defined as the most typical member of a particular category. **Prototype theory** states that prototypes form the central characteristic in our representation of categories. In prototype theory, we compare examples that we encounter in the real world to a constructed mental prototype. If the example matches the prototype, we decide it is an example of the category. If it does not match, we reject the category label for that item. For example, we compare an example of a tool to our prototype of a tool. The prototype itself need not be a real member of the category. In fact, it is likely to be an averaged mental representation of the concept (Rosch, 1975). Thus, the prototype may not exist at all in the real world; it is an abstraction. Consider your prototype of a bird. If you live in the Northeast of the United States, your prototype may look something like a robin, but without the specific coloring. If you live farther south, or closer to the ocean, your "bird" may obtain longer legs and a longer beak but is still not yet an egret. When you encounter a new animal, you match the animal to your prototype of a bird. If it is a close enough match, you assign it to the category "bird." If it fails to match, you dismiss that example as a bird.

> **Prototype theory**: states that prototypes form the central characteristic in our representation of categories. A prototype is defined as the most typical member of a particular category.

What evidence is there that we represent categories in terms of prototypes? We will consider two main lines of research. The first demonstrates that prototypes are rapidly remembered and named when a category is supplied. The second shows the effects of semantic priming on prototypical members of a category and nonprototypical members of a category. Each of these points to a strong role for prototypes in our semantic memory.

Prototypes Are Easily Named. In studies done by Eleanor Rosch and her colleagues, participants were asked to judge how prototypical a given instance was of a particular category. For example, "raccoon" might be judged highly prototypical of the category "mammal," but "platypus" might be judged less prototypical. Similarly, "carrot" may be judged more prototypical of the category "vegetable" than "kale." A second group of participants was then asked to generate the names of examples from categories, such as mammal and vegetable. The researchers found that the items named first and more frequently by the participants were the ones that were usually judged as more prototypical (Mervis, Catlin, & Rosch, 1976). Thus, the first and most common vegetables generated included prototypical vegetables like carrots and peas and only later, if at all, did the participants produce items like kale and bok choy.

Prototypes and Semantic Priming. The more prototypical an example is, the more likely it is to be judged more quickly after semantic priming. That is, semantic priming works better if the target words are prototypical rather than nonprototypical. For example, the prime word *feathers* will create faster response speed if it precedes *robin* than if it precedes *cormorant.* Thus, prototypical examples are more locked into the associative structure that creates categories.

Alternatives to Prototype Theory

> **Exemplar theory**: categories are classified by maintaining a large number of specific instances of a category (exemplars) that are associated with each other in semantic memory.

In **exemplar theory,** categories are classified by maintaining a large number of specific instances of a category that are associated with each other in semantic memory. When we encounter a new item, we compare it to each and every exemplar in that category to determine if it matches or not. The individual items that are stored in semantic memory as evidence of a particular category are called exemplars. This contrasts with prototype theory in that prototype theory suggests that we draw an average of all the instances of a category and use that as a comparison. Exemplar theory contends that the category is all of the associated items (Medin & Rips, 2005).

Exemplar theory is successful in accounting for the multidimensional nature of a category. Consider the category "tools." It is difficult to imagine what the prototype tool would look like. Consider the difference between hand tools and power tools. What could possibly represent an average of hand tools and power tools? It is not something about which we can really generate a prototype. At the very least, one would have to have several prototypes to represent different dimensions of the category. However, if each and every exemplar is represented in an associated structure in semantic memory, any new item can be compared against the appropriate match.

What evidence exists for the reality of the exemplar theory? It turns out that priming can be specific to the particular aspect of the exemplar that is being primed (Gagne & Shoben, 2002). That is, if the prime focuses on one aspect of the category (e.g., color), it will better prime those members of the category for which that aspect is salient. Thus, it will be easier to verify what the term *television shows* means if it is preceded by *reality shows* than if it is preceded by *trade shows* since both *television shows* and *reality shows* share a common meaning of the word *shows*.

Some have criticized the exemplar approach because it necessitates a large memory system that can store hundreds, if not thousands, of exemplars for each and every different category. However, as we saw in the chapter on visual memory, the capacity of long-term memory to store information is seemingly limitless. So large demands on capacity alone are not enough to disqualify any particular theory. It is also possible that exemplars and prototypes may be used both in the formation of categories and in comparing new instances to the existing categories.

Another theory as to how categories are represented in semantic memory is the feature comparison theory. **Feature comparison theory** states that we maintain a list of features for each category. According to this view, each category is represented by an associated list of the kinds of characteristics that make up the category. Thus, for example, the category of books might include the following: (1) contains written material; (2) intended to be read; (3) a set number of pages, usually enclosed in covers of paper or cardboard; and (4) intended to last a long time.

> **Feature comparison theory**: we define our categories by maintaining a list of features for any particular category.

New objects are compared neither to a constructed prototype nor to a set of exemplars. Rather, new objects are matched to the list of features. Thus, when one encounters a magazine, it fails to fit into the category of books because it does not fulfill feature 4 of the category books. Your textbook, however, does fulfill the features and would be classified as a book.

E. E. Smith, Shoben, and Rips (1974) distinguished between defining features and characteristic features. **Defining features** are required for any example of a particular category. For example, the defining feature of a book is that it stores words. **Characteristic features** generally accompany an instance of the category but are not required. Characteristic features of books include that they are meant to be read, have covers, are made of paper, and have an author. Most of us would still classify books-on-tape as books because they store words, which can transmit meaning even if they are not printed, not made of paper, and not meant to be read.

> **Defining features**: according to feature comparison theory, defining features are required for any example of a particular category.
>
> **Characteristic features**: according to feature comparison theory, characteristic features generally accompany an instance of the category but are not required.

Feature comparison theory is essentially flawed because so few categories actually have clear defining features. Consider the example of the category "books." Is the defining feature really accurate? What about a children's book that only has pictures but not words? What does that leave as a defining feature of a book when it includes examples of picture books, audio-books, electronic books, and so on? The category "books" becomes multidimensional, and a single set of features no longer defines it. The more classic example of this problem is to think of what the defining feature is of the category "cat." Is it that it is a living thing, that it meows, and that it has cat genes? What about a dead cat, a mute cat, and a stuffed animal cat? All of these exceptions propelled theorists to consider the prototype and exemplar theory as being better able to explain the structure of semantic memory.

SCHEMAS AND SCRIPTS

To this point, our discussion of semantic memory has concerned the topic of concepts, categories, and the connections among them. Semantic memory also includes more general aspects of memory, that is, units of memory that are more complex. For example, think of the concept of parking, that is, the idea that a car can be turned off and left for a while in a safe location where you can return to it later. But in American society, parking one's car is a well-learned ritual. The script for parking a car involves (1) arriving at the parking lot, (2) searching for a spot—get there early or the spots will be all taken, and (3) you may choose to swing around the lot an extra time in the hope that someone with a really good spot is just leaving and you can take that one. (4) Once you have your spot, position your car so that other cars cannot sneak in front of you, (5) place your car in the spot—maximize difference from nearby cars so as to avoid "door dings," and (6) note the location of your car so you can return to it later. Many of us follow this script several times a week. The point is—that we all have this script memorized already—we know what to expect when we enter the parking lot. The script of "how to park your car" is another form of information stored in semantic memory.

Fundamental to this area is the idea of a schema. A **schema** is generalized knowledge about an event, a person, or a situation. That is, schemas are patterns of connected information about a particular topic. The script described above for parking a car can be considered a schema. We have knowledge about the general form of parking a car. We have schemas, for example, as to what you find in a car. We expect seats, beverage holders, controls, and transparent windows. Imagine your surprise if you entered your friend's car and there were no seats, but there was a sink. Think of a car in which all the windows were rendered completely opaque. These cars would violate your schema of a car (and be quite dangerous). We have schemas about what to expect on tests in college. This particular schema is all too familiar to college students. But imagine coming to an exam to find your professor playing loud music from the 1970s on a phonograph player while you were trying to take the exam. Included in our schema of taking an exam is that the professor will be quiet. From the point of view of memory representation, schemas and scripts are well-learned patterns that guide our behavior and organize information in memory (Abelson, 1981).

> **Schema**: generalized knowledge about an event, a person, or a situation.

Scripts refer to a particular kind of schema. **Scripts** are well-learned sequences of events associated with common activities. For example, we have scripts for such common activities as "going to a restaurant." Without having to recall specific instances of restaurant-going, you can describe the common process. A person shows you to a table and gives you menus. You spend several minutes deciding what to eat. Then a waiter comes by, and you give him or her your order (politely, hopefully). Several minutes later, the waiter returns bearing your meal. You eat your meal. And so on and so forth. Our memories abound in such scripts—waiting to board an airplane, checking out at the grocery store, and your morning "getting ready" ritual are just a few of the many scripts you may have stored in your semantic memory. Violations of scripts often turn out to be memorable events. Consider an airplane flight in which the flight attendants decided to forgo boarding by seat numbers. The ensuing crush to board the airplane may prompt you to avoid that airline in the future. Consider a restaurant without menus. This puts a maximal demand on waiter, who must tell you all of the options for the day's meal. It also puts memory demands on the patron as he or she must remember all of these options. However, you may also consider a restaurant without menus an interesting novelty and recommend the restaurant to friends.

> **Scripts**: well-learned sequences of events associated with common activities.

Consider a schema for a dentist's office. There is a waiting room with relatively comfortable chairs. Magazines are available for patients while they wait. These magazines usually include *Newsweek, Sports Illustrated,* and *National Geographic.* A few children's toys lie unused under a television showing *Oprah.* A woman sits behind a glass panel and checks you in. The office is decorated with hokey signs ("A bright smile shines on everyone's day"). An anthropomorphic tooth encouraging kids to brush stands to one side. Beyond a door is a maze of rooms with dental chairs, X-ray machines, and occasionally an actual dentist. These are items we come to expect after a lifetime of visiting dentist's offices. However, consider when an event or item is inconsistent with the schema. Consider sitting down in the waiting room and finding pornographic magazines instead of the expected *Newsweek.* Consider coming to a waiting room that had yoga mats instead of chairs. Consider a dentist office covered in Marxist slogans ("Viva Castro") instead of the usual platitudes. Such variations from the dentist schema would not go unnoticed. Indeed, many of us would find these deviations from the schema sufficient reason to find a new dentist.

A classic study by Brewer and Treyens (1981) illustrates this point very nicely. Participants arrived for an experiment and were asked to wait in a lab room (Figure 5.4). The participants waited in the room a short time and then entered another room for testing. The catch was that the job of the participants was to recall all of the objects that they could remember from the waiting room.

Participants remembered lots of items from the office, which were consistent with the concept of a waiting room. For example, people remembered the desk, the chair, and the typewriter (this was 1981 after all). Some people even false remembered schema-consistent items not present in the room (e.g., books). However, there were several

Figure 5.4 What can you remember from this room?

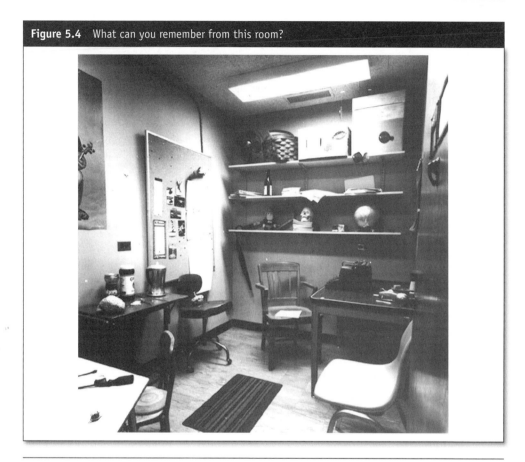

SOURCE: Brewers and Treyens (1981).

items in the room that are generally not found in offices. For example, wine bottles and picnic baskets are seldom found in offices but whose presence here should be surprising, but very few participants remembered these items. Items that violate the office schema were also well recalled. Thus, most participants recalled the skull, even though this is seldom found in academic offices. Thus, we can conclude that schemas help us recall items and events that are consistent with the schema and help us remember violations of the schema.

Once a schema is formed, it is useful in encoding new information. The schema forms the backbone upon which new information can be associated. For example, Bransford and Johnson (1972) presented participants with confusing passages to read, such as the one shown in Box 5.1. Some participants were given schematic information to assist them in understanding the passage. For example, in the passage below, some participants had the title "Washing Clothes" to aid their understanding. Those provided with the title recalled more information from the passage than those who had not.

Box 5.1	Washing Clothes

The procedure is actually quite simple. First arrange items into different groups. Of course one pile may be sufficient depending on how much there is to do. If you have to go somewhere else due to lack of facilities, that is the next step; otherwise, you are pretty well set. It is important not to overdo things. That is, it is better to do too few things at once than too many. In the short run this may not seem important, but complications can easily arise. A mistake can be expensive as well. At first, the whole procedure will seem complicated. Soon, however, it will become just another facet of life. It is difficult to foresee any end to necessity for this task in the immediate future, but then, one can never tell. After the procedure is completed one arranges the material into different groups again. Then they can be put into their appropriate places. Eventually they will be used once more and the whole cycle will then have to be repeated. However, that is part of life.

SOURCE: Bransford and Johnson (1972).

As you can see, the text is written in an ambiguous way. Once you know, however, that it is about washing clothes, most of the ambiguous words should make sense. Therefore, having a schema in mind (in the case, for washing clothes) can help an individual encode new information into memory.

Reconstruction of Events

Schemas are also useful in providing structure in retrieving longer events and information such as stories. Consider describing a recent trip to a restaurant. The distinctive feature about this lunch was getting together with an old friend, who you had not seen in a long time, and perhaps you dined at a restaurant with food you are not accustomed to, perhaps a Middle Eastern restaurant. Thus, what you remember is catching up with your friend, on one hand, and the interesting tastes, on the other, such as humus and baba ghanough. Now consider describing the event. Do you really remember the maitre d' bringing you to the table? Do you remember whether the maitre d' or the waiter brought you the menus? Did the same waiter who took your order bring you your food? In many cases, we may use the schema to help us fill in this information. In telling the story of your visit to the restaurant, what is important is telling your listener the gist of the story: the good food and the good friendship. The listener is not expecting you to get the details of the service accurate, but it may be necessary to insert such information to keep the narrative flow. For example, you might say, "By the time the waiter came to take our order, we were already drinking the most interesting tea," when in fact, you ordered before the waiter brought the tea.

Indeed, one of the classic experiments in all of psychology concerns the use schemas in storytelling. Bartlett (1932) asked his participants to play a "telephone game." In the experiment, he asked one student to read a story derived from a Native

American folktale from the Pacific Northwest. The story was called "War of the Ghosts" and is shown in Box 5.2. Some time after hearing the story, the student was asked to tell another student the story, who then had to tell the story to yet another person. After several such retellings, Bartlett had the student write down the story. He found that changes in the story from the original had to do with making it more consistent with the schema for a story from someone from British culture. For example, "hunting seals" became "going fishing," and often an explanation for the sudden death at the end of the story was included. In short, the British participants transformed the story according to their own schemas. In another experiment, Bartlett had students read the story, and then each student wrote it down 4 months later. As in the telephone game, the errors that students intruded into the story made the story more consistent with British story schemas. For more information on Bartlett himself, go to www.sagepub .com/schwartz.[3]

Box 5.2	The War of the Ghosts

One night two young men from Egulac went down to the river to hunt seals, and while they were there it became foggy and calm. Then they heard war-cries, and they thought: "Maybe this is a war party." They escaped to the shore and hid behind a log. Now canoes came up, and they heard the noise of paddles, and saw one canoe coming up to them. There were five men in the canoe, and they said:

"What do you think? We wish to take you along. We are going up the river to make war on the people."

One of the young men said, "I have no arrows."

"Arrows are in the canoe," they said.

"I will not go along. I might be killed. My relatives do not know where I have gone. But you," he said turning to the other, "may go with them."

So one of the young men went, but the other returned home.

And the warriors went up the river to a town on the other side of Kalama. The people came down to the water, and they began to fight, and many were killed. But presently the young man heard one of the warriors say: "Quick, let us go home: that Indian has been hit." Now he thought: "Oh, they are ghosts." He did not feel sick, but they said he had been shot.

So the canoes went back to Egulac, and the young man went ashore to his house, and made a fire. And he told everybody and said: "Behold I accompanied the ghosts, and we went to fight. Many of our fellows were killed, and many of those who attacked us were killed. They said I was hit, but I did not feel sick."

He told it all, and then he became quiet. When the sun rose he fell down. Something black came out of his mouth. His face became contorted. The people jumped up and cried.

He was dead.

SOURCE: Bartlett (1932).

SEMANTIC MEMORY FOR MUSIC

Most of us have many songs and melodies stored in our memory. You may know the lyrics and music to Bob Dylan's "The Times They Are a-Changin'," Black Eyed Peas' "Imma Be," and Beethoven's "Ode to Joy" (in German). Although some songs may have powerful associations with certain episodic memories (e.g., the song you danced to with your future spouse the first time you met), much of what we store in memory is semantic memory in nature. A professional musician may have thousands of songs accessible in semantic memory. Recently, for example, I attended a concert and watched a young pianist play a complex Rachmaninoff piano concerto. The young man never looked at a sheet of music, having memorized thousands of notes and complex rhythms. It is likely that this was not the only piece of music this man had committed to memory. Now it is likely that his piano skills are procedural memories rather than semantic memory, but the power of our memory to represent music is profound.

It has been argued that the function of music itself is mnemonic (Racette & Peretz, 2007). That is, the rhythms and cadences of music allow for easier encoding of verbal material such as stories. Indeed, we teach our children to learn the alphabet with a song, and many companies sell their products by having us associate their product with a catchy song. However, Racette and Peretz (2007) also showed that trying to remember lyrics and the melody can interfere with each other. It turns out that both can place demands on memory. On the other hand, other studies have shown that melodies can help participants remember words better (Rainey & Larsen, 2002).

INTERIM SUMMARY

Semantic memory is our memory for knowledge. The representational system is thought of as a system of interlocking nodes. Activation spreads from node to node when a cue is given to elicit retrieval. Semantic memory stores many kinds of knowledge, including but not limited to categories and concepts, schemas and scripts, and the music we know (and love). There are a number of models as to how we represent categories in our semantic memory. These include the feature comparison, exemplar, and prototype models. Schemas and scripts serve to organize patterns of connected information about a particular topic. Schemas aid in both the encoding and retrieval of information by serving as a template upon which new information can be connected to.

LEXICAL MEMORY

I have a friend of Turkish ethnic roots who grew up in Iran. He fled political persecution in Iran as a young man and settled in Spain, where he lived for a couple of years. He then moved to Miami to attend college and has not left since. This man is fluent in four languages: Turkish, Farsi, Spanish, and English. This level of multilingual expertise is not uncommon in many cultures, although it is rare among Americans. It is likely that this man knows over

400,000 words between the four languages that he speaks. In addition, this man must have stored in memory literally thousands of grammatical rules that govern how to speak in each of these languages. Even a monolingual knows approximately 100,000 words, still a prestigious amount of information to be stored in memory (English has more words than most languages but relatively easy syntax). This incredibly large number of items requires a memory system to hold it. Thus, language is heavily dependent on memory. Without a strong and easy-to-access memory for language, it would be difficult to become fluent in any language, let alone one's native language.

Language is also learned and remembered at an incredibly fast rate in very young children. By one year of age, many children have already spoken their first word and may know the meanings of several hundred words. In just two years, the average child's vocabulary has increased to 500 words, and he or she may know the meanings of thousands of words (Fenson et al., 2000). In just a few years, some children even know the word *penultimate*.

Although often treated as separate topics in separate courses, language and memory are closely intertwined. Language is heavily dependent on the proper functioning of the memory systems that serve it. We need to remember tens of thousands of words, thousands of aspects of grammar, the way in which to pronounce certain words, and in languages such as English, we also need to memorize the spelling of thousands of irregular words. In other languages, such as French and Spanish, every noun has a gender, and we must memorize that *la mesa* (the table) is feminine, but *el corazon* (the heart) is masculine. This chapter will attempt to unravel the complex memory processes that underlie our language use.

WHAT IS LANGUAGE?

We often take language for granted. It is such an integral part of every part of our life. We wake up talking, we go to sleep talking, and many of us even talk in our sleep. It only becomes an issue in situations in which we fail to retrieve a word that we are sure we know (as in a tip-of-the-tongue state) or when we find ourselves in a situation in which we do not share a language with a person we are trying to communicate with. We sometimes become more aware of the rules and intricacies of language when we write. The written word requires a more explicit knowledge of the rules of language, allowing one to write in precise and grammatical sentences.

Language primarily functions as a mode of communication among human beings. But we also use language for other purposes as well. We express emotion in language (e.g., cursing after you stub your toe). We use language as a means of humor and play (e.g., puns and jokes). We even use language to exert control over the nonhuman environment (e.g., praying). Communication among people, however, remains paramount (see Crystal, 1998).

Psycholinguistics is the study of the psychological processes involved in human language. Psycholinguists study how people produce language, how people understand language, and the relationship between spoken and written language. Cognitive psycholinguists are interested in issues of

Psycholinguistics: the study of the psychological processes involved in human language.

representation, that is, how we store the thousands of words and grammatical rules that we must have in our brains. They are also interested in how we represent the sounds of words and how these sounds are associated with the meanings of those words. For a memory course, this is where our focus will be as well. For more on the topic of psycholinguistics, go to www.sagepub.com/schwartz.[4]

Most psycholinguists think that human language is unique. Many other species, from honeybees to chimpanzees, have complex communication systems, but they do not meet the threshold of any definition of language. Why? Animal communication systems tend to be fairly stereotyped. That is, there is only so much one can communicate in them. They tend to be limited to warnings ("Watch out—predator coming"), information about food ("10 degrees to the left, 1 mile, big patch of flowers"), or sex ("Don't I have a pretty voice—come mate with me"). There is substantial debate as to where to draw the lines and how to consider the complex communication systems of some animals, but even the most complex nonhuman systems pale in comparison to human language. The hallmark of human language is that it is virtually unlimited in its power of what we can communicate. It allows us to speculate on natural beauty ("Doesn't the moon look pretty tonight?"). It allows us to discuss the deep issues of life and death ("What happens to my mind after my body dies?"). It allows us to contemplate the future ("What am I going to do after college?"). It allows us to build complex machinery ("a car's cooling system works by sending a coolant through the passages within the engine block"). These features of human communication seem to set apart language from other forms of animal communication. For a different view of language in nonhuman primates, go to www.sagepub.com/schwartz.[5]

Psycholinguists break down language into a number of features. First and foremost, language is an auditory phenomenon (with the exception of sign languages). Thus, it is important to understand the relation of sound to language. **Phonetics** refers to the details of speech sounds and how we make them. **Phonology** is the study of sounds and how they are used in a language. Thus, someone interested in phonology might study the physical processes of how human mouths produce the "rr" sound in Spanish. Phonologists are also interested how sounds are represented when not being spoken.

> **Phonetics**: the details of speech sounds and how we make them.
>
> **Phonology**: the study of sounds and how they are used in a language.

However, sounds are only as good as they function to communicate ideas. **Semantics** is the study of meaning. Important here is to note the difference in the use of the term *semantic* in what memory researchers call semantic memory and what psycholinguists call semantics. Semantic memory and semantics are two very different concepts. Words carry precise meanings in any particular language. Although a particular word may carry multiple meanings

> **Semantics**: the study of meaning of words in psycholinguistics.

(e.g., "bank"), its meanings are consistent over long periods of time. This is good as it means people can understand each other. Words do shift meaning over time. Try reading a passage from Shakespeare, for example. It is often hard to understand because the same phonological sound (word) may have meant something different to Shakespeare than it does in modern American English.

In all human languages, rules govern how people put words together to form sentences. **Syntax** refers to the word order within a language and other aspects of grammar. For example, in English, subjects come first and verbs follow (e.g., "I throw"). In other languages, such as formal Arabic, verbs come first and then are followed by the subject. Syntax is of great interest to psycholinguists, partially because many rules of syntax are implicitly, not explicitly, learned. For example, most of us could not explain why we refer to more than one leaf as "leaves," but when we go to a hockey game, we watch the Toronto Maple Leafs (see Pinker, 1994). Syntax is also seemingly the most difficult aspect of human language to acquire for nonhuman animals such as chimpanzees.

> **Syntax**: the word order within a language and other aspects of grammar.

Another important aspect of language is called pragmatics. **Pragmatics** refers to language use. This means why we choose the words we do in the particular context we are speaking in. It also refers to the social rules that govern conversation. For example, in one context, you may refer to a neighbor as "Sarah," but in another context, you may refer to her as "Dr. Jones." The first context might be a friendly conversation when you both come home from work. When you see her teaching a class at your university, you refer to her more formally. Humor, irony, and sarcasm also fall into the category of pragmatics. When the pretty girl you have been summoning up the courage to ask out tells you "Yeah right" while laughing and turning away, you know that she has not agreed to go on a date with you but rather has told you that you are not worth her time. Thus, the context here implies different meanings than the standard ones for those words.

> **Pragmatics**: language use, or the context of language.

Finally, **morphology** refers to how words are constructed within a particular language. Morphemes are the smallest unit of meaning in a language. In English, words can contain several morphemes. Thus, a word such as *cat* is a single morpheme. It has just one meaning with nothing attached. But we can then talk about *cats*, which is also one word, but it now has two morphemes, one that tells you the object and one that tells you how many (the letter "s" representing a "z" sound). However, if we want to further modify this concept, we have to add additional words, such as *furry, cute,* or *rabid.* Other languages allow more concepts to be bound together in a single word (e.g., Turkish, Swahili), whereas others only allow one morpheme at a time (Mandarin Chinese). Thus, a literal translation of *cats* into Chinese would be something like "cats many." Despite these differences among languages, words seem to be universal. Every human language seems to parse the world into distinct words. Thus, it also fair to define the word **word** as the smallest unit of grammar that represents a full meaning (see Box 5.3).

> **Morphology**: how words are constructed within a particular language.
>
> **Word**: in psycholinguistics, a word means the smallest unit of grammar that represents a full meaning.

Box 5.3	Linguistic Glossary

Lexicon: our mental "dictionary"; more properly, our word memory system.

Morphology: how words are constructed within a particular language

Phonetics: the details of speech sounds and how we make them

Phonology: the study of sounds and how they are used in a language.

Pragmatics: refers to language use.

Semantics: the study of meaning.

Syntax: refers to word order within a language and other aspects of grammar.

Word: smallest unit of grammar that represents a full meaning.

LEXICAL MEMORY

Episodic memory refers to our memory for individual events from our lives, whereas semantic memory refers to our knowledge of the world. Both of these memory systems are considered declarative memory because we can verbalize the contents of each kind of memory. That is, it is possible to talk about your past experiences and what you know about the world. Thus, both of these memory systems are based on our ability to manipulate and use words. However, to use words, we must have those words represented in memory and easy to access. Lexical memory refers to the memory system that stores words and other linguistic entities in memory. It is also called the **lexicon.**

> **Lexicon**: our mental dictionary.

In theory, lexical memory is a representational system that stores words. But words are not that simple. Words have multiple meanings and many associations in different contexts. They may be pronounced in different ways depending on the context (e.g., "you say tomato, and I say *tomahto*"). In bilinguals, it is important to address the relation in memory between translation equivalents (e.g., *tomato/tomate* or *book/libro* in English and Spanish).

What makes models of lexical memory even more complicated is the speed of access by which speakers must be able to access those words. First, consider how fast most of us speak. We usually can produce 3 to 4 words per second. In order to speak, we must be able to rapidly access our lexical memory. We must also be able to rapidly choose the right word from the potentially 100,000 words in our lexicon. Moreover, at high speed, we must choose the correct syntactical and morphological form of the word pretty much on the fly as we speak. Consider, for example, the sentences "There are media present at the conference" and "There is a medium to express those ideas." In this case, the speaker chooses to make the word *media* plural (as it is in Latin, from whence the word originates rather than the increasingly more common "the media"). In the second sentence, the speaker chooses the traditional singular of the medium/media in a much more rare usage of the term *medium,* which is different from the usual meaning of the word *medium* (that is, something halfway between the best and the worst). Thus, any model of lexical memory must take into account how syntax constrains and changes the particular word to be retrieved at any given point in time (Pinker, 1999). In addition, there must be representation space that stores our basic knowledge of the syntactical rules of our language. For more on Steven Pinker's research, go to www.sagepub.com/schwartz.[6]

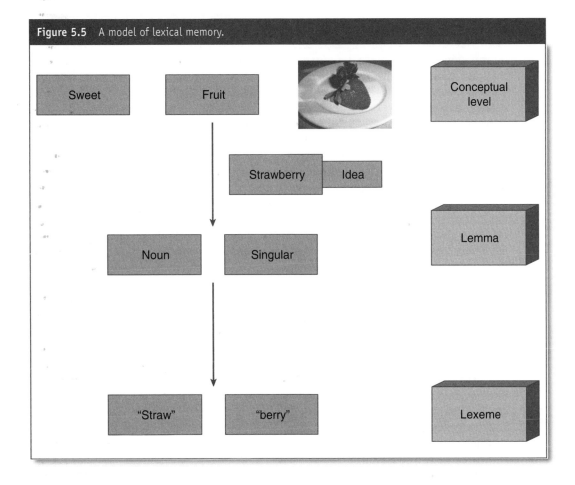

Figure 5.5 A model of lexical memory.

Most models of lexical memory focus on three levels of representation—one at the level of meaning, one at the level of syntax as well as semantic information, and a third level that contains the information about the phonology of the word (see Levelt, 1989; Schwartz, 2002) (see Figure 5.5). The assumption in these models is that there is a network of semantic associations carrying meanings and relating concepts to one another—in essence, a semantic memory system. In this conceptual system, the meaning *tiger* may be represented as an image of a big cat (associated with other concepts such as lion, leopard, etc.), an image of a baseball player from Detroit and its associations, and any other meanings of the word *tiger* (e.g., a sexually charged person). This conceptual-level representation informs a level of representation known as the lemma. A **lemma** is a hypothetical entity containing only semantic and syntactical information without any information concerning the phonology of the word. But, unlike the conceptual level, the lemma is lexical in nature, in that it contains information about language usage, such as the part of speech (noun, verb, etc.), its grammatical gender (in many languages other than English), and other grammatical features. The lemma informs the next highest level, known as the lexeme. The **lexeme** is the level of representation that stores the phonology of a word, that is, how the word sounds. During retrieval, when the lexeme is retrieved, the word can then be sent to the motor system (Caramazza & Miozzo, 1997; Levelt, 1989).

> **Lemma**: a hypothetical entity containing only semantic and syntactical information without any information concerning the phonology of the word.
>
> **Lexeme**: the level of representation that stores the phonology of a word, that is, how the word sounds.

Let's see how this hypothetical system works. Let's say a person asks you a question—"What is the word for the second to last item on any list?" The question starts with the lexical retrieval process from lexical memory. According to the model outlined above, first the person must access information at the semantic level—information such as "toward the end," "part of a list," "fancy word for showing off your vocabulary," and so on. This initial response results in the retrieval of the lemma, which contains both semantic and syntactical information. Here the following syntactical information is added: noun or adjective, derived from Latin, as well as the semantic information from the previous level. However, the lemma does not contain any phonological information about how we say the word.

Once the lemma representation has been retrieved, the next stage begins, and that is the retrieval of the lexeme representation. In retrieving at the lexeme level, the person retrieves the phonological information for the word *penultimate*. The lexeme is still an abstract representation, but it is a representation of sound. The phonological entry *penultimate* is then sent to the motor system so that the person can articulate the answer. Thus, according to this view, every time we retrieve a word (even in normal speech), it passes through these three stages of representation: semantics, lemma, and lexeme. See Levelt (1989) for a detailed description of this theory. Most researchers in psycholinguistics agree on this general model, although, of course, they argue over the specifics (see Harley, 2008).

Much of the research that supports this model comes from errors in ordinary speech. M. Garrett (1992) researched two kinds of **speech errors.** The first are called word exchange errors. Word exchange errors occur when we substitute a word with a similar

> **Speech errors**: errors in ordinary speech.

meaning for another word, regardless of how the words sound. For example, if the word one was trying to retrieve was *sandals,* he or she might accidentally say *heels* instead. People often exchange the names of family members. You know your older sister's name but accidentally call her by your younger sister's name instead. These are errors that occur at the level of the lemma. These errors seldom cross syntactical categories. That is, if the word you want to say is a noun, the substitution will also be a noun. Thus, the correct meaning has been retrieved as well as the correct syntactical information (noun, proper noun, plural or singular, for example), but the wrong lexeme is then activated.

Completely different are errors called sound substitutions (M. Garrett, 1992; Martin & Dell, 2007). Sound substitutions occur when a similar but incorrect phonological structure is retrieved, but the word retrieved has no obvious semantic or syntactical connection to the desired word. For example, if the word you are seeking is *tiger,* you might accidentally retrieve *tirade.* These substitutions appear to happen at the level of the lexeme. The errors involve mistakes in sound but not in meaning and therefore are thought to occur at the last level of retrieval in which sound is retrieved through the lexeme. It is possible to get an error that is both semantic and phonological. In this case, it is difficult to tell if the error is the result of a mistake at the level of the lemma or the lexeme.

Bilingual Lexicon

One of the hotly debated issues in this area is whether bilingual or multilingual people have one lexical memory system for all the languages that they speak or whether each language has its own lexical memory system within the cognitive architecture of that individual. One view is called the **single-store view of bilingual representation.** This view argues that there is a common semantic level of representation—that is, meaning is shared. The shared semantic representational system then connects to lemma-level representations for each language. The alternate view is the **dual-store view (or separate store) of bilingual representation,** which postulates that meaning is represented separately for each language. Much of the recent research on the topic supports the single-store view, that is, that the semantic level is shared across languages (Gianico & Altarriba, 2008; J. F. Kroll, Bobb, Misra, & Guo, 2008). For

> **Single-store view of bilingual representation**: there is a common semantic level of representation—that is, meaning is shared in bilinguals. The shared semantic representational system then connects to lemma-level representations for each language.
>
> **Dual-store view (or separate store) of bilingual representation**: the view that meaning is represented separately for each language in the lexical memory of a bilingual.

more information on this topic, go to www.sagepub.com/schwartz.[7]

Think of a person you know (or yourself) who is bilingual. This person has two phonological forms that may represent any particular concept, one in one language and one in the other. Thus, an English-Spanish bilingual will know both the word *clock* and the Spanish word *reloj.* Obviously, these words will have different phonological representations given that there is no overlap in sound. However, is the semantic representation stored jointly, or is there a separate representation for the meaning in each language? The single-store view states that each concept is stored in a single system and is linked to the phonology in each language. The dual-store view states that we have two separate semantic stores, one for each language (Gianico & Altarriba, 2008).

The view that semantic representations are shared across a multilingual's languages comes from **cross-language semantic priming.** Cross-language semantic priming is similar to semantic priming except that the prime and the target word are in different languages. Consider a lexical decision task in which a participant has to determine if a string of letters is a word. The prime word is presented in Spanish (e.g., *libro,* meaning "book"). Shortly thereafter, the target word appears in English (e.g., *magazine*). The single-store view of lexical memory predicts that *libro* should prime *magazine*. However, the dual-store view argues that meaning is represented separately for both languages. Therefore, the Spanish word should not prime the English word. Studies with cross-language semantic priming typically show that cross-language priming occurs, supporting the single-store view.

> **Cross-language semantic priming**: the effect of priming a word in one language has on a related word in another language in bilinguals or multilinguals.

Meaning is shared, but representation of the lemma and lexeme is clearly separate in a bilingual's representational space. Indeed, when a bilingual is functioning in one language, mechanisms exist to suppress the retrieval of linguistic information from the other language. Rodriguez-Fornells, Rotte, Heinze, Nosselt, and Munte (2002) conducted a study with Spanish-Catalan bilinguals (Catalan is a language spoken in northern parts of Spain, including Barcelona). The participants were asked to attend to words in one language but ignore words in the other language while their brains were being monitored by fMRI. Thus, if they were attending to Spanish words, they were to avoid the Catalan words. If they were attending to Catalan words, they were to avoid the Spanish words. They found that nonwords in the attended language and real words in the nonattended language activated similar areas of the brain. Moreover, these areas of the brain were different from those areas of the brain that were activated by real words in the attended language. This suggests that early in processing, discrimination among languages leads to the suppression of the lemma and lexeme representations of the language not being used.

For many bilinguals, the dual-store view is more naturally intuitive. Many translation equivalents prompt the retrieval of slightly different prototypes or exemplars, depending on which language you are using. To many English-Spanish bilinguals, for example, the word *dog* evokes a different image than does the Spanish word *perro*. However, as we have seen, categories are difficult to describe cognitively, and much of the evidence now points to a single-store view.

HOW ARE LANGUAGES LEARNED BY YOUNG CHILDREN?

None of us come into the world knowing any language. During the first years of our life, we are immersed in a sea of words. Somehow during the first years of life, we begin to sort out meaning from among the stream of sounds we hear coming from our caregivers' mouths. Indeed, by the end of the first year of a baby's life, he or she should be able to recognize the meaning of many words. By 2 years of age, children are learning the syntactical constraints on their native languages. Because babies are born without language but acquire it rapidly during childhood, psycholinguists have argued that there are special mechanisms available to a child to allow him or her to encode the rules of language at that rapid pace (Pinker, 1994). The famous linguist, Noam Chomsky, speculated that such encoding was accomplished by a cognitive module, known as a **language acquisition device (LAD)**. LADs allow young children to extract meaning and start learning words from stimuli that are often ambiguous (Chomsky, 1986). Imagine a 2-year-old child overhearing his mother saying that

> **Language acquisition device (LAD)**: a hypothetical model that allows young children to acquire language quickly and accurately.

"life is a bowl of cherries." Not understanding metaphors yet, this might be very confusing to a child. Even simple utterances like "leave it on the table" are potentially confusing. Which table? And what is "it?"

Even prior to the age of 1, infants are sensitive to distributional information in language. **Distributional information** refers to the patterns of speech that co-occur, that is, an aspect of language that always accompanies each other. For example, a noun always follows the word *the*. Another example is that questions are generally asked with a rising intonation in English (and many other languages). The sound "muh" is frequently followed by the sound "er." Thus, even though most adults include a pause between the syllables in the word *mother*, infants can still detect the regular occurrence of these

> **Distributional information**: refers to the patterns of speech that co-occur, that is, an aspect of language that always accompanies one another.

two sounds together (Mattys & Jusczyk, 2001).

Another feature that appears to be important in the learning of words in infants is the seemingly innate application of the **whole-object assumption**. The whole-object assumption refers to the fact that young infants appear to innately know that words usually refer to an entire object, rather than parts of it or parts of the object and adjacent objects. For example, the word *cat* refers to the entire pet, not just its back legs and tail. Similarly, the word *dad* refers to the entire person, not just his stubbly face. We have few words in any language that refer to things like, "the desk drawer that is sticking out a bit and

> **Whole-object assumption**: refers to the fact that young infants appear to innately know that words usually refer to an entire object, rather than parts of it or parts of the object and adjacent objects.

the contents of that drawer." One could imagine how such a word would be useful, such as when we direct someone to retrieve a calculator for us, but languages seldom "create" words that specific. To adult speakers of a language, this is obvious, but it is not clear a priori that language must be arranged this way. However, young children seldom make mistakes; they seem to know that words refer to whole objects (Waxman & Markow, 1995).

Taxonomic constraint: states that words refer to categories, which share meaning.

Similarly, infants seem to also operate under the taxonomic constraint. The **taxonomic constraint** states that words refer to categories, which share meaning. Thus, a word like *cat* will refer to objects that look alike. A young child may mistakenly call a small dog a "cat" but will seldom call his or her father a "cat." In theory, it is possible to have words that refer to such disjointed categories, but they don't ordinarily exist in languages, and infants appear to be sensitive to this feature (Waxman & Booth, 2001).

Fast mapping: the rules that allow a child to rapidly learn the meaning of words in his or her language.

Together, these principles can be called fast mapping. **Fast mapping** refers to the rules that allow a child to rapidly learn the meaning of words in his or her language. Fast mapping is an encoding mechanism, which appears to be specific to young children learning language. Fast mapping may be part of the cognitive system that allows young children to rapidly and effortlessly learn their native language or languages such that they are fluent speakers in just a few years (and long before they can tie their shoes).

SECOND-LANGUAGE LEARNING IN ADULTHOOD

Second-language acquisition occurs when a person has already mastered his or her native language and then begins learning a second language. Learning a new language as an adult is a very different process than learning one's first language as a child. Instead of the language coming effortlessly through innate language learning mechanisms, mastering a language as an adult is, for most people, the most daunting learning task that they will ever face. Thousands upon thousands of vocabulary words must be learned. Verb endings for different tenses must be mastered.

Second-language acquisition: occurs when a person has already mastered his or her native language and then begins learning a second language.

Thousands of seemingly bizarre syntactic rules must be memorized. Idiomatic usage must be learned thoroughly if the speaker wants ever to be able to converse fluently with native speakers of the language. These idiomatic rules may differ greatly from the formal instruction. And then, as in many aspects of learning, learning a new language epitomizes the cardinal rule of learning a skill: practice, practice, and more practice. Many of us never have the patience to master a second or third language as an adult.

Before we consider the science of second-language learning, let's dispel a standard myth on the topic of learning new languages. Those of us fortunate to be native English speakers still benefit from learning additional languages. Although English has become the international second language, there are billions of people all over the world who cannot speak English. Learning additional languages benefits native English speakers. It is possible to learn a second or third language and be completely fluent as an adult. It may be difficult but is possible with sufficient effort. So your author says: no excuses. Quit smoking and learn a new language and you will be healthier and wiser as a consequence!

One issue that frequently arises with respect to learning new languages is the issue of "having an accent." It is indeed true that often the most difficult part of learning a new language as an adult is learning to speak without an accent that tips off your native language. Americans, for example, learning Spanish as adults tend to elongate their vowels sounds, as we do in English, and mispronounce words with the "rr" sound in them. However, with specific vocal training, it is possible to learn to speak these sounds properly. Think about classically trained actors who can sound like they are from any country, using any accent (e.g., Denzel Washington and Meryl Streep). Using similar training, it is possible to learn to speak with the accent of a native speaker.

Given both the importance and difficulty of learning a second language as an adult, a myriad of language-learning methods have been developed. Many of these can be purchased for a small sum, for use in your CD player, DVD player, iPod, and so on. Each of these commercial products claims to be based on the latest scientific methods, which have "proven" its superiority (the word *proven* is a tip-off; a real scientist would never use that word). Luckily, there are some data out there that bear on this issue.

Harley (2008) describes the main methods that are used in second-language acquisition. In the **traditional method,** words are translated from the speaker's native language into the new language. Grammar is taught in the native language, and reading and writing are emphasized. In the **submersion method,** the language learner is surrounded by native speakers of the to-be-learned language, usually in a foreign country. People are instructed not to use the learner's native language. In the **immersion method,** all instruction is in the to-be-learned language, but outside of the classroom, the student returns to his or her native language. In the **audiolingual method,** speaking and listening skills are taught rather than traditional vocabulary and grammar.

The research comparing these methods is complex. The preferred method depends on a person's age, motivation, and a host of individual differences, including working memory ability. Nonetheless, some studies suggest that the immersion method produces the best second-language learning (Krashen, 1982; see Harley, 2008). Immersion provides the individual with constant practice in speaking and comprehension in the new language but does not overtax the person's ability to function in the new language and helps him or her develop confidence in the new language.

Traditional method: words are translated from the speaker's native language into the new language. Grammar is taught in the native language, and reading and writing are emphasized.

Submersion method: the language learner is surrounded by native speakers of the to-be-learned language, usually in a foreign country. People are instructed not to use the learner's native language.

Immersion method: a method of learning a second language. All instruction is in the to-be-learned language, but outside of the classroom, the student returns to his or her native language.

Audiolingual method: a method of learning a second language. Speaking and listening skills are taught rather than traditional vocabulary and grammar.

Mnemonic Improvement Tip 5.1

According to research, the best way to acquire a second language is to engage in the "immersion technique." Immersion means that all instruction, including subjects not related to the language, will be in the new language. This provides a wide range of topics for which the person can learn vocabulary and strengthens the person's ability to listen and talk in that language.

In the next chapter, the topic of imagery will be introduced. Some researchers have found that imagery techniques can be useful for acquiring vocabulary in a new language. Imagery techniques can be used to focus on particular vocabulary words within any of the major methods of second-language acquisition. This topic will be considered in more detail in the next chapter.

Learning a new language can be one of the most valuable skills you can learn. Using your time wisely while acquiring a new language is therefore important. Immersion may not be possible for all people, as other demands may press on their time. However, the research does show it consistently produces the best long-term language performance.

SUMMARY

Language is a fundamental tool in human cognition. We use language for many cognitive processes in addition to communication. Language requires a large and easily accessible memory system, which has been called lexical memory. Most theorists think of lexical memory as a multilayer system in which semantics (meaning) is stored separately from phonology (sound), but the two are connected. Speech errors reflect this distinction. In bilinguals, the semantic system appears to be shared in the representational system, even though the phonological representations are not. Some theorists also argue that we have innate language-learning devices when we are very young children. These learning mechanisms allow us to rapidly acquire our native language or languages. Later, when learning a language as an adult, we must work very hard at learning new languages, as well as learning words and grammatical rules by slower learning processes. Immersing oneself in a language leads to the most efficient learning.

KEY TERMS

Lexical memory (lexicon)	Semantic priming	Concepts
Associative model	Lexical decision task	Categories
Spreading activation	Sentence verification tasks	Levels of categorization

Family resemblance

Prototype theory

Exemplar theory

Feature comparison theory

Defining features

Characteristic features

Schemas

Scripts

Psycholinguistics

Phonetics

Phonology

Semantics

Syntax

Pragmatics

Morphology

Word

Lexicon

Lemmas

Lexemes

Speech errors

Single-store view of bilingual representation

Dual-store view (or separate store) of bilingual representation

Cross-language semantic priming

Language acquisition device (LAD)

Distributional information

Whole-object assumption

Taxonomic constraint

Fast mapping

Second-language acquisition

Traditional method

Submersion method

Immersion method

Audiolingual method

REVIEW QUESTIONS

1. What is semantic memory? How does it differ from episodic memory and lexical memory?

2. What is meant by the term *spreading activation?* How do experiments on semantic priming support the idea of spreading activation?

3. What is meant by term *levels of categorization?* What empirical evidence suggests that human memory is organized according to these levels?

4. What is meant by the term *family resemblance for categories?* How does it relate to the idea that categories have fuzzy boundaries?

5. What are the differences between prototype theory, exemplar theory, and feature comparison theory?

6. What were the results of Brewer and Treyan's classic experiment on students' memory for a waiting room? What do these results tell us about schemas?

7. What is the difference between a lemma and lexeme? How do speech errors support this conceptual difference?

8. What is the difference between the single-store and dual-store view of a bilingual's lexical memory? Which view do the data on cross-language priming support?

9. How is the concept of whole-object assumptions related to the concept of fast mapping?

10. What is the immersion method of second-language learning?

ONLINE RESOURCES

1. For more on the life of George Berkeley, go to http://www.iep.utm.edu/b/berkeley.htm.

2. The following website allows you to participate in an online lexical decision task experiment: http://www.essex.ac.uk/psychology/experiments/lexical.html.

3. For more information on Frederic Bartlett, go to http://www.ppsis.cam.ac.uk/bartlett.

4. For more on the topic of psycholinguistics, go to http://www.psycholinguisticsarena.com.

5. For a different view of language in nonhuman primates, go to the following website: http://www.IowaGreatApes.org.

6. For more on Steven Pinker's research, go to his website at http://pinker.wjh.harvard.edu/about/index.html.

7. For more information on this bilingual representation, go to http://www.albany.edu/psychology/altarriba.html.

Go to www.sagepub.com/schwartz for additional exercises and study resources. Select **Chapter 5, Semantic Memory** and Lexical Memory for chapter-specific resources.

CHAPTER 6

Visual Memory

Most of the first five chapters have concerned memory for words. However, we remember more than just words. We remember images, sounds, smells, and emotions, to name a few. This chapter will focus on visual memory, our ability to learn and retrieve visual images. Visual memory has many similarities to memory for words and narrative meaning but also significant differences, which will be explored here. We will also discuss how we represent or store images in memory—this has been a major issue in the research literature. First, we will explore the phenomenology (i.e., the experience) of visual memory.

Consider the following exercise. Retrieve from memory an image of the face of President Obama without consulting a photograph (also see Figure 6.1). Once you have the president's face accessible in your mind's "eye," answer the following questions.

1. Does he have any gray hair?

2. Does he have any freckles?

3. Is he wearing a blue tie?

Chances are that you have never intentionally encoded any of these features of President Obama. Yet, you are likely to see him wearing a tie, as he usually dresses formally. Based on your mental image, you can make a decision about the first two questions, even though these may not have been aspects of his appearance that you have ever paid attention to. Now, most adults have spent a fair bit of time watching him on television (or perhaps in person) giving speeches, and thus the image of his face is well known to most Americans. So most of us are likely to have accurate visual images of the president. But there are other iconic images that we may think we know but really do not. A classic (in two ways) example of this is to try to answer the question, "How many columns does the Parthenon in Athens, Greece, have?" Most of us can form a strong visual image of the famous ancient building, still standing on a hillside in Athens. However, actually counting the columns in our mind's eye view is much more difficult than counting the columns from a photograph or from the real thing (see Figure 6.2). If our images are really pictures, this should not be the case. Thus, visual imagery differs from visual perception in important ways. One of the sections in this chapter will address differences between visual perception and visual imagery.

Figure 6.1   Can you fill in the presidents' appearance with your mind's eye?

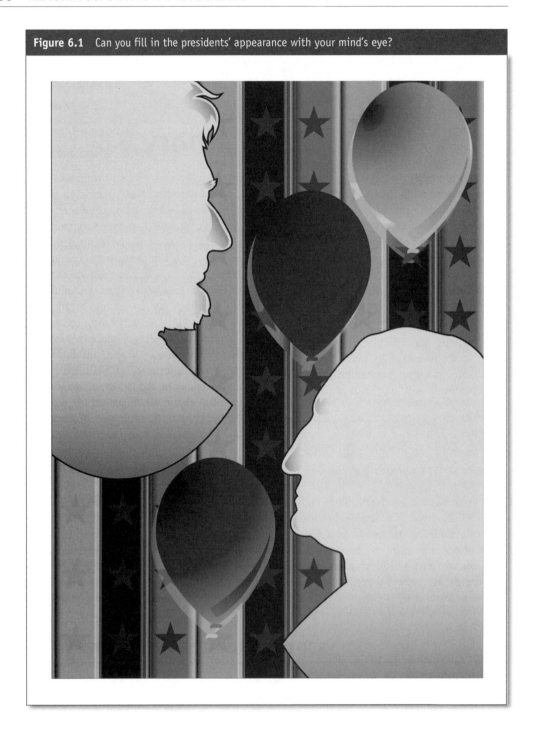

Figure 6.2   The Parthenon—did you correctly count the number of columns in your mind's eye?

VISUAL MEMORY: RECOGNITION AND RECALL

Our eyes are open continuously during our waking hours. We visually perceive the world about 16 hours a day, day in and day out. We are therefore bombarded with a tremendous amount of visual stimulation, not all of which we can attend to at any one time. How much of what you see do you actually remember?

Unlike word memory, in which recall can be measured by asking the participant to speak a word or write a word, visual memory presents some more difficult methodological issues. First, how do you get someone to report a visual image? Do you have him or her describe the image verbally or draw it, or is some kind of recognition test preferable? Consider the example of retrieving what President Obama looks like. You may feel as if you can recall a photograph of the president, but how do we demonstrate that you actually are recalling what he looks like? Some of us might be able to draw him, but many of us never got beyond stick figures. Now consider describing him using words. What words would you use to describe his skin color, for example? Black? Tan? Brown? Do any of these words really capture President Obama's appearance? How would you describe the shape of his head? Thin? Does that word really convey the image you have in your head? Indeed, our verbal descriptions of our images are, for most of us, as poor as our drawing and conveying the content of our actual visual images. In fact, even experienced talented sketch artists only draw rough approximations based on a witness's description. Therefore, both drawing and giving verbal descriptions are problematic because we "feel" as if neither format conveys the information that we think is in our visual memory.

As a consequence, recognition is usually the measure that researchers use when examining long-term visual memory. In particular, old-new recognition tests are used. A picture is presented and the participant is asked whether he or she has seen this particular picture before. If new pictures are interspersed with old pictures, this method can tell us something about visual memory. When recognition measures are used, it is straightforward to demonstrate the power of visual memory. Standing (1973), for example, presented participants with 10,000 pictures over a 5-day period. At the end of the presentation period, a recognition test ensued. During the test, Standing presented some of the original pictures mixed in with pictures that had not been presented. Thus, on half of the trials, the correct answer was "old," whereas on the other half of trials, the correct answer was "new." Participants correctly identified about two-thirds of the pictures, which they had only seen once before. There is a large literature confirming how good we are at remembering faces (Meissner, Sporer, & Susa 2008). In fact, even when people are doing a concurrent task (that is, another cognitive task in addition to looking at pictures), they are still able to recognize pictures that they saw earlier (Wolfe, Horowitz, & Michod, 2007).

The work on recognition memory suggests that people's intuitions are correct. We do have strong visual memories and visual images. It is just that verbal descriptions and drawings do not allow us to express the details in our visual images. Fine recognition distinctions between old and new pictures, however, demonstrate that we are attending to the details in visual images.

One question arises: How does our mind-brain system store visual images? One of the oldest debates in visual imagery is exactly how, at both cognitive and neural levels, we code the images we store and remember. The next section on representation of visual images is one of the more difficult ones in the text. Keep in mind that the goal of the research is to infer—from people's performance—what the exact nature of the representational code is. This representational code is not the visual image itself that we call up in visual working memory. Rather, the code is the manner in which that image is stored when not in use, that is, when it is being stored for future use. With that in mind, we will jump into this topic.

REPRESENTATION AND IMAGERY

Representation means the storage of information in long-term memory when that information is not in use. When we need to retrieve information, we activate it from this long-term representational system. In the case of visual imagery, activating that information means creating a visual image. Once the image is activated, we can inspect it and make decisions about it. For example, at one point in your life, you may have visited your local fire department's station. You may not

Representation: the storage of information in memory when that information is not in use.

have thought of this event in a long time, but the chances are you have some visual memories of the living quarters for the firefighters on duty and perhaps the bay where they keep the big trucks. Representation means the format in which we maintain these images from when we actually perceived them until the time we remember them, forming a mental image.

The problem of studying representation is that scientists cannot directly examine mental images. We cannot pull them out of a person's head and inspect them. They exist only in mental space. Therefore, cognitive psychologists must devise experiments that infer what mental representations are like based on visible behaviors or reports of the person doing the imaging. From the behavior—that is, the recognition judgments that people make about their images—we must infer back to the mode of representation. This presented some serious challenges to early cognitive psychologists.

This was the situation until recently. Neuroimaging allows us to examine what the brain is doing when people are forming visual images. This does not allow us to actually see what the person is remembering, but it does tell us where in the brain that behavior emanates from. Because we know the function of many areas of the brain, we can use neuroimaging to make inferences about cognitive representation as well.

There are two main classes of theories as to how we represent visual information in memory. The first is called **analog representation,** and the second is called **propositional representation.** Analog representation means we store visual images in a manner a lot like pictures. When we retrieve a representation of President Obama, we retrieve the neural equivalent of a photograph. Propositional representation means that we store visual images in terms of a language-like code. When we retrieve an image of the president, what we get is equivalent to a list of features—thin face; short, curly black hair; big ears; and alert eyes.

> **Analog representation**: a theory that argues that we store visual images in a manner similar to actual pictures.
>
> **Propositional representation**: we store visual images in terms of a language-like code.

Our imagery system then re-creates an image in visual working memory (i.e., the visuospatial sketchpad).

Note that the propositional view does not deny that our images appear to us as pictures. We feel like we see a picture. However, the propositional view states that we do not store images in a pictorial format. Rather, we construct a visual image at the time of retrieval. In contrast, the analog representation view argues that the code by which we store images is a sensory one. When we retrieve, we merely have to call up the already stored visual image.

When researchers first began debating this issue, most of them thought that the propositional view would turn out to be correct. They argued that visual memory, if analog, would take up huge amounts of memory within the brain. Just a few pictures, they argued, stored in analog fashion would eat up the memory capacity of the brain itself. Anyone with a large number of high-resolution photographs stored on their disk drive is familiar with this problem. Namely, an average .jpg file takes up a lot more memory space on your hard drive than your average .txt file. Storing information in a descriptive text-like representation requires much less memory on your computer and presumably would require much less memory in your brain. However, just as modern personal computers are more than able to handle many digital pictures, even entire DVDs, it turns out that the brain too has a lot more capacity for storing pictures than had been originally thought. The propositional view, however, does allow more information to be stored in a less-demanding format, which still appeals to some theorists today (see Pylyshyn, 2003).

Nowadays, most researchers today are convinced by the vast amount of data that support the analog view. Yes, it may be memory intensive, but the brain appears to be able to handle the load. Studies using behavioral and neuroscientific methodologies all support the analog view. One of the earliest studies to support the analog view is also one of the most famous studies ever in psychology. It is **Shepard and Metzler's (1971) mental rotation experiment.**

> **Shepard and Metzler's (1971) mental rotation experiment**: an early experiment on visual imagery that showed that representation is analog.

Shepard and Metzler's (1971) Mental Rotation Experiment

Shepard and Metzler (1971) set out to show that, at least in some circumstances, **imagery** was best explained by the analog view. To demonstrate this, they wanted to show that mental images behave like real pictures, at least in some ways. That is, they thought that mental images ought to respond to experimental manipulations in the same or similar way that actually perceiving those objects would. If inspecting a visual image is like inspecting a real picture, then we might be able to answer at least some novel questions about it, if not difficult counting questions. If, however, inspecting images is not like inspecting a real picture, then, as was the view in 1970, the propositional view is the default position. Thus, the goal of the Shepard and Metzler was to determine if we can use mental images in this causal manner. To test this notion, participants were asked to mentally rotate objects, which were shown to them in pictures (see Figure 6.3).

> **Imagery**: the experience of retrieving a memory that is mostly visual or experienced primarily as a sensory experience. Imagery can also refer to the representation of those memories.

The task was relatively simple—decide if two figures were geometrically the same or different. All the participants had to do was decide yes or no as quickly as possible. Shepard and Metzler varied the orientation of one picture relative to the other. That is, in some cases, they were perfectly aligned, but in other sets, they were as much as 180 degrees off from each other. So consider what the participant's task was: For each trial, the participant saw a pair of objects displayed in pictorial format. They were then asked to determine if the two objects were identical or different. Half of the pictures were identical, whereas half were not. But when pictures were identical, one of the objects was rotated to be in a different orientation than its pair.

In order for participants to determine if the two figures were identical, they needed to mentally rotate one of the figures to see if it matched its pair. If, in each participant's mind's eye,

Figure 6.3 Objects to be mentally rotated.

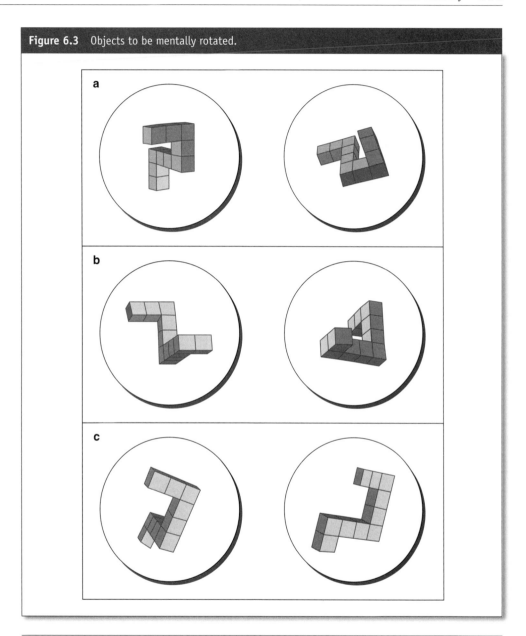

SOURCE: Shepard and Metzler (1971).

the figures matched up, he or she was expected to say "same." If they did not, he or she was expected to say "different." Most people who do this task describe imagining one of the figures and "moving" it in their mind's eye to see if, when rotated, it fits perfectly onto the other figure.

If it does, then you have a match. If not, you say no. If you really had cutout figures, it would take more time to rotate the figure a greater amount than a smaller amount. The question was—if when mentally rotating—would it take longer to rotate a figure more?

Shepard and Metzler (1971) varied the extent to which the two identical figures were rotated. In some cases, one was rotated just 15 degrees to the left or right of its pair. In other cases, however, one figure was rotated as much as 180 degrees to the left or right of its pair. This was true for both pairs that were identical and pairs that were different. This was the main independent variable: the extent to which the two figures were rotated relative to each other. The goal was to see how this would affect the participants' response time when they indicated whether the figures were identical.

Shepard and Metzler (1971) reasoned that if images were stored in an analog manner, then it would take a finite amount of time for the participant to rotate one figure to match the other. If the one figure was rotated only a small amount to the left or right, it should take less time to mentally rotate it than if it had been rotated closer to 180 degrees. This is analogous to how people would do this task if they were given small toy-size objects and asked if the objects were the same shape or different. We would rotate one until it matched the other. If it did, we would say they were identical. If we could not rotate them until they matched, we would say different. Shepard and Metzler's goal was to see if our imagery systems function this way.

Therefore, Shepard and Metzler (1971) measured the amount of time it took participants to come to a decision of same versus different as a function of the degrees of difference between the two figures in a pair (see Figure 6.4). They found that the more the two figures were rotated away from each other, the more time it took participants to make their

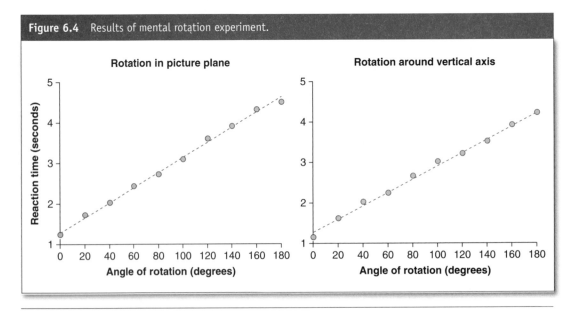

Figure 6.4   Results of mental rotation experiment.

SOURCE: Shepard and Metzler (1971).

decisions. In fact, there was a clear linear relation (straight line) between the degrees of difference between the two figures in a pair and how long the decision took, as can be seen in Figure 6.4. It took—on average—just about two seconds to determine that the images were the same or different when the two figures were rotated 20 degrees off each other but nearly 5 seconds when the figures were 160 degrees different. The Shepard and Metzler data support the analog view; people's imagery systems appeared to be actually manipulating images or pictures and not abstract code-like representations.

Students sometimes have difficulties with the Shepard and Metzler (1971) experiment. Here are some points to keep in mind both to understand the experiment and see why it is so important. First, the participants only see two images per trial. They do not see the figures actually move. They must rotate them mentally. That is, to align them, they must use visual imagery. Since it takes more time to mentally rotate a greater degree than a smaller degree, there must be something similar between mental rotation and actual physical rotation. Because of this, we conclude that the visual images are being used in an analog vision-like representation to do this.

While this may not seem surprising to you, it disrupted the applecart in 1971. Most cognitive psychologist at the time would have not predicted the pattern of results shown in Figure 6.4 ahead of time. For an illustration of this experiment and to participate yourself, go to www.sagepub.com/schwartz.[1]

However, Shepard and Metzler (1971) were not the first to demonstrate the nature of imagery as being a vision-like analog system. In Chapter 3, we described an experiment on the visuospatial sketchpad conducted by Brooks (1968). In the experiment, participants retrieved a mental letter—that is, they imagined a letter, such as *T* in their mind's eye, and then were asked to make decisions about the angles in that letter. That is, what is the nature of the angles that are made when the top of the *t* crosses the vertical line that forms the stem of the *t*? Brooks found that responding on the task using pointing was more difficult than speaking. This is because the visual aspects of pointing interfered with the vision-like processes going on during imagery. This also supports the analog view. If imagery were propositional, it would not require the overlap between real visual tasks and imagery tasks.

Many other researchers subsequently became intrigued by the notion that they could study the nature of imagery. One such prominent researcher was Stephen Kosslyn, who invented many creative ways of studying imagery. Like Shepard, he was restricted to measuring behavior, but also like Shepard, he came up with ingenious ways of inferring how the imagery representation system worked from seemingly ordinary behaviors. In Kosslyn's studies, people are asked to make simple judgments on images but to make them as fast as possible. Thus, in one study, participants were asked to make judgments of details in the picture based on visual image. In Kosslyn's studies, in keeping with the analog view, it took participants less time to verify that a rabbit has soft fur when they imagined the rabbit next to a fly than when they imagined the rabbit next to an elephant. Indeed, the image of the rabbit is relatively bigger when it is the larger animal, and this allows us to make faster response times (Kosslyn, 1975). (See Figure 6.5.) Kosslyn argued that this occurs because the image of the rabbit is likely to be bigger when we contrast it to something smaller, like a fly, than when we contrast it to something bigger, like an

Figure 6.5   Picture of big rabbit/small rabbit.

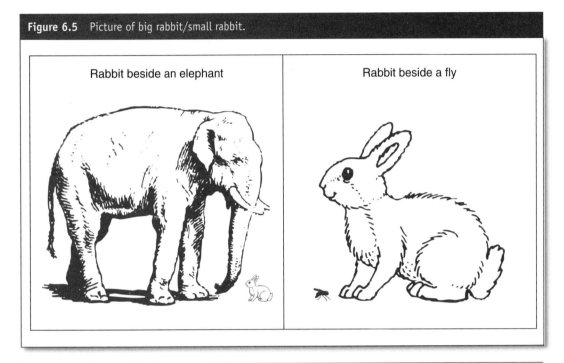

| Rabbit beside an elephant | Rabbit beside a fly |

SOURCE: Kosslyn (1975).

elephant. Therefore, details such as the quality of the fur will be more salient in the bigger image than in the smaller one.

In another now-classic study, Kosslyn, Ball, and Reiser (1978) showed participants a map of an imaginary island (see Figure 6.6). The participants were given ample time to memorize the features of the map. When the participants were satisfied that they had memorized the map, the map was removed. They were then asked to imagine the map and make several decisions based on their mental map. They were asked to imagine a dot moving around the island from various locations to various locations. Kosslyn et al. found that response time from getting the imaginary dot from place A to place B was longer if the two locations were further away on the map, and the response times were faster if the two locations were closer together. Thus, like the Shepard and Metzler (1971) experiment, mental imagery follows the same principles as the real world does—longer distances take longer amounts of time to travel. This suggests that the mental image people made of the island had visual (and spatial) properties, much as a real picture does.

Theorists who argue for the propositional view have criticized much of the data presented here (Pylyshyn, 2003). They argue that we do not need analog visual imagery and that mental propositions or sentences can account for much of the data. For example, when you are asked about the map of the island, you may experience a visual image of the map, but according to the propositional view, that experience is not causal. Rather, that image is a by-product of the proposition that stores the information.

Figure 6.6   Briefly look at this map. Then look away and see if you can make an image.

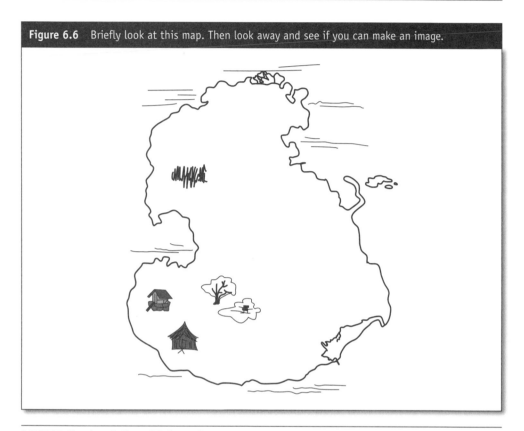

SOURCE: Kosslyn, Ball, and Reiser (1978).

Neuroimaging and the Analog View

The advent of neuroimaging opened up an entire new window into the study of imaging. With neuroimaging, we can look at the regions of the brain directly while people are engaged in imagery tasks. That is, we can look directly at the neural correlates of imagery without having to measure a behavior. With the aid of neuroimaging, a number of researchers have been able to determine the regions of the brain involved in mental imagery. These neuroimaging studies support the view that imagery is analog (Kosslyn, 2005). Kosslyn and his colleagues have found that areas of the visual cortex are excited while people are engaged in visual imagery tasks. In many cases, this activation extends to the primary visual cortex.

The primary areas of vision are located in the back of the brain in the occipital lobe. The **primary visual cortex** (also known as striate cortex, V1 or Area 17) is the first area in the cerebral cortex that receives input from the retina of the eye. Countless studies have shown it to be involved in basic visual processing. Indeed, damage to the primary visual cortex results in blindness (see Figure 6.7). Surrounding V1 are other

Primary visual cortex: the first area in the occipital cortex that processes visual images.

Figure 6.7 The occipital lobe is in the back of the brain.

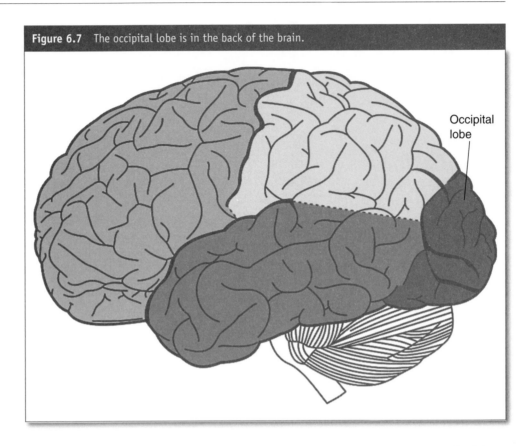

Occipital lobe

areas in the occipital lobe that process visual information (named V2, V3, etc.). All of these areas become activated when people engage in visual imagery (Kosslyn, Ganis, & Thompson, 2006). In fact, the more similar the imagery task is to an actual visual task, the more activation is seen in visual areas of the brain. Finally, those individuals who do better in imagery tasks also show more activity in the primary visual cortex than those who are less good at imagery tasks (Kosslyn, 2005). Thus, it clear that imagery is housed in many of the same areas of the brain that house visual perception.

Research on patients with brain damage also finds that patients with damage to the occipital lobe have deficits in imagery as well as deficits in visual perception (Farah, 1988). Although some patients may have deficits in one area without deficits in the other, most patients have parallel problems with both vision and imagery. That is, if a patient has a deficit in visual imagery, he or she is likely also to have deficits in visual perception. The same is true of the converse. Some but not all patients with visual perception deficits also have deficits in visual imagery. Let's consider one such example.

In one striking demonstration of this, Bisiach and Luzzatti (1978) studied a patient with **hemifield neglect.** Hemifield neglect describes a condition in which patients ignore one half of the visual world. When forced to, they will report that they see what is in that half of the visual world but simply pay it no heed. For example, male hemifield patients will not shave half of their face because they ignore it in the mirror. Hemifield neglect is

> **Hemifield neglect:** a condition in which patients ignore one half of the visual world. It occurs because of damage to the right parietal lobe.

caused by damage to the parietal lobe, usually on the right side of the brain. Luckily, the severe effects of hemifield neglect usually wear off relatively quickly after the brain damage, leaving the patient with a mild tendency to ignore information in that half of the visual world. For more on hemifield neglect, go to www.sagepub.com/schwartz.[2]

The patient studied by Bisiach and Luzzatti (1978) had suffered from a stroke, which resulted in hemifield neglect. The neglect wore off to the point that the patient, a prominent newspaper editor, could return to his professional duties. The researchers had him return to the lab. In the study, they tested his visual imagery, which showed evidence of imagery-based hemifield neglect. Asked to imagine himself walking down the main square from north to south in his native city in Italy, the patient described the monuments and buildings only on the west side (his right). When asked to imagine himself walking up the main square from south to north, the patient described the sites only on the east side (now on his right). Thus, there was nothing wrong with his memory. He successfully retrieved the buildings on either side of the main square. However, regardless of his mental orientation, he ignored the left side of the square. Note that he was doing this in the lab, not in the square. Thus, he was showing neglect for the left side of his visual images rather than visual perception. Thus, the imagery deficit mirrored the perceptual deficit. Both neuroimaging and neuropsychology point to the role of visual areas of the brain as being critical to visual imagery.

Returning to the issue of representation of imagery, the neuroscience data also support the analog view. Remember that the analog view advances the idea that images are stored as "pictures" rather than descriptions. Pictures are most logically stored in the visual areas of the brain, which is, in fact, activated during visual imagery. If representations were more like descriptions, one might expect to see the representation of them in verbal areas of the brain, which does not occur. Thus, the neuroimaging and neuropsychological data are consistent with the analog position.

INTERIM SUMMARY

One of the major issues in visual imagery is the nature of representation. Analog representation essentially means we store visual images in a manner a lot like pictures. Propositional representation essentially means that we store visual images in terms of a language-like code. Much of the early cognitive research on this topic was done to differentiate these two views. At present, almost all data strongly support the analog view. Shepard and Metzler (1971) conducted an experiment on mental rotation, which supported the analog view. When mentally rotating objects, it took participants longer to match objects that were at greater angles relative to each other. Kosslyn's (2005) research has also showed that it takes longer to obtain information from small images than from large images, also consistent with the analog view. More recently, it has been found that visual areas of the brain are active during visual imagery. Even in neuropsychological patients, there is evidence that imagery is analog. A patient suffering from hemifield neglect has deficits in both visual attention and attention in visual imagery.

OTHER TOPICS IN VISUAL MEMORY

The issue of how imagery is represented in the neurocognitive system has been a dominant one over the past three decades. However, many other important aspects of visual memory are also important and perhaps more practically valuable to the nonscientist. In the next few sections, we will consider several of these important topics. We will consider the issue of photographic (or eidetic memory), cognitive maps, memory for faces, and applications of visual memory to mnemonics. Another big topic in visual memory is eyewitness memory. In eyewitness memory, typically, a person must describe what he or she *saw* at the scene of a crime. Although eyewitness memory is clearly an important topic in visual memory, in this book, it will be discussed thoroughly in Chapter 8. First, we consider the facts and myths associated with photographic memory.

PHOTOGRAPHIC MEMORY: REALITY OR FANTASY?

As a professor who teaches courses in memory, students frequently tell me about someone they know who possesses **photographic memory.** Belief in photographic memory is quite common in our society. The student wants to know how that person acquired this photographic-like memory and how he or she might be able to achieve it too. It is often thought that a photographic memory provides a huge advantage in the academic world, as it allows the person with it to memorize vast amounts of materials without effort. I usually reply that "photographic memory" may be correlated with good visual imagery system but is not photographic in the sense that it creates a literal representation of what the person saw. I also add that although photographic memory may seem to help that person, it is no substitute for hard work and understanding.

> **Photographic memory**: very strong visual memories that have a strong feeling of being images.

It is likely that those who claim to possess this "photographic memory" (or eidetic memory, in technical terms) do have extraordinarily good visual imagery systems, which allow them to form strong visual images of the material that they learn. However, it is not truly a photograph. This can be demonstrated empirically. It has been shown that people who have "photographic" memories do remember visual information better than those who do not make this claim. However, they still make errors in memory, and even when they claim to be "reading" off their photograph, their errors tend to be related to meaning, as in normal long-term memory, rather than pictorial (Crowder, 1992).

Surprisingly, very little research has been conducted on people who claim to have photographic memory (but see Bywater, Andrade, & Turpin, 2004). Some has been directed at eidetikers. These are people who are able to maintain an image in visual working memory for anywhere from 30 seconds to up to 5 minutes. It apparently is more common among young children, many of whom lose this ability as they learn to read. But even here the research suggests that eidetic imagery is not purely visual. Errors based on meaning creep in here as well (Crowder, 1992). For more on photographic memory and eidetic memory, go to www.sagepub.com/schwartz.[3]

In those of us who do not claim to have eidetic imagery, it is easy to demonstrate that our memories for even common visual items are less than photographic. During the course of our day, we encounter many objects repeatedly. In many cases, although we see these objects everyday, we seldom attend to them and therefore do not encode certain visual details. For example, consider your neighbor's car. It is probably something you see nearly every day. Can you describe the hubcaps? Where is the radio antenna? For most of us, these features are things we just don't attend to, so they do not become part of our memory. If you don't believe me, consider an experiment done by Nickerson and Adams (1979). They asked people to recognize the "real" penny (that is, how an actually penny appears) from a number of close distractors (see Figure 6.8). They found that, despite people's familiarity with pennies (something we see every day), they were surprisingly poor at picking out the real penny from the distractors (try it for yourself in the demonstration). Also go to www.sagepub.com/schwartz.[4]

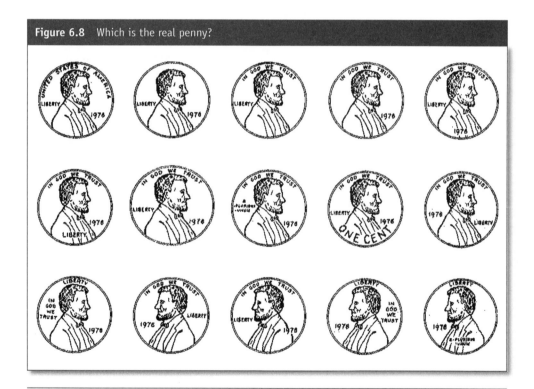

Figure 6.8   Which is the real penny?

SOURCE: Nickerson and Adams (1979).

COGNITIVE MAPS

An important feature of visual memory is that it allows us to learn and remember our physical landscape. We all have "cognitive maps" stored in our visual memory.

> **Cognitive maps**: mental representations of the external world. Based on our spatial representation of the world.

Cognitive maps are mental representations of the external world (Tversky, 2000). These cognitive maps usually refer to the familiar environments we inhabit. We may have a cognitive map of our own homes, the neighborhood, the dorm complex, the campus, and perhaps a few familiar towns and cities. We may have cognitive maps of roads that we use frequently.

Consider the following example. You are asked to give directions to the student center just as you leave your class in the business school. You might consult your cognitive map and then give the following direction: "Go over the bridge on the pond. Then continue on the path past the library. Then make a right, and you'll be at the student center. It should take you about 10 minutes at most." To provide these directions, you must have some representation of what the campus looks like, the relative distances between buildings, and how long it takes to walk these distances. You may also have more specific information, such as the student center is due east of the business school, but providing this information would probably be of little use to a stranger on campus.

Unlike an ordinary map, our cognitive maps are affected by **semantic categories.** That is, places on our cognitive maps that are grouped together are judged to be closer than places that are not grouped together. For example, for most Americans, we would likely judge that the city of Wayne, Michigan, is closer to Detroit, Michigan, than Windsor, Ontario, is. However, Windsor and Detroit are separated by a thin river. Few people who are not familiar with Detroit and Windsor would know this. Semantic categories also affect our judgments of cardinal directions. Our semantic category "the United States" is placed south of our semantic category for "Canada." Thus, most of us would judge Windsor to be north of Detroit. Nope! Detroit—in the United States— is north of Windsor, in Canada. One of the most famous examples of this derives from our semantic categories of the "Atlantic Ocean" and the "Pacific Ocean." Think of your cognitive map. It is pretty easy to determine from that map that the Atlantic Ocean is east relative to the Pacific Ocean. Thus, most people would judge the Atlantic/Caribbean entrance to the Panama Canal as further east of the Pacific entrance to the Panama Canal. Close inspection of a real map reveals the surprising fact that the Pacific entrance is further east. Google the map and see for yourself if you don't believe your memory textbook. The point here is that we use categories, such as the general locations of the Pacific and Atlantic Oceans, to create cognitive maps, which, as a consequence, may lead to inaccuracies (Tversky, 2000).

> **Semantic categories**: meaning affects our cognitive maps. For example, people tend to think of borders between countries as being more straight than they often are.

MEMORY FOR FACES

We humans live in a social world. We interact with other people daily. Being able to identify these people is crucial. Therefore, being able to recognize faces of other people is an important practical skill. Indeed, many researchers argue that we have evolutionarily designed facial recognition mechanisms. Because being able to recognize friend from foe was so important to our early ancestors, it is likely that it shaped our natural selection.

How many times have you had the following experience? You are walking across campus and you see someone you know. However, when you greet that person, you cannot remember the person's name, how you know the person, whether you attended a class together, or if you know the person through some other activity. However, you recognize his or her face. Recognizing faces but failing to retrieve a name is a common experience (Schwartz, 2002). Less common, but also something most people will have experienced, is when someone recognizes you but you fail to recognize him or her at all.. However, despite occasional failures, recognition of familiar faces is a strong skill in human cognition (Bruce, Burton, & Hancock, 2007). Indeed, one of the most important visual stimuli to remember are the faces of the people we come to know in our lives. Imagine arriving at work and not recognizing anyone there. Remember the first day of college before you knew anyone? Not recognizing any familiar faces can be an intimidating experience. Learning new faces and remembering old ones is a critical skill in almost all walks of life.

It turns out that some people are particularly exceptional at identifying faces. Russell, Duchaine, and Nakayama (2009) identified several "super-recognizers," people whose ability to recognize and discriminate faces was several standard deviations above the norm. In keeping with the idea that faces are special, these super-recognizers did not differ from normal controls in other visual recognition tasks. In fact, even when faces were displayed upside down, they lost some of their exceptional ability.

Eyewitness memory: memory for the events that transpire in a single event, usually witnessing a crime.

In some cases, remembering a face correctly can be a matter of life and death. Giving testimony after witnessing a crime (known as **eyewitness memory** in the memory literature) is one such case. Recognizing a face is often considered the strongest piece of testimony (especially in the days prior to memory research and DNA testing) (Loftus, 1979). Because of its significance to eyewitness testimony, face memory has received tremendous research attention over the past 25 years. We have all heard of cases in which, unfortunately, the witness misremembered a face and, as a consequence, someone was erroneously sent to prison. Eyewitness memory is a topic covered in Chapter 8. There are also many other topics relevant to face memory, but just two will be covered here. The first topic is the nature of verbal facilitation and overshadowing in face memory, and the second is the cognitive neuroscience of face memory.

Verbal Facilitation and Overshadowing as It Pertains to Face Memory

Remembering faces and remembering the names that accompany those faces are important in many aspects of human behavior. Consider the professor who must remember the names of dozens and dozens of students each semester, the salesperson who must remember hundreds of clients, or the waiter at the neighborhood restaurant who must remember the faces and names of all of the "regulars" and quickly learn, at least for one meal, the faces of the people that they are serving. At my daughter's elementary school, the principal knows the names of every child, the child's mother, father, and often some grandparents as well.

He is extremely popular among parents because when seeing their faces, they are immediately greeted by name.

We discussed earlier how it is difficult to demonstrate recall from visual memory. I can imagine my father's face, but having no skill at drawing, I cannot demonstrate that I really have a visual image. Thus, if asked about my father's appearance, I must resort to words—somehow convert that visual image into a verbal description. In many situations, we are asked to describe what someone looks like. Asked to describe my father, I might describe him as having "an old but healthy face. Not fat, but not skinny. Balding on top, with hair combed over his bald spot in a way only septuagenarians can get away with. Gray hair. Green eyes. Clean-shaven." As most of you have never seen my father, you now have a rough description of what he looks like. But how many other 78-year-old men also fit that description? It is likely that many do; therefore, at some level, my verbal description is inadequate.

Now consider a situation in which you see someone briefly. For example, if you witness a crime, you just have a minute or less to actually see the thief. Or perhaps you just briefly saw the man your friend is going with on a blind date, and you are describing what the man looks like. Thus, not knowing the person's face well, you are expected to describe the person. It turns out that making such a description impairs your ability to recognize the person's face later. This phenomenon is called verbal overshadowing. In other cases, descriptions can help; this is called verbal facilitation. Indeed, there is a large experimental database on face memory. The results of these experiments are puzzling because in some cases, giving verbal descriptions can help the person remember the face later, but in other situations, giving a verbal description actually impairs one's ability to remember the face later (Meissner et al., 2008). The difference centers on the way in which memory for faces is tested.

Most face memory tests focus on recognition. However, a great deal of face memory research has focused on the differences between two forms of recognition tests. The two forms are multiple-choice recognition (also known as **line-ups**), in which the participant must choose one face from a series of faces, based on the match between the participant's memory and the match to the faces provided (see Figure 6.9). The second form of recognition is old-new recognition (also known as **show-ups**), in which the participant sees only one face and must decide if he or she had seen that face earlier. In legal contexts, the choice of a line-up or a show-up has implications for the likelihood of a witness choosing the correct suspect or the wrong suspect (see Dekle, 2006). Despite the popularity of line-ups, show-ups tend to lead to better overall performance and fewer false alarms (Dekle, 2006).

Line-ups: a multiple-choice form of a face recognition test, often used by police to allow witnesses to identify suspects.

Show-ups: old-new recognition in which the participant sees only one face and must decide if that face was a face that he or she has seen earlier.

In a line-up, the face that you saw earlier will be presented along with several similar faces. The faces are usually matched on such features as gender, age, race, height and weight, the presence or absence of facial hair, and so on. Under these circumstances, participants have to match their memory of the face that they saw to each of the presented faces and then discriminate which is the closest match. Some have argued that

Relative judgment: in a line-up, participants match their memory of what they saw in an event to each of the presented faces in the line-up and then try to determine which is the closest match.

Absolute judgment: in a show-up, the witness matches the particular face to his or her memory of the face seen and decides if this particular face matches the memory.

this leads to a **relative judgment,** that is, which face yields the closest match to the target (Dekle, 2006). In a show-up, the witness matches the particular face to his or her memory of the face seen and decides if this particular face matches the memory. This is called an **absolute judgment.**

Meissner et al. (2008) reviewed the literature to examine what happens if a witness/participant gives a verbal description of a suspect/target face after the initial encounter with the target person. Following this verbal description, the participant is then shown a line-up of faces and asked which one he or she saw. With line-ups, giving a prior description interferes with one's ability to discriminate among the faces, and people's memory for those faces

Figure 6.9 Who done it? A line-up. Faces have been chosen because they are similar in age, gender, hair color, approximate size, and skin color.

SOURCE: Photos by the author.

> **Verbal overshadowing**: when hearing a verbal description makes it more difficult to remember visual features.

will decline. That is, the participant is less likely to identify the correct face. This is the **verbal overshadowing** effect. This is likely because the verbal description is probably similar to more than one of the faces in a line-up. Because the line-up encourages a relative judgment, the description can bias the participant toward one of the faces that matches the description.

Show-ups are affected differently by verbal descriptions (C. Brown & Lloyd-Jones, 2005). In a show-up, the task is matching the presented face with the memory of the previously seen face. Under these circumstances, having given a verbal description of the to-be-remembered face actually improves people's ability to recognize those faces. This is called **verbal facilitation.**

> **Verbal facilitation**: when hearing verbal descriptions makes it easier to remember visual features.

Thus, depending on the kind of test that people will get, providing a verbal description of a face will either facilitate or hurt later memory performance. The theoretical explanation lies in what kinds of processes the actual test situation calls for. The additional stage of having to discriminate among several similar-looking faces results in a comparative analysis of which face best matches the visual memory. However, the verbalization of the description presents a strong memory itself. Given the limits of verbalization of facial features, it is likely that most of the distractors match the verbalization also, and as a consequence, memory suffers. On the other hand, if you are just deciding whether the face is one that you have seen before or one that is novel, the verbal description gives you a second way of recognizing the face. Therefore, and in keeping with encoding variability, verbalization increases memory performance.

This creates a paradox for investigators, such as police interviewing an eyewitness to a crime. They need to get the witness to describe the criminal, as the suspect may be nearby and dangerous, and both police and civilians must be on the lookout for people who look like the suspect. On the other hand, gathering that description will make it more difficult for that witness to correctly identify the suspect in a police line-up (though not a show-up). Thus, the investigator might choose not to ask the witness to describe the criminal if the suspect is already being followed or in custody, as the verbal description may hurt the witness's ability to identify him or her later in a line-up. However, if the suspect is at large and dangerous, the public need for safety may outweigh subtleties of later prosecutions. Many consultants and cognitive psychologists also encourage police to use the show-up procedure rather than the line-up procedure as it produces more accurate memory on the part of the witnesses.

What about for ordinary face memory? That is, how do verbal descriptions affect our ability to remember the faces of students, coworkers, and acquaintances? I argue here that for the normal task of remembering new people we encounter in our lives, it is likely that in most cases, describing the new person to yourself or others allows you an alternate route to recognizing them. It may also provide a deeper encoding of the person's face, thus further strengthening the memory for that person. Nonetheless, providing verbal descriptions of faces can have paradoxical effects on memory.

Cross-Race Bias

One well-studied phenomenon is that people are, by and large, better at recognizing faces from their own "race" than from other racial groups (see Marcon, Susa, & Meissner, 2009). This has been called the **cross-race bias** effect (go to www.sagepub.com/schwartz).[5] That is, when European Americans are asked to study faces of both other European Americans as well as African Americans, the European Americans will perform better on European American faces than they do on African American faces. Perhaps because of their greater familiarity with majority society as the minority, African Americans perform as well on European American faces as do the European Americans. However, African Americans do better than European Americans at recognizing African American faces. Both groups do relatively worse than Hispanic Americans when asked to remember Hispanic faces. These data suggest that there is nothing particular about the physical features of any particular ethnic group that make them more or less memorable, nor do they mean that one group has a better memory than another. Rather, we are better at recognizing features of racial groups for whom we are familiar with. In general, most African Americans have more contact with European American culture than vice versa. Therefore, African Americans do better at recognizing European faces than European Americans do at recognizing African American faces.

> **Cross-race bias:** people are, by and large, better at recognizing faces from their own "race" than from other racial groups.

The idea that this has to do with familiarity is bolstered by Chiroro, Tredoux, Radaelli, and Meissner's (2008) finding that White South Africans performed equivalently to Black South Africans in the identification of Black faces. Because it is those of European ancestry that are in the minority in South Africa, they should have more experience with Black faces than with White Americans. Therefore, their face recognition for Black faces should be better. This is exactly what was found. Black South Africans were also equally good at recognizing White faces. Thus, the pejorative expression that everyone in Group X looks alike is a function of (1) prejudice and (2) lack of familiarity with the facial features of that ethnic or racial group.

Nonetheless, the cross-race bias effect does have some practical implications, especially in eyewitness situations. All else being equal, the witness or victim who is the same race as the criminal will be better at identifying the suspect. While our justice system is predicated on equal treatment to all, police might get more information if they press same-race witnesses to tax their memories to retrieve details of what the perpetrator looked like.

The Neuroscience of Face Memory

There are areas in the temporal lobe of the brain that specialize in face recognition. In particular, a region called the **fusiform face area (FFA)** in the inferior-temporal cortex appears to specialize in face recognition (Kanwisher, 2004). This area of the brain is selectively activated when people are looking at unfamiliar faces and when recognizing familiar faces (Grill-Spector, Knouf, & Kanwisher, 2004). The specialized areas of the brain appear to be evolutionarily determined areas for face recognition. Equivalent areas in

Fusiform face area (FFA): a part of the brain in the inferior-temporal cortex, which appears to specialize in face recognition.

Memory for faces: our ability to encode, represent, and store the visual features of human faces.

Occipital face area (OFA): an area of the occipital lobe has also been identified as crucial to face recognition.

monkeys are also maximally responsive to monkey faces. In addition to the FFA, which is thought to be involved in the recognition of faces and **memory for faces,** an area of the occipital lobe has also been identified as crucial to face recognition. This area in the occipital lobe is known as, aptly, the **occipital face area (OFA)** (Large, Cavina-Pratesi, Vilis, & Culham, 2008). Both of these areas are activated during face recognition tasks in functional magnetic resonance imaging (fMRI) studies (Grill-Spector, 2004) and are also associated with deficits in face recognition when these areas are damaged.

Damage to the FFA results in a neuropsychological condition called **prosopagnosia.** Prosopagnosia is defined as an acquired deficit in recognizing faces (see Shlomo, DeGutis, D'Esposito, & Robertson, 2007). It usually results from damage to the FFA and surrounding areas in the temporal lobe, typically as the result of a stroke or other event that prevents oxygen from reaching these areas of the brain. People suffering from prosopagnosia lose the ability to recognize faces. This includes recognizing the faces of familiar people, people they have known for a long time and the learning of new individuals. If the damage is restricted to the FFA, the patient is usually able to recognize familiar people by their voices, their particular way of walking, or other clues, but faces elude them. In some patients, the deficit is strictly related to human faces, but in other patients, the deficit may extend to other familiar stimuli. In one case, a Scottish shepherd lost his ability to distinguish not only human faces but also individuals in his flock (although he could still recognize ordinary objects, such as tools, electronics, etc.).

Prosopagnosia: an acquired deficit in face recognition caused by brain damage.

Prosopagnosia describes a condition of face blindness. Patients can recognize other objects, but they can no longer recognize faces. Most people can recognize a face regardless of context. One can recognize his or her father's face, regardless of where one sees it. If the father's face is in the newspaper, on the "fan-cam" at a sporting event, or in a family album, it can be recognized. A patient with prosopagnosia cannot do this. However, characteristics that are not facial in nature can help the patient recognize a familiar face. For example, if the patient's spouse always wears a trademark hat, recognition can occur by noting the hat.

In summary, face memory seems to be an integrated process involving both areas in the occipital lobe, which we know are involved with the perception and recognition of faces, and areas in the temporal lobe, which we know are involved in recognizing complex objects and memory. Damage to these areas results in a strange condition known as prosopagnosia, which is a selective deficit at recognizing and remembering human faces. In most people, however, these areas are constantly being used as we negotiate our ways through the sea of human faces that surround us.

APPLICATION OF VISUAL IMAGERY TO MNEMONICS

One of the oldest and most "tried-and-true" techniques to aid memory is the use of visual imagery. The use of imagery techniques to improve encoding and memory performance goes back all the way to the ancient Greeks some 2,500 years ago. Perhaps the oldest recorded story involving the use of visual imagery to aid memory was recorded by the Greek poet Simonides in 477 BCE. According to the legend, Simonides gave a speech at a banquet sponsored by a particular nobleman by the name of Scopas. Scopas expected Simonides to praise him, but instead Simonides praised the gods Castor and Pollux. Scopas was upset at the speech and only paid Simonides half of what he was supposed to receive. According to the legend, the gods sent a messenger to the banquet and called Simonides away. While Simonides, who had shown his respect to the gods, was out of the room, the gods destroyed the banquet hall, killing all the guests except Simonides. When family members came to collect their loved one's remains, Simonides was able to direct each person to his or her family member's body, as he had memorized where every guest had been seated that night using the strategy that has come to be known as the **method of loci** (Yates, 1966). Your author does not understand why all of the guests had to die because Scopas had an inflated ego, but that is the way stories used to work back in ancient times. Although this story may seem a bit violent and gruesome for a textbook on memory, it is generally considered the first recorded use of imagery-based learning.

> **Method of loci**: the learner associates a list of new to-be-learned items with a series of well-known physical locations, using visual imagery.

If you visit your college bookstore or any big-name bookstore, you will find many books on memory improvement. A quick check of the Internet will reveal many sites that claim to have found ways in which people can vastly improve their ability to remember information (e.g., go to www.sagepub.com/schwartz).[6] In the popular press on memory improvement, visual mnemonic techniques are often overemphasized at the expense of many of the other mnemonic "hints" that I have provided throughout this book (e.g., Hagwood, 2007; Lorayne & Lucas, 1974, are some of the more popular memory improvement books). In fact, the visual mnemonics are rather limited in their usefulness, as will become apparent in the discussion below. However, they can be quite powerful in certain circumstances.

In imagery-based learning, the goal is often not to actually remember visual information. Rather, we capitalize on our good visual memory to aid us in learning more difficult, usually verbal information. The basic strategy is to associate the difficult to-be-learned information with existing well-known visual memories. Once we do this, we form a strong association between the two, and the new information will be better encoded. Let's look at the oldest method, the method of loci, and see how it works.

Method of Loci

In the method of loci, the learner associates a list of new to-be-learned items with a series of well-known physical locations, using visual imagery. To use this technique, you must be really familiar with a particular landscape. This might be your house and yard, the central square of a college campus, or perhaps a favorite trail through the woods. You designate a series of landmarks as the memory loci and then associate the new items with each location. The new to-be-learned items can really be anything, but the technique is particularly useful for remembering lists of unrelated items, such as grocery lists. For example, there have been times when my wife has called me up while I am in the car and asked me to pick up items at the grocery store. Being unable to write them down in this situation, I must memorize them. The method of loci is useful here. I've also heard of medical students using it successfully to remember the names of the bones or nerves of the body.

When you get the items on the list, you associate each one with a well-known location in your mental landscape. Thus, if your loci are located in the front yard of your house, you might place the "loaf of bread" in the mailbox, the "butter" in front of the petunias growing under the window, the "salad dressing" right under the doorknob (don't trip on it), the "toilet paper" hung in the tree by the front window, and so on. When you get to the grocery store, you re-create the mental landscape and walk through it in your imagination. You visit each of the landmarks and "find" the item you need to buy for your family. Each landmark should remind you of what you need to purchase, and as you walk through the order of landmarks, you should be able to retrieve your entire list.

What is particularly useful about this list is its portability. When you use it the next time, you may still remember the previous items "left" in each landmark. In your mind's eye, simply remove the loaf of bread left in the mailbox and replace it with the new item ("tomato sauce"). In this way, the same landmarks can be used over and over again for different lists. The method of loci also helps you preserve order information. Because each item is associated with a spot on your mental walk, which you go through the same way every time, you can also remember where in a list an item is, if this information is important.

Mnemonic Improvement Tip 6.1

The method of loci: For learning arbitrary lists of unrelated items, the method of loci can be very effective. Mentally associate each of the to-be-learned items with a well-known physical location in a well-known landscape. When it is time to retrieve, imagine again the physical location and mentally walk through it. Look for the to-be-learned item in each location.

There is not a lot of recent research on the method of loci (see Verhaeghen & Marcoen, 1996) because this is such an old and well-established technique. But older studies support the idea that the method of loci is useful for memory. For example, Groninger (1971) instructed college students to imagine a sequence of 25 spatial locations on their college campus. He then gave a list of 25 unrelated words to learn using the method of loci. He compared them to students who were not given instructions in how to use the method of loci. Students who used the method of loci outperformed those who did not. More recently, Kondo et al. (2004) showed that the method of loci improved memory. This improvement was correlated with increased activity in a variety of areas in the right prefrontal lobe.

Keyword Technique

The **keyword technique** (also known as the linkword) is a common mnemonic technique that also employs visual imagery. It is particularly useful for learning new vocabulary words, especially for foreign-language vocabulary (see Bellezza, 1996). More generally speaking, the keyword technique is useful for paired-associate learning. We use paired-associate learning when we learn new vocabulary or vocabulary in another language. It involves creating an image that links two items in memory. With respect to language learning, it means creating an image that links the word in the language you know to the word in the language

> **Keyword technique:** involves creating an image that links two items in memory. With respect to language learning, it means creating an image that links the word in the language you know to the word in the language you are learning.

you are learning. For example, if you are learning words in Spanish, you will have to study many English-Spanish pairs to master a sufficient Spanish vocabulary. Consider studying the Spanish word *arbol,* meaning "tree." From the word *arbol,* you might think of the English word *arbor* (meaning a grove of trees, both words come from the same Latin root). And arbor, of course, conjures up images of trees. It also works for items that do not necessarily have the same roots. For example, if you are learning the Tagalog word *salamin,* meaning glasses, you might imagine a fish wearing glasses (Tagalog is a widely spoken language in the Philippines). Think of this image, and you will always know at least one word in Tagalog (see Wang & Thomas, 1995, for this example). The keyword technique can also be used to learn other kinds of paired-associate information. For example, at some point, you might need to memorize the capitals of all the countries of Europe. When learning that Tallinn is the capital of Estonia, you might imagine a cat with its "Tail" stuck "In" a refrigerator (because it is so cold there). Asked to learn the capital of Estonia's neighbor, Finland, you might visualize a "sink on fire" to help you remember that Helsinki is the capital of Finland. Some names may be resistant to this technique. It is harder to think of an image such as the ones just given for a capital city like London, which does not have any phonological overlap with other English words. A common problem with the linkword is interference. If the same image is used to learn more than one item, interference can result.

According to A. Y. Wang and Thomas (1995), the keyword technique is particularly useful for the initial encoding of new language vocabulary. That is, they recommend the keyword technique for the first time you encounter the new vocabulary. However, they contend the subsequent study should follow using meaning-based study. That is, after the initial study session, you should use elaborative encoding or some other deep level of processing to help you remember the vocabulary. Wang and Thomas reasoned that the keyword technique is good at forming initial connections between disparate items (such as arbitrary associations such as Estonia-Tallinn or salamin-eyeglasses). But they also noticed that most studies testing the keyword mnemonic tested it at relatively short retention intervals. Earlier studies in their own lab suggested that with time, forgetting occurred just as rapidly with the keyword technique as with other methods. As a consequence, Wang and Thomas were concerned about the educational implications of this finding.

This is a clear concern because most of us want to remember information that we learn not just for a few minutes but for much longer periods of time. I may choose to study a little Tagalog for a half hour a day for weeks before my anticipated trip to the Philippines. Remembering the words in Tagalog is only useful for me if I can use them some time much later than studying, when I find myself in the Philippines with someone who only speaks that language. I want to remember that Tallinn is the capital of Estonia not just now but in several weeks when I appear on *Jeopardy*. So we want to use mnemonic techniques that produce long-term retention, not just a temporary boost, although such boosts may be appreciated just in advance of a big exam.

A. Y. Wang and Thomas (1995) observed that the keyword technique runs contrary to the principles of levels of processing. This troubled them because, as memory scientists, they were aware of how important meaning-based processing was. And yet, here were all these memory experts promoting the keyword technique. In the keyword technique, the linking keyword is usually something that relates the appearance of a word to a similar-looking word in English. This would be classified as shallow processing in the levels-of-processing framework. Therefore, the levels-of-processing framework suggests that the keyword technique may be a temporary artifact of the overlap in visual appearance (or sound overlap) between the words in the two languages. For this reason, they decided to do some experimental work to resolve these issues.

A. Y. Wang and Thomas (1995) conducted an experiment comparing the keyword technique to standard semantic context encoding. In the experiment, participants were taught words in Tagalog along with their English translation (as in *salamin–eyeglasses*). This language was chosen because there are few speakers of it in central Florida (as opposed to Los Angeles, where it is widely spoken among Filipino immigrants). Half of the participants were given instructions in how to use the keyword technique and were given an intermediary word to help them form a visual image (*salamin–salmon–eyeglasses*). In the semantic context, the participants saw an English-language sentence with the Tagalog word substituted in the place in which its language equivalent would appear ("The woman returned from the optometrist with a new pair of reading salamin"). Wang and Thomas gave their participants two tests: one 5 minutes after learning, the next 2 days later. The tests consisted of giving the Tagalog word and asking the participants to supply the English equivalent.

The results are seen in Figure 6.10. A. Y. Wang and Thomas (1995) found that at the 5-minute delay, more items were recalled if they had been encoded via the keyword method. However, at the 2-day delay, many of these items had been forgotten, whereas there was comparatively less forgetting from the semantic context condition. Indeed, recall was better at the 2-day delay overall in the semantic context condition than it was in the keyword condition. These results suggest that the keyword technique may not be all that it is cracked up to be. After all, in most cases, we want to remember the words in a new language not just 5 minutes from now but much later, perhaps when our travels bring us to the Philippines.

A. Y. Wang and Thomas (1995) take a more optimistic take on their data, however. They suggest that the keyword technique leads to good initial encoding, as indicated by the good performance in the 5-minute condition seen in Figure 6.10. They suggest that the keyword technique is a good way to initially encode items. However, after one or two study sessions

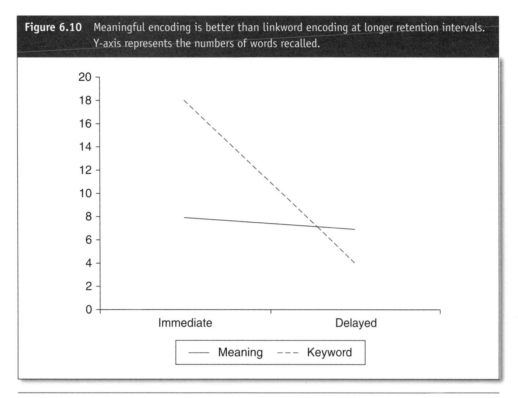

Figure 6.10   Meaningful encoding is better than linkword encoding at longer retention intervals. Y-axis represents the numbers of words recalled.

SOURCE: Based on A. Y. Wang and Thomas (1995).

with the keyword, it is advisable to switch to deeper levels of processing, as exemplified by the semantic encoding in this experiment. This way, the student can capitalize also on the long-term advantages provided by the semantic encoding. Because most students will study any particular item several times before they are actually tested on it, the keyword method can create good initial learning, and the semantic encoding can cement that knowledge.

Mnemonic Improvement Tip 6.2

Keyword technique: An especially strong way to encode paired associates, such as new language vocabulary, is to use the keyword technique. This method provides good initial encoding but should be followed by deeper processing. The keyword technique involves finding a visual image that bridges one word to the other. For example, if you are studying the English-French pair *pen- stylo*, you might imagine a fancy pen in the latest styles. This will provide a vivid visual image that will emphasize the sound of the word *stylo*.

For more information on the keyword technique, go to www.sagepub.com/schwartz.[7]

Pegword Mnemonic

Unlike the method of loci and the keyword technique, the pegword mnemonic is not just a visual memory aid. Rather, it takes advantage of our natural auditory memory system as well as our visual imagery system. To use this technique, an individual must begin by knowing an auditory list. For example, if you are a baseball fan, you may know the batting order for your favorite team. Alternatively, you may remember all the teachers from elementary school, ordered from kindergarten to fifth grade. Once you have such a list memorized, you associate the name of the to-be-remembered item with the name of the baseball player or the teacher. You could then supplement the sounds by forming images to relate the name of the item on the list (perhaps "salad" on a grocery list) with the name on the well-learned list (Ms. Green). In this example, the association of salad-Green is easy and straightforward. "Salad–Ms. Milacio" might invoke a fancy endive salad covered in Italian dressing. When you need to retrieve the list, you simply go through your well-established list (i.e., first grade, Ms. Green; second grade, Ms. Milacio; etc.) and retrieve the novel item that has been associated with each teacher or each baseball player. Empirical research has demonstrated that the **pegword technique** is helpful in memory (Paivio, 1969).

> **Pegword technique**: a mnemonic technique that takes advantage of our natural auditory memory system as well as our visual imagery system. We associate new items with words in a known rhyme scheme.

A standard list that many have used successfully with the pegword technique is the following list:

One–bun	Five–hive	Nine–mine
Two–shoe	Six–sticks	Ten–hen
Three–tree	Seven–heaven	
Four–door	Eight–gate	

The numbers help you remember the words in order, and the rhymes give you easy access to the pegword. You can then pair the word to be remembered with the word in the above sequence. So if the first item on your shopping list is "salad," you can visually imagine a nice tossed salad sitting in a baked bun instead of a salad plate. Similarly, if the second item on your list is a pineapple, you can imagine the pineapple running around with shoes on it. Use each word to generate an image when you are learning the list. Later, you use the well-learned list as a set of cues for remembering your new list, in this case, your grocery items. The following website nicely illustrates this method: go to www.sagepub.com/schwartz.[8]

••

Mnemonic Improvement Tip 6.3

Pegword technique: This technique combines visual and auditory memory into a powerful memory mnemonic for remembering ordered lists. First, you need a well-established word list. Then associate, using visual imagery, the new to-be-learned item with an item from the well-established list. At the time of test, go through your well-established list, and the associated items should be retrieved.

••

Interactive Versus Bizarre Imagery

Although not considered a formal mnemonic as the above three are, the use of **bizarre imagery** can be a memory aid as well. Bizarre imagery means that rather than construct an image that conforms to our general way of thinking, we construct an image that is strange. Essentially, we create a visual von Restorff effect and simultaneously take advantage of both the power of visual imagery and the power of distinctiveness to improve our memory. Make the images interact and you can even boost the memory strength more.

> **Bizarre imagery**: forming strange visual images based on to-be-learned information can lead to good memory for that information.

For example, Wollen, Weber, and Lowry (1972) asked participants to use bizarre interactive imagery in learning new paired associates, such as piano-cigar. They found that the interacting images, even if not bizarre, led to the best memory recall relative to noninteracting images or rote encoding. Thus, they recommend that interactive images are better than bizarre ones at producing good memory (see Figure 6.11). Interestingly, N. E. Kroll, Schepeler, and Angin (1986) replicated this finding but found that people thought they had done better on the bizarre items than they actually did. Thus, when using this technique, it is good to test oneself (as in all mnemonics) to ensure that you have mastered the material.

In this section, we have discussed a number of visual-based mnemonics to add to the growing list of study suggestions, tricks, strategies, and aids that can help each of us become more efficient at remembering information. Keep in mind, of course, that even these visual mnemonics require work and that they are useful in some circumstances but not in others. I repeat the warning that there is no memory pill or magic bullet that will ensure you remember everything all the time (nor would this be desirable). Nonetheless, the visual mnemonic techniques are useful for the kinds of arbitrary lists of items that we have been discussing here.

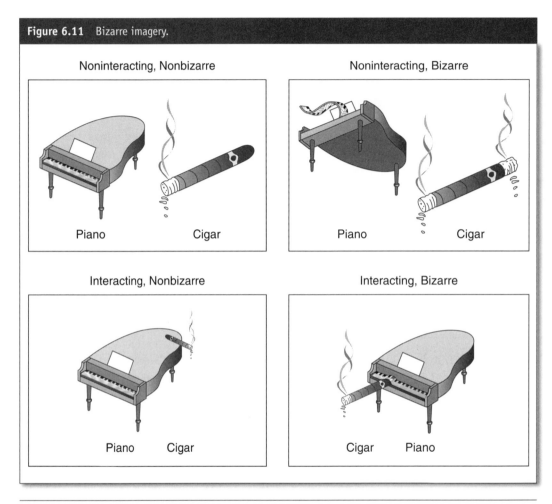

Figure 6.11 Bizarre imagery.

SOURCE: Wollen, Weber, and Lowry (1972).

SUMMARY

Visual memory refers to our ability to remember the visual world, from pictures to faces, from perception to imagery. Much early research on visual memory focused on how we represent visual information in long-term memory. Analog viewpoints eventually won out over propositional viewpoints. One of the turning points in this debate was when Shepard and Metzler (1971) showed that it took more time to match mental images when the angle of rotation was greater. More recent cognitive neuroscience research shows that visual areas of the brain are active when people are activating visual memories. We discussed some issues in photographic memory and cognitive maps. By and large, photographic memory is a myth. Even people with very strong visual memories make errors that are based on meaning. Cognitive maps are visual representations of space that guide our navigation through the world. As visual as both of these kinds of memory are, we still see the heavy hand of meaning in them, that is, the meaning of stimuli influences our visual memory. The chapter then covered face memory. We are good at recognizing familiar faces, and this seems to have a neural basis. In particular, the FFA (fusiform face area) in the temporal lobe and OFA (occipital face area) in the occipital lobe are fundamental areas associated with face recognition. Finally, we discussed the advantages and disadvantages of the classic visual mnemonics, including the method of loci, the keyword technique, and the pegword technique. These techniques use visual imagery to promote memory but should be supplemented with meaning-based techniques.

KEY TERMS

Representation	Cognitive maps	Cross-race bias
Analog representation	Semantic categories	Fusiform face area (FFA)
Propositional representation	Eyewitness memory	Memory for faces
Shepard and Metzler's (1971) mental rotation experiment	Line-ups	Occipital face area (OFA)
	Show-ups	Prosopagnosia
Imagery	Relative judgment	Method of loci
Primary visual cortex	Absolute judgment	Keyword technique
Hemifield neglect	Verbal overshadowing	Pegword technique
Photographic memory	Verbal facilitation	Bizarre imagery

REVIEW QUESTIONS

1. What is meant by the term *visual memory?* Why are recall measures hard to test when assessing visual memory?

2. What are the theoretical differences between a visual memory system that uses analog representation and one that uses propositional representation?

3. Describe the Shepard-Metzler experiment. What was their hypothesis? How was the experiment conducted? What results did they get? And how were these results interpreted?

4. Why does the finding that engaging in visual imagery activates the primary visual cortex support the analog view of imagery representation?

5. What is meant by verbal overshadowing in face memory? How does it occur? When does the opposite (verbal facilitation) occur?

6. What is cross-race bias? Why do minorities have better ability to recognize cross-race faces than majority groups?

7. What is prosopagnosia? What areas of the brain is it associated with?

8. What is the method of loci? How it used and what kinds of materials is it good for?

9. What is the keyword technique? How is it used? Why do Wang and Thomas only recommend it for initial studying?

10. What is the pegword technique? How does it differ from the method of loci and the keyword technique?

ONLINE RESOURCES

1. For an illustration of this experiment and to participate yourself, go to http://psychexps .olemiss.edu/InstrOnly_Page/mentalrotation.htm.

2. For information on hemifield neglect, go to http://psych.ucalgary.ca/PACE/VA-Lab/Visual%20 Agnosias/hemi-neglect.htm.

3. For more on photographic memory and eidetic memory, go to http://www.straightdope.com/ columns/read/2350/is-there-such-a-thing-as-photographic-memory.

4. For a demonstration of Nickerson and Adams (1979), go to http://www.dcity.org/braingames/pennies.

5. For more on the cross-race bias effect, go to http://works.bepress.com/christian_meissner.

6. For memory improvement resources, based on imagery, go to http://www.mindtools.com/ memory.html.

7. For information on the keyword technique, go to http://www.memory-key.com/language/ mnemonics.htm.

8. The following website nicely illustrates this pegword method: http://www.vcld.org/pages/ newsletters/00_01_fall/mnemonic4.htm

Go to www.sagepub.com/schwartz for additional exercises and study resources. Select **Chapter 6, Visual Memory** for chapter-specific resources.

CHAPTER 7

Autobiographical Memory

I was driving in my car, my old Honda Civic, on my way from my home to my university on a hot sunny Tuesday morning, typical of mid-September in Miami. As I usually do, I was listening to the news on NPR. I was just passing Miami airport when the newscaster announced that a plane had crashed into the World Trade Center. They did not have much more news, but when I arrived at the university, the department secretary was in tears. Someone found a portable television, and we started monitoring the news. That is my recollection of my personal whereabouts for the morning of September 11, 2001.

Most people who were adults on 9/11 can vividly remember the personal details of how they heard the news, where they were, and what they were doing during the attacks on the United States. This is true for people who, like myself, had nothing directly to do with the attacks. I was in Miami, a thousand miles away from the attacks, safe in my car and, later, in my office. My whereabouts had no impact on the tragedy unfolding that day or the courageous efforts ongoing to rescue survivors. I had no decision making in how to respond and whether or not to scramble fighter jets. This same sentiment is true for most people that day. For more thoughts on memories of 9/11, go to www.sagepub.com/schwartz.[1]

Yet nonetheless, we remember the personal details of what we did that day, how we learned the news, and where we were at the time. This kind of memory is called a **flashbulb memory.** Most people are certain that their flashbulb memories are accurate. The memories are detailed, and the confidence is strong. Try telling someone that they misremember, and you will be met with surprise and concern. Earlier generations of Americans have equally strong flashbulb memories of the assassination of John F. Kennedy or the attack on Pearl Harbor, which launched the United States into World War II. British may have flashbulb memories of the auto accident that killed Princess Diana. Spanish may have flashbulb memories of hearing the news of the Madrid train bombings. Israelis may have flashbulb memories of the assassination of Prime Minister Rabin. In general, flashbulb memories are studied by examining these public tragedies. We also have flashbulb memories of personal

> **Flashbulb memories**: highly confident personal memories of surprising events. In order to study them, researchers have focused on the memory of public tragedies.

events, but public events have several advantages for researchers. Flashbulb memories are a form of autobiographical memory, the topic of this chapter.

Not all autobiographical memories need be so traumatic and weighty. Sometimes they are highly personal, such as the memory of one's first day of first grade, one's first romantic kiss, one's first day at a new job, or recital of one's wedding vows. In many cases, it will surprise you that you can remember such an event. It may also come as a surprise that you cannot remember other such events. Some of you may remember your first day at your college, whereas others may not. Other memories may arise without having any particular importance. When we remember them, it may surprise us in that we remember them at all, such as the memory of seeing a skinny raccoon on a vacation in Everglades National Park 25 years ago. People often wonder why such memories are still accessible so many years later, when their meaning is seemingly so inconsequential. Some memories we have now, even though we suspect that they will fade shortly. Most of can still remember what we had for breakfast this morning, although that particular meal will be forgotten shortly. Try remembering what you had for breakfast on the same day of the week last week. Unless you eat the same breakfast every Tuesday, chances are you don't remember last Tuesday's breakfast. However, you can give a summary of what you usually eat for breakfast. The contention here is that we stitch together a series of episodic memories with semantic memory to create a life narrative that defines who we are as individuals (Conway, 2005).

Autobiographical memory refers to our specific memories and self-knowledge. As such, autobiographical memory combines information from episodic events ("falling out of a tree at Aunt Beulah's when I was 10 years old") and semantic knowledge ("I was born in the small town of Ottaqueechee, Vermont"). Because we cannot remember episodically events from our earliest infanthood, information that we have about ourselves from this early period is semantic in nature. However, both episodic memories and semantic memories can be about our individual life story, so both are relevant to the topic of autobiographical memory.

In this chapter, we will cover the major theory that organizes research on autobiographical memory—namely, the hierarchical model of autobiographical memory and the working self, advanced by Martin Conway and his colleagues (Conway, 2005; Conway & Pleydell-Pearce, 2000). We will then consider a number of important phenomena in autobiographical memory, including infant or childhood amnesia, flashbulb memories, diary studies, the reminiscence bump, shared memories, perspective in autobiographical memory, the interaction between odor and autobiographical memory, and the neuroimaging of autobiographical memory.

CONWAY'S THEORY OF REPRESENTATION IN AUTOBIOGRAPHICAL MEMORY

Martin Conway is a prominent British memory researcher who has been interested in the nature of autobiographical memory for many years (see Figure 7.1). His theory concerns the representation of autobiographical memory, that is, how our memories are stored and organized for retrieval. For example, when I was in graduate school, I often played basketball with friends at lunchtime. At one basketball game, a professional basketball player joined us.

Figure 7.1   Noted memory theorist Martin Conway. Note George Bush in the background.

This serves as a good example of some of the ideas Conway brings to our attention with respect to autobiographical memory. First, my memory is of a specific event—that is, it is an episodic memory of a particular time (playing basketball with the professional) and place (college gym). Second, there is a "general-event" script that can be used to fill in details—that is, I often played basketball at lunchtime. Third, Conway talks about our use of lifetime periods to organize our memory ("when I was in middle school," "while I worked for GEICO") and how important these are for autobiographical memory. Thus, Conway's organizational schema can neatly catch the nature of how we discuss autobiographical memory. You can hear Dr. Conway talk about his research at www.sagepub.com/schwartz.[2]

So now we will examine the formal model of autobiographical memory described by Martin Conway and his colleagues. Paramount to this model is the idea that levels of autobiographical memory correspond to (1) **event-specific memories**, (2) **general events**, and (3) **lifetime periods.** These levels create an interacting but hierarchical representation structure in our memory system (Conway & Pleydell-Pearce, 2000) see Figure 7.2. Specific events are organized together

Event-specific memories: individual events stored in episodic memory.

General events: include the combined, averaged, and cumulative memory of highly similar events. General events also include extended events, which are long sequences of connected episodic events.

Lifetime periods: the idiosyncratic, personal ways in which we organize our autobiographical past. These lifetime periods are usually organized by a common theme and may overlap in the actual physical time periods that they cover.

into general events, which in turn are organized into cohesive units as lifetime periods. Accessing a lifetime period ("when I was in college"), for example, should unlock a host of general events and specific events associated with that lifetime period.

Any particular memory should be able to fit this schema. For example, "playing volleyball by the dorm building" is a memory that might be activated by the lifetime period of when you were in your first year of college, living in a college dorm. This is a general event, synthesizing many such late afternoons during that year. Or it could activate a specific volleyball event, such as when you dived for the volleyball and cut a deep gash in your elbow. Another person might have a lifetime period of "when I was training hard for the marathon." This lifetime period will activate general events, that is, the combined and synthesized memory of many days spent in uneventful and monotonous running. Furthermore, specific events might be activated, such as the time the runner almost got hit by a car, the time the runner twisted an ankle and had to hitchhike home, or the exact moment when this runner passed the finish line at the marathon. Let's look at each component of Conway's model in more detail.

Event-Specific Memories

In Conway's scheme, part of the representational system of autobiographical memory is the vast reservoir of episodic memories that we accumulate over our lifetimes. Events are the fundamental units of cognitive memory. Thus, an event can be the briefest moment in time, such as the instant you sat down on and immediately broke your aunt's glass coffee table or the time you saw a hammerhead shark while scuba diving. Or, an event can be extended in time, such as your first date with your spouse or the time you drove on the California freeway in a rented convertible. Both the instant events and the extended events refer to particular and unique events; they simply differ in the extent to which they last.

For this reason, some researchers find that the term *episode* is too vague, as it can either mean an isolated instant or an extended event. Linton (1986), for example, suggests that any particular event can be broken down into elements called *details*. Details refer to precise moments in time, whereas events refer to extended but continuous memories. For example, think of the episodic memory of seeing a hammerhead shark while scuba diving. The detail is the exact moment when the dangerous fish flashed by. It lasted only a second, and the shark was gone. However, the event includes the subsequent adrenaline rush in your body, the concern about air supply, and the relaxation induced by subsequently watching a peaceful angelfish.

General Events

For Conway, general events include two different forms of memory. First, general events include the combined, averaged, and cumulative memory of similar events. For example, you may go grocery shopping once a week. Normally, grocery shopping is unexciting, but it is also an important, if repetitive, event. Over time, the specific visits blend into one schema-driven memory. Indeed, it may be impossible to recall any specific visit to the grocery store, but that is not to say that you have forgotten that you ever do it. Rather, the specific events combine in memory into a general event of what you do when you go grocery shopping. This contrasts with the event-specific memory, which might be the time you saw your old gym teacher shopping at your grocery store. This is a one-time event that remains memorable above and beyond the general event.

Figure 7.2   Conway's model.

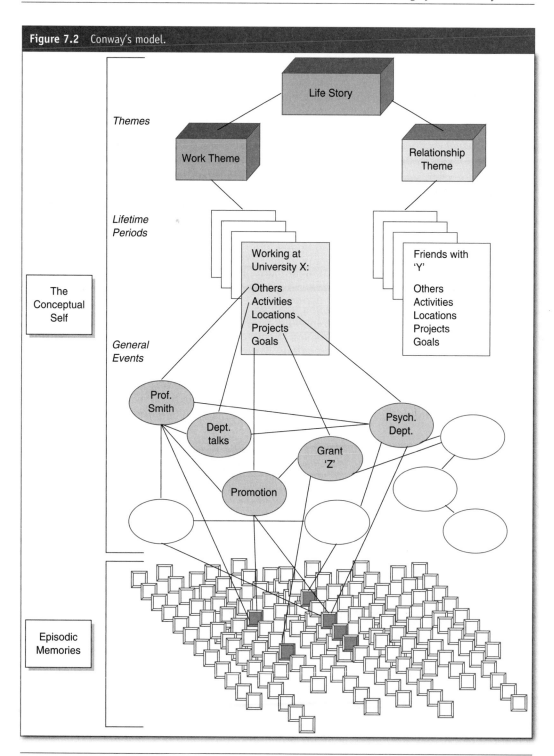

SOURCE: Conway (2005).

We encode many such general events. Encoding events as general events follows general principles of memory, such that meaningful encoding creates stronger general events. You might have a similar general event memory for a class you took a year ago. You don't remember any specific classes, but you have a generalized memory of the classroom, where you sat, what the professor generally wore, and what you learned in the class (hopefully). Our lives are filled with such repeating cycles of work, school, exercise, bedtime rituals, and so on. The ability to form such memories requires that the individual be able to integrate and interpret across individual events, an important skill for creating an autobiography. Thus, cognitive schemata guide us in forming these generalized events. For example, we probably form generalized events of our trips to the grocery store, but when we switch to a new store, we start a new generalized script, even if we are basically doing the same activities at each store.

The second form of "general" event, according to Conway, is an *extended event*. An extended event is a long sequence of connected episodic events. It is different from the averaged memory in that it is the memory of a single sequence of events that occurred only once. However, it is similar in that it requires integrative processes to join the units together into a coherent schema. For example, a 2-week vacation might be remembered in terms of a "general event." It is composed of individual episodes, such as skinning your knee on the steps of the Lincoln Memorial, getting stuck in traffic on the Beltway, sweating in the hot sticky weather while waiting to get into the Smithsonian, or waiting to visit the White House. Each of these is a unique event, but they are joined together to form the memory of your wonderful vacation in the nation's capital. Like the other form of general event, these extended memories require integrating the individual events into the general memory (see Burt, Kemp, & Conway, 2003). Robinson (1992) studied a pattern of general memories called "mini-histories," which are the integrated sequence for activities with a straightforward goal and timeline, such as "learning to drive a car" or "my first romantic relationship" (see Figure 7.3).

Figure 7.3 Do you remember the very first time you drove a car on your own? Despite the many thousands of times you may have driven since, most people remember this coming-of-age act.

Lifetime Periods

We use lifetime periods to organize our autobiographical memories (both event-specific and general events). Lifetime periods are the idiosyncratic, personal ways in which we organize our autobiographical past. These lifetime periods are usually organized by a common theme and may overlap in the actual physical time periods that they cover. For example, such lifetime periods might be "when I was in college," "when I lived, as a child, in Cincinnati, Ohio," "before I got married," or "when I had the summer job as tennis instructor." These labels tend to activate a common set of memories associated with each theme. Thus, the "when I was in college" period might evoke memories of long nights of studying, fraternity parties, college football games, and so on. "Before I got married" might evoke memories of the joys and frustrations of dating. "When I lived in Cincinnati, Ohio" might evoke memories of attending baseball games with your father or going to Girl Scout camp with your troop.

Lifetime periods need not be linear. They also can overlap. For example, it is possible that "when I was in college" coincides with "before I got married," but each is associated with a different set of general and specific event memories. Similarly, "when I worked as a tennis instructor" may overlap with "when I lived in Cincinnati," but each lifetime period evokes different sets of specific and general events. Lifetime periods can provide direction and a sense of goals and accomplishments for some. These lifetime periods can also serve as good cues to retrieve general events or episodic events. When lifetime periods are used as cues, people retrieve autobiographical memories faster (Conway & Pleydell-Pearce, 2000).

The Working Self

The final component of autobiographical memory is the **working self.** The working self is not a level of representation. Rather, it is a monitoring function that controls the retrieval of information from the levels of representation. The working self includes the goals and self-images that make up our view of ourselves. It is a complex collection of autobiographical knowledge, goals, and self-monitoring processes. Thus, you may think of yourself as being a light sleeper, setting high goals, but sometimes being lazy when you should work hard. This "working self" is the function of your aspirations and expectations, combined with your actual memory. Many nights of being woken by the slightest sound has formed a general event in your memory of being a light sleeper. Many evenings spent watching television shows when you thought you should be working on your schoolwork contributes to your working self-perspective that you are lazy.

> **Working self**: the monitoring function that controls the retrieval of information from the levels of representation. The working self includes the goals and self-images that make up our view of ourselves.

With respect to autobiographical memory, the working self functions to keep two features of memory intact, **coherence** and **correspondence** (Conway, 2005). Coherence means the processes that yield autobiographical memories that are consistent with the working self. For example, if one's working self includes the image of oneself as an animal

Coherence: the processes that yield autobiographical memories that are consistent with the working self.

Correspondence: the match between the retrieved memory and the actual event from the past.

lover, the working self will work to yield coherent autobiographical memories of instances in which one was kind to animals. When this aspect of yourself is invoked, you will recall the time when you stopped to help a turtle cross the road and not the time you accidentally ran over a wild rabbit. Correspondence, by contrast, means the requirement that the retrieved memory match the actual event from the past. That is, the retrieved autobiographical memories should actually correspond accurately to the reality of the past. For example, even if one thinks of oneself as a good baseball player, it is important to accurately remember that it was you who struck out with the bases loaded to end your team's opportunity to advance to the playoffs.

This can, as the above example may indicate, lead to conflicts between coherence and correspondence. Coherence works to keep memories consistent with our views of ourselves, whereas correspondence works to keep memories accurate. In some circumstances, these may work at cross-purposes. For example, we may want to remember our vacations as relaxed and enjoyable events. However, you may have also spent a long unpleasant wait in a crowded and hot bus station. The working self integrates these two conflicting aspects of the vacation into the construction of autobiographical memory.

CHILDHOOD AMNESIA

Childhood amnesia refers to our poor to nonexistent memory of early childhood (poor) and infancy (nonexistent). In this sense, the term itself is a misnomer. It is not that young children and infants are amnesic. It is adults who are amnesic for events that occurred to them when they were young children. The amnesia covers the first 2 years of life, and then, depending on the individual, we start to have memories of episodes from our life, sometimes as early as age 2 but more often age 3 or 4. These memories are rare and fragmented. These earliest memories tend to be fragments, bits and pieces of memory largely unconnected to the narratives that form later memories (K. Nelson, 1989). Usually, memories of our lives from age 6 or 7 become more common and have more details to them. Figure 7.4 shows the childhood amnesia phenomenon and its offset by 5 or 6 years of age. It is also at this age that adults remember childhood events in terms of the structure just described in Conway's theory. Indeed, early memories tend to be disjointed—not connected with anything, whereas memories from the early elementary school years often feel like they occurred to us—our current selves. Think about your own earliest memories. What are they about? How do they differ from memories from later in childhood or of recent events? Do they feel somehow different or fragmented?

Childhood amnesia: (also known as infantile amnesia) refers to the observation that adults have almost no episodic memories from the first 3 to 5 years of their lives.

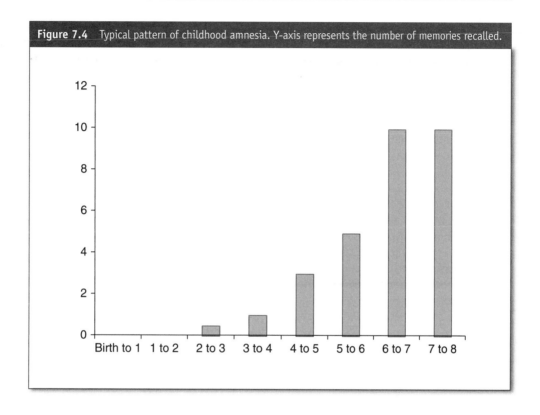

Figure 7.4   Typical pattern of childhood amnesia. Y-axis represents the number of memories recalled.

Childhood amnesia has been a topic of interest to psychologists from a number of perspectives. Early psychoanalysts thought that childhood amnesia reflected the turbulent nature of the unconscious mind. Henri and Henri (1898) were the first to describe childhood amnesia in the scientific literature. Freud (1905/1953) gave a description of the phenomenon and noted its relevance to topics such as repression. Freud thought the first few years of life were so inherently traumatic that adults had to repress. The psychiatrist Ernest Schachtel (1947/2000) also noted its importance in unraveling theories of the unconscious mind. Schachtel argued that this period extended to the age of 6, although most contemporary researchers argue it is by and large over at an earlier age. For most adults, it is surprising when we first encounter this idea. Two to 3 entire years of our life are not accessible to our consciousness. We know we lived them, but they are cut off from us. For a website on childhood amnesia, go to www.sagepub.com/schwartz.[3]

Some people do report memories from earlier ages. However, it is likely that many of these memories are not truly episodic memories. Rather, it is likely that they are stories people heard about themselves, which later because illusory self memories, or they may be memories of pictures they saw when they were somewhat older. They may also be false memories, the topic of the next chapter. In fact, although it is hard to test the reliability of such memories, most researchers studying the area would agree that any memories from the first 2 years of life are not true episodic memories, regardless of whether they reflect an event that happened or not.

In many cases, having a clear life boundary around the age of 2½ can prompt the first memory of early childhood (Eacott & Crawley, 1998; Usher & Neisser, 1993). That is, some obvious transition or big event at that age can leave a lasting episodic memory. For example, moving to a new house or a different city, the birth of a younger sibling, or some other big change can prompt the first memory. For example, one student described moving from San Antonio to Miami when she was 2½ years old. They drove the whole way—but all she remembers from the drive was seeing a shiny 18-wheeler truck with a picture of a baby on it. She has no idea why this image has stuck in her mind but feels certain that it occurred while they were on the road, moving to a new city. Another student of mine recently described being just over 2 years old, waiting for his little sister to be born, but then was sent to his grandfather's house because his mother went into labor just as Hurricane Andrew was approaching Miami. Most of the storm he does not remember, but he does remember listening to records at his grandfather's house while the storm raged outside. All those significant events—the hurricane and the birth of his sister—but what he remembers is the old-style turntable record player. This memory is consistent with the data in this area. According to Eacott and Crawley, adults who are 2.1 years or older than their younger sibling tend to remember the younger child's birth. Those younger have no conscious memory of their life before their sibling arrived. Eacott and Crawley find, however, that most people do not remember the birth of a sibling if the younger sibling is less than 3 years younger than the older sibling, but some do report it during that third year of life.

It is important to keep in mind that childhood amnesia refers to the memory of adults, not the memory of young children. Indeed, young children do remember events from earlier in their life. Indeed, 2-year-olds can describe events from several months earlier (Bauer, 2006). The issue of memory in childhood and memory development will be the focus of Chapter 11. However, specific events from this time period are just not accessible to the adult brain. We learn many things during this time period, not least of which are walking and talking. But nobody remembers their first step or first word in the way that they remember their first day of first grade or their first day of riding a bicycle.

Childhood amnesia is a difficult topic to investigate from an experimental point of view. First, the researchers can rarely verify the accuracy of the memories themselves. In some cases, parents or teachers can be contacted to verify that the event described really did occur, but in most studies, that is simply impossible. Indeed, new research on false memories suggests it is not difficult to induce a false memory of an early childhood experience (Strange, Sutherland, & Garry, 2006). Second, even if the event is verified, the researcher must rely on the subjective judgment by the participant that the memory is a real episodic memory and not the memory of a story told by someone else. Third, in some cases, these early memories may be associated with trauma or abuse. Therefore, the researcher needs to advise participants of the risks involved in the studies. Fourth, participants may have trouble dating an early memory. In some cases, such as the birth of a sibling, the information is datable by knowledge of the sibling's birthday and history, but other memories (a bad dream, a trip to the beach, an angry babysitter) may be much harder to place in time. Thus, even with a memory that can be considered true, it may sometimes be difficult to place it in, for example, the third, fourth, or fifth year of life. Fifth, it also appears that cultural factors influence the offset of childhood amnesia. Some cultural groups emphasize remembering events from childhood, and these cultures tend to have earlier offsets. Memory talk is most common among American parents and children relative to other cultures, which is correlated with an earlier offset of childhood amnesia among American participants than those from other cultures (Q. Wang, 2006). Therefore, researchers must track the cultural backgrounds of their participants as well.

Luckily, researchers have identified a number of methods for examining the offset of childhood amnesia (see Jack & Hayne, 2007). The simplest method is, of course, to ask people about their earliest memory. Across a number of studies, this procedure produces an average of about 3.1 years of age for the first reported memory by adults. This estimate of 3.1 comes from the participants themselves, not from objective sources that might be able to verify the memory. A second and more involved way of examining the offset of childhood amnesia is to target particular memories, such as the birth of a younger sibling, an illness, or a move to a new home or city. This method will only work for a subset of people who have such clear transitions, and it is not always clear how these people differ from those who do not have such transitions. Nonetheless, targeting transition memories actually yields a slightly younger estimate as most adults just a bit over 2 years older than their siblings remember their births. A third method involves asking for exhaustive searches of memory. In this technique, the participant must remember as many memories as possible from the earliest date forward. As adults retrieve childhood events, one sees a steady increase in the number of memories produced as they recall from age 3 and older (Jack & Hayne, 2007). Usually, there is just a smattering of memories from the earliest childhood years, but around 7 years old or so, the memories increase greatly. Fourth, and finally, some researchers have used the cue-word method. A particular word (e.g., *church, river, raccoon*) is provided, and the adult must remember the earliest memory associated with the particular word. Like the other methods, this method has a bottom limit of 2 years of age. In addition, the cue-word technique yields only a smattering of early childhood memories, although it is often quite successful at producing memories from later childhood and adolescence.

Childhood amnesia—age-related changes in self-concept: the view that childhood amnesia is caused by the development of a coherent psychological self.

Childhood amnesia—influence of language on memory development: the view that childhood amnesia is caused by the growth of language ability in the young child provides the structure and narrative schemas necessary to support episodic memories.

Childhood amnesia—neurological transitions in memory systems: the view that childhood amnesia is caused by changes in the brain as it matures.

Childhood amnesia—psychodynamic view: the view that childhood amnesia is caused by active repression.

Why do adults fail to recall events from their earliest years, and what changes that allows them to start remembering events from age 3 and more events from older years? A number of explanations have been offered with varying degrees of success at explaining the phenomena. These include but are not limited to the following:

1. **Psychodynamic view**

2. **Age-related changes in self-concept**

3. **Neurological transitions in memory systems**

4. **Influence of language on memory development**

We consider each in turn.

Psychodynamic View

Starting with Freud (1905/1953), some theorists considered that memories of early childhood were repressed. For Freud, this repression is important to personal development because early on, young children go through a period of sexual thinking and wishing with respect to their parents. (In light of what we know now about development, Freud's view on this is, of course, ridiculous.) As we grow older, however, we realize the rules and norms of our society, which make such wish fulfillment disgusting, vulgar, and inappropriate. Rather than acknowledge such incestuous thoughts, our subconscious blocks out all access to the first 5 or 6 years of our lives. In the Freudian view, psychoanalysis can unlock these early childhood memories, even for the youngest of ages. Thus, these memories are not completely lost; they are only lost to those who have not gone through psychoanalysis. No serious memory researcher takes any of this seriously anymore because there are absolutely no empirical data to support it. Yet, Freudian thinking is surprisingly still influential outside of academic psychology. Most memory researchers focus on the remaining explanations for childhood amnesia.

Age-Related Changes in Self-Concept

In this view, infants lack a coherent view of the self as differentiated from their surrounding environment. Therefore, there is no working self around which to associate episodic memories (Conway, 2005). Individual events do not become organized in the autobiographical memory schema described earlier. It is for this reason, perhaps, that our earliest memories often feel so fragmented. Around the age of 1.5, infants start to develop a sense of self, which continues to mature as the child starts his or her third and fourth year. For example, it is only at 18 months that infants start responding to their mirror image as if they are looking at themselves (Rochat, 2003). Before then, it is unclear what infants perceive when they look in the mirror. But they do not use the mirror to self-explore until after 18 months. In this view, as the sense of self develops, it allows the individual to code his or her memories into this developing sense of self. Thus, once this sense of coherent personhood begins to develop, only then can episodic memories be stored in such a way that we can retrieve them later in life. To summarize, it is not until this sense of self has been established that the person can begin to establish truly autobiographical memories (Howe & Courage, 1993).

Neurological Transitions in Memory Systems

Until recently, this view was the leading contender among serious memory researchers. Recently, however, this view has fallen into disfavor as evidence suggests that some neurological changes necessary for episodic memory occur much earlier than the offset of childhood amnesia, and others appear not to be online until after the offset of childhood amnesia. The neurological view argues that the relevant neural structures for forming episodic and hence autobiographical memories are not fully mature until a child reaches about age 3. Therefore, long-term episodic memories cannot be maintained for the simple reason that the neural machinery is not yet in place (see Hayne, 2004). Two areas of the brain have become the focus of this explanation. First, the learning area of the limbic system known as the hippocampus continues to mature in infants until the age of 3. However, memory studies often yield ages of the offset of childhood amnesia before then. We also know that the prefrontal lobes are still maturing well into childhood, perhaps still changing and growing in adolescence. However, this growth cannot account for the offset of childhood amnesia, which occurs much earlier.

Influence of Language on Memory Development

In this view, the growth of language ability in the young child provides the structure and narrative schemas necessary to support episodic memories. As our ability to speak and communicate grows, we are able to start forming episodic memories that will be retrievable as adults. That is, before we have sufficient language abilities, we do not encode information in words or in narrative form. The forms that we do encode information at an early age are nonlinguistic and without narrative form. As adults, we do not have access to these early forms of memory, but we do have access to our growing linguistic representations.

Although this is not as intuitively straightforward as some of the other explanations are, there are considerable data to support this view (see Hayne, 2004). First, women tend to have an earlier offset of childhood amnesia than do men, and women develop linguistically earlier than men do. Second, studies on memory in children show that, regardless of gender, those with stronger linguistic abilities at 3 or 4 years of age are more likely to recall events from that age later in childhood (Simcock & Hayne, 2002). Third, information that is encoded in nonverbal forms in early childhood tends to stay that way and is not later converted into a verbal format in later childhood (Hayne, 2004).

An interesting experiment done with children supports the importance of language development in the causes of childhood amnesia. Simcock and Hayne (2002) presented 2-, 3-, and 4-year-old children with a demonstration of their "incredible shrinking machine" (see Figure 7.5). An object, such as a beach ball, is placed at the top of the machine. It drops in and the machine makes a lot of noise. After a minute of noise making, a smaller beach ball emerges from the bottom of the machine. Simcock and Hayne "shrunk" a number of objects for the children who watched the machine with rapt attention. Simcock and Hayne then tested the verbal abilities of the children and tested to see if they knew all of the words that described the shrunken objects. And, in case you were worried, they did not shrink any heads for the children.

Simcock and Haynes then tracked down the children a year later. Many of the children still remembered the "incredible shrinking machine" and described the event from a year earlier. This is consistent with other research that suggests that young children do not immediately forget complex events—it is only later as adults that these events are forgotten. However, the children only remembered those objects for which they possessed the vocabulary for when they witnessed the event. That is, if they knew the word *beach ball* when they were 2, they would often recall seeing a beach ball being shrunk a year later. However, if they did not know the word *beach ball* at age 2, they would not recall that object being shrunk a year later. They found no exceptions to this pattern—if the child did not know the word at the time of seeing the event, he or she did not recall that object a year later. This supports the idea that language is critical to the offset of childhood amnesia.

Figure 7.5 The magic shrinking machine.

SOURCE: Simcock and Hayne (2002).

Childhood Amnesia May Result From Multiple Causes

Indeed, the true explanation for childhood amnesia probably requires some mix of developing brains, developing self-concept, and developing language (though probably not the Freudian explanation). The development of a self-reflective episodic memory system is a complex piece of machinery, one that, as far as we know, only exists in humans (see Hampton & Schwartz, 2004). Thus, it is likely that the development of such a system is complex. Childhood amnesia may simply be a symptom of the complexity of a system that requires episodic memory, a sense of self, and language skills all to be operational at once.

FLASHBULB MEMORIES

The shocking news of the attack on the World Trade Center in 2001, the attack on Pearl Harbor in 1941, the assassinations of John F. Kennedy, Robert Kennedy, and Martin Luther King Jr. in the 1960s, and the death of Princess Diana in the 1997. These momentous events in the history of our culture provide people of certain ages with strong memories of where they were and what they were doing during these events, even if they had nothing to do with them directly. To each generation, a different event may have the power of commanding such vivid personal memories. Indeed, think of an older adult who may have been a young child during the attack on Pearl Harbor, a young adult when JFK was assassinated, and approaching retirement when 9/11 occurred. Other cultures have had their share of events creating flashbulb memories, from tsunamis to earthquakes to assassinations.

To start off with, however, we will define what a flashbulb memory is. Flashbulb memories are highly confident personal memories of surprising events. Typically, they have been studied by looking at public events. This is advantageous because many people will have flashbulb memories in response to the same event. We may also have flashbulb memories for other surprising events, such as, on the positive side, when you got the letter of acceptance to your first-choice college or, on the negative side, when you got the news that a close family member had suddenly died. Because not everyone gets accepted to college at the same time, the public events provide a nice benchmark to study flashbulb memories. For the neuroimaging of flashbulb memories, go to www.sagepub.com/schwartz.[4]

The first empirical study on flashbulb memories concerned Americans' memories for the spate of dreadful assassinations in the 1960s (R. Brown & Kulik, 1977), including President John F. Kennedy and civil rights leader Martin Luther King Jr. This first study was done several years after the murders, so there was no possible way of verifying the memory reports of individuals. However, some interesting facts emerged from the study. First, despite the passage of time, people still claimed to have vivid, confident, and detailed flashbulb memories of some of the events. Second, the older memories (the death of JFK) were just as strong as later ones (the death of MLK). Third, the more relevant the event was to an individual, the more likely the person was to have a flashbulb memory of the event. Thus, for example, African Americans were much more likely to have a flashbulb memory of the assassination of Martin Luther King Jr. than were European Americans. For these reasons, Brown and Kulik (1977) argued that the term *flashbulb* "fit." It was as if people recorded the event and hit the "now, print" button in their memory. More recently, evidence suggests that it is not necessary for the news to be surprising. Indeed, many French citizens have flashbulb memories of the death of their former president, François Mitterand, even though his death did not come as a surprise (Curci & Luminet, 2009).

In a large multicity experiment, William Hirst and his colleagues examined flashbulb memories for the terrorist attacks of 9/11 (Hirst et al., 2009). In initial reports, participants reported strong negative emotions. However, 1 year later and nearly 4 years later, when participants were recontacted and asked about the event, they remembered where and when they heard the news but tended to forget their strong emotional reactions. Most of this forgetting was apparent 1 year after the event. After that, the memories stabilized. Thus, although a strong emotional impact appears to be a prerequisite for a flashbulb memory to form, remembering the emotional response itself seems to be less important than remembering the details that people speak about (where and when you heard the news).

Accuracy of Flashbulb Memories

As in many areas of autobiographical memory, there is an issue of correspondence. How do flashbulb memories correspond to the actual situation in which people "heard the news"? Think about your own flashbulb memories. Each person is likely to have strong feelings about these memories. You remember the events vividly, and you feel strongly that our memories are accurate. However, a series of studies suggests that as vivid as our flashbulb memories are and as confident as we are that they are real, they are subject to the same distortions and inaccuracies as normal memories. We will consider a few of the studies that address this issue.

Weaver (1993) conducted a study comparing an ordinary memory and a flashbulb memory. Weaver was teaching a class on cognitive psychology and wanted to do a demonstration of autobiographical memory. He asked each of his students to write down the details of an ordinary interaction with a college roommate or friend. This was in class on January 16, 1991. That evening, the United States Air Force began bombing Baghdad, Iraq, to start the first Gulf War in 1991. Many Americans who were adults at the time formed flashbulb memories of that evening and can still remember where they were when they heard the news of the start of that war (e.g., "I was in graduate school at the time and heard the news while working the shot clock at a college basketball game"). Two days later (January 18, 1991), Weaver's students wrote down as many details as they could remember from the ordinary interaction with their roommate and their memory of hearing the news of the war.

At the end of the semester, 3 months later, Weaver asked the students to describe the contents of each memory. The students answered questions concerning the events and indicated their confidence in the accuracy of their memories. Eight months after that (or nearly a year after the original events), some students were contacted again and asked to describe their memories yet again. This allowed Weaver to compare the accuracy of the memories over time. He assumed that the report given the next day after the event would be the benchmark with which to measure memory accuracy. He could then compare what people reported 3 months and 11 months after the event with the initial report and determine the correspondence.

Weaver (1993) found more similarities between the regular memory and the flashbulb memory than he did differences. The amount and detail in the memory reports declined over time at about the same rate. Moreover, the students remembered about the same amount of details from each event. Accuracy of the two memories was equivalent, meaning that discrepancies between the original description and later descriptions were about the same for both the roommate memory and the flashbulb memory. Notice here that Weaver found that flashbulb memories contained errors. They were not indelibly inscribed into people's memory as Brown and Kulik (1977) had originally thought.

The lack of correspondence between the initial report and the later report could be either small discrepancies or, in some cases, completely different versions of the event. A small discrepancy might be originally reporting that the event happened just before dinner, then later reporting it happened just after dinner. They could also be bigger discrepancies, such as reporting originally you heard the about the news from a professor and then later remembering that you heard it on the television news. One might think that flashbulb memories would be immune to such discrepancies, but in fact, Weaver's (1993) study and many studies since have demonstrated that errors do creep into flashbulb memories and at about the same rate as they occur in normal memories. Nor are inaccuracies in flashbulb memories only found in the Weaver study. Studies now consistently find errors in flashbulb memories. For example, in a study of flashbulb memories for the acquittal of O. J. Simpson, errors in flashbulb memories were clear as well (Schmolck, Buffalo, & Squire, 2000). Thus, despite our beliefs that our flashbulb memories are potent and strong, evidence suggests that they are not more accurate than normal memories. Indeed, it is likely that the studies overestimate accuracy because the studies require participants to make original reports of the event. Participants may, therefore, recall making the original report.

One critical difference did exist between regular memories and flashbulb memories. The confidence that the memory was accurate remained high in flashbulb memories 11 months after the event. Confidence in flashbulb memories did decline over time, but not nearly as much as the confidence in the roommate event. Thus, Weaver (1993) argued that the true hallmark of a flashbulb memory was not how accurate it was but rather the confidence that we assert that our memories are accurate. In other words, something about the flashbulb experiences and talking about them later form a subjectively strong memory even when it does not correspond to the actual events that we witnessed or participated in (see Figure 7.6).

In fact, more recently, some researchers have begun to think that the aspect of flashbulb memories that does make them unique is the vividness with which we remember them and the confidence that we feel, even if they are no more accurate than ordinary memories (Talarico & Rubin, 2007). Talarico and Rubin (2007), for example, compared memories of their personal whereabouts when they heard the news of 9/11 and an ordinary event around the same time. Like Weaver, they found that the flashbulb memories were no more accurate than the ordinary memory, but vividness ratings, confidence ratings, and other subjective ratings were all higher for the flashbulb memory than for the normal memory. Regardless of the actual accuracy of flashbulb memories, they feel more accurate to us.

However, some more recent studies suggest that there is, indeed, a higher degree of accuracy for flashbulb memories than normal memories, if one looks only at the specific memories of personal context. In most of the studies discussed so far, people could report both their personal whereabouts as to where they heard the news but also information pertaining to the event itself—which most participants do not actually witness firsthand or participate in. For example, you might remember that you were on vacation in the mountains when you heard the news that Princess Diana had died, but you can also remember that she died in a car crash and that others were killed as well. The memory of your own situation is considered the memories for personal context.

In one study of the flashbulb memory of an earthquake in Turkey, Turkish subjects had high recall and low inaccuracies in their later report when only personal context was considered (Er, 2003). Furthermore, flashbulb memories of 9/11 have also been shown to be highly accurate when only personal context information is considered (Tekcan, Ece, Gulgoz, & Er, 2003). In this study, Turkish participants' memory for the actual events of 9/11

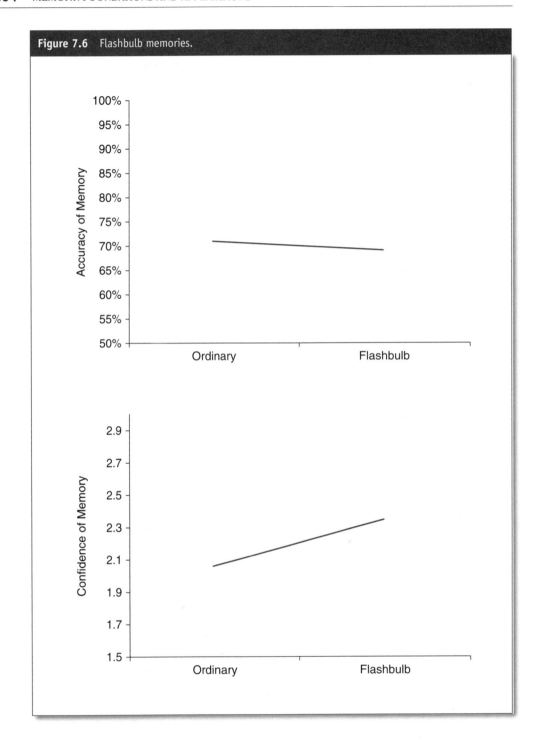

Figure 7.6 Flashbulb memories.

shifted from the original report, but there were almost no deviations in their reports of personal whereabouts. Thus, it is possible that in the earlier studies, context memory might have remained accurate, but the researchers did not differentiate between the two types of information.

An additional consideration is what kinds of events evoke flashbulb memories. They must be surprising and important. This may vary by proximity and relevance. Therefore, it is likely that more Americans have flashbulb memories for when and where they were when the levies broke in New Orleans flooding the city during Hurricane Katrina than they do for the Christmas tsunami that destroyed many areas in southeast Asia. Conversely, it is likely that more Thais have flashbulb memories of the tsunami than they do of Hurricane Katrina. Consistent with this view, Conway et al. (1994) found high consistency across time in the flashbulb memories of British citizens to the sudden resignation of Prime Minister Margaret Thatcher. On the other hand, Danish and American participants showed much fewer flashbulb reports and much less consistency and more error in their memories of the event. Even though the resignation of a leader may be different than earthquakes and other tragedies, it still reached a level of importance to induce an accurate flashbulb in the British but not in non-British. As surprising and relevant as her resignation was to British citizens, it simply did not reach the level of flashbulb induction for either the Americans or the Dutch.

In another interesting take on flashbulb memories, Kensinger and Schacter (2006) examined memories of baseball fans in New York and Boston for the surprise Game 7 victory of the Boston Red Sox over the New York Yankees in the American League Championship in 2004. This is an interesting study because the event was extremely positive for fans of the Boston team but very negative for the fans of the New York team. Thus, using the same event, Kensinger and Schacter were able to examine the effect of emotional valence (that is, if we have positive or negative feelings about the event) on the memories of those individuals. To ensure that the New York fans and Boston fans did not differ in other ways with respect to their memories, Kensinger and Schacter also tested their memory for a personal event and for their memory of the 2004 presidential debates, which took place during the same month as the baseball game. First, the fans of both teams did not differ with respect to their memories of the personal event and the presidential debate. However, when it came to the game, differences emerged. For the New York fans, there was decidedly more consistency between an initial report and a later report than for the Boston fans. However, the Boston fans showed considerable overconfidence in the accuracy of their memories, which the New York fans did not. Kensinger and Schacter suggest that this supports the idea that positive events lead to more distortion and overconfidence, whereas negative events lead to less overconfidence and more accuracy.

Theories of Flashbulb Memory Formation

Special Mechanism Approach. In this view, there is a unique and special mechanism responsible for flashbulb memories only. Originally called the "Now, print" mechanism by R. Brown and Kulik (1977), it stipulates that flashbulb memories are virtually literal representations of the what, how, and where of the original event. In theory, when an event of great emotional impact and importance occurs, the system immediately encodes it as it occurred with great detail and vividness. The implication of this model is that the flashbulb memories created will be subjectively strong. As we have seen, this is true. But the other implication of the model is that flashbulb memories will be accurate. The majority of the research does support the idea that errors do enter our flashbulb memories and are not always veridical.

Ordinary Mechanism Approach. This view claims that flashbulb memories are simply normal memories but memories of emotionally charged and socially significant events. In this view, normal encoding mechanisms create the flashbulb memories. As such, they are subject to the same forgetting processes and the same likelihood of becoming distorted as ordinary memories. Accordingly, in this view, errors will occur in flashbulb memories, and those errors will be consistent with the meaning of the event rather than literal features of the event. Indeed, the research that shows inconsistencies in flashbulb memories tend to show that people's later recall is more schema consistent (Talarico & Rubin, 2003; but see Tekcan et al., 2003). The difficulty for this approach is explaining why flashbulb memories are so vivid and held with such confidence.

To summarize, flashbulb memories are the highly salient memories that we have of surprising events. The paramount feature of these memories is that we feel that they remain strong even after much time elapses between the event and the retrieval. They have typically been studied by examining memories of tragic public events. Of course, we also may have flashbulb memories of the momentous events in our private lives. Studying the public events provides a better method of evaluating flashbulb memories.

INTERIM SUMMARY

Autobiographical memory refers to the memories we have of ourselves, both individual events from our lives and the facts of our lives. An important theory developed by Martin Conway and his colleagues examines the representation of autobiographical memory. In the theory, there are four overlapping levels of organization in autobiographical memory: event-specific memories, general events, lifetime periods, and the working self. Childhood amnesia refers to the observation that adults remember little to nothing from the first 3 to 4 years of life. A number of theories have been advanced to account for amnesia for early childhood. Flashbulb memory refers to our vivid personal recollection of surprising and emotional public events. In general, people have a great level of confidence in their flashbulb memories, but the memories are no more or less accurate than other memories of ordinary events.

DIARY STUDIES AND AUTOBIOGRAPHICAL MEMORY

Go into a bookstore or a stationery store, and one can find dozens of different kinds of diaries. Some have austere black binders, whereas others have kittens, hearts, or superheroes on them. You can usually find more diaries in a typical Barnes and Noble bookstore than you can find books about science. This suggests that, at one time or another, many people keep diaries, which essentially are written-down memories and records of a person's life. Some people use the diaries to schedule their days, whereas others choose to write down their feelings. In memory research, we can use diaries to keep a near-veridical record of a person's life so that we can test his or her autobiographical memory later.

Diaries provide a written record by which memories can be compared. As such, diaries are extremely useful tools in the study of autobiographical memory. A memory diary is a bit different from the diary in which you record your feelings. In a memory diary, the participant must record facts and then attempt to quantify his or her feelings. In particular, an individual records events from his or her everyday life in a diary, usually of a specific form. An entry in the diary will include information about the what, where, when, and who of an event. This record is then turned in to an experimenter who can later devise questions based on each record for the participant to answer.

For example, on a particular day, let's say September 19, 2008, the participant will have to record one event from that day. Here's what it might look like, based on your author's memory diary.

Date: September 19, 2008

What: had a tire with a leak. I went the gas station and put air in the tire after dropping my daughter at school.

Where: in the car, near home.

When: in the morning, when I was taking my daughter to school.

Who: I didn't tell my daughter about it, as she had to get to school. After filling my own tires, I helped a woman fill her car's tires with air as she was dressed in fancy work clothes and did not want to get dirty.

Pleasantness: mildly unpleasant.

Emotion: low; just a tire low on air.

Importance: minor.

Diary studies: the experimenters or participants record events from their own lives and keep track of events over long periods of time. Later, their memory for these events can be tested.

In some **diary studies** aimed at autobiographical memory, the experimenters themselves recorded events from their own lives and kept track of events over long periods of time. In one study, a researcher went back and tested his memory after 20 years since the original events (White, 2002). In contrast, other studies ask volunteers to keep diaries. These studies, typically with student populations, tend to be of shorter duration (e.g., 5 months) because of the difficulty of contacting people after a longer period of time (Larsen & Thompson, 1995). These studies have the advantage of measuring memory for events that really happen in a person's life and that are recorded that day in a veridical format. The disadvantage is that, at least, at the longer retention intervals, they depend on the memories of interested parties, that is, the memory researchers themselves or their willing students.

In one landmark diary study, Willem Wagenaar, a Dutch psychologist, recorded over 2,400 events over the course of 6 years (Wagenaar, 1986). Each event was record in terms of four major features: what happened, where it happened, when it happened, and who was present in addition to the diarist. In addition, each memory was coded in terms of pleasantness, emotion, and importance. After each entry was made, it was turned over to a colleague who did not allow Wagenaar to see them during the "retention interval." Six years later, Wagenaar's colleague used different features of his record as cues for recalling the memory. For example, if "what" was the cue, his colleague would present him with "saw the famous painting *The Scream,*" and he would attempt to remember with whom we went to the art museum, when he made the visit, and, in this case, where the art museum was. If he could not recall based on one cue, he gave himself another cue. If this was not successful, he was given another cue. Each memory prompt could receive up to three cues. If he could not retrieve the fourth feature, based on the first three, Wagenaar admitted to forgetting the event. For other items, Wagenaar's colleague would tell him where an event occurred, and Wagenaar would start with that as the cue to remember the event. For yet other items, the "who" was used, whereas for other items, the "when" was used as the cue.

Wagenaar found that he could, given enough cues, recall 80% of the events he had recorded. However, in some cases, it took him multiple cues to do so. And not all cues were equally successful at prompting the memory of the event. "What," "where," and "who" were all equally good cues to retrieving an event, but "when" was much worse than the other three classes of cues. In addition, highly emotional and pleasant events were remembered better than less emotional and less pleasant events.

One problem with this diary study (and others that followed) is that it tests only one person's memory. In particular, this study examined the memory of a professional memory researcher. Although being a memory researcher does not immediately imply that the person has an exceptional memory, it is likely that a deep interest in the processes of memory might affect the keeping of a memory diary. However, most of the results seem to hold up when nonspecialists are asked to keep diaries (Larsen & Thompson, 1995). In these studies, the researchers recruited college undergraduates to keep memory diaries. And the college students' abilities to recall events differ little from Professor Wagenaar. The astonishing observation from these studies is that people can recall so many of the events. More recent diary studies tend to focus on the "when" aspect of autobiographical memory, that is, how people place the event in time (i.e., Burt, Kemp, & Conway, 2001).

One of the themes of this text is to emphasize the many ways in which we can improve our own memory abilities. From this perspective, diaries are useful memory devices. They do not help us learn material for school, but they do help us retrieve the events from our lives. With them, they provide powerful cues to retrieve the events from our lives. Without them, we are left to the whims of the retrieval cues we can generate or are present around us. Thus, for people who value their own autobiographical memories, diaries can be very useful memory aids. Many people complain that they can no longer remember vacations, fancy dinners, and the like. Keeping a memory diary is one way to combat this. Recording the what, where, and who of an event provides strong retrieval cues to unlock the memory of that event. For example, if someone is trying to remember who was at your 20th birthday party and asks you (after all, it was your party), you might be hard-pressed to remember all the people there. But you can check your diary. In today's world, this might also be accomplished online by keeping a memory blog. Seeing the name of your first cousin might prompt the memory of her actually being there and spilling some ketchup onto your mother's dress. This memory might not have been retrieved unless you had your cousin's name written down in your memory diary. Thus, maintaining a memory diary is a helpful chore if you want to improve your ability to remember autobiographical events.

Mnemonic Improvement Tip 7.1

Keep a memory diary or memory blog. Maintaining a memory diary/blog allows you to later return to that diary and cue your memory. The diary itself serves as an external memory aid, storing the events of your life. But more significantly, the memory diary triggers our own episodic memory of particular events. Diaries can be very powerful memory aids.

THE CUE-WORD TECHNIQUE FOR ELICITING AUTOBIOGRAPHICAL MEMORIES AND THE REMINISCENCE BUMP

The **cue-word technique** is a common tool for investigating autobiographical memory. In the cue-word technique, an ordinary word is provided to participants, and they are asked to provide the first memory—from any point in their life—that the word elicits. The cue-word technique has been used to explore childhood amnesia when the memories are directed toward early experiences. But it can also be done in which the person is also free to choose memories from any point in his or her life. Consider the following words and the memories that they elicit for you:

> **Cue-word technique:** an ordinary word is provided to participants and they are asked to provide the first memory—from any point in their life—that the word elicits.

1. bird
2. whisper
3. wrinkle
4. lazy
5. saddle

Chances are that each word quickly elicited an event from your life. Perhaps you thought about the time you fed the pigeons at a park with your significant other or the time a crazy swan attacked you. Perhaps you remember whispering to your friend about a party during memory class last week. In some cases, the memories may be strong and painful, such as the time you slid off your saddle and broke your leg. Some may be important, but others may be unimportant, such as remembering bringing your dry cleaning back when the cleaner failed to get out the wrinkles that were in your clothes. Most memories are relatively recent, like the recent evening when you felt lazy and ordered out for food instead of cooking yourself. Most people can report events pretty quickly after being given a cue word, although occasionally a particular word will fail to elicit any memory at all.

In one version of the cue-word technique, participants are asked to think of any memory from any point in their life elicited by the cue word. When this cue word technique is used on people older than age 35, an interesting phenomenon occurs. The memories that people describe are not evenly spaced over their lifetime (see Figure 7.7). First, there is the period of childhood amnesia from which no events are reported. Then reported memories

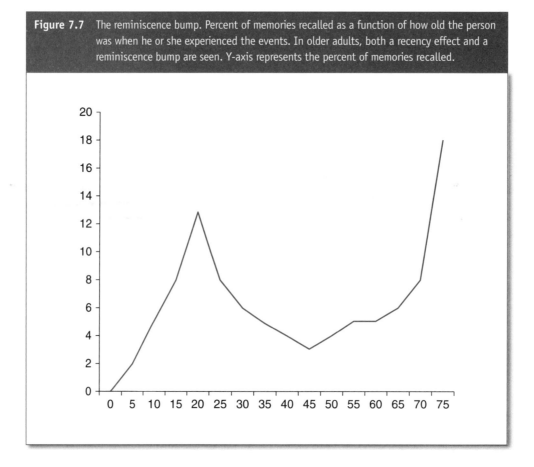

Figure 7.7 The reminiscence bump. Percent of memories recalled as a function of how old the person was when he or she experienced the events. In older adults, both a recency effect and a reminiscence bump are seen. Y-axis represents the percent of memories recalled.

Reminiscence bump: the spike in recalled memories corresponding to late adolescence to early adulthood, or roughly between the ages of 16 and 25.

increase through later childhood. Reported memories then peak in the range between ages 16 and 25. There is then a decline, and memories after 25 are not as likely to be retrieved in response to cues than those before 25. Finally, there is a recency effect, reflecting that lots of memories are recalled from the past 2 years or so. The **reminiscence bump** refers to a spike in recalled memories corresponding to late adolescence to early adulthood, or roughly between the ages of 16 and 25.

The reminiscence bump refers to the number of memories from early adulthood recalled in response to cue words given to relatively older adults. That is, when given a word such as *river,* a 50-year-old will be more likely to recall an event involving a river from when he or she was 18 than when that person was 8 or 38 years old. As seen in Figure 7.7, the reminiscence bump is quite strong, although not as strong as the recency effect. Thus, when middle-aged adults or older adults are given the cue-word method, there are more autobiographical events retrieved from this period of life than the period before it or after it. When older adults are asked to retrieve memories in response to cue words, they do show a preponderance of recent events, as do younger adults. However, they also show a tendency to report older memories from the 16 to 25 age range than they do more recent memories. That is, a 60-year-old will recall more events from 40 years ago than he or she will from 20 years ago. Thus, it is not recency that drives the reminiscence effect. It is rather something about the memories we form during this particular period of time that makes them particularly accessible later in life.

In some studies, participants are given sets of cues relating to specific topics, such as words that are only about music, films, book, or public events. Regardless of the type of stimuli, a robust reminiscence effect is still seen (see Conway, 2005). The effect is also robust across cultures. Despite the differences among American, British, Chinese, Bangladeshi, and Japanese cultures, all show reminiscence bumps in the same age range (Conway, Wang, Hanyu, & Hasque, 2005). However, Gabston (2008) found that African Americans showed a shift toward earlier in life for the reminiscence bump, down to age 11, in comparison with a European American population whose bump does not start until a few years later. Gabston looked at several factors that might explain this difference but was unable to find any conclusive explanation. Nonetheless, it does suggest that cultural differences might affect the reminiscence bump after all.

Another interesting feature of the reminiscence bump is that it illustrates the Pollyanna principle. The Pollyanna principle refers to the observation that people tend to focus on positive aspects of events rather than negative ones. This principle applies to memory. People are more likely to recall positive events and positive aspects of complex events. In reminiscence bump experiments, most of the memories reported tend to be positive ones (Walker, Skrowronski, & Thompson, 2003). Because people with more optimistic outlooks on life tend to have better psychological outcomes, remembering more positive events than negative events can be seen as adaptive.

There are several explanations for why the reminiscence bump occurs, although no single view is without problems. The views can be divided into memory-fluency views, neurological fluency views, and sociocultural views. Let's consider each in turn.

Memory-Fluency. This view is based on the idea that the period between ages 16 and 25 is simply a time period with many "first experiences," that is, events that are unique and novel. Many studies show that which is unique and novel tends to be better remembered. These include but are not limited to first romantic encounters, first jobs, first time away from home, and the first day of college. In this view, these years are a time of rapid change, which render the events that take place during this time period highly memorable (Conway, 2005). The problem with this view is that typically only 20% of the memories retrieved are actually of "first experiences." Furthermore, we find it in cultures where many of these events typically happen on the earlier side of the 16 to 25 age range and on the older side of the range and regardless of whether there are big changes in place of residency and occupation. Third, the reasoning itself is a bit circular. That is, we already know from the data that memory during this time period is more accessible. Accounting for that by arguing that memories are more fluent this time is just deferring an explanation.

Neurological Views. This view centers on the idea that young adults have the most efficient encoding system based on optimal maturation of brain mechanisms of memory before the inevitable decline in memory abilities associated with age. For example, it is well known that young adults are better than both children and older adults in working memory. Perhaps older memories are more salient from this period because the brain mechanisms responsible for their creation were working optimally at the time to create the strongest memories. Conway (2005) speculated that the 16 to 25 age range represents the maximal maturity of the fronto-hippocampal circuitry, which maximally encodes information. Conway also points out that this view is supported by the cultural universality of the phenomena. That is, we all have the same brains, even if different cultures emphasize different time courses for dating, sex, and marriage, on one hand, and learning an occupation, on the other.

Sociocultural Views. In this view, the 16 to 25 age range is associated with changes in identity formation of the individual. During this time period, people make decisions about who they are and where they are going as an individual. The particular decisions a person makes may vary from culture to culture, but the time period of these decisions is the same. The fluency, therefore, espoused in the first view is merely a symptom of the changes occurring in a person's life. This view suggests that that the reminiscence bump should consist of many memories that are consistent with a culture's particular set of transitions. Indeed, this turns out to be the case. Thomsen and Berntsen (2008) found that, among Danish elders, the bump was particularly noticeable for the memory of events that were consistent with cultural life scripts, such as first jobs, dating, and leaving home, whereas it was less noticeable for less socially marked memories, such as travel, memorable meals, or political memories. That is, the older adults showed a bigger reminiscence bump for their memories of culturally consistent events than for their memories of culturally inconsistent events. Thomsen and Berntsen argue that these scripts themselves, culturally defined, provide the set of cues to rehearsal and experience, forming the bulwark of autobiographical memory. One culture may emphasize educational landmarks, another culture may emphasize family milestones, but for both, life scripts emphasize the importance of young adulthood. Gabston's (2008) finding of differences between two cultural groups in the United States supports this view.

To summarize, the reminiscence bump means the large number of memories from late adolescence to early adulthood remembered by older adults (well, 35+) when they are given cue words and asked to remember events from any point in their lives. Scholars have varied in their interpretation of this phenomenon, but its existence seems to be real and not limited to those from Western cultures (Berntsen & Rubin, 2004). The explanation for this phenomenon remains elusive, but the most recent theories focus on how events from this life period fit into a particular culture's view of how lives are defined.

SUBJECTIVE EXPERIENCE AND AUTOBIOGRAPHICAL MEMORY

Recall an event from early childhood. Imagine the event in your mind. Don't read on until you have this image in your mind's eye (that is, activate a visual memory in working memory). What do you see? Where are you in the memory? Are you seeing the event as if through your own eyes or are you looking at the "memory" from another vantage point, that is, seeing yourself in the memory?

Many people report "observer memories" from early childhood (Nigro & Neisser, 1983). **Observer memories** are memories in which we take the vantage point of an outside observer and see ourselves as actors in our visual memory. In contrast, from later childhood and more recent adult memories, most people report "field memories." **Field memories** are autobiographical and visual memories in which we see the memory as if we were looking at the event through our own eyes.

> **Observer memories**: autobiographical memories in which we take the vantage point of an outside observer and see ourselves as actors in our visual memory.
>
> **Field memories**: autobiographical and visual memories in which we see the memory as if we were looking at the event through our own eyes.

It turns out that these points of view in memory are flexible. Once alerted to this difference, people can move back and forth from field and observer memories as they think about an event from the past (Robinson & Swanson, 1993). However, initially, a larger proportion of memories from early childhood do take the observer form than do the field memories. Interestingly, however, observer memories are associated with less emotional content and reduced sensory vividness of the memory. Even when participants consciously shift from field to observer memories, their ratings of emotionality decrease (Berntsen & Rubin, 2006).

The relation between field and observer memories is an important one. People suffering from posttraumatic stress disorder (PTSD) are often bothered by recurrent memories of the traumatic event that haunts them. McIsaac and Eich (2004) found that when patients suffering from PTSD retrieved memories as field memories, their emotional response was more negative and more intense. However, retrieving from an observer perspective lowered the negative emotional response. It is possible that switching to the observer perspective puts some emotional distance between one's sense of self and the memory. McIsaac and Eich argue that this is potentially useful in the treatment of PTSD.

Training participants to recall their traumatic memories in observer mode will allow them to think and cope with their past without that memory eliciting the full weight of negative emotions that it is associated with.

Little is known about the relation between observer and field memories and how they are enacted in the brain. Both involve visual imagery, and therefore, it is likely that the occipital lobe will be active when remembering from either perspective. It is clear, however, that observer memories are necessarily reconstructive. We cannot see our entire bodies when we perform an action, unless we do so in front of a mirror. Thus, the observer mode of seeing yourself carrying out the event from a vantage point other than your eyes is not a veridical representation. How we transform our memories from field into observer is still a subject not yet properly investigated.

Involuntary Memories

Even though you are on a date with your new girlfriend/boyfriend, you hear a song on the radio that reminds you of your old flame. You try to push it out of your mind because you want to be in the moment with the new person. More seriously, a soldier returning from war may want very much to not be reminded of his or her war experiences. However, **environmental cues may still trigger an unpleasant and involuntary memory.** We all experience involuntary memories, but it is only in PTSD that we get overwhelmed with involuntary memories. In one study, Berntsen and Rubin (2008) asked participants to record involuntary memories in a memory diary. In particular, participants were asked to record involuntary memories that referred to a serious (or traumatic) event in their lives. They found that involuntary memories are frequent but decline somewhat with age. There was no particular pattern, however, that predicted a person's involuntary memory of a traumatic event.

Borrowed Memories

Does our autobiographical memory only come from our own life? Consider the issue of **borrowed memories.** As an example, a friend (call him Joe) once told me a story that he had a clear memory of being bitten by a mean dog that lived in the house behind his when he was a child. Yet Joe's parents claim that it was his older brother who was actually bitten by this dog when he was about 6 and his brother was about 8. Somewhere along the line, Joe misattributed his memory of having seen and later heard about his brother's injury as his own. The older brother has the scar to prove that the bite was really on his hand, not Joe's.

> **Borrowed memories**: when we feel a memory is our own when it actually corresponds to an event in another's past.

It turns out that "borrowed memories" are more common among twins than among others. Only 8% of siblings have memories such as the one I described above, but the percentage rises to about 70% among twins (Sheen, Kemp, & Rubin, 2001). Among identical twins, the percentages are even higher (Kuntay, Gulgoz, & Tekcan, 2004). Like the memory above, for twins, these borrowed events tend to come from early in childhood. Because twins spend so much time together, it is likely that the borrowed memories are the result of source monitoring confusions. Memories of the twin's events are remembered, but then source monitoring failures misattribute the memory to oneself rather than the twin.

MUSIC AND AUTOBIOGRAPHICAL MEMORY

For many of us, music is an integral part of our life. Many of us listen to music for large portions of our waking life. A common experience for most people is hearing an old song on the radio. The song elicits a memory, perhaps a memory of dancing with your date at the prom or "your song" with an old boyfriend or girlfriend. The song seems to transport us back in time, and we relive the happy moment. Thus, anecdotally, it appears that music is a powerful cue for autobiographical memories. This issue was investigated experimentally by Janata et al. (2007). They collected a large selection of music from the popular literature by downloading songs from the iTunes top 100 songs from the past few years. They then played 30-second excerpts from these songs to students and asked the students to report any autobiographical memories cued by the song. They found that more than 30% of songs elicited autobiographical memories from the participants. Most of these memories were emotional memories, with a majority being positive in affect. They found that most memories were of event-specific memories, but some songs elicited general events or lifetime periods. Many of the songs also elicited feelings of nostalgia (a longing for an earlier better time). The study confirms the idea that music, particularly popular songs, can be powerful retrieval cues for autobiographical memories.

SENSE OF SMELL AND AUTOBIOGRAPHICAL MEMORY

The famous writer Marcel Proust was fascinated by the relation between the sense of smell and memory. He wrote several famous novels, which fundamentally deal with how one's memory affects one's sense of self. In one of his most vivid and famous passages, the main character (named Marcel) describes how the smell and taste of a small French pastry called a madeleine evokes a memory of his peaceful childhood (Proust, 1928). This description captures the strong connections between odors and memory. Indeed, as we discussed in Chapter 2, odors can be powerful cues to retrieve events from our lives. On a neural level, the strong connections between the olfactory bulb and the limbic system may drive this phenomenon. But what exactly is the relation of the sense of smell to autobiographical memory? For Proust's description of this experience, go to www.sagepub.com/schwartz.[5]

Take a moment and visit your spice cabinet. Pick a jar at random and don't look at the name on the jar or at what the contents look like. Just open it and bring it under your nose. Does it elicit a memory? From what time period in your life? Does it bring back any emotions? If the first jar you select does not work, try another one. Sooner or later as you go through a well-stocked spice shelf, you, like Proust, may be transported back to your grandmother's kitchen and will have a powerful emotional memory in the process. Hopefully, at any rate, you will be transported back to your grandmother's kitchen and not, say, to your elementary school cafeteria, with probably less warm and emotionally satisfying feelings. Let's turn now to the empirical studies done on this topic.

Willander and Larsson (2007) conducted a fascinating study on the role odors play in autobiographical memory, finding that odors alone can create powerful memory effects. They tested three conditions to explore the role of odors in autobiographical memory. In one condition, they presented odors alone and asked participants to report the first autobiographical memory that they experienced. In the second condition, they presented the names (as words) without the smell accompanying it. In the third condition, they presented the name of the odor and the actual odor. As expected, the name-only condition produced the fewest and the least emotional autobiographical memories. However, the odor-alone condition actually produced more, older, and more emotional autobiographical memories than did the odor-and-name condition. That is, not only did odors elicit more autobiographical memories than the odor names did, but including the names along with the odors actually interfered with the retrieval of memories.

Odors also seem to create different patterns in autobiographical memories than does presenting cue words to participants. As discussed earlier, the cue-word technique produces the reminiscence bump, the characteristic increase in memories for late childhood to early adulthood. Presenting odors, however, has a different effect on memory. Willander and Larsson (2006) found that presenting odors and asking for the first memory that came to mind produced mostly memories from earlier in childhood, with most of the memories clustering before the age of 10. In another study, Herz (2004) showed that autobiographical memories produced by odor cues were given higher emotion ratings than were autobiographical memories elicited by either visual cues or auditory cues. Thus, the bottom line is this: It is true—odors elicit old and emotional memories.

THE NEUROSCIENCE OF AUTOBIOGRAPHICAL MEMORY

Autobiographical memory is a complex process. It is not simply the retrieval of episodic memories. Specific events must be organized in terms of generalized events, lifetime periods, semantic knowledge of the self, and sociocultural expectations. Imagine, for example, a participant in an autobiographical memory study. Even though he or she has been given specific instructions to retrieve the first event that comes to mind given a particular cue, most of us might edit even this. Suppose the cue word is *school,* and what comes to mind is sneaking out to smoke marijuana in the schoolyard with one's friends while in high school. It is likely that you may think (a) this is not a good memory to have in response to the word *school,* and (b) you may not want to share this memory with an authoritative stranger, that is, the researcher. So you may quickly shift your memory to a more socially acceptable memory of, say, attending a wedding at a church. In an earlier chapter, we discussed the importance of inhibition in memory. In this example, the socially undesirable memory is inhibited and a more socially acceptable memory is retrieved and described.

As we have seen, specific events are placed into a hierarchy of overlapping lifetime periods, transformed into generalized events, and are subject to all the processes of forgetting, change, and reconstruction that all memories are. Therefore, we should expect to see the neural correlates of autobiographical memory to be complex as well. Indeed, during the course of retrieving an autobiographical memory, many areas of the brain become active. As a consequence, neuroscientists have become interested in not only which areas are active but the sequence of activity in the brain as an autobiographical memory is being recalled.

We next consider a representative study. Daselaar et al. (2008) used a standard cue-word technique—that is, participants heard a word and were asked to think of the first autobiographical memory that came to mind. They pressed a button when they felt like they had the memory in mind. Exactly 24 seconds after the participants heard the word, they were asked to rate the emotion that went along with the memory and the extent to which they felt they were "reliving" the memory as they recalled it. During retrieval, a functional magnetic resonance imaging (fMRI) machine monitored the participants' brains.

The fMRI technique allows the researchers to obtain a detailed map of where activity in the brain is taking place. It also allows the researchers to track changes in brain activity over time, as it is able to take a new image of the brain every .5 second. Thus, Daselaar and colleagues (2008) were able to track both the areas of the brain involved in autobiographical recall and how activity shifts from one area to another.

So, if we start tracking time when the cue word is presented, we can say the cue word is presented at 0.0 seconds. By 1.5 seconds after the presentation of the word, there was activity in three known memory areas of the brain: the medial temporal lobe, the hippocampus, and right prefrontal cortex. The right prefrontal cortex is associated with going into "retrieval mode," that is, initiating the memory search. This is the area that initiates the active search for a memory. The hippocampus and the medial temporal lobe are associated with activating the memory itself. This initial activity is brief. By about 3 seconds after the presentation of the word, activity in all of these areas is decreasing.

At 3 seconds after the cue word, activity in the occipital cortex (visual cortex) and the left prefrontal cortex starts occurring, and these increase until about 12 seconds, and then they level off. The occipital cortex is associated with the visual imagery that usually accompanies autobiographical memories, and the left prefrontal activity is probably related to verbal aspects of the memory, including any elaboration or interpretation of the memory (Daselaar et al., 2008). The activity in this area remains high as long as the person is still thinking about the memory.

What about emotion? What were the neural correlates of emotion? Those memories that were given high judgments of emotionality were correlated with greater activity in the hippocampus and the amygdala in the limbic system. Both of these areas were active early on, even prior to the point in which the person indicated that he or she had retrieved the memory. Thus, it is likely that the feeling of emotion associated with the memory occurs before the actual memory itself. An area in the prefrontal lobe, called the frontopolar cortex, was also more activated in high-emotion memories than in low-emotion memories.

The neural correlates of "reliving" the memory were seen later in the time course of remembering. Starting around 12 seconds after presentation of the cue, memories with strong "reliving" scores showed greater activity in the visual cortex, especially areas in the occipital lobe next to areas involved in primary visual processing. In addition to the increased activity in the visual cortex, memories with high "reliving" score also were correlated with heightened and prolonged activity in the right prefrontal cortex. According to

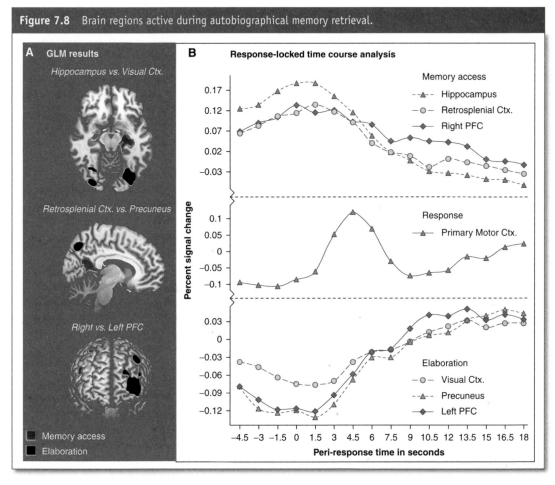

Figure 7.8   Brain regions active during autobiographical memory retrieval.

SOURCE: Daselaar et al. (2008).

Daselaar et al. (2008), this right prefrontal activity is probably correlated with attentional focus on these particular memories.

Thus, Daselaar et al.'s (2008) study and others (see Botzung, Denkova, Ciuciu, Scheiber, & Manning, 2008, for similar studies with similar results) show the complexity of autobiographical memory. They also show the detailed relation of memory areas with memory function. Many areas of the brain are active, and there is a flow of information from the front of the brain to the back of the brain and then, at least for emotional and relived memories, back up to the front. These studies are also consistent with the early electroencephalogram (EEG) studies on the time course of memory retrieval conducted by Conway and his colleagues (see Conway et al., 2003, discussed in Chapter 1).

NEUROPSYCHOLOGY OF AUTOBIOGRAPHICAL MEMORY

Conway (2005) described several patients with déjà vécu. **Déjà vécu** means that these patients had persistent feelings that they had lived the present moment before. Déjà vécu is different from déjà vu in that **déjà vu** refers to a feeling that you feel like you have been somewhere before or seen something before and are seeing it again now, even though you know you could not have seen it earlier. In déjà vécu, you believe you are reliving an earlier experience. In other words, you feel like you have traveled back in time and the event is recurring. In déjà vu, you only have a feeling that an event has occurred before but not that you are reliving the event. That is, you feel like what you are doing in the present has reduplicated something that you did already in the past. Déjà vu occurs in all people and has been tied to unidentified feelings of familiarity (Cleary, Ryals, & Nomi, 2009).

> **Déjà vécu**: the persistent feelings that people get that they have lived the present moment before; seen in neuropsychological patients.
>
> **Déjà vu**: the experience we get when we think we have seen or heard something before but objectively know that we have not.

In patient populations, it can change from being a rare experience to a common experience. For example, when one patient was being interviewed, he described a similar interview with the same psychologist wearing the same clothes in the same place but some time in the past, even though the patient had never met the psychologist before. When given a list of words to remember and a subsequent old-new recognition test, the participant showed a large number of false positives on old items, that is, recognized items as being on the list when they actually were not. Conway explains this phenomenon in terms of mistaking the fluency of the present for information from the past. That is, the present experience erroneously feels like a memory of the past. These patients tend to have deficits in the medial-temporal lobe. This condition is very rare, and Conway and colleagues have just examined a few patients, but it yields an interesting pattern of autobiographical memory failure. For more information on the déjà vu experience, go to www.sagepub.com/schwartz.[6]

SUMMARY

Autobiographical memory refers to memory of our own lives. Information in autobiographical memory can be either episodic (that is, referring to particular events from our lives) or semantic (that is, our knowledge of our own life). Semantic knowledge includes information we learn about ourselves from others (e.g., our birthday), generalized knowledge (e.g., what I usually do on Sundays), and the themes we use to organize our memories ("since I moved to the suburbs"). In fact, Conway and his colleagues divide autobiographical memory into a hierarchy that starts with specific events, builds to generalized events, and uses life themes as an organizing principle.

As adults, we have limited episodic access to the events of early childhood. Childhood amnesia refers to the inability of adults to retrieve events from before the age of 3 and the limited memory of events from early childhood. The latest explanations for this amnesia focus on the need to develop the language to encode these early memories. As adults, we tend to remember our earliest memories in observer mode, that is, as if we were watching ourselves from a vantage point outside ourselves. Memories of our adult life and later childhood tend to be remembered as field memories, as if we were watching the event through our own eyes. Memories, especially among twins, can also be "borrowed" from others. A number of studies with twins show that many falsely "remember" an event that happened to their sibling as happening to themselves.

A particularly salient form of autobiographical memory is the flashbulb memory. These memories are the personal memories of surprising public events. For example, if you remember where you were and what you were doing when you heard about the tragic events of 9/11, you are experiencing a flashbulb memory for that event.

Autobiographical memory is examined in a number of ways. In one well-used paradigm, participants are given ordinary words (e.g., *cupcake*) and asked to generate the first autobiographical memory that they can think of. Studies with adults older than age 35 reveal a pattern called a reminiscence bump. This refers to the observation that memories from late childhood to early adulthood are remembered more frequently than are memories from earlier in childhood or later in adulthood. Recent memories are also well remembered, but early adulthood memories show a bump in almost all studies of adult populations.

Finally, a neuroscience of autobiographical memory is becoming possible. Recent fMRI studies of autobiographical memory show that early in retrieval of autobiographical memory, areas in the hippocampus and right prefrontal cortex are active. As we retrieve the memory, activity spreads to the visual areas of the brain and left prefrontal cortex. To conclude this chapter, let me add that remembering the autobiographical details of our lives is often one of the most subtle and enjoyable pleasures. Those of us who are fortunate enough to be able to relive the past should keep this in mind.

KEY TERMS

Flashbulb memories

Event-specific memories

General events

Lifetime periods

Working self

Coherence

Correspondence

Childhood amnesia

Childhood amnesia—
psychodynamic view

Childhood amnesia—
age-related changes in
self-concept

Childhood amnesia—
neurological transitions in
memory systems

Childhood amnesia—
influence of language on
memory development

Diary studies

Cue-word technique

Reminiscence bump

Observer memories

Field memories

Borrowed memories

Déjà vécu

Déjà vu

REVIEW QUESTIONS

1. What are the three levels of Conway's theory of autobiographical memory representation? How do the levels interact?

2. What does Conway mean by an extended event? How does it differ from an episodic memory?

3. What is childhood amnesia? What are the four explanations for it? Which explanation works best?

4. What is a flashbulb memory? How do they differ from ordinary memories? How are they similar to ordinary memories?

5. Why does keeping a diary help you remember important events from your life?

6. What is the cue-word technique? How can it be used to study autobiographical memory?

7. What is the reminiscence bump? What three explanations have been put forward to explain it?

8. What is the difference between a field memory and an observer memory?

9. What are borrowed memories? Who is most likely to have them?

10. What area of the brain is associated with visual imagery in autobiographical memory? What area of the brain is associated with emotion in autobiographical memory?

ONLINE RESOURCES

1. For more thoughts on memories of 9/11, go to http://scienceblogs.com/cortex/2008/09/flashbulb_memories.php.

2. You can hear Dr. Conway talk about his research at http://www.bbc.co.uk/sn/tvradio/programmes/horizon/broadband/tx/memory/senses.

3. For more on childhood amnesia, go to http://www.apa.org/science/about/psa/2008/03/wang.aspx.

4. For the neuroimaging of flashbulb memories, go to http://www.telegraph.co.uk/scienceandtechnology/science/sciencenews/3350048/911-Study-Reveals-How-Flashbulb-Memories-Form.html.

5. For Proust's description of this experience, go to http://www.haverford.edu/psych/ddavis/p109g/proust.html.

6. For more on the déjà vu experience, go to http://discovermagazine.com/2005/sep/psychology-of-deja-vu and http://castroller.com/podcasts/PriToThe/1179696.

 Go to www.sagepub.com/schwartz for additional exercises and study resources. Select **Chapter 7, Autobiographical Memory** for chapter-specific resources.

CHAPTER 8

False Memory

Donald Thompson is a prominent memory researcher from Australia. He has been studying applications of memory research to eyewitness memory and legal proceedings for years. He worked with Endel Tulving for his dissertation at the University of Toronto and then returned to Australia to become a university professor in his homeland. He frequently testifies as an expert witness in many cases that have to do with eyewitness memory.

One particular evening some years ago, Dr. Thompson appeared on live television, discussing issues of eyewitness memory on a talk show. Also on the talk show was the chief of police of a major city in Australia. Dr. Thompson explained to the television audience how, in some cases, eyewitnesses can be mistaken in their identifications. Shortly after he returned home, police arrived at his door and brought him to the station for questioning. A rape victim had identified him as the culprit. After what must have been a terrifying evening for all involved, Thompson was released. After all, he had a foolproof alibi. At the time of the crime, he had been on live television and could not possibly have committed this awful crime. Subsequent questioning of the victim revealed that she had been watching the program that Dr. Thompson was appearing on just prior to the crime. Apparently, the woman had confused the face of the actual rapist with the face she was seeing at the same time or just prior on television, that is, Dr. Thompson. Dr. Thompson was released, and the real criminal was never brought to justice. This woman had been through a horrible ordeal, made worse by the strange memory error that led to the false accusation of an innocent man and allowed a terribly guilty one to get away. For more on Dr. Thompson's ordeal, go to www.sagepub.com/schwartz.[1]

In another case, the United States government turned over a man named John Demjanjuk to the Israeli government to stand trial for Nazi war crimes. The Israeli government accused Demjanjuk of being "Ivan the Terrible," a bloodthirsty Nazi executioner during World War II, personally responsible for perhaps hundreds of thousands of murders. Five Holocaust survivors came forward and swore that they remembered Demjanjuk's face from 40 years earlier and confirmed that he was "Ivan." Demjanjuk claimed to be innocent. However, the Israeli court went with the compelling testimony of the survivors. Demjanjuk was convicted and sentenced to death for genocide and murder. However, shortly before his scheduled execution, the Russian government found documents that proved—without a shadow of doubt—that Demjanjuk was not "Ivan." The Israeli Supreme Court overturned the verdict and eventually allowed Demjanjuk to return to his home in Cleveland. How had this happened? Presumably, the witnesses were working in good faith and thought that they recognized the actual criminal, yet this turned out to be another case of mistaken eyewitness identification (Loftus & Ketcham, 1991). Demjanjuk was subsequently deported to Germany to be tried for other crimes associated with his Nazi past. Though evidence wound up pointing him out as war criminal, he was not the war criminal he had originally been accused of.

In both cases, people who had been horribly violated by the worst of criminals came forward to identify their assailants. Despite their fundamental honesty and desire to do right, these witnesses "fingered" the wrong person. How can people form these erroneous memories of what happened in an event? How do people come to believe that their memories are accurate when they are not? That is one of the topics of this chapter.

In the cases described above, real crimes were committed, and the victims involved remember them. Their problems were that they falsely identified the wrong person as the criminal. Thus, in these cases, the issue is as much memory accuracy as it is false memory. In other cases, entire fictional events are made up and then later remembered as if they were truth. Consider the strange phenomenon involved in the memory of alien induction, studied by Susan Clancy and explored in her 2005 book (Clancy, 2005). Clancy describes the memories of abductees, normal people who come to believe that their obviously false memories are true. Abductees are people who believe they have been kidnapped by aliens from outer space. Abductees tell similar stories about being removed from their beds in the middle of the night, taken to a spaceship, and then experimented on, usually involving sexual abuse. Clancy claimed that abductees truly believe that these events really happened. She inferred that the memories must arise when people with vivid visual imaginations who believe in alien visits experience sleep paralysis. Sleep paralysis occurs when the brain emerges from REM sleep but the body is still paralyzed. This experience can be very distressing for some people. This is often combined with hypnosis therapy, which we will see later is a major source of false memories. For Clancy's research, the abductees constitute a sample of individuals who have come to believe their strong false memories. Therefore, they make excellent candidates for studying the origin of false memories. These false memories differ from that of the eyewitnesses. The crime victims are real; the witnesses in the Demjanjuk case really did see horrible crimes committed—they only misremembered the face of the man who did it. In the abductees' case, entire events are confabulated. For the transcript of an interview with Dr. Clancy, go to www.sagepub.com/schwartz.[2]

False memory: memories that people have that do not correspond to events as they actually happened.

Correspondence: the match between the retrieved memory and the actual event from the past.

False memories refer to memories that people have that do not correspond to events as they actually happened. Notice that this definition is a loaded sentence. First, to be a false memory, it has to be something that feels like a memory—that is, a person has a recollective experience of an event that took place in the past. This notion of having to feel "real" means that lies and made-up stories do not count as false memories. Second, the memory cannot refer to a real event or at least did not take place as the person remembered it. This includes a range of possibilities from small distortions, such as a blue car being recalled as a green car, to completely made-up events, such as the alien abductions. **Correspondence** is also an important part of the definition. A true memory is one in which the recollective experience corresponds to an actual event that actually occurred in the past, whereas a false memory is one in which the recollective experience does not correspond to an actual event.

Historically, the study of false memories has come in two waves. In the 1970s, a memory scientist at the University of Washington named Elizabeth Loftus introduced a paradigm known as the "misinformation effect" into the memory literature (see Figure 8.1). This effect refers to false memories created by postevent misinformation. That is, participants witness an event and then later receive false information about what occurred during that event. If they later remember the false information, a "misinformation" effect is said to have occurred. Loftus used these data to demonstrate the unreliability of eyewitness memory, and indeed, throughout her career, Loftus has emphasized the role that memory science played in the field of eyewitness testimony. In the 1990s, memory scientists turned their attention to another battle being waged in the courtrooms, clinics, and newspapers of the time—namely, the reality of recovered memories of repressed childhood abuse. On one side, there were people claiming that they had "recovered" memories of abuse after having forgotten for many years. On the other side, there were people claiming that the recovered memories were false and were a function of leading and misleading therapeutic techniques. Elizabeth Loftus took up the cause of those who thought of recovered memories as false memories and was soon developing experimental methodologies to study the issue. This battle raged through much of the 1990s (see Schwartz, 2000), but a middle ground based on solid science was eventually recognized.

Figure 8.1 Dr. Elizabeth Loftus.

The plan for this chapter is to first provide some basic background memory science on the issue of false memory. Then we will look at the issue of how false memories are formed and contrast them with how real repressed memories are recovered. Then we will outline how false or distorted memory has been examined in the context of legal applications. We will discuss the landmark work on the misinformation effect. Memory researchers have also designed protocols to help investigators limit false memories but promote accurate memory. This "cognitive interview" will also be discussed in this chapter.

CORRESPONDENCE, ACCURACY, AND AMOUNT

In some situations, what matters is the amount of information a person remembers. In semantic memory, the sheer bulk of memory is often important. How many names for the bones of the body can you remember? How many kings and queens of Great Britain do you know? How much black pepper should you put into your hot and sour soup? However, in autobiographical memory, correspondence is more important, that is, the relation between the memory of the event and the actual event. For example, on a walk through the park, you saw five swans, three ducks, two squirrels, and seven bicycle riders. Later you report that you saw a bunch of birds and some people on bicycles; your memory is accurate (corresponds to the event) even if you do not recall a lot of details. However, the person who reports pigeons, deer, and ATVs is showing poor correspondence to the point of false memories. In legal settings, correspondence is paramount. It is seldom relevant if a witness remembers lots of details, if the person's memory turns out to be erroneous. Of course, the best testimony is both accurate and complete. But completeness only matters if there is a high degree of correspondence between the witness's testimony and the events that unfolded (Goldsmith & Koriat, 2008).

Suggestibility: the tendency to incorporate information from sources other than the original witnessed event. These other sources may be potentially misleading. Other sources include other people, written materials, or pictures.

Experimental psychologists are interested in the causes of memory phenomena. Therefore, naturally, it is important to try to understand the processes that produce false memory. **Suggestibility** is one—that is, the tendency to incorporate suggestions or postevent information into one's memory of an event. But that topic will be covered later when the misinformation effect is introduced. First, we will introduce one of the other culprits—source monitoring failures.

SOURCE MONITORING

A critical feature of retrieval is determining where your memory comes from, that is, what is its source. That is, how do we know what we are remembering is, in fact, true? Try to remember what you had for breakfast this morning. Are you sure that is what you actually had for breakfast, or are you remembering what you had for breakfast yesterday? Or are you remembering what you wished you had for breakfast? We have to make decisions on the source and veracity of our memories quickly. Now think about the memory you have of your younger sibling being born. Do you know this story because you remember based on your own experience at his or her birth? Or do you know it because you have heard stories of it throughout your life from others? In this case, a source monitoring decision involves determining if your memory is of your own experience or if your memory is based on stories from your parents.

Attributing a memory to the wrong source can have potentially negative consequences. For example, I often tell my students that I have a vivid memory of scoring the winning three-point shot with time ticking out in the seventh game of the NBA finals. Luckily, especially for my friends and family, I am well aware that the source of this memory is my active fantasy. I know the memory is of an imagined event and not a real event. This is the essence of source monitoring: knowing where your memories come from. Another example: You may remember that your friend "Betty" just broke up with her boyfriend. But before you send her flowers, you might consider how you heard of the breakup. If you heard it from an unreliable gossip, you might make certain first by asking Betty herself. If she confirms it, you get her the flowers and take her out for lunch. If you heard it directly from Betty originally, then you will go ahead and order those flowers without calling her again. Thus, when we retrieve the fact, "Betty and her boyfriend broke up," we automatically make a judgment of source—reliable or unreliable—and act accordingly. The ability to distinguish between sources in memory is called source monitoring.

Failures in source monitoring can potentially lead to false memories. Some researchers have argued that many false memories are the result of failures of source monitoring (Meissner, Brigham, & Kelley, 2002). Imagine if somehow I were to fail to source monitor effectively and realize that my memory of basketball greatness is only a fantasy. If I assert to you that I really was a professional basketball hero, I am committing a false memory. Thus, if I forget the source of a memory (in this case, my own fantasy), I run the risk of generating a false memory. Many students might decide I was really weird and take someone else's course.

How do we successfully source monitor? The current theory is that source monitoring occurs at the time of retrieval. When a memory is brought to mind, source monitoring processes unconsciously examine the memory for clues to its origin. Memories with lots of sensory details are usually judged to be real, as are those with strong emotional associations (Johnson, Hashtroudi, & Lindsay, 1993). Note, however, a strongly imagined and plausible memory (say, hitting the winning shot in a pickup basketball game at the local schoolyard) may pass this source monitoring test and be retrieved as a memory of a real event.

> **Reality monitoring**: refers to our ability to distinguish whether our memory is of a real event or of an imagined event.

Reality monitoring (source monitoring between real and imagined sources) has been implicated in false memories concerning both childhood abuse and failures in eyewitness memory.

METHODS OF STUDYING FALSE MEMORY

Deese-Roediger-McDermott Procedure (DRM)

Before you read the rest of this paragraph, test yourself on the demonstration in Figure 8.2. Now look at the words you wrote down. You probably got most of the words on the list. Now check to see if there are any words that you wrote down that were not on the original list. About 55% of people who recall the words from the list shown below will falsely recall the word *sleep.* Examine the list, and you will see. The word *sleep* is not there. Thus, if you wrote down *sleep* on your list, you have made at least one false memory in your life. You are not alone. Almost every individual will make a critical intrusion if given enough of these lists. The word's presence is strong implied by the associations of the words on the list, and as a consequence, it is likely to be falsely recalled. The word *sleep* is called a critical intrusion. **Critical intrusions** are the false memories created by a list in which all of the words are related or associated with the absent but suggested word. Roediger and McDermott (1995) devised a number of lists with a similar theme in mind (but also see Deese, 1959). Go to www.sagepub.com/schwartz[3] and copy some of the lists—then try this experiment on some of your friends.

The **Deese-Roediger-McDermott procedure** (DRM) procedure rapidly induces a false memory.

> **Critical intrusions**: the false memories created by a list in which all of the words are related or associated with the absent but suggested word.

> **Deese-Roediger-McDermott procedure (DRM)**: a procedure used to induce false memories for items on word lists. It involves presenting associates to an unpresented word in the list. The unpresented word is often recalled because of its associations to the other words.

Figure 8.2	Read the following words aloud at a rate of one word every three seconds. After you have read all the words, close your book, take out a piece of paper, and write down as many of these words as you can.

Bed	Dream	Slumber
Drowsy	Awake	Snore
Rest	Tired	Wake
Yawn	Doze	Snooze
Peace	Nap	Blanket

SOURCE: Roediger and McDermott (1995).

That is, people recalled the word *sleep,* but it was not on the list. Therefore, it is, by defin-ition, a false memory. In fact, you may feel certain it was on the list. This is not unusual (Roediger & McDermott, 1995). Many people recall the word *sleep,* ascribe it to a source, and describe its retrieval as a "recollective experience." Moreover, you can then try the person on the next list and see if he or she produces the critical intrusion on that list. Thus, the DRM procedure provides an excellent experimental window on false memories. It is quick and easy to do, reliably produces false memories, involves no misinformation and no questionable ethical procedures, and can lend itself to a great number of experimen-tal manipulations.

There are two standard explanations of the false memories in the DRM procedure. One explanation focuses on the nature of the contextual associations. **Contextual associa-tions** means that all of the presented words are linked or associated to, in some way, the critical intrusion. In the example, all of the words are related to the critical intrusion, "sleep." The context allows for the associations between sleep and all of the words to strongly activate the word *sleep* in the person's memory. Thus, at the time of recall, the word *sleep* is highly acti-vated. This activation is then mistakenly con-fused with episodic memory. Many experiments support this particular point of view (Barnhardt, Choi, Gerkens, & Smith, 2006; Jou, 2008).

> **Contextual associations**: an explanation for the retrieval of critical intrusions in the DRM. It states that all of the presented words are linked or associated to, in some way, the critical intrusion.

Thus, for example, when the list is relatively small (e.g., *nurse, sick, lawyer, medicine*), the critical intrusion (*doctor*) is less likely to be recalled than if the list is relatively long (e.g., *nurse, sick, lawyer, medicine, health hospital, dentist physician, ill, patient, office, stetho-scope, surgeon, clinic, cure*) (Roediger, Watson, McDermott, & Gallo, 2001). That is, longer lists result in a greater likelihood of remembering the critical intrusion as a word on the list. This is likely because the greater number of associations is more likely to strongly activate the absent but associated word. Pictures also produce strong associations (think of why polit-ical candidates want to have their faces constantly seen on television prior to an election). In fact, when pictures of the items are presented instead of the words, the recall of critical intrusions is even larger (Hege & Dodson, 2004).

An alternate explanation of false memories in the DRM procedure focuses on the idea that memory representation is not exact. This has been labeled **fuzzy-trace theory** (Brainerd, Wright, Reyna, & Mojardin, 2001). I prefer the term *gist of the list,* as what is encoded refers to the primary meaning of the list rather than its individual examples. In this view, when items are encoded, they are not encoded literally but rather in terms of their meaning, a reasonable hypothesis given what we know about long-term memory. Thus, for example, when a person encodes words such

> **Fuzzy-trace theory**: an explanation for the retrieval of critical intrusions in the DRM. It states that when items are encoded, they are not encoded literally but rather in terms of their meaning, a reasonable hypothesis given what we know about long-term memory.

as *physician, surgeon, hospital,* these words may be transformed into the word *doctor* at encoding, as the correct meaning is extracted rather than the literal words. This theory explains why participants are good at recognizing the actual words that were on the list, as they are consistent with the gist of fuzzy trace. However, when participants are asked to recall items, the critical intrusion is likely to be recalled as it is the word most strongly encoded by the meaning or gist of the list.

The DRM is a good experimental paradigm for looking at false memories induced by associative structures. However, there is some concern as to whether it serves as a model for real-world false memories. For example, do people who develop false memories for alien abductions produce more critical intrusions in DRM experiments? Many think that there is a large gap between false memories for words and the kinds of false memories that disrupt people's lives. Although there appear to be clear differences among individuals in their propensity to produce critical intrusions (Watson, Bunting, Poole, & Conway, 2005), it is unclear how DRM predicts false memories in real-world situations. Individual differences appear to be related to differences in working memory ability rather than such factors as suggestibility.

False Memory Induction Procedure

The DRM procedure allows for careful experimental manipulation and allows researchers to study false memories in a large-scale way, as the procedure can induce many false memories in ordinary participants. However, it has been criticized in terms of the extent to which it generalizes to real-world false memories and, in particular, the controversial topic of the recovery of repressed memories. That is, the issue of ecological validity has been raised. How does one go from false memories for words on categorized lists to the kinds of false memories about which we are concerned in the outside world, that is, the recovered memories of abuse? For many, it is a far cry to go from a false memory of the word *sleep* on the list above to a false memory of having been attacked as a young child. To counter this criticism, Elizabeth Loftus and her colleagues invented another way of examining false memories in experimental participants. In this technique, Loftus was able to better model the kinds of false memories that are of concern outside the laboratory. This new method is called the **false memory induction procedure,** originally devised by Elizabeth Loftus (Loftus, Coan, & Pickrell, 1996). In this method, false memories of events are induced in participants. Of course, for ethical reasons, abuse memories are avoided, but Loftus and her crew have been able to show that ordinary college students will generate false memories of episodic events when put in this procedure. For an article on this topic by Elizabeth Loftus, go to www.sagepub.com/schwartz.[4]

> **False memory induction procedure**: false memories of events are induced in participants by repeatedly asking them about events they never experienced.

Before discussion of the false memory induction procedure, the controversy over the debate about the recovery of repressed memories though psychotherapy needs to be briefly introduced. I will note at the beginning of this section that the debate is not between cognitive psychology and evidence-based clinical psychology. Rather, the debate arises from different views of memory between cognitive psychology and schools of psychotherapy still largely grounded in Freudian theory, which has never had much scientific support within clinical psychology. The controversy concerns the explanation of recovered repressed memories. Cognitive-based memory researchers argue that many of these recovered memories may, in fact, be false memories brought about by the processes described in this chapter. Freudian psychotherapy argues that these recovered repressed memories are almost always true.

Loftus and Davis (2006) describe several controversial psychotherapy techniques that have been used by some therapists to promote the recovery of repressed memories of childhood abuse, usually sexual abuse. It is their contention that many of these techniques are also powerful at inducing false memories. Loftus and Davis are quick to point out that these techniques do not derive from mainstream science-based clinical psychology. Nonetheless, some, but not all, licensed therapists use the techniques. These techniques include hypnosis, guided imagery (that is, imagining oneself in an abuse situation to see if it is real), the writing in journals, and even more strange activities such as "trance writing." Laboratory studies show that each of these techniques can lead to false memories. **Hypnosis,** for example, leads to a strong increase in the number of reported false memories with a small, if any, increase in the number of reported true memories. With respect to "guided imagery," some therapists believe that it will help clients remember abusive events from their childhood. However, empirical research also links it with false memories. Thus, Loftus and Davis argue that rather than help these people confront what is really causing them the psychological distress, which leads them to seek psychotherapy in the first place, these techniques simply instill false memories in them. Thus, for Loftus and Davis, these techniques are a double-edged sword. They induce false memories, which may have negative repercussions in a person's life, and the techniques distract attention away from the root causes of the person's problems.

> **Hypnosis**: hypnosis increases the number of false memories without increasing the number of accurate memories.

The false memory induction procedure is modeled on these psychotherapy techniques, except that the goal is not to provide insight and relief to people suffering from psychological distress. Rather, the goal is to determine if these techniques induce false memories in healthy normal adults. We shall turn now to this procedure.

In the false memory induction procedure, the experimenters ask participants about particular events from their childhood, which, in fact, never happened. They tell the participant that they have spoken to a parent or an older sibling and received information about the childhood event and that they want to see how much the individual can remember from the event. In fact, the experimenters do contact a family member but just to confirm that a similar event did not happen to the participant. For example, the participants might be asked about the time, as a young child, they spilled punch on the bride's wedding dress at a family wedding. They might be asked about the time they took a ride in a hot air balloon while on vacation. They might be asked about the time that they got lost at the mall. They might be asked about the time a school nurse took a skin sample. Since the events never took place, almost all participants initially deny remembering the event. However, in the false memory induction procedure, the experimenters will repeatedly and leadingly question the participants about such memories. In some cases, people strangely do start to remember details of events that never took place.

For example, Loftus and Pickrell (1995) recruited 24 parents who tried to convince their children that they had been lost in the mall as a child, when, in fact, they had not. No hypnosis was used to induce memories, but repeated and insistent questioning was. Participants were also asked to imagine themselves back in the mall. Although most of the participants never generated false memories of being lost in the mall, 25% did. That is, 6 of the 24 participants "remembered" partial or complete details of the never-experienced event. Hyman, Husband, and Billings (1995) found a similar percentage of people generated false memories in a similar paradigm.

There is a strong parallel between this procedure and the **recovery of repressed memories**. In the criticized forms of psychotherapy, the therapist will repeatedly suggest that current psychological problems are a function of repressed childhood trauma and will repeatedly ask the client to try to remember such trauma. Now, neither the therapist nor the client actually knows whether repressed abuse occurred. However, the therapist strongly believes it to be the case and conveys this expectation to his or her patient. Moreover, the client may put particular weight to the therapist's point of view because the person is regarded as an expert. As such, it may be possible for the therapist to induce a false memory of childhood abuse (Loftus & Davis, 2006). The false memory induction procedure essentially replicates this procedure, although the false memories that are actually induced are far less traumatic.

> **Recovery of repressed memories**: the ability to recover previously forgotten memories that had been repressed.

Returning to the false memory induction procedure, repeated questioning combined with the authority of a close family memory leads some participants to create false memories. The rate of false memory induction is relatively low. At best, it reaches rates of about 50% for memories that are ordinary and not traumatic (i.e., taking a ride in a hot air balloon). For some items, it remains at 0% (being treated with an enema at the doctor's office; see Pezdek, Finger, & Hodge, 1997). In most cases, it takes the form of accepting the wisdom of the parent or sibling, that is, the belief that the event must be true if Mom says it is true, without any recollective experience. However, in some cases, the participants wind up not just believing that the event occurred but elaborating on the event, providing details that were not presented to them by the researchers. In these cases, the participant truly has an autobiographical episodic memory that just happens to not correspond to a real event (e.g., Hyman & Pentland, 1996). In this study, for example, 25% of participants wound up elaborating on and describing new details to events that never happened.

Individual variation abounds in this paradigm. Some participants begin having false memories immediately, whereas others are resistant and eventually give in. Furthermore, still others still never have false memories (Loftus & Davis, 2006). Those with good visual imagery are actually more likely to have false memories, as are those prone to hypnosis.

We can conclude from the above data that human memory is susceptible to false memory. Not all the time, not for all events, and perhaps not even for everybody, but by and large, false memories can and do occur. A question remains—can false memories of truly traumatic memories occur? Is it possible to induce these false memories in unsuspecting participants?

All memory researchers have considered it unethical to attempt to falsely induce memories of childhood abuse, but memory researchers have pushed the limits of ethically acceptable false memory induction to demonstrate the power of false memory induction. Thus, Heaps and Nash (2001) induced false memories of childhood near-drowning events, and Porter, Yuille, and Lehman (1999) induced false memories of vicious animal attacks in childhood. In both cases, false memories were produced at rates similar to those of the earlier studies with less traumatic memories. I will hasten to add that in both of these studies, participants went through rigorous debriefing sessions. So it is likely that these kinds of false memories come closer to demonstrating that at least some recovered memories of childhood abuse are really just false memories. In conclusion, strong data suggest that it is possible to implant false memories of traumatic events in at least some individuals. This strongly supports the assertion that some leading psychotherapy can lead to the creation of false memories of childhood sexual abuse.

The false memory induction procedure has also led to some other interesting findings. In particular, the induction of false memories can lead to changes in patterns of food preferences (Bernstein & Loftus, 2009). For example, Bernstein and Loftus (2009) describe experiments in which participants were induced to have false memories of getting sick from eating particular foods, such as egg salad. Later, participants expressed an aversion to egg salad that they had not had before. In contrast, Laney, Morris, Bernstein, Wakefield, and Loftus (2008) induced false memories of food preferences. They induced participants to remember how much they enjoyed eating asparagus as children. Later, these participants demonstrated increased desire and liking of asparagus. They suggest that inducing false memories may be a way of getting people to eat a healthier diet.

Imagination Inflation

Imagine that, when you were a 6-year-old child, your parents took you on a trip in a hot air balloon while on vacation. It was a warm and sunny day in Napa Valley, California. You were a little bit scared, but once you were aloft, it was a bit boring. You could not see out over the basket, and when you tried, your father pulled you back, fearing you would fall out. So you just counted the number of people in the balloon who were wearing "Crocs" on their feet. Afterward, you told your parents the hot air balloon ride was boring, and they scolded you, explaining they had spent a lot of money so that you could have that experience. You decided it was better not to talk about the balloon ride after that because all you remember of it anyway are being pulled away from the side and the blue Crocs the tall weird-looking man with the mustache was wearing (see Figure 8.3).

Figure 8.3   Is that you in the hot air balloon? See text for explanation.

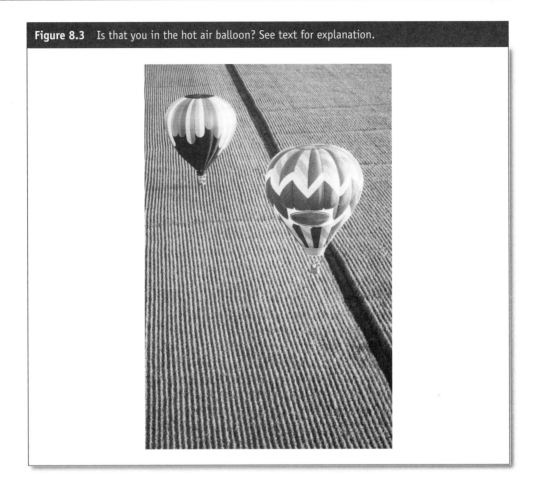

Sound plausible? I am not saying this really happened to you, just that you should imagine it. Try to imagine it vividly—try to see the excitement of the morning, the giant colorful balloon, the disappointment at not being able to see anything, and the image of the blue sandals. Amazingly, research shows that imagining a scenario such as this increases the likelihood that you will falsely remember an event of that type.

In **imagination inflation,** researchers induce false memories by simply having the participant imagine the event. False memories can be induced without any deception on the part of the researcher. The researcher simply asks the participant to imagine an event, such as taking a hot air balloon ride. The simple act of imagining it influences the rate at which those participants later report whether they have ever experienced that event (Mazzoni & Memon, 2003).

For example, Mazzoni and Memon (2003) asked people to rate the likelihood that each of several events had happened to them. Some of the events were plausible, such as finding

> **Imagination inflation**: researchers induce false memories by simply having the participant imagine the event.

money in the back of a taxicab or having a tooth removed by a dentist, and others were impossible, such as having a skin sample taken by a school nurse, something not done in Great Britain, where the experiment took place. Participants were asked the likelihood that each of these events took place to them before they were 6 years old. One week later, the participants returned and imagined the plausible event or the impossible event. As a control, they read a brief description of the other event. For the memory test, participants returned a week after that. Here, they were asked to judge whether various events had happened to them, including both the plausible and impossible event. Participants used a scale that ranged from "no memory of the event" to one that included "vivid memory of the event with details."

In this study, there was no attempt to convince the person that the event actually occurred. The researchers only asked for the participant to imagine an event. Nonetheless, this procedure can and does induce false memories. More participants believed that they had a skin sample taken from them as children than if they had not imagined the event. More important, more participants now reported new details of their memory of the event, convinced that it was real, than if they had not imagined the event. Note here that in this paradigm, the experimenters never tried to convince the participant that the event occurred. They simply asked first to estimate its likelihood and then imagine the event. This alone is sufficient to induce a false memory.

One of the questionable psychotherapeutic techniques criticized by Loftus and her colleagues is guided imagery. In guided imagery, a therapist who suspects a client might have been abused as a child may ask the client to imagine such an event and see if it "feels real." This is exactly what is happening in the imagination inflation paradigm except that the experimenter does not give implicit suggestions that the memory is real. This research suggests that therapists must be careful about what they suggest that their clients imagine because their more suggestible clients might soon have false memories. And these false memories might have devastating consequences for the client and his or her relationship to other people. Consider the following study. Scoboria, Mazzoni, and Josee (2008) suggested to participants that they had gotten sick eating peach yoghurt as a child. One week later, the participants returned for what they thought was a different experiment on food preferences. Compared to control participants, those who thought that they had gotten sick on spoiled yogurt rated their preferences for yogurt lower and were less likely to choose yogurt than crackers when offered food. Thus, a false memory of a food reaction can create an aversion to that food. To find out more about imagination inflation, go to www.sagepub.com/schwartz.[5]

Altered Evidence

Consider looking at a photograph of yourself in a hot air balloon. There you are, 8 years old, smiling from above the railing of the balloon. There's the proof—you may not remember it now—but you definitely were in the balloon. Recent studies have used programs like Photoshop to alter photographs to provide false evidence that false events took place. The question, then, is whether these doctored photographs (or videos) can induce false memories in the people who view them. Nash, Wade, and Lindsay (2009) altered videos of participants interacting with experimenters and then showed the videotapes to participants. Two weeks later, the participants returned for a memory test. Compared to participants who had not seen altered videotapes, those who had seen the altered videotapes had far more false memories. The effect of doctored videos was increased when those participants were also asked to imagine the false events. Thus, fabricated visual evidence can also induce false memories.

HYPNOSIS AND MEMORY

Research suggests that hypnosis does not increase the number of true memories produced. Indeed, to the contrary, all it succeeds in doing is increasing the possibility of succumbing to false memories. Yes, more information is retrieved during hypnosis than when the witness is in his or her normal state, but most of the additional information is false. In some instances, a new and true memory can be produced by hypnosis. However, the increase in memories produced by hypnosis is dominated by false memories (Kirsch, Mazzoni, & Montgomery, 2007).

Hypnosis itself is a real phenomenon. In hypnosis, an individual is placed in an altered state of consciousness in which he or she is more likely to incorporate suggestions into his or her behaviors, beliefs, and memories. People tend to vary with respect to the extent to which they can be hypnotized. Some people are highly suggestible and easily hypnotized. Others are highly resistant and are practically impossible to hypnotize. As shall be seen shortly, suggestibility is another method whereby people can incorporate false information into autobiographical memory. Thus, hypnosis is not a good option when trying to elicit more information from a confused witness.

This is not to say suggestibility is not always a bad thing. In some circumstances, being suggestible has its advantages, and hypnosis does have practical value. Suggestions can be made to people under hypnosis to help them overcome medical conditions, especially with respect to pain tolerance (e.g., Otani, 1992). A highly suggestible person can be hypnotized and made to feel less pain, while the less suggestible person has to bear the more intense pain. But for memory, the contention here is simply that hypnosis is another means of suggestibility, which increases the possibility that false memories will be created (Mazzoni & Lynn, 2007).

RECOVERED MEMORIES: THE REALITY OF REPRESSION

False memories are a real phenomenon. They are relatively straightforward to demonstrate in the lab, and we have evidence that they exist in the real world. It is almost *certain* that some recovered memories of childhood abuse are the result of false memories induced by shaky therapeutic procedures. This has led some to conclude that all recovered memories of repressed events are essentially false memories (Loftus & Ketcham, 1994). Is it possible to show that forgotten memories of childhood trauma can later be retrieved? This has been an important topic in recent years. Nowadays, the consensus is that there is evidence that some childhood trauma is forgotten, only to be remembered much later. Thus, not all recovered memories are therapy-induced false memories. First, the data that suggest that repression and recovery are possible will be discussed. Second, two explanations for this phenomenon will be offered, and experiments will be discussed that support them.

In a landmark study, Williams (1995) tracked down 129 women who had been abused as children and, as children, sent to the hospital for treatment. Thus, these were cases in which the abuse was documented. Williams used this sample to satisfy potential critics who questioned if the abuse had occurred. It would be hard to argue later that the recovered memories of the abuse were completely false, given that these were women who, as children, had been admitted to a hospital for treatment for that abuse. The age at the time of the abuse ranged from less than 1 year to 12 years old. Williams contacted them after they had all reached adulthood.

Williams (1995) found that 12% of the women did not remember the abuse. Some of these women were younger than age 5 at the time of abuse, and for those, this may have just been normal childhood amnesia. But for the women who were older at the time of the abuse, the explanation for forgetting is more complex. Thus, strange as it may seem, it is possible to forget being the victim of such awful crimes and had even been hospitalized as a result of it. Possible reasons for forgetting such traumatic events will be discussed shortly. Furthermore, 16% of women reported that there was a time when they had forgotten about the abuse even when they remembered it at the time of the interview. Indeed, they reported that an external cue triggered their memory of the abuse. Thus, it is also possible to first forget and then recover these memories. Other studies have also shown that some well-documented abuse victims lost their memory of the event and later recovered it (Shobe & Schooler, 2001).

Critics have argued that the Williams (1995) data are not foolproof. There have been critiques of the methodology and the data analysis. Yes, these women have a documented history of abuse, but that does not preclude the possibility that the memory of the abuse is false or something other than a true episodic memory. Indeed, the memory may be true, but it may be a function of reconstructive processes and stories that the woman had heard rather than a true episodic memory. Thus, some memory theorists, like Loftus and Davis (2006), remain skeptical of the Williams study.

Can we do better? Can we distinguish between a recovered memory that is a real episodic memory and a recovered episodic memory that is false (even if it captures a historically true event)? The key here is in looking at features that typically appear in false memories and in true memories. For example, research suggests that memories that are *gradually* recovered during suggestive therapy share many properties with false memories. They tend to be more vague, have more to do with thought processes, are less emotional, and have fewer sensory details. This suggests that memories that arise in this way during therapy may, in fact, be false memories. On the other hand, some recovered memories of childhood abuse are spontaneous and happen all at once. These spontaneous sudden memories are more likely to be correlated with documented histories of abuse (Geraerts, Raymaekers, & Merckelbach, 2008). These spontaneous sudden memories are also more likely to be highly charged emotionally and have more sensory detail. Thus, it appears that the hallmark of the true recovered memory is the spontaneous nature of it, usually brought on by a seemingly random retrieval cue. Memories recovered by the leading nature of a therapist's inquiry are more likely to be false.

In Freudian psychology, it is important for the patient to become aware of the childhood trauma that is now causing psychological distress in adulthood. It is for this reason that many psychotherapists probe for these hidden memories of abuse. However, some research in modern clinical psychology tells us that preventing traumatic memory from entering our conscious awareness can have positive benefits (Philippot, Baeyens, Douilliez, & Francart, 2004), directly contradicting the Freudian view. So for some clinical psychologists, recovering repressed memories may not be a desirable outcome for their clients. But whichever clinical school one adheres to, it is relevant to find out the mechanism whereby repression and recovery take place.

For cognitive psychologists, emotional memories are generally thought to be better remembered than less emotional memories, under normal circumstances (Reisberg &

Heuer, 2004). Thus, situations that produced repressed-but-recoverable memories may result from complex processes operating on those memories. Thus, from the point of view of memory science, the riddle of repression and recovery is equally important. Lately, some intriguing experimental paradigms have been developed to explore this issue.

Mechanisms of Repression and Recovery

What does it mean to repress an event? Repression is usually thought of as the blocking out of traumatic memories of childhood trauma, particularly the trauma associated with sexual abuse. This view of repression dates back to the work of Freud. **Repression** is defined here as forgetting highly emotional memories, usually from childhood. Because the evidence suggests that it is a real phenomenon, there must be a psychological explanation for it. Thus, we can also ask, what cognitive mechanisms can account for repression? As memory scientists, it is necessary to examine what may be such mechanisms, especially given that in most circumstances, highly distinctive and emotional (if negative) events tend to be well remembered and not forgotten. Recent theory has focused on two potential mechanisms. The first is the **failure-to-rehearse** explanation. Because memories of childhood trauma are highly negative, often private, and potentially embarrassing, they are not likely to be rehearsed often. We often reflect and think back on positive events, but for some, negative events may not do so. However, if we do not rehearse the event, the normal processes of updating and elaboration will not be evoked, leading to a poor and less accessible memory trace. So simply failing to rehearse a memory can have a passive effect, leading to that memory becoming inaccessible. Second, **active suppression** may account for some repression. Active suppression here means that people may deliberately force themselves to not remember the item. That is, every time the memory is activated, people will distract themselves or force themselves to think about something else, so as not to think about the traumatic memory. Although this sounds paradoxical at first, research suggests that people can inhibit particular memories from growing stronger. We will consider the data for both of these ideas.

Repression: the active forgetting of highly emotional memories, usually from childhood.

Failure to rehearse: a theory that explains repression. It argues that because memories of childhood trauma are highly negative, often private, and potentially embarrassing, they are not likely to be rehearsed often.

Active suppression: a theory that explains repression. People may deliberately force themselves to not remember the item.

S. M. Smith and Moynan (2008) conducted a study that examined the failure-to-rehearse hypothesis. They wanted to demonstrate that rehearsal failure could account for some initial forgetting and then later subsequent recovery of memory, much like the process of repression. However, they did the experiment in a lab setting with the goal of demonstrating powerful forgetting and equally strong recovery with simple word stimuli. The experiment served as a basis for speculating about the nature of repression and recovery. Here is what Smith and Moynan did.

First, participants viewed a long series of categorized lists. For each list, the participants saw the category label (e.g., fish) and many exemplars (e.g., salmon, halibut, trout, snapper).

Participants wrote down each word and made a judgment as to the fit that each word made to the category. Thus, "trout" would be a good fit to the category of "fish," but perhaps "seahorse" might be less so. Three of these lists were called critical lists, whereas the rest were filler lists. The three critical lists were composed of two word lists designed to elicit emotional responses (e.g., curse words, deadly diseases) and one neutral list (e.g., tools). Critical lists were the ones in which forgetting was to be induced. The fillers were all neutral categories (e.g., fish). Participants were not told about any future memory tests (see Figure 8.4).

Following the category judgments, participants were given one of two filler tasks. In one filler task, the control group was given nonverbal problems to solve, such as math problems. In the other filler task, the "forget" group was given tasks that involved doing semantic tasks with the filler categories. These tasks involved making judgments of the pleasantness of the items on the list, the size of the items on the list, or the number of syllables in each word on the list. What is important here is that these additional tasks were done with the filler categories, that is, the ones that were not critical to later memory for the critical lists. The idea was that retrieval practice of the filler categories would make the critical categories less accessible later on.

The goal was to create a **retrieval bias.** Retrieval bias means that some information is easier to recall than other information. Retrieval bias can be induced by requiring a participant to retrieve certain information (i.e., examples of fish). This makes the fish information easier to retrieve but also makes it more difficult to retrieve the other categories. The filler categories are rendered more accessible and thus more likely to be retrieved. The critical lists are not rehearsed, become less accessible, and, therefore, are less likely to be retrieved. There is analog to this in politics. Think about a recent political election. Political candidates repeat their own "message" over and over, so that their issues are easy to think about, even when the real critical issues lie elsewhere. When a person enters the voting booth, those political pronouncements spoken over and over on the politicians' commercials are what come to mind, rather than other issues about which the candidate might be weak. The politician, of course, wishes to influence your vote, but his or her strategy does so by influencing what you retrieve from memory.

> **Retrieval bias**: a technique used to make some information easier to recall than other information.

Retrieval bias is also relevant in the situation of repressing memories of childhood abuse. These memories are painful, confusing, and embarrassing both to a child and to an adult. It is likely that some people will spend much more time thinking of other things and as little time as possible focusing on the abuse. Eventually, as the other events that are rehearsed continue to grow in accessibility, the memory of the abuse, through lack of retrieval, is rendered inaccessible and hence repressed. S. M. Smith and Moynan (2008) describe a situation in which a long continuous event or set of events occurred (i.e., summer camp), filled mostly with positive recurring events (soccer, campfires), which are described and retold many times (that is, rehearsed), and a single isolated negative event (the abuse), which occurs once and then is never spoken about (that is, failure to rehearse).

Returning to S. M. Smith and Moynan's (2008) experiment. Think of the experimental conditions. First, we have the critical emotion-inducing lists and nonemotional control lists. Second, we have a variable in which one group does a nonverbal distractor task and a second

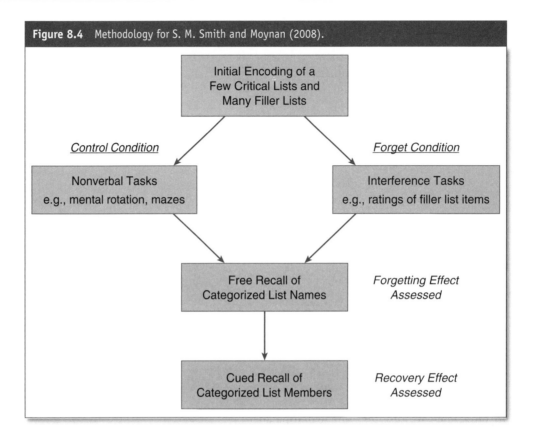

Figure 8.4 Methodology for S. M. Smith and Moynan (2008).

group who does a verbal task with the filler lists, designed to induce retrieval bias. Smith and Moynan followed these experimental variables with two memory tests. In the first test, participants were asked to recall the names of the *categories* presented during the initial phase. That is, the experimenter simply asked the person to recall as many categories as possible without providing any clues, cues, or hints. The participants were expected to recall the category names, not the exemplars within a category. Second, following the free recall of categories, the category names were given as cues to remember the exemplars from each list. In the category-cued list, participants were expected to recall the exemplars from each category, including the critical lists.

The results reveal some interesting features about the critical lists. First, consider the recall of category names. In the "forget" condition (verbal filler task), participants were much less likely to recall the category names of the critical emotional items than they were in the control condition (nonverbal task; see Figure 8.5). Indeed, for the category "diseases," the level of category recall fell from over 20% in the control condition to just about 2% in the "forget" condition. That is, only 2% of participants recalled the category name "disease" in the condition in which the filler lists received semantic practice.

However, in the category-cued retrieval of list exemplars, there was no difference in recall between the control and "forget" conditions in the number of exemplars from the any

Figure 8.5   Results from S. M. Smith and Moynan (2008).

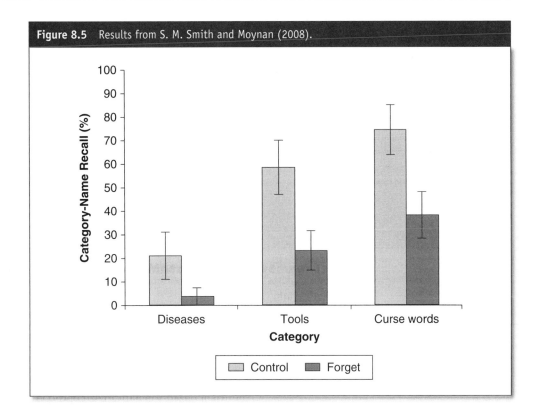

critical categories (disease, curse words, tools). Thus, once the category had been activated, then it was possible to retrieve the words that had been presented in that category. S. M. Smith and Moynan (2008) point out that it was not that the participants were generating words that fit the category. Participants rarely included intrusions, that is, words from the same category that were not on the list (about 1 %).

Let's see how closely this paradigm fits the pattern of repression and recovery of abuse. First, amid a large number of neutral categories, two categories were emotional and negative in nature (diseases, curse words). This is like a normal childhood (neutral categories) shattered occasionally by an abusive event (the negative emotional categories). Then, in the "forget" condition, the neutral categories are rehearsed (as we tell stories of the positive events of childhood), but the emotional critical categories are not rehearsed (as some individuals and families may steadfastly refuse to discuss the abuse and its consequences). Then, when people are asked to recall the categories (or remember the important events of their lives), they are good at remembering the practiced categories but often fail to remember the critical categories (i.e., the abuse). However, when given the appropriate retrieval cue (in this case, the category name, such as "curse words"), the participants have no difficulties in retrieving the items from that list (just as, once the right cue is given, abuse victims spontaneously recall the abuse). This method potentially explains why repressed memories may be recovered in therapy, as therapy may provide just the right retrieval cues. Thus, the S. M. Smith and Moynan (2008) experiment may serve as a good model of the significance of rehearsal or lack of it in producing repressed memories. That is, although the experiment is complex, it provides a manner in which we can study the forgetting and later recovery of information in memory.

Active Suppression

Another mechanism whereby repression might occur is active suppression of the unwanted memories. Active suppression means that people may actively work to push the memory out of consciousness, eventually leading to the event being completely forgotten, at least until the appropriate retrieval cue is given. Think about something really terrible—the horrors of the Holocaust, the images of the Twin Towers tumbling down, or perhaps even the fact that you, like all people, will eventually die. Think about what you do when asked to think about your own death. Most people prefer not to think about it and quickly focus their attention and working memory elsewhere. Similarly, people will try to direct attention away from thinking about unpleasant events in the past. Many people prefer not to think about such topics and do whatever they can to refocus their conscious attention on something less depressing. Thus, even for healthy nonabused normal people, it is not unusual to attempt to suppress unpleasant thoughts or memories. In the case of 9/11, the public images, discussions in schools, news programs, and other venues will always remind you that this event did take place. But a personal tragedy may not receive the same public attention. Thus, actively working to avoid remembering a personal tragedy might just succeed.

A landmark study on this topic was conducted by M. C. Anderson and Green (2001). They were specifically interested in whether repression could be simulated in the laboratory and modeled on active suppression. First, they trained participants on simple word pairs (they used the example of *ordeal–roach*). When the participants had mastered a list of 40 word pairs (i.e., improved to the point where they could recall all the target words when given the cue word), they moved on to the next phase of the experiment.

They were given what M. C. Anderson and Green (2001) called a "think/no think" procedure. On some trials, they were given "think" instructions. This meant when the cue word (*ordeal*) was presented, they were supposed to recall the target word that went with it and say it aloud. On other trials, they received "no think" instructions, which meant they were meant to actively avoid thinking about the target word. Saying it aloud, as in the think condition, led to a loud buzzing sound. In some cases, items in the no-think condition occurred as many as 16 times—that is, people were asked to suppress the target on 16 different opportunities. Note, unlike the S. M. Smith and Moynan (2008) study, the participants were actively suppressing instead of simply not having opportunities to rehearse.

The suppression worked! When M. C. Anderson and Green (2001) gave a final recall test after all of the suppression and practice trials were over, they found that the suppressed items were recalled much worse than control items that were neither practiced nor suppressed as well as being worse than the practiced items. Moreover, the more suppression per item (16 times vs. fewer), the worse recall was. Anderson and Green were afraid that expectations might inhibit some people from reporting recall for some of the suppressed items, so they added a 25-cent-per-item payment for each item recalled. Nonetheless, that incentive failed to increase the number of recalled targets in the suppressed conditions.

Figure 8.6 Experimental paradigm from M. C. Anderson and Green (2001).

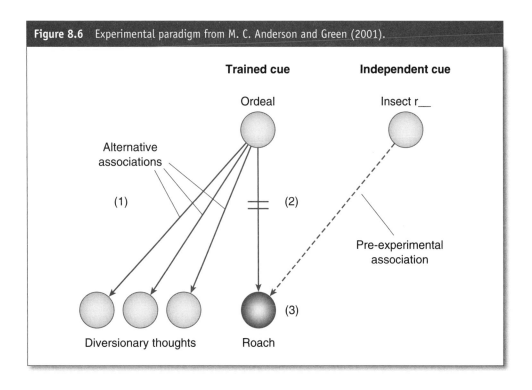

Anderson and his group replicated the study with the same basic behavioral methodology but also employed a functional magnetic resonance imaging (fMRI) scanner to examine what was happening in the brains of participants when they were actively suppressing information (in the "no-think" condition). Thus, when people studied or suppressed the word pairs, they did so under an fMRI scanner (M. C. Anderson et al., 2004). Suppression was associated with a decrease in activity in the hippocampus, a key memory-encoding region of the brain. It was also associated with increased activity in the dorsolateral regions of the prefrontal cortex, an area of the brain associated with control of behavior and attention. The prefrontal cortex was driving the conscious suppression of the no-think item and working to inhibit memory connections being made by the hippocampus. Thus, the neuroscience also supports their view—people are actively attending to the action, and the action is inhibiting memory.

What does this mean? Well, at least in a laboratory simulation, people can actively suppress items and that this active suppression of items later makes those items more difficult to recall. Is this similar to what happens in repression of traumatic events? It is not clear. The material used in this experiment is a far cry from memories of traumatic events in childhood. Nonetheless, people who have suffered from a traumatic event may actively work to not recall that event. This experiment shows that such active suppression works. We do remember less of the items we suppress. Thus, we have two mechanisms that may each explain aspects of repression. On one hand, a failure to actively rehearse information may lead to that information becoming inaccessible, as in the S. M. Smith and Moynan

(2008) experiment. On the other hand, active suppression may also lead to information becoming lost.

INTERIM SUMMARY 1

False memory refers to the observation that people do misremember events. The cognitive study of false memory attempts to determine the how and the why of false memory. Psychologists who study false memory are interested in the correspondence between the actual event and the person's memory of it. One mechanism that produces false memory is the failure to source monitor. If you remember something but attribute to the wrong source, it may wind up as a false memory. False memories have been investigated with a number of techniques, including the Deese-Roediger-McDermott procedure (DRM), the false memory induction procedure, imagination inflation, and altered evidence. One of the debates in the area concerns the nature of the recovery of repressed memories. Are such recovered memories real or false? Although the data suggest that many of them are false, new research attempts to explore the cognitive mechanisms that could produce both initial repression and subsequent recovery. S. M. Smith and Moynan (2008) investigated the hypothesis that repression occurs because of failures to rehearse, whereas M. C. Anderson and colleagues (2004) have conducted experiments on active suppression.

FALSE MEMORIES AND LEGAL PSYCHOLOGY

Increasingly, psychology is contributing to many aspects of how we view the law and our legal system. Think about how many aspects of the legal system reflect important psychological processes. Witnesses to crimes must rely on memory to help police with their investigations. Police detectives themselves must engage in any number of problem-solving skills to solve and catch the criminals they seek. How we interrogate criminal suspects also depends heavily on psychological research. In the courtroom, attorneys must influence jury decision making, and judges must make decisions as to what juries should or should not know about the case. During deliberation, jury members must convince each other of the logic and correctness of their views on a particular trial. All of these aspects of legal behavior are now under investigation by one team of psychological researchers or another.

As such, psychologists are studying the cognitive and social processes involved in these activities and offering their expertise in ways in which the system can be improved. There are scholars studying the process of how juries make decisions, how jurors interpret evidence that they are told to discard, how juries and judges interpret scientific evidence, how police can maximize the evidence they can obtain from an honest witness, how police can detect dishonest testimony, how police conduct line-ups, how children differ from adults when giving testimony, and, of course, the unreliability of eyewitness memory. In this chapter, we will consider eyewitness memory and what processes can lead eyewitness to incorrectly remember aspects of a crime.

EYEWITNESS TESTIMONY

Many years ago, on a cold winter New Hampshire day, a friend offered to drive me home. It was freezing and snowing, and my boots were already soaked through, so I was not looking forward to my usually relaxing mile walk home. We pulled out of my friend's parking spot and were just about to make a right turn, when, out of nowhere, a large truck with a snowplow smashed into my friend's car. Surprisingly, neither my friend nor I was hurt, and there was little damage to either car. The snowplow driver, a large man, stepped out of his car, checked his truck for damage (there was none) and started belligerently swearing at my friend and me. He then got back into his truck and drove off without exchanging insurance information or waiting for the police. I quickly wrote down his license plate tag. My friend and I then drove to the police station to report the incident. After my friend described what happened, a police officer pulled me aside and politely asked me to describe the snowplow driver. "He was tall, almost your height," I responded. But then I was silent. I couldn't describe one more thing about him. The best the police officer could put down on his report was "a tall white man between the ages of 30 and 50," which probably fit the description of every snowplow driver in the state of New Hampshire. I could not recall one detail about his face. Did he have a big nose? Was his hair light colored or dark colored? I could not even recall if he had facial hair. Now this was a minor accident, and my friend had insurance, so a massive manhunt was not ordered for this crime. But what if it had been? Was I worthless as a witness? I was a graduate student studying memory and well versed in the literature on eyewitness memory. But it did me no good. Would I have been able to pick him out of a line-up? I seriously doubted it. I failed as a witness.

I started off the chapter with a number of cases in which eyewitnesses identified a person as a criminal, and later evidence exonerated that person. Here is another. In 1985, Kirk Bloodsworth was convicted and sentenced to death for the brutal rape and murder of a young child. Much of the evidence of his guilt was based on an eyewitness who claimed she saw him with the girl just prior to the crime. Almost immediately, his lawyers started working on the testimony of the witness, which changed considerably from her first encounter with police investigators to the time she testified in court. But her firm assertion that she saw Bloodsworth with the girl convinced the jury. Eight years later, Bloodsworth was pardoned and released after DNA evidence demonstrated he could not possibly have been the killer. For more on this case, go to www.sagepub.com/schwartz.[6]

What leads people to misremember such important information? It turns out that one of the flaws of human memory is suggestibility—that our memories readily incorporate information from other sources into our original memory of an event. Think of the witness who may have misidentified the man that she saw with the doomed girl. The witness wants to help bring the guilty to justice, and the police thought they had the man. The police, even if trying their best to be fair and impartial, may have said things that led the witness to imagine Bloodsworth's face for the man that she really saw. She may have found out that other witnesses had already identified Bloodsworth. These subtle factors may lead to a subtle but steady altering of the memory. By the time the witness reaches the courtroom many weeks after witnessing the event, she is convinced that her memory was of the indicted suspect.

In most of these cases, the witnesses are being honest; it is just that their memory has been altered during the process. Suggestibility is a major source of false memories and is a major factor in errors in eyewitness testimony.

Let's start examining some of the psychological research on this topic.

Effects of Wording on Memory of an Accident

Suggestibility includes incorporating information from leading questions. People assume that there is certain "given" information in questions, particularly when they come from authority figures, such as police officers or lawyers. This information contained in the questions then subtly influences the nature of the witness's memory. Loftus and Palmer (1974) demonstrated this in what is now considered a classic experiment on eyewitness memory (see Figure 8.7). They asked participants to watch a short film depicting a motor vehicle accident. After the film, the participants were asked one of five questions:

1. How fast were the cars going when they *smashed* each other?

2. How fast were the cars going when they *collided* each other?

3. How fast were the cars going when they *bumped* each other?

4. How fast were the cars going when they *hit* each other?

5. How fast were the cars going when they *contacted* each other?

They found that the estimates of speed given by participants were different depending on which question they were asked. Using the term *smashed* led to estimates nearly 10 miles per hour faster than when the word *contacted* was used. Everyone had seen the same crash, but the way in which the question was asked affected the estimate of speed. Thus, a subtle difference in wording affected people's memory enough to bias their report of the accident (see Table 8.1).

Table 8.1   Speed estimates from Loftus and Palmer (1974).

Verb Used	Estimated Speed
Smashed	41
Collided	39
Bumped	38
Hit	34
Contacted	32

Figure 8.7   Stimulus for Loftus and Palmer (1974).

Recall instructions	Schema	Response
"How fast were the cars going when they **smashed** into each other?"		"About 42 mph"
"How fast were the cars going when they **contacted** each other?"		"About 32 mph"

Sometimes a single little word can influence people's memory. Indeed, Loftus and Zanni (1975) found that the subtle difference between the words *the* and *a* can have a strong effect on memory. In their study, participants viewed a film of an automobile accident. Later, they answered a series of questions about the accident. Half of the participants received the following question: "Did you see *a* broken headlight?" whereas the other half of the participants received this question: "Did you see *the* broken headlight?" In fact, the film did not depict an accident with a broken headlight. In these sentences, "*the* broken headlight" implies that there was a broken headlight and inquires if the person noticed it. When the sentence includes "*a* broken headlight," the sentence implies that it is not known if the headlight was broken and asks the witness whether there was one or not. Only 7% erroneously reported a broken headlight when the word *a* was used. However, 18% reported that they had seen a broken headlight when the word *the* was used. Thus, a simple word like *the* can raise the rates of false memory from 7% to over 10% to 18%.

THE MISINFORMATION EFFECT

Misinformation effect: the presenting of postevent misinformation about a witnessed event can obscure, change, or degrade the memory of the original event.

Probably the most influential experiment ever in cognitive psychology is the **misinformation effect** technique developed by Elizabeth Loftus (see Loftus, 1979). It has changed the way memory researchers think about memory and the way the legal system handles witnesses. The basic methodology of the misinformation effect is as follows. People witness an event, usually a crime event—nowadays, it is most often done by having people watch a videotape of a simulated crime. Following the event, they receive written information about the event, either implied through questions ("Did you see the criminal's gang tattoos?") or by reading a description ("The thief had a tattoo of the Skull gang"). Loftus embedded in these descriptions some factual information (consistent with actual event) and some misleading information (contradictory to the actual event). The critical independent variable is the presence or absence of misleading information for any particular detail of the crime. Thus, some witnesses will receive misinformation about the tattoo, whereas others will receive consistent information about the tattoo. The third stage is a memory test, usually recognition, but sometimes recall. The critical dependent measure is the performance of participants on questions referring to the misleading information compared to control conditions. The results consistently show that providing misleading information leads to worse memory performance (see Table 8.2).

Table 8.2   Misinformation procedure.
1. Witnesses view crime film.
2. Receive Condition 1 (some factual information) and Condition 2 (some misleading information).
3. Memory test.
4. Performance on Condition 2 is worse than on Condition 1.

Consider the following experiment from Loftus's work (Loftus, Miller, & Burns, 1978). This experiment was actually done by having the participants view a slide show rather than a filmed version. Later experiments have determined that the effect works equivalently with video. Participants saw a slide show of a small red sports car moving toward an accident with another car. One group of participants saw a slide showing a yield sign, whereas the other group saw a stop sign (see Figure 8.8). Immediately after seeing the slides, the two groups were asked to answer questions about what they had seen in the slides. The important misinformation manipulation went as follows. Regardless of which sign participants had seen, half of each group was asked a question using the term *stop sign,* and half were asked a question using the term *yield sign.* Thus, if you had seen a stop sign but then were asked about a yield sign, this was the misinformation condition. If you had seen a yield sign but then were asked about a stop sign, this was also the misinformation condition. The consistent condition referred to when you witnessed and then were asked about the same sign.

A few minutes later, the participants saw slides with pictures of the event on them. The participants' task was to choose the slide that they had seen during the original presentation. For the critical question, the participants had to choose between the photograph with the yield sign and the photograph with the stop sign (see Figure 8.8). When the

Figure 8.8   Stimuli used to examine the misinformation effect.

SOURCE: Loftus, Miller, and Burns (1978).

original slide and the postevent question were consistent, participants chose the correct slide 75% of the time. However, when misinformation was present, the percent correct dropped to 40%. That is, the introduction of misinformation caused 60% of the participants to choose what they had heard after the event rather than what they had actually seen. The difference in accuracy based on whether the postevent information was accurate or not was 35%.

The misinformation effect is a robust finding. It is easily found and easily replicated. It can work on people's memory of people in an event or on objects. It can work on central or peripheral details of an event. It works with details that arouse emotion (such as the presence of a gun) and with details that do not (whether the victim was eating potato chips or cookies). It can work at short and long retention intervals. It works when recall is the final test and when recognition is the final test (Loftus, 1979; Paz-Alonzo & Goodman, 2008).

Explanations for the Misinformation Effect

The data from misinformation effects experiments show that people's memories are influenced by the misinformation, leading them to falsely report what they witnessed during the crime scene. One question concerning the explanation for this phenomenon is what happens to the representation of the event in memory. Is the memory representation altered by the misinformation, or does the postevent information set up a second memory representation and the participant does not know which one to report? This is the issue of source monitoring described earlier in the chapter. Consider what happens when a person receives misinformation after viewing an event. On one hand, it is possible that the person retrieves the memory of the event and then inserts the misinformation into the original record of the event. On the other hand, the person may form a second memory, that is, a memory of hearing the postevent information. When the person goes to retrieve the original memory and finds it lacking in the information sought by the question, the person instead retrieves the information from the second memory. These are essentially the two theories that have been advanced to explain the misinformation effect.

Loftus (1992) argued that the original memory is altered by the misinformation. This view is known as the **trace impairment view.** The trace impairment view states that the misinformation distorts or alters the memory for the original event. It has also been called the "blending" view because the new memory is a blending of the original event and the memory of the later information, including the misinformation. In contrast, McCloskey and Zaragoza (1985) presented the **coexistence hypothesis.** This is the view that participants form one memory about the original event and then form a second memory of reading the questions or summary after the event. The second memory is composed of both retrieved information from the first event and any new information derived from the postevent questions. In this view, each retrieval attempt generates its own new memory. Moreover, it is the retrieval of these later memories that leads to the misinformation effect. Note that both views agree that suggestibility has a strong effect on the production of false memories. The difference between the two views is the nature of memory representation.

> **Trace impairment view**: a theory that explains the misinformation effect. In this view, the original memory is altered by the misinformation.
>
> **Coexistence hypothesis**: a theory that explains the misinformation effect. Participants form one memory about the original event and then form a second memory of reading the questions or reading the summary after the event.

To test these two theories, McCloskey and Zaragoza (1985) came up with a straightforward experiment. It involved a simple variation of the misinformation paradigm. The variation was to examine the kind of incorrect distractors on the recognition test. In one condition, McCloskey and Zaragoza presented two choices, an object seen in the original event (i.e., a Coke can) and the object suggested in the misinformation (i.e., a Budweiser can).

This is identical to how Loftus originally measured the misinformation effect. However, in the second condition, McCloskey and Zaragoza presented the object from the original event (i.e., the Coke can) with a distractor that was not part of the misinformation (i.e., a 7-Up can). Thus, the comparison is the number of times participants are incorrect when the suggested but wrong item is present and the number of times participants are incorrect when the suggested but wrong item is novel.

If the trace impairment view is correct, then the misinformation should alter and distort the original memory representation. That is, during misinformation, the original memory is retrieved, and the misinformation replaces or changes the correct information. In the example, in the person's memory of the crime, the "can" becomes a visual image of the Budweiser can instead of the Coca-Cola can. The memory is changed. If this is true, performance on the recognition test should be worse in the misinformation condition regardless of the type of test used because the memory is altered. The alternatives now—that is, the original "Coke" and novel "7-Up"—are equally at odds with the "Budweiser" in the person's memory. The item presented as a distractor at the time of the recognition test should not matter. The memory trace is impaired, and therefore, recognition performance should be impaired even when the distractor is a totally novel item, just as it is when the distractor is the misinformation item.

In contrast, if the coexistence hypothesis is correct, two memories are formed, one for the original event and one for the misinformation. That is, there are two memories side by side, one of the original event and a second memory caused by the postevent information, which contains the misinformation. At the time of test, when the recognition test is a choice between the original item and a novel item, there is no cue to induce retrieval of the second memory. Thus, there should be no inducement to select the distractor item that was not part of the misinformation. Thus, under these circumstances, the coexistence view argues that the misinformation effect should disappear. This is exactly what McCloskey and Zaragoza (1985) found. In the recognition test in which there was a novel distractor, there was no misinformation effect. This has some positive applications. If there is good reason to suspect misinformation was given to witnesses at some point during an investigation, the police should avoid presenting that misinformation again later in the investigation. If the witnesses are incorrectly retrieving the event of receiving misinformation, then when the misinformation is not part of the retrieval cue, they may recall the original memory trace (see Figure 8.9).

The McCloskey and Zaragoza (1985) study looks like it supports the coexistence hypothesis. This means that when we answer with the misinformation, it is because we are recalling the misinformation from the time of its presentation rather than a distorted view of the original event. However, subsequent work cast this interpretation into doubt. For example, at short retention intervals, the McCloskey and Zaragoza results replicate, but at longer retention intervals, misinformation reduces correct performance even when the final recognition test does not include the suggested item (Belli, Windschitl, McCarthey, & Winfrey, 1992).

There are also data that support the trace impairment view. Evidence for the trace impairment view comes from research on blending. For example, in one study, participants saw a blue car during a short film of an accident. Later, it was erroneously suggested that the car was green. At the time of test, the participants had to choose the color of the car. Participants

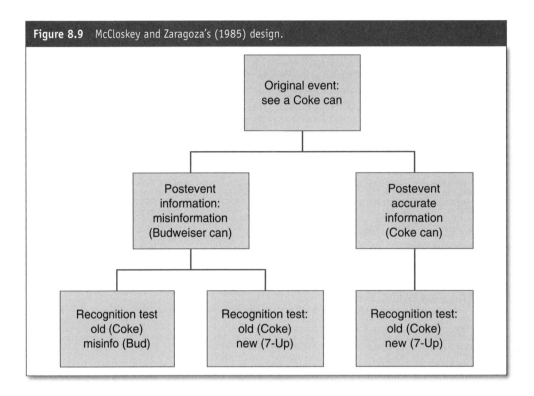

Figure 8.9 McCloskey and Zaragoza's (1985) design.

tended to choose a blue-green when given a palette of colors. The blue-green represented something intermediate between the blue that they saw and the green that was suggested. If the coexistence view is correct, then the participants would have chosen either blue or green but not the intermediate. However, if trace impairment is correct, then the colors might mix in memory, and you would anticipate that the participants would choose the intermediate color. You originally form a memory of a blue car when you see it in the film. However, that memory is altered or distorted at the time of misinformation. The suggested green then interacts with the memory of the original item, which leads to the blend or intermediate color (Loftus, 1992).

INTERIM SUMMARY 2

Witnessing a crime is a rare and emotionally laden event. Memory for that event is often important for the police in helping them solve a crime and for the court system in prosecuting an accused criminal. However, the research on eyewitness memory tells us that such memories are not always accurate. Like other memories, they may be false. In particular, memory researchers have looked at the effect of suggestibility on eyewitness memory. First, subtle differences in words can affect people's memory reports. Second, the introduction of misinformation can also distort or alter people's memory for a crime. Elizabeth Loftus introduced a procedure, called the misinformation effect, to measure suggestibility in eye-witness memory. In the procedure, a person witnesses an event but then sees misinformation about it later. The misinformation impairs memory relative to appropriate controls. It is likely that this decrement in performance is caused by a change to the original memory as a result of its interaction with the misinformation.

THE COGNITIVE INTERVIEW:
MORE INFORMATION WITHOUT SUGGESTION

We know that all of us may have false memories from time to time. We also know that we all my fall prey to suggestion, even in sensitive legal proceedings. Is there anything we can do about it? When the witness confidently proclaims, "I'll never forget that day—it was that man over there who committed the crime," can we ever really put confidence in that statement? Should we ever really trust such a statement? Are there ways of gathering information from witnesses that do not run the risk of inadvertently providing misinformation?

> **Cognitive interview**: a protocol designed to help police investigators obtain the maximum amount of information from witnesses with the least likelihood of inducing false memories.
>
> **Amount of information**: the quantity of information retrieved while recalling an episodic event.

Ron Fisher and Ed Geiselman devised something they called the **cognitive interview** (Fisher & Geiselman, 1992). The cognitive interview is a protocol designed to help police investigators obtain the maximum **amount of information** from witnesses with the least likelihood of inducing false memories. The cognitive interview is based on several principles of memory retrieval that we have discussed earlier in this book. It has also been tested empirically itself to substantiate its claim to boost memory without increasing the rate of false memory. The cognitive interview succeeds in passing these tests (Fisher & Schreiber, 2007). Let's see how the cognitive interview works.

> **Open-ended questions**: retrieval questions that contain very few cues, which allow the participant to describe his or her memory without suggestions. Open-ended questions limit the possibility of introducing inadvertent misinformation.

First, the police officer or other initial investigator is instructed to ask **open-ended questions.** Open-ended questions limit the possibility of introducing inadvertent misinformation. For example, an open-ended question is simply, "What did you see?" rather than "Did you see the man who pulled out a gun?" It is possible that it was a woman who pulled out a gun, two men who had guns, and or there was no gun at all. So unless the investigator saw the crime himself or herself, there is the possibility of introducing misinformation with the directed question, however plausible it may seem. The open-ended questions provide no opportunity for the introduction of misinformation.

However, open-ended questions may not provide sufficient cues for witnesses to remember certain details, which might be important for an investigation. Thus, in the past, open-ended questions have been avoided because they typically generate less total amount of information than a series of directed questions. To counter this, in the cognitive interview, witnesses are encouraged to report everything they can remember, regardless of how inconsequential they may think it is. This may occasionally be a waste of a police officer's time with a particularly longwinded witness, but if the case is important enough, it is time well spent. Therefore, Fisher and colleagues recommend a set of cue-inducing principles to assist the witness in remembering.

The cognitive interview uses three such retrieval-enhancing principles. First, witnesses are encouraged to think about the physical context of the witnessed event. Notice that asking a person to think about the physical context cannot lead to the introduction of misinformation, but it is designed to allow the witness to find context-based retrieval cues to bolster his or her memory. In fact, witnesses are asked to imagine themselves at the scene of the crime and to report what they see. Second, the witness is encouraged to remember the event from different time sequences—most recent to most distant, then from the beginning of the event until the end of the event. Third, witnesses are asked to mentally visualize the crime scene from a variety of perspectives—from their own and from that of someone looking from the outside. The hope is that different perspectives will provide different retrieval cues and more information will be provided. Again, it is especially important to avoid any suggestions, especially as participants will be imagining themselves at the scene of the crime. Indeed, research shows that the cognitive interview can boost the report of recalled information by 30% compared to a standard police interview without raising the percentage of information that is inaccurate (Fisher & Schreiber, 2007).

Mnemonic Improvement Tip 8.1

The cognitive interview: When trying to recall details of a particular event, use the three principles of the cognitive interview: (1) context reinstatement, (2) different temporal patterns, (3) different spatial patterns. Recall as much as possible and sort out what is relevant later.

You might wonder why the cognitive interview does not increase the rate of false memories. Some of these methods look very similar to the therapeutic methods criticized for the likelihood of inducing false memories. There is, however, a critical difference. In the criticized therapy, clients are asked to imagine or visualize a particular event—namely, that they were sexually abused as young children. It is about one particular cause of adult psychological distress, but there are many others. Moreover, the therapist has no real basis for the certainty that abuse occurred. Thus, the therapist runs the risk of being suggestive that this is the cause. In the cognitive interview, witnesses are asked open-ended questions, intended to not bias the witness in any way. Moreover, they do remember the event happening and that they witnessed the event is not in doubt. The goal is simply to get them to remember more details of a remembered event, not to reveal a repressed memory. Keeping the questions open-ended also avoids the suggestions of details that were not present. For example, "Try to think about the physical context of the event and tell me everything you can" is different from "Try to imagine the large man with the gun. Tell me everything you can about his mustache and the semi-automatic handgun he was carrying." Now this second sentence may be an exaggeration, but it is loaded with the potential to suggest misinformation that may affect the witnesses' recall. The cognitive interview question, however, does not. Thus, it leads to an increase in correct recall without an increase in the rate of false memories.

Ron Fisher and Ed Geiselman have worked with police departments all over the world, including Miami, Los Angeles, and London. As a consequence, the cognitive interview has been tested and used successfully in real-world settings. Some police investigators now swear by it. It is also possible that the cognitive interview will be useful for other kinds of investigations. For example, doctors could use it to maximize the amount of information that they get from their patients. In many kinds of illnesses, it is still the symptoms that serve as the best diagnostic tool for doctors. The technique could also be used by historians trying to investigate a historical event by probing the details of remaining witnesses to the event. If you are interested in more information on the cognitive interview, the two cognitive psychologists who devised it also wrote a book, which is designed as a "how-to" for investigators in getting the maximum out of eyewitnesses (Fisher & Geiselman, 1992). For the transcript of an interview with Ron Fisher, go to www.sagepub.com/schwartz.[7]

A recent study on eyewitness memory suggests a simple but potent means of increasing the ability of eyewitnesses to accurately recall an event: Close your eyes while you remember the event. Perfect et al. (2008) showed that simply closing one's eyes allowed witnesses to remember more information about a witnessed crime with no increase in false memories. Because it led to an increase in the recollection of many visual details, they suspect that the improved memory likely occurs because closing one's eyes removes an important part of memory interference—namely, the currently visible world and its impingement on working memory. Thus, closing one's eyes allows retrieval processes to eliminate at least one source of interference. Perfect and his colleagues suggest that eye closure ought to be incorporated into the cognitive interview.

Mnemonic Improvement Tip 8.2

Close your eyes when trying to remember episodic events such as eyewitness memory. It allows you to recall more details without a cost in false memories.

SUMMARY

False memory refers to the relatively small amounts of information that we recall that do not correspond to reality. Accuracy or correspondence is the measure of the extent to which retrieved memories correspond to the factual past. False memories have been highly controversial and well studied in two domains, the recovery of repressed memories of childhood abuse and eyewitness memory. Because of the controversies surrounding these two areas, cognitive psychologists have devised a number of ways of studying false memory in the laboratory. These methods include the Deese-Roediger-McDermott procedure (DRM), the false memory induction procedure, imagination inflation, and the misinformation effect. Explanations for false memories vary, but some center on source monitoring, remembering gist instead of specific details, and suggestibility. Hypnosis can also lead to an increase in false memories. New research suggests, however, that repressed memories may be real. Two mechanisms for repression may be the failure to rehearse the information combined with active suppression. In the legal context, eyewitness memory is fallible, and the dangers of misinformation are well documented. The cognitive interview provides a way for witnesses to recall lots of details from a crime scene without increasing the risk of false memories.

KEY TERMS

False memory

Correspondence

Suggestibility

Reality monitoring

Critical intrusions

Deese-Roediger-McDermott procedure

Contextual associations

Fuzzy-trace theory

False memory induction procedure

Hypnosis

Recovery of repressed memories

Imagination inflation

Repression

Failure to rehearse

Active suppression

Retrieval bias

Misinformation effect

Trace impairment view

Coexistence hypothesis

Cognitive interview

Amount of information

Open-ended questions

REVIEW QUESTIONS

1. What are false memories? Do they only happen to people who have been traumatized, or are they a more general phenomenon?

2. What does correspondence mean? Why is reporting the amount that people recall not enough to fully describe memory ability?

3. What is the Deese-Roediger-McDermott procedure (DRM) procedure? What does it measure, and how does it do so?

4. What is the false memory induction procedure? What does it measure, and how does it do so?

5. What is hypnosis? Why it is not considered advisable to help eyewitnesses remember more information from a crime scene?

6. What evidence exists to show that repression is a real phenomenon? Why would cognitive scientists have doubted repression in the first place?

7. What cognitive mechanisms have been postulated to explain repression? What experimental data support that these cognitive mechanisms are real?

8. What is suggestibility? What evidence exists to show how it influences eyewitness memory?

9. What are the two explanations for the misinformation effect? What evidence supports each one?

10. What is the cognitive interview? How is it used to prevent false memories but still produce good recall?

ONLINE RESOURCES

1. For more on Dr. Thompson's ordeal, go to http://www.spring.org.uk/2008/02/how-memories-are-distorted-and-invented.php.

2. For the transcript of an interview with Dr. Clancy, go to http://www.nuforc.org/npr.html.

3. For more on the Roediger-McDermott illusion, go to http://memory.wustl.edu/McDermott_Lab/MCL.html and http://memory.wustl.edu/Pubs/1995_Roediger.pdf.

4. For an article on this topic by Elizabeth Loftus, go to http://faculty.washington.edu/eloftus/Articles/sciam.htm.

5. To find out more about imagination inflation, go to http://faculty.washington.edu/eloftus/Articles/Imagine.htm.

6. Visit the website of the Innocence Project for other cases in which people have been wrongly convicted (http://www.innocenceproject.org).

7. For the transcript of an interview with Ron Fisher, go to http://www.au.af.mil/au/awc/awcgate/gov/ntsb_cognitive_interview.pdf.

 Go to www.sagepub.com/schwartz for additional exercises and study resources. Select **Chapter 8, False Memory** for chapter-specific resources.

CHAPTER 9

Metamemory

Many of you have probably seen the popular game show, *Who Wants to Be a Millionaire?* In the game show, contestants are asked trivia questions. They see the question with four possible answers in front of them, one of which is the correct answer. It is the contestants' job to select the correct answer from among the four possibilities. With each trivia question they answer correctly, they win more money. If they answer a question incorrectly, however, they lose half or more of their money, and their "15 minutes" of fame comes to an end. However, the rules of the game allow each contestant several options if he or she does not know the answer or is unsure of the answer to a particular question. All of these options rely on the use of metamemory, our ability to introspect on our own memory system. For example, a contestant can choose another question instead of the one originally presented. The contestant must recognize that he or she does not know the answer to the first question before opting for a new question. If this question is also beyond the contestant, he or she can choose to not answer at all and keep all the money he or she has won. However, before a participant opts out and keeps the money already won, the contestant can also choose a "lifeline." He or she can call up a knowledgeable friend and ask for his or her opinion. The contestant only gets one of these, so it has to be used strategically. The contestant must feel unsure of himself or herself and confident that the friend will know. Another choice the contestant can make is to eliminate two of the four multiple-choice answers for one question only. The contestant must make a metacognitive decision as to when and for which question he or she wants to use this option.

Now most of us will never be on a game show, but the show is similar to situations in which a student is in when he or she takes an exam. Indeed, metamemory has a role in the ordinary studying that every college student must engage in. Imagine a student studying for two exams, both scheduled for the following day. She has an exam in social psychology, her favorite class in her intended major. The second exam is in statistics, a difficult class that is required for her major but not the most interesting subject to this student. What should she study? The answer is "It depends." It depends on a host of factors that the student must actively consider. First, how important is it for her to get a really good grade in social psychology? Perhaps she wants to work on an honors thesis with the professor. If so, it is worth putting all of the study time into social psychology, even if that means doing poorly on statistics. But statistics is an important class for graduate school. Should that class get more study time because of the consequences of having a bad grade in that class for likely admission to graduate school? Second, if the student has, by and large, mastered the social psychology, should she instead focus her study on the harder statistics class? Her yoga instructor, however, suggested, on the night prior to the exam, that she simply relax, take a bath, get a good night's sleep, and trust that she knows the material well. These real-life dilemmas are the domain of metamemory.

> **Metacognition**: our knowledge and awareness of our own cognitive processes.
>
> **Metamemory**: our knowledge and awareness of our own memory processes.

Metacognition refers to our knowledge and awareness of our own cognitive processes. Research suggests that based on our metacognitive awareness, we often make quite sophisticated decisions about how to go about learning, remembering, or probably finding our way when lost. The area of metacognition that deals with memory is called metamemory, the subject of this chapter. **Metamemory** means our knowledge and awareness of our own memory processes. Although we do not normally talk about metamemory, it is an important component of memory, as the next example will illustrate.

Metamemory is defined as the knowledge and awareness of one's own memory processes, including the abilities to both monitor one's own memory abilities and control them. It allows human beings to reflect on their own memory processes and to actively and expertly self-regulate their own memory processes. It may be that some animals have rudimentary metamemory processes (Kornell, 2009a; J. D. Smith & Washburn, 2005), but, by and large, metamemory abilities are processes unique to humans. Metamemory allows us to reflect on what we know and what we do not know. For example, when I state, "I know the names of every person who has been president of the United States but just a handful of the people who have been prime minister of Great Britain," I am making a metamemory statement—the knowledge of what is or is not in my memory. I can do this without mentally listing all the presidents; I know I know them. We can also apply this metamemory thinking to our learning and remembering. That is, we can focus our study on what we are unsure of and avoid what we are confident is beyond our abilities. Metamemory allows us to focus on the most difficult items if those are what we need to focus on or informs us we have studied enough and can take that warm bath.

WHAT IS METAMEMORY?

Like most of the topics we have been considering, metamemory is of interest because of both its theoretical importance in understanding the science of human memory and its practical importance for understanding human learning and memory improvement. It is for this reason that metamemory has become one of the hot topics in memory research of the first decade of the 21st century (Son & Vandierendonck, 2007). For information on active research on metamemory, go to www.sagepub.com/schwartz.[1]

Here are the important terms, definitions, and brief descriptions of a few critical ideas concerning metamemory.

Monitoring: our ability to reflect and become aware of what we know and what we do not.

Monitoring occurs whenever we take measure of our own mental states. This means when we judge whether or not we think we can remember something, when we feel more or less confident that we know something, and when we feel more or less confident when we have understood something. Thus, for example, if you state that you are confident that you will remember the vocabulary you just studied when you take your French test tomorrow, you are demonstrating metamemory monitoring. You are confident that you know the words. Similarly, when you are sure you will not recall something, that is also metamemory monitoring.

With respect to memory, monitoring can occur at either the time of learning or the time of retrieval. It can occur for either semantic or episodic information. T. O. Nelson and Narens (1990) likened monitoring to a thermometer—a thermometer tells us the ambient temperature, and metamemory tells us the state of our personal memories. What is essential about monitoring is that the person becomes consciously aware of whether or not the information is accessible in memory. Monitoring can be as simple as noting, "I am not going to remember that phone number." For example, if I am experiencing a tip-of-the-tongue state for the name of the cellist who played at President Obama's inauguration, I have become aware that I may remember that fact soon. If monitoring did not occur, I would not know that I knew the name of the famous cellist. Similarly, if you hear a sentence spoken in a strange language, such as Mongolian, you are certain you did not understand it. This is a form of metacognitive monitoring as well.

Accuracy here means that when you think you know something, you do know it, and when you think you do not know something, you indeed do not know it. If you think you can remember something, then fail to do so, your monitoring has failed you as well as your memory. And if you think you cannot remember something but then do so, your monitoring has also failed. If that sounds confusing, just keep in mind that accuracy here refers to whether or not monitoring correctly reflects our internal state. In our thermometer example, if you have a thermometer that measures cold temperatures too hot and hot temperatures too cold, it is not that useful (unlike the scales that tell us that we weigh less than we actually do). Thus, monitoring is only helpful if it accurately reflects what we do or do not have represented in our memory system. Remember the game show participant. If, after announcing that he is taking the money and leaving an unanswered question on the board, he realizes that he does know the answer, it is too late. He has already made his "final answer." The money is lost, and the participant must pack his bags and go home. If I have a tip-of-the-tongue state for the famous cello player and then recognize the name, then my monitoring is accurate. If I don't recognize the cello player, then my monitoring is inaccurate (Yo-Yo Ma, if you have not remembered it or looked it up yet).

Self-regulation is important in many aspects of human behavior. When self-regulation is directed at memory, we call it "control processes." These processes take the output of monitoring and use that information to inform decisions we make about learning and remembering. In T. O. Nelson and Naren's (1990) analogy, the control device is the thermostat. Based on the temperature reading of the thermometer (monitoring), the thermostat

Control (in metamemory): our ability to regulate our learning or retrieval based upon our own monitoring.

device will either kick in the heat, if the room has gotten too cold, or trigger the air conditioning if the room is too warm. Control is only as good as it responds to the monitoring correctly and adjusts behavior properly. A thermostat that turned on the heat when it reached 80 degrees inside or turned on the air conditioning when it cooled to 55 degrees would require an immediate call to the electrician. In terms of memory, **control** involves the behaviors we engage in to ensure learning. For example, when the student studying for two exams elects to focus her attention and study time on the social psychology class, she is engaged in control. Based on her monitoring, she may come to realize that statistics is hopeless—so she better do well in social psychology. As a result, she spends all of her study time on that class. For another example, think of cooking a special dinner. If you are confident you have the recipe memorized, you will start accumulating the ingredients and turning on the oven. However, if you are uncertain (a metamemory judgment) that you remember the recipe, you will engage in a control behavior—namely, looking for the cookbook on your bookshelf.

T. O. Nelson and Narens (1990) divided metamemory judgments into those that occurred at various stages of the memory process (see Figure 9.1). As you can see in Figure 9.1, just as memory is divided into encoding, representation, and retrieval, metamemory can be divided along similar lines. During encoding or learning, people can make two kinds of metamemory judgments. **Ease-of-learning judgments** are estimates of how likely an item will be remembered in advance of actual studying and are predictions about how difficult that item will be to learn. **Judgments of learning** are made during study and are judgments of whether the item has been learned already. During retrieval, people can make **feeling-of-knowing judgments** on unrecalled items. Feeling of knowing refer to an estimation of the likelihood that an unrecalled item will be recognized. **Tip-of-the-tongue states (TOTs)** refer to the feeling that an unrecalled item will be recalled soon. After an item has been retrieved, the person can make a variety of metamemory judgments, including **retrospective confidence judgments,** which refer to an estimation that the retrieved answer is indeed correct. Source monitoring judgments refer to the likely source from where the person learned the information.

Ease-of-learning judgments: estimates of how likely an item will be remembered in advance of actual studying. They are predictions about how difficult that item will be to learn.

Judgments of learning: are made during study and are judgments of whether the item has been learned already.

Feeling-of-knowing judgments: an estimation of the likelihood that an unrecalled item will be recognized.

Tip-of-the-tongue states: the feeling that an unrecalled item will be recalled soon.

Retrospective confidence judgments: an estimation that a retrieved answer is indeed correct.

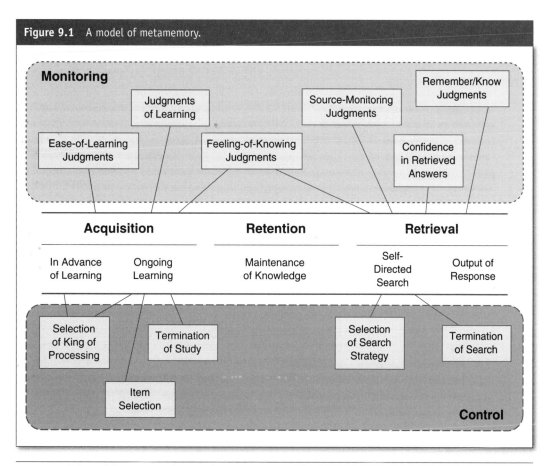

Figure 9.1   A model of metamemory.

SOURCES: Adapted from T. O. Nelson and Narens (1990) and Dunlosky, Serra, and Baker (2007).

THEORIES OF METAMEMORY

Metamemory concerns our awareness of memory processes. But it is also a cognitive process itself and therefore can be studied with the same tools that are applied to other areas of memory research. In this section, we will examine the classes of theories that researchers have advanced to account for metamemory. As it turns out, the different theories all have some success at predicting how metamemory judgments are made, but they don't equally apply to all metamemory judgments. Indeed, it is becoming important to distinguish the mechanisms that drive judgments at the time of encoding, such as judgments of learning, from those that affect judgments at the time of retrieval, such as feeling-of-knowing. The different mechanisms that underlie judgments of learning and feeling-of-knowing judgments have a number of important implications. First, it suggests that they may have different neural substrates. If so, they may be differentially affected by brain damage. Second, different techniques may be required to use these judgments to improve our memory performance.

Direct-Access Theories

Direct-access theories refer to the idea that the judgments we make are based on the same processes that allow us to remember in the first place. That is, the metamemory judgments measure the strength of the stored memory even if that memory cannot be recalled. Thus, when you look at a word pair that you are studying (*sometimes–quelquefois*), you judge your confidence by directly accessing how strong that pair is stored in your semantic memory. Similarly, when you are in a tip-of-the-tongue state (TOT) for the name of the cello player, it is the actual strength of the name itself that is driving the feeling of the TOT. For feeling-of-knowing judgments and TOTs, direct-access views argue that the judgments arise from sensitivity to the unretrieved target. Although items have insufficient memory "strength" to be recalled, they are strong enough to signal their presence as a metacognitive state. For judgments of learning, direct-access views argue that the judgments are caused by a person's ability to gauge how strong an item has become in memory.

To illustrate this concept, consider the following example. A person is asked a game show question, such as, "Who was the first person on the moon?" If the person fails to recall the name of the astronaut, he or she can supply a feeling-of-knowing judgment regarding the likelihood that he or she will recognize the correct name if it was given on multiple-choice test. Direct-access theories postulate that the feeling-of-knowing judgment is driven by unconscious activation of the unrecalled target name (*Neil Armstrong*). That is, the memory (the knowledge that Neil Armstrong was the first man on the moon) and the metamemory ("I will recognize the name") are a function of the same cognitive process.

Indirect or Inferential Theories

Indirect or inferential theories: the idea that we use a variety of clues, cues, tricks, and heuristics to estimate the strength of an item in memory, which we cannot measure directly.

Cue familiarity: stored information about the cue or the sense to which we recognize the cue influences our metamemory judgment for the to-be-remembered target.

Retrieval of related information: when we retrieve information related to a target, that information can influence our metamemory judgment for learning or remembering the target.

Indirect or inferential theories are based on the idea that we use a variety of clues, cues, tricks, and heuristics to estimate the strength of an item in memory, which we cannot measure directly. It is like estimating the temperature on a cold day by seeing if your breath is visible. This does not directly measure temperature (as a thermometer might) but can give you reliable information about the temperature indirectly. If you can see you breath, you may know the temperature is below 45 degrees. If your nostrils start to freeze, then you know it is below zero degrees. Your physiological characteristics do not directly measure the temperature, but you can use them as proxy for temperature. Many scuba divers can estimate the temperature of the ocean within a degree Fahrenheit just by feeling the water. With respect to metamemory, a host of other cognitive processes estimate how well we have learned or how likely we are to remember information. If these clues point to success, we give strong metamemory judgments. If these clues point to failure, we give low metamemory judgments. Applied to feeling-of-knowing judgments, for example, this theory tell us that we may use information about the general topic ("I know a lot about the history of space travel"), **cue familiarity** ("who was the first man on the moon is a question that I have seen frequently"), **retrieval of related information** to the target ("Buzz Aldrin was on the trip but was not first"), and partial information about the target ("I know his last name started with an 'A' and had two syllables"). That is, it is not the exact memory ("Armstrong") that drives the feeling of knowing. Instead, it is other kinds of information that correlate with the likelihood that we do have that memory.

> **Direct-access theory**: the idea that the judgments we make are based on the same processes that allow us to remember in the first place. That is, the metamemory judgments measure the strength of the stored memory even if that memory cannot be recalled.

Both direct and indirect theories have a short but venerable history in memory science (see Dunlosky & Metcalfe, 2009). Each is supported by a number of findings to be discussed shortly. To foreshadow, **direct-access theory** is a better fit for judgments of learning, whereas the inferential theory is a better fit for feeling-of-knowing judgments.

TYPES OF JUDGMENTS

Tip-of-the-Tongue States

TOT is defined as the feeling of temporary inaccessibility. Inaccessibility here means that an item is stored (available) in memory but cannot be retrieved at present. Remember that **availability** means all the information that is stored in memory, whereas **accessibility** refers to that information that is currently retrievable (see Bjork & Bjork, 1992; Tulving & Pearlstone, 1966). In a TOT, we feel as if an item is inaccessible but eventually recoverable (R. Brown & McNeill, 1966; Schwartz, 2006). Note here that there are two components to the TOT; first, the feeling—it is a subjective state—in a TOT can feel quite strong. And then, second, there is the referent of that feeling—namely, that a particular item is there in our memory. It is the feeling of the TOT that concerns metamemory. For an interesting overview on tip-of-the-tongue states from prominent science writer Jonah Lehrer, go to www.sagepub.com/schwartz.[2]

> **Availability**: all information present in the memory system.
>
> **Accessibility**: that part of our stored memories that we can retrieve under the present conditions.

Researchers have examined TOTs by prospecting for them (A. S. Brown, 1991; R. Brown & McNeill, 1966). Researchers present participants with a series of general-information questions. If the participant knows the answer, he or she moves on. If the participant cannot recall the answer, however, he or she may be in a TOT for that item. If so, the experimenter can then probe for different variables that may arise during TOTs. Consider the following questions. Do any of them elicit a TOT in you?

1. What is the largest planet in the solar system?

2. Which precious gem is red?

3. What is the capital of Jamaica?

4. What is the capital of Chile?

5. What is the name of the legendary one-eyed giants in Greek mythology?

6. What is the last name of the author of the James Bond novels?

7. What is the last name of the author who wrote under the pseudonym of Mark Twain?

8. What is the city in Italy that is known for its canals?

9. What is the last name of the composer who wrote the opera *Don Giovanni?*

10. What is the last name of the author of *Little Women?*

Did you experience a TOT? What happens when you are in a TOT? Do you feel frustrated that you cannot recall the answer? Do you feel like you are about to get the answer or do you think it will come later? Do you have the first letter of the missing word and just can't seem to fill it out? All of these are common experiences during TOTs. The answers to each question are presented below.

Answers: 1. Jupiter 2. Ruby 3. Kingston 4. Santiago 5. Cyclops 6. Fleming 7. Clemens 8. Venice 9. Mozart 10. Alcott

When a participant reports a TOT in an experiment, the researcher can then make a number of inquiries into the mental state of the participant and the knowledge possessed during the TOT. In many cases, the participant may know the word for the item in another language (Gollan & Brown, 2006) if the TOT is for a name, whether or not that person has a middle name (Hanley & Chapman, 2008), the first letter and how many syllables are in the word (A. S. Brown, 1991; Koriat & Lieblich, 1974), words that sound similar to the target and words that mean something similar to the target (Kornell & Metcalfe, 2006; S. M. Smith, 1994), even tastes associated with the word (Simner & Ward, 2006), and many other aspects of the word other than the actual word itself (Schwartz, 2006). Indeed, it is likely that the accessibility of this related information feeds back and makes the TOT all the more frustrating.

After this information has been gleaned from the participant, usually the researchers present a final recognition test. The likelihood of recognition can then be compared for TOTs and for items for which the participant simply does not know. By and large, TOTs are highly accurate at predicting subsequent memory. If the participant is in a TOT, the person will be more likely to recognize the correct answer than for those items for which the person was not in a TOT.

Theoretical Mechanism

To most of us, when we experience a TOT, it feels as if we have direct access to the unretrieved answer. Because we are so sure that we know the answer and we can just feel it right there below the surface, the experience is often quite frustrating. Originally, it was assumed that the TOT was caused by unconscious access to the unrecalled item. This assumption forms the basis of some work using TOTs to investigate processes of word retrieval (see A. S. Brown, 1991). However, much of the empirical research points to the cause of TOTs being elsewhere. It is not unconscious access to the target but rather a host of clues that participants pick up on that direct the experience of a TOT. This is sometimes called the heuristic view of metacognition—namely, that we use cues and clues to infer that we will remember or learn a particular item.

The research supports the idea that TOTs are caused by inferential or indirect processes (see Schwartz, 2002). That is, it is the clues and cues that we can recognize and retrieve that allows us unconsciously to infer that the item is likely to be remembered. This unconscious inference is experienced as a TOT. Research has suggested that both cue familiarity and the partial retrieval of related information play a role in this inference. One experiment that demonstrated both of these factors examined TOTs for the names of newly learned fictional animals (Schwartz & Smith, 1997).

Schwartz and Smith (1997) presented participants with lists of fictional animal names (see Figure 9.2). Each name was paired with the name of a country, and some of the names were also accompanied by line drawings of fictional animals. For example, participants might have seen "Yelkey–Panama," which indicated that the "yelkey" is an animal that lives in Panama. Of the animals for which line drawings were provided, half were also accompanied by information pertaining to the size and diet of the animal. The three encoding conditions were minimum information (just the name–country pair), medium information (the name–country pair and line drawing), and maximum information (the name–country pair, line drawing, and diet and size information). The conditions were designed to allow different amounts of information to be retrieved when the participants were given the country name as a cue for the retrieval of the animal name. If the participants could not retrieve the name of the animal associated with a given country cue, they were then asked for a TOT judgment and asked to guess at the first letter of the animal's name. The participants were also asked to retrieve as much related information as they could.

The encoding manipulation (amount of related information) did not affect recall of animal names or the recognition of unrecalled names. This suggests that three conditions were composed of roughly equivalent items for which possible TOTs could exist. However, the rates of TOTs differed among the conditions. There were more TOTs reported in both the medium and maximum information conditions than in the minimum information condition. In addition, the number of reported TOTs was correlated with the amount of related information retrieved. Thus, when more information was accessible to participants, they were more likely to experience TOTs. This supports the inferential theory because it was not the strength of the target name that was driving the number of TOTs reported but rather the amount of related information accessible to that participant.

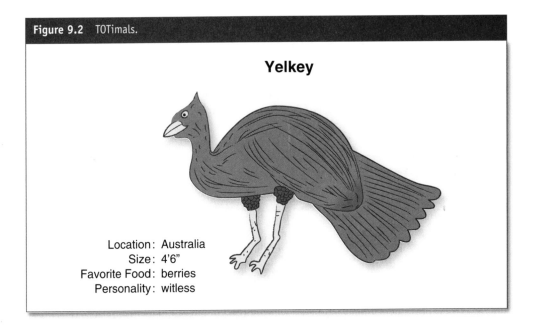

Figure 9.2 TOTimals.

Yelkey

Location: Australia
Size: 4'6"
Favorite Food: berries
Personality: witless

In the same experiment, Schwartz and Smith (1997) also asked participants to judge whether they would like to take vacations to different countries. Some of these countries (i.e., Panama) were then later the habitats of the fictional animals. The question was whether the priming of the countries, which would make these countries more familiar to the participants, would also induce more TOTs. Indeed, they did, at least in the minimum-information condition. Thus, priming the cues themselves also increased the number of TOTs, also independent of the likelihood of actually remembering the target.

Brain Mechanisms

Circuits in the prefrontal lobes of the cerebral cortex appear to be important for metamemory (Pannu & Kaszniak, 2005; Shimamura, 2008). Monitoring appears to be linked to areas of the prefrontal cortex known as the dorsomedial prefrontal cortex, whereas control is linked to the dorsolateral prefrontal cortex (Shimamura, 2008). Both appear to be activated during TOTs. That these areas are clearly activated is evidence that TOTs should be considered metamemory and not simply an issue of word retrieval. Much of the data has come from the work of Anat Maril at Harvard University. She and her colleagues have shown that there are areas of the brain unique to TOTs in the prefrontal lobe (see Figure 9.3). In particular, the anterior cingulate (considered part of the dorsomedial prefrontal cortex) is activated during TOTs (Maril, Simons, Weaver, & Schacter, 2005). This area is associated with a number of experiential components associated with surprise and novelty as well as cognitive monitoring (Botvinick, 2007), of which the TOT qualifies. In addition to the anterior cingulate, the dorsolateral cortex is also activated during TOTs. This area has been associated with metacognitive control (Shimamura, 2008) and perhaps is responsible for guiding the behaviors that people engage in to resolve TOTs when they occur.

Figure 9.3   Functional magnetic resonance imaging results from Maril, Simons, Weaver, and Schacter (2005).

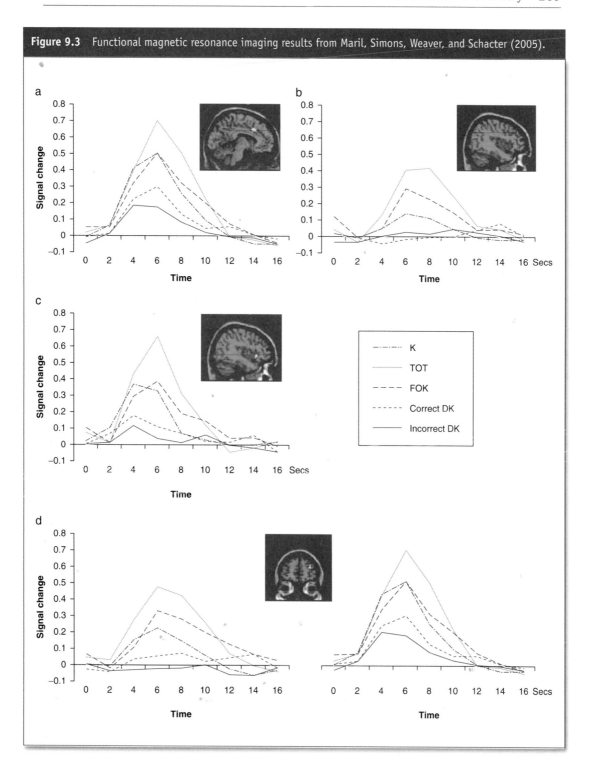

Feeling of Knowing

Feeling-of-knowing judgments, like TOTs, are predictions of the future retrievability of a particular item. Unlike TOTs, they can be made without the feeling that the person will recall the answer. This is a subtle difference but easily explained. For example, I may be reasonably sure that I will not recall my seventh-grade science teacher's name but may be confident that I could recognize it among a multiple-choice format. In a TOT, I am sure I could recall it, but a feeling-of-knowing judgment is a prediction of likely recognition. The feeling of knowing has been studied in two ways. One is similar to the prospecting technique with TOTs. With feeling-of-knowing judgments, though, it is called the RJR (recall-judgment-recognition) and was first used by Joseph Hart to initiate the formal study of metamemory (Hart, 1965). That is, the participant tries to recall the answer to general-information questions or the target of a cue-target pair. If unsuccessful, the participant provides a feeling-of-knowing judgment for recognition of that item. A recognition test then is given to measure accuracy.

Another way of examining feeling of knowing is the "game show" paradigm developed by Lynne Reder and her colleagues in the 1980s (Reder, 1987; Reder & Ritter, 1992). In the game show paradigm, the participant is given a question and, as fast as possible, must either indicate the answer or simply that he or she knows the answer. For example, if the question is, "What was the name of the first person on the moon?" some participants would have to say "Armstrong" as fast as possible, whereas others would have to simply say "know it" as fast as possible. Reder and her colleagues discovered that people could make the "know it" response faster than they could actually retrieve the name. This suggests that we have an initial and rapid feeling of knowing, which we can actually act on even before we recall the target word. That we can determine that we know an answer faster than we can actually recall the answer also strongly supports the view that our metamemory judgments are heuristic and based on clues to the correct answer rather than nonconscious access to that answer.

Cue Familiarity and Feeling of Knowing

One of the inferential mechanisms thought to be responsible for metamemory is cue familiarity. Cue familiarity means that if we recognize or are familiar with the question (in a general-information question) or if the cue in a cue-target pair elicits a sense of familiarity, this will increase our feeling of knowing that we can recognize the answer. For example, at this point, the man on the moon question should be quite familiar to you. The feeling of familiarity that the question now evokes will drive higher your feeling of knowing that you know the astronaut's name. In an experiment, Schwartz and Metcalfe (1992) asked participants to study randomly selected cue-target pairs, such as *captain–carbon* and *pasture–dragon*. Before the participants were tested on their ability to retrieve the second word when given the first as cue, they were given a long list of words and asked to rate whether or not these words were pleasant. Some of the words on the pleasantness rating task were also cues in the cue-target pairs (*captain*, for example). The cue words that had been primed to be more familiar in the pleasantness rating task were, on average, given higher feeling-of-knowing judgments when the participants could not recall the target word that went with them. This experiment supports a role for cue familiarity in feeling-of-knowing judgments. As a practical matter, given that feeling-of-knowing judgments are based on familiarity of the cue and also correlated with memory performance, one can rely on these feelings of familiarity. They do predict what we know. Many students mark the questions on an exam that feel familiar in order to come back to them after they have finished the rest of the test. This research suggests that returning to the familiar items is a good test strategy.

Brain Mechanisms of Feeling of Knowing

You might expect that the areas of the brain responsible for feeling of knowing would be similar to those in TOTs. The answer is yes and no. Both TOTs and feeling-of-knowing judgments appear to be produced in the prefrontal lobe. But, in fact, they appear to be a function of different areas within the prefrontal lobe (see Figure 9.4). Feeling-of-knowing judgments also appear to activate areas in the parietal lobe. Whereas TOTs are more concentrated in the right hemisphere, feeling-of-knowing judgments are more concentrated in the left hemisphere. Maril, Simons, Mitchell, Schwartz, and Schacter (2003) showed that the inferior frontal gyrus was activated when participants reported feeling-of-knowing judgments, an area not activated during TOTs. Nonetheless, there have been only a few neuroimaging studies done, so research may yet indicate some more direct overlap between the two. Figure 9.4 shows the areas of the brain activated during feeling-of-knowing judgments.

Neuropsychology and the Feeling of Knowing

Feeling-of-knowing judgments have also been examined in amnesic patients. Amnesic patients are people who suffer problems with memory as a function of brain damage. Not all amnesic patients, however, have the same symptoms. Shimamura and Squire (1986) compared the ability of temporal lobe amnesiacs (i.e., patients with damage to their temporal lobe) to patients with Korsakoff's syndrome (who have damage to the diencephalon as well as damage in frontal areas of the brain). Both groups of amnesic patients scored very low on the learning of new information. However, the temporal lobe amnesiacs were no different from controls in the accuracy of their feeling-of-knowing judgments. For them, the feeling-of-knowing task was easy. They knew that they would not remember. However, in patients with Korsakoff's syndrome, their feeling-of-knowing judgments were essentially random. There was no relation between their feeling-of-knowing judgments and which items they would recognize, and as a function, their accuracy was much lower than controls. Given that patients with Korsakoff's syndrome have damage to the frontal lobe and the temporal lobe amnesiacs did not, the patient data also support the idea that metamemory is housed in the frontal lobes (also see Schnyer et al., 2004). Later, we will discuss how awareness of one's memory deficits is a critical component for patients' ability to cope with neuropsychological problems. The temporal lobe amnesiacs, therefore, usually respond better to neuropsychological therapy than do patients with Korsakoff's syndrome.

Figure 9.4 Feeling of knowing results from Maril, Simons, Weaver, and Schacter (2005).

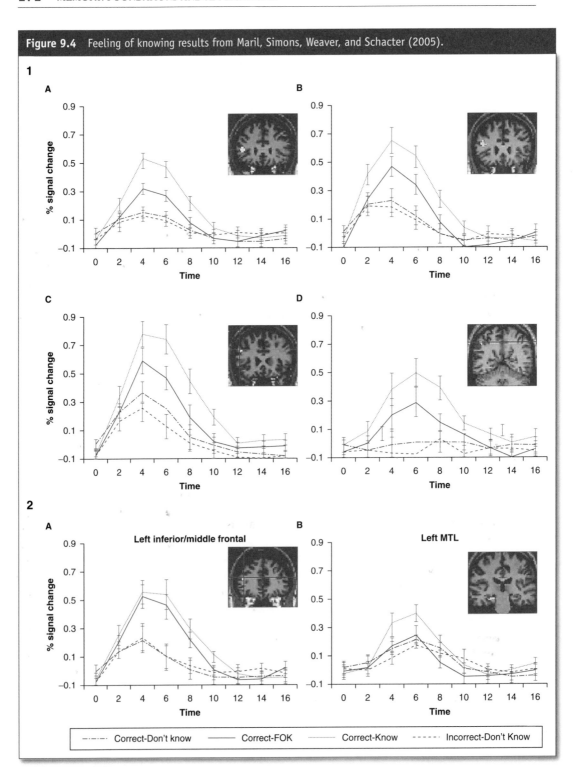

Judgments of Learning

Judgments of learning are made during study and are predictions of future memory performance (see Arbuckle & Cuddy, 1969, for the origins of this research area). These judgments can inform the individual as to which items being studied are likely to be remembered later and which items will not be remembered later. The judgments can also be directed at which items will be forgotten and which will not be forgotten. Finn (2008) has shown that judgments of forgetting tend to be more accurate than judgments of learning—so it may be advisable for people who are studying to actually predict what items they will forget rather than what items they will remember. However, aside from Finn's study, all of the other research has been directed at predictions of remembering, not predictions of forgetting.

Judgments of learning are important for a number of reasons. First, they are the main judgment that researchers use to study metacognition during the encoding process. Second, it is likely that many people implicitly make judgments of learning during learning and that judgments of learning directly affect our choices when we sit down and decide how we are going to learn or prepare for an exam. Third, if people naturally use judgments of learning to guide their study, it is important to know if they are accurate and if that accuracy can be improved. Fourth, for experimentalists, judgments of learning offer an advantage over feeling-of-knowing judgments and TOTs—namely, that judgments of learning can be made on all items, not just the subset that remains unrecalled.

Consider the role of judgments of learning in normal studying. We can imagine a student studying for a vocabulary test in French class. During the quiz, the student will be given words in French and will have to provide the meaning in English. Presumably, anyone who will be reading this book for a college course has had to take such a quiz (if not in French, then in some other language) at some point in his or her life. Consider that the following items are on the to-be-studied list.

Le mur–the wall

La tache–the stain

Le chant–the song

Le porte-voix–the megaphone

Le singe–the monkey

As we study each pair, we make an implicit judgment of learning. For example, you might judge *le chant–the song* as an easy one because the word *chant* in English has some overlap with its meaning in French. However, *le porte-voix–the megaphone* may be judged to be difficult as it is unlikely that most English-speaking students have seen this French word before, and the compound nature of the word suggests that it may be more difficult to remember.

When experimenters elicit judgments of learning, we can do so in one of two ways. Cue-target judgments of learning involve presenting the participant with both the cue and the target and asking the participant to predict if that item will be recalled later when presented with only the cue. This would look something like this:

How likely are you to remember the English meaning of the French word when presented with only the French word on tomorrow's test?

Le singe—the monkey

0   20   40   60   80   100

In contrast, cue-only judgments of learning involve presenting the participant with only the cue and asking the participant to predict if that item will be recalled later when presented with only the cue. This would look something like this:

How likely are you to remember the English meaning of the French word when presented with only the French word on tomorrow's test?

La tache—?

0   20   40   60   80   100

Research by John Dunlosky and his colleagues has demonstrated that cue-only judgments of learning are more accurate at predicting future test performance if there is a delay between the initial study of the pair (*la tache–the stain*) and the judgment of learning (*la tache—?*) (e.g., Dunlosky & Nelson, 1994). Just a few minutes of delay can raise the accuracy of the judgment of learning to something close to perfect. This is called the delayed judgment of learning effect (Dunlosky & Nelson, 1992, 1994). It has been studied quite extensively both because of its theoretical interest and because it is of some practical import (Scheck, Meeter, & Nelson, 2004), which we will get to shortly.

Dunlosky and Bjork (2008) summarized the explanations for the increase in accuracy in delayed judgments of learning. Dunlosky and his group have argued that it occurs because if participants retrieve the target at the time of making the judgment, then they are also likely to retrieve the target at the time of test. Conversely, if you cannot recall the target at the time of test, you are unlikely to get it later. So the judgment of learning serves as a dry run for the final test. This is called the monitoring dual-memories hypothesis. The retrieval from long-term memory that occurs during a delayed judgment of learning is more likely to predict future performance than the retrieval from short-term memory that occurs during an immediate judgment of learning. This cannot occur with the cue-target judgment of learning because the target is already provided to you, so you must rely on other, perhaps inferential mechanisms to predict your test performance. Spellman, Bloomfield, and Bjork (2008) argued that, as we have seen earlier, testing yourself is a powerful learning method. Thus, whenever we engage in a judgment of learning, we are implicitly testing ourselves. If we recall the target during the judgment of learning, we are giving that item a huge boost in memory strength. This strength will carry over to the test. This is similar to the testing effect (a testing trial produces better learning than a study trial), which will be discussed in Chapter 13. Thus, those items that are successfully retrieved during the judgment of learning process are then stronger in memory than they otherwise would be, and this ensures the accuracy of the judgment of learning itself. Either mechanism, however, points to the possibility that the strategic use of judgments of learning can be advantageous for efficient learning and memory improvement.

Mnemonic Improvement Tip 9.1

Use judgments of learning to help you study. After you've studied an item, make an index card with a question on one side and an answer on the other. Ten to 30 minutes later, pick up the card with the question on it and make a judgment of learning. If your judgment of learning is high, say the answer and then check to make sure you are correct. Put these in one pile as you will not need to restudy them. If your judgment of learning is low, check the answer, and put the low judgments-of-learning cards in a separate pile for later study.

Factors That Influence Judgments of Learning

One puzzle that has driven researchers is to determine what causes judgments of learning to increase or decrease in strength, not the factors that concern their accuracy to get better or worse. Note that the delayed judgment of learning effect concerns the accuracy at predicting recall. The factors below do not affect accuracy at predicting recall but whether the person is more or less confident. One factor that influences judgments of learning is the fluency and speed of retrieval (Son & Metcalfe, 2005). Think of retrieving an easy item such *song* in response to *le chant*. It is likely that *song* is retrieved quickly and effortlessly when the French word is given as a cue. However, in response to *le porte-voix*, the word *megaphone* may take a bit longer and require more thought. Son and Metcalfe (2005) showed that judgments of learning were affected by these factors. High and low judgments of learning were made fluently and quickly. Intermediate judgments of learning—those that might be hard but possible to retrieve—received the longest response times. Metcalfe and Finn (2008) found that when cue-only judgments of learning were made under speeded conditions, the judgments were influenced by cue familiarity (that is, how easy it was to recognize the cue word), but when participants were not timed, the factors that influenced the memorability of the target also influenced the judgments of learning.

In another study, Koriat (2008) demonstrated that "easily learned" is "easily remembered." This means that items that we learn more quickly are objectively easy and, as a consequence, are more likely to be remembered. People's judgments of learning appear to be sensitive to this feature, and judgments of learning are related to the speed at which particular items are acquired during study. While this generally is helpful to the person studying, it can be misleading. For example, Benjamin, Bjork, and Schwartz (1998) showed that in some cases, fluently generated answers are given less attention than more hard to retrieve items. Because the harder items receive more attention, they are better remembered later. Still, it is the fluency of generating the answer that produces the higher judgment of learning. Finally, another factor that appears to influence judgments of learning is where the item is along the serial position curve (Castel, 2008). In this study, Castel (2008) showed that judgments of learning were higher for items learned in the primacy and recency parts of the serial position curve than they were for the items in the middle of the curve. Thus, it appears that people combine a number of factors to determine their judgments of learning, some related to the properties of what they are studying and some related to the properties of their own memory systems.

Because of the importance of judgments of learning to study, it is important to understand the factors that can affect judgments of learning. In particular, it is important to understand those factors that can create artificially high judgments of learning, as these illusory feelings may affect study. Recently, Rhodes and Castel (2008) showed that a host of perceptual features can increase the judgments of learning given to studied items even though they do not help recall. They found that words written in larger font sizes were given higher judgments of learning, even though they were no more likely to be free recalled than other words. So do not be confused by sentences like this—it is no easier to remember than the one before it.

Brain Mechanisms for Judgments of Learning

Like feeling of knowing and tip-of-the-tongue states, the areas of the brain that are activated during judgments of learning reside in the prefrontal lobe of the cerebral cortex. Kao, Davis, and Gabrieli (2005) conducted a functional magnetic resonance imaging (fMRI) study and showed that the areas of the brain unique to judgments of learning were located in ventromedial, lateral, and dorsomedial prefrontal cortex (see Figure 9.5). Vilkki, Servo, and Surma-aho (1998) also showed that patients with damage to their frontal lobes were less accurate on judgments of learning tasks than were controls.

For more on judgments of learning, you can read the excellent chapters in Dunlosky and Metcalfe's (2009) book on metamemory. It can be found at www.sagepub.com/schwartz.[3]

INTERIM SUMMARY

Metamemory means our knowledge and awareness of our own memory processes. In a broader sense, metacognition refers to our knowledge and awareness of our cognitive processes. Monitoring refers to the ability to reflect on our own memory processes, whereas control means the ability to direct our memory processes in advantageous ways. Two main theories have organized research on the mechanism of metamemory. In direct-access theory, we make metamemory judgments by a mechanism, which directly measures the strength of a memory. In inferential theory, people make metamemory judgments by measuring a host of accessible information that is correlated with the strength of the memory. Three major judgments are the tip-of-the-tongue state, the feeling of knowing, and the judgment of learning. TOTs and feeling-of-knowing judgments are particularly sensitive to inferential factors. Judgments of learning are excellent predictors of whether an item will be recalled.

CONTROL PROCESSES IN METAMEMORY

Metamemory has two important components. Monitoring allows us to become aware of what items we will and will not remember and what are our mnemonic strengths and

Figure 9.5   Functional magnetic resonance imaging results from Kao, Davis, and Gabrieli (2005).

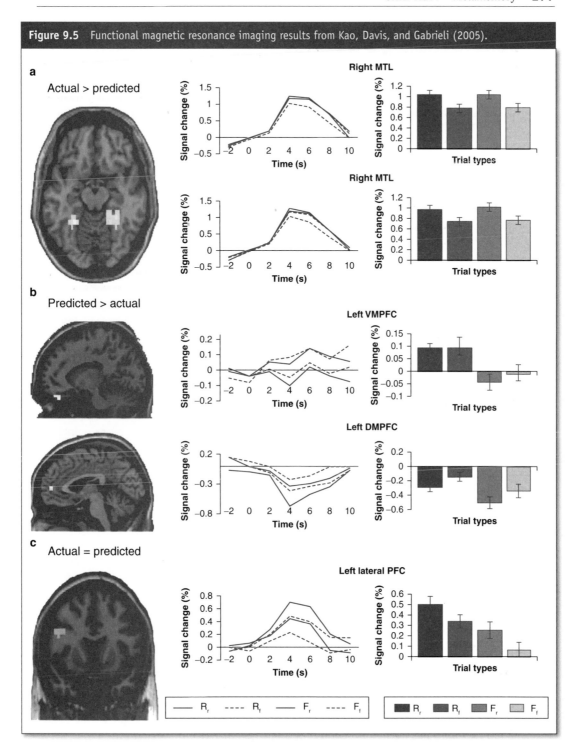

weaknesses. Control processes involve the decisions and behaviors that we engage in to improve or alter or memory processes. Control processes include such things as "googling" a name, to ensure one's retrieved name matches the real name. Control processes include asking someone to repeat a name because the rememberer is not sure that he or she heard that person correctly. Indeed, any behavior one engages in that is a consequence of cognitive uncertainty can be thought of in terms of metacognitive control. For students, engaging in an "all-nighter" in preparation for an exam in the morning is an example of how metacognition can control our behaviors. The student knows that he or she has not tried to learn the information and, in this case, may be aware how little about the topic he or she knows and therefore decides to study all night long. In this section, the relation of monitoring and control will be discussed as will the topic of how successful metamemory control can be.

Consider the student studying for two exams, one in social psychology and the other in statistics. First, she must decide which exam to study for first. Following this, she must decide how much to time to allocate to each course. Both of these are metamemory control decisions. But metamemory control extends beyond that. During study for each subject, she then must allocate study time among the various concepts, definitions, and examples. For example, does she know the definition of *cognitive dissonance* well enough to answer the test questions without mistakes? Should she devote her study time to the difficult statistical concept of "multivariate analysis," or should she make sure that she has *t* tests down pat? Researchers study **allocation of study time** because it lends itself to careful experimentation.

> **Allocation of study time**: the decisions participants make about which items to study during an experiment.

Metamemory control can also take place at the time of retrieval. Consider the student taking a standardized exam like the SAT. If the student answers incorrectly, more points are deducted than if the student leaves it blank. Thus, a student who can assess his or her feeling of knowing at this point has an advantage. If one has a feeling of knowing, one might be tempted to guess at the most appealing answer. However, if the student is sure that his or her answer would be a pure guess, then it is better strategically to leave it blank. Therefore, metamemory control means the strategic decision to guess, if one can eliminate a few of the multiple-choice answers as wrong or leave it blank and not risk the penalty. Another example of metacognitive control at the time of retrieval is a decision to self-cue during a TOT state. Many people report mentally running through the alphabet in order to cue themselves to the forgotten name when they are in a TOT (Schwartz, 2002). If they did not feel the TOT, they might not choose to self-cue. We will now consider the experimental literature on this topic.

Allocation of Study Time

Allocation of study time is the manner in which people choose to direct their study. In the example above, the student chose to allocate her study time to the social psychology exam and not to her statistics exam. One of the major questions concerning allocation of study time is how judgments of learning and allocation of study time relate to each other. Researchers interested in metamemory are interested in the allocation of study time because it both tells us something about the nature of metamemory and has practical implications in terms of memory improvement strategies. The first question that we can ask about this relation is whether students allocate their study time based on the judgments of learning they give to items and if this leads to improvements in performance.

Labor-in-Vain Effect

Remember that a correlation measures the statistical relation between two quantities. For example, if you correlate people's height in inches and in centimeters, you will get a perfect correlation because each measurement assesses the same quantity. Height and weight will be somewhat correlated. T. O. Nelson and Leonesio (1988) found that there was a correlation between judgments of learning and the allocation of study time. They found that the lower the judgments of learning given to an item, the more time that person spent studying it. Here's how they did it. Nelson and Leonesio asked participants to study language translation pairs (e.g., *monkey–le singe*). Participants made judgments of learning and then chose the amount of time to study each item. After the initial judgment of learning phase, the participants then saw all the translation pairs again and chose the ones that they wanted to study.

T. O. Nelson and Leonesio (1988) made two important discoveries. First, in this experiment, the relation between judgments of learning and study time was negative. That is, the items that were given the lowest judgments of learning (i.e., the most difficult items) received the most study. In other words, the participants focused on learning the most difficult items and gave them the most attention. However, the second finding was equally revealing. When the participants were tested on the vocabulary at the end of the experiment, participants still remembered more of the items for which they had given high judgments of learning. Even though they spent most of their time studying the difficult items, they were still better at remembering the easy ones. For this reason, Nelson and Leonesio labeled the effect **labor in vain** because their experiment showed that participants were unable to compensate for the difficulty of those items. Nonetheless, because they did show that participants studied the low judgment of learning items, it was assumed for about 10 years that this was the way in which people allocated study time all the time.

> **Labor in vain**: when extra study does not guarantee that difficult items will be mastered.

T. O. Nelson and Leonesio (1988) and a number of other studies found that people choose to study the most difficult items, that is, the ones for which the participants gave the lowest judgments of learning. This makes sense because the easier items are already learned and therefore do not require subsequent study. But think about how you study—do you always choose the hardest items to study? Think about a particularly difficult test you are preparing for that you need to pass to keep your scholarship. At some point, completely mastering the material or getting an "A" no longer becomes the goal—you just want to pass! Under these circumstances, many students will opt to forgo the most difficult material and instead concentrate on what they think they can master in the shortest time period. This particular intuition led Lisa Son and Janet Metcalfe (2000) to challenge the notion that there will always be a negative correlation between judgments of learning and study time. They thought that in some circumstances, people will choose to study the easy items (high judgments of learning) if the material is particularly difficult or they are constrained for time. So they set out to do an experiment on this topic.

Region of Proximal Learning

Son and Metcalfe (2000) conducted an important study that challenged the ideas of T. O. Nelson and Leonesio (1988) concerning allocation of study time. They argued that, in some situations, as in the Leonesio and Nelson experiment, participants will choose to focus on the hardest items, but in other situations, they will choose to focus on the easiest items. The key variable for Son and Metcalfe was the norm of study. If time is limited or the goal of mastery is limited, a student may choose to concentrate on the easier items, guaranteeing his or her success even if it means simply getting a C (at least you pass!). If time is not an issue or the goal is complete mastery, then one chooses more difficult items to study (allowing that student to "go for the A").

In their study, participants were given several short passages of text to study and told to master all of them. The topics varied—some were about the use of bacteria in making beer, whereas others were about Shakespeare's difficulties getting his first plays produced. Among other judgments, the participants gave judgments of learning as the degree of learning on an initial run-through for each passage. After the participants had read all of the passages, some were told that they would have 30 minutes to study the passages for an upcoming test, whereas others were told that they would have 60 minutes to study the passages. In both groups, participants were told that, in general, it required students 60 minutes to master this material. Each group was free to use the 30 or 60 minutes as they saw fit. They could divide that time among the different passages as they saw fit. That is, they could choose to study difficult passages or easy passages. Therefore, the question was whether the norm of study, as indexed by the amount of time each group had, would dictate study patterns.

Son and Metcalfe (2000) found that the students who had 60 minutes to study for the test choose the hardest passages to review. For them, as in the T. O. Nelson and Leonesio (1988) experiment, there was a negative correlation between judgments of learning and study time. The lower the judgment of learning (that is, the harder the item), the more study time was allocated to those items. However, for the students who only had 30 minutes to study for the test, the pattern reversed. For these students, there was a positive correlation between judgments of learning and study time. The higher the judgment of learning (that is, the easier the item), the more study time was allocated to those items (see Figure 9.6). Therefore, the norm of study is important. When time is short, we focus on consolidating what we already know. When we have more time, we can focus on the edge of our learning, the most difficult items.

Metcalfe (2002) introduced the idea of the **region of proximal learning,** which argues that an adaptive strategy is to study those items that have not yet been learned but are not too

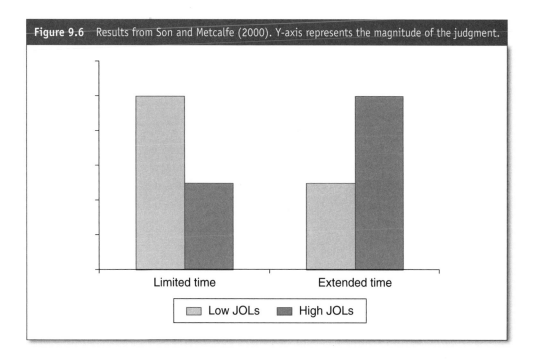

Figure 9.6   Results from Son and Metcalfe (2000). Y-axis represents the magnitude of the judgment.

| Limited time | Extended time |

Low JOLs   High JOLs

Region of proximal learning: a theory of metamemory that advances that an adaptive strategy is to study those items that have not yet been learned but are not too difficult. We maximize our learning by studying the leading edge of difficulty. That is, we maximize our learning by studying the easiest items we have not mastered yet.

difficult. This seems to go against both the results from T. O. Nelson and Leonesio (1988) and Son and Metcalfe (2000). This view suggests that we choose to study items of intermediate difficulty—under ordinary circumstances. However, when we have lots of time to study, as in Nelson and Leonesio, we can study the difficult items, but when time is limited, we study the easier ones. But usually, we are somewhat but not completely time limited. Under normal studying conditions, our studying would be optimal if we do study the easiest items that we have not yet learned.

Using this strategy, participants should allocate study time not to easy items that they have already mastered or to the extraordinarily difficult items but to learnable items, only those that have not yet been learned. In an experiment in which participants made multiple judgments of learning and had multiple opportunities to study items, participants consistently followed this strategy, choosing the items judged least difficult that had not yet been committed to memory (Metcalfe, 2002). Thus, the items that were given high judgments of learning were not studied, nor were the items given the lowest judgments of learning. Instead, they were the items with the highest judgments of learning that were not yet retrievable. Metcalfe (2002) called this the "region of proximal learning" because the participants realized that the items that would most benefit from additional study were those items that were easiest to learn but had not been learned yet. This strategy proved also to be the most successful strategy in terms of mastering all of the information. For more on Janet Metcalfe's research, go to www.sagepub.com/schwartz.[4]

Mnemonic Improvement Tip 9.2

As you study, make judgments of learning on the items you need to remember for your test (or job). When you have completed your initial review, start with the easiest ones you don't know as of yet, and start working your way to the harder items. Once you have mastered all the items, then you can go back and review the easier ones.

Control Processes at Retrieval

Conscious control over our memory system allows us to tailor our memory to our needs at any particular time. We have just seen how judgments of learning can be used as a guide as to what to study. Contrary to what you might have thought, it turns out the most adaptive way to study is to focus on the least difficult items that you have not yet mastered. What about retrieval? Sometimes it feels as if we have no control over our retrieval. When we are stymied in a TOT, we are frustrated because the item is seemingly blocked. However, it turns out we can use our metamemory judgments to affect control at the time of retrieval.

TOTs and Retrieval Time

Most often, we experience TOTs as frustrating. We know the person's name, and yet, we cannot recall it. It appears to be a quirky annoying error in our memory systems. But the experience of TOTs also serves an important monitoring function. It makes us aware of retrieval failure (temporary inaccessibility). This allows us to exert metacognitive control. If we are experiencing a TOT, then we should be able to recall the actual word. Thus, one possible metacognitive function of the TOT is to cause one to search longer for an item that is currently inaccessible. To be more specific, the TOT tells us that the unrecalled word is both in memory store and likely to be recalled, so we devote more time in our attempt to retrieve the item. One study that tested this idea examined the relation of TOTs to the time it took people to retrieve answers or decide that they could not retrieve the answers (Schwartz, 2001). TOTs were associated with longer retrieval times than were n-TOTs, suggesting that the TOT state indicated to participants that the item was likely in memory and that they should keep looking. Similarly, research on feelings of knowing found that feeling-of-knowing judgments are related to the amount of time people spend attempting retrieval of the target (Costermans, Lories, & Ansay, 1992; T. O. Nelson, Gerber, & Narens, 1984). Items that are high in feeling of knowing will elicit longer retrieval attempts because participants think they can retrieve the time if they keep trying. Interestingly, TOTs have also been linked to motivation to learn. Ryan, Petty, and Wenzlaff (1982) and Schwartz (2008) found that when people were in TOTs, their performance on other tasks was slowed, suggesting that the motivation to recall the TOT item interfered with the other tasks. In another study, Litman, Hutchins, and Russon (2005) showed that people were more likely to look up in a dictionary or an encyclopedia those items for which they had experienced TOTs. In other words, despite the sense of frustration that accompanies TOTs, they do serve vital control functions. Thus, at retrieval, we can use metamemory judgments to help us. A TOT serves as a warning light—we can recall this item eventually if we keep working. A person not experiencing a TOT is more likely to give up.

A Note on Accuracy

In this chapter, we have focused on the mechanisms that produce judgments of metamemory and on how these judgments direct our behavior, particularly study behavior. Equally important from the point of view of research and practical consideration is that our metamemory judgments are accurate at predicting our learning and performance. Accurate metamemory means two things: that we know what we will learn or remember and that we know what we will not learn or remember. Typically, this accuracy is measured by correlating the metamemory judgments with performance on some later test (Benjamin & Diaz, 2008; T. O. Nelson, 1984). Accurate metamemory judgments best serve our needs to control and direct our behavior. Imagine if our metamemory was perversely inaccurate, for example, if what we thought we had learned was what we actually forget and what we thought we would not learn was what we actually did learn. Thus, it is important to know which kinds of judgments are accurate, as these are the ones that are best used to drive our learning behavior. Luckily, almost all studies on metamemory show that the judgments are accurate at predicting future behavior.

OTHER KINDS OF METAMEMORY

Retrospective Confidence

Retrospective confidence refers to the metacognitive judgment of certainty after you have recalled an item. Strong retrospective confidence means that you think the answer that you have recalled is correct. Weak retrospective confidence means that you think the answer that you have recalled is incorrect. Have you ever recalled something only to doubt that what you have recalled is accurate or not? For example, if you are asked which actress played the character "Alex Rover" in the movie *Nim's Island*. Helen Hunt may come to mind, but you may realize that this is incorrect. You may google the information and learn that it was actually Jodie Foster.. This is retrospective confidence, or our judgments as to whether the information we do retrieve is indeed correct (Koriat & Goldsmith, 1996).

It is important to note that retrieval can be covert. That is, you can retrieve the name "Helen Hunt" but then opt not to report it or say it aloud, if you are unsure you have recalled the correct actress's name. Or you may retrieve the name that you think goes with a person you think you should know. But you may want to spare yourself embarrassment if you are wrong and forgo saying the person's name.

Koriat and Goldsmith (1996) were interested in the issue of whether one should say what they think. They investigated this by looking at retrospective confidence judgments. They thought that control mechanisms exist at the time of retrieval that screen out unlikely answers that pop into our mind. For example, given a question such as, "Who is the only man who died on the moon?" the name "Tommy Lee Jones" might be retrieved as his character in the movie *Space Cowboys* (2000) dies on the moon. However, as this answers pops out, we are able to screen it out as something fictional, not fact, and so we answer, "Nobody; all the astronauts returned safely from the moon." There are also social situations in which we might think better than to output an answer. The honors student in high school may know the answer to the teacher's question but answers "I don't know" so as not to show up his or her classmates. Thus, there are a number of situations in which output monitoring is important. Koriat and Goldsmith examined these postretrieval decisions as to whether to output a retrieved item by asking people trivia or general-information questions.

In Koriat and Goldsmith's (1996) study, some participants were told that they had to report an answer (the forced-recall condition), whereas other participants were allowed to report only those answers that they were confident were the correct answers (free-recall condition). This allowed Koriat and Goldsmith to look at two aspects of the students' performance: both the quantity (that is, how many items they remembered in total) as well as the quality of their output (that is, what percentage of their answers was indeed correct). Not surprisingly, the participants in the forced-recall condition reported more items, but the free-recall condition participants showed a better accuracy rate. This difference is important. It means that when participants have control over their output, not all retrieved answers actually will be reported. In other words, participants can and do screen their own answers for accuracy. The free-recall participants were able to selectively eliminate some of the items that they did retrieve and then rejected as incorrect. Thus, people can discard information considered inaccurate. This provides another example of the use of metamemory in the control of memory performance.

Retrospective confidence is important in eyewitness situations. First of all, we expect witnesses to give testimony only if they are highly confident that they are correct. The costs of misremembering are high, so we want witnesses to screen answers for accuracy. Second, if a witness is highly confident that his or her memory is correct, this is given substantial weight by juries (Cutler, Penrod, & Dexter, 1990). Fortunately, research shows that most of what we retrieve is correct. Incorrectly retrieved information represents only about 10% of responses (Dunning & Stern, 1992). However, legal psychologists have struggled to demonstrate a relation between retrospective confidence and the accuracy of eyewitness identification. This is in part because juries must frequently distinguish between two witnesses, one who expresses strong confidence ("I'll never forget that face!") and another who may not speak as demonstratively ("I think it was him"). Most of us would be more likely to believe the witness who expresses strong confidence. However, the data do not show that more confident witnesses are more accurate witnesses (Perfect, 2002). However, if one looks at confidence within each witness—that is, the confidence that some of his or her memories are more likely to be accurate than others—then retrospective confidence predicts performance quite well (Perfect, 2002).

Students often emerge from an exam feeling that they did well, only to find out that their performance was less than they expected. Why does this occur, given the general high accuracy of individual retrospective confidence judgments? It turns out that although retrospective confidence judgments discriminate well between correct and incorrect answers, we also have a tendency to be overconfident (Dunlosky & Metcalfe, 2009). Thus, if we rate a number of answers as likely to be 90 % correct, it is likely that only 80 % will be correct. This general overconfidence leads to the illusion that we did better than we actually did.

We will end this chapter with one interesting research question. Recently, research has begun to address whether humans are the only beings on the planet with the ability to monitor and control our memories. Metamemory certainly seems like a complex cognitive task that, as we have seen, requires our huge human frontal lobes. Is it possible that other animals too can show metamemory, even its must rudimentary forms? A number of highly inventive researchers are asking just that question.

Metamemory in Nonhuman Animals

Until quite recently, it was assumed that metamemory was something only human beings possessed (Kornell, 2009a). Even the few studies that suggested that, with sufficient training, monkeys could show evidence of metamemory-like behaviors (J. D. Smith et al., 1995), it was assumed that it was more a function of massive training and unintended shaping of the behavior than actual metacognition (see Terrace & Metcalfe, 2005). However, over the past few years, a number of studies have shown various degrees of metamemory ability in primates and perhaps other species as well. The breakthrough was in developing a method that could ask nonverbal animals to report on their metamemory experiences. This method, developed by David Smith and his colleagues, has now been applied to rats, rhesus monkeys, pigeons, capuchin monkeys, bottlenosed dolphins, and orangutans (see J. D. Smith & Washburn, 2005). The method involves asking the animal to judge difficulty during a perceptual task or memory task. The animal indicates that a trial is difficult by opting out on difficult trials. If the trial is easy, the animal can receive reinforcement for choosing the correct response, but on difficult trials, the animal can avoid the negative consequences of choosing incorrectly by opting out of a particular trial, by pressing a particular button or pulling a particular lever. Thus, the animal can tell us how difficult a memory trial "feels" by choosing not to answer those questions and instead selecting the "opt-out" button.

Suda-King (2008) trained several orangutans at the National Zoo in Washington, D.C., to perform in a simple memory experiment. The orangutans watched two grapes placed under one of two cups. After a short retention interval of about 10 seconds, the orangutans were allowed to point to one of the cups. If they were correct, they received the grapes, whereas if they were incorrect, they received a short time-out before the resumption of the experiment, thus delaying the next opportunity to receive a tasty snack. On some trials, however, Suda-King placed a large wooden block in front of the cups when she placed the grapes in one of the cups, completely occluding the orangutan's view of the cups. On these trials, the orangutan did not know where the grape was hidden and could only guess. Suda-King then introduced another cup, which was a different color and always had one, but only one, grape. This one-grape cup would serve the purpose of being the "opt-out" cup. The orangutan could forgo the two-grape cup if it did not remember or see where the grapes had been put and always get one grape by choosing this cup. However, two grapes are always more desirable to the orangutans than one, so if they did remember where the grapes were, they would choose those.

Therefore, on trials in which the orangutans saw and remembered where the two grapes were, they could choose that one and receive a larger reward. On the unseen or forgotten trials, the orangutans could still receive food, just a lesser amount. The orangutans successfully chose the correct cup with two grapes on more than 90% of the seen trials. However, on the occluded trials, some but not all orangutans often (about 50%) chose the escape option rather than risk getting nothing at all. In other words, it appeared as if the orangutans were aware that they did not know where the two grapes were and therefore opted for the safe bet of one grape. One orangutan could even opt out before the memory test was actually given, thus approximating a judgment of learning. This orangutan choose a single cup with a single grape in it before the memory test was presented—that is, the array of two cups, one with two grapes in it and the other empty. Hampton (2001) found similar results for a rhesus macaque. Therefore, at least some individuals of nonhuman primate species can demonstrate metamemory awareness and avoid guessing on difficult trials when the outcome of guessing is potentially aversive.

The research on animal metacognition is still new, and much remains to be seen if the behavior in animals is really equivalent to the metamemory seen in people. However, it is provocative to think that monitoring and control of memory may not be limited to human beings. Indeed, news that rats were engaging in metacognition recently brought some controversy to the area (Foote & Crystal, 2007). However, on closer examination, most researchers concluded that the rats were really just being conditioned to the contingencies of the experimental situation (Metcalfe, 2008). But research continues apace. It is likely that as more studies similar to Suda-King's appear, that there will be a growing consensus that metamemory may indeed be a skill shared with our primate cousins.

SUMMARY

Metamemory is an important component of the memory system because it concerns our awareness of our own memory processes. We can monitor what it is we are learning and remembering and use that information to control what we do. As such, metamemory is an important aspect of memory improvement. Metamemory is studied by asking participants in experiments to make judgments, such as feeling-of-knowing judgments, tip-of-the-tongue judgments, and judgments of learning. Most of the research suggests that these judgments are indeed accurate and therefore can help us guide our learning behaviors and strategies.

KEY TERMS

Metacognition	Monitoring	Ease-of-learning judgments
Metamemory	Control	Judgments of learning

Feeling-of-knowing judgments

Tip-of-the-tongue states

Retrospective confidence judgments

Indirect or inferential theories

Cue familiarity

Retrieval of related information

Direct-access theory

Availability and accessibility

Allocation of study time

Labor in vain

Region of proximal learning

REVIEW QUESTIONS

1. What is metamemory and how does it differ from memory?

2. What are monitoring and control? How do they work together to form an efficient metamemory system?

3. What do each of the following judgments measure?

   a. ease of learning

   b. judgments of learning

   c. feeling of knowing

   d. tip of the tongue (TOT)

   e. retrospective confidence

4. What is the difference between direct-access theory and inferential theory in how explain metamemory judgment?

5. What is a TOT? How is it best explained?

6. How does the cue familiarity hypothesis explain feeling-of-knowing judgments?

7. How can delayed judgments of learning be used by individuals to improve their learning?

8. What is allocation of study time? How can it be used to make learning more efficient?

9. What is the region of proximal learning?

10. How is metamemory measured in nonhuman animals?

ONLINE RESOURCES

1. For information on active research on metamemory, go to the website of the International Association for Metacognition at http://www.personal.kent.edu/~jdunlosk/metacog.

2. For an interesting article in the popular press on the tip-of-the-tongue phenomenon, go to http://www.boston.com/bostonglobe/ideas/articles/2008/06/01/whats_that_name.

3. For more on judgments of learning, you can read the excellent chapters in Dunlosky and Metcalfe's (2009) book on metamemory at http://www.sagepub.com/booksProdDesc.nav? prodId=Book229322&.

4. For more on Janet Metcalfe's research, go to http://www.columbia.edu/cu/psychology/ metcalfe/jm.html.

Go to www.sagepub.com/schwartz for additional exercises and study resources. Select **Chapter 9, Metamemory** for chapter-specific resources.

CHAPTER 10

Memory Disorders

In movies, amnesia varies from a source of humor to a minor inconvenience to a life-altering experience. In the children's movie *Finding Nemo,* a good-natured but amnesic fish named Dory helps a father save his son. Her frequent forgetting of names provides the bulk of the laughs in the movie. In the Adam Sandler movie *50 First Dates,* the character played by Drew Barrymore suffers a dense, albeit unrealistic, amnesia. She forgets all postaccident information when she goes to sleep each night, although she remembers the events of the day throughout the day (I know of no real cases of amnesia following this pattern). Nonetheless, for Drew Barrymore's character, these symptoms present only minor problems for her in finding love and ultimately traveling the world aboard a yacht with her husband and child. Indeed, that her husband, played by Adam Sandler, must woo and win her each new day is portrayed as romantic. In *Memento,* an amnesic widower is bent on revenge for his murdered wife, which he believes is unsolved. Because his dense amnesia prevents him from learning anything new, he must tattoo himself with the evidence he discovers, lest he forget an important clue. Unlike the first two movies, *Memento* is realistic in its portrayal of anterograde amnesia (if not in how to investigate a crime). Indeed, to emphasize the disorder of time in amnesia, *Memento* starts in the middle and then simultaneously goes forward and backward. Nonetheless, the main character, "Leonard," despite his amnesia, "gets things done." Thus, in each movie, amnesia does not prevent the character from fulfilling an important mission. In reality, amnesia can be extremely debilitating. See the following video to get a sense of this: www.sagepub.com/schwartz.[1]

As an example, I will describe a case of amnesia within my own family. This account is not unique. Many families can describe similar stories of amnesic symptoms. Some years ago, I visited my then 80-year-old grandmother in the assisted-living facility she had just moved to. My grandmother has spent most of her adult life as a music teacher and had only retired a few years earlier. Unfortunately, by the age of 80, she had suffered from a series of small and undiagnosed strokes and was no longer able to work or live on her own. I told her that I just finished my Ph.D. and would be moving to Florida soon to start a job as an assistant professor. "Mazel tov," she replied ("Mazel tov" is Yiddish for "congratulations"), and I told her about how excited I was to be moving to Miami. I then told her my younger brother had just gotten engaged, and we talked about that for a while. She was excited about hearing of my brother's engagement and the eventual prospect of great-grandchildren. She then said, "Enough about your brother—I want to hear about you. When are you going to finish at that school of yours?" I told her that I just finished my Ph.D. and would be moving to Florida soon to start a job as an assistant professor. "Mazel tov," she replied, completely unaware that we had just had this conversation not more than 15 minutes earlier. Like some other older adults, my grandmother had suffered a stroke, which had left her with strong anterograde amnesia, leaving her with a deficit in encoding new information. Notice that, at this point, my grandmother had lost only episodic memory. She forgot the specifics of the conversation, but her lexical memory was intact; that is, her ability to talk and communicate was not affected. In addition, her semantic memory was unaffected; she knew what a Ph.D. was, for example, and was able to talk intelligently about my job opportunity. Anterograde amnesia, restricted to episodic memory, is a quite common result of strokes and also the first symptoms seen in Alzheimer's disease, also a disease that disproportionately affects older adults.

Memory disorders are devastating, both for the person who has lost his or her memory and for that person's family. Amnesia frequently results from brain damage that occurs in strokes or motor vehicle accidents. Memory impairment can also result from tumors, near-drowning experiences (apoxia), brain surgery, bullet wounds, and other damage to the brain. Psychological conditions can also cause memory deficits. In this chapter, we will consider psychogenic amnesia (specific amnesias caused by psychological trauma) but not memory deficits that occur in other psychological disorders such as schizophrenia. The most common form of amnesia is associated with Alzheimer's disease. Approximately 360,000 new cases are diagnosed every year (Brookmeyer et al., 2007). In this chapter, we will sort out the various forms of amnesia and define what they are and who they affect. We will discuss the areas of the brain affected and the behavioral deficits that result from this brain damage.

WHAT IS AMNESIA?

Amnesia can be considered any impairment of memory abilities beyond normal forgetting. In most cases, the term *amnesia* refers to an acquired condition brought about by trauma to the brain. A whole host of separable disorders can be classified as amnesia. In most, the major deficit is encoding new information into episodic memory, but there are amnesias that affect retrieval from episodic memory, access to semantic memory, access to working memory, and deficits in the executive control of memory. We will mostly focus on organic amnesias, that is, amnesia that results from physical destruction of different regions of the brain. We will touch on psychogenic amnesias, much heralded by Hollywood but quite uncommon in the real world. These amnesias do not result directly from brain damage but seem to be elicited by psychological trauma.

> **Amnesia**: memory deficits acquired through brain damage.

CASE STUDIES OF AMNESIA

Patient HM

In Chapter 2, we introduced the patient HM. The study of HM's memory initiated the modern study of amnesia. In 1953, neurosurgeon William Scoville removed HM's hippocampuses as a treatment for epilepsy. Much of the surrounding medial temporal tissue was excised as well. The surgery was, in one sense, successful, as HM's seizures decreased. His measured IQ remained stable before and after surgery. Indeed, it appeared to rise from a normal 101 to an above-average 112. He continued to enjoy crossword puzzles. His working memory was normal. His ability to speak, understand, read, and write was not impaired. He was also able to remember much of his life from before the surgery. That is, his stored episodic memories were still accessible. However, the effect on his ability to encode new information was devastating. For the next 55 years of his life, HM never learned anything new in a direct and conscious manner. For example, if he was given a list of words to recall, he could read them and tell you what they meant. However, 5 minutes later, he would have forgotten both the words on the list and the experience of reading them. Despite his inability to encode information episodically, he was able to learn some information, but only after countless repetitions. For example, he eventually learned that family members (such as his parents) had died. HM died in December 2008 at the age of 82. Go to the following website for HM's obituary: www.sagepub.com/schwartz.[2]

In addition, other forms of memory, such as implicit memory, were largely intact in HM. For example, he learned various skills, including mirror writing (that is, writing that can only be read by looking at the text in a mirror). When asked to write in mirror style, he would often report that he could not do so. He could not remember any episode of such writing, even though he had learned to do it since his surgery. Thus, he found it a surprise when he could mirror write. When shown a word list, he remembered none of the items later in an episodic memory test but did show implicit memory when tested via priming techniques later on. Therefore, it is likely that his deficit was simply a profound anterograde amnesia, that is, the inability to encode new information into episodic memory. Because of his symptoms, anterograde amnesia was originally attributed to deficits in the hippocampus and surrounding temporal lobe areas. However, more recent magnetic resonance imaging (MRI) on HM also shows damage to other areas of the brain, including the amygdala (Corkin, Amaral, Gonzalez, Johnson, & Hyman, 1997). It is likely that the widespread bilateral damage to HM's memory areas in his brain is responsible for the very strong amnesia he was stricken with.

Clive Wearing

Clive Wearing was born in 1938 in England and went on to have a successful musical career, as a singer, piano player, conductor, and composer. Indeed, he composed and conducted the music played at the wedding of Princess Diana and Prince Charles. However, in 1985, Wearing contracted viral encephalitis, which caused massive damage to his brain, including damage to his medial temporal lobes and prefrontal lobes. Viral encephalitis is a rare but dangerous disease that causes massive swelling of the brain. In Wearing's case, it was associated with a herpes infection. Wearing has severe anterograde amnesia; in the 23 years since his illness, he has not learned a single new thing about the world. He also has severe retrograde amnesia; he cannot remember a single event from his past. He lives in a perpetual present. In fact, he writes over and over in his "diary" that he has just returned to consciousness after a long illness. He has written this entry several times a day for many years. His wife estimated that if his attention is distracted, his working memory maintains information for about 10 seconds, and then that experience is lost forever. Indeed, his wife can leave the room for 30 seconds and return, at which point Wearing will greet her joyously and emotionally as if he had not seen her for years. Unlike HM, Wearing also cannot remember events from before his illness. Ask him about a concert or some other important event, and he cannot retrieve.

Like HM, Wearing has profound amnesia—in the episodic domain. Again, like HM, the problem seems restricted to memory. His amnesia does not extend to lexical memory. He is still articulate and has full command of spoken language. Nor does it extend to procedural memory; he is still an accomplished piano player. Nonetheless, he does not remember a single event from his life, and he has learned nothing new in 23 years (see B. A. Wilson & Wearing, 1995, for a complete description of this case). To observe his symptoms yourself, go to www.sagepub.com/schwartz.[3]

These two individuals are cases of extreme amnesia. The typical amnesiac who does not become the subject of many years of psychological testing will have less severe anterograde amnesia and less severe retrograde amnesia. R. Campbell and Conway (1995) have some poignant descriptions of the problems faced by people with less severe amnesia. Often these problems involve finding ways for them to turn off the stove, remember what needs to be purchased at the store, and when to pick up the children from their soccer game.

ANTEROGRADE AMNESIA

Anterograde amnesia refers to an inability to form new memories following brain damage. It varies from mild impairment, in which a person simply requires more time to encode information than normal individuals do, to the severe impairment seen in patients like HM, in which the person may remember little of anything new, essentially leaving him or her frozen in time. Severe anterograde amnesiacs need round-the-clock supervision—as they may forget where they live if they have moved since their accident or injury. In almost all cases, severe impairment means the person also cannot continue at a job and must be dependent on others. Mild amnesiacs may be able to compensate for their deficit, return home, and, in some cases, even resume their careers.

> **Anterograde amnesia:** an inability to form new memories following brain damage.

In many cases, the deficit can be quite specific; that is, the person is impaired in the learning of new information and the encoding of episodic events, but other aspects of memory are intact. Anterograde amnesiacs can remember information that they learned

Hippocampus: an area of the brain associated with learning and memory. Damage can cause anterograde amnesia.

Medial temporal lobes: a cortical area of the brain in the temporal lobes associated with learning and memory. Damage can cause anterograde amnesia.

Mammillary bodies: a subcortical region of the brain associated with learning. Damage can cause anterograde amnesia.

from before their accident, have no deficits in speech or intelligence, and have no deficits in working memory. Damage in the brain tends to be in the **hippocampus** and **medial temporal lobes.** There is a second locus in the brain that also causes the amnesic syndrome—namely, the **mammillary bodies** of the diencephalon. Damage to the adjacent fornix can also induce anterograde amnesia (Aggleton, 2008). At this point, it is not clear if there are differences in the symptoms experienced by patients with damage to the hippocampus and medial temporal lobe compared to patients with damage to the mammillary bodies or to the fornix.

Damage to these areas of the brain produces the **amnesic syndrome** so called because many patients suffer a common set of problems (and spared abilities), regardless of whether the amnesia was induced by stroke, auto accident, head injury, brain tumors, viral infections, or even neurosurgery (see Table 10.1). Characteristic of the amnesic syndrome patient is specific impairment of encoding new information into both episodic and semantic memory, while most other cognitive functions remain intact.

Amnesic syndrome: characteristic of the amnesic syndrome patient is specific impairment of encoding new information into both episodic and semantic memory, while most other cognitive functions remain intact.

If patients with the amnesic syndrome are given a list of words to recall, they will remember few, if any, of the words if there is more than a 30-second delay between the time of learning and the time of recall. This is also the case if the test is recognition. Indeed, any test that calls on the patient to consciously remember new information from episodic memory will result in poor performance. By contrast, patients can recount events from their preinjury life in a normal manner.

Table 10.1 Symptoms of the amnesic syndrome.

1. Anterograde amnesia for both episodic and semantic memory
2. Intact working memory
3. Intact language and intelligence
4. Intact implicit memory
5. Damage to hippocampus and surrounding medial temporal lobe

One hint of a difference between patients with hippocampal damage and patients with damage to the diencephalon is the difference between recall tests and recognition tests. Patients with damage to the hippocampus and to the surrounding medial temporal lobes will show deficits on both recall and recognition tests. Patients with damage to areas of the diencephalon will show relatively preserved performance on tests of recognition. Thus, if the test asks the patients to distinguish between new words and old words, the hippocampus patients will show an amnesic pattern, but the diencephalon patients do not (Tsivilis et al., 2008).

Implicit Memory in the Amnesic Syndrome

Implicit memory refers to the preserved ability to perform tasks that are influenced by a past event without the person being aware of the event experience. For example, after hearing and then forgetting a sentence such as the "The grizzly bear scared the campers," you will still be more likely to spell the word *bear/bare* as *bear* than if you had not heard the sentence. It turns out that amnesic patients will sometimes show the influence of earlier events, even when they do not recall those events. What happens here is that the brains of the amnesic patients process this information, and it influences their thinking. However, because it is not registered by the episodic memory system, the amnesiac does not return a conscious memory.

> **Implicit memory**: the preserved ability to perform tasks that are influenced by a past event without the person being aware of the event experience.

Here's how implicit memory is tested in amnesic patients. Consider an experiment in which an amnesic individual is given a list of words to recall. Immediately following the presentation of the list, the amnesiac is asked to recall as many words as possible from the list. Given that the patient is amnesic, he or she may recall very few, if any at all, and certainly far less than a nonamnesic control. In cases like Clive Wearing, the patient may promptly forget that he or she had even been given a list of words. Now, the patient is given an implicit test of memory. In implicit memory tests, participants are not required to retrieve an answer from memory—the tests can be done without remembering a particular event. They can be done by general cognitive reasoning skills. For example, one classic test of implicit memory is **word fragment completion.** In this task, a participant is given some letters of a word but not all of them and must figure out the word. For example, "S_h_l_r" is a word fragment. The task can be completed without any reference to the past (that is, the episodic past). The participant can simply determine what letters are needed to insert into the fragment to make it an acceptable word. Indeed, amnesiacs may be just as good as normal individuals in completing this task. However, **repetition priming** studies show that a prior experience with the word *scholar* will make it easier to later

> **Word fragment completion**: in this task, a participant is given some letters of a word but not all of them and must figure out the word.
>
> **Repetition priming**: the effect of presenting a stimulus on the processing of that same stimulus at a later date. Amnesiacs will show repetition priming even if they do not consciously recall the target.

solve the word fragment. Normal participants will be more likely to solve "S_h_1 _r" if they saw *scholar* in another context, sometimes as much as a year earlier. Because participants may not always be aware of the connection between their earlier experience and the present task, researchers have called the effects of repetition priming to be implicit memory. Certainly, this term applies to amnesiacs who do not consciously remember the words from the list but benefit similarly from the earlier experience as normal individuals do when they are tested with an implicit test. What is relevant here is that even when amnesiacs do not recall the word they just saw (e.g., *scholar*), they show normal repetition priming effects. That is, even though the word does not register in their episodic memory, it is processed at some level, as their behavior in the implicit memory test is later affected by that experience. Many studies have documented this preserved implicit memory in amnesic patients (Tulving & Schacter, 1990).

Awareness in the Amnesic Syndrome

Do amnesic patients know that they are amnesic? The answer to this question is, it depends. It depends on the form of amnesia they have acquired. In the amnesic syndrome, patients tended to be keenly aware of their deficits. They are aware of how it has changed their lives and struggle to overcome it. In some ways, this is an important feature as it gives clinical neuropsychology a manner in which to help these patients by focusing them on ways to compensate for their memory loss. Diaries, index cards, Post-it notes, portable computers, iPhones, and BlackBerries can all be kept close by to record events and appointments. In this way, neuropsychological interventions can help patients with mild to moderate anterograde amnesia. Although, even then, many of the memory feats most of us take for granted elude these amnesiacs.

Although external memory can be used to compensate for some aspects of amnesia, being amnesic can be frustrating both for the amnesiac and his or her family. For example, consider the pride and satisfaction you may have had today after having successfully climbed a new route at the rock climbing gym. You worked on it for weeks and finally mastered the moves. Today, you are basking in the feeling of pride that comes with that success. An amnesiac would feel just as much pride at having succeeded at the task but a few minutes later would have completely forgotten not just the accomplishment but also the ensuing feeling of pride. Similarly, think back on your last summer vacation. Perhaps the highlight was going jet-skiing, something you had never done before. Remembering that event may result in bolstering your mood and reminding you that all the hard work you do pays off, as it allows you to afford your vacations. An amnesiac may thoroughly enjoy the jet-skiing trip but will not remember it later or be able to mentally time travel to that event later to get the enjoyment that the rest of us get from revisiting our pleasant memories.

Medved (2007) interviewed a number of patients with anterograde amnesia with the goal of understanding what it was like to be amnesic. The patients had suffered brain damage from a variety of causes about a year prior to the interview. Medved was interested in the coping strategies that amnesiacs use to discuss past events with others when their ability to retrieve such events is impaired. More specifically, Medved's goal was to understand how these people approached **memory conversations.** Memory conversation refers to the discussions we have with others about the past. Normal individuals frequently have memory

Memory conversations: The discussions we have with others about the past. Normal individuals frequently have memory conversations.

Memory importation: when amnesiacs describe a memory from before their injury as if it had happened after.

Memory appropriation: an amnesiac may be able to retrieve an event based on someone else's repeated retelling of the event.

Memory compensation: rather than trying to answer a question about the past, amnesiacs talk instead about the issues that they are having with their amnesic syndrome.

conversations. Think of a woman coming home from work and sharing her aggravations of the day with her spouse. Medved found that amnesiacs used three major coping strategies when discussing memories. First, many used **memory importation.** This means that the amnesiacs described a memory from before their injury as if it had happened after the injury. One patient interviewed by Medved described having a job interview—even though he was no longer able to work at his old job. After more questioning, he realized that this event was in his preinjury past, not his present. Second, because semantic memory is almost always less severely affected than episodic memory, in many cases, events can be remembered from semantic memory rather than episodic memory. Thus, a person may be able to retrieve an event based on someone else's repeated retelling of the event. Medved calls this strategy **memory appropriation.** Finally, amnesiacs engage in **memory compensation,** in which rather than trying to answer a question about the past, they talk instead about the issues that they are having with their amnesic syndrome. Conversationally, this may convey to the listener that they would like to talk about their memory, but the memories are simply lacking. According to Medved, these three strategies help amnesiacs fit in with their families and in other conversational situations.

Patients with the amnesic syndrome are usually aware that they have memory deficits. This can make the suffering more profound, as is clear in the cases above, but it also provides an avenue for people to find ways of compensating (see Campbell & Conway, 1995). Patients are encouraged to maintain memory books, in which they write down the events of each day. They can also use electronic devices such as cell phones or laptop computers to record events from their life and to plan events for the future. In this way, even if they cannot recall them episodically, they can always consult their book or iPhone to determine what they did on a particular day. Patients can also structure their lives in ways that are helpful. Common objects (keys, kitchen utensils, etc.) can always be returned to the same location for easy finding. People can place Post-its or program their cell phone to beep when they have to remember to do something. Patients can stay close to home, so they do not get lost. Some patients can return to a job, provided the job calls upon well-learned skills from the past or involves simple skills that can be learned. Amnesiacs are particularly good at doing repetitive tasks that might bore others as they do them over and over again. The amnesiac forgets the previous repetitions so he or she can do the task the next time with more attention than the ordinary person might (Campbell & Conway, 1995).

There have also been specific programs designed to help patients with the amnesic syndrome cope with their condition. These patients can learn through classical and operational conditioning, and as we have shown, they also have intact implicit memory. A number of

Method of vanishing cues: this technique uses the spared implicit memory of amnesiacs to help them learn new skills.

remediation programs have been developed to take advantage of these skills to help these patients resume normal functions. Schacter (1996) described a technique he called the **method of vanishing cues** to train an amnesic woman to perform a simple but new computer task required by her employer. This technique uses the spared implicit memory of amnesiacs to help them learn new skills. Schacter presented the woman with the definitions of tasks she would be required to carry out along with their name. Thus, "run the antivirus program: Norton" might be her first trial of learning. Schacter would then slowly remove letters from the name "Norton." After many trials, the participant might be able to generate the word *Norton* from simply "run the antivirus program: No. . . ." Eventually, Schacter could remove all cues. Even though the patient did not remember learning about Norton antivirus software, she would know to apply it when the topic came up. This and other intervention strategies help people suffering from amnesia learn new skills and allow them to continue to be productive members of society.

Simulated Anterograde Amnesia

Unfortunately, amnesia induced by permanent brain damage is permanent, with recovery relatively limited. However, there are forms of amnesia that are temporary. One such amnesia resembles anterograde amnesia seen in the amnesic syndrome but wears off. Certain drugs temporarily mimic the symptoms of anterograde amnesia. In particular, a class of drugs called **benzodiazepines,** which are frequently prescribed by doctors as sedatives, also have strong amnesic affects on memory. Benzodiazepines, such as diazepam (Valium), lorazepam, triazolam, and midazolam, are given for their effects on anxiety, insomnia, and muscle relaxation (Kaplan, 2005). However, they are also amnesia-inducing drugs, especially within the episodic memory domain.

Benzodiazepines: drugs that are used usually because of their effects on anxiety, insomnia, and muscle relaxation. However, they are also strong amnesia-inducing drugs, especially within the episodic memory domain.

Benzodiazepines have achieved notoriety with respect to their amnesic effect. Attackers, particularly in date rape situations, give benzodiazepines to potential victims. When combined with alcohol, the benzodiazepines leave the victims more vulnerable to attack and amnesia for the event later. Given the prevalence of benzodiazepines as legally prescribed drugs, people should be alert as to what goes into their drink, particularly at raucous parties. Go to the following website to read about a heroic waiter who saved a woman from a potential benzodiazepine-linked date rape: www.sagepub.com/schwartz.[4]

All benzodiazepines impair episodic memory, but their effects on short-term memory and semantic memory are mixed, depending on the specific drug and the specific task (Bacon, Schwartz, Paire-Ficout, & Izaute, 2007; Izaute & Bacon, 2006). In experiments, when volunteers take benzodiazepines, they have poor memory of word lists, paired associates, and other materials when tested later. Once the drug wears off, the amnesic effects do so also. Indeed, some have argued that part of the reason why these drugs relax stressed-out patients is that they cause impairment of memory. However, the data suggest that benzo-diazepines produce anterograde amnesia only. When the benzodiazepine wears off, the patient's memory returns to normal, as there seem to be no long-term impairments in memory. However, information seen or heard while the drug was in the patient's blood-stream will not be recovered.

However, observations indicate that patients who develop a transient amnesia following administration of benzodiazepine are unaware of their episodic memory deficit. This con-dition is called **anosognosia,** the failure to become aware of a cognitive deficit. This distin-guishes them from the amnesic syndrome patients who are aware of their amnesia. In the case of benzodiazepine-linked temporary amne-sia, it is not a long-term problem as the amnesia wears off. However, patients will overestimate the likelihood that they will remember stud-ied material while under the influence of the benzodiazepine (Weingartner et al., 1993).

> **Anosognosia**: the failure to become aware of a cognitive deficit.

RETROGRADE AMNESIA

Retrograde amnesia occurs when patients lose the ability to retrieve memories of events prior to brain damage. This means that the patient can learn new facts and encode new events but cannot remember experiences or events that happened prior to the brain damage. Typically, the retrograde amnesia is not com-plete, as it is in Clive Wearing. Rather, it extends back in time from the injury to a particular point in the past. In most cases of retrograde amnesia, the inability to retrieve from memory is limited to episodic memory. Recalling facts about the world (and the person himself or herself) is not impaired as often (although it can occur; this condition is called semantic amnesia). People with retrograde amnesia will have periods of their lives in which they cannot recall any specific events. When given autobiographical cueing, all of their reported memories (if any) will come from a different period of their life.

> **Retrograde amnesia**: when patients lose the ability to retrieve memories of events prior to brain damage.

Keep in mind that for most patients, the retrograde amnesia is not total. There is a period starting with just before the brain damage and then extending backward in time in which events cannot be recalled from memory. This period of time may be small and the conse-quences relatively inconsequential or may stretch back for many years. Or, as we saw with Clive Wearing, the retrograde period may stretch back for an entire lifetime.

A well-known person with a relatively short window of retrograde amnesia is Trevor Rees-Jones, the only survivor of the tragic car crash that killed Princess Diana of Britain and her boyfriend, Dodi Fayed. Rees-Jones, Mr. Fayed's bodyguard, suffered severe injuries, including a blow to his head. Rees-Jones eventually made a full recovery from the auto accident, which included no long-term deficits in his cognitive abilities. The head injury did create a window of retrograde amnesia from the time of the accident to several hours before. Mr. Rees-Jones does not remember any of the events of the evening leading up to the crash, although he can remember events from earlier that day as would an uninjured person. In this case, this was unfortunate, as his testimony would have been useful in piecing together the events that led to the crash. It is worth noting (however irrelevant to this subject of this book) that Mr. Rees-Jones was the only one in the car wearing a seatbelt and the only one to survive.

In almost all cases of retrograde amnesia, the loss of memory occurs for events closest to the point of brain damage. Older memories are more difficult to dislodge from memory in patients with retrograde amnesia. Indeed, this observation has been called **Ribot's law,** which means the newer memories will be more affected by retrograde amnesia than older memories. This has led some researchers to argue that a process called **consolidation** is disrupted in retrograde amnesia. Consolidation refers to a neurological process whereby memory traces are made permanent in a person's long-term memory. That is, many memories may be held in a temporary state (in long-term memory) and only preserved if they turn out to have significance for the individual. For example, the many hours you spend working on a paper for your English class are typically lost to memory once the paper has been handed in. The goal is to produce the paper; the memory of drinking coffee and eating pizza while you spent hours in front of your computer are generally forgotten, as they are seldom relevant. However, if your computer crashes and you lose all your work, you are more likely to remember all that now wasted time. Although consolidation cannot explain retrograde amnesia over periods of years, it can account for the retrograde amnesia seen in cases like Trevor Rees-Jones.

> **Ribot's law**: newer memories will be more affected by retrograde amnesia than older memories.
>
> **Consolidation**: to a neurological process whereby memory traces are made permanent in a person's long-term memory.

In minor injuries, such as concussion, the period of retrograde amnesia can be quite short, often for just a few minutes before the injury. Lynch and Yarnell (1973), for example, found that football players who suffered from concussions during games could no longer remember the play in which they had gotten injured, although remembered the rest of the game prior to their injury. In some cases, the retrograde period will initially be somewhat longer, perhaps several days or even a month, but as the person recovers from the head trauma, provided there is no permanent damage to the brain, the retrograde period will shrink over time. Older memories return first, followed by more recent memories. In most cases, however, a small window of time, anywhere from 5 minutes to an hour, will remain permanently lost to the accident victim. It is worth noting that brain damage from concussions, however, is cumulative. Each concussion brings a greater and greater risk of permanent brain damage. For this reason, many neurologists often advise athletes to retire from such sports as football, soccer, and boxing if they have had too many concussions.

With permanent damage to the brain, however, the retrograde period can remain lengthy and remain unchanged for the rest of the person's life. Consider the case of KC (Rosenbaum et al., 2005). KC was a college-educated man living near the city of Toronto in Ontario, Canada. He worked as a foreperson in a factory. He was also a motorcycle enthusiast who spent most weekends driving around the countryside outside of Toronto. He was not a newcomer to injury, having had a head injury as a child and a major motorcycle accident, which fractured his leg. However, in 1981 at the age of 30, he suffered a major head trauma in a single-vehicle motorcycle crash, which destroyed large amounts of brain tissue in his frontal and temporal lobes, including extensive damage to his left hippocampus. As a result of these injuries, KC was left with profound anterograde and retrograde amnesia. Like Clive Wearing, KC remembers no events from his life at all. He has no episodic memory, as he can neither recall any events from his life nor encode any new events. However, the amnesia only affects his episodic memory. His lexical memory and semantic memory are largely intact. Because of these spared skills, KC, after recovering from his physical injuries, has spent the past 25 years living with his family at home and working at the local library, filing and reshelving books. For a series of interviews with KC by the prominent memory researcher Endel Tulving, go to www.sagepub.com/schwartz.[5]

Rosenbaum et al. (2005) and the other researchers who have studied KC have found that his retrograde amnesia for episodic memory is complete. He does not remember any of his motorcycle crashes (i.e., the ones where his head was not injured) and does not remember attending hockey games or going out with friends. He cannot remember holiday dinners with family, any of the times where he changed a flat tire, or having played a game of chess with Endel Tulving. Even more monumental events escape his memory, including having been evacuated when a train derailed spilling toxic chemicals in his neighborhood or the tragic drowning death of his brother. However, he has not lost preaccident semantic memory, which is largely intact. For example, KC can tell you how to change a tire, which team won the Stanley Cup every year up until 1981, and the address where he grew up. Moreover, he maintains his sense of personal identity, and his verbal abilities and his intelligence remain intact as well.

The exact locus in the brain that causes retrograde amnesia is elusive. Retrograde amnesia is seen in cases of amnesia related to damage to the diencephalon (as in Korsakoff's disease, to be discussed shortly), damage to the frontal lobes, and damage to the medial temporal lobes. There is some debate as to the role of the hippocampus in retrograde amnesia. Some argue that damage to the hippocampus results in a restricted time-limited retrograde amnesia, similar to that seen in concussions (although anterograde amnesia may be extensive). Others argue that the retrograde amnesia in these cases is due to the damage to the surrounding medial temporal lobe (Lah & Miller, 2008).

A less severe form of retrograde amnesia can be seen in patients with temporal lobe epilepsy. Epilepsy is a disease in which damaged brain tissue (usually as the result of brain trauma) results in abnormal neuronal discharging, resulting in seizures. In most cases, epilepsy can be controlled by medications, but in some cases, it requires surgery. The focal point of the brain damage that causes epilepsy is often the temporal lobe. These patients will often demonstrate retrograde amnesia. The more frequent the seizures, the more retrograde amnesia seen (Bergen, Thompson, Baxendale, Fish, & Shorvon, 2000).

Just a note to students concerned about their own memory: All of us forget events from our past, including the recent past. There is nothing abnormal about that. The patients we are discussing have suffered extensive damage to their brain, resulting in the retrograde amnesia. If you are concerned about your own memory, perhaps having had a recent auto accident, a trip to the neuropsychologist can be illuminating.

Clinical neuropsychologists will run you through a battery of tests to examine your cognitive and emotional skills. If you score poorly on tests of remote memory (memory for the past) relative to your other tests, the neuropsychologist may diagnose memory problems. However, in most cases, people's concerns about their own memory are unfounded. We are often concerned about our forgetting, but forgetting is normal. Keep that in mind as we continue our discussion of amnesia.

Electroconvulsive Therapy

Electroconvulsive shock brings up images of torture or barbaric medical practices of the past. Indeed, its use has been quite controversial in psychiatry for many years. Most psychiatrists no longer think it is appropriate for schizophrenia, bipolar disorder, or a host of other psychiatric disorders. However, most clinical psychologists agree that the evidence shows it is actually beneficial for patients with clinical depression. For clinically depressed patients, usually with suicidal thoughts, a last course of action may involve **electroconvulsive therapy (ECT).** It involves delivering a strong electric shock to the head of a patient. Drugs are administered to prevent convulsions and injury during the treatment. As strange as it sounds, a repeated course of ECT actually successfully works to heighten mood and reduce suicidal tendencies among the clinically depressed (O'Conner et al., 2008).

> **Electroconvulsive therapy (ECT):** an effective treatment for depression that involves delivering a strong electric shock to the head of a patient. It also creates periods of retrograde amnesia.

One of the side effects of the ECT is that it induces retrograde amnesia. This retrograde period is not trivial—it may extend to up to a year or more prior to the shock, mostly for episodic events, but often for semantic memories as well. In most cases, it wears off once the sessions are complete but usually remains intact for the ECT procedure itself and a short period before it. Some have even speculated that it is the memory loss itself that creates the improved mood—the patients can no longer recall what is depressing them so much. However, ECT appears not to cause anterograde amnesia (O'Conner et al., 2008). Patients can encode new information soon after their ECT treatment. Despite its negative impact on remote memory, ECT continues to be used because of its beneficial effects on alleviating depression.

Korsakoff's Disease

> **Korsakoff's disease:** a severe form of amnesia brought on by long-term alcoholism. Characterized by anterograde amnesia, retrograde amnesia, anosognosia, and confabulation.

One of the most life-shattering forms of amnesia is Korsakoff's disease. Named after the Russian physician who first categorized the disease, **Korsakoff's disease** mostly affects older adults with a history of chronic alcohol abuse. As such, the etiology of Korsakoff's disease differs from other forms of amnesia. It is not the result of stroke or a sudden accident.

Rather, Korsakoff's disease begins with a vitamin B1 (thiamine) deficiency, which results from the long-term chronic alcohol abuse. Long-term deficiencies in vitamin B1 can damage parts of the brain, including the diencephalon (mammillary bodies and thalamus), as well as the basal forebrain and sometimes connections to the frontal lobes (see Figure 10.1). Most Americans have little difficulty acquiring enough vitamin B1 in their diets and so are not at risk of developing Korsakoff's disease. However, alcohol interferes with the synthesis of vitamin B1. Thus, alcoholics may develop B1 deficiencies, which can lead to brain damage. In rare cases, Korsakoff's disease can also develop because the patient has a genetic deficit in processing vitamin B1.

Similar symptoms can also arise from stroke damage to the diencephalon or genetic disorders that prevent the synthesis of vitamin B1, but in most patients with Korsakoff's disease, the symptoms arise from alcoholism. Despite the gradual accumulation of the brain damage, the onset of the symptoms is sudden, usually occurring after a period of illness, including delirium tremens. In some cases, immediate reintroduction of thiamine back into the bloodstream can alleviate symptoms. If thiamine is not given immediately, the effects are devastating. In most cases, the damage is irreversible, and there is often very little a neuropsychologist can do to foster improvement in a patient with Korsakoff's disease.

Figure 10.1 Illustration of the location of the diencephalon.

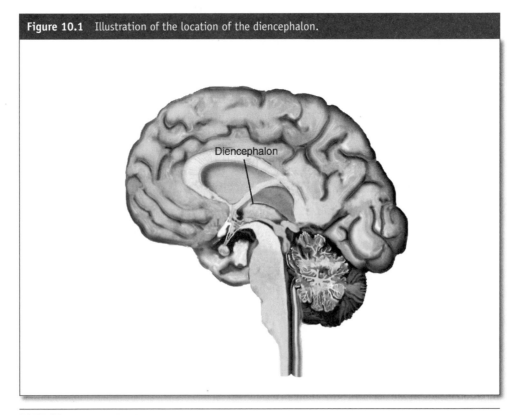

SOURCE: B. Garrett (2009).

Diencephalon: the part of the brain that includes the thalamus and hypothalamus. It serves as an important relay point in the human memory circuit.

The **diencephalon** (i.e., thalamus) is a major relay center connecting different areas in the brain. In particular, it serves as a relay point, gathering information from the hippocampus and medial temporal lobes and sending them to the prefrontal lobe. Thus, because of the difficulty that the brain has in communicating internally, Korsakoff's disease is characterized by deficits associated with damage to both the temporal lobes and to the frontal lobes.

Korsakoff's patients generally present both anterograde and retrograde amnesia. Their anterograde amnesia can often be as dense as that of a patient with damage to the medial temporal lobes. However, they perform differently on different kinds of memory tests. Both Korsakoff's patients and medial temporal lobe patients do equally poorly on recall tests, but Korsakoff's patients may do better on recognition tests, consistent with the idea that they encode information but have difficulties processing and retrieving it (Hirst et al., 1986).

Korsakoff's patients may also have quite severe retrograde amnesia, sometimes dating to some significant event in their life, in many cases years prior to the onset of the Korsakoff's disease. The retrograde amnesia is similar to that discussed earlier, except that it is combined with the other deficits seen in Korsakoff's disease. Sacks (1985) described a Korsakoff's patient who has retrograde amnesia extending back to his return from military service in World War II. The patient, "Jimmy" (not his real name), was a career naval sailor, hospitalized in 1975, 30 years after the end of the war. Jimmy's retrograde amnesia period is complete for that 30-year period, although he remembers information prior to 1945 with a great degree of accuracy. Sacks's eloquent description of a Korsakoff's amnesia patient is as poignant as it is revealing. The following interview took place in 1975, when Jimmy was 49 years old.

He [Jimmy] was a genial soul, very ready to talk and to answer any questions I asked him. He told me his name and birth date, and the name of the little Connecticut town where he was born. He described it in affectionate detail, even drew me a map.... He remembered the names of the various submarines on which he had served [during World War II], their missions, where they had been stationed, the names of his shipmates. He remembered Morse code, and was still fluent in Morse-tapping and touch-typing.

"What year is this, Mr. G.?" I asked, concealing my perplexity under a casual manner.

"Forty-five, man. What do you mean?"

He went on, "We've won the war, FDR's dead. Truman's at the helm. There's great times ahead."

"And you, Jimmy, how old would you be?"

(Continued)

(Continued)

Oddly, uncertainly he hesitated a moment, as if engaged in calculation.

"Why, I guess I'm nineteen, Doc. I'll be twenty next birthday."

The retrograde amnesia is obvious from his words. "Jimmy" believes he is 19, not 49, and he does not know that 30 years have passed without his having any memory for them. However, unlike patients with simply retrograde amnesia, there is an additional problem with "Jimmy" and many patients with Korsakoff's disease. They have anosognosia, meaning a lack of awareness of their own memory deficits. At best, Korsakoff's patients have only a very dim awareness of their memory problems. Indeed, their lack of insight into their own condition makes treatment and intervention extremely difficult. Often, when patients are confronted with their poor memory performance or inconsistencies in their story, they make countless excuses, blaming the situation or the tester. This contrasts with the medial temporal lobe amnesiacs, who are often aware of their own memory deficits. Consider the following dialogue of Sacks and "Jimmy."

"Okay," I said. "I'll tell you a story. A man went to his doctor complaining of memory lapses. The doctor asked him some routine questions, and then said, 'These lapses. What about them?' 'What lapses?'" the patient replied.

"So that's my problem," Jimmy laughed. "I kind of thought it was. I do find myself forgetting things, once in a while, things that have just happened. The past is clear, though."

This is not the comment of a person deeply troubled by having lost the memory of the past 30 years of his life. The patient, Jimmy, is clearly without any awareness of the severity of his memory loss. Even his comments suggest that he thinks he has mild anterograde amnesia, not profound retrograde amnesia.

Most Korsakoff's patients are also unaware of their anterograde amnesia as well (also known as anosognosia). They think they can remember anything and then deny that they have forgotten when they do so. Indeed, Shimamura and Squire (1986) showed that the metamemory accuracy of patients with Korsakoff's disease was at chance, meaning that they did not know what they did know and they did not know what they did not know. In contrast, temporal lobe amnesiacs were accurate in this task.

Confabulation: when amnesic patients lie about their past. They do not know they are not telling the truth because of deficits in source monitoring.

Another identifying characteristic of Korsakoff's is confabulation. **Confabulation** is defined as honest lying. This paradoxical definition is not an oxymoron; rather, it reflects both the falsehood of the stories and the belief on the part of the patients that the stories they tell are true. Confabulation means that the person will make up stories and identify them as personal memories (Moscovitch, 1989). Korsakoff's patients believe these false memories while they are generating them, even if they forget them moments later and confabulate entirely new ones.

Confabulated memories appear to be the function of confusion between imagination and memory, which allows patients with Korsakoff's disease to fill in inconsistencies in their life narrative. In this sense, confabulation is considered a failure of source monitoring. Korsakoff's patients are unable to screen out their wistful imaginations as being imagination and instead believe that they are accurately recalling their past. Because they lack insight into their own memory deficits, they then often fail to recognize the inconsistency in what they are saying.

Moscovitch (1989) argued that confabulation also arises from an inability to order events in memory, that is, temporal sequencing. Combined with the failure to screen out false memories, many memory reports from Korsakoff's patients will appear extremely odd to friends, family, and doctors, not to mention students. Consider this conversation between Morris Moscovitch and a patient (HW) who suffers from Korsakoff's (taken from Moscovitch, 1989). MM stands for Morris Moscovitch.

HW: I'm 40, 42, pardon me, 62.

MM: Are you married or single?

HW: Married.

MM: How long have you been married?

HW: About four months.

MM: What's your wife's name?

HW: Martha.

MM: How many children do you have?

HW: Four. (He laughs). Not bad for four months.

MM: How old are your children?

HW: The eldest is 32; his name is Bob; and the youngest is 22; his name is Joe.

MM: (He laughs again.) How did you get these children in four months?

HW: They're adopted.

MM: Who adopted them?

HW: Martha and I.

MM: Immediately after you got married you wanted to adopt these older children?

HW: Before we were married we adopted one of them, two of them. The eldest girl, Brenda, and Bob, and Joe and Dina since we were married.

In this conversation, you can see a vivid example of confabulation, as the patient has to square the knowledge of his four adult children with the confabulated memory of being a newlywed. This kind of confabulation is relatively common among Korsakoff's patients. Sacks (1985) described a patient who thinks he is still running his butcher shop from his hospital bed. Also apparent in the conversation is that the Korsakoff's patient has no insight into his memory deficit. It does not seem to bother them that there are incongruities between the stories they tell and the reality around them. For more on Dr. Moscovitch's research, go to www.sagepub.com/schwartz.[6]

To summarize, Korsakoff's disease is a devastating illness. Korsakoff's patients suffer from both anterograde amnesia and retrograde amnesia. They may also confabulate and lack awareness of their amnesia. Korsakoff's disease is caused by damage to the diencephalon (in particular, the thalamus), the part or the brain that connects the temporal lobes to the frontal lobes. The damage to this area of the brain is usually the result of chronic long-term alcohol abuse.

INTERIM SUMMARY

Amnesia refers to memory deficits, usually brought about by damage to the brain. Anterograde amnesia refers to deficits in learning new information, whereas retrograde amnesia refers to deficits in retrieving already learned information. The amnesic syndrome is a common form of amnesia brought about by damage to the hippocampus and other areas in the surrounding temporal lobe. Even though conscious learning is impaired in the amnesic syndrome, there still is evidence that amnesiacs show normal implicit memory. Retrograde amnesia can be induced by electroconvulsive shock, which is still considered a good treatment for depression. A debilitating form of amnesia is Korsakoff's disease, which is usually brought on by chronic alcohol abuse. Korsakoff's patients have anterograde amnesia, retrograde amnesia, and anosognosia, which means a deficit in recognizing their own deficits. Korsakoff's patients also have a tendency to confabulate, that is, to tell lies without knowing they are doing so.

FRONTAL LOBE AMNESIA

Selective memory deficits can also arise from damage to the frontal lobes of the brain. Many of the symptoms of frontal lobe damage are similar to those seen in Korsakoff's amnesia. For example, both anosognosia and confabulation are typical of both forms of brain damage. On the other hand, unlike Korsakoff's disease, anterograde amnesia is usually only a minor issue in frontal lobe injuries. Retrograde amnesia is also a frequent symptom of damage to the frontal lobes. **Frontal lobe amnesia** is characterized by damage to the frontal lobes and behavioral symptoms, which include retrograde amnesia, anosognosia, and confabulation.

Frontal lobe amnesia: people show some evidence of anterograde amnesia, although it tends to be much less severe than in other patients. They may also show anosognosia and confabulation.

The frontal lobes are enormous areas in the human brain, encompassing regions responsible for many cognitive, emotional, motor, and behavioral functions. The areas of the frontal lobe that are correlated with memory deficits are the areas most anterior (that is, to the front) of the human brain, known collectively as the prefrontal cortex. Prefrontal areas in both the left and right hemispheres are associated with memory functions. Within the prefrontal cortex, the specific areas associated with memory deficits include the dorsolateral, ventrolateral, anterior, and anterior cingulate (Shimamura, 2008).

Behavioral Issues in Frontal Patients

Frontal patients may show some evidence of anterograde amnesia, although it tends to be much less severe than in amnesic syndrome patients or Korsakoff's disease patients. Like the Korsakoff's disease patients, anterograde amnesia in frontal patients appears related to difficulties in processing and accessing information rather than with its initial encoding. Thus, when tested on recognition tests, frontal lobe patients will show relatively small deficits relative to control patients, although they will show more evidence of anterograde amnesia when tested in free recall. Frontal lobe patients will also show a high rate of false alarms (saying old to new items) in recognition (Parkin, Bindschaedler, Harsent, & Metzler, 1996). This suggests that frontal lobe patients are likely to accept false information as self-experienced episodic memory.

Some frontal lobe patients also confabulate in a manner similar to that of the Korsakoff's patients. Like their high false alarm rates, confabulation appears to be a function of the inability of frontal lobe patients to screen or monitor the contents of their retrieval. For normal people, when an image comes to mind, we make a near automatic judgment as to the source of that image. If we conclude it comes from imagination, we immediately discount it as a memory. For example, if an image arises of yourself having a drink with Justin Timberlake (or some other pop star), you may discredit it as not being a real memory. In frontal lobe patients, like the Korsakoff's patients, this reality monitoring process is lacking, leading to the confabulation and false memories.

This monitoring deficit extends to source information as well. Frontal lobe patients have deficits in correctly attributing the source of a memory as well, sometimes known as **source amnesia.** That is, the frontal lobe patients can acquire new information but forget where they heard the information at rates much greater than those of control patients. Thus, an event the person read about might be misremembered as the patient actually witnessing the event. Or something a spouse or close friend said might be attributed to the self. In experiments, participants might hear a list of words in which two narrators alternate the reciting of each word. Then at test, the person must remember the words from the list and who said each one. Relative to controls, the frontal patients will make many more errors in source monitoring, even when their recall of words is roughly equivalent to the normal participants. Normal people make source memory errors as well, but they are much more common among frontal lobe patients (Shimamura, 2008).

> **Source amnesia**: deficits in correctly attributing the source of a memory.

Frontal lobe patients have selective difficulties with temporal order information. This means they have relative difficulty in organizing past events into the correct order of events. This includes both semantic and autobiographical information. For example, a frontal lobe patient might have difficulties reporting whether her visit to the hospital came before or after her weekly golf match. She might forget if she had taken her medicines already for the day or had not taken them since the previous evening. In some cases, temporal order may also play into the source confusions. Therefore, one patient may complain that visits to the hospital took place before the accident that injured his brain. In addition, frontal patients do have difficulties with ordering semantic memory. Thus, they might report that Bill Clinton was president prior to Ronald Reagan. Normal individuals also forget the order of information of events, but not to the extent to which frontal lobe patients do.

Damage to the prefrontal lobe can create other cognitive deficits in addition to problems with memory. Frontal lobe patients may have deficits with planning, problem solving, language, and emotion. Damage to the orbital frontal area in the frontal cortex can also change personality. The orbital frontal cortex appears to be a part of the brain that inhibits impulsive behavior. Damage to this area can, depending on the damage and the situation, make someone more impulsive or, in other cases, extremely passive. Thus, typically, the memory deficits in frontal lobe patients are accompanied by a number of other cognitive and behavioral problems (see Table 10.2).

Table 10.2 Symptoms of frontal lobe amnesia.
1. Damage to prefrontal areas of cortex
2. Anosognosia (lack of awareness of deficits)
3. Confabulation
4. Frequent false memories
5. Deficits in source monitoring
6. Deficits in temporal ordering

TRANSIENT GLOBAL AMNESIA

Transient global amnesia: a rare form of amnesia, in which the amnesic affects are short-lived, usually on the order of hours.

Transient global amnesia (TGA) is a rare form of amnesia in which the amnesic affects are short-lived, usually on the order of hours. TGA is rare and seldom recurs in the individual who gets it. However, it can provide quite a jolt of fear into the victim and his or her family. In TGA, the amnesic effects are extremely strong but last a short time and then, by and large, vanish. Apparently, there is also no long-term damage to any part of the brain.

TGA is characterized by a dense anterograde amnesia—new information is simply not encoded during the TGA episode. A person may repeatedly ask the same questions, such as, "Where am I?" "Who drove me to the hospital?" or "When did I put on these clothes?" Because the person does not remember the answers to these questions, he or she may ask them just a few minutes later and then continue to repeat them. Because the onset of TGA is so unexpected and the offset so fast, there are few comparative studies of the extent of the anterograde amnesia in TGA relative to other neuropsychological syndromes and to normal controls, but the reports from patients and their doctors point to a strong anterograde amnesia. It is also characterized by retrograde amnesia. The TGA patient may suffer a retrograde period from a few hours into the past to several years into the past during the TGA episode (A. S. Brown, 1998). Once the TGA episode is over, almost all of the retrograde amnesia disappears except a small window just before the onset and often concerning the TGA episode itself.

TGA onset is sudden; there is usually no warning or physical cues that an attack of TGA is about to occur. Despite the robustness of both the anterograde and retrograde amnesia, there is typically no loss of personal identity, and other aspects of cognition appear unimpaired. That is, language, reading, attention, and problem solving all appear unimpaired. Working memory also appears unimpaired.

TGA attacks tend to occur in people from mid-age to early old age (roughly 50 to 70) and then decreases among older adults. For younger people, a history of migraines is associated with TGA attacks. Neither men nor women are more or less likely to have TGA attacks. The onset is often triggered by rigorous exercise or physical stress. This can include physical exertion, sexual intercourse, a hot bath after being cold, or an immersion in cold water after being hot, as well as psychological stress, such as an argument with a spouse or bad news at work. This covers a lot of ground, but all of these activities are associated with an increased heart rate.

The etiology of TGA is less than clear. Once hospitalized, a patient will undergo screening for stroke, seizure, or head injury, but none of these are associated with TGA. According to A. S. Brown (1998), the most likely explanation for TGA is temporary disruption of blood flow within the brain (technically known as ischemias). Compression of veins preventing the proper flow of blood from the brain back to heart has also been suggested as a potential cause. However, it is not clear which explanation is best or whether both contribute to TGA.

The good news with TGA is that it wears off. By the next day, the patient is feeling fine and is only left with a small retrograde amnesia period just prior to the attack. There is no residual anterograde amnesia; by the next day, the person is learning and remembering normally. Most people who get TGA attacks will never get another.

SHORT-TERM MEMORY AMNESIA

In each form of amnesia so far discussed, the deficit has been in long-term memory. These forms of amnesia are much more common than deficits in short-term memory. Nonetheless, there are some cases in which short-term/working memory is impaired and long-term memory appears to be relatively intact. In this form of amnesia, people have deficits keeping larger amounts of information stored or rehearsed in working memory. Thus, a patient might have difficulty remembering a phone number long enough to dial. In the lab, the patient would have difficulties with digit spans, being able to hold far fewer of them in working memory than a control patient. However, encoding of information into long-term memory is not affected.

Short-term memory amnesia was first studied by Shallice and Warrington (1970), studying a patient known by the initials KF. KF was a young man who injured his head in a motorcycle accident. He suffered from a selective impairment of short-term memory even though he experienced neither anterograde nor retrograde amnesia. He learned paired associates just as rapidly as did control participants. However, on digit span tasks, KF was severely impaired. Whereas normal adults can recall seven digits, KF was unable to maintain more than two digits when tested in the auditory modality and four when tested with visual presentation.

> **Short-term memory amnesia**: when patients have deficits keeping larger amounts of information stored or rehearsed in working memory.

KF suffered extensive damage to the frontal lobe of the left hemisphere. Localization of the lesion revealed that it was close to the Sylvan fissure, which separates the frontal lobes from the temporal lobes. This is an area of the brain closely associated with language formation and processing. For this reason, KF's deficit might have been limited to the phonological loop or auditory working memory with less damage to visual working memory.

A similar patient was studied some years later by Vallar and Baddeley (1984). This patient, PV, seemed to have selective damage to the phonological loop. PV was intellectually normal in most areas and showed no evidence of impaired long-term memory. However, she showed impairments on all tests that made use of the phonological loop. PV showed deficits in digit span tasks but only when the items were presented in an auditory format. Her visual working memory appeared unimpaired. She also showed deficits remembering lists of words, which were presented to her in the auditory modality. When the same stimuli were presented to her visually, she showed no differences from normal control patients.

PV had damage not to the frontal lobes but to an area of the brain in the parietal lobe in the left hemisphere, near the back of the frontal lobes. Belleville, Caza, and Peretz (2003) have also documented a case of a patient with selective deficits to the phonological loop with damage in this area of the brain. So it remains to be seen if it is the parietal lobe, the frontal lobe, or both that is the culprit in short-term memory amnesia.

REDUPLICATIVE PARAMNESIA AND CAPGRAS SYNDROME

Many of us experience **déjà vu** from time to time. Déjà vu is the experience we get when we think we have seen or heard something before but objectively know that we have not. For most of us, this experience is rare and fleeting. However, for patients with reduplicative

Déjà vu: the experience we get when we think we have seen or heard something before but objectively know that we have not.

Reduplicative paramnesia: a condition in which patients believe that places or locations have been duplicated and that the two locations exist simultaneously. It is caused by brain damage.

Capgras syndrome: patients come to believe that other people have been duplicated and that two sets of identical people may exist. It is caused by brain damage.

paramnesia, this experience is with them constantly. **Reduplicative paramnesia** is defined as a condition in which patients believe that places or locations have been duplicated and that the two locations exist simultaneously. Its closely related cousin is **Capgras syndrome**, in which patients come to believe that other people have been duplicated and that two sets of identical people may exist (Budson, Roth, Rentz, & Ronthal, 2000).

Reading the above definitions of reduplicative paramnesia and Capgras syndrome might leave you utterly confused. What could these definitions actually mean? The best way to illustrate this is with examples. Let's start with reduplicative paramnesia. In one case of reduplicative paramnesia, a patient agreed that his hospital room looked just like ones found in the hospital in the local city. Moreover, the patient agreed that the view out the window revealed a view of a town just like the small city near his home. But the patient insisted that the hospital was a different one, and the city, although a lookalike of the patient's home city, was actually a fake (Benson, Gardener, & Meadows, 1976). Thus, although the patient recognized the surroundings, they appeared to lack a feeling of familiarity. To explain this, the patient thinks the world around him is a fake, made to look like the world he knows. These symptoms appear delusional, and indeed they are. But reduplicative paramnesia occurs after traumatic brain damage, not from schizophrenia or other psychiatric disorders.

Consider another case of reduplicative paramnesia reported more recently. Hinkebein, Callahan, and Gelber (2001) described a case of reduplicative paramnesia in which the patient was a 67-year-old man who had recently undergone brain surgery to repair a damaged artery. The man had no history of psychiatric disorder, was a high school graduate, and had owned a small business most of his adult life. He was hospitalized in a small hospital in southern Illinois. He insisted, however, that he was in a hospital in Southern California, which was an exact duplicate of the hospital located in Illinois. He believed that his visitors were commuting from the Illinois to California. He often wondered aloud why "they" were trying to trick him into thinking he was in Illinois, when he "knew" that he was in California. Therapists subtly and repeatedly tried to convince the patient that he really was in Illinois, to no avail. He was eventually released to a rehabilitation center because he was normal in all other respects other than his paramnesia. Nine months after the brain injury, his reduplicative paramnesia seemed to have passed, and he reliably reported that he was, in fact, at home in Illinois. Although he rationally agreed that he must have been hospitalized near home, he continued to report that it *felt to him* like he had been in California. A similar case was reported in Japan recently. Yamada, Murai, and Ohigashi (2003) reported a case of a 73-year-old woman with the same basic set of symptoms. This woman needed 2 years of treatment to dispel the paramnesia symptoms.

Hinkebein et al. (2001) argued that two neurological deficits combine to create the symptoms seen in reduplicative paramnesia. First, damage to areas in the right parietal lobe creates impaired visual perception and visual memory. This damage creates the feeling that well-known places are no longer familiar. It may also induce the experience that familiar places have something peculiar or different about them (that is, they are in California instead of Illinois). Second, bilateral damage in the prefrontal lobes prevents the individual from inhibiting the false familiarity or dismissing it as an illusion. Thus, when normal people get a sense of déjà vu, we are able to dismiss it as a "trick" our brain is playing on us. However, the patient with reduplicative paramnesia is unable to screen out these delusional senses of familiarity and winds up believing in the strange duplication.

Capgras syndrome involves the delusional belief that people have been duplicated. In general, it occurs when the patient believes that his or her family members and close friends have been duplicated and replaced by imposters or robots (Young, 2008). A striking case was described by Hermanowicz (2002). The patient was a 73-year-old man suffering from retinitis pigmentosa, leaving him nearly blind, and Parkinson's disease. He began suffering from visual hallucinations at age 71, usually of strange people approaching his wife. He came to believe that his wife was variously replaced by a series of men and women who dressed up to impersonate her. He believed he could always tell the difference between his wife and the imposters. As such, he frequently angrily turned away from his wife, believing she was a male imposter. Various changes to his medications were made with no success. Brain scans revealed minor scattered damage in his frontal lobes but nothing major.

Relative to reduplicative paramnesia, Capgras syndrome is more associated with psychiatric conditions, such as schizophrenia, than it is with traumatic brain injuries. Indeed, most cases of Capgras syndrome occur in schizophrenics. In cases where it does occur because of brain damage, it often occurs in conjunction with deficits in face recognition (prosopagnosia). Ramachandran and Blakeslee (1998) have argued that Capgras syndrome arises from a breakdown in the connections between the temporal lobe areas involved in face recognition and the limbic system involved in emotion. Thus, the patient will see a familiar face but not feel any of the associated sense of familiarity and emotion that seeing one's spouse, parents, or children might evoke. Left without an explanation for this, the brain presupposes duplication. In some advanced cases, the patient no longer recognizes himself or herself in the mirror and may ask who has altered the mirror to portray someone else (Lucchelli & Spinnler, 2007). In this case, there is a complete breakdown of connections between the areas responsible for face recognition and the production of familiarity.

PSYCHOGENIC AMNESIA

Psychogenic amnesia is a broad term that covers all forms of amnesia that are not directly linked to disruption or injury to the brain. Psychogenic amnesias are caused by psychological disorders or trauma rather than physical insult to the brain. Because of this, psychogenic amnesia is much more difficult to classify and also exceedingly rare. However, it is often the symptoms of psychogenic amnesia that capture the public attention concerning amnesia, reflected in how amnesia is portrayed in movies. In particular, in psychogenic amnesia, we occasionally see a loss of personal identity. This means that, although patients are verbal, responsive to surroundings, and socially aware, they do not know their name or very much about themselves. They are unable to recall any events from their life. This loss of identity may occur without anterograde amnesia. That is, the patient may be learning new information, including autobiographical information starting from the time of the onset of the amnesia. This puzzling condition is often dramatized in movies (i.e., Goldie Hawn's character in *Overboard*). I will start with a well-reported and well-documented real case of psychogenic amnesia.

Schacter (1996) described the fascinating story of the patient Lumberjack. Lumberjack (an alias chosen by Schacter) was admitted to a hospital in Toronto, Canada, in 1980. He had been discovered by a police officer roaming the streets of Toronto in mid-winter. Lumberjack was not wearing a coat and looked freezing, so the police officer questioned him. When the officer was unable to obtain information from him, Lumberjack was brought to the hospital for testing. Lumberjack was suffering from a dense and complete psychogenic amnesia. His amnesia was so dense that he did not know his own name or where he lived. Indeed, Lumberjack could remember nothing from his personal past, except for the events just prior and subsequent to his interaction with the police officer. Local newspapers printed his photograph in a vain effort to locate relatives who could identify him. During the next few days, Lumberjack remained in a dense amnesic state. Then, while watching television at the hospital, some images from a movie he was watching triggered his memory. The specific image that triggered his memory was the depiction of a funeral in the movie *Shogun*. This caused him to remember the funeral of his own grandfather, which was the traumatic event that triggered the amnesic episode. Within a matter of hours, he had recalled not just his name and home, but complete autobiographical memory returned as well.

This form of amnesia is called psychogenic amnesia. **Psychogenic amnesia** is caused by psychological problems rather than neurological problems. In most cases, a traumatic event of one kind or another causes a strong block, preventing access to episodic and autobiographical memories, in some cases, including issues of self-identity. In the case of Lumberjack, the funeral of his grandfather triggered his psychogenic amnesia. His grandfather had raised Lumberjack and was his only committed relative. The shock of his grandfather's death apparently was sufficiently traumatic to induce the amnesia. For most people, a grandparent's funeral would not be as terribly traumatic, but for Lumberjack, it apparently was sufficient to induce the amnesic state. Psychogenic amnesia is extraordinarily rare. Some argue that the amnesia is one way in which the person copes with the tragedy of the trauma.

> **Psychogenic amnesia**: a broad term that covers all forms of amnesia that are not directly linked to disruption or injury to the brain.

Psychiatrists, rather than neurologists and neuropsychologists, are the ones who typically study psychogenic amnesias. They have identified a number of different forms of psychogenic amnesia. Although psychogenic amnesias have a psychological cause, Schacter (1996) points out that a large proportion of documented cases of psychogenic amnesia are in people who have a history of brain injury, as indeed was the case with Lumberjack. But because of the rareness of this state, little empirical data exist on this topic.

Dissociative Amnesia

Dissociative amnesia is a condition in which only the traumatic event or events closely related to that trauma are not remembered. For example, a veteran may have selective amnesia for the event in which he or she lost a limb in combat. **Dissociative amnesia** is

> **Dissociative amnesia**: a condition in which only the traumatic event or events closely related to that trauma are not remembered.

a retrograde amnesia, as it refers to the inability to remember a specific past event or events. Most patients suffering from dissociative amnesia have equivalent semantic knowledge of the traumatic event. But they have lost episodic access to the trauma. This distinguishes dissociative amnesia from "repression," in which both episodic and semantic access is lost. Because dissociative amnesia is a psychological amnesia, there can be a great deal of variation from patient to patient. Some will experience amnesia only for the event, whereas others will also be amnesic for events that surround the trauma in time or that are related to the trauma (Kihlstrom & Schacter, 1995).

Dissociative Fugue

Dissociative fugue is a psychogenic amnesia in which the patient forgets his or her personal identity in addition to access to his or her autobiographical past. The case of Lumberjack involved a dissociative fugue state. **Dissociative fugue** is therefore also a retrograde

> **Dissociative fugue**: the psychogenic amnesia in which the patient forgets his or her personal identity in addition to access to his or her autobiographical past.

amnesia. Characteristic of dissociative fugue is forgetting one's name, occupation, place and date of birth, and where one currently lives. In most documented cases of dissociative fugue, the fugue state wears off in a matter of days. But there are some reports of dissociative fugues lasting years. In some cases, something, often either a word or an image, serves as a cue or trigger for the person in a fugue to remember his or her past. With that one cue, the person's entire past seems to return in a flood of memories. However, in one recently documented case, much retrograde amnesia remained even after the fugue state had worn off and the patient regained his identity (Hennig-Fast et al., 2008). Thus, not all dissociative fugue states end in the flood of memories from the past. Future research will be required to determine if these two types of recovery from dissociative fugue differ with respect to the psychological and neurological origins of the amnesic state.

Posttraumatic Stress Disorder

> **Posttraumatic stress disorder**: psychological problems caused by exposure to extremely dangerous or stressful situations.

Memory deficits in **posttraumatic stress disorder** (PTSD) differ greatly from memory deficits in other neurological or psychological disorders. This is mainly because the deficit in PTSD is not with having amnesia but in not being able to inhibit the retrieval of unwanted memories. In PTSD, harmless events can cue the retrieval of traumatic ones, such as the memory of being a victim of a violent crime or a wartime tragedy. For example, a veteran might be reminded of a violent explosion on the battlefield when his or her shopping cart accidentally bumps into a cart of another shopper. Treatment usually involves trying to desensitize these cues (B. A. Wilson, 2009).

Repression

> **Repression**: the active forgetting of highly emotional memories, usually from childhood.

The standard view of **repression** is that psychological mechanisms (defense mechanisms) act to block out access to memory of traumatic events. In this sense, repression can be defined as a psychogenic retrograde amnesia for selective events. This view of repression is generally associated with Freudian theory. Much debate concerns if this condition exists at all. However, to the extent that it does, it should be classified as a psychogenic amnesia.

In general, psychogenic amnesia is exceedingly rare. It occurs because of psychological trauma instead of organic damage to the brain. It is seldom confused with organic brain damage because the symptoms are usually quite different. In the final section of this chapter, we will tackle the biggest producer of amnesic patients, Alzheimer's disease.

ALZHEIMER'S DISEASE

Alzheimer's disease is a frighteningly common condition that attacks mainly older adults. As medical technology has improved and people live longer lives, more people are suffering from Alzheimer's disease. With increasing age, a person's likelihood of being diagnosed with Alzheimer's disease increases. However, it is important to note that not all older adults will get Alzheimer's disease. In fact, the vast majority of older adults never get Alzheimer's disease. Even among people 90 years old and older, there is only a 7% rate of Alzheimer's (Bermejo-Pareja, Benito-León, Vega, Medrano, & Román, 2008).

> **Alzheimer's disease**: one of many dementia-type illnesses that are more common in older adults than they are in younger adults. Memory is the first deficit detected in this disease.

This still represents a large number of people in a country such as the United States with an aging population. However, the simple fact is that most older adults *do not* get Alzheimer's disease. For more information and statistics on Alzheimer's disease, go to www .sagepub.com/schwartz.[7]

Alzheimer's disease is a terminal illness. At present, medical science has various ways of slowing the progress of the disease and, at least during the early phase of the illness, slowing the development of symptoms. Unfortunately, a cure for the disease is still not in our reach, and Alzheimer's disease is inevitably fatal.

Although each individual may follow a unique course of decline once the person has been diagnosed with Alzheimer's disease, there is a pattern typically seen with most patients with the disease (Brandt & Rich, 1995). With almost all victims of Alzheimer's disease, issues of memory decline are the first symptom noticed by the patient and his or her family. Memory deficits are followed by more general cognitive problems, requiring the person to find help for even simple tasks. As the disease progresses, more and more cognitive systems fail, and then in the latest stages, physical systems decline rapidly as well, requiring nursing home care until the disease finally results in the death of the patient.

In the earliest stage of the disease, the patient will recognize that his or her memory is "not what it used to be." Complaints include misplacing items, forgetting people's names, and requiring more time in acquiring new information. In the earliest states, such memory deficits may be difficult to distinguish behaviorally from normal age-related declines in memory. However, neuropsychological tests can often distinguish between the two. Alzheimer's patients will show deficits in short-term memory performance relative to age-matched controls. Although digit spans may be normal, Alzheimer's disease patients do not show normal recency effect on free-recall tasks (Germano, Kinsella, Storey, Ong, & Ames, 2008). Usually, by the end of the early phase, an individual will have sought medical attention and have a diagnosis of Alzheimer's disease. We will turn later to the steps that can be taken to alleviate the progress of the disease. For now, we will continue with its natural progression.

In the intermediate stages, the cognitive deficits begin to mount. The anterograde amnesia grows stronger, and retrograde amnesia may also occur, although usually for only relatively recent events. The patient may begin to experience difficulties in naming familiar people. Problem solving and decision making may also be impaired. Language problems may also surface. These tend to be a decreasing vocabulary and a lower word fluency—that is, the person's speech may be characterized by frequent word-finding difficulties, similar to tip-of-the-tongue experiences. At this point, the patient may also begin to experience motor deficits (called apraxias). These are deficits in implementing complex motor patterns, such as dressing, writing, threading a needle, or even loading a dishwasher. At first, these tasks may just become difficult, and the person will appear clumsy to others, but eventually the patient will need help with these tasks.

With respect to memory, the intermediate stage is characterized by both anterograde amnesia and the beginnings of retrograde amnesia. Because of this, some argue that the chief deficit at this stage is an encoding deficit. However, as Alzheimer's disease progresses, there is more and more retrograde amnesia. There is usually a temporal gradient to the retrograde amnesia, with more recent information being lost before older information. With the progression of Alzheimer's disease, the failures of retrograde amnesia stretch farther back in time. By the later stages of Alzheimer's disease, there may be little from a person's past that the patient can remember.

In the late stages of Alzheimer's disease the patient is completely dependent on caregivers, as even basic motor movement may be difficult. Muscle mass declines as the person neither is capable nor wants to exercise. Memory declines to the point in which it no longer appears as if the patient recognizes even close family members such as a spouse, his or her children, or his or her siblings. In many cases, the patient will no longer respond to hearing his or her own name. In late stages of Alzheimer's diseases, the patient may also lose all access to

Table 10.3   Alzheimer's disease.
Initial stage: forgetfulness; may last for several years before diagnosis
Early stage: deficits in episodic memory; mild anterograde amnesia; lexical retrieval difficulties
Intermediate stages: deficits begin in reasoning and problem solving; deficits in understanding speech; help often needed in daily living skills, including feeding, dressing, and bathing
Late state: loss of language skills, failure to recognize close family members, loss of personal identity; round-the-clock care necessary

language and be unable to either speak or understand others. Death is usually the result of external factors, such as pneumonia, rather than the Alzheimer's disease itself (see Table 10.3).

Causes of Alzheimer's Disease

The cause of Alzheimer's disease is still largely unknown, although what happens inside the brain of people with Alzheimer's is relatively well understood. At present, there is a tremendous amount of research investigating the cause of Alzheimer's. Perhaps within a decade, we will know the causes of the disease, which might allow us to prevent or cure it.

It is known that there is a genetic component to Alzheimer's disease. If you have a close relative with Alzheimer's disease, for example, your likelihood of someday getting it is larger than someone without a close relative with Alzheimer's disease. However, its cause is not entirely genetic. Indeed, even for a person who has an identical twin, the risk of developing Alzheimer's disease is "only" 50 % if the twin has already developed the disease. This is a high coincidence, but given that identical twins are 100 % genetic, it disproves the idea that Alzheimer's disease is completely genetic.

The brains of Alzheimer's disease patients come under incredible stress. Neurons and synapses between the neurons start to degenerate and die in Alzheimer's disease. This neuronal degeneration begins in the cerebral cortex, including the temporal lobes, frontal lobes, and parietal lobes. In later stages of the disease, it spreads to subcortical areas as well. Furthermore, dense **amyloid plaques** form throughout the cortex. These plaques are gooey masses of unwanted proteins, which interfere with normal brain function. They twist around the neurons, causing **neurofibrillary tangles,** which lead to more neuron death by interfering with the function of the axons (Wenk, 2003). Thus, one clear goal of medical science is to determine how and why the amyloid plaques form and how their formation can be prevented.

Amyloid plaques: masses of unwanted proteins, which interfere with normal brain function.

Neurofibrillary tangles: the twisting of amyloid plaques around neurons, which cause destruction of those neurons.

Furthermore, there appear to be changes to the brain's cholinergic system. The brain appears to have difficulty producing the neurotransmitter acetylcholine. Acetylcholine is used by the brain in many of its learning and memory circuits (Wenk, 2003). Thus, as the amyloid plaques and neurofibrillary tangles grow and cholinergic production declines, the brain shuts down more and more function, leading to the progressive loss of cognitive function seen in Alzheimer's disease patients.

Treatment of Alzheimer's Disease

At present, there is no known way to prevent the development of Alzheimer's disease, nor is there any known way to cure it once someone develops it. However, a number of factors reduce the likelihood that someone will develop Alzheimer's disease, and a number of treatments are available to ease or delay some of the symptoms in the earlier stages of the disease. This section will briefly review each of these considerations.

Prevention

First of all, there is no 100% guaranteed manner in which to prevent Alzheimer's disease. Any individual may engage in all of the behaviors that lower the rate of the illness and still develop it. However, a number of factors are associated with lower rates of Alzheimer's disease. First, lifelong involvement in intellectually challenging activities lowers the risk of Alzheimer's disease. These activities can vary from crossword puzzles to playing musical instruments to engaging in quantum physics research. An active social life is also associated with a lower risk of developing Alzheimer's disease (Bennett, Schneider, Tang, Arnold, & Wilson, 2006). It is thought that these activities spur the growth of synapses in the brain, which may act to reduce the development of plaques. Diet also plays a role in Alzheimer's disease prevention. Healthy low-cholesterol diets are also correlated with lower rates of Alzheimer's disease. A variety of other conditions such as hypertension, high cholesterol, diabetes, and smoking are all correlated with higher rates of Alzheimer's disease.

Treatment

A number of drugs are now available in the United States to combat symptoms in early Alzheimer's disease. These drugs work by reducing the rate at which acetylcholine is broken down (destroyed) in the brain. Because acetylcholine production is decreased in Alzheimer's disease, lowering its rate of destruction in the brain will leave more of it around in the brains of Alzheimer's disease patients. These drugs lead to temporary improvements in memory and cognitive processes in patients with early Alzheimer's disease. However, in the long run, these drugs do not slow down the progress of the disease because they do not interfere with the processes that lead to neuron death. Current research is directed at finding drugs that will inhibit, reverse, or prevent the forming of the amyloid plaques (Ait-Ghezala et al., 2005).

MEMORY REHABILITATION

Memory rehabilitation is the domain of the burgeoning field of clinical neuropsychology. Neuropsychologists are tasked with the job of helping the many people who

> **Memory rehabilitation**: the interventions that clinical neuropsychologists use to promote improved memory performance in memory-impaired individuals.

suffer memory loss from stroke, accidents, warfare, and disease. For many patients, memory recovery will come either spontaneously or not at all, but for some, rigorous intervention by neuropsychologists is crucial in regaining memory skills (B. A. Wilson, 2009). Some patients, like Korsakoff's disease patients, seldom regain memory function, but memory rehabilitation can benefit those in the early stages of Alzheimer's disease and those with the amnesic syndrome.

Memory rehabilitation focuses on compensation. For example, amnesic syndrome patients will be taught to make use of external memory aids. These can include clock alarms, cell phones, and keeping a notebook handy. Patients also can be taught mnemonic strategies, including many of the hints listed throughout this book. In addition, intact skills can be used to transfer function from episodic memory to existing memory systems. For example, many patients can learn new skills by capitalizing on their intact implicit memory system (B. A. Wilson, 2009).

One of the most important neuropsychological interventions is called errorless learning. **Errorless learning** refers to a technique that trains a patient to learn a particular fact or skill while preventing that person from making errors during training. Because much of learning in amnesic patients requires the use of implicit or procedural memory, it is important for the patient to avoid developing bad habits. If she or he is guided such that mistakes are avoided, bad habits will not develop. In practice, it means providing immediate and constant feedback, lots of

> **Errorless learning**: a technique that trains a patient to learn a particular fact or skill while preventing that person from making errors during training.

cues, and lots of repetitions. For example, if a patient must learn "red pill, green pill, white pill," he or she will first start off by repeating these phrases over and over. Then the patient will have to complete exercises in which more and more cues are removed. At first, he or she will see "red pi__, green pi__, white pi___," and more and more parts of the phrase will be removed as the patient successfully gets the phrase. After training, the patient will then know the sequence of medications that he or she must take. Clare, Wilson, Carter, and Hodges (2003) have shown that errorless learning leads to better retention of sentences in patients with early stage Alzheimer's disease, and Evans et al. (2000) found it to be successful with other amnesic patients. For more on this topic, please see Barbara Wilson's (2009) book, *Memory Rehabilitation*.

SUMMARY

Amnesia is a catch-all term that refers to a wide diversity of acquired memory deficits. Amnesia results from damage to the brain, particularly the hippocampus in the limbic system, medial temporal lobes, the diencephalon, and parts of the prefrontal cortex. Anterograde amnesia refers to deficits in acquiring new information, whereas retrograde amnesia refers to deficits in retrieving already learned information. Anterograde amnesia occurs after damage to the medial temporal lobe and/or hippocampus, whereas retrograde amnesia is associated with the temporal lobes, the diencephalon, and the prefrontal cortex. Korsakoff's disease is a devastating amnesia, marked by anterograde amnesia, retrograde amnesia, and confabulation. Frontal lobe patients also have demonstrated confabulation and have deficits in source monitoring and temporal order information. Other forms of amnesia include transient global amnesia, reduplicative paramnesia, Capgras syndrome, and psychogenic amnesia. Alzheimer's disease is a degenerative and terminal illness. Memory deficits are the first noticeable symptom of Alzheimer's. Memory rehabilitation refers to interventions that neuropsychologists attempt to help patients improve their memory performance.

KEY TERMS

Amnesia	Benzodiazepines	Déjà vu
Anterograde amnesia	Anosognosia	Reduplicative paramnesia
Hippocampus	Retrograde amnesia	Capgras syndrome
Medial temporal lobes	Ribot's law	Psychogenic amnesia
Mammillary bodies	Consolidation	Dissociative amnesia
Amnesic syndrome	Electroconvulsive therapy (ECT)	Dissociative fugue
Implicit memory		Posttraumatic stress disorder
Word fragment completion	Korsakoff's disease	
Repetition priming	Diencephalon	Repression
Memory conversations	Confabulation	Alzheimer's disease
Memory importation	Frontal lobe amnesia	Amyloid plaques
Memory appropriation	Source amnesia	Neurofibrillary tangles
Memory compensation	Transient global amnesia	Memory rehabilitation
Method of vanishing cues	Short-term memory amnesia	Errorless learning

REVIEW QUESTIONS

1. What is amnesia? What is the main difference between anterograde and retrograde amnesia?

2. Describe the amnesic symptoms of HM and Clive Wearing. Describe at least two differences in their memory profile following the onset of their amnesia.

3. What is the amnesic syndrome? What cognitive functions are preserved? What cognitive functions are impaired? What parts of the brain are typically impaired?

4. What is implicit memory? How is it studied in amnesic patients? What outcomes are typically seen with anterograde amnesiacs?

5. What is Ribot's law? How does it apply to cases of retrograde amnesia?

6. What causes Korsakoff's disease? What are the primary symptoms of Korsakoff's disease? How does it differ from the amnesic syndrome?

7. What is anosognosia? How does it affect the outcome of neuropsychological treatment? In what forms of amnesia is there evidence of anosognosia?

8. What is confabulation? Why does confabulation occur in both Korsakoff's disease patients and in frontal lobe patients?

9. What are the causes of psychogenic amnesia? What symptoms differ from organic amnesia caused by brain injury?

10. What are the stages of Alzheimer's disease? How is memory affected during each stage?

ONLINE RESOURCES

1. See the following YouTube video for an overview of amnesia: http://www.youtube.com/watch?v=wDNDRDJy-vo.

2. For an article about HM, go to http://www.nytimes.com/2008/12/05/us/05hm.html?_r=3&adxnnl=1&partner=rss&emc=rss&adxnnlx=1228579234-xC4tWoMNrhmvyjdYptsa1g.

3. For more on Clive Wearing, go to http://www.youtube.com/watch?v=Vwigmktix2Y&feature=related.

4. Go to the following website to read about a heroic waiter who saved a woman from a potential benzodiazepine-linked date rape: http://www.cbsnews.com/stories/2008/02/21/earlyshow/main3855974.shtml?source=RSSattr=HOME_3855974.

5. For a series of interviews with KC by the prominent memory researcher Endel Tulving, go to http://www.youtube.com/watch?v=tXHk0a3RvLc or go to http://video.healthhaven.com/Tulving.htm.

6. For more on Dr. Moscovitch's research, go to http://psych.utoronto.ca/Neuropsychologylab/morris2.html.

7. For more information and statistics on Alzheimer's disease, go to http://www.alz.org/index.asp.

Go to www.sagepub.com/schwartz for additional exercises and study resources. Select **Chapter 10, Memory Disorders** for chapter-specific resources.

CHAPTER 11

Memory in Childhood

In this chapter, we consider the development of memory in infants and young children. This is a broad topic. As we have seen, the term *memory* covers a great many different kinds of information processing. However, there are some parallels among the development of memory systems in early life. Early childhood is a time of rapid cognitive growth. However, some systems grow more quickly than others. When examining the development of memory in infants and young children, we can learn about memory by examining the differences in how separate memory processes develop and change. For example, by the end of the first year of life, infants are rapidly adding words to their lexical memory. Some evidence, however, suggests that there is no or little encoding into episodic memory at this point in a person's life. Thus, by studying development, we gain insight into the memory processes of children and gain some understanding of the nature of memory systems.

We will not cover procedural learning in this chapter. Procedural learning refers to the acquisition of complex motor tasks. Almost all infants, for example, learn to walk during the first 18 months of life. This takes practice and learning—the learning involves memory. This chapter instead focuses on the development of declarative memory systems, that is, those memory systems such as episodic, semantic, and lexical memory that can eventually be reported on verbally once an infant has started to acquire language. We will discuss, albeit briefly, how language is learned in infants.

MEMORY IN INFANCY

Human infants are born in a precocious state. As such, for several months after birth, human infants are completely dependent on caregivers and have little motor control. This lack of motor control presents a problem for memory researchers. Moreover, human infants cannot make any verbal responses until they are about 1 year old. Thus, without an obvious set of behaviors that psychologists can observe, and with infants' limited means of communication, the study of infant memory has had to rely on a series of clever innovations. We review the methods that researchers use to ask what infants remember of what they experience (see Figure 11.1).

Figure 11.1 Infants learn rapidly.

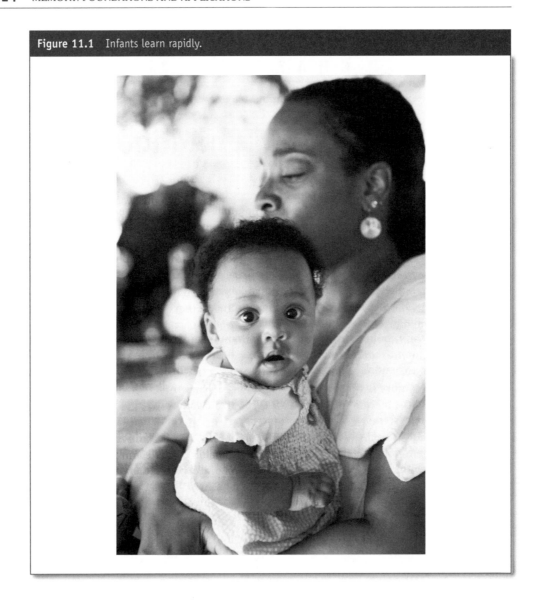

Visual Recognition

Although newborns are restricted in their ability to move their limbs, they can move their eyes. And they do spend a lot of time looking around their worlds with seeming curiosity. This allows researchers to observe behavior in young infants. That is, we can use gaze direction as a proxy for memory. Consider a colorful mobile placed over an infant's crib. The mobile may grab the infant's attention, and he or she may direct his or her gaze toward it. Eventually, the novelty wears off, and the infant's attention is directed elsewhere. The mobile is removed and stored out of the infant's view. Later, the mobile is again placed above the infant's crib. If the infant now does not attend to it or spends less time attending to it, this may be evidence of memory. Because the infant has already examined it, it does not appear novel. This could only occur if at some level, the infant recognizes the mobile (Hayne, 2004; Luo, Baillageon, Brueckner, & Munakata, 2003). This recognition is evidence that there is some memory of the earlier experience. For more on eye tracking in infants, go to www.sagepub.com/schwartz.[1]

Newborns are also equipped with a functioning auditory system. This allows researchers to examine auditory recognition as well as visual recognition. Studies have shown that newborns already can discriminate their mother's voice from that of other women. Similar to the visual recognition studies, infants will look more toward the source of the mother's voice than to that of a control woman. This functioning auditory system appears to support recognition of the mother's voice even before birth. A startling study showed that fetuses can recognize their mother's voice. Kisilevksy et al. (2003) showed that fetuses 1 to 2 weeks before birth recognized their mother's voice. Heart rate monitoring showed an increase in the fetuses' heart rate when a tape recording of the mother's voice reading a story was compared with a tape recording of another women reading the story.

Nonnutritive Sucking

Another behavior that young infants, almost from birth, do naturally is sucking. This is a natural reflexive behavior biologically necessary for obtaining milk. Infants can suck on pacifiers, which have no nutritive value, but can be monitored by sensitive electronic equipment, which can measure how fast or slow the infants are sucking. Their rate of sucking may increase or decrease depending on what they see or hear in the environment around them. Memory researchers can measure the increase or decrease in sucking in response to presented stimuli. A novel stimulus will usually elicit an increase in sucking most likely because the stimulus is new and exciting. Familiar stimuli will either not affect the rate of sucking or decrease it (Eimas, Siqueland, Jusczyk, & Vigorito, 1971). Thus, the infant can tell us something about what is novel or what is familiar by adjusting his or her sucking rate. Because we cannot tell the infant to suck faster when he or she sees something novel, researchers must measure baseline sucking rates in response to different stimuli, so that any difference in sucking rates is a function of memory.

Visual recognition: infants will look selectively at novel stimuli over familiar stimuli.

Nonnutritive sucking: a natural reflexive behavior biologically necessary for obtaining milk. Infants will suck differentially to the presence of a novel stimulus compared to a familiar stimulus. A novel stimulus will usually elicit an increase in sucking most likely because the stimulus is new and exciting.

Conjugate reinforcement technique: a ribbon is attached to the infant's foot, which will eventually be attached to a mobile placed overhead. When the infant moves or kicks his or her foot, it will make the mobile move and jiggle. After a delay, the infant is again given the opportunity to move the mobile. If the infant does so in less time, learning has occurred.

Imitation: mimicking the actions of another.

Conjugate Reinforcement Technique

This clever technique is useful to study memory in infants approximately age 2 months to about 6 months. In the technique, an infant lies on his or her back in a crib, usually the baby's home crib. A ribbon is attached to the infant's foot, which will eventually be attached to a mobile placed overhead. At first, however, the ribbon is not attached to the mobile. During this phase, a baseline measure of kicking is made. That is, how often does the infant make kicking movements with the foot that has the ribbon attached to it? The ribbon is then attached to the mobile. In this way, whenever the infant moves or kicks his or her foot, it will make the mobile move and jiggle. This is very exciting and entertaining for the infant. Within a few minutes, most infants will be shaking their feet and kicking repeatedly to get the mobile to move. The researchers measure how long it takes for the infant to learn that moving the foot results in the reinforcing display of the moving mobile. In behavioral terms, the response behavior is the kicking, and the movement of the mobile is the reinforcement (Rovee-Collier & Cuevas, 2008).

To test memory, researchers may impose a retention interval of a few minutes or wait several weeks. During this retention interval, the infant does not have access to the ribbon or the attached mobile. At the end of the retention interval, the ribbon is again attached to both the infant's foot and to the mobile. Given the intrinsically rewarding nature of the moving mobile, an infant who remembers the game will begin kicking immediately. However, an infant who has forgotten the relation between the ribbon and the mobile will have to relearn it again, and this may take several minutes. Thus, memory can be measured by counting the number of kicks or by recording the time until above-baseline kicking begins.

Rovee-Collier and her colleagues have shown that babies as young as 3 months will remember the relation between kicking and reinforcement up to 1 week later. As infants get older, the amount of time that they will retain such information increases. For instance, a 6-month-old infant will remember the relation as long as 2 weeks later. The researchers have used this technique to look at a number of memory variables. For instance, they have demonstrated a spacing effect. Two practice trials close in time to each other will not be as effective at producing good remembering as two practice trials more effectively spaced in time (Bearce & Rovee-Collier, 2006). In another experiment, Rovee-Collier demonstrated a "misinformation" effect. Exposure to a second mobile reduced the likelihood that the infant would remember the first mobile (Rovee-Collier & Cuevas, 2008). Thus, there are parallels between early memory in infants and later memory in adults. However, none of these studies demonstrates conscious memory in infants. Rather, they demonstrate that learning has taken place, but it may be more similar to implicit memory than to conscious recall.

By the time infants are 7 months old, they are no longer interested in the mobiles or in kicking them to make them move. As a consequence, Rovee-Collier developed a parallel technique to work with older infants. Hartshorn and Rovee-Collier (1997) found that older infants learned the relation between pressing a lever and following a toy train move around a track. The infants remembered to press the lever even several weeks after they last saw the relation between the train and the lever.

Imitation

Although most adults tend to reject the cognitive sophistication of "mere imitation," it can be used as a marker of memory. Indeed, studies with nonhuman primates demonstrate that imitation is more complex than most of us might think. To be able to duplicate the motor patterns of another, one must be able to remember those patterns. Imitation is more similar to recall than to recognition. Thus, demonstrating that infants cam imitate behavior suggests complex memory abilities. Bauer (2002) has examined the ability of infants (usually closer to a year old than birth) to imitate actions of experimenters up to 1 month later. Most infants can duplicate simple actions by an adult experimenter by the age of 9 months old (Hayne, 2004).

These methods have allowed memory development researchers to examine a host of issues with largely nonverbal infants. Using these methods, researchers have been able to explore the origins of many of the memory systems that will come to dominate cognition in older children and adults. Perhaps no memory system develops sooner and faster than does lexical memory. We will address lexical memory first.

Memory for Language in Infancy

One of the most monumental achievements of each and every infant is his or her success in breaking the code of language. Think of a 1-year-old infant. He or she may have just learned to walk, certainly cannot use keys to open a door, cannot tie shoes, and certainly cannot balance a checkbook. Yet that infant is well on the way to producing speech and likely understands some speech already. We know that infants are learning and storing language-related information early on in development. Indeed, a massive amount of language-related information is learned by a baby's first birthday, even if that infant is not actually talking yet.

Infants hone in on the phonemes (sounds) of their native language very early, within the first few months. Eimas et al. (1971) showed that babies as young as 1 month habituated to a particular phoneme, that is, their sucking rate decreased after hearing the phoneme over and over. When a new phoneme was played, their sucking rate increased again. By 6 months of age, infants are distinguishing between phonemes of their native language and similar sounds that are not present in their native language (Werker & Tees, 1999). Some of these distinctions can be quite subtle (think of the difference in the "p" sound in English and the "p" sound in Spanish, if you are bilingual), and yet infants are able to distinguish the sounds.

Infants are also learning the symbolic meanings of words by the end of the first year. As most parents know, 1-year-old infants recognize many common words, such as *mommy, daddy, cookie, milk, doggie,* and so on. Tincoff and Jusczyk (1999) demonstrated this empirically in a clever way. They placed two videotapes side by side in front of 6-month-old infants. One video depicted their mothers and the other video depicted their fathers. After hearing the word *mommy,* infants looked for a greater amount of time at the video of their mothers, whereas after hearing the word *daddy,* the infants looked for a greater amount of time at the video of their fathers. They did not show this preference when the adults depicted were strangers. Thus, even 6-month-old infants have learned a few important linguistic concepts.

Semantic Memory

Semantic memory is developing rapidly during the first year of life. Research suggests that by age 3 to 4 months, infants are starting to understand categorization and to group objects together into specific concepts, such as the cat/dog distinction (Eimas & Quinn, 1994). Early semantic memory appears limited. For example, infants cannot acquire superordinate categories, but semantic memory, perhaps in association with lexical memory, appears to develop early in infancy.

Episodic Memory

Performance in the conjugate reinforcement tasks suggests that infants can learn based on a single event and maintain that knowledge across a long-term memory retention interval. Similarly, infants can imitate behavior even when the model is no longer engaging in the behavior after seeing that behavior only once. Therefore, infants satisfy one of the conditions whereby memory is considered to be episodic. They can learn based on unique single events. However, given their lack of verbal abilities, it is difficult to determine if infants are aware of the past event when they begin kicking at the sight of the mobile or engaging in the imitation behavior. It is possible that these memories are mediated by conditioning and not by a cognitive mechanism of episodic memory. Given that young children are unable to remember events from their first year of life (as are adults), it is likely that most learning that takes place during the first year of life is not episodic in nature. Thus, it is likely that true episodic memory is not online until at least the second year of a person's life.

MEMORY IN EARLY CHILDHOOD

By the time children are 2 years old, most have entered the world of language and can both understand and produce speech. This makes the task of the memory research easier, as experimenters can use verbal commands and children can produce verbal reports. This allows many more aspects of memory to be examined than during the first year of life. In particular, verbal abilities allow researchers to explore the origins of the declarative memory systems—semantic memory and episodic memory. Nonetheless, it is often a challenge to examine memory in young children as they may not understand instructions that older children or adults will understand, and children younger than 5 years of age cannot use any written instructions or written responses. In this section, we will consider a few topics in the development of memory in early childhood.

Why Does Memory Improve During Early Childhood?

It is not surprising that research shows that 5-year-old children are better at a variety of memory tasks than are 2-year-old children (Flavell, Miller, & Miller, 1993). They have a greater capacity in working memory, learn more quickly when learning semantic memory materials, and begin to show clear evidence of functioning episodic memory systems.

A 2-year-old has little knowledge or understanding of the greater world around him or her; a 5-year-old is ready to begin formal schooling. What changes during this critical period that allows children to start learning the materials that they will need to master in school? As cognitive psychologists, memory researchers want to explore how these developmental changes occur.

There are two basic theories as to how and why memory improves during this period. In one view, the **memory efficiency view,** memory improves because the processes of memory themselves improve as a child grows. That is, working memory capacity increases, learning processes become faster and more efficient, and episodic memory processes start functioning. Hence, better memory systems allow young children to learn more rapidly. In contrast, the **memory strategies view** argues that as children grow, they learn strategic behaviors (e.g., elaboration, rehearsal, organization) that allow them to use their memory better. Thus, it is their knowledge of the tools they have available to them that leads to faster learning in young children (see Flavell et al., 1993). Like most contrasting views, the reality of human memory is that both are important features in memory development. Because an earlier generation simply assumed that the improvement was due to greater memory efficiency as children grow, much of the research has concentrated on the extent to which young children learn and use memory strategies.

> **Memory efficiency view**: the efficiency of learning new information and storing it in long-term memory.
>
> **Memory strategies view**: the conscious activities a person engages in to assist the remembering of information.

We will first consider how young children develop memory strategies, that is, the conscious activities a person engages in to assist the remembering of information. Memory strategies include reminding oneself of things that need to be remembered, rehearsing unlearned information, allocating cognitive resources, and using retrieval strategies.

Memory strategies start to develop early, perhaps as early as around 2 years of age. For example, in one study, children as young as 18 months verbally rehearsed the location of a toy more often when it was hidden than when it was in open view. In particular, Deloache, Cassidy, and Brown (1985) asked children between the ages of 18 and 24 months to watch as an experimenter hid a desirable stuffed animal (Big Bird) somewhere in the room. The experimenter told the children to remember where Big Bird was so that they could play with him later. Despite the availability of other toys, children frequently verbally reminded themselves of the hidden location of Big Bird, thus inhibiting the potential to forget his location. In control conditions, in which Big Bird was visible during the retention interval, the children did not engage in verbal reminders. Thus, in this study, children as young as 1.5 years are showing evidence of using memory strategies (see Figure 11.2). For more information on Judy DeLoache's research, go to www.sagepub.com/schwartz.[2]

Younger children have not fine-tuned their study strategies. Think of a 7-year-old and a 12-year-old studying for a spelling test. The 7-year-old is not yet ready to realize that he or she needs to study difficult items more than easy items, that reading through the words does not guarantee that the words will be spelled correctly on the test. The older child already knows that doing well in school means applying himself or herself. Indeed, adult college students have fine-tuned their memory strategies. Failure to do so may mean that a college student will need to spend far more time studying new information than he or she has time for in a day. Thus, the vast majority of college students use a number of sophisticated memory strategies. One of these is elaboration. Elaboration means connecting the new to-be-learned material to well-learned material by looking for meaningful connections between the two. The question can be posed—at what age do young children learn to use elaborative encoding?

Younger children do not spontaneously use elaboration. When children are asked to encode paired associates, younger children (ages 3–6) do not use elaborative encoding, although their performance benefits when researchers impose these strategies on the children. However, at age 7 or 8, children are using and benefiting from elaborative strategies (Beuhring & Kee, 1987). Similar patterns are seen in the use of organizational strategies—they do not seem to be used by children until they are in third grade (Pressley & Hilden, 2006).

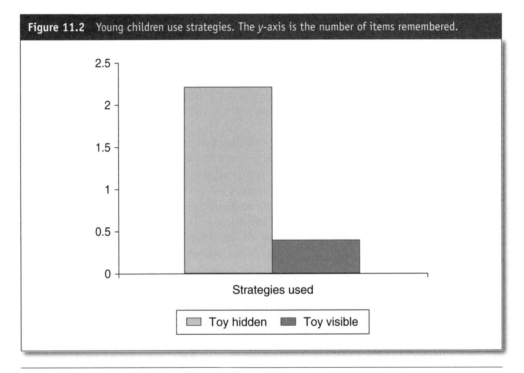

Figure 11.2 Young children use strategies. The y-axis is the number of items remembered.

SOURCE: Based on Deloache, Cassidy, and Brown (1985).

Imagery can also be a powerful tool to assist in the learning of new information. With training, adults can use imagery to remember long lists of unrelated items. Many adults spontaneously use imagery to assist their memory, but some will not use them at all. Thus, it should not be surprising that young children do not use imagery to boost their memory. Nonetheless, when children are trained to use imagery, they too can benefit from it (Howe,

2006). For example, de Graaff, Verhoeven, Bosman, and Hasselman (2007) showed that kindergarten-age children who were taught visual mnemonics to help them learn the letters of the alphabet had quicker acquisition of those letters.

To summarize, children do start using strategies at an early age. However, some of the most sophisticated memory strategies, such as the use of imagery, elaborative encoding, and organization skills, do not develop until much later in childhood. Although children can be trained to use these techniques at early ages, they do not spontaneously use them until they are around 7 to 8 years old. Other techniques, such as imagery, do not spontaneously develop at all, but young children can also benefit from being trained with them.

Memory Efficiency

Memory efficiency means that memory improves during development because memory capacity, the speed of learning, and the ability to retain information in long-term memory increase. Memory efficiency could be a function of more efficient cognitive processes or more mature neurological mechanisms. In this section, we will consider the evidence that supports the view that memory capacity increases during early childhood. Memory capacity is defined here as the amount of information that can be stored in working memory.

Improved working memory capacity means that older children have a larger buffer to store information than do younger children. To demonstrate this, Kail (1991) compared digit spans of younger children (age 2) and older children (age 9). The digit spans of the younger children were only two items, whereas the older children had digit spans of six, not much different from adults. Improved working memory capacity is important for children as they mature—as countless studies have correlated working memory capacity with reading ability. Indeed, children who perform well on tasks that tap into the phonological loop also score high on tests of reading and writing (Alloway et al., 2005).

Working memory efficiency is related to the ability to screen out irrelevant information. For example, if you want to be able to use the full capacity of your working memory on the digit spans, you need to be able to inhibit other thoughts or ideas from entering working memory and "crowding" out the digits. Research shows that older children are better able to inhibit irrelevant information in working memory. For example, Harnishfeger and Pope (1996) tested school-age children on a directed forgetting task. In directed forgetting, participants are told to inhibit or ignore items that they have already studied, that is, to forget them. After they are instructed to forget certain materials, they are then asked to learn new materials. To maximize performance on the new material, you must inhibit the to-be-forgotten information as it may interfere with the new learning. Adults in directed forgetting will show poor recall for items that they were directed to forget. Harnishfeger and Pope found that older children (age 10) were better at directed forgetting than the younger participants (age 6).

Long-term memory also improves in efficiency in early childhood, although it is usually quite difficult to tease apart the changes that derive from improved strategic use of memory and the changes that derive from efficiency. But there are studies that show that given an equal amount of study time, older children will retain more information than younger children. For example, Myers and Perlmutter (1978) examined the ability of children to remember objects shown to them. The 4-year-olds remembered twice as many objects (40% to 20%) as did the 2-year-olds. We know that 4-year-olds already use complex memory strategies, but the test in this experiment was a recognition test. Recognition tests are less sensitive to memory strategies use than are recall tests. So it is likely that some of the improvement of the older children is because of better strategies in encoding.

Episodic Memory

Episodic memory refers to the memory of individual events from our lives. Adults remember no events from the first 3 years of life (by and large) and few from the next 2 years. This is the phenomenon of childhood amnesia (or infantile amnesia) discussed in Chapter 7. This led some researchers to speculate that episodic memory does not develop until a child is around 3 years of age. However, as any parent will tell you, young children do discuss the past. Many 3-year-olds will discuss events that may have happened to them as much as a year earlier. These events will be forgotten later as adults but are retained for long periods of time in young children (Ornstein, Haden, & Elischberger, 2006). Thus, young children have something very similar or identical to episodic memory at quite young ages. The explanation for childhood amnesia lies elsewhere. For more on the relation on early childhood memory and later childhood amnesia, go to www.sagepub.com/schwartz.[3]

In an important study, Tessler and Nelson (1994) examined the memory of 3½-year-old children who visited a museum. Mothers and children attended a visit to a museum in New York City. One week later, the children were asked to describe the event. Despite the fact that this event is unlikely to be remembered when the children become adults, at 7 days later, the children remembered the event in some detail, clearly demonstrating episodic remembering. However, some interesting features distinguished the memory reports from those of adults. For example, the manner in which the mothers interacted with their children influenced the amount and accuracy of their recall. We will see shortly that young children's episodic memory is prone to distortion. In this case, the mothers were probably not distorting information, but their talk influenced the children's reports. The point here is that the young children remembered a specific event 1 week later, demonstrating the beginnings of episodic memory.

Other research points to the hypothesis that young children can retain autobiographical events over retention intervals of years rather than simply days. Sutcliffe Cleveland and Reese (2008) showed that young children (age 5) accurately recall events that happened to them before the age of 2. They asked children about events that they also had reports on from the parents. Thus, the researchers had a manner in which to corroborate the narratives of the children. In the study, the children were given an actual event, such as "remember the time you went on a hayride in the country," and children were given the opportunity to describe the event. Sutcliffe Cleveland and Reese showed that some 5½-year-olds reported remembering events from before age 2 but made many errors in accuracy. However, 5½-year-olds accurately recalled more events from age 3½ and older. In another study, Van Abbema and Bauer (2005) were able to get children to visit the lab at age 3 and then again around the age of 8 (varied from 7 to 9). In their first visit, the 3-year-olds described six events that had recently happened to them. Approximately 5 years later, the children returned to the lab and were asked again about those events. The researchers also found that the older children were able to remember some (about 50%) of the original events and did so in an accurate manner.

Thus, this research suggests that, at least early on, children can reach across the "childhood amnesia" barrier and remember events from before they reached 2 years of age that they certainly would not be able to remember later, as adults. This suggests that childhood amnesia may be an issue of retrieval from episodic memory in adults rather than encoding into episodic memory in young children.

Memory Conversations and Episodic Memory

What influences the kinds of episodic events young children will remember? To many parents, what their children remember is often a mystery. The salient events that adults remember may not be the salient events that young children remember. For example, a parent may ask a child about an event that the parent thought would be very salient, such as a visit to a theme park, only to find that the child does not recall the event at all. Then, later the child asks about an event—stopping the car to help a turtle cross the road safely—that the parent has long since forgotten about. Parents might be tempted to argue that they have little influence on what their children remember from childhood. But in fact, research suggests that parents do have a strong influence on their children's episodic memory development. This conclusion comes from studies on parent-child **memory conversations.**

> **Memory conversations**: the talk that goes back and forth between a parent and a child concerning past events. The discussions we have with others about the past. Normal individuals frequently have memory conversations.

Memory conversations are the kinds of verbal exchanges that go back and forth between a parent and a child concerning past events. Most research suggests that parents often dictate the kinds of recollections that the children have and direct the recall in particular directions. However, not all parents employ the same styles while discussing past events with their young children. Some parents spend more time talking about past events with their children than do other parents. And among the parents who do speak of the past with their young children, some encourage their children to elaborate on the past events and what they mean and encourage their children to participate in much of the memory talk. Other parents correct their young children when they make a mistake and provide much of the details of the earlier event themselves. These parental styles have been correlated with the amount and accuracy of children's recollection—the more open-ended and elaborative the conversation between parent and child, the more the child will remember later (C. Peterson, McDermott Sales, Rees, & Fivush, 2007). Parents' style affects the recall of young children in both formal and informal settings.

For example, returning to the study Tessler and Nelson (1994), the researchers varied the kinds of interactions the parents had discussing the museum visit with their children. In the study, some parents were directed to discuss the events at a museum in a more interactive participatory style, and other mothers were instructed not to discuss the events at all. The children of the parents who discussed the event together remembered more of the event. These findings show that not only do children report more information if their parents adopt the more interactive style of memory conversation, but they actually remember more. This has been corroborated in a number of recent studies. In another study, C. Peterson et al. (2007) showed that open-ended and elaborative styles even helped young children (ages 2–5) remember more from a stressful event. Children recalled more of a hospital emergency visit if they later discussed the events in an elaborative style with their parents. Thus, elaborative discussions, in general, lead to children with better autobiographical memory. It also works in specific cases; an open-ended elaborative memory conversation increases recall of that particular event.

Mnemonic Improvement Tip 11.1

Memory conversations increase recall from episodic memory with young children.

Some research suggests that not all cultures equally emphasize the role of autobiographical memory. Q. Wang and Fivush (2005) point out that parent-child interactions in the United States are much more likely to be discussions of past events than are parent-child interactions in China. Chinese families are much more likely to stress moral precepts and family standards, whereas American families revel in sharing past experiences. Therefore, American families have more memory conversations in general and more that are elaborative and open-ended. This suggests that American children might show better recall of episodic events than do Chinese children. Indeed, Wang and her colleagues have shown in a number of different contexts that young American children are more likely to remember recent events than young Chinese children. Wang also speculates that this may account for why American adults remember events from childhood better than do Chinese adults. A number of studies demonstrate that the offset of childhood amnesia is earlier for Americans than it is for Chinese (see Q. Wang, 2001). For more on Qi Wang's research, go to www.sagepub .com/schwartz.[4]

INTERIM SUMMARY

Infancy and early childhood are times of rapid cognitive growth. Memory develops rapidly during this time. Studying infant memory is fraught with difficulties because infants cannot yet use language. To study memory in infancy, researchers use **visual recognition, nonnutritive sucking, conjugate reinforcement technique,** and **imitation.** Language learning takes place quickly, and by 1 year old, most infants are starting to understand language. Two theories have been advanced to explain the growth of memory in early childhood. In the memory efficiency view, memory improves because the processes of memory themselves improve as a child grows. In contrast, the memory strategies view argues that as children grow, they learn strategic behaviors that allow them to use their memory better. Episodic memory starts to develop in early childhood, particularly in the context of memory conversations between parent and child. Cultures that spend more time engaged in memory conversations have children that form autobiographical representations earlier.

CHILDREN'S EYEWITNESS MEMORY

In many legal proceedings, children may be the victim of a crime or the only witness to a crime. Therefore, some court cases are dependent on the accuracy of a young child's memory of a stressful event. In our society, we consider crimes against children as most despicable, and we reserve our harshest criminal sentences for those who commit crimes against children. Therefore, we place great weight on convicting the perpetrators of violence against children. However, research has determined that young children are highly suggestible and therefore prone to false memories (Melnyk, Crossman, & Scullin, 2007). This can often make it quite difficult to prosecute people accused of harming children.

Back in the late 1980s, several high-profile criminal trials that relied heavily on testimony from young children thrust the issue of children's eyewitness memory into the spotlight. For example, in one high-profile case in California, a woman who ran a child care center was accused of sexually molesting numerous children (see www.sagepub.com/schwartz).[5] In this case, repeated and suggestive questioning led to what were surely many instances of false memory in the child witnesses. Some children claimed that the accused could fly, whereas others reported that famous actors had participated in the abuse. Because of the confused and clearly false memories on the part of the children who had been through the questioning procedures, much of the evidence against the accused was suspect and eventually dismissed. What actually happened is anyone's guess, as suggestive questioning rendered the children's testimony invalid, and the accused was not required to testify. Because of this preschool abuse case and a few other similar cases, police are now much more careful about leading questions when questioning child witnesses. In the wake of this trial and others, developmental psychologists rushed in to examine the nature of the child as a witness.

In a classic study on this topic, Leichtman and Ceci (1995) investigated the suggestibility of child witnesses. They used children ages 3 to 6 as participants. In the study, a man—a confederate of the researchers—named "Sam Stone" came to visit the children's preschool class. Sam Stone wandered around the classroom for a couple of minutes, made a couple of innocent comments, and then left. Three conditions defined what happened just prior to or after Sam Stone's visit. In a control condition, nothing else happened either before or after. In the next condition (the stereotype condition), a research assistant visited the class several times starting 3 weeks before Sam Stone's visit. The research assistant described how Sam Stone was a nice man but clumsy. In a third condition (suggestibility condition), children were interviewed after his visit. The interviewer incorrectly mentioned that Sam Smith had spilled a drink and ripped a book while visiting the classroom. Leichtman and Ceci were curious to know what the effect of the biasing information would be, whether it occurred before Sam Stone's visit, as in the stereotype condition, or after Same Stone's visit, as in the suggestibility condition.

Some 10 weeks later, a new interviewer came to class. This interviewer asked a number of things about Sam Stone's visit, including whether the children had seen Sam Stone spill his drink or had seen Sam Stone rip up a book. In the control condition, children's recall was quite accurate. That is, few children reported seeing Sam Stone spill or rip anything.

Among the 5- and 6-year-old kids, there were no inaccuracies in their reports and only a marginal one for the 3- and 4-year-olds. That is, the false memory rate in the control condition was practically zero (see Figure 11.3). However, in the stereotype condition in which children had been told that Sam Stone was clumsy, the false memory rate increased to about 20% for the younger children and about 10% for the older children. In the suggestibility condition, in which the children had been told that Sam Stone ripped a book and spilled a drink, the false memory rate was even higher. About 40% of the younger kids and 10% of the older kids reported *seeing* Sam Stone do these things (Leichtman & Ceci, 1995).

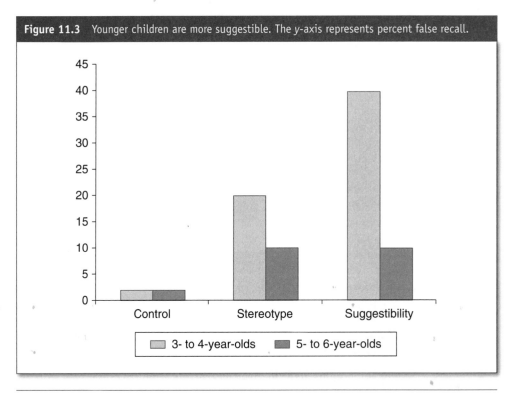

Figure 11.3 Younger children are more suggestible. The *y*-axis represents percent false recall.

SOURCE: Based on Leichtman and Ceci (1995).

In this study, 40% of the 3- and 4-year-olds reported seeing Sam Stone rip a book apart, something the actual Sam Stone had not done. Given the large number of false memories based on a simple suggestion spoken only once, it is likely that it is easy to induce false memories in young children. This effect has now been documented in a great many studies (see Melnyk et al., 2007, for a review). Certainly 40% is beyond any conceivable definition of "beyond a shadow of a doubt." Therefore, unless the prosecution in court cases can document that no misleading procedures have been introduced in the interviewing of child witnesses, courts should use extreme caution in evaluating the testimony of very young children. For the transcript of an interview with Dr. Ceci, go to www.sagepub.com/schwartz.[6]

Memory and Stress in Children's Episodic Memory

In real crime situations, any person—especially a young child—may be stressed and anxious while witnessing a crime. Thus, it is important to understand how stress affects memory, especially in the context of eyewitness memory. In the Leichtman and Ceci (1995) study, there was no attempt to duplicate the real stress a child might experience in a situation that would later lead that child to testify in court. Even the alleged crimes that Sam Stone was accused of—spilling a drink and ripping a book—are not uncommonly witnessed events in a preschool classroom.

The problem, of course, is that intentionally putting children into a stressful situation is unethical. Nor would many parents sign a consent form to put their child in a stressful situation or one in which he or she witnessed a simulated crime. However, a number of studies have used naturalistic settings—that is, by examining memory for real-life trauma. These can include memory tests for painful but necessary medical procedures, memory of natural disasters, and actual crime witnesses. The problem with these studies is that it is difficult to control the stress level—as it depends on the procedure or event. It is also difficult to compare across studies. Thus, the only solid evidence to come from these studies is that young children can recall events even if they are highly stressful, but how stress affects memory is not clear (H. L. Price & Connolly, 2008). However, one study was able to examine children's memory under three levels of stress, which can allow a comparison of low and high stress to a middle condition. We will consider this study in detail.

Fivush, McDermott-Sales, Goldberg, Bahrick, and Parker (2004) examined the memories of children who had experienced Hurricane Andrew in 1992. Hurricane Andrew was a Category 5 storm that ripped through Miami on August 24, 1992, destroying homes and knocking out power all across the city. Shortly after the storm, the researchers interviewed over one hundred 3- to 4-year-old children about their experiences in the storm. In the first interview, the sample was divided into children who had experienced low, medium, and high stress, as indicated by the amount of damage sustained to the child's home. In the low-stress condition were families whose homes had received no damage or minor damage. In the medium-stress condition were families whose homes had received considerable damage but had not been destroyed. In the high-stress condition were families who had seen their homes collapse around them.

The children's memory was measured in a number of ways—but the findings were consistent across measurement. The children who remembered the most details and gave the most spontaneous descriptions of the hurricane were the children in the moderate-stress condition. For the children in the low-stress condition, Hurricane Andrew may not have been any different than the many ordinary thunderstorms that come through Miami every summer and may not have been distinctive enough to remember. The high stress caused by extensive damage may have interfered with children's ability to accurately encode the events in these heaviest hit homes. As with adults, extreme stress may impair memory. With all measures, the best memory performance was seen in the moderate-stress condition (see Figure 11.4).

Fivush et al. (2004) followed up with a second interview some 6 years later, when the children were about 10 years old. Again, the children were divided into those who had experienced low stress, medium stress, or high stress during the hurricane. All of the children still remembered some details from Hurricane Andrew. However, the effect of initial stress

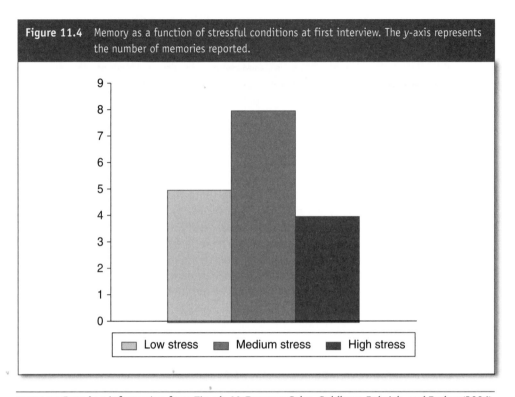

Figure 11.4 Memory as a function of stressful conditions at first interview. The *y*-axis represents the number of memories reported.

SOURCE: Based on information from Fivush, McDermott-Sales, Goldberg, Bahrick, and Parker (2004).

was no longer obvious. The high-stress children recalled as much as the lower stress children. The high-stress children were actually also more accurate in their recall than the lower stress children.

Based on this analysis, it is clear that stress can influence children's memory. In the young children who experienced the hurricane, high stress led to worse memory than medium stress. This is similar to patterns of memory observed with adults under stress. Why the high-stress children's memory caught up to the lower stress kids when tested 6 years later is less easily interpreted. It is possible that in families that sustained extensive damage to the family home, there was more continued focus on remembering the storm and the consequences of the storm for that family.

In the past 10 years, a huge number of studies have attempted to examine the effects of stress, especially those associated with being a witness to or victim of a crime. Within this area are those who argue that children's memory is reliable and can be trusted in cases of great import and those who argue that stress increases the likelihood of memory distortion and false memory. However, the bulk of the data supports the view that (a) children are at greater risk of false memories than adults, and (b) high-stress situations can increase that risk while lowering the amount of veridical recall (see H. L. Price & Connolly, 2008). Thus, criminal investigators must proceed with caution when interviewing a child who has experienced a stressful event.

MEMORY IN OLDER CHILDREN

By and large, the previous section has focused on children as they make the transition from preschool (age 3) to elementary school (ages 6–7), although the studies have addressed memory as young as 2 and as old as 10. This section will address changes in the human memory system that occur later in childhood. This transition to middle childhood begins around the age of 7 and ends as the teenage mind becomes essentially adult-like, at least with respect to memory, around the age of 14 or 15.

Consider working memory. Younger children are not able to maintain more than two or three digits in the phonological loop. However, by the age of 9, most children average around six digits, just a little bit under the adult average of seven, which is in place by age 12 (Dempster, 1981). As we discussed earlier, data suggest this improvement is both a function of improved strategic regulation of memory and improved fluency of memory processing. For example, older children are both more likely to report using chunking strategies (strategic regulation) and respond faster in reaction time experiments (fluency) (Hale, 1990).

Episodic memory also changes as it matures during this period. Many studies indicate that older children can remember more information and in greater detail than can younger children. One of the key contributors to this improvement is that older children elaborate on the to-be-learned information or tie new events to already existing knowledge structures. Thus, starting around the age of 7, the meaning of an event becomes increasingly important. By the age of 13, meaning is the central aspect in a memory. Think about your own memory for a moment. Think of an event that happened to you before the age of 6 or so. What often strikes us about these memories is that they are often of complete trivia—a random snapshot out of our childhoods. Consider this with memory for events after the age of 8. These memories seem to fit into the thematic constraints of our lives—that is, we remember that which is personally meaningful.

There is, however, a paradoxical effect of the transition from literal memory to meaning-based memory in this time period. Several studies have shown that older children are more susceptible to a number of memory illusions than are younger children because they are now encoding for meaning, whereas the younger children are not. For example, consider the Deese-Roediger-McDermott illusion (DRM illusion; see Chapter 8). As a reminder, in the DRM illusion, participants are given a list of related words. The critical word, however, that relates all the other words to each other is missing. At recall, many participants will include this critical intrusion when they recall the list from memory. Holliday, Reyna, and Brainerd (2008) examined the DRM effect in children ages 7 to 13. They found that the older the children were, the better they did on the recall test. That should not come as a surprise—the overwhelming majority of developmental studies find that older children perform better than younger children in tests of recall. However, older children also made more critical intrusions than did younger children. That is, the younger children were more accurate and less likely to include a false memory in their memory report. Metzger et al. (2008) also found that older children recalled more correct information but also recalled more critical intrusions than did younger children. Metzger et al. found that by age 11, the children's pattern of responses was essentially the same as those of college students. The explanation here is that because the older children are more likely to encode for meaning, they are more likely to produce meaning-based critical intrusion when they recall the list. Thus, this study supports the assertion that older children increasingly process for meaning—this has the advantage of producing more correctly recalled items but also leaves older children (and adults) more susceptible to meaning-based memory errors. For more on this topic and its relation to eyewitness memory, go to www.sagepub.com/schwartz.[7]

Other studies show similar reverse effects with respect to false memory. Fazio and Marsh (2006) looked at memory for false facts embedded in stories given to children varying from ages 5 to 7. Even though the age range was relatively narrow, Fazio and Marsh found the older children remembered more in total from the stories than did the younger children. However, the older children were also more likely to make mistakes on a general-information test based on the errors they heard in the story. Again, the increasing attention to meaning drives the increase in false memories. Ceci, Papierno, and Kulkofsky (2007) found a similar pattern with a greater range of ages. Comparing children from ages 4 to 9, he found that older children were more likely to have story-based false memories, again pointing to the importance of meaning in memory as children move from early childhood into middle childhood.

These data should not mean that older children are always more susceptible to false memories. It simply shows that older children have more meaning-based memory errors. But there are other sources of false memories. Thus, when meaning helps disambiguate truth from falsehood, older children will have fewer false memories than younger children. Strange et al. (2006) conducted an interesting study on autobiographical memory. They compared memories of 6-year-olds and 10-year-olds for events from their lives. Most of the events were real events gathered from interviews with parents. However, they doctored some photographs to show the children in events that they had never experienced. Some of these false events were plausible (going on a hot air balloon ride at a fair), and others were less plausible (having tea with the Queen of England). False memories occurred for both types of events with both ages of children. Nonetheless, in this paradigm, the older children were much less susceptible to false memories. Thus, the effects of greater false memories in older children are not a general characteristic of being older but a function of the increased focus on meaning.

This pattern was recently confirmed in an interesting study examining memory in children ages 7 to 12. In this study, Otgaar, Candel, Merckelbach, and Wade (2009) found that many children ages 7 to 8 developed false memories of being abducted by a UFO when it was suggested that this actually occurred to them. In fact, a *majority* of children in this age range developed false memories when it was also suggested that UFO abductions were common. In contrast, the 11- to 12-year-old children were much less likely (although some still did) to develop false memories of UFO abduction. Moreover, the suggestion that UFO abductions were common did not increase the rate of false memories. Therefore, in this case, more knowledge and greater coding for meaning meant fewer, not more, false memories for the older children. For more on Dr. Otgaar's research, go to www.sagepub.com/schwartz.[8]

A recent study has found a neural basis for the change from literal-based memory to meaning-based memory in children. Chiu, Schmithhorst, Brown, Holland, and Dunn (2006) examined memory in children while scanning those children using functional magnetic resonance imaging (fMRI) technology. Children were given two incidental memory tasks. In one task, they generated verbs in response to nouns. In the second task, they were given a story comprehension task. Later, a recognition memory test was given. There were no differences in brain activation for the verb generation task between 8- and 10-year-old children. However, in the story comprehension task, activation in the left prefrontal lobe was associated with correct recognition in the older children but not in the younger children. The left prefrontal lobe is associated with the extraction of meaning. Thus, this study provides a neural correlate of the increased meaning-based processing in older children.

METAMEMORY IN CHILDREN

Metamemory is our knowledge and awareness of our own memory processes. We discussed this topic at length in Chapter 9 with a focus on metamemory in adults, but it is also of interest to know how and when it develops. Indeed, researchers studied metacognition in children before they turned their attention to adults. In this way, the study of metacognition got its start in developmental psychology rather than cognitive psychology because some researchers interested in the development of memory thought that metacognition was the key to understanding the development of memory in children. For example, Flavell et al. (1993) argued that metacognition was the basis of children's improvements in memory over the years of early childhood. It turns out that metacognition develops earlier than was originally thought but does play a role in memory improvement in young children.

> **Metamemory**: our knowledge and awareness of our own memory processes.

How early in a person's life can we see evidence of metamemory processes? Well, at least one study suggests that children are experiencing tip-of-the-tongue (TOT) states during their third year of life. Elbers (1985) recorded conversations with her 2½-year-old son concerning a difficult retrieval in Dutch, their native language. On the previous day, Elbers and her son had visited the aquarium, where the child saw some dolphins. The next day, when trying to retrieve the word for dolphins, the boy could not do so. Elbers suggested that her son was in a genuine TOT state, that he was aware of failed retrieval and was trying to recall the word anyway. If this anecdote is true, then metamemory develops early. This is consistent with the idea that other memory strategies start appearing early in childhood. Before, however, we discuss metamemory in children, it is important to understand the development of an important cognitive process called theory of mind in order to think about metamemory development. Metamemory development and the development of a theory of mind have often been linked conceptually. Therefore, we will take a brief look at theory of mind.

Theory of mind refers to the awareness that other individuals have separate states of awareness different from that of our own. A person with theory of mind can contemplate that another may know (or not know) information that he or she does not know. For example, when you order at a restaurant, you are aware that the waiter does not know what you want to eat. Looking up blankly at the waiter because you assume that she knows what you want just

> **Theory of mind**: the awareness that other individuals have separate states of awareness different from that of our own.

won't do! As simple and obvious as it is, you must tell the waiter what you want to eat in order for the waiter to know. Therefore, the simple interaction of ordering food at a restaurant involves theory of mind. The customer must understand that the waiter needs information from him or her that the waiter does not yet have (waiters will tell you, however, that their customers seldom have theory of mind and that customers expect all kinds of miracles from them). The waiter must have theory of mind too. She must understand that she does not know what you want in order to fulfill her job and must ask you what you want. Think about any human interaction you might have—almost all of them involve an assumption that you need to know something you don't about another person. Of course, to adults, theory of mind seems self-evident. But developmental psychology suggests that children are not fully equipped with theory of mind until about the age of 4 (Perner, 2000).

Theory of mind is tested in young children with the **false-belief test.** The false-belief test capitalizes on the simple fact that you may know something another person does not.

> **False-belief test**: a child learns something that another person does not have the opportunity to learn. The child must then decide if the other person knows what he or she knows. Three-year-olds seldom succeed, whereas most 5-year-olds have mastered it.

For example, you may have hid your grandmother's cigarettes in the cookie jar. When your grandmother goes to look for her lung cancer–causing cigarettes, they are not in her cigarette box because she does not know that they are actually in the cookie jar. Because she does not know what you know, she cannot do further damage to her body, at least for the time being. Now, you know that by hiding the cigarettes, your grandmother will not know their location. But a young child who has not yet developed theory of mind will think that because he knows where the cigarettes are, so too will his grandmother. Children under the age of 4 will assume that the other person has access to the same knowledge that they do, even when objectively they do not.

In the false-belief test (see Figure 11.5), a child learns something that another person does not have the opportunity to learn. The child must then decide if the other person knows what he or she knows. Consider the following experiment by Wimmer and Perner (1983). Children ages 3, 4, and 5 served as participants. The children were shown a bag of M&M's. While a child was watching, the M&M's were poured out of the M&M bag and into a bag marked "crayons." Both boxes were then sealed up so that no one could see what was inside. At this time, a research assistant entered the room, and the child was asked where the new person thinks the M&M's are. Because the research assistant did not see the M&M's placed in the crayon box, the child should indicate that the research assistant still thinks that they are in the M&M bag. However, all of the 3-year-olds and some of the 4-year-olds incorrectly answered that the research assistant knew that the M&M's were in the crayon box. Most of the 5-year-olds were correct and realized that because the research assistant had not seen the switch, he would not know the actual location of the M&M's. Thus, at the age of 3, children cannot separate what they know from what others know. This ability to do so, which develops in the 4 to 5 age range, is called theory of mind. The 5-year-old child is now aware that mental states of others differ from his or her own. In keeping with this knowledge, deception begins around this age as well. Behavioral variants of this test have been done on nonhuman animals, and at present, no experiment has shown that even chimpanzees can "pass" the false-belief test. Like 3-year-olds, chimpanzees assume that others know what they know.

Figure 11.5   An illustration of the false-belief test.

SOURCE: Illustration by Jack Frazier.

In understanding false belief, the child realizes that other minds have content different from their own and that others may not have access to the same information that they do. Thus, theory of mind refers to our knowledge of other minds. Metacognition refers to our understanding of our own minds. The rudiments of metacognition appear to develop around the same time in development as does theory of mind. This applies to both metamemory knowledge (explicit information about how memory works) and metamemory experience (the subjective feelings that accompany memory, such as confidence).

With respect to metamemory knowledge, consider a few of the "mnemonic hints" included in this textbook. Many of them are rather self-evident to an experienced college student. For example, that related items are easier to remember together than unrelated items is obvious to most college students. This leads to the hint that students seek out relations among the material they are studying because this elaboration improves memory. A fair developmental question is, "At what age do children become aware of the advantage of related information over unrelated information?" Another fair question might be, "At what age do children become aware that elaborative encoding leads to better memory performance than rote encoding?" Research suggests that children younger than 7 years old have little awareness of these obvious memory strategies but that by the second or third grade, most children have incorporated an accurate theory of memory (Schneider & Pressley, 1997). Moreover, recent research suggests that first-grade teachers who emphasize the development of metamemory skills wind up with students who learn faster by the end of first grade (Coffman, Ornstein, McCall, & Curran, 2008).

Children start to show the ability to monitor and control their memory based on metacognitive judgments in the early school-age years. Clearly, by the time most children are in second grade, they know which material is easy or difficult for them. But it is also around this age that metacognitive experiences can be channeled into explicit judgments such as judgments of learning. As we discussed in the chapter on metamemory, judgments of learning are predictions that people make as to the likelihood that they will remember an item later when asked to do so on a test. Judgments of learning are usually studied in the context of paired-associate learning. A person is given a pair of items (e.g., *leaf–city*) and later will have to remember the second word (*city*) when provided with the first word (*leaf*). Research shows that children are able to make accurate judgments of learning by the time they are in kindergarten, although older children tend to be more accurate. Remember here that accuracy means the relation between the magnitude of the judgment (high or low) and the correctness of the answer. A high-magnitude judgment followed by a correct answer is accurate, as is a low-magnitude judgment followed by an incorrect answer. Let's consider a representative study.

Schneider, Vise, Lockl, and Nelson (2000) examined the ability of kindergartners, second graders, and fourth graders to make judgments of learning. The children studied paired associates (pictures instead of words). The children made immediate judgments of learning for half of the picture pairs and delayed judgments of learning for the other half. Following study and judgments of learning on all items, the children were given a cued-recall test. Interestingly, all three groups of children showed the delayed judgment of learning effect—that is, their accuracy for the delayed judgments of learning was greater than it was for immediate judgments of learning. Also of interest and perhaps a surprise, there were no differences in accuracy among the age groups. All groups were above chance in predicting performance, but the kindergartners were as good as the older children. Other studies have, however, found developmental trends in the accuracy of judgments of learning. Koriat and Shitzer-Reichert (2002) found that fourth-grade children gave more accurate judgments of learning than did second-grade children. The conclusion that can be made from these studies is that judgments of learning are accurate by the early elementary years and probably improve in accuracy as children move from first grade through fourth grade. But because this accuracy increase is in dispute, it is likely that accuracy improvements are, at best, small and that judgments of learning are "on-line" by the time a child is in second grade.

Metacognitive control is defined as the ability to use metacognitive knowledge or experience to influence learning behaviors. Thus, a college student who does not feel that she has sufficiently mastered the material for an exam will choose to spend more time studying the material in advance of the test. Data were just presented that show that young children can accurately monitor their learning. But can they also use that monitoring to successfully control their learning? We discussed the strengths and weaknesses of adult metacognitive control in Chapter 9. Indeed, even elementary school age children show evidence of metacognitive control. That is, they use the output of their monitoring to control their study behavior. Children in the second grade will spend more time studying items that they gave low judgments of learning to (i.e., judged to be more difficult) than items that they gave high judgments of learning to (i.e., judged to be easier items). In one study, children were given the opportunity to allocate study time after initially making judgments of learning. Both second- and fourth-grade children chose the more difficult items to restudy (Schneider & Lockl, 2008).

Overconfidence in Judgments

Overconfidence in judgments means that people's judgments overestimate the likelihood that they will remember a to-be-learned item or set of items. It can refer to either a judgment that a person will answer a particular question correctly or a judgment as to how well that person will master a large set of materials. If the judgments are greater than the actual performance, overconfidence has occurred.

> **Overconfidence in judgments**: people's judgments overestimate the likelihood that they will remember a to-be-learned item or set of items.

You do not have to spend much time with a 6-year-old to see evidence of overconfidence. Many young children will assert that they possess skills that they could not possibly have yet. For example, some time ago, I played chess with a 6-year-old relative. I assured him before we started that I knew he was a good chess player and I would not go easy on him. He assured me that he would win every game. His overconfidence was such that he thought he could reliably beat an experienced adult chess player.

Metacognition researchers have examined this issue in a number of important experiments. For example, Shin, Bjorkland, and Beck (2007) asked children in kindergarten to estimate how many pictures they would be able to remember out of a set of 15 pictures. Following judgment and study, the children tried to recall the names of the pictures they had seen. They then repeated the process on a new set of pictures. Despite the experience and feedback they received on the earlier sets, their judgments of learning were equally overconfident on all trials. That is, not only were they overconfident on the first set, but they did not learn from the feedback that their actual performance was likely to be lower, and the children continued to give high judgments. Such overconfidence is not unusual—it has been demonstrated in a variety of situations in children (see Dunlosky & Metcalfe, 2009).

Shin et al. (2007) argued that—in children at any rate—overconfidence is adaptive. Young children must learn how to do a great many things, many of which they will fail at initially. Consider whether or not my 6-year-old relative would have wanted to play chess with me if he was certain that he would lose every game. Overconfidence provides children with a psychological buffer to deal with failure. Even though they may not be successful, they still think they will be the next time. To support this position, Shin et al. point out that those children who showed the greatest level of overconfidence in the initial trial also showed the greatest level of improvement in their actual performance. Alternatively, Dunlosky and Metcalfe (2009) label this overconfidence the "wishful-thinking" hypothesis, in which children substitute their desire to do well for their actual performance.

Metamemory and the Strategic Use of Memory

In this chapter, we have discussed the development of memory strategies and the development of metamemory. These two concepts are closely related. Recall that memory strategies are the conscious activities a person engages in to assist the remembering of information, where metamemory is the awareness and knowledge of our own memory. Defined in this way, metamemory should provide information that would be helpful to the development of memory strategies. Siegler (1999) argued that some memory strategies are based on simple associations; that is, children continue to engage in behaviors that have been successful. However, Siegler also argued that other memory strategies are based on metamemory. To support this proposition, Cavanaugh and Borkowski (1980) found that elementary school-age students who demonstrated greater metamemory knowledge also showed a more effective use of memory strategies.

A GUIDE TO DEVELOPING MEMORY SKILLS IN YOUNG CHILDREN

Memory is often viewed as an innate ability; some people are good at it, others are poor at it, and these cannot be changed. However, the research suggests otherwise. People of all ages can train their memories, using strategies and metamemory to facilitate their learning. Moreover, practice itself improves the efficiency of memory systems.

This is certainly true for young children. We have seen in this chapter that memory conversations between parents and children can strengthen children's episodic memory (Peterson et al., 2007). Cultural differences in autobiographical memory clearly reflect cultural leaning, not innate differences among ethnic groups (Q. Wang & Fivush, 2005). By and large, episodic memory is not trained in the school setting, as is information in semantic memory, such as concepts and categories that are more relevant in school. Nonetheless, frequent practice rehearsing information from episodic memory helps build a strong episodic memory system.

Although some of the improvement in memory across childhood has to do with the maturation of the child's brain (Bauer, 2002) and the speed of cognitive processing (Hale, 1990), much of it has to do with the learning of memory strategies and the development of metacognition (Dunlosky & Metcalfe, 2009). Certainly, in the later elementary school years, memory strategies can be taught, and children who use them learn faster (Pressley & Hilden, 2006).

Coffman et al. (2008) compared two groups of teachers in a naturalistic study. One group of teachers seldom referred to memory strategies and ways in which their first-grade children could learn faster. Rather, this group of teachers focused on content rather than process. A second group of teachers often referred to such strategies. Although this group also focused on content, there was more attention to process. When Coffman et al. tested these children at the end of first grade, the ones in the process-oriented classrooms acquired new information more quickly.

SUMMARY

We do not come into the world with our memory systems fully operational. They grow and develop as we do. Evidence suggests that learning and memory processes operate very early on, perhaps even before birth. There is a great amount of learning during the first year of life, although very little of it is actually declarative memory. Nonetheless, data show infants before the age of 1 year are learning words, rules of syntax, concepts, and categories, as well as a myriad number of perceptual associations. These are further strengthened in the second year of life with an incredible surge in the memory of words in the infant's native language.

Preschool years are marked by the beginnings of episodic memory. Although many researchers previously thought that episodic memory did not begin to develop until the school years, ample data suggest that young children can learn and retain event information. In the preschool years, we see the continued growth of working memory and the beginnings of the use of memory strategies. As children begin school, their memory processes are becoming faster and more efficient, and they are learning to use memory strategies and developing their metamemory skills. Events are encoded into episodic memory in such a manner as they can be retrieved later when the child becomes an adult. As children enter adolescence, their memories are more guided by the use of meaning-based strategies at encoding. This further strengthens their ability to encode and retain information. However, it also leads older children to experience more meaning-based false memories. Research shows that children, especially younger children, are highly prone to suggestion. This has led to the claim that young children should not be treated as reliable witnesses.

Metacognition also develops over the childhood years. The beginning of metamemory parallels the beginnings of theory of mind. Children around the age of 5 years pass the false-belief test. It is about the same age that children start making accurate metamemory judgments. Metamemory judgments, such as judgments of learning, improve over the first few years of grade school. Metamemory control also improves over this period. Overconfidence is often seen in young children's judgments. Improvement in metamemory predicts improvement in memory recall in children, suggesting that metamemory is important to the development of memory.

KEY TERMS

Memory efficiency view	Nonnutritive sucking	Metamemory
Memory strategies view	Conjugate reinforcement technique	Theory of mind
Memory conversations		False-belief test
Visual recognition	Imitation	Overconfidence in judgments

REVIEW QUESTIONS

1. Describe three methods that are used to investigate memory in infancy. How does each attribute learning to the growing infant?

2. Why is episodic memory nearly impossible to examine in infants younger than 1 year of age?

3. What is meant by the terms *memory strategies* and *memory efficiency?* How does each shape the development of memory in young children?

4. Describe a study that supports the idea that young children have episodic memory. Does this study support the idea that young children can remember over the childhood amnesia barrier?

5. What are memory conversations? How do they shape the development of episodic memory in young children?

6. Why is testimony from young children not considered reliable? What evidence supports this claim?

7. Why do older children show more false memories in the DRM paradigm?

8. What is meant by the term *theory of mind?* How is it tested in young children?

9. At what age do children start making accurate judgments of learning? Do judgments of learning accuracy continue to improve with age?

10. What is meant by the term *overconfidence?* How might it be adaptive for young children to be overconfident?

ONLINE RESOURCES

1. For more on eye tracking in infants, go to http://www.psychology.uiowa.edu/labs/maclab/references.asp#infantet.

2. For more information on Judy DeLoache's research, go to http://www.faculty.virginia.edu/deloache.

3. For more on the relation of early childhood memory and later childhood amnesia, go to http://www.apa.org/science/psa/sb-bauer.html.

4. For more on Qi Wang's research, go to http://www.human.cornell.edu/che/HD/socialcognition.

5. For more on the high-profile case in California in which a woman who ran a child care center was accused of sexually molesting numerous children, go to http://www.law.umkc.edu/faculty/projects/ftrials/mcmartin/mcmartin.html.

6. For the transcript of an interview with Dr. Ceci, go to http://www.pbs.org/wgbh/pages/frontline/shows/terror/interviews/ceci.html.

7. For more on this topic and its relation to eyewitness memory, go to http://www.nsf.gov/news/news_summ.jsp?org=NSF&cntn_id=111230&preview=false.

8. For more on Dr. Otgaar's research, go to http://www.personeel.unimaas.nl/henry.otgaar.

Go to www.sagepub.com/schwartz for additional exercises and study resources. Select **Chapter 11, Memory in Childhood** for chapter-specific resources.

CHAPTER 12

Memory in Older Adults

Jane Y is 75 years old. She retired 5 years ago after teaching art education at the high school level for over 40 years. She also taught art instruction at the local community college and wrote a book on art instruction, which is still used in the public schools in her state. Since retiring, she has kept active by gardening, reading a novel a week, taking courses at the local community college in the "seniors in education" program with her husband, also retired, and by baby-sitting her various grandchildren whenever possible. What bothers Jane is that she seems to be forgetful. She forgets appointments, she forgets if she has reordered her cholesterol medicine, and she sometimes pauses before calling each grandchild by the right name. She visited a highly respected neurologist in the closest big city, who did a scan of her brain and told her everything looked good and that she should not worry about her memory. The doctor told her that being a little forgetful is normal for someone her age. Nonetheless, the worries persist.

Should Jane be concerned? Is Jane really more forgetful than she was when she was younger, or is she simply more aware of the failures of her memory when they occur? Or is her forgetfulness a harbinger of bad things to come? Is poor Jane Y going senile or succumbing to Alzheimer's disease? Should she be worried despite the clean bill of health given her by the neurologist? Is there anything she can do to restore her memory to its youthful vigor and strength? These are just some of the questions seniors ask themselves when they feel that their memory is "not as good as it once was" (see Figure 12.1).

For most of us, preserved memory function is seen as vital to maintaining health and competence in older adults. The ability to remember is so crucial to so many aspects of human life. Memory provides us with our sense of identity, an ability to keep track of the things that are vital to our survival (money, food, medicines, clothing, etc.), and a way of avoiding deception (older adults are often the target of scammers). Thus, the prospect of having diminished memory abilities can cause concern in even the least hypochondriacally challenged older adult. So it should come as no surprise that many older adults are themselves most concerned with memory loss. When they find themselves unable to recall a specific word or event when called upon to do so, they worry about the consequences. Indeed, they may worry that each memory failure is an omen of further decline to come. Thus, it is important to separate fact from fiction in this chapter. Thus, again, our focus is on the science of memory, and in this case, that means examining the empirical findings on aging and memory.

Figure 12.1 Healthy older adults have functional memory systems.

This chapter will discuss change in normal healthy aging only. In Chapter 10, we considered the many forms of memory loss that accompany brain damage. Many of these forms of brain damage, particularly an increased risk of stroke and increased likelihood of developing Alzheimer's disease, are associated with being older. These conditions and illnesses can be devastating to older adults. But most old adults have healthy brains, albeit older brains, and the majority of seniors will never develop Alzheimer's. This chapter concerns the developmental changes that occur in healthy older adults. For a comparison of healthy and unhealthy brains, go to www.sagepub.com/schwartz.[1]

Certainly, in our culture, we have a stereotype of older adults as being more forgetful and having memory deficits relative to younger adults (Zacks & Hasher, 2006). How many movies have you seen in which a joke is made about an older person forgetting a vital piece of information? What this chapter will consider is in what domains older adults really do have worse memories than their juniors and in what ways they are equal or superior to those younger than themselves.

As memory scientists, we want to know: Is this stereotype true? Are there memory deficits associated with old age? Do all older adults experience them or only some people? It is probably unavoidable in American culture not to have some negative stereotypes about memory and cognition in older adults. The student reading this textbook might consider writing down some of his or her own before continuing with the text. Then, you can compare your views before reading the chapter to those afterward. Most readers of this book are younger adults, but college students hopefully will become senior citizens in time. Thus, the issue of memory and aging will eventually affect of all of us.

By this point, you should also know that memory comes in many flavors (e.g., working memory, autobiographical memory, episodic memory, lexical memory, semantic memory). You should also know that there are many processes involved in producing and retrieving memories (encoding, retrieval, source monitoring, etc.). Thus, it is sensible to suspect that older adults may have declines in some aspects of memory (e.g., ease of retrieval) but may have no declines or even advantages in other areas (general semantic knowledge). In reviewing the science, we will see areas in which older adults show declines relative to their younger peers. But we will also examine areas in which age-related declines are seldom seen in normal aging. In some areas, in fact, older adults outperform younger adults (word knowledge, for example).

Table 12.1 lists some of the areas in which older adults can expect declines relative to their younger peers or to when they themselves were younger. It also lists areas in which age either has little to no effect (implicit memory and metamemory) or improvements continue with age (semantic memory and lexical knowledge). Each of these areas will be discussed at length. First, however, the theories that guide memory and aging research will be introduced. These theories attempt to explain how memory changes in older adults and why it does so. That is, these theories are developmental in nature. They attempt to explain the changes that occur to memory as we grow older.

Table 12.1   Most older adults are healthy with healthy memories.
Memory declines:
Working memory
Encoding into and retrieval from episodic memory
Source monitoring
Prospective memory
Constant or improvements:
Implicit memory
Metamemory
Lexical knowledge
Semantic memory

THEORIES OF AGING AND MEMORY

Processing Speed

Processing speed theory postulates that age-related declines occur because the older person's cognitive processing does not work as quickly as those of younger adults. Because the speed of processing slows down, it will take people longer to learn new information, and it will take longer to retrieve information already stored in memory. Both of these slowed processes can result in relatively weaker memory performance. This general slowing leads to deficits in those memory-specific domains that require encoding of new information and rapid retrieval of existing information. The processing view does not predict deficits in memory performance that is untimed and does not require recall. For example, self-paced recognition tests should not show any deficits.

> **Processing speed**: age-related declines are caused because the older person's cognitive processing does not work as quickly as those of younger adults.

This view likens memory to a physical skill. In general, younger adults have quicker reflexes and stronger muscles than do older adults. As one grows older, one loses quickness, and it takes longer to build muscle. The processing speed hypothesis suggests that this slowing also occurs with respect to cognitive processes. In this view, memory declines occur because the individual can no longer process new information as fast, leading to declines in working memory and declines in the speed of encoding. However, it also suggests that when older adults have ample time to study or process information, their performance may be no weaker than those of younger adults. In fact, in many cognitive tasks, older adults can perform just as accurately as younger adults, but each response takes them a bit more time.

Studies that measure reaction time show age-related declines (J. McCabe & Hartman, 2008). For example, in tasks in which participants must make speeded decisions, such as lexical decision tasks, older adults will perform more slowly than younger adults (see Figure 12.2). Salthouse (1996) asked younger and older adults to make perceptual comparisons as fast as possible. These involved deciding whether two letters in different fonts (c, C) are the same or whether two pictures are the same. The participants were expected to make these judgments as fast as they possibly could. When reaction times were examined, there was a consistent advantage for younger adults over older adults. Speed of processing also predicted performance on a host of memory tasks within each age group. Those older adults who were faster at the perceptual comparison tasks also did better in working memory and episodic memory tasks (Salthouse, 1996).

In order for any theory to be useful, it must be predictive across a range of situations. The processing speed theory meets this expectation. Consider memory for music. Older adults, relative to younger adults, have more difficulty recognizing melodies when they are played at a fast tempo than when they are played at a slower tempo (Dowling, Bartlett, Halpern, & Andrews, 2008). That is, when the melody is played slowly, there are no differences in recognition between younger and older adults, but when the music is sped up, older adults cannot follow it as well, and their performance goes down relative to the younger adults. Indeed, on a great many other cognitive tasks, younger adults can react more quickly (see Salthouse, 1996). For more on Dr. Salthouse's research, go to www.sagepub.com/schwartz.[2]

Figure 12.2 Younger adults make faster lexical decisions than do older adults. The y-axis represents reaction time measured in seconds.

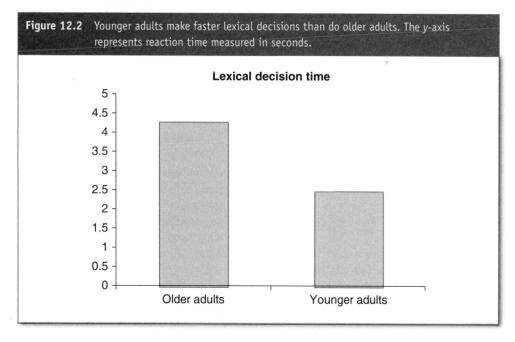

Figure 12.3 Recognition as a function of age and speed of tempo. The y-axis represents percent recognized.

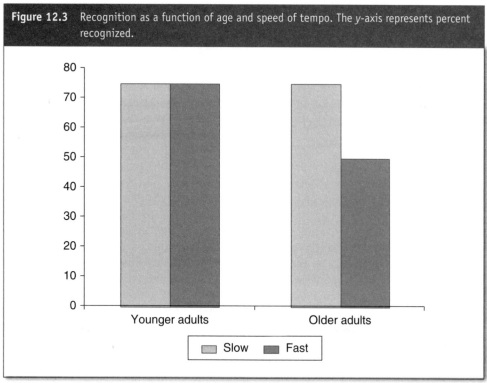

Inhibition Theory

Inhibition theory argues that older adults do not have a good ability to block out irrelevant stimulation. This means that the memory declines seen in old age are a consequence of poor attentional processes. Younger adults can more easily block out competing sources of information, such as background noise, and focus on the task at hand. Older adults, by contrast, cannot direct their attention as well among a host of competing sources of information. This is perhaps why parents tell their teenage or college children to put away the headphones while studying—because the parents can no longer concentrate on learning with music in the background. By contrast, listening to music may be less distracting for the teenager or college student. Although this example simplifies both the cognitive aspects of inhibition and the complexity of parent-child interactions, it gives a sense of what inhibition means. Younger adults are better at blocking out irrelevant stimuli than are older adults.

> **Inhibition theory**: older adults do not have a good ability to block out irrelevant stimulation. This means that the memory declines seen in old age are a consequence of poor attentional processes. Inhibition also means the ability to suppress the retrieval of irrelevant information.

Inhibition also means the ability to suppress the retrieval of irrelevant information. For example, when older adults attempt to retrieve a name, such as the name of a grandchild, they have difficulties in inhibiting other names (of other grandchildren). Thus, the grandparent may need extra time to sort through the additional names that are accidentally retrieved, or it may lead to the older adult inadvertently using the wrong name. It is not that the older adult does not know the name of his or her grandchild; it is just that it is harder to suppress the other names that are also retrieved. Younger adults are less plagued by the accidental retrieval of related but incorrect information.

Evidence of inhibition problems come from directed forgetting studies. In **directed forgetting,** participants are asked to remember some information but are explicitly told to forget other information (Bjork & Woodward, 1973). Directed forgetting experiments require participants to first study some items and then try to forget them. In experiments, it usually involves the presentation of a list of words for participants to study. After the participants study the words, the experimenters "apologize" and tell the participants that they gave the participants the wrong

> **Directed forgetting**: the inhibition in memory that occurs when people are asked to forget some information but not other information.

list. Forget that list, the researchers say, because you need to study this other list. Surprisingly, most people will succeed at this task, and recall of the to-be-forgotten list is worse than it is in control conditions. However, there are differences between younger and older adults. Younger adults are better able to inhibit the to-be-forgotten words than are older adults. Older adults have difficulties with directed forgetting, ironically, leading to better recall of the to-be-forgotten information (Andrés, Van der Linden, & Parmentier, 2004).

A powerful demonstration of the success of inhibition theory to explain age-related memory declines comes from Darowski, Helder, Zacks, Hasher, and Hambrick (2008). Darowski et al. asked younger and older participants to read short texts. Some of these texts contained irrelevant and distracting words embedded in otherwise meaningful sentences. For example, consider the following sentence: "Jane Goodall has studied chimpanzee behavior for many years at Gombe Stream National Park in the African nation of Tanzania." Hopefully, this is an easy and informative sentence. Now compare your fluency in reading that sentence as compared to this one: "Jane Goodall *clerk* has studied *Kansas* chimpanzee *definition* behavior *lunch* for many *clones* years at Gombe *blanket* Stream National *whisker* Park in the *pine* African nation *reverse* of Tanzania." Obviously, the insertion of irrelevant words in italics makes the sentence more difficult to decipher. With some work, most of us can figure out what the sentence about Jane Goodall is about. However, Darowski et al. found that older adults were more affected by the irrelevant stimuli than were younger adults. Their reading times were slower than younger adults, and they remembered less from the passages than did younger adults. In essence, the younger adults were better able to screen out or inhibit the irrelevant words, allowing them to process the information in the sentences. The older adults struggled with the irrelevant stimuli. Thus, deficits in inhibition, like slower processing speed, may account for some of the age-related declines in memory in aging.

Decline in the Strategic Use of Memory

A third theory of memory and aging argues that declines in memory are a function of a declining use of appropriate memory strategies (e.g., Craik, Morris, & Gick, 1990; Navah-Benjamin, Cowan, Kilb, & Chen, 2007). This means that older adults are less likely to explicitly use strategies that will help their encoding and retrieval, such as elaboration, imagery, mnemonics, and appropriate distribution of study time. It is based on the finding that older adults have control deficits with respect to working memory that might interfere with strategy use. Craik et al. (1990) claimed that older adults engage in less self-initiated strategies. When instructed to use memory strategies, they will, but left on their own, they use them less often than do younger adults. Navah-Benjamin et al. (2007) showed that older adults used less chunking than did younger adults in a working memory task. They suspected that relative impairment in the frontal lobe may lead to few memory strategies being used and a decrease in metamemory ability. For more on this topic, go to www.sagepub.com/schwartz.[3] However, this view is no longer in favor. In particular, many studies now show that metamemory shows no or very few declines in older adults. Dunlosky and Metcalfe (2009) argued that there are domains in which older adults show decreased metamemory, but in general, preserved metamemory abilities allow older adults to maintain high functioning. With respect to both judgments of learning and feelings of knowing, older adults are as accurate as younger participants. Thus, metamemory monitoring remains excellent among older adults. Preserved metamemory function suggests that older adults continue to maintain good strategic use of memory.

As in most issues in human memory, the answer is complex. Therefore, age-related memory declines are likely to be a combination of slower processing speed and reduced ability to inhibit irrelevant stimuli, although probably not because of declining use of memory strategies. With that in mind, we will turn our focus to specific components of memory and how they are affected by aging.

AGE-RELATED CHANGES IN WORKING MEMORY

Working memory is the short-term memory system that maintains information for conscious introspection over relatively short time intervals (up to 15 seconds). Although working memory is generally considered a separate neurocognitive system from long-term memory systems, information must be held in working memory during encoding and also during retrieval. Therefore, it is possible, and indeed many researchers have argued, that deficits in working memory in older adults are also responsible for the deficits seen in long-term memory (Craik & Byrd, 1982; Salthouse, 2000). These deficits in working memory may arise from the general reduction in processing speed seen in older adults. Then, because older adults may be slower with respect to working memory, it may mean that information is less likely to reach the long-term memory systems.

To review from Chapter 3, working memory is composed of three major systems. The phonological loop maintains information about auditory stimuli, whereas the visuospatial sketchpad maintains information about visual stimuli. When task difficulty increases or simultaneous processing is required, the central executive allocates attentional resources to the appropriate system. It is the central executive system that seems to be most negatively affected by age. In working memory tasks that require central executive components (i.e., directing attention among competing stimuli), older adults find themselves at a disadvantage. Thus, in dual-processing tasks, older adults are impaired relative to younger adults. Central executive deficits may also be the function of reduced ability to inhibit competing sources of information. Because in dual tasks, participants must figure out a manner in which to attend to two or more competing sources, being able to inhibit one while focused on the other is important. Deficits in the ability to inhibit competing sources will show up as executive deficits.

In some working memory tasks, particularly those that tap the phonological loop, older adults perform just as well as younger adults. Consider the standard digit span task. A participant hears a list of numbers and must repeat them back immediately in order, as in the famous magic-number-seven experiment (Miller, 1956). Most young adults can maintain about seven items in working memory. However, older adults do just as well as younger adults in this task (Dixon & Cohen, 2003). It is likely that because the digit span task mostly uses the phonological loop, it requires little input from central executive processes in working memory. This leads to equivalent performance between healthy old and young participants.

However, in tasks for which the central executive is an important component, age becomes an issue, with older adults performing less well than younger adults. Consider the following experiment by Göthe, Oberauer, and Kliegl (2007), which nicely illustrates the deficits in older adults. They compared younger and older adults in two tasks. One task was a visuomotor task in which participants had to mentally track the location of an arrow as it moved to various marked locations on a computer screen. When the arrow reached a predetermined location, the participants were expected to press the space bar. This task is fairly easy to do, but it does require attention. When older and younger adults were tested on this task, both were able to learn it and perform it at a criterion level, although younger adults were faster at learning it than were the older adults. The second task was a simple numerical task, that is, to add a number to a preexisting sum every time the participant heard a tone. Certain tones were associated with certain numbers. Thus, a high-pitch tone might mean 8, whereas a low-pitch tone might mean 5. A high-pitch tone followed by a low-pitch tone would mean a sum of 13. Another high-pitch tone would mean 21. This task employs the phonological loop as the participants had to maintain the sums in their head without writing them down. Again, the task is relatively easy but requires attention and some problem-solving ability. Both older and younger adults learned this task with equal ease, although younger adults were faster in performing the task, consistent with their general advantage in processing speed. Note that the first task involves using the visuospatial sketchpad, and the second task requires the use of the phonological loop. Thus, both tasks involve working memory processes. In each task, despite a speed advantage for the younger adults, the older adults were able to learn the task and perform it accurately. Once the task had been learned, there were no differences in performance between the older and younger adults—as long as the tasks were done individually.

A second group of participants, both old and young, was asked to learn the two tasks simultaneously and then asked to perform the tasks simultaneously. After considerable practice, the younger adults were able to learn the task and to perform the task simultaneously without any costs in speed at either task. This took much more practice than had been necessary to learn the tasks individually—but they did learn the task. That is, they could perform both tasks at the same time as fast as they could each task when doing it alone. However, not one of the older adults could reach this level of performance! The demands on their central executive were just too great. Whereas the older adults were as good as the younger adults when the tasks were done alone, they were at a huge disadvantage when the tasks were required to be completed together. In fact, the older adults could only complete the study by alternating from one task to the other, whereas the younger adults appeared to be successfully dual tasking, essentially doing both tasks at once. Göthe et al. (2007) conclude that the differences reflect differences in executive control on working memory tasks. Many other studies find similar findings between old and young adults in dual-task performance (see Riby, Perfect, & Stollery, 2004).

This experiment appears quite complicated and removed from real-world experience. If you did not get the procedures and conclusions, reread the above paragraph and make sure you understand what Göthe et al. (2007) were doing. Study it until you understand—your professor just may ask a question about it on the next exam. But, in fact, it does have some real-world applications too! Think about how often you engage in dual tasks, trying to do two or more things at once. Perhaps you have listened to music while studying for class or watched the football game on television while cooking for your family. Perhaps the most ubiquitous dual processing occurs when we drive. Driving a car is a visuomotor task; it requires your eyes on the road and your hands on the steering wheel. However, it leaves your mouth and ears free to do other things. Many of us listen to music or speak on our cell phones while we are driving. Research suggests that speaking on a cell phone can cause driving failures even in young adults (Strayer & Drews, 2007), as attentional resources must be redistributed from driving to talking. The Göthe et al. (2007) study suggests that older adults might even be more at risk when trying to talk and drive at the same time because they have a reduced ability to allocate attention to multiple sources. Older people may be just as good at driving (and just as good at speaking) as younger adults are. But when the two tasks are combined, their performance may suffer relative to younger adults.

Cell phone use while driving is an obvious application of the dual-task findings, but there are other implications for older adults as well. Consider the busy life of a medical doctor. He or she might have to examine magnetic resonance imaging (MRI) scans while simultaneously giving advice to a resident walking alongside. The data on dual-task performance suggest that older doctors might want to do one task, then the other task, in a linear fashion to remain competent. The resident, on the other hand, still in his or her late 20s, might be able to do both. The point here is that older adults can do tasks equally well as younger adults but that multitasking can be more difficult.

To summarize, older adults have deficits in working memory, but these deficits tend to be related to the reduced capacity of the central executive. The visuospatial sketchpad and the phonological loop are less affected by age-related declines.

SEMANTIC MEMORY AND LEXICAL MEMORY

Aging has little effect on **semantic memory** tasks. Most studies point to the preserved nature of representation of information in semantic memory. Indeed, in studies in which general knowledge is tested (politics, history, sports, etc.), older adults typically outperform younger adults (Dixon, Rust, Feltmate, & See, 2007). The one caveat here is that older adults do report more memory blocks in which they cannot recall an item of information that they are sure they know and can later recognize. That is, older adults find that they cannot recall information that they think they should know—even though they can correctly recognize the

> **Semantic memory:** the neurocognitive memory system that encodes, stores, and retrieves information concerning knowledge of the world.

item they are searching for. In addition, older adults are slower in accessing information, but this probably has little to do with semantic memory per se but rather general processing speed. Similarly, older adults tend to have larger vocabularies than do younger adults. A lifetime of learning new words appears to be resistant to forgetting (Dahlgren, 1998). Thus, semantic memory and lexical memory are domains in which older adults outperform younger adults.

EPISODIC MEMORY

"I can't remember if I took my blood pressure pill or not." "I forgot my lunch date with my cousin Estelle." "I forgot to turn the stove off, and if it wasn't for my son coming over to visit, I might have burned the house down." These are some of the complaints older adults have

Episodic memory: the neurocognitive memory system that encodes, stores, and retrieves memories of our personal individual experiences.

about their memory problems. You will note that all of these are failures of episodic memory. **Episodic memory** is the domain of memory in which older adults most often complain of declines. In fact, these self-perceptions are validated by the research. Even in healthy older adults, episodic memory declines do occur, both in encoding and retrieval (N. Anderson & Craik, 2000). But what is the nature of these declines? Even within episodic memory, there are some areas in which performance is preserved, but there are declines in other areas.

Recall Versus Recognition

Recall involves the ability to produce the correct answer by generating that answer from retrieval. Recognition only requires one to match a presented stimulus to one's memory of the original event. In general, recognition is therefore considered the easier test, as it can be done on the basis of familiarity without necessarily requiring specific recollection from the original event. Familiarity seems to be unaffected by aging, but recollection is impaired in aging. Therefore, it is likely that recognition will be relatively spared in older adults, whereas recall may show impairments. In general, the research supports this, suggesting that the ability to recall information declines with age but that recognition performance remains relatively stable (see Figure 12.4). This is true for information learned earlier, such as autobiographical memory. It is also true for new learning. That older adults do as well as younger adults on recognition tests of newly learned information suggests that encoding processes can be as good in older adults as they are in younger adults. However, recall involves the inhibition of competing responses. Thus, recall will show more age-related deficits. In other words, older adults are encoding information; it is just more difficult for them to access that information relative to younger adults. Although with respect to recall, the total amount declines, the accuracy of older adults' memory reports does not decline. Let's look at each of these claims in turn.

Most studies find that older adults show roughly equivalent performance on recognition tests relative to younger adults. For example, Rhodes, Castel, and Jacoby (2008) asked both older and younger adults to study pairs of faces with the goal of being able to recognize that the two faces go together. In each pair, the participants studied a male and female face paired together. Later, the participants were given a recognition test. The cue was one of the faces from the male-female pairs, and the test choices were two faces, one of which was the actual pair seen at the time of study. The participant chose the face that matched his or her memory for the original pair. Older adults and younger adults performed at the same level in this task. Both groups of participants were good at identifying the matching face. Thus, this study demonstrates the similar performance of older and younger adults in a recognition task.

However, when recall tests are used to evaluate episodic memory, older adults typically have deficits relative to younger adults. In general, the findings here show that starting around age 40, adults tend to do progressively worse at recall tests than those younger than

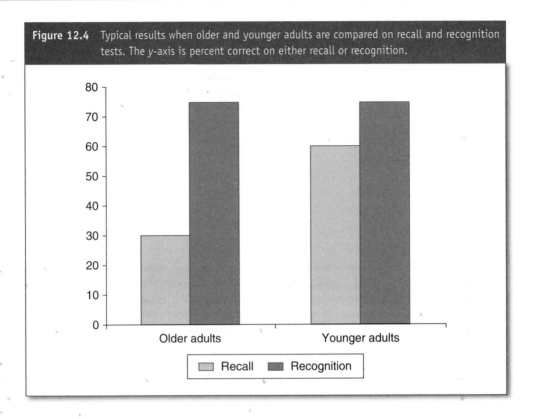

Figure 12.4   Typical results when older and younger adults are compared on recall and recognition tests. The *y*-axis is percent correct on either recall or recognition.

them. The effect may not be statistically large, but it is found in nearly every study. In one study, Dunlosky and Hertzog (1998) asked older and younger adults to study unrelated word pairs (*cat–fork*). Participants studied the items until all participants had mastered the items; this took a bit longer for the older participants. Later, when they returned for a recall test, the younger participants remembered more of the target words than did the older participants, even though all participants had learned all of the associations during initial learning. This study is one among many studies that point to age-related declines in recall from episodic memory.

Age differences occur in recall but not in recognition because recognition is largely based on familiarity, a process that may not be affected by the slowing associated with aging, nor is it likely to be affected by problems with inhibition. Recall, on the other hand, may suffer because the older adult has a more difficult time screening out other answers that come to mind that would be inhibited by younger adults. Given that, in a recall task, the person must generate the answer, it is also possible that the slower speed of retrieval in older adults means that less information will be recovered.

Memory Accuracy

Although the total amount of information in recall decreases in older adults, the accuracy of what older adults recall is not impaired relative to younger adults. What does this mean?

Well, if a younger adult recalls 20 words from a list, but two items are errors, he or she has a 90% hit rate. That is, 18 out of 20 are correct. The older adult may remember only 10 items, but 9 of those are correct. This gives the older adult the same hit rate—90%. Thus, even though the older adult has remembered fewer correct items, his or her accuracy remains the same. In simple free recall and cued recall tests, older adults and younger adults exhibit the same level of accuracy (Rhodes & Kelley, 2005).

Consider the implications of the above findings for eyewitness testimony. Because younger adults remember more details, they make better witnesses for the initial phases of investigation. The police investigators may get more leads from younger witnesses, although numerically more of these leads may be errors. However, in a courtroom, an older witness is as likely to remember as accurately as the younger witness. Thus, what an older witness reports during testimony is as likely to be accurate as the testimony of a younger adult.

There is a caveat here—older adults are more susceptible to misleading and deceptive information, and this has a greater effect on their accuracy than it does on younger adults (Rhodes & Kelley, 2005). Thus, as with young children, investigators must be careful not to make suggestive statements to their oldest witnesses. As long as one is certain that the witnesses were not tampered with, then the older witness is as good as the younger witness.

It is important to note that older adults are individuals, and each individual is unique. And, as in every domain of psychology, there are individual differences. In this sense, one should never judge an individual's memory abilities by his or her age. The distributions overlap—and any individual older adult may outperform an individual younger adult. In cognitive psychology, we do our best to make generalizations about trends and patterns while remembering that individual differences exist. Indeed, there are factors that lead some older adults to have more memory loss than others. Education and verbal ability, for example, mitigate age-related declines (Manly, Touradji, Tang, & Stern, 2003).

FALSE MEMORY IN OLDER ADULTS

When nonsuggestive methods are used, older adults will demonstrate equivalent memory accuracy to younger adults. However, older adults are more susceptible to a host of memory illusions caused by suggestive statements, misattribution of source, and associative meaning. Each of these memory illusions can result in lower accuracy of the older adult's memory report. We will consider each of these forms of memory illusions in this section.

Suggestibility

One of the major sources of false memories is suggestibility. A generation of research has shown how misleading information can affect people's memory for an event (Loftus, 1979, 2004). These findings were discussed in detail in Chapter 8. In the misinformation paradigm, a person witnesses a crime by watching videotape or some other media and then later receives postevent information about the event, often via a questionnaire. Some of the questions on the questionnaire contain misleading information about the event. The misinformation effect comes about because people are more likely to falsely remember the event if they received misinformation.

Older adults are more likely to make errors based on misleading suggestions. In one study using the classic misinformation paradigm, Karpel, Hoyer, and Toglia (2001) showed older and younger participants a slideshow depicting a crime. Later, the participants were given questions about the event. Some of the questions had misleading information, such as, "Did you see the thief kick the garbage can in anger?" when no garbage can had been actually present in the slideshow. Following questioning, the participants were given a recognition test in which they had to select the correct answer from alternatives. In the recognition test, older participants showed a bigger misinformation effect than did younger participants. The older adults were more likely to misremember, for example, that they had seen a garbage can. Thus, older adults are more susceptible to suggestive information and are more likely therefore to demonstrate false memories when misinformation is presented. For more on this topic, go to www.sagepub.com/schwartz.[4]

Misattribution of Source

Source memory refers to the ability of an individual to remember from whom or where

> **Source memory**: refers to the ability of an individual to remember from whom or where (that is, what source) they learned something.

(that is, what source) he or she learned something. For example, you may know that your cousin is coming to visit next week. That is the basic memory; that you heard this tidbit of information from your mother is the source memory. Many studies have shown that older adults have a deficit in source monitoring. For example, they are more likely to think that an imagined event was real and more likely to confuse the source of a real memory (Henkel, Johnson, & De Leonardis, 1998).

Source monitoring deficits in older adults are widespread. For example, older adults have a more difficult time than younger adults in distinguishing perceptually similar sources as well as conceptually similar sources. Perceptually similar sources would include remembering hearing a story from one person with a similar voice to another. Conceptually similar sources would include remembering hearing in one newspaper rather than another. Older adults are also more likely to make source errors if their attention is divided (Henkel et al., 1998). However, these source errors do not extend to all kinds of tasks. One study found that when older and younger adults had to make judgments of whether statements were true based on where they had heard the statements (i.e., from someone they knew was telling the truth or someone they knew was lying), older adults performed just as well as younger adults (Rahhal, May, & Hasher, 2002).

This last study is important because it is well known that scammers often target older adults thinking that they will be more likely to be deceived. Given the prevalence of identity theft in today's digital world, attributing falsehood to remembered statements that are, in fact, false is important. That older adults are not more likely to think a false statement is true than do younger adults is fortunate. It suggests that older adults may not be more vulnerable than younger adults to scams that capitalize on a person's willingness to believe others.

Nonetheless, source errors can have negative consequences for older adults. If their memory for taking their medicine is based on an imagined memory of yesterday's pills, older adults may jeopardize their health by not taking their medicine. Moreover, if they cannot correctly attribute medical advice to their doctor and instead think it comes from the gossipy neighbor, they may follow incorrect health plans. Older adults, like younger adults, must be especially vigilant to attend to source in order to avoid these errors.

Associative Meaning

Associative meaning means the links that form among related concepts in semantic memory and how these associations can influence episodic memory. This avenue to false memories has typically been studied with the Deese-Roediger-McDermott (DRM) illusion, discussed in Chapter 8. Researchers have compared the rate of critical intrusions in the DRM illusion in younger and older participants. In the DRM illusion, participants study a list of words, all of which are related to an absent critical intrusion. Many people will falsely report the critical intrusion as being on the list. A large number of studies support the conclusion that older adults are more likely to recall the critical intrusion than are younger adults. In addition, when participants are warned of the likelihood of misremembering a critical lure, older adults are less able to resist recalling it anyway than younger adults (Jacoby & Rhodes, 2006; D. P. McCabe & Smith, 2002), consistent with the general deficit in inhibiting incorrect alternatives.

INTERIM SUMMARY

Many older adults are concerned about deficits in memory, and there are popular beliefs that memory declines in old age. However, the research shows that although there are some declines, mostly associated with episodic memory, other memory domains, such as semantic and lexical memory, remain intact. Three theories have been advanced to account for declines in memory. Decline in processing speed is supported by reaction time studies, which show slower reaction times for older adults. Inhibition theory is supported by showing that older adults have a more difficult time dividing their attention and blocking out irrelevant stimuli. Little data support the theory that the strategic use of memory declines in healthy older adults. Working memory shows age-related declines because of decreases in processing speed. Older adults are more susceptible to false memories, most likely because of older adults' deficits in source monitoring.

METAMEMORY IN OLDER ADULTS

Metamemory is our knowledge and awareness of our own memory. In the last chapter, we discussed how metamemory develops in children. In the section, we will examine metamemory in older adults. To review, metamemory consists of two main functional

Monitoring: our ability to reflect and become aware of what we know and what we do not.

Control (in metamemory): our ability to regulate our learning or retrieval based upon our own monitoring.

components: monitoring and control. **Monitoring** means the awareness or knowledge of whether our cognitive systems are successfully engaging in a particular task. Thus, if a person is confident that he or she is going to remember something, that confidence reflects his or her metacognitive monitoring. **Control** means the behaviors a person engages in to ensure encoding or retrieval. Thus, an older adult who wants to remember more of what he reads in the newspaper may choose to read more slowly than he used to and read without music playing in the background like he used to.

An important component of metamemory concerns beliefs that we have about our own memory systems. If people, for example, believe that they remember everything they read based on a single reading, they may be less inclined to reread chapters in advance of an exam. If they believe that they are not good at remembering names, they may make an extra effort to learn them. If older adults believe that they are having memory difficulties, they may make adjustments in the way they encode information. On the other hand, older people who believe that their memory is impaired may also choose to not try to remember new information. Thus, it is important to assess memory beliefs among older adults and then determine to what extent these beliefs correlate with actual memory performance. It is also important to consider how the beliefs themselves affect memory.

Dunlosky and Metcalfe (2009) summarized the results of numerous studies that assess older adults' beliefs about memory. These studies confirm a few assertions that many of us might assume to be self-evident with respect to memory and aging. These studies confirm that older adults believe that their memories are not as good as those of younger people, that their memories are not as good as they used to be when they were younger, and that they have less control over the efficiency of their memory than they did when they were younger. Thus, in terms of their metacognitive beliefs about memories, Dunlosky and Metcalfe conclude that older adults tend to be pessimists; they believe in memory decline. However, as we have seen, memory does not universally decline in old age. Many areas of memory, such as semantic and lexical memory, remain intact in healthy older adults.

Do beliefs matter? Does it matter that older people think that their memories are better or worse than they once were or compared to that of other people? Yes, it does. It turns out that older adults do make decisions based on their self-perception of their own memory abilities. Consider two older adults—one who is confident in his or her memory ability and another who is not. The confident individual may be more likely to engage in memory-intensive pursuits, such as crossword puzzles or senior learning courses, than the person who is less confident in his or her memory abilities (Dunlosky & Metcalfe, 2009). Moreover, the older adults who believe that their memory is impaired may be less likely to engage in strategic memory behaviors, believing that it is pointless to work to remember something (Lachman & Andreoletti, 2006). Thus, there is some value in working to promote better memory beliefs among older adults; if they believe their memory is better, they will work harder to remember information. Working harder to learn and remember is obviously beneficial to people of any age. Of course, overconfidence is not desirable, but the belief that, with effort, information can be learned and mastered is certainly within the grasp of every healthy older adult.

Metamemory is also concerned with the monitoring of learning on individual to-be-learned items. Metamemory judgments can be made to assess whether we have learned a particular item or whether we think we are going to retrieve information. These are measured by the various judgments introduced in Chapter 9.

Judgments of Learning

One of the common metamemory judgments is the judgment of learning. **Judgments of learning** are made at the time of study and are predictions of the likelihood of remembering that item in the future. Generally, high judgments of learning indicate a prediction

> **Judgments of learning**: are made during study and are judgments of whether the item has been learned already.

that the item will be remembered, whereas low judgments of learning indicate a prediction that the item will not be remembered. Judgments of learning are important for several reasons—first, in younger adults, they have been shown to be highly accurate in some circumstances but less accurate in others. Judgments of learning have also been shown to be highly predictive of study behavior. That is, people use judgments of learning to allocate their study efforts to the difficult or to the easy items, depending on study constraints. Therefore, if we can direct people to situations in which their judgments of learning are predictive of performance, then their study behaviors will be effective.

Older adults, in general, believe that their memory ability is worse than it used to be when they were younger. But that is a global judgment. Do these beliefs affect older adults' ratings of individual items? We can use judgments of learning to ask if older adults also feel that they are less likely to remember each item. Furthermore, it is of interest if older adults are more, equal, or less accurate in their judgments relative to younger adults. If metamemory is largely intact in older adults, one might expect that older adults will give lower judgments of learning to most items, reflecting their impaired ability to learn, but that their accuracy will remain high and equivalent to younger adults, reflecting their preserved metamemory. We now turn to some empirical studies that have addressed these issues.

Hertzog, Kidder, Powell-Moman, and Dunlosky (2002) asked younger and older adults to study word pairs. Some of the word pairs were related (e.g., *cat–dog*), whereas other word pairs were unrelated (e.g., *buffalo–rocket*). During the study, both the younger and older adults made judgments of learning on the likelihood of recalling the second word when given the first word later as a cue. Subsequently, the participants were given a recall test for all of the pairs. Not surprisingly, given that all participants had the same amount of study time, the younger adults remembered more of the pairs than did the older adults. In keeping with this finding, the older adults gave lower judgments of learning overall than did the younger adults. This makes sense given that their overall ability to learn the items was less. Indeed, when Hertzog et al. looked at the accuracy of the judgments at predicting recall, the older adults showed just as good accuracy as the younger adults, and their accuracy equally benefited from a delay between study and test. This means that those items that were given high judgments of learning tended to be recalled, and those given low judgments of learning tended to be forgotten. This ability to accurately predict performance was equivalent for both groups. A number of other studies also confirm the observation that older adults' judgment of learning accuracy is equivalent to younger adults (see Dunlosky & Metcalfe, 2009) (see Figure 12.5). Thus, the bottom line here is that older adults' lower judgments of learning are adaptive—they remember fewer items than do younger adults. However, they know they will remember less, and therefore their judgments are just as accurate as the younger adults' judgments.

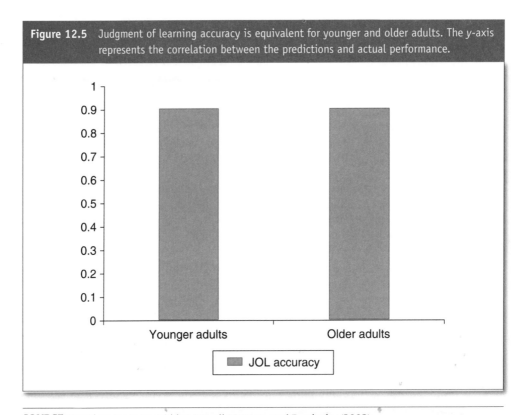

Figure 12.5 Judgment of learning accuracy is equivalent for younger and older adults. The *y*-axis represents the correlation between the predictions and actual performance.

SOURCE: Based on Hertzog, Kidder, Powell-Moman, and Dunlosky (2002).

The above results support the claim that older adults are just as good as younger adults in determining what they will learn and what they will not learn. This is the essence of metacognitive monitoring, the ability to predict one's performance. However, monitoring is only half of the metamemory equation. For metamemory to be functional, older adults must be able to use their monitoring accuracy as input for making sound decisions about learning and remembering; this is metacognitive control. That is, if older adults know that a particular item is difficult, will they spend more time studying that item than easier items? Will they do this similar to or different from younger adults?

It turns out that, although older adults are as good as younger adults at monitoring what they know and what they don't know, they are not as good at metacognitive control as younger adults (although this conclusion is debated). For example, in one study, Souchay and Isingrini (2004) asked a group of younger adults and a group of older adults to study a list of paired associates. For each pair, the participants also made a judgment of learning. After making judgments of learning for all the pairs, the participants were given an opportunity to restudy items. In the restudy phase, participants had control over how much time they would spend on each item. In other words, this study phase was self-paced. The question was whether older adults would restudy the items in the same way that younger adults do. And if older adults differed from the younger adults, would they be more or less successful in directing that control?

Souchay and Isingrini (2004) found that the younger adults remembered more of the word pairs than did the older adults. Obviously, this was expected. They also found that the older adults were equally accurate at predicting their performance as the younger adults, also in keeping with earlier studies. The critical measurement in this experiment, though, was the relation of the judgments of learning to the amount of time for which each item was restudied. Assuming that easy items require less study and more difficult items require more study, people should study items that are given lower judgments of learning for more time than the items given high judgments of learning. That is, a difficult pair such as *refuse–button* will receive a lower judgment of learning but require more time to associate in memory than an easier pair, such as *black–sheep*. Souchay and Isingrini found a negative correlation between judgments of learning and study time for both older and younger adults, but the effect was larger among the younger adults. That is, younger adults spent more time restudying the items with the lowest judgments of learning relative to the older adults. Older adults were more likely to choose items with higher judgments of learning for restudy.

Does this mean that the older adults have a deficit in metacognitive control? Well, probably not. First, both the older adults and the younger adults restudied more difficult items; the effect was greater in the younger adults but present in both groups. Second, other studies have shown smaller or no differences in the allocation of study time (see Dunlosky & Metcalfe, 2009). Third, it is not always the case that studying the most difficult items is the most adaptive pattern of restudy (Metcalfe & Kornell, 2005). If the items are particularly difficult, it is possible that no amount of restudy will guarantee that they will be remembered. Thus, especially difficult items, despite their low judgments of learning, should be avoided during restudy. Indeed, it is more efficient to restudy a known item to ensure you will not forget it than to study an item you have no chance of learning. Given the general better ability of younger adults to encode novel associations relative to older adults, there will be more of these self-judged impossible pairs for the older adults than for the younger adults. Avoiding the study of these difficult items will lower the correlation for the older adults but not for the younger adults, who may think these items are learnable. Then, the older adults can concentrate their study on relatively easier items that they might, in fact, be better able to remember. This was referred to as the region of proximal learning model in Chapter 9. Thus, the decision to study items with higher judgments of learning may be adaptive after all in older adults. Thus, it also possible to interpret the results of Souchay and Isingrini (2004) as supporting the hypothesis that older adults are as good at metacognitive control as are younger adults.

TOTs and Aging

Many studies show that, as people age, they experience more tip-of-the-tongue states (TOTs; see Gollan & Brown, 2006; Schwartz & Frazier, 2005). Indeed, many older adults can find TOTs to be a frustrating condition. Increased numbers of TOTs can occur because of two possible reasons. First, it may be that older adults have more retrieval failures for known words. This is consistent with the findings that older adults have difficulties in the recall of information. Second, older adults may be more aware of the retrieval failures they do have, consistent with the findings that older adults are more sensitive or pay more attention to memory failures and consistent with their beliefs about memory. There are data that suggest both come into play. The first theory is in line with the various memory declines that we have discussed in this chapter—that is, older adults have increased difficulty in word retrieval. Many studies show that the number of TOTs increases with age, as the ability to rapidly retrieve words declines (Heine, Ober, & Shenaut, 1999). The second view—that TOTs increase with age because older adults are more self-conscious of memory failures—is consistent with the view that older adults have strong metamemory beliefs concerning the decline of their memory. There is a third theory that has been advanced to explain the increase in TOTs with age. This view suggests that older adults experience more TOTs because they have bigger lexical and semantic memories. Because they know more, there are more items for which TOTs can occur (Dahlgren, 1998; Schwartz & Frazier, 2005). Indeed, Dahlgren showed that TOTs increased with vocabulary scores to a greater extent than TOTs increased with respect to age. Regardless of the explanation, all researchers agree that older adults are experiencing more TOTs than are younger adults.

However, from a metamemory perspective, TOTs serve an important function. TOTs alert the person that an unretrieved item may be stored in memory but may be temporarily inaccessible. Thus, experiencing a TOT may serve an important function for an older adult. By alerting the older adult that the item is still in memory, the person can engage in a number of memory strategies to trigger retrieval. If the awareness of the block did not occur, the person would not be able to engage in these behaviors. Therefore, that older adults experience more TOTs is an advantage that older adults have—they are more aware of their retrieval failures than younger adults. In order to investigate this issue, it is important to know if older adults TOTs are accurate at predicting later memory recall. If TOTs are accurate at predicting the future recall, then TOTs can be considered an adaptive adjustment to the increase in memory failures in older adulthood. Indeed, analysis of people's ability to resolve (recall the originally unrecalled item) shows that older adults are better at resolving TOTs than are younger adults (see Schwartz & Frazier, 2005). Thus, with respect to metamemory, TOTs can be seen as another area in which older adults have preserved metamemory, at least as well, if not better than, younger adults.

We can also draw on studies that use feeling-of-knowing judgments to address retrieval failures in older adults. In feeling-of-knowing experiments, people first attempt recall. If they are unable to recall the target word, they are asked to make a feeling-of-knowing judgment, which is a prediction of future recognition. Then, they receive a multiple-choice recognition test and must pick out the correct target from a number of other items. In younger adults, feeling-of-knowing judgments are highly accurate at predicting correct recognition. Most of the research also suggests that older adults are highly accurate at feeling-of-knowing judgments too (see Souchay, Moulin, Clarys, Taconnat, & Isingrini, 2007). Thus, like with judgments of learning, older adults are equally able to use metamemory monitoring to arrive at accurate predictions of memory performance. The one caveat here is that Souchay and her colleagues (2007) find that when the feeling-of-knowing test is directed at episodic memory, there is a slight deficit in accuracy with older adults. With semantic memory, however, the older adults' feeling-of-knowing judgments are just as accurate as the younger adults'.

To summarize: Healthy older adults perform just as well in metamemory tasks as do younger adults. Their accuracy in predicting performance is as good as younger adults in judgments of learning, TOTs, and feelings of knowing. Some evidence suggests that older adults have slight deficits in control, but it may also be the case that good metamemory control may be different for older adults who do have weaker abilities to encode new information. Older adults correctly believe that their memory is not as good as that of younger adults. Unfortunately, this may lead to decisions to avoid learning or remembering contexts, which may have negative outcomes. Nonetheless, the general message here is that metamemory is an area of preserved function in older adulthood.

USE IT OR LOSE IT: MAINTAINING MEMORY ABILITY IN OLDER ADULTS

Is the decline in memory in old age inevitable, or are there behaviors that older adults can engage in to preserve their memory? The answer is no and yes. First, all of us do lose a bit in terms of the speed of our responses as we get older. In fact, this aspect of cognition can be shown to start declining in adults in their 30s. There is no single thing a person can do to preserve his or her memory, nor do any combination of the activities described below ensure that memory will not decline. Moreover, age-related diseases that affect memory may occur regardless of the behaviors that older adults engage in to prevent them. However, numerous studies show statistically that certain behaviors tend to alleviate some age-related memory declines (Dixon et al., 2007; Salthouse, 2006).

Education and lifestyle are buffers against memory declines and other cognitive declines in old age. Those who are more educated maintain cognitive skills longer and later into older adulthood. Shimamura, Berry, Mangels, Rusting, and Jurica (1995), for example, found that college professors (a group that certainly qualifies as educated, some might say, overeducated) showed no decline in story recall as a function of age, although they did show declines in working memory tasks. It is likely that the declines in working memory simply reflect diminished speed of processing, which even the educated cannot avoid. However, a lifetime of learning provides many associative structures with which to process new stories. Thus, the college professors showed no declines in their recall of these stories. More educated adults are also less likely to experience some forms of abnormal aging, such as Alzheimer's disease, than are their less educated peers. Physical fitness is also correlated with fewer declines. Older adults who exercise routinely show greater cognitive abilities as well (Dixon et al., 2007).

However, older adults without advanced degrees who cannot exercise regularly need not despair. Other behaviors appear to be related to a decreased likelihood of excessive declines of memory and cognitive skill in aging. Those older adults who engage in mental activity regularly are also less prone to memory loss. Salthouse (2006) calls this the **use it or lose it hypothesis** because it states that older adults who engage in complex mental activity on a regular basis are more likely to preserve function, whereas those who do not engage in complex mental activity are more likely to suffer declines. This mental activity can include reading the newspaper, performing in musical groups, doing crossword puzzles, or taking college-level courses, to name a few. The important component is that the tasks need to be challenging. In one important study, for example, the researchers tracked a group of nuns as they grew older (Snowdon, 2003). The nuns who spent more time engaged in mentally demanding exercises such as crossword puzzles maintained cognitive function to an older age and were also less likely to develop

> **Use-it-or-lose-it hypothesis**: older adults who engage in complex mental activity on a regular basis are more likely to preserve function, whereas those who do not engage in complex mental activity are more likely to suffer declines.

Alzheimer's disease than the nuns who engaged in less cognitive activity. Given that all the nuns had similar habits (no pun intended) in terms of diet, living arrangements, and personal health, it is likely that it really was the mental activity driving the effect rather than some other unidentified correlate of mental activity. Nonetheless, some researchers such as Salthouse (2006) argue that there is still insufficient evidence that the use-it-or-lose-it hypothesis is indeed true. Thus, although this hypothesis seems plausible, it remains to be seen if the data will support it. For advocates of this position, go to www.sagepub.com/schwartz.[5]

MEMORY REHABILITATION AMONG OLDER ADULTS

Some research suggests that memory training can improve memory in older adults, just as it can for younger adults. Focused emphasis on memory skills can improve memory in everyday domains in normal older adults. If older adults practice memory skills, such as chunking, using encoding strategies, and processing for meaning, they should be able to improve memory, just as younger adults do. For long-term memory, this is generally true. Craik et al. (2007) found that memory training led to improvements in the recall of stories. However, Craik et al. also found out that working memory practice does not lead to significant improvement in working memory tasks in older adults. This study suggests that aspects of memory that are primarily dictated by processing speed, such as working memory tasks, are less easily changed

> **Memory rehabilitation**: the interventions that clinical neuropsychologists use to promote improved memory performance in memory-impaired individuals.

because older adults probably cannot increase processing speed. But tasks that rely on strategic or controlled processing, such as story recall, can be improved by greater attention to strategic use of memory. Thus, Craik et al. demonstrated an improvement in story recall. For more on **memory rehabilitation,** go to www.sagepub.com/schwartz.[6]

MNEMONIC TIPS FOR OLDER ADULTS

First, metamemory is just as good in older adults as it is in younger adults. Thus, older adults can use their metamemory as a guide for what has been learned already and what requires further study. When an older adult needs to learn something new, he or she should self-test and make judgments of learning. If the person has not learned it, he or she will benefit from restudy. If the person has already learned it, he or she will have the confidence that the item is now known. The person may require more restudy than a younger peer but may get to the same level of learning eventually. If one spends more time restudying than do younger persons, he or she may wind up outperforming them. If the older adult is having retrieval difficulties, he or she should remember that a TOT is not just a time to be frustrated. It means that the person is likely to recall the item, if the older adult figures out the right way to cue himself or herself. So the older adult should keep working at it before giving up. Thus, the first mnemonic tip is to let metamemory be the guide.

Second, semantic memory and lexical memory are not impaired in normal aging. Therefore, even though it may take on older adult a split second more to retrieve information than it used to, the older adult still has a lifetime's worth of learning at his or her disposal. This may still give the person a competitive advantage over a younger adult who may still have to learn what the older adult already knows.

Third, know thy weaknesses. As an older adult, it takes more time and is more difficult to encode new information, particularly episodic knowledge. Older adults should compensate for this by taking the slow and steady approach. Older adults should spend more time trying to learn the information that they will need to know. They should write it down just to be sure and go back to it more often. But they should not give up: Older adults do learn and remember, and the deficits are usually relatively minor in episodic memory. Thus, older adults can compensate for their deficits. They should take especial care with routine but important aspects of memory. For example, a problem many older adults report is not remembering if they have already taken their medications that day. This routine activity is easily forgotten. But this problem is easily remedied. Older adults should keep a log by their medicine cabinet. After they take their medications, they should check off that medication for that day. This externalizes the memory; it is down on paper, so there is no longer any need to trust one's slightly rusty episodic memory.

Fourth, mnemonic techniques are effective in older adults as well as in younger adults. Older adults can learn and successfully apply mnemonic techniques, and they will create equal boosts in memory performance relative to younger adults. In one study, Robertson-Tchabo, Hausman, and Arenberg (1976) taught older adults the use of the method of loci. The method of loci involves associating to-be-learned items with locations in a well-known spatial layout. They found that all of their older adults were able to acquire the use of the technique and deploy it successfully to improve their recall. Unlike the proverbial old dog, you can teach old folks new tricks! More recently, J. Price, Hertzog, and Dunlosky (2008) showed that older adults benefit from the training and use of imagery mnemonics, although older adults often underestimate the effectiveness of this training. Thus, older adults, especially those who become concerned about problems in memory, can avail themselves of the mnemonic techniques, which will benefit them to a similar extent to which it benefits younger adults.

OSCIENCE OF MEMORY AND AGING

Significant changes occur in the brain even in normal adults as they age. The changes are widespread, and therefore it is difficult to pin down exactly which brain areas cause the changes associated with memory and aging. Nonetheless, this is an area with a tremendous amount of research directed toward it, and some progress has come from it. As it turns out, many of the brain regions known to be associated with memory show changes as the brain itself ages (Head, Rodrigue, Kennedy, & Raz, 2008).

The **hippocampus** has long been known to be a part of the memory circuit, particularly with respect to encoding into episodic memory. A number of studies have shown that the hippocampuses show a general shrinkage of size in older adults. Indeed, Head et al. (2008) showed that hippocampal volume (that is, the size of the hippocampus) was correlated with episodic memory performance in older adults. They showed that the smaller the hippocampal volume was, the greater the memory deficit seen.

Hippocampus: an area of the brain associated with learning and memory. Damage can cause anterograde amnesia.

Other studies have come to similar conclusions (e.g., Jernigan et al., 2001). Thus, one effect of aging is that the hippocampus may, in effect, shrink. This shrinkage then causes the deficits in encoding.

Areas in the prefrontal lobe have been shown to be associated with a number of memory functions, including working memory and memory for source information, two areas in which older adults often exhibit declines. The prefrontal areas are particularly vulnerable to minor damage in older adults as well, both in terms of reduction of volume of prefrontal areas and small structural damage in the prefrontal lobe. Head et al. (2008) correlated decreased prefrontal tissue with problems in working memory. Decreased prefrontal volume was also associated with failures to inhibit competing sources of information, another age-related decline. Rabbitt et al. (2007) also found that decreased prefrontal volume was correlated with deficits in retrieving information from episodic memory. Indeed, in these studies that measure volume reduction, age, and memory performance, once the volume reduction is factored out, age has no continued influence on memory performance. Thus, it is the reduction of cortical space that really predicts memory decline rather than age per se. Nonetheless, it is becoming increasingly clear that age-related declines in memory are based on selective reduction of size and efficiency in the areas of the brain responsible for those memory functions. At present, there is nothing than can be done about reduced cortical volume, but it is possible that this will be a tractable issue for medical science in the future. If medical science could find ways to prevent the reduction of cortical volume or reverse it, it might be possible to ameliorate some of the effects of age-related memory problems.

SUMMARY

Normal aging is much more common that age-linked memory disorders. Normal older adults do, however, show some deficits in memory performance relative to younger adults. There are a number of hypothetical reasons for memory decline in older adults. They include decreased speed of processing, difficulties in inhibiting competing sources of information, and failures in the conscious control of memory. The declines in memory, however, are not uniform. Some areas are spared, but others do show deficits. In particular, encoding and retrieval from episodic memory decline. In addition, working memory, particularly central executive functions in working memory, decline in older adults. In normal older adults, neither of these declines approaches a clinical level. Moreover, older adults show more source memory errors than do younger adults and do not do as well in prospective memory tests. As a consequence of source memory errors and declines in episodic memory, older adults are more at risk of creating false memories than are younger adults. However, other memory abilities are preserved in older adults. Semantic and lexical memory are generally unaffected by age-related declines. In addition, metamemory is unimpaired in older adults. Many myths about memory and aging have arisen. This chapter attempts to debunk some of those myths. Normal aging includes a healthy memory, albeit perhaps a bit slower. Older adults can benefit from memory rehabilitation and from mnemonic techniques. Finally, we reviewed how reduction of volume of areas critical to memory, such as the hippocampus and the prefrontal cortex, is correlated with age-related memory declines.

KEY TERMS

Processing speed	Episodic memory	Judgments of learning
Inhibition theory	Source memory	Use-it-or-lose-it hypothesis
Directed forgetting	Monitoring	Memory rehabilitation
Semantic memory	Control	Hippocampus

REVIEW QUESTIONS

1. What stereotypes exist with respect to the effects of aging on memory? What parts of the stereotype are true and what parts are false?

2. Describe two memory components that decline in older adults and two memory components that remain stable in healthy older adults.

3. What is the processing speed theory? What memory phenomena does it predict?

4. What is the inhibition theory of memory decline? What memory phenomena does it predict?

5. What working memory components are spared in aging, and what components suffer declines in memory? Describe an experiment that supports this view.

6. What evidence exists to suggest that older adults are more susceptible to false memories? What mechanisms can account for this?

7. What are metamemory beliefs? How do they change among older adults?

8. Souchay and Isingrini (2004) examined the effects of aging on metamemory control of self-paced study. What did they find?

9. What does the phrase "use it or lose it" mean with respect to memory and aging? What evidence is relevant to testing this theory?

10. What areas of the brain are associated with which memory problems in older adults?

ONLINE RESOURCES

1. For more on normal aging, go to http://memory.ucsf.edu/Education/Topics/normalaging.html.

2. For more on Dr. Salthouse's research, go to http://www.faculty.virginia.edu/cogage/index.shtml.

3. For more on Dr. Navah-Benjamin's research on memory and aging, go to http://macal.missouri.edu/researchers.html.

4. For more on the misinformation effect and aging, go to http://www.apa.org/news/press/releases/2005/05/misinformation.aspx.

5. For advocates of this position, go to http://www.memorylossonline.com/use_it_or_lose_it.htm.

6. For more on memory rehabilitation, go to http://www.apa.org/research/action/memory-changes.aspx.

Go to www.sagepub.com/schwartz for additional exercises and study resources. Select **Chapter 12, Memory in Older Adults** for chapter-specific resources.

Memory Improvement

A User's Guide

Learning and remembering are ubiquitous human activities. Learning starts almost from the moment a child is born, and evidence now suggests it already occurs in the developing fetus. In Western countries, most children are in school settings by the time they are 3, with formal instruction already taking place. Indeed, studies now show that children who do not attend pre-K are "behind" when they get to first grade. And this is just the beginning of life-long learning. Many years of formal schooling ensue—and then in order to function in today's world requires constant retraining, regardless of whether you are a plumber, a nurse, an auto mechanic, or an experimental psychologist. For example, an auto mechanic who trained in the late 1970s is likely to be still working today. However, the increased computerization of auto mechanics, the introduction of hybrid engines, and cleaner engines means that fixing today's engines requires knowledge that did not exist in 1979. Even retired people may retrain to learn how to use cell phones and set up their computer printers. In this chapter, some evidence-based methods of improving memory are discussed.

In almost all nations in the world, most children engage in some form of formal education. In most Western countries, many young adults then attend college with the goal of learning new skills and new knowledge. In 2009, there were approximately 19 million people enrolled in American higher education institutions (National Center for Education Statistics, 2009). Millions of people every year receive formal on-the-job training; thus, education is a part of business as well. And it does not stop there—consider the five branches of the U.S. military; they train additional tens of thousands every year from basic training to specialist training to the elite military academies. In terms of money, billions of dollars are spent annually to promote learning and remembering in the United States alone (and the United States spends less of its gross domestic product on education than many other Western countries do). Thus, making learning more efficient is financially expedient and vital to national security as well.

Now think of all the informal learning that goes on every day—in businesses, in homes, and nowadays, very often, on our computers, forever connected to the Internet. Many people assert that we now need to know more than ever before in our information age.

Think about some of the things you may not have known about a few years ago—as they did not exist—that have nothing to do with formal training or education. These include but are not limited to learning how to rent movies over the Internet, how to set up your own webpage, how to set your new digital watch, and where to find the best bargains in the new mall in your town. If you are a sports fan, you may have learned LeBron James's scoring average; if you follow the gossip, you may have just learned on what day Oprah Winfrey was born. Then there are your daily activities that must be remembered. Did you remember to call your mother and tell her about your aunt's visit? Did you remember to tell your boyfriend or girlfriend about the concert tickets you just bought? Our lives are filled with acts of learning and remembering.

Given how much time we all spend learning and remembering, you might expect that at some point, you might get some specific instruction in how to maximize your learning and memory abilities. Unfortunately, such instruction is usually lacking. Very seldom do high school age students receive specific instructions in how best to master new material. Even when it is done, it is usually done as an "extra," letting the typical high school student know that attention is not required. Even some college courses on human memory often skip the topic of memory improvement—you will not find an equivalent chapter in most of the competitors for this textbook.

It is the goal of the last chapter of this book to remedy that oversight on the part of our educational system. This chapter is intended as a guide to memory improvement. It will outline how one can improve one's memory as well as the science behind these assertions. It cannot, however, guarantee improvement. Each individual will need to figure out what works best for him or her and then apply that technique assiduously. However, following some of the principles outlined in this book and emphasized in this chapter will certainly be part of any person's success at improving his or her memory skill. But before we start, let me reiterate one of the key themes of memory improvement: Memory improvement does not come for free—it requires work and intelligence.

Thus, hard work is incumbent even on the "memory elite." In this chapter, we will discuss memory performers—these are people with truly fantastic innate memory abilities. Yet, they too must work hard to maximize their memory performance. So, yes, there are clearly individual differences in the ability to learn, process information, and remember it later, but even the most intelligent and gifted must work to learn. This chapter will provide some guidelines as to how to make the work you put in give you the most learning for the time spent. In other words, this chapter offers hints as to how to make your study time more efficient. The chapter will do so by reviewing and summarizing the various mnemonic hints that you have already read in the earlier chapters.

Over the course of the first 12 chapters, 22 mnemonic improvement hints have been offered to help readers bolster their ability to learn and remember. All 22 can be found in abbreviated form in Table 13.1 at the end of the chapter. However, by now, you should recognize 22 hints puts quite a bit of strain on a person's memory to remember. How many of you could list all 22 hints? It is likely that few of you can, despite the fact that you studied each one in advance of your exams for your memory course. The paradox here is that to use the mnemonic hints, you must be able to remember them. And 22 hints is a lot to retain. In addition, each hint applies under slightly different situations. Thus, you also have to remember which hint is appropriate under which set of circumstances. The point here is that 22 hints is a lot to remember. Proposed here is way to organize the 22 hints into four broad principles.

There are four broad principles to be drawn from the 22 hints, which are a lot easier to remember than all 22 hints. The first principle is to **process for meaning.** That is, as you learn new material, focus on what it means. Several of the hints are related to the importance of meaning-based processing in learning. For example, Mnemonic Improvement Hint 4.1 advises you to use elaborative encoding. By relating new information to knowledge we already have, we focus on the meaning of the stimuli. The second principle is to **make use of retrieval cues.** Many of the hints promote the generation of strong and multiple retrieval cues for a particular item of information in memory. Think of Mnemonic Improvement Hint 1.2, the spacing effect. By spacing or distributing the study of new items, you allow the development of a different set of retrieval cues to be established at each study trial. Then, at test, you have a number of different retrieval cues to fall back on. The third principle is to use **metamemory.** By careful and deliberate monitoring of what you have learned and what you still need to know, you can guide your learning in efficient ways. For example, Mnemonic Improvement Hint 1.3 reminds you that memory does not come for free—you have to work at it. This is metacognitive knowledge, which compels you to spend more time engaged in study behaviors. Finally, the fourth principle is that **distributed learning or practice** is superior to massed learning or practice. This means that spreading your studying out over time is superior to cramming. With busy schedules, students have a tendency to cram, but it shortchanges them. A little distributed practice goes a long way to improved memory efficiency. Mnemonic Improvement Hint 1.2 embodies this principle. Many cognitive psychologists interested in learning efficiency would concur with these four broad principles (see Willingham, 2009). For a related approach to memory improvement, based on Daniel Willingham's ideas, go to www.sagepub.com/schwartz.

Let's examine each of these principles in detail.

> **Process for meaning**: as you learn new material, focus on what it means.
>
> **Make use of retrieval cues**: generate effect cues to help you remember. Test yourself frequently to practice retrieval.
>
> **Metamemory**: our knowledge and awareness of our own memory processes.
>
> **Distributed learning or practice**: spacing one's study over time can lead to faster acquisition of information.

1. PROCESS FOR MEANING

Think about the "washing clothes" story introduced in Chapter 5. Bransford and Johnson (1972) asked two groups of participants to read a story. One group had few clues as to what the story was about, whereas the other group knew the title of the story, namely, "Washing Clothes." The group that knew the title remembered more details from the story than the group that did not have the title, even though both groups had the same amount of time to learn the material. Why did the title group do better? Because the group that knew the title was better able to process for meaning. The title provided meaning and therefore structure to the otherwise confusing passage. The title allowed for the person to process the confusing sentences in terms of what they actually meant, for which we already have existing knowledge bases for which to associate the new material. Thus, the meaning implied in the title led to efficient memory. Both groups had the same amount of study time, but the group that was also better able to process for meaning remembered more from the story.

As human beings, we must often need to attend to the meaning of what a person is saying, something we are watching, and certainly what we are reading. Therefore, we are tuned to be sensitive to meaning. Certainly, in school settings, it is meaning that is important. This becomes apparent when we are asked to attend to sensory details instead of meaning. Consider the famous **Stroop effect.** The classic Stroop effect is an example of this—we find it difficult to identify the color of words that refer to colors when the words are written in different color ink than what the word means (e.g., what is the color of green?). For most fluent adult readers, we process "red" first—because that is what the word means. When we have to say "green," we are slower because it interferes with what the word means. The Stroop effect works because by the time we are adults, we have automatized the attention to meaning rather than sensory characteristics of a stimulus (MacLeod, 2005; Stroop, 1935). The same holds true for memory. Go to www.sagepub.com/schwartz for an interesting demonstration of the Stroop effect.

> **Stroop effect**: interference in identifying the color of a stimulus if the stimulus is a word denoting another color.

Now apply this to the learning one typically does in a college course. In college course, even facts (e.g., Berlin is the capital of Germany) are less crucial than concepts (Berlin was made the capital after the unification of Germany in 1990 following the fall of the Berlin Wall in 1989. Berlin was also the capital of a united Germany before the end of World War II. What do these facts tell us about German nationalism?). In our technological urban Western world, meaning is far more a significant aspect of our world than sensory characteristics. Thus, our teachers generally focus on meaning. This is a critical point—that is, mostly what we are tested on is meaning based. Textbook authors do not put some terms in bold and dark lettering like **this** because we want you to remember which words are in boldface. We use boldface because those words carry important meaning in a particular section, and we want to draw your attention to them. We do not put words in bold because we want you to remember that the print was darker. Similarly, your dive instructor does not care if you remember whether he or she was wearing a blue wetsuit or a black wetsuit during your practice dive. Rather, the instructor wants you to remember why you need to ascend slowly (avoiding decompression sickness) and why you can only stay a few minutes at depths of over 100 feet (buildup of nitrogen in the blood) but much longer when you are diving at 30 feet. Thus, in general, process for meaning works because it conforms to the demands of the teacher—who generally emphasizes meaning.

A review of the mnemonic hints in Table 13.1 will demonstrate just how many are related the principle of "process for meaning." Mnemonic Improvement Hints 4.1 to 4.4, 5.1, 6.1 to 6.3, 7.1, and 11.1 all make use of process for meaning to one degree or another. Hints 4.1 through 4.4 are all about processing for meaning. Thus, one of the most reliable ways of improving your memory is to focus on levels of processing. Processing for meaning (or thinking of its survival value) focuses our attention on meaning, which then leads to better memory performance. Organization also helps learners process for meaning. Although this concept was introduced in Chapter 4, it was not fully examined there. We shall do so now.

Consider the mnemonic improvement hint that advises you to organize what you are learning (4.3). Organization has a long and distinguished history of helping memory (Tulving, 1962). But some organizational schemes are better than others. Consider the dilemma faced by the sitcom character Miley Stewart in the Disney show *Hannah Montana*. To get her father's approval to go on a trip to France, she must first pass her biology class. This is made difficult by her inability to remember the names of the bones of the body. Struggling to remember the names (i.e., metacarpal, frontal, etc.), she hits upon a musical organizational scheme by singing a song that reviews the formal names of the bone and which ones they are "connected" to. This allows her to pass the test and win her father's approval to visit France. For Disney's version of musical mnemonics, go to www.sagepub.com/schwartz.

Although this story is fictional, it hits upon an important part of the use of organization in memory. Organization is personal! What works for one person may not work for another; the best way to organize material is in relation to oneself, known as **subjective organization** (Tulving, 1962). Thus, in studying, you may want to vary from the standard way in which information is organized and make up your own organization. For a budding musician, using musical principles to organize biology or history may indeed be helpful. Because, for a young musician, music is a well-learned and meaningful body of knowledge, it can be used as an organizing principle for scaffolding on new information—namely, the bones of the body. Conversely, a doctor attempting to learn the cello as an adult may want to use this process in reverse. The names of the bones may help the doctor as an organizational scheme for remembering musical notation.

> **Subjective organization**: in studying, you may want to vary from the standard way in which information is organized and make up your own organization.

Indeed, research shows that when students are forced to organize the material themselves, they remember more than when someone else provides the organization. This is true even when the external organization derives from an expert on the subject matter. In one experimental demonstration, Mannes and Kintsch (1987) gave to one group of students well-organized outlines of material for which they would be tested. The outlines, prepared by professionals, provided a logical and coherent manner in which to study for the test. A second group was given a disorganized outline. It contained all of the same facts and did not contain any errors, but there was no logical and coherent sequence to it. This forced the students into deriving their own organizational schemes while they were studying. There were two interesting outcomes. First, the organized outlines were judged as more helpful by the students. Students liked the well-organized outlines better than the disorganized ones. Second, the first group did better on simple memory tasks such as recognition, but the second group learned in a deeper, more flexible way that gave them an advantage when they were asked to solve problems and make inferences. Why? Well, the second group, students had to employ their own personalized organizational strategies to learn the material rather than rely on the already prepared outlines. This forced them into using self-organization and focusing on the meaning of the stimuli in a way not required of the other students. The self-organization that they supplied to the learning of the material led to better performance than the logical, professional, but impersonal outline provided by the experimenters. This study demonstrates the need for students to organize material themselves into meaningful patterns (see Christina & Bjork, 1991) (see Figure 13.1).

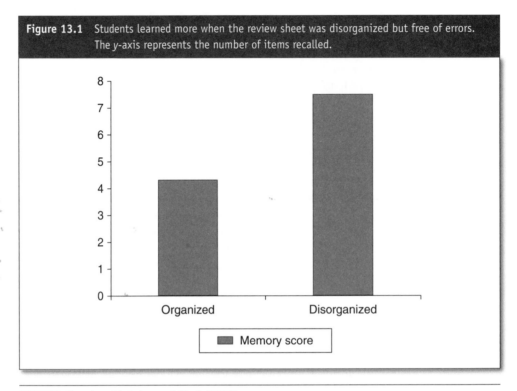

Figure 13.1 Students learned more when the review sheet was disorganized but free of errors. The y-axis represents the number of items recalled.

SOURCE: Based on Christina and Bjork (1991).

This presents a conundrum for some teachers. If you want students to like you and give you good evaluations, you should provide them with careful, well-organized notes and outlines. This will make the students feel like they are learning easily. However, if you want the students to learn more, you will give them disorganized outlines that will force them to learn the material themselves. They will be less satisfied with your teaching but will understand more information from your class.

Subjective Organization and Mnemonics

Technical mnemonics: ready-made methods of learning information such as acronyms or acrostics.

A few technical mnemonics take advantage of subjective organization. These mnemonics can often be quite useful in remembering arbitrary lists. By and large, they employ simple meaning-based schemes that are useful for the memory of items unrelated to that scheme. **Technical mnemonics** refer to ready-made methods of learning information.

Acronyms can be used to help learn lists of information not obviously linked together. Acronyms involve taking the first letter of each word from a list and forming them into

Acronyms: a mnemonic device in which the first letter of each word from a list is formed into an easily remembered word. For example, "HOMES" is a common acronym for remembering the Great Lakes of the United States and Canada (Huron, Ontario, Michigan, Erie, and Superior).

easily remembered words. For example, "HOMES" is a common acronym for remembering the Great Lakes of the United States and Canada (Huron, Ontario, Michigan, Erie, and Superior). "FACE" represents the musical notes in the open spaces on the musical staff on the treble clef. When the information is needed, all one needs to remember is the acronym, and each letter then serves as a cue to recall the information. That is, "H" cues Huron, "O" cues Ontario, and so on. The famous, if silly, ROY G BIV stands for the colors of the spectrum (red, orange, yellow, green, blue, indigo, violet). Acronyms are easy to generate and helpful for remembering arbitrary information.

Acrostics can also serve as memory aids. Acrostics involve taking the first letter from each item in the list and forming a sentence with an easily remembered visual image or auditory connection that makes the sentence memorable. When the information needs to be retrieved, it can be unpacked from the acrostic. For example, a famous acrostic is "Every Good Boy Does Fine." The first letter specifies the musical note on the line in the treble clef in musical notation. "Beautiful People Wear Clothes" is your author's personal acrostic to remember that Broca's area (B) of the brain is involved with the production of language (P), and Wernicke's area (W) is responsible for comprehension (C) of language.

Acrostics: a mnemonic that involves taking the first letter from each item in the list and forming a sentence with an easily remembered visual image or auditory connection that makes the sentence memorable.

Both of these mnemonics employ organizational principles that may be lacking in the material itself. For example, the naming of the parts of the brain is a historical accident—nor is the logic apparent in the names of the Great Lakes. When we devise our acronym or acrostic, we supply organization that helps us encode that information.

A Note About Imagery-Based Mnemonics

You will note that imagery-based mnemonics have been largely left out of this chapter. Indeed, the principle upon which they are based—namely, that use of perceptual imagery can boost memory—runs counter to the first principle reviewed in this chapter (process for meaning). Don't let this confuse you—memory is complex—the more techniques we use, the more efficient memory can become. Therefore, processing for meaning and using imagery-based mnemonics will be superior to using either by itself. It is also important to consider encoding variability and setting up retrieval routes for subsequent retrieval. In some cases, imagery techniques, such as the method of loci, will help do this. Imagery-based mnemonics can be quite useful in remembering lists of arbitrary items, names, and especially new language vocabulary (see Verhaeghen & Marcoen, 1996).

2. MAKE USE OF RETRIEVAL CUES

The second broad principle in improving memory is to make proper use of retrieval cues. Retrieval cues are the stimuli present at the time of retrieval that spur our memories. In Chapter 4, we discussed the importance of retrieval cues in many aspects of human memory. Because of the associative structure of human memory, retrieval cues are necessary keys to eliciting information from long-term memory.

Think about the following familiar situation. You are in your English literature class. You are sitting in front of a blank piece of paper, trying to remember something about the character of Horatio in Shakespeare's play *Hamlet*. Your exam essay is to write a short description of the character Horatio and comment on his influence on the main character Hamlet. But you are drawing a blank. You know you read the play, and you think you got the gist out of it: a man trying to avenge his father's murder but bogged down in uncertainty about whether to believe a ghost. But there were so many funny names that it was hard to keep track of them all. Was Horatio one of the friends who betrayed him to his evil uncle? Or was Horatio Polonius's son? The failure here is not one of learning but one of retrieval. You do not have the correct retrieval cue. If the question had contained information about Horatio's role, such as, "Hamlet's friend Horatio, who also witnessed seeing the ghost, influences Hamlet in certain ways," this ought to instantly trigger the associations of Hamlet's close friend and his role in the play, and then you are able to tackle the essay without any difficulty. This additional information now gives you a cue to remember his role in the play that simply his name could not provide. Armed with the extra information, you are now able to write a stellar essay on the play.

Cues are bits of information, provided by either the environment outside of yourself or through your own imagination. Cues are triggers that help us recall the information that is associated with them. As we discussed in Chapter 4, the right cue can bring back a long-lost memory. You might not have thought of the vacation you took to the woodlands of Minnesota when you were a child for a long time. But when your father or mother says, "Remember when we were staying at the fishing lodge, and you caught a large trout?" This cue then elicits your memory of yourself as a young child struggling to land the feisty fish. You may not have known you could have remembered this until your parent provided the correct retrieval cue.

Students can also rely on the structuring of retrieval cues in a number of different ways. That is, if we learn in such a way that we know what the relevant retrieval cues will be later, we can perform better by ensuring that those retrieval cues are present at the time of test. Thus, this means controlling the encoding environment so that it produces usable cues that will be present at the time of retrieval. Therefore, the first manifestation of the importance of retrieval cues will be the research on **encoding variability.** Encoding variability means that multiple encoding conditions produce good recall because encoding under a variety of conditions provides lots of different cues, which can then be taken advantage of at the time of retrieval. By chance, it is more likely that one of

> **Encoding variability**: this principle claims that if you study an item of information under several different mental and physical conditions, you will be more likely to remember it than if you had studied for the same amount of time or trials but under uniform conditions.

these conditions will be present at the time of retrieval than if the encoding had taken place under homogeneous conditions. Thus, encoding variability produces good memory (Verkoeijen, Rikers, & Ozsoy, 2008).

The encoding variability principle claims if you study an item of information under several different mental and physical conditions, you will be more likely to remember it than if you had studied for the same amount of time or trials but under uniform conditions. This means that if I want to remember a particular piece of information (i.e., Julius Caesar lived from 100 BCE to 44 BCE), it is best to study it under a variety of conditions, such as when you are tired, angry, in your dorm room, and in the library. Then, when you are asked about the facts of Julius Caesar's life in your history class, you have a number of different cues to remember this information. You may be tired when you take the test, in which cases the cues acquired when you studied when tired will be useful. You may be feeling angry for one reason or another when you take the test, and therefore your "angry" cues will be useful. Consider the scenario when you study only when you are well rested, happy, and only in your dorm room. You may establish a series of cues that are associated with each of those states. When you take the exam, you may be tired, unhappy about something or other, and in the classroom. Not having studied in different states will leave you with fewer retrieval cues to rely on than if you had studied under more diverse conditions. Therefore, encoding variability can be used by students to boost memory performance. Your study is more efficient if you do it under a variety of encoding conditions (Soraci et al., 1999).

Thus, encoding variability ensures that you will have created a range of cues for the information. At the time of test, the **encoding specificity** principle applies; that is, if retrieval conditions match encoding conditions, recall will be maximized. The problem is that you may not always know what the retrieval conditions will be. It may be that the test will take

> **Encoding specificity**: retrieval of information from memory will be maximized when the conditions at retrieval match the conditions at encoding.

place on a sunny day in which you are a bit tired but feel good about the world. The test may also take place on a rainy day in which you are agitated and angry because you just had an argument with your boyfriend or girlfriend. If you studied under both sets of conditions—that is, encoding variability—you will be able to make use of the encoding specificity principle at the time of test, as either condition at test was preceded by study in the same condition. Therefore, if you want to maximize your retrieval during a test, make sure to study under a variety of mental and physical conditions.

Retrieval Practice

Retrieval practice means to learn by testing oneself. That is, making yourself retrieve information is a superior method learning than simply rereading that information. As such, it fits into the second rubric of memory improvement (make use of retrieval cues). Retrieval practice is currently an important topic of cognitive research, but it is also an easily applied principle of learning and remembering. Research shows that a trial of testing oneself is superior to a trial of restudy (see Kornell & Bjork, 2007). As an example, consider a student who must memorize a lengthy passage from a Shakespeare play. Once the information has been studied to the

> **Retrieval practice**: this means to learn by testing oneself. That is, making yourself retrieve information is a superior method of learning than simply rereading that information.

point where the student is beginning to memorize the lines but is still shaky with them, he or she can consider two options: continue to read over the lines or practice saying them, and when he or she makes a mistake, a listener can provide feedback. A volume of research demonstrates that retrieval practice or the generation of the lines themselves produces quicker learning than reading them.

Learning a new vocabulary word in French is quicker when you repeatedly test yourself (as in, *monkey–*) than when you simply read the association (*monkey–singe*). The act of retrieving creates stronger associations between cues and targets than does simply restudying the items (Karpicke & Roediger, 2008; Roediger & Karpicke, 2006) (see Figure 13.2).

Roediger and Karpicke (2006) have focused attention on the advantages of retrieval practice. They asked participants to read short prose passages concerning scientific information. One group of participants simply restudied the items several times. A second group read the same passage but then was asked to recall information about the story on three practice tests. One week later, the participants returned and were retested on the information. The testing group outperformed the restudy group. In fact, the testing group recalled 50 % more information than did the restudy group. This study clearly shows how important testing yourself is to acquiring information.

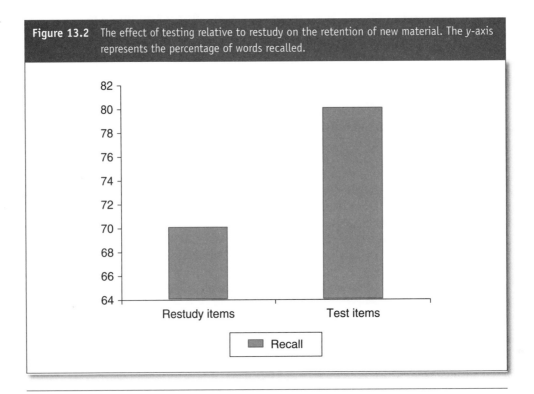

Figure 13.2 The effect of testing relative to restudy on the retention of new material. The *y*-axis represents the percentage of words recalled.

SOURCE: Based on Karpicke and Roediger (2008).

Recently, there has been a great deal of attention devoted to the idea that testing produces better learning than studying. Testing here means presenting the cues or questions without the answers and having the student generate the answer. Many professors, for example, provide practice tests to their students. In general, these practice tests are given to provide students with the opportunity to see what kinds of materials will be tested on the actual exam. But research shows that a trial of testing produces more learning than a trial of study (McDaniel, Roediger, & McDermott, 2007). That is, if you measure later learning or retention, the student who spends a minute testing himself or herself will remember more later than a student who simply reviews the material. In another demonstration of this, J. Campbell and Mayer (2009) tested college students during classes. In one condition, students in an educational psychology class received a PowerPoint presentation in which questions were included as part of the presentation. In another set of PowerPoints, only statements were made. The students who saw the questions later remembered more from the lecture than those who had only read statements.

> **Generation effect**: memory is better when we generate associations ourselves than when we simply read them.

This is similar to the **generation effect**, discussed in Chapter 4 (Slamecka & Graf, 1978). In the generation effect, a person generates the to-be-remembered target either by following a rule (e.g., generate a word that rhymes with *head* and starts with a *b*) or by simply reading the association (e.g., *head–bed*). The data show that participants remember the generated associations better than the read associations. Again, here the act of producing the to-be-remembered item oneself produces cues that will later be useful in recall.

Thus, a generalization we can make about memory improvement is the following: Test thyself. Repeatedly generating target answers and testing your knowledge base produces the cues that lead to good memory later. This is a pretty easy rule to follow. Most textbooks have test banks that go along with them or review questions at the end of the chapter. The memory-conscious student can employ these educational tools. Ten minutes spent answering the review questions at the end of this chapter will promote better long-term learning of the material in this chapter than 10 minutes spent rereading various sections. If the questions are not provided to you by your textbook, you can also make flashcards that have a question on one side and the answer on the back. Try answering the question first before you check the back. This can be done on regular index cards or on the equivalent in computer files. This allows students to benefit from the generation effect—the student produces the answer and retrieval practice; this act of generation can be repeated to ensure stronger learning of the items. Making your own flashcards has an additional advantage—writing down the questions and the answers when you make the cards also provides an additional study trial. For more on the advantages of self-testing and other mnemonic techniques, go to www.sagepub.com/schwartz.

Retrieval Cues and Autobiographical Memory

In this chapter, the focus is on learning and remembering that is relevant in educational settings, such as the college classroom. However, many people also would prefer to have stronger memory performance in other domains as well, such as the memory of personal events from each of our lives. Autobiographical memory is also heavily cue dependent. Thus, if you want to be able to improve your ability to recall the events of your life, increased attention to the development of good retrieval cues is important in this domain as well. Because this topic has been thoroughly discussed in Chapter 7, it will be only briefly touched on here. But methods to improve autobiographical memory mostly revolve around the structuring of cues. Keeping a diary, for example, involves providing cues for later memory. Rereading your diary later provides a powerful boost to recall the events of that day. In most cases, people can remember details of the event not included in the diary, whereas they may not have the right cues to retrieve anything without the diary entry. Thus, within the domain of autobiographical memory, retrieval cues are paramount. Structuring your retrieval cues in advance of retrieval promotes good recall of autobiographical events.

3. USE METAMEMORY: THE ADVANTAGES OF SELF-REGULATED LEARNING

The importance of metamemory is generally underestimated in memory improvement programs and books. These books emphasize imagery and other memory tricks and seldom mention the important role of conscious control over the learning environment. However, cognitive psychology is showing an increasing understanding of the role that metamemory plays in ordinary learning and remembering and the role it plays in memory improvement (Son & Vandierendonck, 2007; Willingham, 2009). Metamemory means our awareness and knowledge of our own memories. This awareness ("I know this material really well") and knowledge ("I am good at remembering names" or "I know very little about dog shows") can be used to structure our learning and remembering. For example, when asked to recall the mailing address of my third cousin twice-removed, I know immediately that I do not know this bit of information. This awareness can spur a number of responses. I can look up the number in my address book or call another cousin to get the number. But my awareness of the knowledge allows me to make a decision. A student studying can quickly assess whether he or she has learned all of the vocabulary items to be studied. On the basis of this assessment, he or she can decide to continue studying or get a good night's rest. Metamemory can play a role in memory improvement both at the time of encoding and at the time of retrieval.

Judgments of Learning as Mnemonic Improvement Tools

Judgments of learning are made during study and are judgments concerning the likelihood of remembering an item later. As reviewed in Chapter 9, judgments of learning are both accurate at predicting future performance and useful as a guide to which items to restudy. Consider the use of judgments of learning in encoding. While studying, you can assess how well you have learned particular items. For example, while studying for a Spanish

> **Judgments of learning**: are made during study and are judgments of whether the item has been learned already.

vocabulary test, you can make judgments of learning on the various English-Spanish word pairs (e.g., *railroad–ferrocaril*). Making judgments of learning can offer a number of distinct memory advantages. First, if you use the delayed judgment of learning effect (that is, wait a few minutes after studying the item and then cue yourself only with the cue word, in this case, the English word), you can make more accurate judgments of learning as well as benefit from the retrieval practice. Second, assessing judgments of learning provides you with feedback as to what you have learned and what you have not. Having assessed your judgments of learning for the various items, you are in a position to now make decisions about what you need to restudy. For those items that you gave high judgments of learning to, you probably do not need to restudy those items further. However, for those items that you gave lower judgments of learning, these are the items you must restudy. More time and more study trials should be devoted to those items for which you gave low judgments of learning too.

How does this improve memory? The act of making a judgment of learning itself appears not to improve memory more than the equivalent amount of time spent studying the item, although this has been the subject of a great deal of debate within the field (see Dunlosky & Metcalfe, 2009). Instead, judgments of learning can be used to improve memory by allowing us to direct our time, energy, and effort toward those items for which we need the most study. Consider if you studied all the items a second time for an equal amount. You would essentially be wasting study time on the easy items that you have already mastered and might not study the more difficult items for enough time. Instead, by making judgments of learning and knowing the easy items and the difficult items, you can concentrate your study on the items you need to learn. Thus, in the same amount of time, you can learn more information by not focusing on items you already know. Thus, making judgments of learning allows us to sort out the easy and more difficult items for us.

The output of judgments of learning can also inform our learning in a second manner. It can allow us to adaptively control our study behavior, depending on our goals and our circumstances. For one class, for example, you may be aiming for an "A" because you really want to do well in that class. In another class, you may be satisfied to just get by, perhaps because it is a requirement, perhaps because it is just plain difficult, and perhaps because it is less interesting. Thus, the goal of one class is perfection, but for the other class, it is just to master enough to pass the course. Judgments of learning can be used to help adjust to these different goals. In the class where you want the "A," you must study even the most difficult items, but in the other class, you

Region of proximal learning: a theory of metamemory that advances that an adaptive strategy is to study those items that have not yet been learned but are not too difficult. We maximize our learning by studying the leading edge of difficulty. That is, we maximize our learning by studying the easiest items we have not mastered yet.

might just study the easier items and perhaps a few difficult items to master enough information to earn a "C" on the exam. Interestingly, this approach to study has now been formalized in a model of memory study called the **region of proximal learning,** developed by Janet Metcalfe and her colleagues (see Metcalfe & Kornell, 2005). For more on this topic, go to www.sagepub.com/schwartz.

In this theory, we maximize our learning by studying the leading edge of difficulty. That is, we maximize our learning by studying the easiest of the items we have not mastered yet. We do not need to restudy the items we have learned already—this would be an inefficient use of our time. We do not exactly know how much time we will have to prepare, so we might sacrifice too much if we focus on the most difficult items first. So we study the least difficult of the ones we have not yet mastered. But then we should direct our attention to those items that we think we can master in the shortest amount of time and retain for the longest. We can only do so by focusing on the judgments of learning we have made about these items.

The region of proximal learning stipulates that the most efficient manner of studying is to study the easiest items we have not yet learned. This is illustrated by the relation of judgments of learning to study time decisions in Figure 13.3.

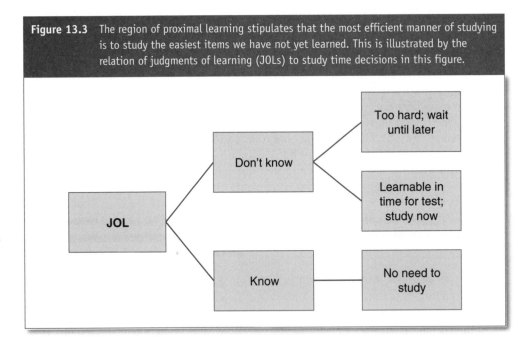

Figure 13.3 The region of proximal learning stipulates that the most efficient manner of studying is to study the easiest items we have not yet learned. This is illustrated by the relation of judgments of learning (JOLs) to study time decisions in this figure.

The advantage to this strategy is that we seldom know exactly how much time we need to study or how much time we have to study. You don't know when you are going to have to drive to the airport to pick up your cousin or when a friend needs to speak to you after a bad breakup with a boyfriend or girlfriend. Thus, at times, our ability to learn or prepare for a test will be cut off before we are satisfied. If our study time turns out to be limited, and we cannot study all the items, we are better off learning as many items as possible in the time that we have. Thus, by focusing on the easiest of the not-yet-mastered items, we can learn more of these items than if we had started with the most difficult of the not-yet-mastered items and then progressed to easier items. If it then turns out we do have more time, then we can focus on the most difficult items. But these items are attempted only if all other items have been learned.

Thus, judgments of learning can be used as a screen to determine the difficulty of items—easy items require less study than difficult items. However, moderately difficult items ought to be studied before the most extremely difficult items. Depending on how much total study time we have, we can master more and more of the difficult items. The efficient way to study is to always study the easiest item not yet learned. This means we can master the most amount of the material if our study time is suddenly curtailed.

These aspects of metamemory involve the continuous monitoring of one's own knowledge and the continuous use of this monitoring to make informed decisions about learning and memory. This approach to memory improvement is called **self-regulated learning.** Research shows that self-regulated learning is superior to learning in which others, even experts, are making the decisions as to which items a person should study (Kornell & Bjork, 2008). This is because only each individual can know which items are distinctive (and therefore easy) or confusing for that individual. We now turn to the next broad principle that drives memory improvement.

> **Self-regulated learning**: the continuous monitoring of one's own knowledge and the continuous use of this monitoring to make informed decisions about learning and memory.

4. DISTRIBUTED PRACTICE AND THE SPACING EFFECT

Distributed practice means that long-term retention is enhanced when we spread out our study over time as compared to studying all at once. This particular principle applies across many learning domains, not just studying for exams or mastering a new language. Distributed practice is superior to massed practice in learning new skills varying from learning to play a musical instrument, learning to type, learning to sew, learning to play basketball, and even learning to drive a tank. However, this section will focus on the advantages of distributed practice for encoding information, such as school-related learning, into long-term memory.

> **Distributed practice**: space your study out over time.

Avoid Cramming: Massed Versus Distributed Practice

Every college student has found himself or herself in this situation. It is the night before the big test, and you have not yet even started reading the textbook chapters that will be covered on the exam. Because of practice and other commitments, you have also missed class. So you are essentially starting to prepare for this exam from scratch—but you do have all night to prepare for the exam. Students call this "cramming." It is a staple of college life, yet it is a remarkably inefficient manner of learning. The memory improvement tip offered here is to avoid cramming.

> **Massed practice**: when all study occurs in one block of time.

The technical term for cramming is massed practice. **Massed practice** means when all study occurs in one block of time. Alas, massed practice has its place. It should not be completely rejected. In fact, massed practice can be employed with some success right before an exam (or performance). The practice immediately before the exam will leave some information highly accessible. This may help on test performance. Think of the time you quickly glanced over your notes just before a professor started handing out exams. You may have noticed something in your notes, which turned up on the exam. The advantage of massing is that if you do it just before the test, some information will be highly accessible and may be on the test. The disadvantage of massing is that although it may render a few items highly accessible, it does little for availability. Since a student cramming for an exam is focused on short-term issues—passing the test—it is easy to forget that the long-term goal is learning. Thus, students often fall into a pattern of cramming because it gets them through their tests, but then they remember little of the course once it is over.

Massed practice promotes little long-term retention of the practiced material. That is, cramming may result in enough learning to get you a passing grade on the test, but you will have to restudy it all over again to prepare for the cumulative final, almost as if it was brand-new material. More important in the long run is that you will not remember the information later—in the real world—when it might come in handy. A handy rule is that massed practice promotes accessibility—good if the material is already well learned and you are about to be tested on it. But distributed practice promotes availability—so that the information is in your memory when you may need it later. In this sense, distributed practice is more efficient—it creates more total learning than does massed practice in less time.

Distributed practice means that practice is spread out over time. In this way, distributed practice is based on the **spacing effect**; two trials produce better retention if they are more separate in time than if they are less separate in time. For the college student, distributed practice means that you might spend a half-hour period every morning reading your text-

> **Spacing effect**: more learning occurs when two study trials on the same information are spread out over time than when they occur successively.

book and perhaps 15 minutes reviewing the major concepts. If you do this, you may need only a short study session the night prior to the exam because you would have already mastered the material. The short study test accomplishes the same goal as the "cramming"; it renders the material accessible. Thus, you will do better on the test than the "crammers" and remember it years from now. In addition, when your friends are busy cramming and feeling really stressed, you can go out for dinner with other friends, get a good night's sleep, be relaxed the next day, and still do better than your cramming friends on the exam the next day. And then go to the beach or to a party while your crammer friends are sleeping off the all-nighter. Moreover, you will remember the material better for the final exam and when daily life calls on you to use that information. The only negative side to distributing your practice—your friends will be jealous! For more on the differences between massed and distributed practice, go to www.sagepub.com/schwartz.

There is ample research to support this assertion in many studies (except the part about jealous friends and partying at the beach). In one recent study that employed methods very much akin to the learning students must do for school, Kornell (2009b) asked participants to study difficult GRE-type words and their more common synonyms (e.g., *effulgent: brilliant*). Each word definition was presented on a computerized version of a flashcard. The "flashcards" had the difficult word on one side, and if you pressed a key, you could see the "back" of the flashcard, which had the definition or more common word. Kornell used this paradigm to compare learning under massed or distributed practice.

Kornell's (2009b) participants were divided into two groups. One group learned by massing first, the other group by distributing practice first. In both the massed and the spaced conditions, participants studied each definition four times throughout the course of study. However, in the distributed condition, the group studied one big stack of flashcards, thereby maximizing spacing. A particular word definition was not restudied until all of the other definitions had already been studied. In the massed condition, the group studied four small stacks of flashcards and was tested after each one. Thus, there was much less time between two successive study sessions of the same word definition. The total number of items was the same for the big stack of flashcards and the four smaller ones. Therefore, the difference was the amount of spacing between successive study of a particular definition.

Kornell (2009b) found that the distributed items led to better cued recall than did the massed items. And the distributed condition produced about 50% more items recalled. This is a huge effect! Imagine just by employing this one memory improvement technique, you can improve your memory ability by 50%! And it is remarkably consistent across individuals. The advantage of distribution over cramming was present in over 90% of the students tested. Thus, the effects of distributed practice are strong and consistent across individuals. Regardless of whether we use old-fashioned index cards or computer programs to help us learn efficiently, the spacing effect is important. Kornell's study is one of a long line of studies that demonstrates just how much better distributed practice is than massed practice. What makes Kornell's study particularly compelling is that it deals directly with materials that many students must master—if they want to be accepted into graduate school—and it deals with the manner in which many students do study.

In another study, Landauer and Bjork (1978) attempted to maximize the advantages of both massed and distributed practice by using both in a study paradigm. They devised what they called optimum rehearsal patterns. In their study, Landauer and Bjork compared standard spaced practice to something they called **expanded retrieval practice.**

Expanded retrieval practice: expanded retrieval practice means that initially you space your study of a particular item very close together to maximize learning and the advantages of retrieval practice, but then your subsequent trials get further and further apart.

Expanded retrieval practice means that initially you space your study of a particular item very close together to maximize learning and the advantages of retrieval practice, but then your subsequent trials get further and further apart. Thus, you might study *book-livre,* then study the same item again. Then you might intersperse three other French-English word pairs before you study *book-livre* again. Then, you might intersperse eight more French-English word pairs before you study *book-livre* again. In this way, you continually remind yourself of the items, keep the pairs easily accessible, but don't waste study time by short spacing.

The expanded retrieval practice takes advantage of the effects of "cramming"—that is, that studied items become easily accessible in the early phases of study—and then it takes advantage of distributed practice by the expanding spacing, which allows for restudy and permanent storage in an efficient way. This phenomenon is also one of a select few in memory science that has actually inspired a limerick:

> You can get a great deal from rehearsal
>
> If it just has the proper dispersal
>
> You would just be an ass
>
> To do it *en masse*
>
> Your remembering would turn out much worsal.
>
> —Bjork (1988, p. 399)

A caveat to the advantages of distributed practice (spacing effect) over massed practice is that people prefer to mass their practice. Indeed, in Kornell's (2009b) study, even though 90% of people did better when using distributed practice, 72% *thought* that they did better when massing their practice. This metamemory error can be persuasive. In another study, Baddeley and Longman (1978) also showed that distributed practice produced better learning, in this case, in a program to teach employees to type on typewriters quickly and accurately. However, the employees who learned via a massed program rated their learning experience as more positive than those who had learned via distributed practice. Thus, it is important for those who want to maximize their memory efficiency to keep distributed practice in mind when they begin learning because it is both counterintuitive and less pleasant than massed practice.

MYTHS AND METHODS TO AVOID

A few widely practiced mnemonic techniques and memory improvement strategies are not based on good science and, in some cases, may work against good memory performance. These will be described briefly because it is often as important to avoid bad the techniques as it is to embrace good technique in many endeavors, memory included.

First, there is no such thing as a memory drug—at least, as of yet. If you go to your local health food store, you may see "ginkgo biloba" advertised as a memory-enhancing herbal supplement. However, there is no scientific evidence that ginkgo biloba actually boosts memory (Canter & Ernst, 2007). Harmless, perhaps, but it will not give your memory the boost that the advertisements on the bottles claim. Second, many students rely on caffeine to help them study. Caffeine does allow one to remain alert for longer, but there is no evidence that it helps memory abilities. In fact, if anything, people who have caffeine in their bloodstreams are less efficient learners than those who do not have caffeine in their blood (Mednick et al., 2008). So drink your cappuccino if you like it, but don't expect it to help you remember. However, it is likely that memory-enhancing drugs are not far off in the future. For more on this topic, go to www.sagepub.com/schwartz.

Second, there is no science behind the claim that you can learn new information by subliminal methods or by playing tapes while you sleep (Druckman & Bjork, 1991). Subliminal learning means presenting information below the threshold of consciousness. Although such subliminal presentation can affect some behaviors (e.g., implicit memory), it does not seem to promote the learning and remembering of explicit information, such as the knowledge we acquire in college courses. Furthermore, there is no research to support the claim that playing tapes while sleeping will have any positive impact on later learning or remembering (Willingham, 2009).

Thus, by careful and intelligent use of these memory principles, it is possible to improve your memory. Repetition and distributed practice are important to the learning process—so we'll repeat them again: (1) Process for meaning, (2) use good retrieval cues, (3) use metamemory, and (4) distribute your practice and use the spacing effect.

MNEMONISTS

For the overwhelming majority of us, even when we follow all the recommendations in this chapter, memory will still be hard work and take time. However, through a combination of innate ability and practice, there are people with extraordinary memory. By and large, these people use memory techniques similar to the ones described in this chapter, but they often heavily rely on imagery and remember new information much more effortlessly than do the rest of us. In this section, we will consider some of these famous **mnemonists** and how they remember or remembered so well.

> **Mnemonists**: people with extraordinary memory. One becomes a mnemonist through a combination of innate ability and practice.

S

The famous Russian psychologist, A. R. Luria, wrote a book about his study of a young Russian man named Solomon Sherashevsky (Luria, 1968/1987). Luria refers to his subject by his initial S, but since Mr. Sherashevsky was also a public memory performer, there is no need for anonymity. Sherashevsky was born into an educated Jewish Russian family, growing up learning Hebrew and Yiddish as well as Russian. He would later use his multilingual abilities to help him remember large lists when giving demonstrations of his memory.

As Luria describes the history of this mnemonist, Mr. Sherashevsky was working as a reporter for a newspaper in Soviet-era Moscow when his editor noticed that, despite the fact that Sherashevsky never took notes, he seemed to remember everything: his assignment, the assignments of other reporters, indeed everything the editor said. On the urging of his editor, Sherashevsky visited the neuropsychologist Luria, who then began probing his memory, a collaboration that lasted years. In one study, Luria showed that he could give Sherashevsky a list of 70 items just one time, and Sherashevsky could repeat the list *in any order!*

One thing that became clear to Luria was that Sherashevsky's great memory was in part dependent on his unusual sensory characteristics. Sherashevsky had a condition called **synesthesia.** Synesthesia means that sensory qualities from one sense (e.g., vision) are perceived as being sensory qualities in another sense (e.g., sound) in addition to the actual modality that they are perceived in. Synesthesia does not involve hallucinations; people with it know where the perceptions are coming from in the environment and behave normally in most circumstances. However, they have interesting perceptual responses. Many people with synesthesia, for example, see words as colored. Thus, the word *image* may be purple, but the word *book* may be bright red. They know that the word *image* may be printed in any particular color and they perceive that too. But when they read the word *image,* a sensation of "purpleness" appears. Most people with this condition consider it an advantage, and many of them use it to become successful artists (see Ward, 2008). For more on synesthesia, go to www.sagepub.com/schwartz.

> **Synesthesia**: sensory qualities from one sense (e.g., vision) are perceived as being sensory qualities in another sense (e.g., sound) in addition to the actual modality that they are perceived in.

Sherashevsky employed his synesthesia to remember just about everything in his world throughout his life. He could remember a single list memorized for Luria a year later without any loss of details. He claimed to be able to remember events from very early in his infancy, well before the offset of childhood amnesia in most people. Sherashevsky parlayed his memory abilities into a career, as he toured Russia showing off his memory abilities. But Luria claims there was also a price to pay: Because of his vivid synesthesia and attention to sensory details, Sherashevsky would often become confused about the meaning of even the simplest stories. Sherashevsky was an intelligent man who could eventually figure out the meanings, but it was difficult for him at times because the sensory characteristics would always overwhelm the meaning intended by the storyteller. Thus, a particular metaphor by an author would elicit a synesthesiac reaction from him, which was often counter to the intended meaning of the metaphor. He also picked up on the slightest errors in text—such as when a blue coat is later referred to as "navy." The change in color would completely throw off his imagery of the story. Such conflicts were confusing to Sherashevsky.

Most of the empirical work done by Luria concentrated on Sherashevsky's extraordinary ability to encode meaningless information on the very first trial, such as his ability to hear and then recall a long list of numbers. Luria does express interest in Sherashevsky's seeming inability to forget information from autobiographical memory. However, Luria did not extend his research into this domain. Recently, there have been a number of cases of people reported with superior autobiographical memory, including people who claim to be able to remember everything they have done on every day of their life. Parker, Cahill, and McGaugh (2006) could find no events for which their mnemonist participant could not remember from her life. This woman claims no effort in encoding the events of her life; in fact, there are events that she wishes that she could forget, but she simply cannot. However, documented cases of such superior autobiographical memory are rare indeed. For more on the case investigated by Parker et al., go to www.sagepub.com/schwartz.

Rajan Mahadevan

Mr. Mahadevan entered the **Guinness Book of World Records** in 1984 by reciting over 30,000 digits of the irrational number pi (this record has since been broken several times). From an early age, Mr. Mahadevan showed an extraordinary ability to remember numbers. His parents, part of the educated elite, in India, fostered his ability and helped him practice it. Even better than Sherashevsky, Mr. Mahadevan has a digit span of close to 80 numbers. Unlike Sherashevsky, Mr. Mahadevan does not have synesthesia. Rather, any particular sequence of digits will remind him of some already memorized sequence, usually from pi. Thus, he uses his incredible long-term memory of digit sequences as the basis of remembering new sequences. Interestingly, Mr. Mahadevan's superior memory is confined to numbers. In other respects, his memory is normal, although like S, Mr. Mahadevan is a highly educated and intelligent individual. Mr. Mahadevan is currently a psychology instructor in the United States (see C. P. Thompson, Cowan, & Frieman, 1993, for a more detailed description of Mr. Mahadevan's memory abilities).

Many other mnemonists have been studied by experimental psychologists. Some seem similar to Sherashevsky in that they have synesthesia (Yaro & Ward, 2007) or are unique to numbers like Mahadevan (Takahashi, Shimizu, Saito, & Tomoyori, 2006). Because this chapter is more about ordinary individuals, we will leave our discussion of mnemonists here. But it is worth pointing out the title of one of the most recent scientific reports on a mnemonist—namely, "One percent ability and ninety-nine percent perspiration" (Takahashi et al., 2006). That is, even most individuals who claim to have great memory, demonstrate great memory, and even work as professional mnemonists need to put a great deal of work into it.

Exceptional memory has actually become a competitive sport. Every 2 years, at the Memory Olympics, participants compete in remembering names, remembering digits, and many other memory-dependent games. Maguire, Valentine, Wilding, and Kapur (2003) were able to study some of these competitors using functional magnetic resonance imaging (fMRI). Relative to control participants, the "olympians" showed more activity in areas of the right prefrontal cortex, which are associated with spatial memory and navigation. This is consistent with the report by more than 90% of the memory experts that they use the method of loci to aid their memory. For more on memory competitions, go to www.sagepub.com/schwartz.

COLLABORATIVE MEMORY

Memory is not strictly a solitary activity. Many students form study groups and meet together to learn new material and prepare for exams. Graduate students and faculty have group meetings where they discuss new research—the goal might not be specifically to memorize the new research, but learning the hypotheses, methods, and findings of new studies is a constant task for scientists in any field. Coaches have group meetings with their teams so that the team members can learn new plays and practice them together. Businesses may call joint strategy sessions in which a number of employees must remember old strategies and generate new ones. Thus, in many instances, remembering can be a collaborative enterprise.

We often play games, which involve collaborative remembering. "Trivial Pursuit" is more fun when two or more people are on the same team, trying to remember the same facts. Imagine a game in which each person is asked to remember a list of related items. Thus, each person might be asked to recall as many names of U.S. presidents as he or she can think of. One person might generate "Washington, Adams, Jefferson," whereas the other person might generate, "Obama, Bush, Clinton." Now think of it as an experiment. In one condition, three people are placed in separate rooms and are asked to generate as many names of U.S. presidents as possible. When they have completed the task, the number of presidents generated in total (not counting duplicates) can then be tallied. In a second condition, three people are placed in the same room and asked collaboratively to generate the names of as many U.S. presidents as possible. The collaborating triads can then be matched and compared to triads working alone. Who remembers more?

It turns out that **collaborative memory** leads to collectively less recall than individuals remembering alone. Numerous experiments model the game described above. In one study, triads working separately recalled more information than triads working collaboratively (Blumen & Rajaram, 2008). That is, the study shows that recall is impaired when we do it collaboratively compared to when we do it by ourselves. Thus, if you want to maximize recall, you are better off working separately during retrieval of already learned items.

> **Collaborative memory:** working together with other people to remember information.

However, a study session is often a mix of studying new items and remembering already studied items. Does collaboration help when we are studying new items? There is some evidence that collaboration at the time of study (or encoding) does help memory (Rajaram & Pereira-Pasarin, 2007) but newer evidence that it does not (Barber, Rajaram, & Aron, 2010). Studying together has advantages, sometimes called the social facilitation effect. Members of a group may work harder to impress each other, to be competitive with each other, and may be more interested in studying longer because of the social aspect to it. Indeed, Rajaram and Pereira-Pasarin (2007) found that collaborative study led to better individual recognition memory than did individual study. However, when Barber et al. (2010) tested recall, there was a negative effect of collaborative study relative to individual study. Thus, it may be that collaborative study depends on the circumstances, but remembering together actually impairs performance. In addition, collaborative memory has implications for eyewitness memory (D. B. Wright, Memon, Skagerberg, & Gabbert Current, 2009). D. B. Wright et al. (2009) showed that the testimony of one witness can alter that of another.

SUMMARY

This chapter focuses on how each of us can improve our memory by learning and remembering more efficiently. Four major principles have been emphasized: (1) Process for meaning, (2) make use of retrieval cues, (3) use metamemory, and (4) make use of distributed practice. Each of these individually can improve memory, and certainly in combination, they can make your learning and remembering far more efficient. In this chapter, the various mnemonic improvement hints given throughout the book are organized according to these four memory principles. Moreover, it is possible to contrast normal memory and how to make it efficient with the exceptional memory seen in rare individuals. For the most part, these individuals combine a natural gift for memory with the same principles that improve normal memory. We closed the chapter with a discussion of the disadvantages and advantages of collaborative learning and remembering. Collaboration hurts recall but helps encoding. The author personally wishes each and every reader the best of luck in applying these cognitive principles to your own learning and remembering.

Table 13.1   Twenty-two mnemonic hints.

- Mnemonic Improvement Hint 1.1: **Overlearning:** study past the point where you have mastered the material. Promotes long-term retention.
- Mnemonic Improvement Hint 1.2: **Spacing effect or distributed practice.** Space your study over time—don't study all at once. Promotes long-term retention.
- Mnemonic Improvement Hint 1.3: **Think of learning as work:** There is no magic bullet for memory. Good memory requires hard work. Strategic planning.
- Mnemonic Improvement Hint 1.4: **External cues can help.** Structure your environment to help you remember. Prospective memory and memory for ordinary objects.
- Mnemonic Improvement Hint 3.1: **Chunking:** group information in working memory. Promotes good short-term retention.
- Mnemonic Improvement Hint 3.2: **Practice working memory tasks.** Train your working memory. Promotes good short-term retention.
- Mnemonic Improvement Hint 4.1: **Deep processing:** Use elaborative encoding. Promotes rapid encoding of new information.
- Mnemonic Improvement Hint 4.2: **The Generation Effect:** Produce your own associations and practice recalling the items you need to remember. Promotes rapid encoding of new information.
- Mnemonic Improvement Hint 4.3: **Organization:** Apply meaningful categories to to-be-learned information. Promotes rapid encoding of new information.
- Mnemonic Improvement Hint 4.4: **Distinctiveness:** Focus on a distinctive aspect of to-be-learned information. Promotes rapid encoding of new information.
- Mnemonic Improvement Hint 4.5: **Retrieval cues:** Create powerful retrieval cues. Ensures access to learned information.
- Mnemonic Improvement Hint 4.6: **Encoding specificity principle:** Match testing environment to learning environment. Ensures access to learned information.
- Mnemonic Improvement Hint 5.1: **Immersion technique:** All instruction for a to-be-learned language is in the to-be-learned language. Fastest way to learn new languages.

(Continued)

Table 13.1 (Continued)

- Mnemonic Improvement Hint 6.1: **The method of loci:** Use well-learned landscape to encode new items. Promotes rapid encoding of new information.
- Mnemonic Improvement Hint 6.2: **Keyword technique:** Make visual images that link to-be-learned items. Promotes rapid encoding of new information.
- Mnemonic Improvement Hint 6.3: **Pegword technique:** Use both visual and auditory imagery to learn new items. Promotes rapid encoding of new information.
- Mnemonic Improvement Hint 7.1: **Keep a memory diary.** Record events from your life every day. Promotes good retention of autobiographical events.
- Mnemonic Improvement Hint 8.1: **The cognitive interview:** Use cognitive principles when retrieving eyewitness events. Allows for maximum retrieval of event detail.
- Mnemonic Improvement Hint 8.2: **Close your eyes:** It allows you to recall more details from episodic memories without a cost in false memories.
- Mnemonic Improvement Hint 9.1: **Judgments of learning:** Assess what you know and don't know. Use this as a guide as to what to study. Promotes rapid encoding of new information.
- Mnemonic Improvement Hint 9.2: **Degree of mastery:** Study easy or difficult items based on time constraints and learning goals. Maximizes study efficiency.
- Mnemonic Improvement Hint 11.1: **Memory conversations:** Frequent discussions with young children about past events promote later recall of those events. Promotes good retention of autobiographical events.

KEY TERMS

Process for meaning	Encoding variability	Distributed practice
Make use of retrieval cues	Encoding specificity	Massed practice
Metamemory	Retrieval practice	Spacing effect
Stroop effect	Generation effect	Expanded retrieval practice
Subjective organization	Judgments of learning	
Technical mnemonics	Region of proximal learning	Mnemonists
Acronyms		Synesthesia
Acrostics	Self-regulated learning	Collaborative memory

REVIEW QUESTIONS

1. What are the four broad principles of memory improvement?

2. What is the Stroop effect, and what principle does it demonstrate with respect to memory improvement?

3. What is subjective organization? What evidence exists that subjective organization is superior to other forms of organization?

4. What is encoding variability? How can it be employed to improve memory?

5. What is retrieval practice? How can it be employed to improve memory?

6. How can the judgments of learning be used by students to improve the efficiency of their study? What is the region of proximal learning, and how can judgments of learning inform it?

7. When is massed practice helpful? Why is distributed practice generally a better study strategy?

8. Kornell (2009b) conducted a study to examine the differences between massed and distributed practice. What was his methodology, and what did he demonstrate?

9. What is a mnemonist? How do their memories differ from those of normal individuals?

10. What is collaborative memory? When is it an advantage and when is it a disadvantage?

ONLINE RESOURCES

1. For a related approach to memory improvement, go to Daniel Willingham's website at http://www.danielwillingham.com.

2. Go to http://faculty.washington.edu/chudler/java/ready.html for an interesting demonstration for the Stroop effect.

3. For Disney's version of musical mnemonics, go to http://www.youtube.com/watch?v=BdGxOB9J2t0.

4. For more on the advantages of self-testing and other mnemonic techniques, go to http://bps-research-digest.blogspot.com/2008/02/how-to-study.html.

5. For more on the region of proximal learning, go to http://www.columbia.edu/cu/psychology/metcalfe/Research.html.

6. For more on the differences between massed and distributed practice, go to http://www.psychologicalscience.org/observer/getArticle.cfm?id=2425.

7. It is likely that memory-enhancing drugs are not far off in the future. For more on this topic, go to http://www.newyorker.com/reporting/2009/04/27/090427fa_fact_talbot?currentPage=all. Also see http://www.scientificamerican.com/article.cfm?id=the-quest-for-a-smart-pil.

8. For more on synesthesia, go to http://www.syn.sussex.ac.uk.

9. For more on the case investigated by Parker et al., go to http://www.universityofcalifornia.edu/news/article/7952.

10. To learn more about the USA memory championships, go to http://www.usamemorychampionships.com.

 Go to www.sagepub.com/schwartz for additional exercises and study resources. Select **Chapter 13, Memory Improvement: A User's Guide** for chapter-specific resources.

Glossary

Absolute judgment: in a show-up, the witness matches the particular face to his or her memory of the face seen and decides if this particular face matches the memory.

Accessibility: that part of our stored memories that we can retrieve under the present conditions.

Acronyms: a mnemonic device in which the first letter of each word from a list is formed into an easily remembered word. For example, "HOMES" is a common acronym for remembering the Great Lakes of the United States and Canada (Huron, Ontario, Michigan, Erie, and Superior).

Acrostics: a mnemonic that involves taking the first letter from each item in the list and forming a sentence with an easily remembered visual image or auditory connection that makes the sentence memorable.

Action potentials: the electrochemical process of transmission in an axon.

Active suppression: a theory that explains repression. People may deliberately force themselves to not remember the item.

Allocation of study time: the decisions participants make about which items to study during an experiment.

Alzheimer's disease: one of many dementia-type illnesses that are more common in older adults than they are in younger adults. Memory is the first deficit detected in this disease.

Amnesia: memory deficits acquired through brain damage.

Amnesic syndrome: characteristic of the amnesic syndrome patient is specific impairment of encoding new information into both episodic and semantic memory, while most other cognitive functions remain intact.

Amount of information: the quantity of information retrieved while recalling an episodic event.

Amygdala: a part of the brain critical in emotional learning, fear, and memory.

Amyloid plaques: masses of unwanted proteins, which interfere with normal brain function.

Analog representation: a theory that argues that we store visual images in a manner similar to actual pictures.

Anosognosia: the failure to become aware of a cognitive deficit.

Anterograde amnesia: an inability to form new memories following brain damage.

Articulatory suppression: a concurrent task that prevents the participants from engaging in rehearsal within the phonological loop.

Associative model: we represent information in semantic memory in terms of connections among units of information. A node is the unit of memory, which is then connected to other nodes.

Audiolingual method: a method of learning a second language. Speaking and listening skills are taught rather than traditional vocabulary and grammar.

Availability: all information present in the memory system.

Axons: the part of the neuron that sends information to other neurons.

Behaviorism: a school of psychology that focused on only the relation of environmental inputs and the observable behavior of organisms, including human beings.

Benzodiazepines: drugs that are used usually because of their effects on anxiety, insomnia, and muscle relaxation. However, they are also strong amnesia-inducing drugs, especially within the episodic memory domain.

Bizarre imagery: forming strange visual images based on to-be-learned information can lead to good memory for that information.

Borrowed memories: when we feel a memory is our own when it actually corresponds to an event in another's past.

Capacity: the amount of information that can be maintained in working memory.

Capgras syndrome: patients come to believe that other people have been duplicated and that two sets of identical people may exist. It is caused by brain damage.

Category: mental construct referring to a set of objects or ideas that are grouped together or are associated with each other.

Central executive: the attentional mechanism of working memory.

Cerebral cortex: the outer layer of the brain most associated with higher cognitive and emotional functioning.

Characteristic features: according to feature comparison theory, characteristic features generally accompany an instance of the category but are not required.

Childhood amnesia: (also known as infantile amnesia) refers to the observation that adults have almost no episodic memories from the first 3 to 5 years of their lives.

Childhood amnesia—age-related changes in self-concept: the view that childhood amnesia is caused by the development of a coherent psychological self.

Childhood amnesia—influence of language on memory development: the view that childhood amnesia is caused by the growth of language ability in the young child provides the structure and narrative schemas necessary to support episodic memories.

Childhood amnesia—neurological transitions in memory systems: the view that childhood amnesia is caused by changes in the brain as it matures.

Childhood amnesia—psychodynamic view: the view that childhood amnesia is caused by active repression.

Cholinergics: drugs prescribed to patients with Alzheimer's disease that alleviate memory loss in early phases of the disease.

Chunk: memory unit consisting of related components.

Classical conditioning: a situation in which a relation exists between a stimulus (e.g., a ringing bell) and an outcome (e.g., getting food); the organism demonstrates behavior or response (e.g., salivating) that shows that the organism has learned the association between the stimulus and the outcome.

Clinical neuropsychology: the practice of helping brain-damaged patients recover and cope with their injuries.

Coexistence hypothesis: a theory that explains the misinformation effect. Participants form one memory about the original event and then form a second memory of reading the questions or reading the summary after the event.

Cognitive interview: a protocol designed to help police investigators obtain the maximum amount of information from witnesses with the least likelihood of inducing false memories.

Cognitive maps: mental representations of the external world. Based on our spatial representation of the world.

Cognitive neuroscience: the study of the role of the brain in producing cognition.

Cognitive psychology: an approach to psychology that emphasizes hidden mental processes.

Coherence: the processes that yield autobiographical memories, which are consistent with the working self.

Collaborative memory: working together with other people to remember information.

Concept: mental construct that contains information associated with a specific idea.

Concurrent tasks: tasks to be done simultaneously.

Confabulation: when amnesic patients lie about their past. They do not know they are not telling the truth because of deficits in source monitoring.

Conjugate reinforcement technique: a ribbon is attached to the infant's foot, which will eventually be attached to a mobile placed overhead. When the infant moves or kicks his or her foot, it will make the mobile move and jiggle. After a delay, the infant is again given the opportunity to move the mobile. If the infant does so in less time, learning has occurred.

Consolidation: to a neurological process whereby memory traces are made permanent in a person's long-term memory.

Contextual associations: an explanation for the retrieval of critical intrusions in the DRM. It states that all of the presented words are linked or associated to, in some way, the critical intrusion.

Control (in metamemory): our ability to regulate our learning or retrieval based upon our own monitoring.

Correspondence: the match between the retrieved memory and the actual event from the past.

Critical intrusions: the false memories created by a list in which all of the words are related or associated with the absent but suggested word.

Cross-language semantic priming: the effect of priming a word in one language has on a related word in another language in bilinguals or multilinguals.

Cross-race bias: people are, by and large, better at recognizing faces from their own "race" than from other racial groups.

Cue familiarity: stored information about the cue or the sense to which we recognize the cue influences our metamemory judgment for the to-be-remembered target.

Cue-word technique: an ordinary word is provided to participants and they are asked to provide the first memory—from any point in their life—that the word elicits.

Deep processing vs. shallow processing: when we process more deeply, that is, using elaborative or meaningful processing, we will be more likely to remember the information processed. When we process more shallowly, that is, using maintenance rehearsal or processing for sensory characteristics, we will remember less of the information processed.

Deese-Roediger-McDermott procedure (DRM): a procedure used to induce false memories for items on word lists. It involves presenting associates to an unpresented word in the list. The unpresented word is often recalled because of its associations to the other words.

Defining features: according to feature comparison theory, defining features are required for any example of a particular category.

Déjà vécu: the persistent feelings that people get that they have lived the present moment before; seen in neuropsychological patients.

Déjà vu: the experience we get when we think we have seen or heard something before but objectively know that we have not.

Dendrites: the part of the neuron that receives information from other neurons or from sensory receptors.

Dependent variable: dependent variables are the observations that we measure or record in response to the independent variable.

Developmental amnesia: a congenital memory deficit, usually restrictive to episodic memory.

Diary studies: the experimenters or participants record events from their own lives and keep track of events over long periods of time. Later, their memory for these events can be tested.

Diencephalon: the part of the brain that includes the thalamus and hypothalamus. It serves as an important relay point in the human memory circuit.

Digit span task: a task in which a person must remember a list of digits presented by an experimenter.

Direct-access theory: the idea that the judgments we make are based on the same processes that allow us to remember in the first place. That is, the metamemory judgments measure the strength of the stored memory even if that memory cannot be recalled.

Directed forgetting: the inhibition in memory that occurs when people are asked to forget some information but not other information.

Dissociation: brain damage (or an experimental variable) can affect one cognitive system but leave another one intact.

Dissociative amnesia: a condition in which only the traumatic event or events closely related to that trauma are not remembered.

Dissociative fugue: the psychogenic amnesia in which the patient forgets his or her personal identity in addition to access to his or her autobiographical past.

Distinctiveness: we search for the unique meaning for each item. Focusing on distinctive aspects of a stimulus causes comparatively good memory performance.

Distributed practice: space your study out over time.

Distributional information: refers to the patterns of speech that co-occur, that is, an aspect of language that always accompanies one another.

Double-blind procedure: neither the tester nor the participant should know what condition that participant is in.

Dual-store view (or separate store) of bilingual representation: the view that meaning is represented separately for each language in the lexical memory of a bilingual.

Duration of information in working memory: the amount of time in which information will remain in working memory if not rehearsed.

Ease-of-learning judgments: estimates of how likely an item will be remembered in advance of actual studying and are predictions about how difficult that item will be to learn.

Echoic memory: auditory sensory memory.

EEG (electroencephalography): using electrodes to measure the electrical output of the brain.

Elaborative rehearsal: processing the meaning of information in working memory.

Electroconvulsive therapy (ECT): an effective treatment for depression that involves delivering a strong electric shock to the head of a patient. It also creates periods of retrograde amnesia.

Empirical evidence: the product of scientific research. In order to be empirical evidence, it must be verifiable; that is, another scientist should be able to get the same results if he or she does the same or similar experiment.

Enactment effect: performed tasks are remembered better than those that are simply read about.

Encoding: the learning process, that is, how information is initially encountered and learned.

Encoding specificity: retrieval of information from memory will be maximized when the conditions at retrieval match the conditions at encoding.

Encoding variability: this principle claims that if you study an item of information under several different mental and physical conditions, you will be more likely to remember it than if you had studied for the same amount of time or trials but under uniform conditions.

Engram: the hypothetical physical unit of storage of a memory.

Episodic buffer: coordinates overlap between the auditory and visual systems.

Episodic memory: the neurocognitive memory system that encodes, stores, and retrieves memories of our personal individual experiences.

Errorless learning: a technique that trains a patient to learn a particular fact or skill while preventing that person from making errors during training.

Event-specific memories: individual events stored in episodic memory.

Exemplar theory: categories are classified by maintaining a large number of specific instances of a category (exemplars) that are associated with each other in semantic memory.

Expanded retrieval practice: expanded retrieval practice means that initially you space your study of a particular item very close together to maximize learning and the advantages of retrieval practice, but then your subsequent trials get further and further apart.

Experiment: set of observations that occur under controlled circumstances determined by the experimenter.

Eyewitness memory: memory for the events that transpire in a single event, usually witnessing a crime.

Failure to rehearse: a theory that explains repression. It argues that because memories of childhood trauma are highly negative, often private, and potentially embarrassing, they are not likely to be rehearsed often.

False-belief test: a child learns something that another person does not have the opportunity to learn. The child must then decide if the other person knows what he or she knows. Three-year-olds seldom succeed, whereas most 5-year-olds have mastered it.

False memory: memories that people have that do not correspond to events as they actually happened.

False memory induction procedure: false memories of events are induced in participants by repeatedly asking them about events they never experienced.

Family resemblance: membership in a category may be defined by each item's general similarity to other members in the category rather than by a specific list of features.

Fast mapping: the rules that allow a child to rapidly learn the meaning of words in his or her language.

Feature comparison theory: we define our categories by maintaining a list of features for any particular category.

Feeling-of-knowing judgments: an estimation of the likelihood that an unrecalled item will be recognized.

Field memories: autobiographical and visual memories in which we see the memory as if we were looking at the event through our own eyes.

Flashbulb memories: highly confident personal memories of surprising events. In order to study them, researchers have focused on the memory of public tragedies.

fMRI: magnetic fields create a three-dimensional image of the brain, which can capture both the structure and function of the brain.

Frontal lobe: the most anterior part of the cerebral cortex associated with higher emotion, decision making, metacognition, and memory.

Frontal lobe amnesia: people show some evidence of anterograde amnesia, although it tends to be much less severe than in other patients. They may also show anosognosia and confabulation.

Fusiform face area (FFA): a part of the brain in the inferior-temporal cortex, which appears to specialize in face recognition.

Fuzzy-trace theory: an explanation for the retrieval of critical intrusions in the DRM. It states that when items are encoded, they are not encoded literally but rather in terms of their meaning, a reasonable hypothesis given what we know about long-term memory.

General events: include the combined, averaged, and cumulative memory of highly similar events. General events also include extended events, which are long sequences of connected episodic events.

Generation effect: memory is better when we generate associations ourselves than when we simply read them.

Hemifield neglect: a condition in which patients ignore one half of the visual world. It occurs because of damage to the right parietal lobe.

HERA (hemispheric encoding/retrieval asymmetry): the theory that the right hemisphere is more involved in the retrieval of events from episodic memory and that the left hemisphere is more involved in the retrieval of events from semantic memory.

Hippocampus: an area of the brain associated with learning and memory. Damage can cause anterograde amnesia.

Hypnosis: hypnosis increases the number of false memories without increasing the number of accurate memories.

Hypothalamus: an area of the brain associated with basic emotions.

Iconic memory: visual sensory memory.

Imagery: the experience of retrieving a memory that is mostly visual or experienced primarily as a sensory experience. Imagery can also refer to the representation of those memories.

Imagination inflation: researchers induce false memories by simply having the participant imagine the event.

Imitation: mimicking the actions of another.

Immersion method: a method of learning a second language. All instruction is in the to-be-learned language, but outside of the classroom, the student returns to his or her native language.

Implicit memory: the preserved ability to perform tasks that are influenced by a past event without the person being aware of the event experience.

Implicit memory tests: tests that draw on the nonconscious aspects of memory.

Incidental learning: people encode information not by actively trying to remember but rather as by-product of perceiving and understanding the world.

Independent variable: independent variables are the factors that the experimenter manipulates among different conditions.

Indirect or inferential theories: the idea that we use a variety of clues, cues, tricks, and heuristics to estimate the strength of an item in memory, which we cannot measure directly.

Inhibition: mechanism that actively interferes with and reduces the likelihood of recall of particular information.

Inhibition theory: older adults do not have a good ability to block out irrelevant stimulation. This means that the memory declines seen in old age are a consequence of poor attentional processes. Inhibition also means the ability to suppress the retrieval of irrelevant information.

Intentional learning: people actively engage in learning information because they know that their memories may be tested.

Interference: new information enters working memory and displaces information already present.

Judgments of learning: are made during study and are judgments of whether the item has been learned already.

Keyword technique: involves creating an image that links two items in memory. With respect to language learning, it means creating an image that links the word in the language you know to the word in the language you are learning.

Korsakoff's disease: a severe form of amnesia brought on by long-term alcoholism. Characterized by anterograde amnesia, retrograde amnesia, anosognosia, and confabulation.

Labor in vain: when extra study does not guarantee that difficult items will be mastered.

Language acquisition device (LAD): a hypothetical model that allows young children to acquire language quickly and accurately.

Lemma: a hypothetical entity containing only semantic and syntactical information without any information concerning the phonology of the word.

Levels of categorization: categories are nested structures in which the level of organization is important in defining the category. There are three such levels: basic, subordinate, and superordinate.

Levels of processing: more meaningful handling of information leads to better encoding of that information.

Lexeme: the level of representation that stores the phonology of a word, that is, how the word sounds.

Lexical decision task: a cognitive task in which participants judge if a string of letters is a word as quickly as they can.

Lexical memory (lexicon): our mental dictionary, a representational system for the words of our language.

Lexicon: our mental dictionary.

Lifetime periods: the idiosyncratic, personal ways in which we organize our autobiographical past. These lifetime periods are usually organized by a common theme and may overlap in the actual physical time periods that they cover.

Limbic system: set of brain structures, located just beneath the cerebral cortex. It includes the hypothalamus, the hippocampus, and the amygdala. The limbic system functions as an important area for both memory and emotion.

Line-ups: a multiple-choice form of a face recognition test, often used by police to allow witnesses to identify suspects.

Long-term potentiation: the lowering of the threshold at which a postsynaptic dendrite will begin sending an electric signal.

Maintenance rehearsal: repeating information over and over.

Make use of retrieval cues: generate effect cues to help you remember. Test yourself frequently to practice retrieval.

Mammillary bodies: a subcortical region of the brain associated with learning. Damage can cause anterograde amnesia.

Massed practice: when all study occurs in one block of time.

Medial temporal lobes: a cortical area of the brain in the temporal lobes associated with learning and memory. Damage can cause anterograde amnesia.

Memory appropriation: an amnesiac may be able to retrieve an event based on someone else's repeated retelling of the event.

Memory compensation: rather than trying to answer a question about the past, amnesiacs talk instead about the issues that they are having with their amnesic syndrome.

Memory conversations: the talk that goes back and forth between a parent and a child concerning past events. The discussions we have with others about the past. Normal individuals frequently have memory conversations.

Memory efficiency view: the efficiency of learning new information and storing it in long-term memory.

Memory for faces: our ability to encode, represent, and store the visual features of human faces.

Memory importation: when amnesiacs describe a memory from before their injury as if it had happened after.

Memory rehabilitation: the interventions that clinical neuropsychologists use to promote improved memory performance in memory-impaired individuals.

Memory strategies view: the conscious activities a person engages in to assist the remembering of information.

Metacognition: our knowledge and awareness of our own cognitive processes.

Metamemory: our knowledge and awareness of our own memory processes.

Method of loci: the learner associates a list of new to-be-learned items with a series of well-known physical locations, using visual imagery.

Method of vanishing cues: this technique uses the spared implicit memory of amnesiacs to help them learn new skills.

Misinformation effect: the presenting of postevent misinformation about a witnessed event can obscure, change, or degrade the memory of the original event.

Mnemonists: people with extraordinary memory. One becomes a mnemonist through a combination of innate ability and practice.

Monitoring: our ability to reflect and become aware of what we know and what we do not.

Mood congruence: people are more likely to remember events or information that is positive when they are in a positive mood and more likely to remember events or information that is negative when they are in a negative mood.

Morphology: how words are constructed within a particular language.

Multiple sclerosis: a disease caused by the loss of myelin along human axons.

Neurofibrillary tangles: the twisting of amyloid plaques around neurons, which cause destruction of those neurons.

Neuroimaging: refers to a set of techniques that allows researchers to make detailed maps of the human brain and assign functions to particular regions in the brain.

Neurons: biological cells that specialize in the transmission and retention of information.

Neuropsychology: the study of patients with brain damage.

Neurotransmitters: chemicals (such as dopamine), which cross the synapse and induce an electric flow in the next neuron.

Nonnutritive sucking: a natural reflexive behavior biologically necessary for obtaining milk. Infants will suck differentially to the presence of a novel stimulus compared to a familiar stimulus. A novel stimulus will usually elicit an increase in sucking most likely because the stimulus is new and exciting.

Nonsense syllables: meaningless phrases that can be given to participants to study that avoid the effect of meaning on memory (e.g., *wob*).

Observer memories: autobiographical memories in which we take the vantage point of an outside observer and see ourselves as actors in our visual memory.

Occipital face area (OFA): an area of the occipital lobe has also been identified as crucial to face recognition.

Olfactory bulb: the primary organ in the brain for processing odors.

Open-ended questions: retrieval questions that contain very few cues, which allow the participant to describe his or her memory without suggestions. Open-ended questions limit the possibility of introducing inadvertent misinformation.

Operant conditioning: organisms learn to emit responses or behaviors (e.g., pressing a bar), in response to a stimulus, to achieve desirable outcomes (e.g., getting food) or avoiding undesirable outcomes (e.g., getting electric shock).

Organization: imposing a meaningful structure on to-be-learned material.

Orienting tasks: directs the participant's attention to some aspect of the stimuli—either deep or shallow—but does not alert the participant to the potential of a later memory test.

Overconfidence in judgments: people's judgments overestimate the likelihood that they will remember a to-be-learned item or set of items.

Overlearning: studying after material has been thoroughly learned.

Paired-associate learning: learning the association between two items, such as in language learning (e.g., learning the association between *monkey–le singe*).

Part-set cueing: occurs when people study some of the information in a set of already learned information but not all of it.

Pegword technique: a mnemonic technique that takes advantage of our natural auditory memory system as well as our visual imagery system. We associate new items with words in a known rhyme scheme.

PET (positron emission tomography): radioactive chemicals are placed in the blood, which allows scientists to obtain a three-dimensional image of the intact brain.

Phonetics: the details of speech sounds and how we make them.

Phonological loop: auditory working memory.

Phonology: the study of sounds and how they are used in a language.

Photographic memory: very strong visual memories that have a strong feeling of being images.

Posttraumatic stress disorder: psychological problems caused by exposure to extremely dangerous or stressful situations.

Pragmatics: language use, or the context of language.

Prefrontal cortex: the part of the frontal lobe most associated with higher emotion and memory.

Primacy effect: the observation that memory is usually superior for items at the beginning of a serial position curve; thought to be caused by the encoding of those items into long-term memory.

Primary memory: a term used to mean short-term memory.

Primary visual cortex: the first area in the occipital cortex that processes visual images.

Process for meaning: as you learn new material, focus on what it means.

Processing speed: age-related declines are caused because the older person's cognitive processing does not work as quickly as those of younger adults.

Pronunciation time: the amount of time it would take to say aloud the items being rehearsed in working memory.

Propositional representation: we store visual images in terms of a language-like code.

Prosopagnosia: an acquired deficit in face recognition caused by brain damage.

Prospective memory: memory for the things we need to do in the future.

Prototype theory: states that prototypes form the central characteristic in our representation of categories. A prototype is defined as the most typical member of a particular category.

Psychogenic amnesia: a broad term that covers all forms of amnesia that are not directly linked to disruption or injury to the brain.

Psycholinguistics: the study of the psychological processes involved in human language.

Random assignment: any particular participant is equally likely to be assigned to any of the conditions.

Reading fluency: the ability to read at speeds sufficient to process and understand written material.

Reality monitoring: refers to our ability to distinguish whether our memory is of a real event or of an imagined event.

Recall: a person must generate the target memory based on cues, but without seeing or hearing the actual target memory.

Recency effect: the observation that memory is usually superior for items at the end of a serial position curve; thought to be caused by the maintenance of those items in working memory.

Recognition: person must identify the target memory from presented item(s).

Recovery of repressed memories: the ability to recover previously forgotten memories that had been repressed.

Reduplicative paramnesia: a condition in which patients believe that places or locations have been duplicated and that the two locations exist simultaneously. It is caused by brain damage.

Region of proximal learning: a theory of metamemory that advances that an adaptive strategy is to study those items that have not yet been learned but are not too difficult. We maximize our learning by studying the leading edge of difficulty. That is, we maximize our learning by studying the easiest items we have not mastered yet.

Rehearsal: actively maintaining the items in working memory by repeating them over and over (maintenance rehearsal) or by elaborating on the item to some other concept (elaborative rehearsal).

Rehearsal prevention task: a task that prevents a participant from maintaining information in working memory.

Relative judgment: in a line-up, participants match their memory of what they saw in an event to each of the presented faces in the line-up and then try to determine which is the closest match.

Remember/know judgments: a task in which participants determine the feeling of memories by assigning them categories of "remember" or "know."

Reminiscence bump: the spike in recalled memories corresponding to late adolescence to early adulthood, or roughly between the ages of 16 and 25.

Repetition priming: the effect of presenting a stimulus on the processing of that same stimulus at a later date. Amnesiacs will show repetition priming even if they do not consciously recall the target.

Representation: the storage of information in memory when that information is not in use.

Repression: the active forgetting of highly emotional memories, usually from childhood.

Retention interval: the amount of time that transpires between the learning of an event or material and when recall for that event or material occurs.

Retrieval: the process of how we activate information from long-term memory and access it when we need it.

Retrieval bias: a technique used to make some information easier to recall than other information.

Retrieval cues: we use information present in our current environment, that is, retrieval cues, to trigger our memories of past events.

Retrieval of related information: when we retrieve information related to a target, that information can influence our metamemory judgment for learning or remembering the target.

Retrieval practice: this means to learn by testing oneself. That is, making yourself retrieve information is a superior method of learning than simply rereading that information.

Retrieval-induced inhibition: when recently retrieved information interferes with the retrieval of other related information.

Retrograde amnesia: when patients lose the ability to retrieve memories of events prior to brain damage.

Retrospective confidence judgments: an estimation that a retrieved answer is indeed correct.

Ribot's law: newer memories will be more affected by retrograde amnesia than older memories.

Right hemisphere/left hemisphere: the brain is divisible into two symmetrical halves, oriented in the left-right direction.

Savings score: the reduction in time required to relearn a previously mastered list.

Schema: generalized knowledge about an event, a person, or a situation.

Script: well-learned sequences of events associated with common activities.

Second-language acquisition: occurs when a person has already mastered his or her native language and then begins learning a second language.

Self-reference effect: the observation that linking to-be-learned information to personally relevant information about oneself creates strong encoding.

Self-regulated learning: the continuous monitoring of one's own knowledge and the continuous use of this monitoring to make informed decisions about learning and memory.

Semantic categories: meaning affects our cognitive maps. For example, people tend to think of borders between countries as being more straight than they often are.

Semantic memory: the neurocognitive memory system that encodes, stores, and retrieves information concerning knowledge of the world.

Semantic priming: the effect of one word or idea on the processing of a related word or idea. A related word will activate a target item and allow it to be processed more quickly.

Semantics: the study of meaning of words in psycholinguistics.

Sensory memory: a very brief memory system that holds literal information for a fraction of a second to allow cognitive processing.

Sentence verification tasks: participants are asked to decide as quickly as possible if a sentence is true or false.

Serial position curve: the observation that participants remember items well from the beginning and end of a list but not from the middle.

Shepard and Metzler's (1971) mental rotation experiment: an early experiment on visual imagery that showed that representation is analog.

Short-term memory: an older term used to describe the memory system that holds information for a short period of time, up to 15 seconds.

Short-term memory amnesia: when patients have deficits keeping larger amounts of information stored or rehearsed in working memory.

Show-ups: old-new recognition in which the participant sees only one face and must decide if that face was a face that he or she has seen earlier.

Single-store view of bilingual representation: there is a common semantic level of representation—that is, meaning is shared in bilinguals. The shared semantic representational system then connects to lemma-level representations for each language.

Source amnesia: deficits in correctly attributing the source of a memory.

Source judgments: our attributions of where of from whom we learned something.

Source memory: refers to the ability of an individual to remember from whom or where (that is, what source) they learned something.

Spacing effect: more learning occurs when two study trials on the same information are spread out over time than when they occur successively.

Speech errors: errors in ordinary speech.

Spreading activation: refers to the transfer of activation from one node to an associated node.

State-dependent memory: when encoding specificity is applied to internal human states such as drug state or mood states.

Stroop effect: interference in identifying the color of a stimulus if the stimulus is a word denoting another color.

Submersion method: the language learner is surrounded by native speakers of the to-be-learned language, usually in a foreign country. People are instructed not to use the learner's native language.

Substantia nigra: a part of the brain that produces dopamine. In Parkinson's disease, this brain region does not produce enough dopamine.

Suggestibility: the tendency to incorporate information from sources other than the original witnessed event. These other sources may be potentially misleading. Other sources include other people, written materials, or pictures.

Survival processing: processing information in terms of its value to surviving the wild is a surprisingly effective manner in which to encode information.

Synapses: gaps between the axon of one neuron and the dendrite of the next neuron, in which transmission occurs via neurotransmitters.

Synesthesia: sensory qualities from one sense (e.g., vision) are perceived as being sensory qualities in another sense (e.g., sound) in addition to the actual modality that they are perceived in.

Syntax: the word order within a language and other aspects of grammar.

Taxonomic constraint: states that words refer to categories, which share meaning.

Technical mnemonics: ready-made methods of learning information such as acronyms or acrostics.

Temporal lobe: a part of the cerebral cortex associated with learning, memory, audition, and language.

Terminal buttons: the ends of axon that hold neurotransmitters.

Thalamus: an area of the brain heavily connected to other areas of the brain. It appears to serve as a routing center, connecting disparate parts of the brain.

Theory of mind: the awareness that other individuals have separate states of awareness different from that of our own.

Tip-of-the-tongue states: the feeling that an unrecalled item will be recalled soon.

Trace impairment view: a theory that explains the misinformation effect. In this view, the original memory is altered by the misinformation.

Traditional method: words are translated from the speaker's native language into the new language. Grammar is taught in the native language, and reading and writing are emphasized.

Transfer-appropriate processing: retrieval will be stronger when the cognitive processes present at the time of retrieval are most similar to the ones that were present at the time of encoding.

Transient global amnesia: a rare form of amnesia, in which the amnesic affects are short-lived, usually on the order of hours.

Traumatic brain injuries: sudden and devastating injuries to the brain.

Use-it-or-lose-it hypothesis: older adults who engage in complex mental activity on a regular basis are more likely to preserve function, whereas those who do not engage in complex mental activity are more likely to suffer declines.

Verbal facilitation: when hearing verbal descriptions makes it easier to remember visual features.

Verbal fluency: the ability to talk without pausing or stopping.

Verbal overshadowing: when hearing a verbal description makes it more difficult to remember visual features.

Visual recognition: infants will look selectively at novel stimuli over familiar stimuli.

Visuospatial sketchpad: visual working memory.

von Restorff effect: advantage in memory that distinctive items have over less distinctive items.

Whole-object assumption: refers to the fact that young infants appear to innately know that words usually refer to an entire object, rather than parts of it or parts of the object and adjacent objects.

Word: in psycholinguistics, a word means the smallest unit of grammar that represents a full meaning.

Word fragment completion: in this task, a participant is given some letters of a word but not all of them and must figure out the word.

Word length effect: longer words are more difficult to maintain in working memory than shorter words.

Working memory: the neural structures and cognitive processes that maintain the accessibility of information for short periods of time in an active conscious state.

Working self: the monitoring function that controls the retrieval of information from the levels of representation. The working self includes the goals and self-images that make up our view of ourselves.

References

Abelson, R. P. (1981). Psychological status of the script concept. *American Psychologist, 36,* 715–729.

Aggleton, J. P. (2008). Understanding anterograde amnesia: Disconnections and hidden lesions. *Quarterly Journal of Experimental Psychology, 61,* 1441–1471.

Ait-Ghezala, G., Mathura, V. S., Laporte, V., Quadros, A., Paris, D., Patel, N., . . . Mullan, M. (2005). Genomic regulation after CD40 stimulation in microglia: relevance to Alzheimer's disease. *Molecular Brain Research, 140,* 73–85.

Alloway, T. P., Gathercole, S. E., Adams, A.-M., Willis, C., Eaglen, R., & Lamont, E. (2005). Working memory and phonological awareness as predictors of progress towards early learning goals at school entry. *British Journal of Developmental Psychology, 23,* 417–426.

Amaral, D., & Lavenex, P. (2007). Hippocampal neuroanatomy. In P. Andersen, R. Morris, D. Amaral, T. Bliss, & J. O'Keefe (Eds.), *The hippocampus book* (pp. 37–115). Oxford, UK: Oxford University Press.

Anderson, M. C. (2007). Inhibition: Manifestations in long-term memory. In H. L. Roediger III, Y. Dudai, & S. M. Fitzpatrick (Eds.), *Science of memory: Concepts* (pp. 295–299). New York, NY: Oxford University Press.

Anderson, M. C., Bjork, R. A., & Bjork, E. L. (1994). Remembering can cause forgetting: Retrieval dynamics in long-term memory. *Journal of Experimental Psychology: Learning, Memory, and Cognition, 20,* 1063–1087.

Anderson, M. C., & Green, C. (2001). Suppressing unwanted memories by executive control. *Nature, 410,* 366–369.

Anderson, M. C., Ochsner, K. N., Kuhl, B., Cooper, J., Robertson, E., Gabrieli, S. W., . . . Gabrieli, J. D. E. (2004). Neural systems underlying the suppression of unwanted memories. *Science, 303,* 232–235.

Anderson, N., & Craik, F. I. M. (2000). Memory in the aging brain. In E. Tulving & F. I. M. Craik (Eds.), *The Oxford handbook of memory* (pp. 411–426). New York, NY: Oxford University Press.

Andrés, P., Van der Linden, M., & Parmentier, F. B. R. (2004). Directed forgetting in working memory: Age-related differences. *Memory, 12,* 248–256.

Arbuckle, T. Y., & Cuddy, L. L. (1969). Discrimination of item strength at time of presentation. *Journal of Experimental Psychology, 81,* 126–131.

Bacon, E., Schwartz, B. L., Paire-Ficout, L., & Izaute, M. (2007). Dissociation between the cognitive process and the phenomenological experience of the TOT: Effect of the anxiolytic drug lorazepam on TOT states. *Cognition and Consciousness, 16,* 360–373.

Baddeley, A. D. (1986). *Working memory.* Oxford, UK: Clarendon.

Baddeley, A. D. (2000). The episodic buffer: A new component of working memory? *Trends in Cognitive Sciences, 4,* 417–423.

Baddeley, A. D. (2007). *Working memory, thought and action.* Oxford, UK: Oxford University Press.

Baddeley, A. D., & Hitch, G. J. (1974). Working memory. In G. Bower (Ed.), *Recent advances in learning and memory* (Vol. 8, pp. 47–90). New York, NY: Academic Press.

Baddeley, A. D., & Longman, D. J. A. (1978). The influence of length and frequency of training session on the rate of learning to type. *Ergonomics, 21,* 627–635.

Baddeley, A. D., & Wilson, B. A. (2002). Prose recall and amnesia: Implications for the structure of working memory. *Neuropsychologia, 40,* 1737–1743.

Bahrick, H. P. (1984). Semantic memory content in permastore: Fifty years of memory for Spanish learned in school. *Journal of Experimental Psychology, 113,* 1–29.

Barber, S. J., Rajaram, S., & Aron, A. (2010). When two is too many: Collaborative encoding impairs memory. *Memory & Cognition, 38,* 255–264.

Barnhardt, T. M., Choi, H., Gerkens, D. R., & Smith, S. M. (2006). Output position and word relatedness effects in a DRM paradigm: Support for a dual-retrieval process theory of free recall and false memories. *Journal of Memory and Language, 55,* 213–231.

Bartlett, F. C. (1932). *Remembering: A study in experimental and social psychology.* Cambridge, UK: Cambridge University Press.

Basden, B. H., Basden, D. R., & Morales, E. (2003). The role of retrieval practice in directed forgetting. *Journal of Experimental Psychology: Learning, Memory, and Cognition, 29,* 389–397.

Bauer, P. J. (2002). Long-term recall memory: Behavioral and neuro-developmental changes in the first two years of life. *Current Directions in Psychological Science, 11,* 137–141.

Bauer, P. J. (2006). Constructing a past in infancy: A neuro-developmental account. *Trends in Cognitive Sciences, 10,* 175–181.

Bearce, K. H., & Rovee-Collier, C. (2006). Repeated priming increases memory accessibility in infants. *Journal of Experimental Child Psychology, 93,* 357–376.

Belleville, S., Caza, N., & Peretz, I. (2003). A neuropsychology argument for a processing view of memory. *Journal of Memory and Language, 48,* 686–403.

Bellezza, F. S. (1996). Mnemonic methods to enhance storage and retrieval. In E. L. Bjork & R. A. Bjork (Eds.), *Memory* (pp. 345–380). San Diego, CA: Academic Press.

Belli, R. F., Windschitl, P. D., McCarthey, T. T., & Winfrey, S. E. (1992). Detecting memory impairment with a modified test procedure: Manipulating retention interval with centrally presented event items. *Journal of Experimental Psychology: Learning, Memory, and Cognition, 18,* 356–367.

Benjamin, A. S., Bjork, R. A., & Schwartz, B. L. (1998). The mismeasure of memory: When retrieval fluency is misleading as a metamnemonic index. *Journal of Experimental Psychology: General, 127,* 55–68.

Benjamin, A. S., & Diaz, M. (2008). Measurement of relative metamnemonic accuracy. In J. Dunlosky & R. A. Bjork (Eds.), *Handbook of memory and metamemory* (pp. 73–94). New York, NY: Psychology Press.

Bennett, D. A., Schneider, J. A., Tang, Y., Arnold, S. E., & Wilson, R. S. (2006). The effect of social networks on the relation between Alzheimer's disease pathology and level of cognitive function in old people: A longitudinal cohort study. *Lancet: Neurology, 5,* 406–412.

Benson, D. F., Gardner, H., & Meadows, J. C. (1976). Reduplicative paramnesia. *Neurology, 26,* 147–151.

Bergen, P. S., Thompson, P. J., Baxendale, S. A., Fish, D. R., & Shorvon, S. D. (2000). Remote memory in epilepsy. *Epilepsia, 41,* 231–239.

Bermejo-Pareja, F., Benito-León, J., Vega, S., Medrano, M. J., & Román, G. C. (2008). Incidence and subtypes of dementia in three elderly populations of central Spain. *Journal of the Neurological Sciences, 264,* 63–72.

Bernstein, D. M., & Loftus, E. F. (2009). The consequences of false memories for food preferences and choices. *Perspectives on Psychological Science, 4,* 135–139.

Berntsen, D., & Rubin, D. C. (2004). Cultural life scripts structure recall from autobiographical memory. *Memory & Cognition, 32,* 427–442.

Berntsen, D., & Rubin, D. C. (2006). Emotion and vantage point in autobiographical memory. *Cognition & Emotion, 20,* 1193–1215.

Berntsen, D., & Rubin, D. C. (2008). The reappearance hypothesis revisited: Recurrent involuntary memories after traumatic events and in everyday life. *Memory & Cognition, 36,* 449–460.

Beuhring, T., & Kee, D. W. (1987). Developmental relationships among metamemory, elaborative strategies, and associative memory. *Journal of Experimental Child Psychology, 44,* 377–400.

Bisiach, E., & Luzzatti, C. (1978). Unilateral neglect of representational space. *Cortex, 14,* 129–133.

Bjork, R. A. (1988). Retrieval practice and the maintenance of knowledge. In M. M. Gruneberg, P. E. Morris, & R. N. Sykes (Eds.), *Practical aspects of memory II* (pp. 396–401). London: John Wiley.

Bjork, R. A. (1992). William Kaye Estes as mentor, colleague, and friend. In A. Healy, S. Kosslyn, & R. Shiffrin (Eds.), *From learning theory to connectionist theory* (Vol. 1, pp. vii–x) and *From learning processes to cognitive processes: Essays in honor of William K. Estes* (Vol. 2, pp. viii–xi). Hillsdale, NJ: Lawrence Erlbaum.

Bjork, R. A., & Bjork, E. L. (1992). A new theory of disuse and an old theory of stimulus fluctuation. In A. F. Healy, S. M. Kosslyn, & R. M. Shiffrin (Eds.), *From learning processes to cognitive processes: Essays in honor of William K. Estes* (Vol. 2, pp. 35–67). Hillsdale, NJ: Lawrence Erlbaum.

Bjork, R. A., & Woodward, A. E. (1973). Directed forgetting of individual words in free recall. *Journal of Experimental Psychology, 99,* 22–27.

Blaney, P. H. (1986). Affect and memory: A review. *Psychological Bulletin, 99,* 229–246.

Blumen, H. M., & Rajaram, S. (2008). Influence of re-exposure and retrieval disruption during group collaboration on later individual recall. *Memory, 16,* 231–244.

Botvinick, M. (2007). Conflict monitoring and decision making: Reconciling two perspectives on anterior cingulate function. *Cognitive, Affective and Behavioral Neuroscience, 7,* 356–366.

Botzung, A., Denkova, E., Ciuciu, P., Scheiber, C., & Manning, L. (2008). The neural bases of the constructive nature of autobiographical memories studied with a self-paced fMRI design. *Memory, 16,* 351–363.

Bower, G. H. (2000). A brief history of memory research. In E. Tulving & F. I. M. Craik (Eds.), *The Oxford handbook of memory* (pp. 3–32). New York, NY: Oxford University Press.

Brainerd, C. J., Wright, R., Reyna, V. F., & Mojardin, A. H. (2001). Conjoint recognition and phantom recollection. *Journal of Experimental Psychology: Learning, Memory, and Cognition, 27,* 307–327.

Brandt, J., & Rich, J. B. (1995). Memory disorders in the dementias. In A. D. Baddeley, B. A. Wilson, & F. N. Watts (Eds.), *Handbook of memory disorders* (pp. 243–270). New York, NY: John Wiley.

Bransford, J. D., & Johnson, M. K. (1972). Contextual prerequisites for understanding: Some investigations of comprehension and recall. *Journal of Verbal Learning and Verbal Behavior, 11,* 717–726.

Brewer, W. F., & Treyens, J. C. (1981). Role of schemata in memory for places. *Cognitive Psychology, 13,* 207–230.

Brookmeyer, R., Johnson, E., Ziegler-Graham, K., & Arrighi, M. H. (2007). Forecasting the global burden of Alzheimer's disease. *Alzheimer's and Dementia, 3,* 186–191.

Brooks, L. (1968). Spatial and verbal components of the act of recall. *Canadian Journal of Psychology, 22,* 349–368.

Brown, A. S. (1991). A review of the tip-of-the-tongue experience. *Psychological Bulletin, 109,* 204–223.

Brown, A. S. (1998). Transient global amnesia. *Psychonomic Bulletin & Review, 5,* 401–427.

Brown, C., & Lloyd-Jones, T. J. (2005). Verbal facilitation of face recognition. *Memory & Cognition, 33,* 1442–1456.

Brown, J. (1958). Some tests of the decay theory of immediate memory. *Quarterly Journal of Experimental Psychology, 10,* 12–21.

Brown, R., & Kulik, J. (1977). Flashbulb memories. *Cognition, 5,* 73–99.

Brown, R., & McNeill, D. (1966). The "tip of the tongue" phenomenon. *Journal of Verbal Learning and Behavior, 5,* 325–337.

Bruce, V., Burton, M., & Hancock, P. (2007). Remembering faces. In R. C. L. Lindsay, D. F. Ross, J. D. Read, & M. P. Toglia (Eds.), *The handbook of eyewitness psychology: Vol II. Memory for people* (pp. 87–100). Mahwah, NJ: Lawrence Erlbaum.

Brunel, F. F., & Nelson, M. R. (2003). Message order effects and gender differences in advertising persuasion. *Journal of Advertising Research, 42,* 330–341.

Buchanan, J. P., Gill, T. V., & Braggio, J. T. (1981). Serial position and clustering effects in a chimpanzee's free recall. *Memory & Cognition, 9,* 651–660.

Budson, A. E., Roth, H. L., Rentz, D. M., & Ronthal, M. (2000). Disruption of the ventral visual stream in a case of reduplicative paramnesia. *Annals of the New York Academy of Sciences, 911,* 447–452.

Burt, C. D. B., Kemp, S., & Conway, M. A. (2001). What happens if you retest autobiographical memory 10 years on? *Memory & Cognition, 29,* 127–136.

Burt, C. D. B., Kemp, S., & Conway, M. A. (2003). Themes, events, and episodes in autobiographical memory. *Memory & Cognition, 31,* 317–325.

Butler, A. C., & Roediger, H. L., III. (2007). Testing improves long-term retention in a simulated classroom setting. *European Journal of Cognitive Psychology, 19,* 514–527.

Bywater, M., Andrade, J., & Turpin, G. (2004). Determinants of the vividness of visual imagery: The effects of delayed recall, stimulus affect and individual differences. *Memory, 12,* 479–488.

Cabeza, R., & Nyberg, L. (1997). Imaging cognition: An empirical review of PET studies with normal subjects. *Journal of Cognitive Neuroscience, 9,* 1–26.

Calkins, M. W. (1894). Association: I. *Psychological Review, 1,* 476–483.

Campbell, J., & Mayer, R. E. (2009). Questioning as an instructional method: Does it affect learning from lectures? *Applied Cognitive Psychology, 23,* 747–759.

Campbell, R., & Conway, M. A. (1995). *Broken memories: Case studies in memory impairment.* Malden, MA: Blackwell.

Canter, P. H., & Ernst, E. (2007). Ginkgo biloba is not a smart drug: An updated systematic review of randomized clinical trials testing the nootropic effects of G. biloba extracts in healthy people. *Human Psychopharmocology, 22,* 265–278.

Caramazza, A., & Miozzo, M. (1997). The relation between syntactic and phonological knowledge in lexical access: Evidence from the tip-of-the-tongue phenomenon. *Cognition, 64,* 309–343.

Castel, A. D. (2008). Metacognition and learning about primacy and recency effects in free recall: The utilization of intrinsic and extrinsic cues when making judgments of learning. *Memory & Cognition, 36,* 429–437.

Cavanaugh, J. C., & Borkowski, J. G. (1980). Searching for the metamemory-memory connections: A developmental study. *Developmental Psychology, 16,* 441–453.

Caza, N., & Belleville, S. (2008). Reduced short-term memory capacity in Alzheimer's disease: The role of phonological, lexical, and semantic processing. *Memory, 16,* 341–350.

Ceci, S. J., & Bronfenbrenner, U. (1985). "Don't forget to take the cupcakes out of the oven": Prospective memory, strategic time-monitoring, and context. *Child Development, 56,* 152–164.

Ceci, S. J., Papierno, P. B., & Kulkofsky, S. (2007). Representational constraints on children's suggestibility. *Psychological Science, 18,* 503–509.

Centers for Disease Control and Prevention. (2010). *Traumatic brain injury.* Retrieved May 16, 2010, from http://www.cdc.gov/traumaticbraininjury/

Chiroro, P. M., Tredoux, C. G., Radaelli, S., & Meissner, C. A. (2008). Recognising faces across continents: The effect of within-race variations on the own-race bias in face recognition. *Psychonomic Bulletin & Review, 15,* 1089–1092.

Chiu, C.-Y. P., Schmithorst, V. J., Brown, R. D., Holland, S. K., & Dunn, S. (2006). Making memory: A cross-sectional investigation of episodic memory encoding in childhood using fMRI. *Developmental Neuropsychology, 29,* 321–340.

Chomsky, N. (1986). *Knowledge of language.* New York: Praeger Special Studies.

Christina, R. W., & Bjork, R. A. (1991). Optimizing long-term retention and transfer. In D. Druckman & R. A. Bjork (Eds.), *In the mind's eye: Enhancing human performance* (pp. 23–56). Washington, DC: National Academy Press.

Cinel, C., Boldini, A., Fox, E., & Russo, R. (2008). Does the use of mobile phones affect human short-term memory or attention? *Applied Cognitive Psychology, 22,* 1113–1125.

Clancy, S. (2005). *Abducted: How people come to believe they were kidnapped by aliens.* Cambridge, MA: Harvard University Press.

Clare, L., Wilson, B. A., Carter, G., & Hodges, J. R. (2003). Cognitive rehabilitation as a component of early intervention in Alzheimer's disease: A single case study. *Aging and Mental Health, 71,* 15–21.

Cleary, A. M., Ryals, A. J., & Nomi, J. N. (2009). Can déjà vu result from similarity to a prior experience? Support for the similarity hypothesis of déjà vu. *Psychonomic Bulletin & Review, 16,* 1082–1088.

Coffman, J. L., Ornstein, P. A., McCall, L. E., & Curran, P. J. (2008). Linking teachers' memory-relevant language and the development of children's memory skills. *Developmental Psychology, 44,* 1640–1654.

Cohen, G. (1996). *Memory in the real world.* Hove, UK: Psychology Press.

Collins, A. M., & Loftus, E. (1975). A spreading activation theory of semantic memory. *Psychological Review, 82,* 407–428.

Collins, A. M., & Quillian, M. R. (1969). Retrieval time from semantic memory. *Journal of Verbal Learning and Verbal Behavior, 8,* 240–247.

Colombo, M., & Broadbent, N. (2000). Is the avian hippocampus a functional homologue of the mammalian hippocampus? *Neuroscience and Biobehavioral Reviews, 24,* 465–484.

Conway, M. A. (2005). Memory and the self. *Journal of Memory and Language, 53,* 594–628.

Conway, M. A., Anderson, S. J., Larsen, S. F., Donnelly, C. M., McDaniel, M. A., McClelland, A. G., . . . Logie, R. H. (1994). The formation of flashbulb memories. *Memory & Cognition, 22,* 326–343.

Conway, M. A., Cohen, G., & Stanhope, N. (1992). Very long-term memory for knowledge acquired at school and university. *Applied Cognitive Psychology, 6,* 467–482.

Conway, M. A., & Pleydell-Pearce, C. W. (2000). The construction of autobiographical memories in the self-memory system. *Psychological Review, 107,* 261–288.

Conway, M. A., Pleydell-Pearce, C. W., Whitecross, S. E., & Sharpe, H. (2003). Neurophysiological correlates of memory for experienced and imagined event. *Neuropsychologia, 41,* 334–340.

Conway, M. A., Wang, Q., Hanyu, K., & Hasque, S. (2005). A cross-cultural investigation of autobiographical memory: On the universality and cultural variation of the reminiscence bump. *Journal of Cross-Cultural Psychology, 36,* 739–749.

Cowan, N. (2001). The magical number 4 in short-term memory: A reconsideration of mental storage capacity. *Behavioral and Brain Sciences, 24,* 87–185.

Corkin, S. (2002). What's new with the amnesic patient H.M.? *Nature Reviews Neuroscience, 3,* 153–160.

Corkin, S., Amaral, D. G., Gonzalez, R. G., Johnson, K. A., & Hyman, B. T. (1997). H.M.'s medial temporal lobe lesions: Findings from magnetic resonance imaging. *Journal of Neuroscience, 17,* 3964–3979.

Costermans, J., Lories, G., & Ansay, C. (1992). Confidence level and the feeling of knowing in question answering: The weight of inferential processes. *Journal of Experimental Psychology: Learning, Memory, and Cognition, 18,* 142–150.

Craik, F. I. M., & Byrd, M. (1982). Aging and cognitive deficits: The role of attentional resources. In F. I. M. Craik & S. Trehub (Eds.), *Aging and cognitive processes* (pp. 191–211). New York, NY: Plenum.

Craik, F. I. M., & Lockhart, R. S. (1972). Levels of processing: A framework for memory research. *Journal of Verbal Learning and Verbal Behavior, 12,* 671–684.

Craik, F. I. M., Morris, R. G., & Gick, M. L. (1990). Adult age differences in working memory. In G. Vallar & T. Shallice (Eds.), *Neuropsychological impairments of short-term memory* (pp. 247–267). New York, NY: Cambridge University Press.

Craik, F. I. M., & Tulving, E. (1975). Depth of processing and the retention of words in episodic memory. *Journal of Experimental Psychology: General, 104,* 268–294.

Craik, F. I. M., Winocur, G., Palmer, H., Binns, M. A., Edwards, M., Bridges, K., . . . Stuss, D. T. (2007). Cognitive rehabilitation in the elderly: Effects on memory. *Journal of the International Neuropsychological Society, 13,* 132–142.

Crowder, R. G. (1992). Eidetic memory. In L. R. Squire (Ed.), *Encyclopedia of learning and memory.* New York, NY: Macmillan.

Crystal, D. (1998). *Language play.* Harmondsworth, UK: Penguin.

Curci, A., & Luminet, O. (2009). Flashbulb memories for expected events: A test of the emotional-integrative model. *Applied Cognitive Psychology, 23,* 98–114.

Cutler, B. L., Penrod, S. D., & Dexter, H. R. (1990). Juror sensitivity to eyewitness identification evidence. *Law and Human Behavior, 14,* 185–191.

Dahlgren, D. J. (1998). Impact of knowledge and age on tip-of-the-tongue rates. *Experimental Aging Research, 24,* 139–153.

Daneman, M., & Carpenter, P. A. (1980). Individual differences in working memory and reading. *Journal of Verbal Learning and Verbal Behavior, 19,* 450–466.

Daneman, M., & Hannon, B. (2001). Using working memory theory to investigate the construct validity of multiple-choice reading comprehension tests such as the SAT. *Journal of Experimental Psychology, 130,* 208–223.

Danion, J. M. (1994). Drugs as a tool for investigating memory. *European Neuropsychopharmacology, 4,* 179–180.

Darowski, E. S., Helder, E., Zacks, R. T., Hasher, L., & Hambrick, D. Z. (2008). Age-related differences in cognition: The role of distraction control. *Neuropsychology, 22,* 638–644.

Daselaar, S. M., Rice, H. J., Greenberg, D. L., Cabeza, R., LaBar, K. S., & Rubin, D. C. (2008). The spatiotemporal dynamics of autobiographical memory: Neural correlates of recall, emotional intensity, and reliving. *Cerebral Cortex, 18,* 217–229.

de Graaff, S., Verhoeven, L., Bosman, A. M. T., & Hasselman, F. (2007). Integrated pictorial mnemonics and stimulus fading: Teaching kindergartners letter sounds. *British Journal of Educational Psychology, 77,* 519–539.

Deese, J. (1959). On the prediction of occurrence of particular verbal intrusions in immediate recall. *Journal of Experimental Psychology, 58,* 17–22.

Dekle, D. J. (2006). Viewing composite sketches: Lineups and showups compared. *Applied Cognitive Psychology, 20,* 383–395.

Deloache, J. S., Cassidy, D. J., & Brown, A. (1985). Precursors of mnemonic strategies in very young children's memory. *Child Development, 56,* 125–137.

Dempster, F. N. (1981). Memory span: Sources of individual and developmental differences. *Psychological Bulletin, 89,* 63–100.

Dixon, R. A., & Cohen, A. L. (2003). Cognitive development in adulthood. In R. M. Lerner, M. A. Easterbrooks, & J. Mistry (Eds.), *Handbook of psychology* (pp. 443–461). Hoboken, NJ: John Wiley.

Dixon, R. A., Rust, T. B., Feltmate, S. E., & See, S. K. (2007). Memory and aging: Selected research directions and application issues. *Canadian Psychology, 48,* 67–76.

Dowling, W. J., Bartlett, J. C., Halpern, A. R., & Andrews, M. W. (2008). Melody recognition at fast and slow tempos: Effects of age, experience, and familiarity. *Perception & Psychophysics, 70,* 496–502.

Druckman, D., & Bjork, R. A. (Eds.). (1991). *In the mind's eye: Enhancing human performance.* Washington, DC: National Academy Press.

Duñabeitia, J. A., Carreiras, M., & Perea, M. (2008). Are coffee and toffee served in a cup? Orthophonologically mediated associative priming. *Quarterly Journal of Experimental Psychology, 61,* 1861–1872.

Dunlosky, J., & Bjork, R. A. (2008). The integrated nature of metamemory and memory. In J. Dunlosky & R. A. Bjork (Eds.), *Handbook of memory and metamemory: Essays in honor of Thomas O. Nelson* (pp. 11–28). New York, NY: Psychology Press.

Dunlosky, J., & Hertzog, C. (1998). Aging and deficits in associative memory: What is the role of strategy production? *Psychology and Aging, 13,* 597–607.

Dunlosky, J., & Metcalfe, J. (2009). *Metacognition.* Thousand Oaks, CA: Sage.

Dunlosky, J., & Nelson, T. O. (1992). Importance of the kind of cue for judgments of learning (JOL) and the delayed-JOL effect. *Memory & Cognition, 20,* 373–380.

Dunlosky, J., & Nelson, T. O. (1994). Does the sensitivity of judgments of learning (JOLs) to the effects of various study activities depend on when JOLs occur? *Journal of Memory and Language, 33,* 545–565.

Dunlosky, J., Serra, M., & Baker, J. M. C. (2007). Metamemory applied. In F. Durso, R. S. Nickerson, S. T. Dumais, S. Lewandowsky, & T. J. Perfect (Eds.), *Handbook of applied cognition* (2nd ed., pp. 137–159). New York, NY: John Wiley.

Dunning, D., & Stern, L. B. (1992). Examining the generality of eyewitness hypermnesia: A close look at time delay and question type. *Applied Cognitive Psychology, 6,* 643–658.

Eacott, M. J., & Crawley, R. A. (1998). The offset of childhood amnesia: Memory for events that occurred before age 3. *Journal of Experimental Psychology: General, 127,* 22–33.

Ebbinghaus, H. (1965). *Memory: A contribution to experimental psychology.* New York, NY: Dover. (Original work published 1885)

Eich, E. (1984). Memory for unattended events: Remembering with and without awareness. *Memory & Cognition, 12,* 105–111.

Eich, E. (In press). Mood and memory at 26: Revisiting the idea of mood mediation in drug-dependent and place-dependent memory. In M. A. Gluck, J. R. Anderson, & S. M. Kosslyn (Eds.), *Memory and mind: A Festschrift for Gordon Bower.* New York, NY: Psychology Press.

Eich, E., & Metcalfe, J. (1989). Mood dependent memory for internal versus external events. *Journal of Experimental Psychology: Learning, Memory and Cognition, 15,* 443–455.

Eich, J., Weingartner, H., Stillman, R., & Gillian, J. (1975). State-dependent accessibility of retrieval cues and retention of a categorized list. *Journal of Verbal Learning and Verbal Behavior, 14,* 408–417.

Eimas, P., Siqueland, E. R., Jusczyk, P., & Vigorito, J. (1971). Speech perception in infants. *Science, 171,* 303–306.

Eimas, P. D., & Quinn, P. C. (1994). Studies on the formation of perceptually-based basic-level categories in young infants. *Child Development, 65,* 903–917.

Elbers, L. (1985). A tip-of-the-tongue experience at age two? *Journal of Child Language, 12,* 353–365.

Ellis, N. C., & Hennely, R. A. (1980). A bilingual word-length effect: Implications for intelligence testing and the relative ease of mental calculation in Welsh and English. *British Journal of Psychology, 71,* 43–52.

Elsabagh, S., Hartley, D. E., Ali, O., Williamson, E. M., & File, S. E. (2005). Differential cognitive effects of Ginkgo biloba after acute and chronic treatment in healthy young volunteers. *Psychopharmacology, 179,* 437–446.

Engle, R. W. (2002). Working memory capacity as executive attention. *Current Directions in Psychological Science, 11,* 19–23.

Er, N. (2003). A new flashbulb memory model applied to the Marmara earthquake. *Applied Cognitive Psychology, 17,* 503–517.

Ericsson, K. A. (2003). Exceptional memorizers: Made, not born. *Trends in Cognitive Sciences, 7*(6), 233–235.

Ericsson, K. A., Chase, W. G., & Faloon, S. (1980). Acquisition of a memory skill. *Science, 208,* 1181–1182.

Evans, J. J., Wilson, B. A., Schuri, U., Andrade, J., Baddeley, A. D., Bruna, O., . . . Taussik, I. (2000). A comparison of errorless learning and trial-and-error learning methods for teaching individuals with acquired memory deficits. *Neuropsychological Rehabilitation, 10,* 67–101.

Farah, M. J. (1988). Is visual imagery really visual? Overlooked evidence from neuropsychology. *Psychological Review, 95,* 307–317.

Farah, M. J., & McClelland, J. L. (1991). A computational model of semantic memory impairment: Modality-specific and emergent category-specificity. *Journal of Experimental Psychology: General, 120,* 339–357.

Fazio, L. K., & Marsh, E. J. (2006). Older, not younger, children learn more false facts from stories. *Cognition, 106,* 1081–1089.

Feinberg, T. E., & Farah, M. J. (2000). A historical perspective on cognitive neuroscience. In M. J. Farah & T. E. Feinberg (Eds.), *Patient-based approaches to cognitive neuroscience* (pp. 3–20). Cambridge, MA: MIT Press.

Fenson, L., Bates, E., Dale, P., Goodman, J., Reznick, J. S., & Thal, D. (2000). Measuring variability in early child language: Don't shoot the messenger. *Child Development, 71,* 323–328.

Finn, B. (2008). Framing effects on metacognitive monitoring and control. *Memory & Cognition, 36,* 813–821.

Fisher, R. P., & Craik, F. I. M. (1977). Interaction between encoding and retrieval operations in cued recall. *Journal of Experimental Psychology: Human Learning and Memory, 3,* 701–711.

Fisher, R. P., & Geiselman, R. E. (1992). *Memory-enhancing techniques for investigative interviewing: The cognitive interview.* Springfield, IL: Charles C Thomas.

Fisher, R. P., & Schreiber, N. (2007). Interview protocols for improving eyewitness memory. In M. P. Toglia, J. D. Read, D. F. Ross, & R. C. L. Lindsay (Eds.), *The handbook of eyewitness psychology: Vol I. Memory for events* (pp. 53–80). Mahwah, NJ: Lawrence Erlbaum.

Fivush, R., McDermott-Sales, J., Goldberg, A., Bahrick, L., & Parker, J. (2004). Weathering the storm: Children's long-term recall of Hurricane Andrew. *Memory, 12,* 104–118.

Flavell, J. H., Miller, P. H., & Miller, S. A. (1993). *Cognitive development* (3rd ed.). Upper Saddle River, NJ: Prentice Hall.

Fleischman, J. (2002). *Phineas Gage: A gruesome but true story about brain science.* New York, NY: Houghton Mifflin.

Foley, M. F., & Foley, H. J. (2007). Source monitoring about anagrams and their solutions: Evidence for the role of cognitive operations information in memory. *Memory & Cognition, 35,* 211–217.

Foote, A. L., & Crystal, J. D. (2007). Metacognition in the rat. *Current Biology, 17,* 551–555.

Freud, S. (1953). Three essays on the theory of sexuality. In J. Strachey (Ed.), *The standard edition of the complete psychological works of Sigmund Freud* (Vol. 7, pp. 125–148). London: Hogarth. (Original work published 1905)

Gabston, M. S. (2008). The impact of ethnicity, age, and cue word type on autobiographical memories of African American and European American adults. *Dissertation Abstracts International: Section B: The Sciences and Engineering, 68*(9-B), 6348.

Gagne, C. L., & Shoben, E. J. (2002). Priming relations in ambiguous noun-noun combinations. *Memory & Cognition, 30,* 637–646.

Gardiner, J. M. (2002). Episodic memory and autonoetic consciousness. In A. Baddeley, M. Conway, & J. Aggleton (Eds.), *Episodic memory: New directions in research* (pp. 11–30). New York, NY: Oxford University Press.

Garrett, B. (2009). *Brain & behavior: An introduction to biological psychology* (2nd ed.). Thousand Oaks, CA: Sage.

Garrett, M. (1992). Disorders of lexical selection. *Cognition, 42,* 143–180.

Geraerts, E., Raymaekers, L., & Merckelbach, H. (2008). Recovered memories of childhood sexual abuse: Current findings and their legal implications. *Legal and Criminological Psychology, 13,* 165–176.

Germano, C., Kinsella, G. J., Storey, E., Ong, B., & Ames, D. (2008). The episodic buffer and learning in early Alzheimer's disease. *Journal of Clinical and Experimental Neuropsychology, 30,* 613–638.

Gianico, J. L., & Altarriba, J. (2008). An introduction to bilingualism: Principles and processes. In J. Altarriba & R. R. Heredia (Eds.), *An introduction to bilingualism: Principles and processes* (pp 71–103). Mahwah, NJ: Lawrence Erlbaum.

Godden, D. R., & Baddeley, A. D. (1975). Context-dependent memory in two natural environments: On land and under water. *British Journal of Psychology, 66,* 325–331.

Goldsmith, M., & Koriat, A. (2008). The strategic regulation of memory accuracy and informativeness. In A. Benjamin & B. Ross (Eds.), *The psychology of learning and motivation* (Vol. 48, pp. 1–60). Amsterdam: Academic Press.

Gollan, T. H., & Brown, A. S. (2006). From tip-of-the-tongue (TOT) data to theoretical implications in two steps: When more TOTs means better retrieval. *Journal of Experimental Psychology: General, 135,* 462–483.

Goodwin, D. W., Powell, B., Bremer, D., Hoine, H., & Stern, J. (1969). Alcohol and recall: State-dependent effects in man. *Science, 163,* 1358–1360.

Göthe, K., Oberauer, K., & Kliegl, R. (2007). Age differences in dual-task performance after practice. *Psychology and Aging, 22,* 596–606.

Grill-Spector, K., Knouf, M., & Kanwisher, N. (2004). The fusiform face area subserves face perception, not generic within-category identification. *Nature Neuroscience, 7,* 555–562.

Groninger, L. D. (1971). Mnemonic imagery and forgetting. *Psychonomic Science, 23,* 161–163.

Habib, R., McIntosh, A. R., Wheeler, M. A., & Tulving, E. (2003). Hemispheric asymmetries of memory: The HERA model revisited. *Trends in Cognitive Science, 7,* 241–245.

Hagwood, S. (2007). *Memory power: You can develop a great memory: America's grand master shows you how.* New York, NY: Free Press.

Hale, S. (1990). A global developmental trend in cognitive processing speed. *Child Development, 61,* 653–663.

Hampton, R. R. (2001). Rhesus monkeys know when they remember. *Proceedings of the National Academy of Sciences, 98,* 5359–5362.

Hampton, R. R., & Schwartz, B. L. (2004). Episodic memory in nonhumans: What, and where, is when? *Current Opinion in Neurobiology, 14,* 192–197.

Hanley, J. R., & Chapman, E. (2008). Partial knowledge in a tip of the tongue state about two and three word proper names. *Psychonomic Bulletin & Review, 15,* 156–160.

Harley, T. A. (2008). *The psychology of language: From data to theory* (3rd ed.). New York, NY: Taylor & Francis.

Harnishfeger, K. K., & Pope, R. S. (1996). Intending to forget: The development of cognitive inhibition in directed forgetting. *Journal of Experimental Child Psychology, 62,* 292–315.

Harris, J. E., & Wilkens, A. J. (1982). Remember how to do things: A theoretical framework and an illustrative experiment. *Human Learning, 1,* 123–126.

Hart, J. T. (1965). Memory and the feeling-of-knowing experience. *Journal of Educational Psychology, 56,* 208–216.

Hartshorn, K., & Rovee-Collier, C. (1997). Infant learning and long-term memory at 6 months: A confirming analysis. *Developmental Psychobiology, 30,* 71–85.

Hayne, H. (2004). Infant memory development: Implications for childhood amnesia. *Developmental Review, 24,* 33–73.

Head, D., Rodrigue, K. M., Kennedy, K. M., & Raz, N. (2008). Neuroanatomical and cognitive mediators of age-related differences in episodic memory. *Neuropsychology, 22,* 491–507.

Heaps, C. M., & Nash, M. (2001). Comparing recollective experiences in true and false autobiographical memories. *Journal of Experimental Psychology: Learning, Memory, and Cognition, 27,* 920–930.

Hege, A. C. G., & Dodson, C. S. (2004). Why distinctiveness information reduces false memories: Evidence for both impoverished relational-encoding and distinctiveness heuristics accounts. *Journal of Experimental Psychology: Learning, Memory, and Cognition, 30,* 787–795.

Heine, M. K., Ober, B. A., & Shenaut, G. K. (1999). Naturally occurring and experimentally-induced tip-of-the-tongue experiences in three adult age groups. *Psychology and Aging, 14,* 445–457.

Helstrup, T. (2004). The enactment effect is due to more than guesses or beliefs. *Scandinavian Journal of Psychology, 45,* 259–263.

Henkel, L. A., Johnson, M. K., & De Leonardis, D. M. (1998). Aging and source monitoring: Cognitive processes and neuropsychological correlates. *Journal of Experimental Psychology: General, 127,* 251–268.

Hennig-Fast, K., Meister, F., Frodl, T., Beraldi, A., Padberg, F., Engel, R. R., . . . Meindl, T. (2008). A case of persistent retrograde amnesia following a dissociative fugue: Neuropsychological and neurofunctional underpinnings of loss of autobiographical memory and self-awareness. *Neuropsychologia, 46,* 2993–3005.

Henri, V., & Henri, C. (1898). Earliest recollections. *Popular Science Monthly, 53,* 108–115.

Hermanowicz, N. (2002). A blind man with Parkinson's disease, visual hallucinations and Capgras syndrome. *Journal of Neuropsychiatry & Clinical Neurosciences, 14,* 462–463.

Hertzog, C., Kidder, D., Powell-Moman, A., & Dunlosky, J. (2002). Monitoring associative learning: What determines the accuracy of metacognitive judgments? *Psychology and Aging, 17,* 209–225.

Herz, R. (2007). *The scent of desire: Discovering our enigmatic sense of smell.* New York, NY: HarperCollins.

Herz, R. S. (2004). A naturalistic analysis of autobiographical memories triggered by olfactory, visual, and auditory stimuli. *Chemical Senses, 29,* 217–224.

Herz, R. S. (2005). Odor-associative learning and emotion: Effects on perception and behavior. *Chemical Senses, 30,* 250–251.

Hicks, J. L., Marsh, R. L., & Cook, G. I. (2005). Task interference in time-based, event-based, and dual intention prospective memory conditions. *Journal of Memory and Language, 53,* 430–444.

Hinkebein, J. H., Callahan, C. D., & Gelber, D. (2001). Reduplicative paramnesia: Rehabilitation of content-specific delusion after brain injury. *Rehabilitation Psychology, 46,* 75–81.

Hirst, W., Johnson, M. K., Kim, J. K., Phelps, E. A., Risse, G., & Volpe, B. T. (1986). Recall and recognition in amnesiacs. *Journal of Experimental Psychology: Learning, Memory, & Cognition, 12,* 445–451.

Hirst, W., Phelps, E. A., Buckner, R. L., Budson, A. E., Cuc, A., Gabrieli, J. D. E., & Johnson, M. K. (2009). Long-term memory for the terrorist attack of September 11: Flashbulb memories, event memories, and the factors that influence their retention. *Journal of Experimental Psychology: General, 138,* 161–176.

Holliday, R. E., Reyna, V. F., & Brainerd, C. J. (2008). Recall of details never experienced: Effects of age, repetition, and semantic cues. *Cognitive Development, 23,* 67–78.

Howe, M. L. (2006). Distinctiveness effects in children's memory. In R. R. Hunt & J. Worthen (Eds.), *Distinctiveness and human memory* (pp. 237–257). New York, NY: Oxford University Press.

Howe, M. L., & Courage, M. L. (1993). On resolving the enigma of infantile amnesia. *Psychological Bulletin, 113,* 305–326.

Hyman, I. E., Jr., Husband, T. H., & Billings, F. J. (1995). False memories of childhood experiences. *Applied Cognitive Psychology, 9,* 181–197.

Hyman, I. E., Jr., & Pentland, J. (1996). The role of mental imagery in the creation of false childhood memories. *Journal of Memory and Language, 35,* 101–117.

Izaute, M., & Bacon, E. (2006). Effects of the amnesic drug lorazepam on complete and partial information retrieval and monitoring accuracy. *Psychopharmacology, 188,* 472–481.

Jack, F., & Hayne, H. (2007). Eliciting adults' earliest memories: Does it matter how we ask the question? *Memory, 15,* 647–663.

Jacoby, L. L. (1991). A process dissociation framework: Separating automatic from intentional uses of memory. *Journal of Memory and Language, 30,* 513–541.

Jacoby, L. L., & Rhodes, M. G. (2006). False remembering in the aged. *Current Directions in Psychological Science, 15,* 49–53.

James, W. (1890). *The principles of psychology.* New York, NY: Henry Holt.

Janata, P. (2001). Brain electrical activity evoked by mental formation of auditory expectations and images. *Brain Topography, 13,* 169–193.

Janata, P., Tomic, S. T., & Rakowski, S. K. (2007). Characterisation of music-evoked autobiographical memories. *Memory, 15,* 845–860.

Jernigan, T. L., Archibald, S. L., Fennema-Notestine, C., Gamst, A. C., Stout, J. C., Bonner, J., & Hesselink, J. R. (2001). Effects of age on tissues and regions of the cerebrum and cerebellum. *Neurobiology and Aging, 5,* 356–368.

Johnson, M. K., Hashtroudi, S., & Lindsay, S. (1993). Source monitoring. *Psychological Bulletin, 114,* 3–28.

Jonides, J. (1995). Working memory and thinking. In E. E. Smith & D. N. Osherson (Eds.), *An invitation to cognitive science: Vol. 3. Thinking* (pp. 215–265). Cambridge, MA: MIT Press.

Jonides, J., Lacey, S. C., & Nee, D. E. (2005). Processes of working memory in mind and brain. *Current Directions in Psychological Science, 14,* 2–5.

Jou, J. (2008). Recall latencies, confidence and output positions of true and false memories: Implications for recall and metamemory theories. *Journal of Memory and Language, 58,* 1049–1064.

Kail, R. (1991). Processing time declines exponentially during childhood and adolescence. *Developmental Psychology, 27,* 259–266.

Kanwisher, N. (2004). The ventral visual object pathway in humans: Evidence from fMRI. In L. M. Chalupa & J. S. Werner (Eds.), *The visual neurosciences* (pp. 1179–1190). Cambridge, MA: MIT Press.

Kao, Y.-C., Davis, E. S., & Gabrieli, J. D. E. (2005). Neural correlates of actual and predicted memory formation. *Nature Neuroscience, 8,* 1776–1783.

Kaplan, M. (2005). Benzodiazepines and anxiety disorders: A review for the practicing physician. *Current Medical Research and Opinion, 6,* 941–950.

Karpel, M. E., Hoyer, W. J., & Toglia, M. P. (2001). Accuracy and qualities of real and suggested memories: Nonspecific age differences. *Journals of Gerontology Series B: Psychological Sciences and Social Sciences, 56,* P103–P110.

Karpicke, J. D., & Roediger, H. L., III (2008). The critical importance of retrieval for learning. *Science, 319,* 966–968.

Kelley, W. M., Macrae, C. N., Wyland, C. L., Caglar, S., Inati, S., & Heatherton, T. F. (2002). Finding the self? An event-related fMRI study. *Journal of Cognitive Neuroscience, 14,* 785–794.

Kensinger, E. A., & Schacter, D. L. (2006). When the Red Sox shocked the Yankees: Comparing negative and positive memories. *Psychonomic Bulletin & Review, 13,* 757–763.

Keppel, G., & Underwood, B. J. (1962). Proactive inhibition in short-term retention of single items. *Journal of Verbal Learning and Verbal Behavior, 1,* 153–161.

Kihlstrom, J. F., & Schacter, D. L. (1995). Functional disorders of autobiographical memory. In A. D. Baddeley, B. A. Wilson, & F. N. Watts (Eds.), *Handbook of memory disorders* (pp. 337–364). New York, NY: John Wiley.

Kirsch, I., Mazzoni, G., & Montgomery, G. H. (2007). Remembrance of hypnosis past. *American Journal of Clinical Hypnosis, 49*(3), 171–178.

Kisilevsky, B. S., Hains, S. M. J., Lee, K., Xie, X., Huang, H., Ye, H. H., . . . Wang, Z. (2003). Effects of experience on fetal voice recognition. *Psychological Science, 14,* 220–224.

Klingberg, T., Forssberg, H., & Westerberg, H. (2002). Training of working memory in children with ADHD. *Journal of Clinical & Experimental Neuropsychology, 24,* 781–791.

Kondo, Y., Suzuki, M., Mugikura, S., Abe, N., Takahashi, S., Iijima, T., & Fujii, T. (2004). Changes in brain activation associated with the use of a memory strategy: A functional MRI study. *Neuroimage, 15,* 1154–1163.

Koriat, A. (2008). Easy comes, easy goes? The link between learning and remembering and its exploitation in metacognition. *Memory & Cognition, 36,* 416–428.

Koriat, A., & Goldsmith, M. (1996). Monitoring and control processes in the strategic regulation of memory accuracy. *Psychological Review, 103,* 490–517.

Koriat, A., & Lieblich, I. (1974). What does a person in a "TOT" state know that a person in a "don't know" state doesn't know. *Memory & Cognition, 2,* 647–655.

Koriat, A., & Shitzer-Reichert, R. (2002). Metacognitive judgments and their accuracy: Insights from the processes underlying judgments of learning in children. In P. Chambres, M. Izaute, & P. J. Marescaux (Eds.), *Metacognition: Process, function, and use* (pp. 1–18). Dordrecht, the Netherlands: Kluwer Academic.

Kornell, N. (2009a). Metacognition in humans and animals. *Current Directions in Psychological Science, 18,* 11–15.

Kornell, N. (2009b). Optimising learning using flashcards: Spacing is more effective than cramming. *Applied Cognitive Psychology, 23,* 1297–1317.

Kornell, N., & Bjork, R. A. (2007). The promise and perils of self-regulated study. *Psychonomic Bulletin & Review, 14,* 219–224.

Kornell, N., & Bjork, R. A. (2008). Optimising self-regulated study: The benefits—and costs—of dropping flashcards. *Memory, 16,* 125–136.

Kornell, N., & Metcalfe, J. (2006). Study efficacy and the region of proximal learning framework. *Journal of Experimental Psychology: Learning, Memory, & Cognition, 32,* 609–622.

Koshino, H., Kana, K., Keller, T. A., Cherkassky, V. L., Minshew, N. J., & Just, M. A. (2008). fMRI investigation of working memory for faces in autism: Visual coding and underconnectivity with frontal areas. *Cerebral Cortex, 18,* 289–300.

Kosslyn, S. M. (1975). Information representation in visual images. *Cognitive Psychology, 7,* 341–370.

Kosslyn, S. M. (2005). Mental images and the brain. *Cognitive Neuropsychology, 22,* 333–347.

Kosslyn, S. M., Alpert, N. M., & Thompson, W. L. (1995). Indentifying objects at different levels of hierarchy: A positron emission tomography study. *Human Brain Mapping, 3,* 107–132.

Kosslyn, S. M., Ball, T. M., & Reiser, B. J. (1978). Visual images preserve metric spatial information: Evidence from studies of mental scanning. *Journal of Experimental Psychology: Human Perception and Performance, 4,* 47–60.

Kosslyn, S. M., Ganis, G., & Thompson, W. L. (2006). Mental imagery and the human brain. In Q. Jing, M. R. Rosenzweig, G. D'Ydewalle, H. Zhang, H.-C. Chen, & K. Zhang (Eds.), *Progress in psychological science around the world: Vol 1. Neural, cognitive, and developmental issues* (pp. 195–209). London: Psychology Press.

Krashen, S. D. (1982). *Principles of second-language acquisition.* Oxford, UK: Pergamon.

Kroll, J. F., Bobb, S. C., Misra, M., & Guo, T. (2008). Language selection in bilingual speech: Evidence for inhibitory processes. *Acta Psychologica, 128,* 416–430.

Kroll, N. E., Schepeler, E. M., & Angin, K. T. (1986). Bizarre imagery: The misremembered mnemonic. *Journal of Experimental Psychology: Learning, Memory, and Cognition, 12,* 42–53.

Kuchinke, L., van der Meer, E., & Krueger, F. (2009). Differences in processing of taxonomic and sequential relations in semantic memory: An fMRI investigation. *Brain and Cognition, 69,* 245–251.

Kuntay, A. C., Gulgoz, S., & Tekcan, A. I. (2004). Disputed memories of twins: How ordinary are they? *Applied Cognitive Psychology, 18,* 405–413.

Lachman, M. E., & Andreoletti, C. (2006). Strategy use mediates the relationship between control beliefs and memory performance for middle-aged and older adults. *Journal of Gerontology: Series B: Psychological Sciences and Social Sciences, 61B,* P88–P94.

Lah, S., & Miller, L. (2008). Effects of temporal lobe lesions on retrograde amnesia: A critical review. *Neuropsychological Review, 18,* 24–52.

Landauer, T. K., & Bjork, R. A. (1978). Optimum rehearsal patterns and name learning. In M. M. Gruneberg, P. E. Morris, & R. N. Sykes (Eds.), *Practical aspects of memory* (pp. 625–632). London: Academic Press.

Laney, C., Morris, E. K., Bernstein, D. M., Wakefield, B. M., & Loftus, E. F. (2008). Asparagus, a love story: Healthier eating could be just a false memory away. *Experimental Psychology, 55,* 291–300.

Large, M.-E., Cavina-Pratesi, C., Vilis, T., & Culham, J. C. (2008). The neural correlates of change detection in the face perception network. *Neuropsychologia, 46,* 2169–2176.

Larsen, S. T., & Thompson, C. P. (1995). Reconstructive memory in the dating of personal and public news events. *Memory & Cognition, 23,* 780–790.

Leichtman, M. D., & Ceci, S. J. (1995). The effects of stereotypes and suggestions on preschoolers' reports. *Developmental Psychology, 31,* 568–578.

Lesk, V. E., & Womble, S. P. (2004). Caffeine, priming, and tip of the tongue: Evidence for plasticity in the phonological system. *Behavioral Neuroscience, 118,* 453–461.

Levelt, W. M. J. (1989). *Speaking: From intention to articulation.* Cambridge, MA: MIT Press.

Levitin, D. J. (2006). *This is your brain on music: The science of a human obsession.* New York, NY: Penguin.

Linton, M. (1986). Ways of searching and the contents of memory. In D. C. Rubin (Ed.), *Autobiographical memory* (pp. 50–67). New York, NY: Cambridge University Press.

Litman, J. A., Hutchins, T. L., & Russon, R. K. (2005). Epistemic curiosity, feeling-of-knowing, and exploratory behaviour. *Cognition and Emotion, 19,* 559–582.

Loftus, E. F. (1979). *Eyewitness testimony.* Cambridge, MA: Harvard University Press.

Loftus, E. F. (1992). When a lie becomes a memory's truth: Memory distortion after exposure to misinformation. *Current Directions in Psychological Science, 1,* 121–123.

Loftus, E. F. (2004). Memory of things unseen. *Current Directions in Psychological Science, 13,* 145–147.

Loftus, E. F., Coan, J. A., & Pickrell, J. E. (1996). Manufacturing false memories using bits of reality. In L. M. Reder (Ed.), *Implicit memory and metacognition* (pp. 195–220). Hillsdale, NJ: Lawrence Erlbaum.

Loftus, E. F., & Davis, D. (2006). Recovered memories. *Annual Review of Clinical Psychology, 2,* 469–498.

Loftus, E. F., & Ketcham, K. (1991). *Witness for the defense; the accused, the eyewitness, and the expert who puts memory on trial.* New York, NY: St. Martin's.

Loftus, E. F., & Ketcham, K. (1994). *The myth of repressed memory.* New York, NY: St. Martin's.

Loftus, E. F., Miller, D. G., & Burns, H. J. (1978). Semantic integration of verbal information into a visual memory. *Human Learning and Memory, 4,* 19–31.

Loftus, E. F., & Palmer, J. C. (1974). Reconstruction of automobile destruction: An example of the interaction between language and memory. *Journal of Verbal Learning and Verbal Behavior, 13,* 585–589.

Loftus, E. F., & Pickrell, J. E. (1995). The formation of false memories. *Psychiatric Annals, 25,* 720–725.

Loftus, E. F., & Zanni, G. (1975). Eyewitness testimony: The influence of the wording of a question. *Bulletin of the Psychonomic Society, 5,* 86–88.

Logie, R. H. (1986). Visuo-spatial processing in working memory. *Quarterly Journal of Experimental Psychology, 38A,* 229–247.

Lorayne, H., & Lucas, J. (1974). *The memory book: The classic guide to improving your memory at work, at school, and at play.* New York, NY: Ballantine.

Lucchelli, F., & Spinnler, H. (2007). The case of lost Wilma: A clinical report of Capgras delusion. *Neurological Science, 28,* 188–195.

Luo, Y., Baillageon, R., Brueckner, L., & Munakata, Y. (2003). Reasoning about a hidden object after a delay: Evidence for robust representations in 5-month old infants. *Cognition, 88,* B23–B32.

Luria, A. R. (1987). *The mind of a mnemonist: A little book about a vast memory.* Cambridge, MA: Harvard University Press. (Original work published 1968)

Lynch, S., & Yarnell, P. R. (1973). Retrograde amnesia: Delayed forgetting after concussion. *American Journal of Psychology, 86,* 643–645.

MacLeod, C. (2005). The Stroop task in cognitive research. In A. Wenzel & D. C. Rubin (Eds.), *Cognitive methods and their application to clinical research* (pp. 17–40). Washington, DC: American Psychological Association.

Maguire, E. A., Valentine, E. R., Wilding, J. M., & Kapur, N. (2003). Routes to remembering: The brains behind superior memory. *Nature Neuroscience, 6,* 90–95.

Manly, J. J., Touradji, P., Tang, M., & Stern, Y. (2003). Literacy and memory decline among ethnically diverse elders. *Journal of Clinical and Experimental Neuropsychology, 25,* 680–690.

Mannes, S. M., & Kintsch, W. (1987). Knowledge organization and text organization. *Cognition and Instruction, 4,* 91–115.

Marcel, A. J. (1983). Conscious and unconscious perception: An approach to the relations between phenomenal experience and perceptual processes. *Cognitive Psychology, 15,* 238–300.

Marcon, J. L., Susa, K. J., & Meissner, C. A. (2009). Assessing the influence of recollection and familiarity in memory for own- and other-race faces. *Psychonomic Bulletin & Review, 16,* 99–103.

Maril, A., Wagner, A. D., & Schacter, D. L. (2001). On the tip of the tongue: An event-related fMRI study of semantic retrieval failure and cognitive conflict. *Neuron, 31,* 653–660.

Maril, A., Simons, J. S., Mitchell, J. P., Schwartz, B. L., & Schacter, D. L. (2003). Feeling-of-knowing in episodic memory: An event-related fMRI study. *NeuroImage, 18,* 827–836.

Maril, A., Simons, J. S., Weaver, J. J., & Schacter, D. L. (2005). Graded recall success: an event-related fMRI comparison of tip of the tongue and feeling of knowing. *NeuroImage, 24,* 1130–1138.

Marsh, R. L., & Hicks, J. L. (1998). Event-based prospective memory and executive control of working memory. *Journal of Experimental Psychology: Learning, Memory, & Cognition, 24,* 336–349.

Marsh, R. L., Hicks, J. L., & Cook, G. I. (2006). Task interference from prospective memory interferes covaries with contextual associations of fulfilling them. *Memory & Cognition, 34,* 1037–1045.

Martin, N., & Dell, G. S. (2007). Common mechanisms underlying perseverative and non-perseverative sound and word substitutions. *Aphasiology, 21,* 1002–1017.

Massimini, M., Ferrarelli, F., Huber, R., Esser, S. K., Singh, H., & Tononi, G. (2005). Breakdown of cortical effective connectivity during sleep. *Science, 309,* 2228–2232.

Mattys, S. L., & Jusczyk, P. W. (2001). Phonotactic cues for segmentation of fluent speech by infants. *Cognition, 78,* 91–121.

Mazzoni, G., & Lynn, S. J. (2007). Using hypnosis in eyewitness memory: Past and current issues. In M. P. Toglia, J. D. Read, D. F. Ross, & R. C. L. Lindsay (Eds.), *The handbook of eyewitness psychology: Vol I. Memory for events* (pp. 321–338). Mahwah, NJ: Lawrence Erlbaum.

Mazzoni, G., & Memon, A. (2003). Imagination can create false autobiographical memories. *Psychological Science, 14,* 186–188.

McCabe, D. P., & Smith, A. D. (2002). The effects of warnings on false memories in young and older adults. *Memory & Cognition, 25,* 838–848.

McCabe, J., & Hartman, M. (2008). An analysis of age differences in perceptual speed. *Memory & Cognition, 36,* 1495–1508.

McCloskey, M., & Zaragoza, M. (1985). Misleading postevent information and memory for events: Arguments and evidence against the memory impairment hypothesis. *Journal of Experimental Psychology: General, 114,* 1–16.

McDaniel, M. A., & Einstein, G. O. (2007). *Prospective memory: An overview and synthesis of an emerging field.* Thousand Oaks, CA: Sage.

McDaniel, M. A., Maier, S. F., & Einstein, G. O. (2002). Brain-specific nutrients: A memory cure? *Psychological Science in the Public Interest, 3,* 12–38.

McDaniel, M. A., Roediger, H. L., III, & McDermott, K. B. (2007). Generalizing test-enhanced learning from the laboratory to the classroom. *Psychonomic Bulletin & Review, 14,* 200–206.

McIsaac, H. K., & Eich, E. (2004). Vantage point in traumatic memory. *Psychological Science, 15,* 248–253.

McNamara, T. P. (2005). *Semantic priming: Perspectives from memory and word recognition*. New York, NY: Psychology Press.

McNamara, T. P., & Altarriba, J. (1988). Depth of spreading activation revisited: Semantic mediated priming occurs in lexical decisions. *Journal of Memory and Language, 27,* 545–559.

Medin, D. L., & Rips, L. J. (2005). Concepts and categories: Memory, meaning, and metaphysics. In K. J. Holyoak & R. J. Morrison (Eds.), *The Cambridge handbook of thinking and reasoning* (pp. 37–72). New York, NY: Cambridge University Press.

Mednick, S. C., Cai, D. J., Kanady, J., & Drummond, S. P. A. (2008). Comparing the benefits of caffeine, naps, and placebo on verbal, motor, and perceptual memory. *Behavioral Brain Research, 193,* 79–86.

Medved, M. I. (2007). Remembering without a past: Individuals with anterograde memory impairment talk about their lives. *Psychology, Health, & Medicine, 12,* 603–616.

Meissner, C. A., Brigham, J. C., & Kelley, C. M. (2002). The influence of retrieval processes in verbal overshadowing. *Memory & Cognition, 29,* 176–186.

Meissner, C. A., Sporer, S. L., & Susa, K. J. (2008). A theoretical review and meta-analysis of the description-identification relationship in memory for faces. *European Journal of Cognitive Psychology, 20,* 414–455.

Melnyk, L., Crossman, A. M., & Scullin, M. H. (2007). The suggestibility of children's memory. In M. Toglia, J. D. Read, & R. C. L. Lindsay (Eds.), *Handbook of eyewitness memory* (Vol. 1, pp. 401–451). Mahwah, NJ: Lawrence Erlbaum.

Mervis, C. B., Catlin, J., & Rosch, E. (1976). Relationships among goodness-of-example, category norms, and word frequency. *Bulletin of the Psychonomic Society, 7,* 283–284.

Metcalfe, J. (1993). Monitoring and gain control in an episodic memory model: Relation to event-related potentials. In A. F. Collins, S. E. Gathercole, M. A. Conway, & P. E. Morris (Eds.), *Theories of memory* (pp. 327–354). Hillsdale, NJ: Lawrence Erlbaum.

Metcalfe, J. (2002). Is study time allocated selectively to a region of proximal learning? *Journal of Experimental Psychology: General, 131,* 349–363.

Metcalfe, J. (2008). The evolution of metacognition. In J. Dunlosky & R. A. Bjork (Eds.), *Handbook of memory and metamemory: Essays in honor of Thomas O. Nelson.* Mahwah, NJ: Lawrence Erlbaum.

Metcalfe, J., & Finn, B. (2008). Familiarity and retrieval processes in delayed judgments of learning. *Journal of Experimental Psychology: Learning, Memory, & Cognition, 34,* 1084–1097.

Metcalfe, J., & Kornell, N. (2005). A regional of proximal learning model of metacognitively guided study-time allocation. *Journal of Memory and Language, 52,* 463–477.

Metzger, R. L., Warren, A. R., Shelton, J. T., Price, J., Reed, A. W., & Williams, D. (2008). Do children "DRM" like adults? False memory production in children. *Developmental Psychology, 44,* 169–181.

Meyer, D. E., & Schvanevelt, R. W. (1971). Facilitation in recognizing pairs of word: Evidence of a dependence between retrieval operations. *Journal of Experimental Psychology, 90,* 227–234.

Meyer, D. E., & Schvanevelt, R. W. (1976). Meaning, memory structure, and mental processes. *Science, 192,* 27–33.

Miller, G. A. (1956). The magical number seven, plus or minus two: Some limits on our capacity for processing information. *Psychological Review, 63,* 81–97.

Moscovitch, M. (1989). Confabulation and the frontal system: Strategic vs. associative retrieval in neuropsychological theories of memory. In H. L. Roediger & F. I. M. Craik (Eds.), *Varieties of memory and consciousness: Essays in honour of Endel Tulving* (pp. 133–160). Hillsdale, NJ: Lawrence Erlbaum.

Murre, J. M., & Sturdy, D. P. (1995). The connectivity of the brain: Multi-level quantitative analysis. *Biological Cybernetics, 73,* 529–545.

Myers, N. A., & Perlmutter, M. (1978). Memory in the years from two to five. In P. A. Ornstein (Ed.), *Memory development in children* (pp. 191–218). Hillsdale, NJ: Lawrence Erlbaum.

Nairne, J. S., & Pandeirada, J. N. S. (2008). Remembering with a stone-age brain. *Current Directions in Psychological Science, 17,* 239–243.

Nairne, J. S., Thompson, S. R., & Pandeirada, J. N. S. (2007). Adaptive memory: Survival processing enhances retention. *Journal of Experimental Psychology: Learning, Memory, & Cognition, 33,* 263–273.

Nash, R. A., Wade, K. A., & Lindsay, D. S. (2009). Digitally-manipulated memory: Effects of doctored videos and imagination in distorting beliefs and memories. *Memory & Cognition, 37,* 414–424.

National Center for Education Statistics. (2009). *Digest of education statistics.* Retrieved May 17, 2010, from http://nces.ed.gov/programs/digest/d09

Naveh-Benjamin, M., & Ayres, T. J. (1986). Digit span, reading rate, and linguistic relativity. *Quarterly Journal of Experimental Psychology, 38,* 739–751.

Navah-Benjamin, M., Cowan, N., Kilb, A., & Chen, Z. (2007). Age-related differences in immediate serial recall: Dissociating chunk formation and capacity. *Memory & Cognition, 35,* 724–737.

Neisser, U. (1967). *Cognitive psychology.* New York, NY: Appleton.

Nelson, K. (1989). *Narratives from the crib.* Cambridge, MA: Harvard University Press.

Nelson, T. O. (1984). A comparison of current measures of the accuracy of feeling of knowing predictions. *Psychological Bulletin, 95,* 109–133.

Nelson, T. O., Gerler, D., & Narens, L. (1984). Accuracy of feeling of knowing judgments for predicting perceptual identification and relearning. *Journal of Experimental Psychology: General, 113,* 282–300.

Nelson, T. O., & Leonesio, R. J. (1988). Allocation of self-paced study time and the "labor-in-vain" effect. *Journal of Experimental Psychology: Learning, Memory, & Cognition, 14,* 676–686.

Nelson, T. O., & Narens, L. (1990). Metamemory: A theoretical framework and new findings. In G. Bower (Ed.), *The psychology of learning and motivation* (Vol. 26, pp. 125–141). San Diego, CA: Academic Press.

Nickerson, R. S. (1984). Retrieval inhibition from part-set cueing: A persistent enigma in memory research. *Memory & Cognition, 12,* 531–552.

Nickerson, R. S., & Adams, J. J. (1979). Long-term memory for a common object. *Cognitive Psychology, 11,* 287–307.

Nigro, G., & Neisser, U. (1983). Point of view in personal memories. *Cognitive Psychology, 15,* 467–482.

O'Conner, M., Lebowitz, B. K., Ly, J., Panizzon, M. S., Elkin-Frankston, S., Dey, S., . . . Pearlman, C. (2008). A dissociation between anterograde and retrograde amnesia after treatment with electroconvulsive therapy: A naturalistic investigation. *Journal of ECT, 24,* 146–151.

Olesen, P. J., Westerberg, H., & Klingberg, T. (2004). Increased prefrontal and parietal activity after training of working memory. *Nature Neuroscience, 7,* 75–79.

Ornstein, P. A., Haden, C. A., & Elischberger, H. B. (2006). Children's memory development: Remembering the past and preparing for the future. In E. Bialystok & F. I. M. Craik (Eds.), *Lifespan cognition: Mechanisms of change* (pp. 143–161). New York, NY: Oxford University Press.

Otani, A. (1992). Memory in hypnosis. *The Advocate, 16,* 111–121.

Otgaar, H., Candel, I., Merckelbach, H., & Wade, K. (2009). Abducted by a UFO: Prevalence information affects young children's false memories for an implausible event. *Applied Cognitive Psychology, 23,* 115–125.

Otsuka, Y., & Osaka, N. (2005). Working memory in the elderly: Role of prefrontal cortex. *Japanese Psychological Research, 48,* 518–529.

Paivio, A. (1969). Mental imagery in associative learning and memory. *Psychological Review, 76,* 241–263.

Pannu, J. K., & Kaszniak, A. W. (2005). Metamemory experiments in neurological populations: A review. *Neuropsychological Review, 15,* 105–130.

Parker, E. S., Cahill, L., & McGaugh, J. L. (2006). A case of unusual autobiographical remembering. *Neurocase, 12,* 35–49.

Parkin, A. J., Bindschaedler, C., Harsent, L., & Metzler, C. (1996). Pathological false alarm rates following damage to the left frontal cortex. *Brain & Cognition, 32,* 14–27.

Paz-Alonso, P. M., & Goodman, G. S. (2008). Trauma and memory: Effects of post-event misinformation, retrieval order and retrieval interval. *Memory, 16,* 58–75.

Perfect, T. J. (2002). When does eyewitness confidence predict performance? In T. J. Perfect & B. Schwartz (Eds.), *Applied metacognition* (pp. 95–120). Cambridge, UK: Cambridge University Press.

Perfect, T. J., Wagstaff, G. F., Moore, D., Andrews, B., Cleveland, V., Newcombe, S., . . . Brown, L. (2008). How can we help witnesses to remember more? It's an (eyes) open and shut case. *Law and Human Behavior, 32,* 314–324.

Perner, J. (2000). Memory and the theory of mind. In E. Tulving & F. I. M. Craik (Eds.), *The Oxford handbook of memory* (pp. 285–314). New York, NY: Oxford University Press.

Peterson, C., McDermott Sales, J., Rees, M., & Fivush, R. (2007). Parent-child talk and children's memory for stressful events. *Applied Cognitive Psychology, 21,* 1057–1075.

Peterson, L. R., & Johnson, S. F. (1971). Some effects of minimizing articulation of short-term retention of individual verbal items. *Journal of Verbal Learning and Verbal Behavior, 10,* 346–354.

Peterson, L. R., & Peterson, M. J. (1959). Short-term retention of individual verbal items. *Journal of Experimental Psychology, 58,* 193–198.

Pezdek, K., Finger, K., & Hodge, D. (1997). Planting false childhood memories: The role of event plausibility. *Psychological Science, 8,* 437–441.

Philippot, P., Baeyens, C., Douilliez, C., & Francart, B. (2004). Cognitive regulation of emotion: Application to clinical disorders. In P. Philippot & R. S. Feldman (Eds.), *The regulation of emotion* (pp. 71–97). Mahwah, NJ: Lawrence Erlbaum.

Pinker, S. (1994). *The language instinct: How the mind creates language.* New York, NY: HarperCollins.

Pinker, S. (1999). *Words and rules: The ingredients of language.* New York, NY: Basic Books.

Porter, S., Yuille, J. C., & Lehman, D. R. (1999). The nature of real, implanted, and fabricated memories for emotional childhood events: Implications for the recovered memory debate. *Law and Human Behavior, 23,* 517–537.

Pressley, M., & Hilden, K. (2006). Cognitive strategies. In D. Kuhn & R. Siegler (Eds.), *Handbook of child psychology* (6th ed., pp. 511–556). Hoboken, NJ: John Wiley.

Price, H. L., & Connolly, D. A. (2008). Children's recall of emotionally arousing repeated events: A review and call for further investigation. *International Journal of Law and Psychiatry, 31,* 337–346.

Price, J., Hertzog, C., & Dunlosky, J. (2008). Age-related differences in strategy knowledge updating: Blocked testing produces greater improvements in metacognitive accuracy for younger than older adults. *Aging, Neuropsychology, and Cognition, 15,* 601–626.

Proust, M. (1928). *Swann's way.* New York, NY: The Modern Library.

Purdy, J., Markham, M. R., Schwartz, B. L., & Gordon, W. C. (2001). *Learning and memory* (2nd ed.). Belmont, CA: Wadsworth.

Pylyshyn, Z. W. (2003). Return of the mental image: Are there pictures in the brain? *Trends in Cognitive Science, 7,* 113–118.

Quiroga, R. Q., Reddy, L., Kreiman, G., Koch, C., & Fried, I. (2005). Invariant visual representation by single neurons in the human brain. *Nature, 435,* 1102–1107.

Rabbitt, P., Mogapi, O., Scott, M., Thacker, N., Lowe, C., Horan, M., . . . Lunn, D. (2007). Effects of global atrophy, white matter lesions, and cerebral blood flow on age-related changes in speed, memory, intelligence, vocabulary, and frontal function. *Neuropsychology, 21,* 684–695.

Racette, A., & Peretz, I. (2007). Learning lyrics: to sing or not sing. *Memory & Cognition, 35,* 242–253.

Rahhal, T. A., May, C. P., & Hasher, L. (2002). Truth and character: Sources that older adults can remember. *Psychological Science, 13,* 101–105.

Rainey, D. W., & Larsen, J. D. (2002). The effects of familiar melodies on initial learning and long-term memory for unconnected text. *Music Perception, 20,* 173–186.

Rajaram, S., & Pereira-Pasarin, L. P. (2007). Collaboration can improve individual recognition memory: Evidence from immediate and delayed tests. *Psychonomic Bulletin & Review, 14,* 95–100.

Ramachandran, V. S., & Blakeslee, S. (1998). Phantoms in the brain. New York, NY: William Morrow.

Reder, L. M. (1987). Selection strategies in question answering. *Cognitive Psychology, 19,* 90–138.

Reder, L. M., & Ritter, F. E. (1992). What determines initial feeling of knowing? Familiarity with question terms, not with the answer. *Journal of Experimental Psychology: Learning, Memory, and Cognition, 18,* 435–451.

Reisberg, D., & Heuer, F. (2004). Memory for emotional events. In D. Reisberg & F. Heuer (Eds.), *Memory and emotion* (pp. 3–41). New York, NY: Oxford University Press.

Rhodes, M. G., & Castel, A. D. (2008). Memory predictions are influenced by perceptual information: Evidence for metacognitive illusions. *Journal of Experimental Psychology: General, 137,* 615–625.

Rhodes, M. G., Castel, A. D., & Jacoby, L. L. (2008). Associative recognition of face pairs by younger and older adults: The role of familiarity-based processing. *Psychology and Aging, 23,* 239–249.

Rhodes, M. G., & Kelley, C. M. (2005). Executive processes, memory accuracy, and memory monitoring: An aging and individual difference analysis. *Journal of Memory and Language, 52,* 578–594.

Riby, L. M., Perfect, T. J., & Stollery, B. T. (2004). The effects of age and task domain on dual task performance: A meta-analysis. *European Journal of Cognitive Psychology, 16,* 868–891.

Robertson-Tchabo, E. A., Hausman, C. P., & Arenberg, D. (1976). A classical mnemonic for older learners: A trip that works. *Educational Gerontology, 1,* 215–226.

Robinson, J. A. (1992). First experience memories: Contexts and function in personal histories. In M. A. Conway, D. C. Rubin, H. Spinnler, & W. A. Wagenaar (Eds.), *Theoretical perspectives on autobiographical memory.* Dordrecht, the Netherlands: Kluwer Academic.

Robinson, J. A., & Swanson, K. L. (1993). Field and observer modes of remembering. *Memory, 1,* 169–184.

Rochat, P. (2003). Five levels of self-awareness as they unfold early in life. *Consciousness and Cognition, 12,* 717–731.

Rodriguez-Fornells, A., Rotte, M., Heinze, H. J., Nosselt, T., & Munte, T. (2002). Brain potential and functional MRI evidence for how to handle two languages with one brain. *Nature, 415,* 1026–1029.

Roediger, H. L., III, (1980). Memory metaphors in cognitive psychology. *Memory & Cognition, 8,* 231–246.

Roediger, H. L., III, & Crowder, R. G. (1976). A serial position curve in recall of United States presidents. *Bulletin of the Psychonomic Society, 8,* 275–278.

Roediger, H. L., III, & Karpicke, J. D. (2006). Test-enhanced learning: Taking memory tests improves long-term retention. *Psychological Science, 17,* 249–255.

Roediger, H. L., III, & McDermott, K. B. (1995). Creating false memories: Remembering words not presented in lists. *Journal of Experimental Psychology: Learning, Memory, and Cognition, 21,* 803–814.

Roediger, H. L., III, Watson, J. M., McDermott, K. B., & Gallo, D. A. (2001). Factors that determine false recall: A multiple regression analysis. *Psychonomic Bulletin & Review, 8,* 385–407.

Rogers, T. B., Kuiper, N. A., & Kirker, W. S. (1977). Self-reference and the encoding of personal information. *Journal of Personality and Social Psychology, 35,* 677–688.

Rogers, T. T., & McClelland, J. L. (2004). *Semantic cognition: A parallel distributed processing approach.* Cambridge, MA: MIT Press.

Rosch, E. (1975). Cognitive representations of semantic categories. *Journal of Experimental Psychology: General, 104,* 192–233.

Rosch, E., & Mervis, C. B. (1975). Family resemblances: Studies in the internal structure of categories. *Cognitive Psychology, 7,* 573–605.

Rosch, E., Mervis, C. B., Gray, W. D., Johnson, D. M., & Boyes-Braem, P. (1976). Basic objects in natural categories. *Cognitive Psychology, 8,* 382–439.

Rosenbaum, R. S., Kohler, S., Schacter, D. L., Moscovitch, M., Westmacott, R., Black, S. E., . . . Tulving, E. (2005). The case of K. C.: Contributions of a memory-impaired person to memory theory. *Neuropsychologia, 43,* 989–1021.

Rovee-Collier, C., & Cuevas, K. (2008). The development of infant memory. In M. Courage & N. Cowan (Eds.), *The development of memory in childhood* (pp. 11–42). Hove, UK: Psychology Press.

Ruchkin, D. S., Grafman, J., Cameron, K., & Berndt, R. S. (2003). Working memory retention systems: A state of activated long-term memory. *Behavioral and Brain Sciences, 26,* 709–777.

Russ, M. O., Mack, W., Grama, C.-R., Lanfermann, H., & Knoff, M. (2003). Enactment effect in memory: Evidence concerning the function of the supramarginal gyrus. *Experimental Brain Research, 149,* 497–504.

Russell, R., Duchaine, B., & Nakayama, K. (2009). Super-recognizers: People with extraordinary face recognition ability. *Psychonomic Bulletin & Review, 16,* 252–257.

Ryan, M. P., Petty, C. R., & Wenzlaff, R. M. (1982). Motivated remembering efforts during tip-of-the-tongue states. *Acta Psychologica, 51,* 137–147.

Rypma, D., & D'Esposito, M. (2003). A subsequent-memory effect in dorsolateral prefrontal cortex. *Cognitive Brain Research, 16,* 162–166.

Sacks, O. (1985). *The man who mistook his wife for a hat.* New York, NY: Simon & Schuster.

Sahakyan, L., Waldum, E. R., Benjamin, A. S., & Bickett, S. P. (2009). Where is the forgetting with list-method directed forgetting in recognition? *Memory & Cognition, 37,* 464–476.

Salame, P., & Baddeley, A. (1989). Effects of background music on phonological short-term memory. *Quarterly Journal of Experimental Psychology, 41A,* 107–122.

Salthouse, T. A. (1996). The processing-speed theory of adult age differences in cognition. *Psychological Review, 103,* 403–428.

Salthouse, T. A. (2000). Aging and measures of processing speed. *Biological Psychology, 54,* 35–54.

Salthouse, T. A. (2006). Mental exercise and mental aging. *Perspectives on Psychological Science, 1,* 68–87.

Schachtel, E. G. (2000). On memory and childhood amnesia. In U. Neisser & I. E. Hyman Jr. (Eds.), *Memory observed: remembering in natural contexts.* New York, NY: Worth. (Original work published 1947)

Schacter, D. L. (1996). *Searching for memory: The brain, the mind, and the past.* New York, NY: Basic Books.

Schacter, D. L. (2001). *Forgotten ideas, neglected pioneers: Richard Semon and the story of memory.* Philadelphia, PA: Psychology Press.

Schacter, D. L. (2007). Memory: Delineating the core. In H. L. Roediger, Y. Dudai, & S. M. Fitzpatrick (Eds.), *Science of memory: Concepts* (pp. 23–27). New York, NY: Oxford University Press.

Scheck, P., Meeter, M., & Nelson, T. O. (2004). Anchoring effects in the absolute accuracy of immediate versus delayed judgments of learning. *Journal of Memory and Language, 51,* 71–79.

Schmolck, H., Buffalo, A. E., & Squire, L. R. (2000). Memory distortions develop over time: Recollections of the O. J. Simpson verdict after 15 and 32 months. *Psychological Science, 11,* 39–45.

Schneider, W., & Lockl, K. (2008). Procedural metacognition in childhood: Evidence for developmental trends. In J. Dunlosky & R. A. Bjork (Eds.), *Handbook of metamemory and memory* (pp. 391–409). New York, NY: Taylor & Francis.

Schneider, W., & Pressley, M. (1997). *Memory development between two and twenty* (2nd ed.). Hillsdale, NJ: Lawrence Erlbaum.

Schneider, W., Vise, M., Lockl, K., & Nelson, T. O. (2000). Developmental trends in children's memory monitoring: Evidence from a judgment-of-learning task. *Cognitive Development, 15,* 115–134.

Schnyer, D. M., Verfaellie, M., Alexander, M., LaFleche, G., Nicholls, L., & Kaszniak, A. W. (2004). A role for right medial prefrontal cortex in accurate feeling-of-knowing judgments: Evidence from patients with lesions to frontal cortex. *Neuropsychologia, 42,* 957–966.

Scholl, R. (2002). *Der Papyrus Ebers. Die größte Buchrolle zur Heilkunde Altägyptens* [The Ebers Papyrus: The big book of ancient Egyptian medicine] (Schriften aus der Universitätsbibliothek 7). Leipzig: Universität Leipzig.

Schwartz, B. L. (2000). Skirmishes in the memory wars: A review of Williams and Banyard's (Eds.) *Trauma and Memory. Applied Cognitive Psychology, 14,* 594–595.

Schwartz, B. L. (2001). The relation of tip-of-the-tongue states and retrieval time. *Memory & Cognition, 29,* 117–126.

Schwartz, B. L. (2002). *Tip-of-the-tongue states: Phenomenology, mechanism, and lexical retrieval.* Mahwah, NJ: Lawrence Erlbaum.

Schwartz, B. L. (2006). Tip-of-the-tongue states as metacognition. *Metacognition and Learning, 1,* 149–158.

Schwartz, B. L. (2008). Working memory load differentially affects tip-of-the-tongue states and feeling-of-knowing judgment. *Memory & Cognition, 36,* 9–19.

Schwartz, B. L., & Frazier, L. D. (2005). Tip-of-the-tongue states and aging: Contrasting psycholinguistic and metacognitive perspectives. *Journal of General Psychology, 132,* 377–391.

Schwartz, B. L., & Metcalfe, J. (1992). Cue familiarity but not target retrievability enhances feeling-of-knowing judgments. *Journal of Experimental Psychology: Learning, Memory, and Cognition, 18,* 1074–1083.

Schwartz, B. L., & Smith, S. M. (1997). The retrieval of related information influences tip-of-the-tongue states. *Journal of Memory and Language, 36,* 68–86.

Schweickert, R., & Boruff, B. (1986). Short-term memory capacity: Magic number or magic spell? *Journal of Experimental Psychology: Learning, Memory, and Cognition, 12,* 419–425.

Scoboria, A., Mazzoni, G., & Josee, J. L. (2008). Suggesting childhood food illness results in reduced eating behavior. *Acta Psycologica, 128,* 304–309.

Shallice, T., & Warrington, E. K. (1970). Independent functioning of verbal memory stores: A neuropsychological study. *Quarterly Journal of Experimental Psychology, 22,* 261–273.

Sheen, M., Kemp, S., & Rubin, D. (2001). Twins dispute memory ownership: A new false memory phenomenon. *Memory & Cognition, 29,* 779–788.

Shepard, R. N., & Metzler, J. (1971). Mental rotation of thee-dimensional objects. *Science, 171,* 701–703.

Shettleworth, S. J. (2010). *Cognition, evolution, and behavior* (2nd ed.). New York, NY: Oxford University Press.

Shimamura, A. P. (2008). A neurocognitive approach to metacognitive monitoring and control. In J. Dunlosky & R. A. Bjork (Eds.), *Handbook of memory and metamemory: Essays in honor of Thomas O. Nelson* (pp. 373–390). New York, NY: Psychology Press.

Shimamura, A. P., Berry, J. M., Mangels, J. A., Rusting, C. L., & Jurica, P. J. (1995). Memory and cognitive abilities in university professors: Evidence for successful aging. *Psychological Science, 6,* 271–277.

Shimamura, A. P., & Squire, L. (1986). Memory and metamemory: A study of the feeling-of-knowing phenomenon in amnesic patients. *Journal of Experimental Psychology: Learning, Memory, & Cognition, 12,* 452–460.

Shin, H., Bjorkland, D. F., & Beck, E. F. (2007). The adaptive nature of children's overestimation in a strategic memory task. *Cognitive Development, 22,* 197–212.

Shlomo, B., DeGutis, J. M., D'Esposito, M., & Robertson, L. C. (2007). Too many trees to see the forest: Performance, event-related potential, and functional magnetic resonance imaging manifestations of integrative congenital prosopagnosia. *Journal of Cognitive Neuroscience, 19,* 132–146.

Shobe, K. K., & Schooler, J. W. (2001). Discovering fact and fiction: Case-based analyses of authentic and fabricated memories of abuse. In G. M. Davies & T. Dalgleish (Eds.), *Recovered memories: Seeking the middle ground* (pp. 95–151). Chichester, UK: John Wiley.

Siegler, R. S. (1999). Strategic development. *Trends in Cognitive Science, 3,* 430–435.

Simcock, G., & Hayne, H. (2002). Breaking the barrier? Children fail to translate their preverbal memories into language. *Psychological Science, 13,* 225–231.

Simner, J., & Ward, J. (2006). The taste of words on the tip of the tongue. *Nature, 444,* 438.

Simons, J. S., Scholvinck, M. L., Gilbert, S. J., Frith, C. D., & Burgess, P. W. (2006). Differential components of prospective memory? Evidence from fMRI. *Neuropsychologia, 44,* 1388–1397.

Slameka, N. J., & Graf, P. (1978). The generation effect: Delineation of a phenomenon. *Journal of Experimental Psychology: Human Learning and Remembering, 4,* 592–604.

Smith, E. E., Shoben, E. J., & Rips, L. J. (1974). Structures and process in semantic memory: A featural model for semantic decisions. *Psychological Review, 81,* 214–241.

Smith, J. D., Schull, J., Strote, J., McGee, K., Egnor, R., & Erb, L. (1995). The uncertain response in the bottlenosed dolphin (*Tursiops truncatus*). *Journal of Experimental Psychology: General, 124,* 391–408.

Smith, J. D., & Washburn, D. A. (2005). Uncertainty monitoring and metacognition by animals. *Current Directions in Psychological Science, 14,* 19–24.

Smith, S. M. (1994). Frustrated feelings of imminent recall: On the tip-of-the tongue. In J. Metcalfe & A. P. Shimamura (Eds.), *Metacognition: Knowing about knowing* (pp. 27–46). Cambridge, MA: MIT Press.

Smith, S. M., & Moynan, S. C. (2008). Forgetting and recovering the unforgettable. *Psychological Science, 19,* 462–468.

Snowdon, D. A. (2003). Healthy aging and dementia: Findings from the nun study. *Annals of Internal Medicine, 139,* 450–454.

Son, L., & Vandierendonck, A. (Eds.). (2007). *Bridging cognitive science and education: Learning, memory, and metacognition.* New York, NY: Psychology Press.

Son, L. K., & Metcalfe J. (2000). Metacognitive and control strategies in study-time allocation. *Journal of Experimental Psychology: Learning, Memory, & Cognition, 26,* 204–221.

Son, L. K., & Metcalfe, J. (2005). Judgments of learning: Evidence for a two-stage model. *Memory & Cognition, 33,* 1116–1129.

Soraci, S. A., Carlin, M. T., Chechile, R. A., Franks, J. J., Wills, T., & Watanabe, T. (1999). Encoding variability and cuing in generative processing. *Journal of Memory and Language, 41,* 541–559.

Souchay, C., & Isingrini, M. (2004). Age-related differences in the relation between monitoring and control of learning. *Experimental Aging Research, 30,* 179–193.

Souchay, C., Moulin, C. J. A., Clarys, D., Taconnat, L., & Isingrini, M. (2007). Diminished episodic memory awareness in older adults: Evidence from feeling of knowing and recollection. *Consciousness and Cognition, 16,* 769–784.

Spellman, B. A., Bloomfield, A., & Bjork, R. A. (2008). Measuring memory and metamemory: Theoretical and statistical problems with assessing learning (in general) and using gamma (in particular) to do so. In J. Dunlosky & R. A. Bjork (Eds.), *Handbook of memory and metamemory: Essays in honor of Thomas O. Nelson* (pp. 95–116). New York, NY: Psychology Press.

Sperling, G. (1960). The information available in brief visual presentations. *Psychological Monographs: General and Applied, 74,* 1–29.

Sporer, S. L. (1991). Deep-deeper-deepest? Encoding strategies and the recognition of human faces. *Journal of Experimental Psychology: Learning, Memory, and Cognition, 17,* 323–333.

Standing, L. (1973). Learning 10,000 pictures. *Quarterly Journal of Experimental Psychology, 25,* 207–222.

Strayer, D. L., & Drews, F. A. (2007). Cell-phone-induced driver distraction. *Current Directions in Psychological Science, 16,* 128–131.

Strange, D., Sutherland, R., & Garry, M. (2006). Event plausibility does not determine children's false memories. *Memory, 14,* 937–951.

Stroop, J. R. (1935). Studies of interference in serial verbal reactions. *Journal of Experimental Psychology, 18,* 643–662.

Suda-King, C. (2008). Do orangutans (*Pongo pygmaeus*) know when they do not remember? *Animal Cognition, 11,* 21–42.

Sutcliffe Cleveland, E., & Reese, E. (2008). Children remembering early childhood: Long term recall across the offset of childhood amnesia. *Applied Cognitive Psychology, 22,* 127–142.

Sylwester, R. (2005). *How to explain a brain: An educator's handbook of brain terms and cognitive processes.* Thousand Oaks, CA: Corwin Press.

Takahashi, M., Shimizu, H., Saito, S., & Tomoyori, H. (2006). One percent ability and ninety-nine percent perspiration: A study of a Japanese memorist. *Journal of Experimental Psychology: Learning, Memory, and Cognition, 32,* 1195–1200.

Talarico, J. M., & Rubin, D. C. (2003). Confidence, not consistency, characterizes flashbulb memories. *Psychological Science, 14,* 455–461.

Talarico, J. M., & Rubin, D. C. (2007). Flashbulb memories are special after all; in phenomenology, not accuracy. *Applied Cognitive Psychology, 21,* 557–578.

Teasdale, J. D., Dritschel, B. H., Taylor, M. J., Proctor, L., Lloyd, C. A., Nimmo-Smith, I., & Baddeley, A. D. (1995). Stimulus-independent thought depends on central executive resources. *Memory & Cognition, 23,* 551–559.

Tekcan, A. I., Ece, B., Gulgoz, S., & Er, N. (2003). Autobiographical and event memory for 9/11: Changes across one year. *Applied Cognitive Psychology, 17,* 1057–1066.

Terrace, H. S., & Metcalfe, J. (2005). *The missing link in cognition: Origins of self-knowing consciousness.* Oxford, UK: Oxford University Press.

Tessler, M., & Nelson, K. (1994). Making memories: The influence of joint encoding on later recall by young children. *Consciousness & Cognition, 3,* 307–326.

Thomas, M. H., & Wang, A. Y. (1996). Learning by the keyword mnemonic: Looking for long-term benefits. *Journal of Experimental Psychology: Applied, 2,* 330–342.

Thompson, C. P., Cowan, T. M., & Frieman, J. (1993). *Memory search by a memorist.* Hillsdale, NJ: Lawrence Erlbaum.

Thompson, D. M., & Tulving, E. (1970). Associative encoding and retrieval: Weak and strong cues. *Journal of Experimental Psychology, 86,* 255–262.

Thompson-Schill, S. L., Ramscar, M., & Chrysikou, E. G. (2009). Cognition without control: When a little frontal lobe goes a long way. *Current Direction in Psychological Science, 18,* 259–263.

Thomsen, D. K., & Berntsen, D. (2008). The cultural life script and life story chapters contribute to the reminiscence bump. *Memory, 16,* 420–435.

Tincoff, R., & Jusczyk, P. W. (1999). Some beginnings of word comprehension in 6-month-olds. *Psychological Science, 10,* 172–175.

Tsivilis, D., Vann, S. D., Denby, C., Roberts, N., Mayes, A. R., Montaldi, D., & Aggleton, J. P. (2008). The importance of the fornix and mammillary bodies for human memory: A disproportionate role for recall versus recognition. *Nature Neuroscience, 11,* 834–842.

Tulving, E. (1962). Subjective organization in free recall of "unrelated" words. *Psychological Review, 69,* 344–354.

Tulving, E. (1972). Episodic and semantic memory. In E. Tulving & W. Donaldson (Eds.), *Organization of memory* (pp. 381–403). New York, NY: Academic Press.

Tulving, E. (1983). *Elements of episodic memory.* New York, NY: Oxford University Press.

Tulving, E. (1985). Memory and consciousness. *Canadian Journal of Psychology, 26,* 1–12.

Tulving, E. (1993). What is episodic memory? *Current Directions in Psychology, 3,* 67–70

Tulving, E. (2002). Episodic memory and common sense: how far apart. In A. Baddeley, M. Conway, & J. Aggleton (Eds.), *Episodic memory: New direction in research* (pp. 269–287). New York, NY: Oxford University Press.

Tulving, E., & Lepage, M. (2000). Where in the brain is awareness of one's past? In D. L. Schacter & E. Scarry (Eds.), *Memory, brain, and belief* (pp. 208–228). Cambridge, MA: Harvard University Press.

Tulving, E., & Pearlstone, Z. (1966). Availability versus accessibility of information in memory for words. *Journal of Verbal Learning and Verbal Behavior, 5,* 381–391.

Tulving, E., & Schacter, D.L. (1990). Priming and human memory systems. *Science, 247,* 301–306.

Tversky, B. (2000). Remembering spaces. In E. Tulving & F. I. M. Craik (Eds.), *The Oxford handbook of memory* (pp. 363–378). New York, NY: Oxford University Press.

Usher, J. A., & Neisser, U. (1993). Childhood amnesia and the beginnings of memory for four early life events. *Journal of Experimental Psychology: General, 122,* 155–165.

Vallar, G., & Baddeley, A. D. (1984). Fractionation of working memory: Neuropsychological evidence for a phonological short-term store. *Journal of Verbal Learning and Verbal Behavior, 23,* 151–161.

Van Abbema, D. L., & Bauer, P. J. (2005). Autobiographical memory in middle childhood: Recollections of the recent and distant past. *Memory, 13,* 829–845.

Vargha-Khadem, F., Gadian, D. G., Watkins, K. E., Connelly, A., Van Paesschen, W., & Mishkin, M. (1997). Differential effects of early hippocampal pathology on episodic and semantic memory. *Science, 277,* 376.

Verhaeghen, P., & Marcoen, A. (1996). On the mechanism of plasticity in young and older adults after instructions in the method of loci: Evidence for an amplification model. *Psychology & Aging, 11,* 164–178.

Verkoeijen, P. P. J. L., Rikers, R. M. J. P., & Ozsoy, B. (2008). Distributed rereading can hurt the spacing effect in text memory. *Applied Cognitive Psychology, 22,* 685–695.

Vilkki, J., Servo, A., & Surma-aho, O. (1998). Word list learning and prediction of recall after frontal lobe lesion. *Neuropsychology, 12,* 268–277.

von Restorff, H. (1933). Über die Wirkung von Bereichsbildungen im Spurenfeld [The effects of field formation in the trace field]. *Psychologie Forschung, 18,* 299–234.

Wagenaar, W. A. (1986). My memory: A study of autobiographical memory over six years. *Cognitive Psychology, 18,* 225–242.

Walker, W. R., Skowronski, J. J., & Thompson, C. P. (2003). Life is pleasant—and memory helps us keep it that way! *Review of General Psychology, 7,* 203–210.

Wang, A. Y., & Thomas, M. H. (1995). The effect of keywords on long-term retention: Help or hindrance. *Journal of Educational Psychology, 87,* 468–475.

Wang, Q. (2001). Culture effects on adults' earliest childhood recollection and self-description: Implications for the relation between memory and the self. *Journal of Personality and Social Psychology, 81,* 220–233.

Wang, Q. (2006). Earliest recollections of self and others in European Americans and Taiwanese young adults. *Psychological Science, 17,* 706–714.

Wang, Q., & Fivush, R. (2005). Mother-child conversations of emotionally-salient events: Exploring the functions of emotional reminiscing in European-American and Chinese families. *Social Development, 14,* 473–495.

Ward, J. (2008). *The frog who croaked blue: Synesthesia and the mixing of the senses.* Oxford, UK: Routledge.

Warrington, E. K., & Shallice, T. (1969). The selective impairment of auditory short-term memory. *Brain, 92,* 885–896.

Watson, J. B. (1913). Psychology as the behaviorist views it. *Psychological Review, 20,* 158–177.

Watson, J. M., Bunting, M. F., Poole, B. J., & Conway, A. R. A. (2005). Individual differences in suscepti-bility to false memory in the Deese-Roediger-McDermott paradigm. *Journal of Experimental Psychology: Learning, Memory, and Cognition, 31,* 76–85.

Waugh, N. C., & Norman, D. A. (1965). Primary memory. *Psychological Review, 72,* 89–104.

Waxman, S. R., & Booth, A. E. (2001). Seeing pink elephants: Fourteen-month-olds' interpretations of novel nouns and adjectives. *Cognitive Psychology, 43,* 217–242.

Waxman, S. R., & Markow, D. B. (1995). Words as invitations to form categories: Evidence form 12-13 month-old infants. *Cognitive Psychology, 29,* 257–303.

Weaver, C. A., III. (1993). Do you need a "flash" to form a flashbulb memory? *Journal of Experimental Psychology: General, 122,* 39–46.

Weingartner, H. J., Joyce, E. M., Sirocco, K. Y., Adams, C. M., Eckardt, M. J., George, T., & Lister, R. G. (1993). Specific memory and sedative effects of the benzodiazepine triazolam. *Journal of Psychopharmacology, 7,* 305–315.

Weinstein, Y., Buck, J. M., & Roediger, H. L., III. (2008). Can the survival recall advantage be explained by basic memory processes? *Memory & Cognition, 36,* 913–919.

Wenk, G. L. (2003). Neuropathologic changes in Alzheimer's disease. *Journal of Clinical Psychiatry, 64,* 7–10.

Werker, J. F., & Tees, R. C. (1999). Influences on infant speech processing: Toward a new synthesis. *Annual Review of Psychology, 50,* 509–535.

White, R. (2002). Memory for events after twenty years. *Applied Cognitive Psychology, 16,* 603–612.

Willander, J., & Larsson, M. (2006). Smell your way back to childhood: Autobiographical odor memory. *Psychonomic Bulletin & Review, 13,* 240–244.

Willander, J., & Larsson, M. (2007). Olfaction and emotion: The case of autobiographical memory. *Memory & Cognition, 35,* 1659–1663.

Williams, L. M. (1995). Recovered memories of abuse in women with documented child sexual victimization histories. *Journal of Traumatic Stress, 8,* 649–673.

Willingham, D. T. (2009). What will improve student's memory? *American Educator, 32,* 17–25.

Wilson, B. A. (2009). *Memory rehabilitation: Integrating theory and practice.* New York, NY: Guilford.

Wilson, B. A., & Wearing, D. (1995). Broken memories: Case studies in memory impairment. In R. Campbell & M. A. Conway (Eds.), *Broken memories: Case studies in memory impairment* (pp. 14–30). Malden, MA: Blackwell.

Wilson, T. L., & Brown, T. L. (1997). Reexamination of the effect of Mozart's music on spatial-task performance. *Journal of Psychology: Interdisciplinary and Applied, 131,* 365–370.

Wimmer, H., & Perner, J. (1983). Beliefs about beliefs: Representation and constraining function of wrong beliefs in young children's understanding of deception. *Cognition, 13,* 103–128.

Wolfe, J. M., Horowitz, T. S., & Michod, K.O. (2007). Is visual attention required for robust visual memory? *Vision Research, 47,* 955–964.

Wollen, K. A., Weber, A., & Lowry, D. (1972). Bizarreness versus interaction of mental images as determinants of learning. *Cognitive Psychology, 3,* 518–523.

Wright, A. A., Santiago, H. C., & Sands, S. F. (1984). Visual serial position curves in SPR tasks. *Journal of Experimental Psychology: Animal Behavior Processes, 10,* 513–529.

Wright, D. B., Memon, A., Skagerberg, E. M., & Gabbert Current, F. (2009). When eyewitnesses talk. *Current Directions in Psychological Science, 18,* 174–178.

Yamada, M., Muria, T., & Ohigashi, Y. (2003). Postoperative reduplicative paramnesia in a patient with a right frontotemporal lesion. *Psychogeriatrics, 3,* 127–131.

Yaro, C., & Ward, J. (2007). Searching for Shereshevskii: What is superior about the memory of synaesthetes? *Quarterly Journal of Experimental Psychology, 60,* 681–695.

Yates, F. A. (1966). *The art of memory.* London: Routledge & Kegan Paul.

Young, G. (2008). Capgras delusion: An interactionist model. *Consciousness and Cognition, 17,* 863–876.

Yuille, J. C., & Cutshall, J. L. (1986). A case study of eyewitness memory of a crime. *Journal of Applied Psychology, 71,* 291–301.

Zacks, R. T., & Hasher, L. (2006). Aging and long-term memory: Deficits are not inevitable. In E. Bialystok & F. I. M. Craik (Eds.), *Lifespan cognition: Mechanisms of change* (pp. 162–177). New York, NY: Oxford University Press.

Figure and Photo Credits

Chapter 1

Figure 1.1, page 5. ©2010 Jupiterimages Corporation.

Figure 1.2, page 12. Used with permission of Endel Tulving.

Figure 1.3, page 14. Conway, M. A., Pleydell-Pearce, C. W., Whitecross, S. E., & Sharpe, H. (2003). Neurophysiological correlates of memory for experienced and imagined event. *Neuropsychologia, 41,* 334–340. Published by Elsevier Ltd.

Figure 1.4, page 16. Bennett Schwartz.

Figure 1.5, page 23. ©2010 Jupiterimages Corporation.

Chapter 2

Figure 2.1, page 33. From Garrett, B. *Brain & Behavior: An Introduction to Biological Psychology,* Second Edition. Copyright ©2009 by SAGE Publications, Inc.

Figure 2.2, page 35. From Garrett, B. *Brain & Behavior: An Introduction to Biological Psychology,* Second Edition. Copyright ©2009 by SAGE Publications, Inc.

Figure 2.3, page 36. From Garrett, B. *Brain & Behavior: An Introduction to Biological Psychology,* Second Edition. Copyright ©2009 by SAGE Publications, Inc.

Figure 2.4, page 40. From Garrett, B. *Brain & Behavior: An Introduction to Biological Psychology,* Second Edition. Copyright ©2009 by SAGE Publications, Inc.

Figure 2.5, page 42. Copyright ©2001 Ann L. Myers-Krusznis.

Figure 2.6, page 44. From Garrett, B. *Brain & Behavior: An Introduction to Biological Psychology,* Second Edition. Copyright ©2009 by SAGE Publications, Inc.

Figure 2.7, page 47. Wikipedia (http://en.wikipedia.org/wiki/File:Spike-waves.png).

Figure 2.8, page 50. © Thinkstock.

Chapter 3

Figure 3.1, page 62. © Dick Luria/Photodisc/Thinkstock.

Figure 3.2, page 66. Adapted from Naveh-Benjamin, M., & Ayres, T. J. (1986). Digit span, reading rate, and linguistic relativity. *Quarterly Journal of Experimental Psychology, 38,* 739–751.

Figure 3.3, page 69. Adapted from Peterson, L. R., & Peterson, M. J. (1959). Short-term retention of individual verbal items. *Journal of Experimental Psychology, 58,* 193–198.

Figure 3.4, page 71. Bennett Schwartz.

Figure 3.5, page 75. Adapted from Baddeley, A. D. (2000). The episodic buffer: A new component of working memory? *Trends in Cognitive Sciences, 4,* 417–423.

Figure 3.6, page 78. Based on information from Salame, P., & Baddeley, A. (1989). Effects of background music on phonological short-term memory. *Quarterly Journal of Experimental Psychology, 41A,* 107–122.

Figure 3.7, page 79. Based on Brooks, L. (1968). Spatial and verbal components of the act of recall. *Canadian Journal of Psychology, 22,* 349–368.

Chapter 4

Figure 4.1, page 96. ©2010 Jupiterimages Corporation.

Figure 4.2, page 98. Based on Craik, F. I. M., & Tulving, E. (1975). Depth of processing and the retention of words in episodic memory. *Journal of Experimental Psychology: General, 104,* 268–294.

Figure 4.3, page 101. Based on Nairne, J. S., Thompson, S. R., & Pandeirada, J. N. S. (2007). Adaptive memory: Survival processing enhances retention. *Journal of Experimental Psychology: Learning, Memory, & Cognition, 33,* 263–273.

Figure 4.4, page 102. Bennett Schwartz.

Figure 4.5, page 110. Based on Godden, D. R., & Baddeley, A. D. (1975). Context-dependent memory in two natural environments: On land and under water. *British Journal of Psychology, 66,* 325–331.

Figure 4.6, page 110. ©2010 Jupiterimages Corporation.

Figure 4.7, page 111. Based on Eich, J., Weingartner, H., Stillman, R., & Gillian, J. (1975). State-dependent accessibility of retrieval cues and retention of a categorized list. *Journal of Verbal Learning and Verbal Behavior, 14,* 408–417.

Figure 4.8, page 113. Based on Eich, E., & Metcalfe, J. (1989). Mood dependent memory for internal versus external events. *Journal of Experimental Psychology: Learning, Memory and Cognition, 15,* 443–455.

Figure 4.9, page 116. Based on Anderson, M. C., Bjork, R. A., & Bjork, E. L. (1994). Remembering can cause forgetting: Retrieval dynamics in long-term memory. *Journal of Experimental Psychology: Learning, Memory, and Cognition, 20,* 1063–1087.

Chapter 5

Figure 5.1, page 125. Bennett Schwartz.

Figure 5.2, page 130. Thinkstock.

Figure 5.3, page 131. Thinkstock.

Figure 5.4, page 137. Brewer, W. F., & Treyens, J. C. (1981). Role of schemata in memory for places. *Cognitive Psychology, 13,* 207–230. Published by Elsevier Ltd.

Figure 5.5, page 145. Sarina D. Schwartz.

Chapter 6

Figure 6.1, page 156. © Liquid Library/Thinkstock.

Figure 6.2, page 157. ©2010 Jupiterimages.

Figure 6.3, page 161. From Shepard, R. N., & Metzler, J. (1971). Mental rotation of three-dimensional objects. *Science, 171,* 701–703. Reprinted with permission from AAAS.

Figure 6.4, page 162. From Shepard, R. N., & Metzler, J. (1971). Mental rotation of three-dimensional objects. *Science, 171,* 701–703. Reprinted with permission from AAAS.

Figure 6.5, page 164. Kosslyn, S. M. (1975). Information representation in visual images. *Cognitive Psychology, 7,* 341–370. Published by Elsevier Ltd.

Figure 6.6, page 165. Kosslyn, S. M., Ball, T. M., & Reiser, B. J. (1978). Visual images preserve metric spatial information: Evidence from studies of mental scanning. *Journal of Experimental Psychology: Human Perception and Performance, 4,* 47–60. Published by the American Psychological Association.

Figure 6.7, page 166. Wikipedia (http://en.wikipedia.org/wiki/File:Lobes_of_the_brain_NL .svg).

Figure 6.8, page 169. Nickerson, R. S., & Adams, J. J. (1979). Long-term memory for a common object. *Cognitive Psychology, 11,* 287–307. Published by Elsevier Ltd.

Figure 6.9, page 173. Bennett Schwartz.

Figure 6.10, page 181. Based on Wang, A. Y., & Thomas, M. H. (1995). The effect of keywords on long-term retention: Help or hindrance. *Journal of Educational Psychology, 87,* 468–475.

Figure 6.11, page 184. Wollen, K. A., Weber, A., & Lowry, D. (1972). Bizarreness versus interaction of mental images as determinants of learning. *Cognitive Psychology, 3,* 518–523. Published by Elsevier Ltd.

Chapter 7

Figure 7.1, page 189. © Martin Conway.

Figure 7.2, page 191. Conway, M. A. (2005). Memory and the self. *Journal of Memory and Language, 53,* 594–628. Published by Elsevier Ltd.

Figure 7.3, page 192. ©2010 Jupiterimages Corporation.

Figure 7.4, page 195. Bennett Schwartz.

Figure 7.5, page 200. Simcock, G., & Hayne, H. (2002). Breaking the barrier? Children fail to translate their preverbal memories into language. *Psychological Science, 13,* 225–231. Published by Wiley-Blackwell.

Figure 7.6, page 204. Bennett Schwartz.

Figure 7.7, page 210. Bennett Schwartz.

Figure 7.8, page 218. Daselaar, S. M., Rice, H. J., Greenberg, D. L., Cabeza, R., LaBar, K. S., & Rubin, D. C. (2008). The spatiotemporal dynamics of autobiographical memory: Neural correlates of recall, emotional intensity, and reliving. *Cerebral Cortex, 18,* 217–229. Published by Oxford University Press.

Chapter 8

Figure 8.1, page 225. Courtesy of Elizabeth Loftus.

Figure 8.2, page 228. Bennett Schwartz.

Figure 8.3, page 234. ©2010 Jupiterimages Corporation.

Figure 8.4, page 240. Smith, S. M., & Moynan, S. C. (2008). Forgetting and recovering the unforgettable. *Psychological Science, 19,* 462–468. Published by Wiley-Blackwell.

Figure 8.5, page 241. Smith, S. M., & Moynan, S. C. (2008). Forgetting and recovering the unforgettable. *Psychological Science, 19,* 462–468. Published by Wiley-Blackwell.

Figure 8.6, page 243. Anderson, M. C., & Green, C. (2001). Suppressing unwanted memories by executive control. *Nature, 410,* 366–369. Reprinted by permission from Macmillan Publishers Ltd.

Figure 8.7, page 247. Loftus, E. F., & Palmer, J. C. (1974). Reconstruction of automobile destruction: An example of the interaction between language and memory. *Journal of Verbal Learning and Verbal Behavior, 13,* 585–589. Published by Elsevier Ltd.

Figure 8.8, page 249. Loftus, E. F., Miller, D. G., & Burns, H. J. (1978). Semantic integration of verbal information into a visual memory. *Human Learning and Memory, 4,* 19–31. Published by APA.

Figure 8.9, page 252. Bennett Schwartz.

Chapter 9

Figure 9.1, page 263. Dunlosky, J., Serra, M., & Baker, J. M. C. (2007). Metamemory applied. In F. Durso, R. S. Nickerson, S. T. Dumais, S. Lewandowsky, & T. J. Perfect (Eds.), *Handbook of applied cognition* (2nd ed., pp. 137–159). New York, NY: John Wiley.

Figure 9.2, page 268. Steven M. Smith.

Figure 9.3, page 269. Maril, A., Simons, J. S., Weaver, J. J., & Schacter, D. L. (2005). Graded recall success: An event-related fMRI comparison of tip of the tongue and feeling of knowing. *NeuroImage, 24,* 1130–1138. Published by Elsevier Ltd.

Figure 9.4, page 271. Maril, A., Simon, J. S., Mitchell, J. P., Schwartz, B. L., & Schacter, D. L. (2003). Feeling-of-knowing in episodic memory: An event-related fMRI study. *NeuroImage, 18,* 827–836. Published by Elsevier Ltd.

Figure 9.5, page 277. Kao, Y.-C., Davis, E. S., & Gabrieli, J. D. E. (2005). Neural correlates of actual and predicted memory formation. *Nature Neuroscience, 8,* 1776–1783. Reprinted by permission from Macmillan Publishers Ltd.

Figure 9.6, page 281. Bennett Schwartz.

Chapter 10

Figure 10.1, page 302. From Garrett, B. *Brain & Behavior: An Introduction to Biological Psychology,* Second Edition. Copyright © 2009 by SAGE Publications, Inc.

Chapter 11

Figure 11.1, page 324. ©2010 Jupiterimages Corporation.

Figure 11.2, page 330. Based on Deloache, J. S., Cassidy, D. J., & Brown, A. (1985). Precursors of mnemonic strategies in very young children's memory. *Child Development, 56,* 125–137.

Figure 11.3, page 336. Based on Leichtman, M. D., & Ceci, S. J. (1995). The effects of stereotypes and suggestions on preschoolers' reports. *Developmental Psychology, 31,* 568–578.

Figure 11.4, page 338. Based on information from Fivush, R., McDermott-Sales, J., Goldberg, A., Bahrick, L., & Parker, J. (2004). Weathering the storm: Children's long-term recall of Hurricane Andrew. *Memory, 12,* 104–118.

Figure 11.5, page 343. Created by Jack L. Frazier. © Jack L. Frazier.

Chapter 12

Figure 12.1, page 352. Creatas Images/Thinkstock.

Figure 12.2, page 355. Bennett Schwartz.

Figure 12.3, page 355. Bennett Schwartz.

Figure 12.4, page 362. Bennett Schwartz.

Figure 12.5, page 368. Based on Hertzog, C., Kidder, D., Powell-Moman, A., & Dunlosky, J. (2002). Monitoring associative learning: What determines the accuracy of metacognitive judgments? *Psychology and Aging, 17,* 209–225.

Chapter 13

Figure 13.1, page 382. Based on Christina, R. W., & Bjork, R. A. (1991). Optimizing long-term retention and transfer. In D. Druckman & R. A. Bjork (Eds.), *In the mind's eye: Enhancing human performance* (pp. 23–56). Washington, DC: National Academy Press.

Figure 13.2, page 386. Based on Karpicke, J. D., & Roediger, H. L., III (2008). The critical importance of retrieval for learning. *Science, 319,* 966–968.

Figure 13.3, page 390. Bennett Schwartz.

Author Index

Subject Index

About the Author

Bennett L. Schwartz is Professor of Psychology and Fellow of the Honors College at Florida International University. A native of Long Island, New York, he earned both his bachelor's degree (1988) and Ph.D. (1993) from Dartmouth College in Hanover, New Hampshire. He then moved to Florida International University in Miami, Florida, where he has been ever since. He does research on metamemory, human memory, and nonhuman primate memory. He has published over 40 journal articles in these areas. He authored the book *Tip-of-the-Tongue States: Experience, Mechanism, and Lexical Retrieval* (2002) and coedited the book *Applied Metacognition* (2002, with Timothy Perfect). He is past president of the Southeastern Workers in Memory (2006), and he has served on the editorial boards of several journals in cognitive and comparative psychology, including the *Journal of Experimental Psychology: General* and *Animal Cognition*. He teaches courses in memory, cognitive psychology, sensation and perception, and interdisciplinary honors courses.